2nd edition

A History of Film

JACK C. ELLIS
Northwestern University

PRENTICE-HALL, INC., ENGLEWOOD CLIFFS, NEW JERSEY 07632

Library of Congress Cataloging in Publication Data

Ellis, Jack C.
  A history of film.

    Includes index.
    1. Moving-pictures—History. I. Title.
PN1993.5.A1E4 1985   791.43'09   84-18054
ISBN 0-13-389479-7

Editorial/production supervision and interior design: *Alison D. Gnerre*
Cover design: *George Cornell*
Manufacturing buyer: *Barbara Kittle*

For MK

Printed in the United States of America

10 9 8 7 6 5 4 3 2 1

ISBN 0-13-389479-7 01

PRENTICE-HALL INTERNATIONAL, INC., *London*
PRENTICE-HALL OF AUSTRALIA PTY. LIMITED, *Sydney*
EDITORA PRENTICE-HALL DO BRASIL, LTDA., *Rio de Janeiro*
PRENTICE-HALL CANADA INC., *Toronto*
PRENTICE-HALL HISPANOMERICANA, S.A., *Mexico*
PRENTICE-HALL OF INDIA PRIVATE LIMITED, *New Delhi*
PRENTICE-HALL OF JAPAN, INC., *Tokyo*
PRENTICE-HALL OF SOUTHEAST ASIA PTE. LTD., *Singapore*
WHITEHALL BOOKS LIMITED, *Wellington, New Zealand*

Contents

PREFACE   xi

INTRODUCTION: CHARACTERISTICS OF FILM HISTORY   1

An Industrial Art, 2
A Composite Art, 3
A Collectively Created Art, 4
An Ephemeral and Inaccessible Art, 6
Books on Film Theory and General Histories, 7

1

DEVELOPMENTS PRIOR TO 1895 THAT LED TO THE MOTION PICTURE   10

Projection: The Magic Lantern, 11
Animation: Principle and Practice, 11
Photography: From Still to Stopped Motion, 15
The Motion Picture, 21

Foreshadowings of Motion-Picture Technique in the Nineteenth-Century Theater, 26
Films about the Period before 1895, 30
Books on the Period, 30

2

INTERNATIONAL CHILDHOOD OF A NEW MEDIUM AND ART, 1895–1914   31

Brief Motion-Picture Records of Actuality and of Performances, 31
Telling Stories through Staged and Filmed Pantomime, 35
Telling Stories through Filmic Means, 37
The Language of Film, 43
Increasing Films to Feature Length, 47
Films of the Period, 49
Books on the Period, 50

3

RISE OF THE AMERICAN FILM, 1914–1919   52

The First Masterpieces, 53
A Tradition of Screen Comedy is Established, 65
Emerging Patterns of Industry, 71
Films of the Period, 75
Books on the Period, 75

4

SCANDINAVIAN FILM, 1917–1924   77

Denmark, 77
Sweden, 81
Films of the Period, 85
Books on the Period, 85

5

GREAT GERMAN SILENTS, 1919–1925   86

Predominant Types and Themes, 87
Principal Technical and Stylistic Advances, 94
Mirror of the Culture, 100

Influence on Hollywood, 101
Films of the Period, 102
Books on the Period, 103

6

ART AND DIALECTIC IN THE SOVIET FILM, 1925–1929   104

Historical Setting, 105
Three Silent Masters, 110
Montage: Theory and Practice, 117
Films of the Period, 121
Books on the Period, 122

7

FRENCH IMPRESSIONISTS AND THE AVANT-GARDE, 1919–1929   123

Impressionists, 123
Avant-Garde, 126
Films of the Period, 130
Books on the Period, 131

8

HOLLYWOOD IN THE TWENTIES, 1919–1929   132

Movies Become Big Business, 133
Some Major Directors and Their Films, 136
Popular Genres, 141
Films of the Period, 148
Books on the Period, 149

9

SOUND COMES TO AMERICA, 1927–1935   150

Technological and Economic Problems, 151
Aesthetic Differences, 155
Evolution of Technique, 157
Films of the Period, 162
Books on the Period, 162

10

GOLDEN AGE OF FRENCH CINEMA, 1935–1939   164

Literary, Theatrical, and Painting Traditions, 167
Five Major Directors, 168
Reflections of a Troubled Nation, 174
Films of the Period, 177
Books on the Period, 177

11

HOLLYWOOD IN THE THIRTIES, 1929–1939   178

The Industry, 179
Censorship, Self-regulation, Pressure Groups, 182
Emergent Genres, 184
Major Directors, 199
Films of the Period, 205
Books on the Period, 206

12

BRITISH WARTIME SEMI-DOCUMENTARIES AND POSTWAR COMEDIES, 1939–1955   207

Wartime Semi-Documentaries, 208
Postwar Comedies, 213
Films of the Period, 215
Books on the Period, 216

13

HOLLYWOOD IN THE FORTIES, 1940–1952   217

Film Noir, 218
Realism, 220
Liberalism, Communism, and Anticommunism; the House Un-American Activities Committee and Blacklisting, 222
Six Directors, 225
Films of the Period, 234
Books on the Period, 236

14

ITALIAN NEOREALISM, 1945–1952   237

Three Major Directors, 237
Theory, 243
Practice, 244
Afterwards, 245
Films of the Period, 247
Books on the Period, 247

15

ASIAN FILM, 1951–   248

Japan, 249
India, 264
Films of the Period, 268
Books on the Period, 270

16

HOLLYWOOD IN TRANSITION, 1952–1962   271

Television, 272
New Screen Processes, 274
Fall of the Studios and Rise of the Independents, 279
Internationalization, 280
Loosened Controls on Content, 282
Six Directors, 285
Films of the Period, 297
Books on the Period, 299

17

THE FILM OF THE AUTEUR
AND THE FRENCH NEW WAVE, 1954–   300

Auteurism, 300
Three Auteurs, 303
New Wave, 311
Some Contemporary French Directors, 315
Films of the Period, 324
Books on the Period, 326

18

THE NEW ITALIANS, 1960–   327

Relationships to the New Wave, 327
Roots in Neorealism: Three Film Makers, 329
Other Directors and Subsequent Films, 335
Films of the Period, 341
Books on the Period, 342

19

EASTERN EUROPEAN CINEMA, 1954–   343

Poland, 346
Hungary, 351
Czechoslovakia, 354
Yugoslavia, 357
Films of the Period, 359
Books on the Period, 361

20

BRITISH FILM, 1956–   362

Social-Realist Features, 363
Gothic Tradition, 368
Americans Abroad, 372
Renaissance, 377
Films of the Period, 379
Books on the Period, 380

21

AMERICAN REEVALUATION AND REEMERGENCE, 1963–1977   382

Reevaluation, 382
Reemergence, 394
Films of the Period, 403
Books on the Period, 405

22

THIRD WORLD CINEMA
AND RECENT NATIONAL MOVEMENTS, 1959–   406

Latin America and Africa, 406
West Germany, 412
Spain, 415
Australia, 416
Films of the Period, 418
Books on the Period, 420

23

HERE AND NOW: U.S., 1977–   421

Economics and Technology, 421
Social Content, 422
Artistry, 424
Films of the Period, 430
Books on the Period, 430

INDEX   433

Preface

This is *a* history of film. As in the Jean-Luc Godard title *A Married Woman* (1964), the indefinite article should indicate that this is only one kind of film history. Though it is international in scope, it is limited largely to the narrative fiction film. The avant-garde, documentary, and animated film are dealt with only in part. No two histories of the international narrative fiction film can be the same; there are many valid and illuminating ways to approach the subject. When Godard entitled another of his films *A Film Like All the Others* (1968), he was, of course, being ironic.

Since the first edition of this book, an increasing amount of historical research, especially on the American film, has appeared. Some of it has centered on the very early years in an effort to understand what the film forms and contents of the first decade actually were. Other researchers have looked into the practices of film exhibition in the nickelodeon era or later in the twenties; into the way the motion picture trust functioned and how it faced both competition from the independents and legal action in the courts; into the transition from silence into sound; and the like. This research has involved the screening of films preserved in archives and the scrutinizing of early trade journals, distributors' catalogues, legal and corporate records. In addition to the increased scholarly digging, recent research has brought to film the application of rigorously thought-through ideas about the nature of history (historiography), neoclassical economics, and Marxist theory.

In the revision of this book I have attempted to incorporate the findings of this contemporary research. At the same time, the method and basic structure of the original edition have been preserved. If we have learned that earlier makers of films had motivations we had not previously acknowledged, their contributions were still part of an evolution, the outcomes of which they could not have imagined. If there are underlying economic forces and ideological underpinnings to be understood, they are still determined by men and women whose work can be identified, described, analyzed, and appreciated. Perhaps the approach to film history that, initially anyway, most readily permits us to grasp and remember its parts in relation to its whole remains the sort of historical narrative offered in the following pages.

This is essentially an aesthetic history. The organizing thesis is what Arthur Knight once called the "moving spotlight" view of film history. Among film scholars and critics it is generally agreed that for brief periods certain countries made seminal contributions to the evolution of film form and content. Of course, there are brilliant individual film makers who exist outside the construct, and countries whose achievements are parallel. Even admitting the Procrustean limitations of any kind of historical scheme, this one has proven serviceable and does permit variation and amendment with relative ease.

Part of the present effort is directed toward trying to identify patterns in the unique and rampant growth of film over the past nine decades. If there is anything original in this book, it has grown out of an attempt to understand the evolving practice of this young art. It may be too early to attempt an overall theory of film history (not until the late nineteenth century was one enunciated for English literature by Frenchman Hippolyte Taine), but the historian ought to feel obliged to interpret, clarify, and connect. If our work is to be of value, we must undertake the chancy business of analysis and generalization, as well as assemble information.

Recognizing that you cannot yet take from a shelf the complete works of Robert Altman, or move to a section labeled "The Soviet Film 1925–1929," perhaps what a book like this can most usefully do is to establish contexts for individual films that are usually viewed at random over a period of years. At any rate, the attempt here is to provide observations and inferences related to the films and culture surrounding major works and to note the special contributions and preoccupations of their creators. Throughout, the writing is more interpretive than descriptive or critical.

The early chapters are somewhat like separate essays, the content and structure of each being dictated by the special conditions that prevailed in the national period under consideration. General characteristics receive attention along with particular persons and their films. Later chapters extend from previous periods to the present in order to provide greater inclusivity and currency than a strict application of the thesis would permit. Interspersed are chapters on the American film by the decade—in the twenties, the thirties, the forties, and so on. These chapters are intended to keep track of major ongoing trends and contributions of the dominant Hollywood industry even during those periods when the greatest artistic excitement seemed to be elsewhere.

Set forth within the introduction are criteria and attitudes—means for attempting to come to an understanding of the art and its development—which are operative throughout. There has not been space to do more than refer to the theoretical aspects of film.

Basic works on film theory in English are listed at the end of the introductory chapter, along with previously published international film histories. Following the other chapters are lists of significant films of each period and of books pertaining to the period. This is intended to suggest that many more films and film makers are worth attention than this limited space and the desire to simplify and clarify permit covering, and that books exist that offer additional information and other interpretations.

The films discussed in this text are confined largely to those the author has seen which are also available to the reader on some basis. They are referred to by the titles most commonly used in this country, and the years listed for them are those of release rather than of production. However useful background information and critical interpretation may be, close and repeated viewing of films remains the primary method of film study.

Though the choice of viewpoint and organization for this history is an individual one, my indebtedness to preceding writers about film is evident to me and will be to others. Also requiring conspicuous acknowledgement is my debt to former film students and colleagues—Sharon Russell, Stuart Kaminsky, Paddy Whannel, and the rest—who added information and contributed insights to this book. My thanks again to all of them.

JCE

Permission to use quoted material has been granted by the following companies and persons: Holt, Rinehart and Winston, Inc., for Arthur Edwin Krows, *The Talkies,* Phenakistiscope illustrations, p. 14; Harcourt Brace Jovanovich, Inc., for Sergei Eisenstein, *Film Form* and *The Film Sense* (translated and edited by Jay Leyda), pp. 119–120; University of California Press, for Jean-Louis Rieupeyrout, "The Western: A Historical Genre," *The Quarterly of Film, Radio, and Television,* vol. 7, no. 2 (Winter 1952), p. 141; E. P. Dutton, for Ernest Betts, *Heraclitus; or the Future of Films,* p. 155; A D Peters & Co Ltd, for Liam O'Flaherty, *The Informer* (film script adaptation by Dudley Nichols, published in *Theatre Arts* magazine), p. 160; Rodney Whitaker, for his "The Content Analysis of Film: a Survey of the Field, an Exhaustive Study of *Quai des brumes,* and a Functional Description of the Elements of the Film Language," Ph.D. dissertation, Northwestern University, pp. 174–175; Courtenay Beinhorn, for her *Cinema Texas Program Notes,* vol. 4, no. 1 (January 17, 1973), p. 191; Martin Secker & Warburg, Ltd., and Indiana University Press, for Peter Wollen, *Signs and Meaning in the Cinema,* pp. 202, 204; Donald Richie, for his *Japanese Cinema: Film Style and National Character,* Doubleday & Co., Inc., p. 253; The Gordon Fraser Gallery Limited, for David Pirie, *A Heritage of Horror: The English Gothic Cinema, 1946–1972,* p. 369; The British Film Institute, for "Film Guide," *Sight and Sound,* vol. 43, no. 2 (Spring 1974), p. 370; Andrew Sarris, for his *The American Cinema: Directors and Directions 1929–1968,* E. P. Dutton, pp. 387, 388, 390, 391, 392; Penguin Books Limited, for V. F. Perkins, *Film as Film,* p. 388; Indiana University Press, for Jim Kitses, *Horizons West: Studies in Authorship in the Western,* p. 391.

Introduction: Characteristics of Film History

The motion picture is one of two major arts to have evolved within modern history—the other art being still photography, upon which the motion picture is based. (Television is here regarded simply as a means of distribution and exhibition of moving images accompanied by sound.) We can only guess what first prompted people to express themselves in the various older artistic media, or how early modes and conventions developed and disappeared as aesthetic and social functions changed. The motion picture, however, is clearly the child of nineteenth-century scientific curiosity and technological ingenuity; it has grown up under our twentieth-century noses.

The most important of its original reasons for being had nothing to do with its artistic potential. The theory underlying the motion picture was demonstrated in a succession of optical toys. Its tools and materials were invented out of a desire to make visual records of life and to study the movements of animals, including humans. Its capacity to provide peep-show entertainment attracted impresarios and paying customers to what scientists and inventors had made available. Later, as the novelty of life-like movement began to pale, the technicians and entrepreneurs who had discovered how to project moving images onto screens stumbled onto an old interest latent in audiences—the story. They began to offer simple narratives in a new form.

Commercial viability followed, and an industry began to develop along with what came to resemble an art. Marked from the outset by high cost, this art depended on technology and mass consumption as much as did any other modern industrial undertaking. Business people and artists, temperamentally incompatible, were nonetheless fellow travelers in the progress of this new art-industry—and it wasn't always the artists who led the way, even aesthetically.

Audiences soon became the arbiters of change. Their support of what they liked and rejection of what they did not has determined the overall course of film history. Technological inventiveness, business acumen, and artistic genius only offered possibilities. Immediate and wide response from the public established which of the possibilities would be permanently incorporated into the ongoing development of film. In this art there was no pleasing a single patron, prelate, or noble; no waiting for future generations to discover poems written on scraps of paper left in a garret. Even more than the popular theater and novel—which it supplanted in many ways—the motion picture had to relate closely to contemporary tastes and preoccupations, which it in turn helped to shape.

AN INDUSTRIAL ART

Most of the major changes in this art form have been technological in origin, backed by business and supported by box-office returns. When still pictures became moving pictures in the 1890s, space was extended into time and the moving pictures were hung on narrative lines. Silent film was supplanted by sound film in the late 1920s. Black and white was supplemented with color in the 1930s. In the early 1950s the standard screen, four-by-three ratio, spread wide to five-by-two and sound emanated from many directions. In none of these cases was there complete consensus that the innovation was desirable.

On the contrary, the first film makers thought that to record fragments of life in the street or bits of vaudeville performance was a quite adequate use of the medium. Some of the finest later film makers and the most perceptive of newly arrived critics decried the addition of audible speech to film as inimical to the great visual art that was being forged. Color seemed at first to transform the careful selectivity and balance of monochrome (black-and-white or tinted) into a garish, uncontrollable travesty of the hues of life as observed outside the theater or interpreted in paintings. It was thought that wide screens would suit only spectacles—religious, historical, musical; the very format seemed to preclude intimate personal drama and subtle observation. In every instance, the artists and subsequently the critics had to run to catch up with the engineers, the businessmen, and the audience—turning to new subject matter and introducing techniques and aesthetic criteria that would accommodate the imposition.

With these frequent and radical alterations in the very materials available to the artist, it is risky to ask—as the aesthetician likes to—"What is cinema?" When the question was raised in the late twenties by critics who failed to realize the irrevocable and extreme changes that sound was bringing, their brilliant answers were to have only limited applicability. Given this strange phenomenon of frequent mutation—greater, in degree at least, than that experienced by any other art—a historical approach may be necessary. The great French critic André Bazin used the question *What is Cinema?* as the title for his collected writings. He answered it in part by suggesting that cinema in its fullness exists only in the aggregate: in its historical totality. Each period of film history, Bazin argued, explored only one aspect of cinema (or a complex of aspects). If, then, the only valid description of the motion picture is the sum of what it has been, predictions about where it is going must be based on knowledge of its history—but with an eye on the current *Journal of the Society of Motion Picture and Television Engineers* and *Variety*'s weekly box office figures.

A COMPOSITE ART

Then there is the mongrel nature of this art. It is distinctive, paradoxically, *because* it embodies so many of the other arts and yet does not duplicate any one of them. Film's relationships to and borrowings from the graphic, literary, and dramatic arts are most important and obvious.

The motion picture is a flat, two-dimensional, visual representation, more like photography than painting in its realistic style. Unlike photography or painting, its succession of rapidly projected still photographs creates the illusion of movement taking place in time. In photographs and paintings, subject time is stopped: A single instant from life is fixed and frozen. Viewing time is up to the viewer, who may merely glance at the work or study it for minutes on end. In the motion picture, as one frame follows another, we see not only the single photographic instant but what happened before and what happens afterwards. We view the succession of images in the order and for the duration predetermined by the film maker. The static visual arts require only spatial organization; the moving picture requires temporal organization as well.

To give coherence to a succession of moving images, the film maker employs structures like those common to literature—narrative, expository, descriptive, argumentative. The fiction feature film, the staple of the art, is most like the novel in its construction. But whereas the novelist must evoke a sensory reality using abstract and arbitrary printed signs, the film maker offers sight and sound experience directly to the senses. Novelists tell us what they want us to think about the characters, and what they are thinking. Film makers let us infer ideas and feelings through the visible and the audible, through what the characters do and say. Rarely do they speak in their own voices; in this respect they depend, as do playwrights, upon dramatic action and dialogue.

In the theater, because the stage is distant from most viewers and limited in its visual variety, primary communication is through the actors' spoken words. Movement, gesture, and setting are reinforcements. In film the balance is reversed: we tend to learn as much from how a man enters a room, the way a woman pats a child's head, or the darkening light on water as a thunderstorm approaches, as we do from what the characters say. There is usually more speech on the stage than in life, and it is heightened—dramatic, poetic, dense with ambiguity and innuendo. In film the dialogue tends to be sparse and less demanding of our full attention. Speech becomes a subservient part of a complex artistic entity that includes great visual richness as well as music and sound effects.

One further basic distinction between film and theater involves something of an aesthetic contradiction. Though the conventions of theater are patently artificial, and though film tends to seem much closer to actual life, space and time on the stage are absolutely real, while in film they are always synthetic illusion. On stage the performers move within three-dimensional space, requiring the same time that it would take off the stage to cross a given distance, set a dining room table, and so on. Film is a two-dimensional representation of a three-dimensional reality; it is not the reality itself. In placing pictures together, the film maker can unite things spatially that were never adjacent in life. (In Alfred Hitchcock's *Frenzy,* 1972, the camera tracks down a studio-constructed stairway and then—with an unnoticed cut—out into a real London street.) The film maker can speed up action for excitement or slow it down for suspense. (Cutting back and forth between bank robbers fleeing and police in pursuit may actually prolong the chase, yet make it seem more tense and, yes, even faster.)

The circle of film's main artistic analogues—the pictorial, the literary, the dramatic—should properly be closed with re-emphasis on the primacy of picture. As has been noted, however, these pictures are very different from still photographs or paintings. They move, tell stories, and offer their own special kind of performance.

Finally, even those arts that seem less directly related to film have points of contact. The motion picture camera moves around, peering at people and things from different distances and angles, as one would look at a piece of sculpture. Architecture is an ingredient of film in a more profound way than stage sets are part of a play. Michelangelo Antonioni's films, for example, are about cities as well as the people living in them (Ravenna in *The Red Desert,* 1964; London in *Blow-Up,* 1966; Los Angeles in *Zabriskie Point,* 1969). It seems only fitting that the protagonist of his first international success, *L'Avventura,* 1960, is an architect.

Movement—human and other kinds—gives the medium a balletic quality, which the great silent comedians exploited superbly. Music, of course, from the first nickelodeons onward, has almost always formed part of the total film experience, and some observers have felt that film's flow through time and its direct sensory appeal to the emotions is somewhat like musical form. Yet, for all of its compositeness and indebtedness, the aesthetic experience film offers is unique. The whole is clearly different from any of its parts.

A COLLECTIVELY CREATED ART

Because of the many kinds of artistic materials involved, most films are made by many persons with various skills. One of the historian's jobs is to determine which of the people involved in a production contributed what to its quality, and who the major artists were. We speak of the stage play, another collectively created art, as "the playwright's." The Kabuki theater of Japan, however, is much like film in its compositeness and collectivity; the terse dialogue is only a part of the work in which music, movement, gesture, and costume have something like the integral balance of a good wide-screen color-and-sound film. We sometimes speak of buildings as being works of individual architects—a Frank Lloyd Wright house, a Mies van der Rohe skyscraper—leaving aside Gothic cathedrals that were created anonymously by whole generations of townspeople. If one includes the "performances" that take place and the "props" used within those Gothic buildings, the totalities involve many kinds of artistic media and sensory stimuli.

Whether or not art can be created by a committee, the Western tradition in the last several centuries is to regard the art work as preeminently the expression of one individual through forms which he or she shapes and controls. In film the controlling sensibility is most often and most recognizably that of the director. This now seems obvious in regard to past instances, and we speak of the films *of* D. W. Griffith, F. W. Murnau, Sergei Eisenstein, Jean Renoir, and others. Directorial control has become increasingly characteristic of contemporary cinema. When film historians refer to a Bergman film, they mean Ingmar rather than Ingrid, however important the actress's contribution may have been to films in which she appeared—including *Autumn Sonata,* 1978, which they made together.

Sometimes, however, works bear a consistent personal identification with their producer, particularly in American films during the first three decades of sound. In such cases, directors directed under orders. The productions of Samuel Goldwyn, David Selznick, Walter Wanger, or Carlo Ponti may be examples, as would the marvelous 1940s horror series produced by Val Lewton (including *Cat People* and *The Body Snatcher*).

The script writers, also, may exert an identifiable kind of control over a body of work. Carl Mayer during the German silent cinema and Cesare Zavattini in post-World War II Italian neorealism were strong and frequently dominant creative contributors. A number of actors come to direct themselves, in a sense; whoever else is credited, they carry their *personas* intact from role to role. One is apt to speak of a W. C. Fields movie or a Garbo movie, and perhaps of a Barbra Streisand or Burt Reynolds picture. Though undervalued cinematographers and editors usually work under the close supervision of directors, there are often distinguished craftspeople among them. Some cinematographers bring great skill, artistic integrity, and individual style to their work. Among notable editors, Dede Allen has played an extremely important part in films directed by Arthur Penn, as has Ralph Rosenblum in some of Woody Allen's. Working the camera, Billy Bitzer was to Griffith what Edward Tissé was to Eisenstein or what Karl Freund was to Murnau; Gregg Toland's camera contributions to William Wyler and Orson Welles were as profound as Raoul Coutard's were to Jean-Luc Godard and François Truffaut. The cinematography of Nestor Almendros for *Days of Heaven,* 1978, contributed as much to its special quality as did any other aspect of its production.

Exceptions aside, if personal vision is assumed to be the primary prerequisite for the creation of a work of art, as it will be in this book, the case for the director's ascendancy is a strong one. It consists not only of historical demonstration that the director of enduring films has more often than not assumed that commanding position, but also of argument that the director *should* command. The director is the only member of the creative team, excluding the producer (whose role is generally managerial—supportive to the creative functions), who bridges all three phases of the production process, who is in a position to guide the whole. The director usually enters at the writing stage. Even when the script is someone else's or the director is not listed among the writers, he or she inevitably serves to some degree as collaborator. To give life to the conception, a director must make it his or her own; and he must fully and deeply comprehend the emotions and ideas, the characters, and situations, in order to render them into tangible sights and sounds. Complete understanding and realization of this sort involves shaping the elements to fit his own preconceptions and intentions. The director accomplishes this either by changing words on script pages or by modifying what those words will mean when they move from the writer's conception to the director's, and are translated into instructions to crew and cast.

It is the director who dictates what images and sounds are recorded during the vital shooting phase. The script describes, and others may add suggestions, but it is the director who fixes the meaning and feeling, the exact mood and nuance. The French term for director is *réalisateur*—in literal translation, "realizer." It is the director's view of the world which is brought to life in front of and through the camera and microphone, that film world which she or he evokes and commands.

The final editing and mixing of sight and sound are of as much concern to the film artist as are the preceding phases. Alfred Hitchcock often acknowledged that both his shooting and his cutting were precisely preplanned at the script stage. John Ford is said to have shot films so tightly that they could be put together in only one way. George Stevens, on the other hand, was known to shoot a scene allowing for a maximum number of possibilities from which to select during editing. Most directors reserve many of their final decisions for the editing stage and work closely with their editors. Accordingly, the Directors Guild of America eventually gained for its members the right to approve the rough assemblage—the first cut—as a minimum standard contractual right.

On this matter of the director having control even within the confines of commercial entertainment, we owe a debt to the French critics who inaugurated what has come to be called the auteur (author) theory—from *la politique des auteurs,* a phrase coined by François Truffaut. To simplify for the moment (since the subject will be dealt with at length later), this French critical contingent held that directors usually are and always should be the principal creators of films, and that those directors who leave the strongest individual stamp on their work are to be most valued. This idea is easily acceptable when applied to acknowledged masters of the silent film or to contemporary European "star directors" (Michelangelo Antonioni or Federico Fellini, Robert Bresson or Claude Chabrol). It was when the French, and then some young American and English critics, began to reassess the massive bulk of the Hollywood sound film that their contribution became most original and most controversial.

They argued that within factory-like conditions there had been created some of the most interesting and valuable works in the history of film. Certain previously obscure, or at least disregarded, film makers were seen to have given consistent expression to their own world views in spite of hackneyed scripts and low budgets, in defiance (or owing to the indifference) of the front office. It was to these directors and the body of their work, as well as to those of more obviously serious intent, that the auteurists insisted we must look in order to arrive at a total assessment of film art. Though they discovered no Shakespeares or Rembrandts, the auteurists have made more useful and inclusive lists of directors than those celebrated in standard histories, by calling attention to Howard Hawks, Don Siegel, Robert Aldrich, Samuel Fuller, and others. They have reminded us once again that the history of an art, like the history of anything else, needs to be rewritten for each generation, that the evidence must continually be reexamined and the canons of taste subjected to constant review.

AN EPHEMERAL AND INACCESSIBLE ART

The reevaluation by the auteurists was solidly based on the close and systematic viewing of large numbers of films. This may seem an obvious requirement for the historian, but a final and vexing characteristic of film history is the ephemeral nature of the films themselves and their peculiar inaccessibility for study: They are shown, and then disappear; they may be altered by censorship or for commercial expedience; and, until the late forties they were printed on perishable stock (cellulose nitrate), which disintegrates with time. Of 21,000 American theatrical films created before 1951, more than half have been lost forever. Over 80 percent of the survivors—those existing only on nitrate stock—face a similar fate.

Fortunately, such difficulties are being lessened by increasing efforts to preserve and make available our film heritage. In many countries, selected older films are being transferred by national film archives to more permanent bases (cellulose acetate).

In the U.S. the Library of Congress, the Museum of Modern Art, and the George Eastman House are aided in this work by the American Film Institute. Copies of noteworthy new works are being acquired for preservation. The Museum of Modern Art and a number of commercial distributors make available to film societies and film classes a sampling of the total corpus.

In some cities "art theaters" and "revival houses" offer the foreign, the old, and the otherwise unusual. Commercial television provides a partial repertory of the English-language sound film. Public television occasionally presents the silent and subtitled non-English-dialogue film. Video cassettes and discs, added to 8mm and 16mm copies, begin to offer better prospects for private and institutional study collections of some scope. At present, however, it is extremely difficult to locate and view all of the films of Nicholas Ray (let alone Satyajit Ray or Man Ray), for example, or a representative selection of French cinema of the late thirties, or that of 1939–1945 American and German fiction features with war themes. If the films are in distribution, the rental prices are prohibitive for individuals. If they exist in archives or vaults, one must go where they are and—if permitted—usually pay costs to project them.

It is no accident that auteur criticism began in Paris, where the Cinémathèque Française shows four programs a day covering the widest presently available range of nations, genres, and film makers, and provides additional private screenings for the serious critic and scholar. Even with (and most certainly without) a Cinémathèque, however, endless frustration and considerable expense is often sustained in order to see the films one needs to. No wonder the scholar is sometimes driven into the proliferating underworld of illegal and necessarily inferior copies of copies—duped prints. Like other eccentricities of the art, the problem of inaccessibility is subject to ever constant technological and economic change, and something approaching solution may eventually be achieved, when films will become as readily and inexpensively available as books. The situation can only get better.

BOOKS ON FILM THEORY AND GENERAL HISTORIES

Theory

ANDREW, J. DUDLEY,   *The Major Film Theories.* New York: Oxford University Press, 1976. 278 pp.

ARNHEIM, RUDOLF,   *Film as Art.* Berkeley: University of California Press, 1957. 230 pp.

BALÁZS, BÉLA,   *Theory of the Film.* New York: Arno Press, 1972. 291 pp.

BAZIN, ANDRÉ,   *What is Cinema?* 2 vols. Berkeley: University of California Press, 1967, 1971.

BURCH, NOËL,   *Theory of Film Practice.* New York: Praeger Publishers, 1973. 172 pp.

CAUGHIE, JOHN, ed.,   *Theories of Authorship: A Reader.* London: Routledge & Kegan Paul, Ltd., 1981. 320 pp.

CAVELL, STANLEY,   *The World Viewed: Reflections on the Ontology of Film.* New York: Viking Press, Inc., 1971. 192 pp.

EISENSTEIN, SERGEI,   *Film Form; The Film Sense.* New York: Harcourt, Brace & Co., 1969. 561 pp.

HENDERSON, BRIAN,   *A Critique of Film Theory.* New York: E. P. Dutton & Co., 1980. 233 pp.

KRACAUER, SIEGFRIED,   *Theory of Film.* New York: Oxford University Press, 1960. 311 pp.

LANGER, SUSANNE,   "Appendix: A Note on Film," *Feeling and Form.* New York: Charles Scribner's Sons, 1953, pp. 411–415.

LINDGREN, ERNEST,   *The Art of the Film.* New York: Collier Books, 1970. 340 pp.

MAST, GERALD, and MARSHALL COHEN, eds.,   *Film Theory and Criticism*. New York: Oxford University Press, 1974. 639 pp.

METZ, CHRISTIAN,   *Film Language: A Semiotics of the Cinema*. New York: Oxford University Press, 1974. 268 pp.

NICHOLS, BILL, ed.,   *Movies and Methods*. Berkeley: University of California Press, 1976. 640 pp.

PERKINS, VICTOR,   *Film as Film*. Baltimore: Penguin Books, Inc., 1972. 198 pp.

TUDOR, ANDREW,   *Theories of Film*. New York: Viking Press, Inc., 1973. 168 pp.

TYLER, PARKER,   *Magic and Myth of the Movies*. New York: Henry Holt & Co., 1947. 283 pp.

WOLLEN, PETER,   *Signs and Meaning in the Cinema*. Bloomington: Indiana University Press, 1973. 168 pp.

History

BARDÈCHE, MAURICE, and ROBERT BRASILLACH,   *The History of Motion Pictures*. New York: Arno Press, 1970. 412 pp. (originally published in 1938)

BEAVER, FRANK E.,   *On Film: A History of the Motion Picture*. New York: McGraw-Hill Book Company, 1983. 530 pp.

BOHN, THOMAS W., et al.,   *Light and Shadows: A History of Motion Pictures*. Sherman Oaks, Calif.: Alfred Publishing Co., Inc., 1978. 479 pp.

CASTY, ALAN,   *Development of the Film: An Interpretive History*. New York: Harcourt Brace Jovanovich, Inc., 1973. 425 pp.

COOK, DAVID A.,   *A History of Narrative Film, 1889–1979*. New York: W. W. Norton & Co., Inc., 1981. 721 pp.

COWIE, PETER, ed.,   *A Concise History of the Cinema*. 2 vols. Cranbury, N. J.: A. S. Barnes & Co., Inc., 1971.

COWIE, PETER,   *Eighty Years of Cinema*. Cranbury, N. J.: A. S. Barnes & Co., Inc., 1977. 323 pp.

CROWTHER, BOSLEY,   *The Great Films: Fifty Golden Years of Motion Pictures*. New York: G. P. Putnam's Sons, 1967. 258 pp.

DICKINSON, THOROLD,   *A Discovery of Cinema*. New York: Oxford University Press, 1971. 164 pp.

FELL, JOHN L.,   *A History of Films*. New York: Holt, Rinehart and Winston, Inc., 1979. 588 pp.

FIELDING, RAYMOND, comp.,   *A Technological History of Motion Pictures and Television*. Berkeley: University of California Press, 1967. 255 pp.

FULTON, A. R.,   *Motion Pictures: The Development of an Art*. Norman: University of Oklahoma Press, 1980. 274 pp.

GARBICZ, ADAM, and JACEK KLINOWSKI,   *Cinema, The Magic Vehicle: A Guide to its Achievement. Journey One: The Cinema Through 1949*. Metuchen, N. J.: Scarecrow Press, Inc., 1975. 551 pp.

HOUSTON, PENELOPE,   *The Contemporary Cinema*. Baltimore: Penguin Books, Inc., 1963. 222 pp.

JACOBS, LEWIS, ed.,   *The Emergence of Film Art*. New York: W. W. Norton & Company, 1979. 544 pp.

KNIGHT, ARTHUR,   *The Liveliest Art*. New York: New American Library, 1978. 369 pp.

LENNIG, ARTHUR,   *The Silent Voice—A Text, The Golden Age of the Cinema*. Troy, N. Y.: published by the author, 1969. 367 pp.

LINDGREN, ERNEST,   *A Picture History of the Cinema*. New York: Macmillan Co., 1960. 160 pp.

MACGOWAN, KENNETH,   *Behind the Screen: The History and Techniques of the Motion Picture*. New York: Delacorte Press, 1965. 528 pp.

MAST, GERALD,   *A Short History of the Movies*. Indianapolis: Bobbs-Merrill Co., Inc., 1981. 516 pp.

MUSEUM OF MODERN ART FILM LIBRARY,   *Film Notes: Part 1, The Silent Film*. New York: Museum of Modern Art, 1949. 68 pp.

O'LEARY, LIAM,   *The Silent Cinema*. New York: E. P. Dutton & Co., 1965. 160 pp.

PRATT, GEORGE C., ed.,   *Spellbound in Darkness: A History of the Silent Film*. Greenwich, Conn.: New York Graphic Society, Ltd., 1973. 548 pp.

READER, KEITH,   *The Cinema: A History.* London: Hodder & Stoughton, 1979.

RHODE, ERIC,   *A History of the Cinema from Its Origins to 1970.* New York: Hill & Wang, 1976.

ROBINSON, DAVID,   *The History of World Cinema.* New York: Stein and Day, 1981. 512 pp.

ROTHA, PAUL, and RICHARD GRIFFITH,   *The Film Till Now: A Survey of World Cinema.* New York: Funk and Wagnalls Co., 1949. 755 pp.

ROTHA, PAUL, and ROGER MANVELL,   *Movie Parade, 1888-1949: A Pictorial Survey of World Cinema.* London: Studio Limited, 1950, 160 pp.

SCHICKEL, RICHARD,   *Movies: The History of an Art and an Institution.*. New York: Basic Books, Inc., 1964. 208 pp.

SELDES, GILBERT,   *An Hour with the Movies and the Talkies.* New York: Arno Press, 1973. 156 pp. (originally published in 1929)

TYLER, PARKER,   *Classics of the Foreign Film: A Pictorial Treasury.* New York: Citadel Press, 1962. 253 pp.

WISEMAN, THOMAS,   *Cinema.* Cranbury, N. J.: A. S. Barnes & Co., Inc., 1965. 181 pp.

WOOD, LESLIE,   *The Miracle of the Movies.* London: Burke Publishing Company, Limited, 1947. 352 pp.

WRIGHT, BASIL,   *The Long View.* New York: Knopf, 1974. 709 pp.

1

Developments Prior to 1895 that Led to the Motion Picture

The discoveries and inventions leading up to the first projection of motion pictures for a paying public (December 1895) had developed along three quite separate, though parallel, lines. The first came from a desire to project images onto a surface using an artificial light source. This possibility, when achieved, was called the magic lantern. The second line began with the idea that an illusion of movement might be obtained from a succession of related still images. Many experiments and toys using drawings or paintings applied the theory and improved the illusion. The third line began with the invention of a practicable still photographic process and extended to photographs that could be taken and shown fast enough to make full use of the image-succession theory.

Since all three lines of development were advanced by the work of numerous persons in various countries, patriotic contentions continue about who did this or that first. Simply, it can be said that a great many people over a great many years invented the motion picture, borrowing freely from each other and simultaneously discovering various solutions to the same problems.

Another early development, though not directly connected with the origins of the motion picture, would influence its subsequent contents and forms. The popular nineteenth-century theater, giving emphasis to pictorial and realistic staging, offered extraordinarily precise models for what film would become.

PROJECTION: THE MAGIC LANTERN

The ancient Greeks stumbled onto the basic requirements for a projected illuminated image; Aristotle noted the matter. Passed along by the Arabs, the understanding of the possibility was picked up and forwarded by Leonardo da Vinci. This became what was called in sixteenth-century Italy the *camera obscura*. This ''darkened room'' had a small hole in one side, which permitted an inverted image of what was outside to form on the inside wall opposite the small hole. Though it took many years for the room to shrink, the modern motion picture projector and camera are basically a portable miniature of that room—a light-tight box with a hole in it.

Athanasius Kircher, a seventeenth-century Jesuit priest and mathematician living in Austria, constructed a portable camera obscura operating in reverse in a way—to project the image out of the box onto the wall of a room. He called it a *magic lantern*. In addition to the light-tight box with a small hole, it made use of a candle to provide illumination, a lens to focus the light, and glass slides which were drawn on to provide the images. An account of his understandings and inventions was published as *Ars Magna Lucis et Umbrae* (The Great Art of Light and Shadow) in 1649. The slide projection he pioneered out of scientific curiosity became popular throughout Europe as entertainment. Later, limelight—made by heating lime to its point of incandescence—and electricity replaced the candle and permitted the showing of slides to large audiences. By the nineteenth century quite sophisticated narrative slide shows were being presented, which even continued concurrently with early motion pictures.

ANIMATION: PRINCIPLE AND PRACTICE

It was in 1824 that Dr. Peter Mark Roget, English physician and scholar best remembered for his *Thesaurus,* read before the Royal Society a paper entitled ''Explanation of an Optical Deception in the Appearance of the Spokes of a Wheel seen through Vertical Apertures.'' The ''persistence of vision'' dealt with by Roget involves a quirk in human perception that causes us to think we are still seeing something for about one-tenth of a second after it has disappeared. Roget was, perhaps unknowingly, repeating an observation made by Aristotle and reaffirmed by da Vinci. Why, Aristotle had asked, does a flaming brand whirled overhead seem to form a continuous circle of fire, when at any

Etching of a *camera obscura,* with an inverted image of the exterior view forming on the wall opposite the peephole. Gregory Faller.

Diagrammatic representation of an early magic lantern. National Film Archive London.

given instant the flame can be in only one place? Much later, Leonardo da Vinci observed that if he looked at a bright light and then looked away, he still thought he saw the light. It was through the same kind of accident that Roget arrived at his understanding. Looking through the vertical slats of a fence at the wheels of a moving cart, he noted that the spokes seemed to bend and distort. Only in their vertical position did the spokes appear straight. This illusion was caused by his brain having retained the image of the spokes after they had passed behind the slats—which functioned as a sort of stationary shutter.

Roget's purely scientific explanation of the phenomenon was followed, in 1826, by the appearance in London of a "Thaumatropical Amusement" whose invention is generally attributed to John Ayrton Paris, another English doctor. The Thaumatrope, a fashionably pretentious Greek name meaning "magical turning," consisted simply of a cardboard disk with a drawing on each side—a bird on one side and a cage on the other, for example, or a seated rider and a riderless horse. When the disk was spun,

Thaumatrope, early nineteenth-century optical toy. (This example U.K., 1826). National Film Archive/Stills Library.

the bird would appear to be in the cage; the rider, on the horse's back. The popularity of the device set off a series of disk experiments in Britain, France, and Belgium at the end of the 1820s.

The next step consisted of notching a much larger disk, then peering through the slot at a succession of drawings while the disk was spun. The development of the spinning, notched disk led to the discovery of the crucial moving-shutter principle, which could confer on a series of still pictures the illusion of animated movement. One of the principal contributors to the advance was Joseph Plateau of Brussels; another was Simon Ritter von Stampfer of Vienna. By the end of 1832 both men had separately arrived at similar devices. Plateau's device, which he called the Phenakistiscope, consisted of a disk with slots on the edges, and drawings of successive stages of movement of humans or animals in between the slots on the side facing away from the viewer. When you spun the disk in front of a mirror and peered through the slots, the separate stages formed an appearance of continuous movement. Stampfer put his slotted spinning disk in front of a stationary one with drawings on its front, so the viewer could look directly at the device and get the same illusion without the use of a mirror. (Plateau, dedicated to the study of optical phenomena, later paid a high price for his scientific curiosity: Testing the effect protracted staring at the sun might have, he was blinded.)

Slotted disks led to the development of a topless revolving drum. With a strip of pictures placed around the lower inside, and with vertical slits above to look through, the appearance of continuous movement became even more convincing. When the drum was revolved, horses jumped over fences, sprites leapt in and out of bottles, ballerinas pirouetted. William George Horner, a distinguished English mathematician, seems to have invented the device in 1834. Reinvented in France and introduced into America in the 1860s, it was marketed under the name Zoetrope (''life turning'') and enjoyed wide popularity. Revived periodically, it still can be seen in toy stores.

The disks and drums established a theoretical basis for the moving picture, and led directly to the animated cartoon. This line of experimentation culminated in the painstakingly ingenious work of Emile Reynaud in this Théâtre Optique. In the late 1870s Reynaud revised the Zoetrope, combined its shutter principle with the magic lantern, and achieved the first projection of animated drawings. The use of angled mirrors in his Praxinoscope, as he called the new device, was a great improvement that increased illumination and allowed a smoother flow of images.

By the late 1880s Reynaud was entertaining paying audiences in his Théâtre Optique at the Musée Grevin in Paris with little stories thrown onto a screen. His colored drawings were made at first on strips of translucent material, then on celluloid when it became available. A bright light shone through the quite long strips, which were cranked by hand through a maze of sprockets and reels, offering projected motion picture shows—from 1892 (the year before Edison's Kinetoscope peep show) until 1900 (five years after the first photographic motion pictures had been projected by the Lumières). Though a resourceful mechanic, Reynaud was above all a showman. In this respect, as well as in his stress on story, he presaged the future of the motion picture more closely than did most persons associated with the development from static photographs to recorded and reproduced motion.

Phenakistiscope, early nineteenth-century optical device. Holt, Rinehart & Winston, Inc.

Zoetrope, mid-nineteenth century. National Film Archive/Stills Library.

PHOTOGRAPHY: FROM STILL TO STOPPED MOTION

In 1614, an Italian physician noticed that silver nitrate turned dark on exposure to light. With this discovery the recording of an image formed in the camera obscura—and in smaller, portable versions of it—became possible.

By the early 1800s experimenters were working with silver bromides: Using cameras, they found they could record images of figures or landscapes on paper coated with these light-sensitive particles. There were two difficulties, however. After being removed from the camera, the picture continued to darken from exposure to light until it finally disappeared in blackness. Also, the tonality of the image was reversed: what was light in nature became dark in the emulsion. By the 1830s a way was discovered to chemically "fix" the silver salts so that they would not continue to be affected by light. First to achieve a permanent negative, in 1835, was the Englishman W. H. Fox Talbot. He also found that by using very thin paper for the negative and waxing it, the negative

Artist's rendition of an animated image being watched by an audience in the Théâtre Optique of Emile Reynaud, Paris, 1892–1900. National Film Archive London.

became transparent enough for light to shine through it onto another piece of paper coated with light-sensitive emulsion. The result was a negative of a negative—a positive print, with lights and darks conforming to what was in front of the camera. The dark (opaque) areas of the negative blocked light; the white (clear) areas let it through.

Concurrent with Talbot's work was that of a French scene designer named Louis Daguerre. In partnership with Nicéphore Niépce—the man credited with having made the first true photograph (c. 1816), albeit an impermanent negative—Daguerre invented in 1837 a new and highly successful method of photography which he immodestly called the daguerreotype. Using burnished copper as a base, and a very thin silvered negative emulsion with unexposed particles washed away in solvent, the final effect was that of a positive. With heavy publicity surrounding the announcements and demonstrations of his process, it was Daguerre rather than Talbot who first sparked public interest in photography. Unlike Talbot's system, however, the daguerreotype offered no way of making copies. Each daguerreotype was as unique as it very often was charming. Metal is not the best photographic base; Talbot was right to seek transparency. His waxed paper would be followed by glass (1847) and then by celluloid (1888).

Though Daguerre's method represented an extraordinary refinement over anything preceding it, in terms of the exquisite clarity of its detail and the accuracy of its light and dark shades, it shared with the other early systems a limitation that was even more critical than its incapacity for reproduction: It took as long as thirty minutes to ex-

Daguerreotype, nineteenth century. Jean Bartz.

pose one daguerreotype at first. By 1839, when it was in widespread use, the time had been cut only to twenty minutes. If our ancestors often look carved in stone, no wonder: Their heads were frequently clamped in place from behind. The familiar hand on the shoulder—great-great grandfather standing, with his hand on the shoulder—great-great grandmother's shoulder—may have had as much to do with muscular fatigue as affection.

Daguerreotypes were later replaced by wet plates (1851), which took two minutes to expose, but photography remained severely limited by this slowness of the emulsion. In the justifiably famous Civil War photographs of Mathew Brady and others, there is everything but fighting: Men sit in front of their tents, troops stand in formation, corpses lie on battlefields. The movement of battle had to be left to the artist sketching for lithographs and engravings. Wet plates were finally succeeded by dry plates (1871), which had a ten-second exposure time at first, and then much less. But it wasn't until 1888 that gelatin emulsions became available, emulsions sufficiently rapid (one twenty-fifth of a second) to permit the persistence-of-vision phenomenon to manifest itself.

Faced with the lengthy exposure times, some early photographers had approximated persistence of vision through a technique known as the successive pose: The subject held one position of a movement long enough for exposure, then advanced the movement slightly, paused, and so on. When flipped—or later projected—in rapid succession, the still photos could provide a somewhat jerky impression of movement—this procedure is what we would call ''stop-action photography,'' in motion picture terms.

Photo by Mathew B. Brady's organization, of the Seventh Regiment Wisconsin Volunteers, Arlington, Virginia, 1862. State Historical Society of Wisconsin.

Lithograph in *Harper's Weekly* (February 8, 1862, p. 88). State Historical Society of Wisconsin.

(A hundred years later, Norman McLaren called it ''pixillation'' when he ''animated'' human beings in his short films *Neighbors* and *A Chairy Tale.*)

In the 1860s two Philadelphians, Coleman Sellers and Henry Renno Heyl, used the wet-plate, stop-action method to achieve a semblance of movement. In 1861 Sellers photographed his two sons playing, and mounted the photos on a small paddle wheel. When turned in front of the viewer, the pictures appeared briefly in succession before the eye—like a large ''riffle book'' in which the pages are flipped rapidly to give the illusion of movement. In 1870 Heyl projected two series of photos in life size (of a waltzing couple—Heyl himself and his partner—and of a popular Japanese acrobat) by mounting them on a glass disk which revolved in front of a bright light shining through an opening and closing shutter.

The next major advance was that of capturing a subject in rapid unposed movement. It was made by a colorful and controversial Englishman-turned-American, Eadweard Muybridge, whose private life was tinged with scandal when he shot to death his wife's lover, and whose scientific contributions have frequently been suspected of a certain amount of charlatanism. The part of his career that concerns us occurred in California from 1872 to 1879, and there can be no doubt about his achievement. As a professional photographer, Muybridge was apparently called upon to settle a dispute about whether or not all four feet of a trotter were off the ground at some point in its stride. Muybridge set out to prove that they were, and in this he was financed by Leland Stanford—railroad tycoon, ex-governor of California, founder of Stanford University, and owner of a string of race horses. Stanford reportedly continued to subsidize Muybridge's work, involving an outlay of money well over the $25,000 said to have been won on the initial bet.

In 1878 Muybridge reported that he had set up a battery of cameras—twelve at first, and later twenty-four—alongside a race track at Stanford's Palo Alto estate. Threads to trip the shutters were stretched across the track, and a white background was constructed that would be the same in each image and thus conceal the differing positions of the cameras. As a galloping horse broke the threads, each of the cameras, only a foot apart, caught one phase of its movement. Unlike the effect of twenty-four frames taken rapidly from one camera position, as we experience in the movies we see, the ef-

Re-creation of a series of posed, stop-action photographs like those made by Coleman Sellers and Henry Renno Heyl in Philadelphia in the 1860s. Film Images.

Eadweard Muybridge still photographic motion studies. Museum of Modern Art/Film Stills Archive.

fect would have been more like that of a modern motion picture camera (at twenty-four frames per second) moving (trucking) alongside a galloping horse.

We know that Muybridge even projected his studies of motion. In 1880 *The Scientific American* reported that at a meeting of the San Francisco Art Association, Muybridge's Zoopraxiscope "threw upon the screen apparently the living, moving animals. Nothing was wanting but the clatter of the hoofs upon the turf."[1] According to this and other accounts, in addition to horses the subjects included a bull, greyhounds, deer, and

Sketch of Eadweard Muybridge's experiments with stopped-motion photography, Palo Alto, California, 1878. National Film Archive/Stills Library.

[1] Quoted by Kenneth Macgowan, *Behind the Screen* (New York: Delacorte Press, 1965), p. 49.

Photographic gun developed by Jules Marey, France, 1882. National Film Archive/
Stills Library.

athletes. It may be that Muybridge came closer to solving the ultimately more difficult problems presented by the motion picture projector than he did those connected with the camera. At any rate, in order to make use of persistence of vision, rather than twenty-four cameras taking one picture each, what was needed was a single camera taking twenty-four pictures within two seconds or less. It was a French physician and scientist, Etienne Jules Marey, who took a long step in that direction.

Marey and Muybridge were curiously linked from the outset. Marey's researches into animal locomotion may have influenced Stanford to hire Muybridge in the first place; Muybridge's subsequent work with Stanford's horses inspired Marey to turn to photography. The two men finally met in 1881, when Muybridge put on an exhibition in Paris. During the following year Marey constructed what he called a "photographic gun," which looked like a revolver grafted onto a shotgun. In the muzzle was a lens; the cylindrical chamber contained a dry plate which revolved when the trigger was pressed. With this camera Marey was able to capture birds in flight, with twelve pictures a second on a single plate. By 1887 he was using sensitized strips of paper, then paper-backed celluloid strips. Since his concern was to analyze movement that had been fragmented and stopped, not to record it intact, he had little interest in a projector.

THE MOTION PICTURE

From 1887 on, leading directly to photographed, projected motion pictures, the relative value of various innovations is uncertain: Many claims are bolstered as much by chauvinism as by tangible evidence. For example, between 1886 and 1888 Louis Le

Prince, a Frenchman (working mainly in England and America, however), and William Friese-Greene, an Englishman, separately developed cameras of arguable practicability. Le Prince's system involved sixteen lenses alternately focusing eight frames in succession on two parallel strips of paper; he later used a single lens. Friese-Greene, also using paper at first, seems to have developed a successful camera by 1888; but it appears unlikely to experts that his projector actually functioned.

In 1890 Le Prince confounded posterity and obscured the potential worth of his invention by disappearing from a train traveling between Dijon and Paris. Friese-Greene was later celebrated in a highly conjectural, all-star feature film *The Magic Box* made in 1951 for the Festival of Britain. Friese-Greene is played by Robert Donat; Sir Laurence Olivier appears briefly as a bobby who supposedly witnessed the results of Friese-Greene's early efforts.

Other developments, if not completely free from contention, are at least less mysterious. The manufacture of transparent celluloid in 1888 provided a photographic base considerably superior to what had preceded it; still, it was brittle, thick, and stiff. About a year later there appeared a strong, thin, and flexible "film," an almost ideal base for the motion pictures. Its availability set off a race over the last of the technological hurdles toward practicable machines for recording and presenting photographic images that would seem to move. The contestants are too numerous to list, but the principal front runners in the international competition were Thomas Edison and Thomas Armat in the United States; Marey, Le Prince, and Louis and Auguste Lumière of France; Ottomar Anschütz, Max Skladanowsky, and Oskar Messter for Germany; and Friese-Greene and Robert Paul representing England.

It is not just Americans, of course, who acknowledge the key role played by Edison and admit the crucial nature of his contributions. Yet one feels inclined to enclose his name in quotation marks, since most of the actual motion-picture work at the West Orange laboratory appears to have been undertaken by William Kennedy Laurie Dickson, an emigrant Englishman like Muybridge. If Dickson was the prime mover, that would explain why Edison later seemed vague at times, and even misinformed, about the principles involved in his own motion-picture system. It is surprising that he lacked the imagination to foresee its full commercial potential: Even Edison's detractors don't accuse him of being blind to financial considerations. Apparently, what motivated his initial interest in the motion picture was a desire to supply visual accompaniment, as it were, to his already successful cylinder phonograph.

Beginning in 1888, Dickson worked at mounting spirals of tiny photographs on cylinders, to be viewed through a magnifying eyepiece while they revolved with the audio cylinder. A year later, he claimed to have achieved synchronous sight-and-sound projection experimentally. Edison remained committed to the rotating cylinder idea—until he visited France in 1889, where Marey showed him a working strip camera. Motion picture efforts at the Edison laboratory were then rather quickly redirected toward the flexible film approach. By this time George Eastman (of the Eastman Dry Plate and Film Company in Rochester, New York) had begun to market the amateur Kodak still camera—"You press the button. We do the rest." Dickson bought some of the Kodak film in 1889 and started designing a peep-show machine. At some point between May 1891 and October 1892 the vertical-feed Kinetograph camera was completed. The peep-show machine, named the Kinetoscope, was demonstrated privately in 1891 and publicly in 1893; the first large shipment of machines reached Broadway in 1894.

In supplying the fifty-foot loops of Kinetoscope film, which moved in less than

Kinetoscopes in the Peter Bacigalupi Parlour, San Francisco, c. 1894. National Film Archive/ Stills Library.

half a minute over a series of spools, Dickson became the first motion-picture producer. Though the Edison Kinetograph was probably the first fully efficient camera, with sprockets and perforated 35mm film, it was about the size and at least the weight of an upright piano. Since it was virtually impossible to move it about, Dickson built a studio for it in 1893. Nicknamed the Black Maria because of its tar paper covering, the studio's roof could be raised and the whole structure turned on tracks—to let in maximum sunlight to expose the relatively insensitive emulsion at an excessively rapid, average rate of forty frames per second. Subjects for those first films were thus restricted largely to what could be brought across the Hudson from New York City to appear before the camera: vaudeville and circus performers, trained animals, dancers, celebrities, and comic skits, all of which gave the Edison films a decidedly theatrical tone and made them, to some degree, precedents for the fiction film that would become the staple of the entertainment and the art.

Edison was not thinking in theatrical terms, however; he remained resolutely fixed on the coin-in-the-slot peep show. His interest was in selling machines, and he argued that by accommodating many people at a single showing fewer machines would be needed. Ten projectors would be enough to show moving pictures to everybody in the country, he calculated. At the same time, he refused to spend $150 to secure international protection for his motion picture patents; this opened up all of his work to borrowing and adaptation abroad. Terry Ramsaye, American patriot and Edison booster, asserted in the first large-scale film history, *A Million and One Nights,* that there was no

"Black Maria," the Edison studio in West Orange, New Jersey, c. 1892. National Film Archive/Stills Library.

"motion picture film machine . . . that is not descended by traceable steps from the Kinetoscope."[2] On the other hand, a later court ruling held that there were no features in the Edison patents that had not been in earlier patents.

Other inventors added an arc light and lens to the Kinetoscope, and, more important, went back to the intermittent film movement of the earlier inventors. Dickson was able to get by with continuous movement and a narrowly slotted, rapidly moving shutter disk in the peep-show machine. (The Edison camera had used intermittent movement from the outset.) But for projection, even more light was needed than for exposure. The best way to get it was to stop each frame in front of the aperture for a fraction of a second, and open the shutter wider and for a longer duration than in the Kinetoscope. An important requirement in early projection design was to extend the time during which the frame was stationary in the gate while being illuminated by the arc or limelight, to hold it longer in relation to the time spent in advancing the next frame into position.

By skipping over some lesser figures—mostly Americans—who solved projection problems and added refinements in 1894 and 1895, we arrive at the Lumière brothers, Louis and Auguste. Not only did they adapt the Edison-Dickson inventions most effectively, they moved beyond them to achieve a rival and sustained success. Having become interested in motion pictures when the Kinetoscope arrived in Paris in 1894, Louis Lumière set about devising a system that would correct some of the deficiencies of the Edison machine, particularly those resulting from its feeble and diffused light. In

[2] Terry Ramsaye, *A Million and One Nights* (New York: Simon and Schuster, Inc., 1964), p. 73.

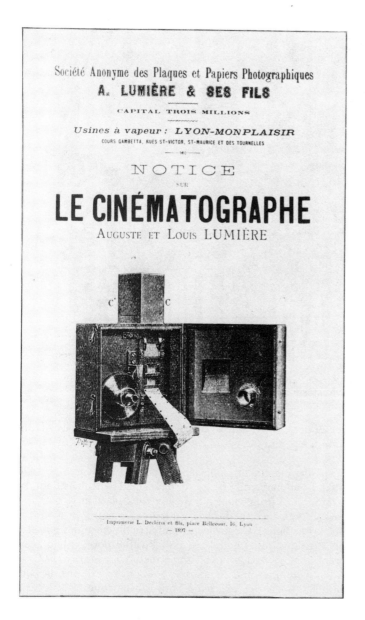

The Cinematographe, motion picture camera-projector-printer invented by Louis Lumière, France, 1895. National Film Archive/Stills Library.

March of 1895 the Lumières demonstrated their projector before the Society for the Encouragement of National Industry, and in December of that year they began paid public performances in a basement café. The machine they used for projecting served as a camera and printer as well. Much smaller and lighter than the Edison equipment (because of his proprietary interest, Edison had insisted that both the Kinetograph and the Kinetoscope be driven by an electric motor), the Lumières's hand-cranked Cinémato-

Poster advertising early Lumière showings; *L'Arroseur arrosé* (France, 1895, Louis Lumière) is the film being shown. Museum of Modern Art/Film Stills Archive.

graphe permitted much greater portability. This is clearly evident in their choice of film subjects: They took the camera out into the world rather than bringing bits of performance into a studio.

The Lumière projection was quickly followed by others. In March of 1896 there was a public screening in London, using a projector developed by Robert Paul. In April, the first American commercial projection in a theater took place at Koster and Bial's Music Hall, New York City. Called the Edison Vitascope (to make promotional use of the Wizard of Menlo Park's fame), the projector had actually been designed by fellow-Americans C. Francis Jenkins and Thomas Armat. Furthermore, it had been demonstrated during the preceding fall (with some Edison Kinetoscope film) at the Cotton States Exposition in Atlanta. Jenkins and Armat had sold out to Edison—in part because they could not manufacture enough projectors, but Edison could.

FORESHADOWINGS OF MOTION-PICTURE TECHNIQUE IN THE NINETEENTH-CENTURY THEATER

Once the technology had become available and had been directed toward entertainment, the question of what films should be about became important for the first time. Paralleling the gestation of the motion picture was a kind of popular theater that seemed to cry out for the screen to give it full form. This theater, which Nicholas Vardac called "realistic-romantic" in his diligently researched and insightful *Stage to Screen,* appeared in those same countries where moving pictures were then being pursued—France, England, Germany—and reached its final flowering in the United States. To the Broadway of that time, David Belasco and Steele MacKaye were more or less what D. W. Griffith and Cecil B. De Mille would later be to Hollywood. (Both film directors, incidentally, came out of that popular theater: Griffith wrote and acted in plays; De Mille was a member of the Belasco company.)

Consisting of melodrama, action, spectacle, and farce, the little-remembered American plays of the late nineteenth century looked remarkably like the films of forty years later. *Looked* is very much the key word. Emphasis was heavily on the visual: Language was stripped away; dialogue scripts were as sparse as screenplays; plot and character were mere vehicles on which the set designers and technicians hung ingeniously realistic and fantastic creations, exhausting and sometimes seeming to surpass the limitations of staging method. "The more romantic the subject matter," wrote Vardac, "the more realistic must be its presentation upon the boards, else the entire effect would be lost."[3]

The plays in this pictorial tradition followed two main patterns which lent themselves to visual effect. First were the action-melodramas, which included dramatic situations that would later become typical of film. For example, when the curtain rose for the last act, the heroine was seen tied to a log in a saw mill, moving toward certain dismemberment; or she was tied across railroad tracks, as a locomotive whistle grew louder (and the train drew nearer); perhaps the villain lurked stage right, stroking his mustache. Then the curtain lowered. When the curtain rose, the backdrop portrayed field and road. The breathless young hero strode forward and climbed over a wall in the foreground, peering off stage right; we heard the buzz saw, or the approaching train. Curtain down. Curtain up: The log had just about reached the saw, or the train noises were very loud; the villain may still have been lurking, or slinking off. Curtain down. Curtain up: The breathless young hero was running along the road (endless belt kept scenery moving by, where possible); the noises were now louder, and perhaps a feminine scream came from offstage right. And so on.

This kind of plot construction frequently included parallel simultaneous lines of action and "cross-cutting"—a simulated chase and last-minute rescue, which one thinks of as originating in film. The transition, curtain down and curtain up, even with amazingly quick set changes, was more awkward and distracting than was film's instantaneous cut. But clearly suggested were the essentials of filmic form: the manipulation of time and space ("Meanwhile, back at the ranch"), and the reliance on simple, strong emotions (fear, joy, anger, remorse) expressed in movement and gesture against realistic settings.

Mack Sennett would later parody the typical dramatic situation in *Teddy at the Throttle* (1917), which had Gloria Swanson as the young woman tied to the tracks, Wallace Beery as the villain, and Bobbie Vernon as the hero. The principal difference in Sennett's treatment is that he was able to show the interiors of the locomotive cab and passenger coach (with all the passengers falling down when the brakes were slammed), and could look out of the moving cab at the tracks ahead. In his film there is also a kind and variety of incident that would be very difficult on the stage: The dog Teddy, for example, leaps out of a second story window, and from a cliff into a river, which he then swims. As in a stage play, Sennett had to depend on theater musicians for the sound of

[3] A. Nicholas Vardac, *Stage to Screen* (Cambridge: Harvard University Press, 1949), p. xx.

Poster advertising a turn-of-the-century stage melodrama. State Historical Society of Wisconsin.

the train whistle; but he could show a dramatic closeup of steam escaping as the whistle is blown.

In touring stage productions, only a silver-painted cardboard saw blade could be used, or a light wooden front end of a locomotive—smoke puffing and bell ringing, to be sure, for the final curtain. In fixed, urban presentations there would be much more elaborate representations of these action-melodrama scenes. An expert theatrical artist like Dion Boucicault would work through a series of inductions and aim for the ultimate in romantic-realistic excitement. It had been established that audiences would turn out to see horses on stage; patrons were also known to like stage Indians; many plays had proved the popularity of boats on water; fires were always a sure thing. It took Boucicault to bring it all together: The climactic scene of his play *The Octoroon* had Indians on horseback attacking a riverboat with flaming arrows! It was a long-run smash, of course, as *The Birth of a Nation, The Iron Horse,* and *The Ten Commandments* would be years later. One of the insurmountable handicaps suffered by theater, in comparison with film, was the expense and difficulty involved in re-staging this sort of extravaganza every night. A long, full-house run at one theater was necessary to earn a profit. Such elaborate stage productions, unlike their filmic counterparts, were consequently confined to a few theaters in the larger cities.

The same was true of the historical and religious spectacles, which were even more dependent on scenic grandeur and realistic detail for their appeal. The big set-pieces advertised in lurid posters drew the crowds; maybe star names would be featured, but nothing much was said about the drama. It was the nineteenth-century stage pro-

Marc Antony's oration in Shakespeare's *Julius Caesar,* as staged by Herbert Beerbohm Tree at The New Theatre, New York City, c. 1903. Performing Arts Research Center, New York Public Library.

ductions of Shakespeare (rather than later films) that established the precedent for removing whole scenes and swatches of dialogue to make way for vast period re-creations. Various stagings of *The Merchant of Venice,* for example (as Vardac quotes from contemporary reviewers), stressed scenes " 'as real as circumstances permit of their being,' " with a " 'succession of striking pictures. . . palaces and prisons, the argosies, gondolas and watery ways, the wealth of marts and frolic mirth of Venice.' "[4] The frolic mirth of Venice indeed! Surely Shakespeare and his tortured Jew would have gotten lost somewhere in this display, and one can think of Shakespearian films that may have been much "stagier." The freest cinematic adaptations of Laurence Olivier and Orson Welles may be positively reverential in comparison.

   Though Vardac's account is informative and suggestive, he tends to exaggerate to prove his thesis. (The book grew out of a Harvard Ph.D. dissertation.) In insisting that film had to be invented at the time it was, that the *Zeitgeist* and demands of those popular theatrical forms called it into being, his argument becomes somewhat mystical in its implications. True, film soon learned to out-chase and out-splendor the theater; and when it did, it took over the popular audience, moving from penny arcades

[4] Vardac, *Stage to Screen,* pp. 94, 95.

and vaudeville houses to converted stores (''nickelodeons'') and later into the empty ''legitimate'' theaters themselves. Every new art has as its content the art that preceded it, Marshall McLuhan observed. (The late nineteenth-century popular theater had itself grown out of the early nineteenth-century popular novel.) But to evoke the motion picture as an artistic form in this way is to minimize the long trail of discovery and invention that led to its technology, and the primarily scientific motivation of those who contributed most to its mechanical possibility.

Also, there was a lag between the actual existence of the motion picture and its adoption of the kinds of theatrical prototypes that Vardac considers. The first films were mere photographic motion recordings of vaudeville acts or views of the everyday world (workers leaving a factory, a train pulling into a station). The slice-of-life record and ''documentary'' thrust of the earliest films was very strong. In the new medium, film makers had to learn to tell stories by using the distinctive limitations of black-and-white, two-dimensional photography and illusory movement. Nothing innate in the motion picture demanded storytelling. On the contrary, the technique of cinematic narrative and the extension of running time to feature length (so that the story could be as significant as one told on the stage) took nearly two decades of accident and experiment before they became pervasive.

FILMS ABOUT THE PERIOD BEFORE 1895

1946

Animated Cartoons: The Toy That Grew Up (France, Roger Leenhardt)—nineteenth-century experiments and toys based on persistence of vision, through Reynaud's Théâtre Optique.

Biography of the Motion Picture Camera (France, Leenhardt)—technological developments from still photography to motion pictures.

BOOKS ON THE PERIOD

BARNOUW, ERIK, *The Magician and the Cinema*. New York: Oxford University Press, 1981. 128 pp.

CERAM, C. W., *Archaeology of the Cinema*. New York: Harcourt, Brace & Co., 1965. 264 pp.

COE, BRIAN, *The History of Movie Photography*. Westfield, N. J.: Eastview Editions, 1981. 176 pp.

COOK, OLIVE, *Movement in Two Dimensions: A Study of the Animated and Projected Pictures which Preceded the Invention of Cinematography*. London: Hutchinson Publishing Group Ltd., 1963. 142 pp.

FELL, JOHN, ed., *Film Before Griffith*. Berkeley: University of California Press, 1983. 352 pp.

HAMMOND, JOHN H., *The Camera Obscura, A Chronicle*. Bristol: Adam Hilger, 1981. 182 pp.

HENDRICKS, GORDON, *Origins of the American Film*. New York: Arno Press, 1972. 592 pp.

HOGBEN, LANCELOT, *From Cave Painting to Comic Strip*. London: Max Parrish & Co. Ltd., 1949. 288 pp.

QUIGLEY, MARTIN, JR., *Magic Shadows: The Story of the Origin of Motion Pictures*. Washington, D.C.: Georgetown University Press, 1948. 191 pp.

RAMSAYE, TERRY, *A Million and One Nights: A History of the Motion Picture*. New York: Simon and Schuster, Inc., 1964. 868 pp. (originally published in 1926)

VARDAC, A. NICHOLAS, *Stage to Screen*. Cambridge: Harvard University Press, 1949. 283 pp.

2

International Childhood of a New Medium and Art, 1895–1914

The motion picture came into being partly as a means for analyzing movement, much as the microscope and telescope had been developed to study visual phenomena inaccessible to the naked eye. The other aspect of its development began with the commercial exploitation of entertaining optical toys and viewing devices that presented a novel illusion of movement.

At first no one considered the storytelling potential of moving pictures, let alone their potential as an art form; but when still pictures began to move, they acquired duration, and the photographer was challenged to deal with that fourth dimension. Temporal organization was demanded in addition to spatial composition. As in the novel, the play, music, or dance, an ordering of events into a beginning, middle, and end was required in even the simplest motion picture.

BRIEF MOTION-PICTURE RECORDS OF ACTUALITY AND OF PERFORMANCES

Initially the moving picture was scarcely more than still photographs extended into motion. The brief duration of the short strips of film demanded little beyond the still photographer's concern that there be an interesting subject appropriately lit and composed.

The early motion picture camera operator sought something that moved, but otherwise the conception was the same. Rather than a fixed instant of Mama and Papa Lumière at breakfast with baby, we see the infant being fed successive spoonfuls of cereal; or we see two trained cats with tiny boxing gloves patting away at each other in a miniature ring, rather than standing in static pose. The novelty of captured motion was intriguing enough at first.

As they chose the actions they would record, film makers soon discovered what painters and still photographers had already known: that some subjects have more intrinsic (or in another sense extrinsic) interest than others. While the motions of knocking down a wall or of a woman feeding chickens satisfied the earliest audiences, such everyday scenes were shortly supplemented by scenes of ships being launched and heads of state addressing large crowds. A strong man flexing his muscles (Edward Sandow) or a sharpshooter rapidly breaking targets thrown into the air ("Little Sure Shot," Annie Oakley) were soon followed by a somewhat more eventful vaudeville skit, *Fun in a Chinese Laundry* (1894), and then by a piece of a popular stage success with Joseph Jefferson, *Rip van Winkle* (1896).

Even with more interesting subjects, however, the film makers' further choices were limited to two: where they set the camera and when they started cranking. They usually chose the ideal position of a human observer—straight in front, at eye level, and far enough back to take in all of the significant action. The length was fixed at half a minute or less.

In offering perfect reproductions of unmanipulated reality, Edison and Lumière succeeded (given the limitations of silence, black-and-white, and two dimensions) as well as anyone has since. The rowboat rounding the pier in early Lumière, or Fatima dancing for the Edison camera, are extraordinarily fresh, revealing the delight the first film makers and audiences must have felt when looking at natural movement in a new way. "It is life itself," one Frenchman is supposed to have exclaimed at a premiere screening; and Lumière's train pulling into the station established at once the definitive way to record such an event—the camera low, stationary, and at an oblique angle.

As stripped to essentials as these primitive films seem, there were seminal differences between the programs of the Grand Café on the Boulevard des Capucines and those at Koster and Bial's Music Hall. These differences suggest, in fact, the two main and divergent aesthetic impulses that have continued up to today, impulses that began in still photography—as Siegfried Kracauer emphasizes in his *Theory of Film: The Redemption of Physical Reality*. One tendency, what Kracauer calls the *formative,* was to strive for the "artistic," to use materials and models from the older arts. Even before the motion picture, certain photographers had begun to pose their subjects, arrange their decor and lights, and manipulate the emulsion in various ways intended to make their photos look more like paintings, less like mere mechanical recordings. The other tendency, the *realistic,* was to take pride in the verisimilitude of photographic reproduction and in its ability to capture and preserve unadulterated actuality of events and views.

Perhaps largely because of the cumbersomeness of his camera, Edison started along the "artistic" way, in that he recorded performances that had been created for the stage or circus ring. The pleasure afforded by a film of this sort depended almost entirely on the quality of the performance. Film merely preserved and made widely available what had been created and offered to the camera. In essence this is the theatrical tradition, characteristic of fiction films in which actors perform roles in scripts that follow the time-honored rules of the earlier forms of storytelling.

Early film taken at the Edison laboratory (U.S. 1890/91, W. K. Laurie Dickson). Museum of Modern Art/Film Stills Archive.

The "realistic" tradition, the documentary impulse, was the more vigorous at first. Louis Lumière, with a portable camera, had no need for a studio or prepared material. He could wander the streets and set up his camera in front of any aspect of observed reality that took his fancy. The large projected image, unlike the image in a peep show, supported the illusion that the viewer was looking out a window (rather than into a room with one wall missing, as on the stage). Another key factor sustaining the illusion was that in Lumière's work the people, animals, and vehicles frequently moved toward and away from the camera, not just laterally in relation to it—as in many Edison films that duplicated stage-bound movement. As a result of his subjects and method, Lumière and his followers have left us a fascinating surface view of what the people and the world they lived in were like at the turn of the century.

Although film as record may not be film as art, these early topical and scenic views pointed to the capacity of film to find or to set its drama within real life. Lumière himself made a kind of fusion of the conceived and the actual, which seems to look way beyond Edison to the nonstudio fiction films of today. In the 1895 *L'Arroseur arrosé* (which means something like "the squirter is squirted") he sets a concocted, vaudeville-like gag outdoors in an actual garden. A gardener is watering the lawn. When a boy steps on the hose, the water stops. The gardner looks into the nozzle to see what the trou-

Workers Leaving the Factory (France, 1895, Louis Lumière). National Film Archive/Stills Library.

ble is. The boy takes his foot off the hose and the gardener is doused. *A Game of Cards* (1896) made a somewhat similar attempt as a visual gag.

Evidently *L'Arroseur* and *A Game of Cards* were flukes, however: what they suggested regarding an acted story in real settings would not be returned to for almost a decade. Instead screens were filled alternately with Lumière-type *actualités* and Edison-like stage attractions, and before the end of the decade both firms were producing both types of films. The films continued to be brief, with single shots from one camera position, and were shown characteristically as part of vaudeville programs. At first they were featured attractions; then, as the novelty began to wear off, they were reduced to the function of "chasers"—shown while one audience was leaving and another was coming into the theater.

It is entirely possible that the art of the motion picture might have died stillborn, along with its capacity for entertainment, if the story ingredient hadn't been added. As with the inventions leading to film technology, the "firsts" in film technique are subject to endless argument, unresolvable because so many of the early films have disappeared. National pride and individual partisanship further affect the writing of film history in this regard. But no one would deny the importance of Georges Méliès's contribution to the advance toward narrative full-length film, even though lesser contributions from his contemporaries must also be acknowledged. One of these was Alice Guy-Blaché, the world's first woman director, who began her career contemporaneously with Méliès when she joined the Gaumont film company in 1896.

TELLING STORIES THROUGH STAGED
AND FILMED PANTOMIME

Unlike other of the earliest film makers, Méliès had a background in the arts, which led him to think of the motion picture in a different way. At the time of the first Lumière showings he operated the Théâtre Robert-Houdin—named in honor of the renowned French magician, who also received homage from the American who called himself Houdini. In Méliès's tiny theater, fantastic sketches and magical acts were performed with the aid of trap doors, mirrors, invisible wires, and all the other trappings of stage illusion. As a magician it was only natural that Méliès would be fascinated by the unprecedented apparitions offered with such seeming ease by the motion picture. Immediately after seeing the first Lumière program in the small café near his theater, he asked the brothers Lumière to sell him one of their camera-projectors. They refused, adding that Méliès would eventually thank them for saving him from a folly certain to be extravagant once the novelty lost public interest. Undeterred, Méliès obtained apparatus from the English pioneer Robert Paul, assembled a machine, and soon was, like the Lumières, out on the streets photographing.

In April 1896 (the month the Vitascope opened in New York) Méliès began showing movies at the Théâtre Robert-Houdin. His brief skits and slices of life on the street were evidently quite indistinguishable from those of others. But according to Méliès's later account, it was during that first year as a film maker that he discovered quite by accident what would make his contribution most distinctive: the capacity of the motion picture to move beyond the real into the fantastic. One day, while photographing in the Place de L'Opéra, the film jammed. When he succeeded in getting the camera functioning again, he indifferently cranked the film on through. Fortunately, he developed it to see if any of the footage would be usable. When projected, the film offered a succession of images that would have brought instant joy to the heart of any conjurer: a horse-drawn tram on the street suddenly metamorphosed into a hearse. What had happened, of course, was that the tram was passing in front of the camera when Méliès had first started cranking; by the time the film had gotten stuck and unstuck the tram had passed on and been followed by a funeral cortege.

Méliès took deliberate advantage of this accidental discovery in *The Vanishing Lady* and *The Haunted Castle* (both in 1896), starting an early genre of "trick films." Within the next few years he mastered most of the technical means for what today are called "special effects." Using fades and dissolves, superimpositions and mattes, fast and slow motion, animation and miniatures, and even hand coloring of each frame, he created a delightful phantasmagoric world. Though he had many imitators, it was years later before film makers were able to figure out how some of his remarkable results had been achieved.

In addition to introducing trickery, Méliès also made the most important beginning steps in the screen narrative techniques and helped increase the standard running time from less than a minute to ten to fifteen minutes—one reel. In 1897 he built France's first permanent film studio and founded Star Film Company, the first French firm devoted exclusively to making movies. By 1912 he had produced over five hundred films of various types, but is best remembered for his fairy tales (beginning with *Cinderella* in 1900) and for a special kind of fantastical science fiction (such as *An Impossible Voyage*, 1904; *The Conquest of the Pole*, 1912). Of the latter genre *A Trip to the Moon* (1902) is generally regarded as the master work; its enduring charm of conception and ingenuity of execution are easily appreciated today. It is one of the few early fiction films that modern audiences laugh with rather than at. This man of the theater brought to film an innate taste for eccentric humor and a developed sophistication of visual embellishment.

A Trip to the Moon is vaguely based upon but also parodies a Jules Verne story; it lampoons scientific presumptions of the day as well. In making the film, an unprecedented thirty separate scenes were acted out by a sizeable professional cast (including Méliès himself as the chief scientist) on the stage of his specially constructed glass-enclosed studio. Each scene was taken with an unbroken run of a stationary camera placed in an ideal position for viewing the whole—twelfth row center, as it were. The performers fully, not to say exaggeratedly, pantomime the action (there were no titles yet), move laterally across the stage, make entrances and exits (who was to know they didn't have to in this new medium?), and occasionally bow and gesticulate directly towards the audience. The decor consists of painted canvas backdrops and highly stylized constructions and props; the robes and conical hats of the scientists, the shorts of the chorus-line guard of honor, and the devil suits of the moon men are all out of theater rather than life. Some of the trick effects are created by cinematic means; for example, the scenes are joined by dissolves in place of opening and closing curtains. Other effects are achieved by such stage devices as scenery flats that are raised and lowered, trap doors, pulleys, and the like. What appears to be a dolly shot as the rocket ship approaches the moon (and lands right in the eye of its papier-mâché face) was achieved by moving the moon toward the camera rather than the camera toward the moon. In an-

A Trip to the Moon (France, 1902, Georges Méliès). National Film Archive/Stills Library.

other shot, a matted drawing of the rocket enters an incongruously real ocean, proceeds down into an animated rendering of undersea life, then surfaces.

Méliès's marvelous contributions and ultimate limitations, in terms of film, are all clearly evident in *A Trip to the Moon*. He did manage to tell a complete story of many incidents in a coherent fashion; script, staging, and performances are carefully controlled to achieve a satisfying whole. The advance of what Méliès himself proudly called ''artificially arranged scenes'' over the single, undirected, and casually planned fragments which preceded him can only be admired. Where he stopped short, however, was in confining his camera to an uninterrupted view, making the photographic frame equivalent to the proscenium arch. Granting his intention ''to push the cinema toward the theatrical way,'' we can say that he succeeded almost too well. Though he achieved a theatrical sophistication of content and style, he failed to discover what the unique tools of the motion picture—camera and cutting shears—were capable of. We would hate to be without those creations of his that remain (hundreds of them no longer exist). But once Méliès had established larger ambitions for storytelling in film, it remained for others to make further contributions by using methods unique to the new medium.

One other aspect of Méliès's importance should be acknowledged before we leave him. With his trick films he established the basis for what would become the avant-garde tradition, which began in France in the 1920s and has continued down to today in the experimental/underground/independent film.

It is possible to say, then, that the three main artistic modes of film were present in embryo form from near the outset: narrative fiction, documentary, experimental. The first represented a desire to tell stories with the new and increasingly rich effectiveness of moving pictures. The second had as its intention capturing the real world in a way that would help us to know and understand it more fully. The third creative impulse would lead beyond physical reality to humorous imaginings or frightful hallucinations, to the terrain of dream and the subconscious. The documentary and experimental possibilities were scarcely explored in the first decades of screen history; they did not evolve into mature forms until the early twenties, when they did so with curious simultaneity. Though given their proper value by the cognoscenti, the documentary and experimental modes have never been as widely popular as the fiction film. It was storytelling that first attracted a loyal audience and built an economic base, and the art continued to move along fictional lines.

TELLING STORIES THROUGH FILMIC MEANS

Edwin S. Porter, an American who began film work in 1896, was much less well equipped in artistic background or sensibility than Méliès. In the history of the motion picture, a lack of experience with the traditional arts has frequently proved an advantage, artistically as well as commercially. In a medium seeking its own way, vigor and vulgarity have often stimulated rather than inhibited valuable innovation. A film maker without preconceptions about the nature of artistic function and form is free to try anything. By his own admission Porter was more mechanic than artist. In choosing a career he had considered both the horseless carriage and the ''flickers,'' coincidental new engineering fields carrying unknown potential of industrial expansion and cultural influence. At the time Porter was hired by Edison, in 1900, film makers were first of all camera operators, valued more for their technical ingenuity to keep the camera operating properly than for their creative imagination. Unconscious genius though he may have been, Porter made the next and crucial step—through primitive and tentative editing—that set film on its main road of advance.

One of the favorite subjects for the early actuality film makers was horse-drawn fire engines rushing to a fire. It may have been commercial expediency that led Porter to use this available and conventional material in a new way, to ''re-tread'' what we would now call stock footage by adding some specially staged bits of action. At any rate, in late 1902 and early 1903 Porter made *Life of an American Fireman,* which raised the possibility of connecting different parts of a total action, all seeming to be happening at the same time but in various places. These segments were edited together in a more complex relationship than existed among Méliès's long, unbroken takes proceeding in strict chronological succession.

By employing a double line of action, Porter was forced into cutting from one setting to another, thus demonstrating for the first time that a film scene didn't have to be played through in its entirety before being followed by another (as is the usual practice in theater). Instead the scene could be left—while its action was still in progress—to go to the next, related scene. Given the greater mobility of film over theater, it is much easier to bring performers from one scene into another, thus joining the parallel lines of action. Furthermore, in Porter's scenes filmed at quite different times and places, the staged and the actual are intermingled to create a synthetic whole that never existed in real space or time. Editing, which appears in rudimentary form for the first time in Porter's films, was a potentiality that would excite the Soviet proponents of *montage* some twenty years later. Through Porter, film became simply but profoundly a new artistic entity rather than a reproduction of another art.

The opening scene of *Life of an American Fireman* is of a fire chief who has fallen asleep in his office and is dreaming (in superimposition) of a mother and baby trapped by fire in a bedroom. The next scene, very brief, is a closeup (perhaps the first, and what would later be called an insert) of a fire alarm box. A hand (and part of a body) enters the frame to send an alarm. The third scene (which begins the stock footage) is of the firemen asleep in their fire station. They leap from their beds, presumably as the alarm is sounded. Note the narrative linkage that Porter has managed to imply with these three separate shots. The fire chief dreaming of a woman and child in danger foreshadows what we will see, economically evoking the tension and responsibilities of his job. At that very moment, we feel, someone has observed such a fire. The alarm turned in goes to the firehouse and awakens the firemen.

This apparently interconnected and simultaneous action is followed by more stock footage: interiors of the firemen sliding down the pole, hitching up their apparatus, and starting off; then, the exterior of an engine house as fire wagons come out; next, a splendid shot (from a moving vehicle) of horses galloping down a wide street with men and equipment. Now there appears what must have been a specially taken shot: A fire engine enters the frame, and the camera pans with it to reveal the house that is on fire. This is followed by a studio interior of the bedroom with mother and child amidst (rather unconvincing) wisps of smoke. There is some question about the extent of the cutting which follows—from firemen on the exterior to victims in the interior, brought together as a fireman rescues first the unconscious mother and then the child. Even if the original strips of exterior and interior were not as fully intercut as in one (possibly re-edited) version that has come down to us, Porter clearly demonstrated a grasp of the cinematic principle of simultaneous parallel lines of action by connectively cutting them together.

Life of an American Fireman (U.S., 1903, Edwin S. Porter). Museum of Modern Art/Film Stills Archive.

Porter's most famous film, *The Great Train Robbery* (1903), also exists in two versions with different amounts of cross-cutting. But even the simpler version represents a substantial advance over *Life of an American Fireman* and everything else that had gone before. It is a remarkable achievement, containing virtually all of the elements that might be needed for a super-Western released tomorrow, and it warrants repeated study. Unlike *Life of an American Fireman,* all of *The Great Train Robbery* was specially shot for the film, exteriors "on location," interiors in the studio. Though using "artificially arranged scenes," Porter dealt with a topical subject much in the headlines and built from realistic materials. In this respect his work was very different from Méliès's stylized theatricality; Méliès offered the first filmed fantasies, but realism became the main artistic style of the fiction film.

The plot of *The Great Train Robbery* progresses in three lines with three principal sets of characters. The first scene is in a railway telegraph office. Bandits enter and force the telegrapher to order the approaching train to stop there for water. After binding and gagging him, the bandits leave. In scene two the desperadoes hide behind the water tank, then sneak aboard the train as it departs. Scene three takes place in the interior of the express car, which the bandits enter and rob. Scene four shows them commandeering the locomotive and forcing the engineer to stop the train. In scene five the engineer is made to uncouple the locomotive, pull ahead, and stop again. Scene six furthers the course of the robbery as the passengers empty out of the train, line up while the bandits collect all their valuables, and then depart. The robbers board the locomotive in scene seven, and it moves off. In scene eight the locomotive comes to a halt and the bandits run off into the countryside. Scene nine shows them moving down a hill and across a stream to mount their waiting horses. Back in the telegraph office, scene ten, the telegrapher's daughter enters and frees her father, who then rushes out. In a dance hall, scene eleven, we see a number of couples square dancing; the telegraph operator staggers in; the men grab their rifles and leave. In scene twelve the robbers, and then the posse in pursuit, gallop by the camera. In the thirteenth and final scene the bandits, thinking they have escaped their pursuers, are inspecting their loot; the posse surrounds them, and shoots them all down. The famous epilogue, a medium closeup of one of the bandits firing directly at the camera, had no narrative function (as did the alarm box closeup in *Life of an American Fireman*); it was added simply to startle. In fact, the Edison catalogue of 1904 suggests that this scene "can be used to begin or end the picture."

Notice how neatly the thirteen scenes dovetail into each other. The bandits enter the telegrapher's life, and then we follow them for the robbery and escape that constitute the bulk of the picture. The dance hall is introduced without explanation, Porter evidently counting on our being patient for a moment until the telegrapher arrives—thus bringing the dance hall men into the story and leading to the final dramatic action, the gunning down of the bandits.

The film's structure and characterization are so basically sound that one can easily imagine how its twelve minutes might be further expanded to ninety. The telegrapher would be a widower, let's say, whose daughter badly wants him to marry the local schoolteacher so she can have a new mother, and so her father won't be so lonely. The Eastern dude who has his heels shot at in the dance hall is really a fearless secret service agent whose job it is to track down train robbers. There is also the possibility of preceding events that may have led the gang's leader into a life of crime. The sturdy bones are all there; only flesh would be needed to give that first western large and full life today.

Note also how time and space are dealt with. Between most scenes brief or longer ellipses are suggested, and the order is straight succession as in *A Trip to the Moon*. When we cut from the mounted bandits back to the telegraph office, however, a reversal in time seems implied—since the bandits are still in the vicinity for the posse to catch them. There are instances of implicit simultaneity as well: In the beginning of scene three, in the express car, the bandits are evidently approaching as we watch the expressman's actions; or, at the start of scene eleven, in the dance hall, the telegraph operator is presumably on the way from his office as we see the dancing.

Each scene is still one continuous take—scene equals shot. Porter does not cut to varying distances or angles within scenes: The camera remains resolutely at eye level in long shot. But there are some interesting beginnings of camera variety, most likely forced on Porter by the exigencies of location shooting. First of all, in photographing the action of the robbers on the topside of a train in motion, a sort of moving camera results; the camera itself is stationary but the scenery passes by. Second, with what I suspect is half the population of West Orange lined up alongside the train, Porter probably couldn't get straight back far enough to include them all in the frame; and the side of the roadbed no doubt sloped down to a ditch. So he may have been required to move up the track for that effective oblique angle emphasized by the man who runs toward the camera to do a little dance of death at closer range. Finally, if horsemen are going to ride down a bluff and then left in front of the camera, the choice is either to pan and tilt with them or to let them leave the frame. Though Porter's camera moves most hesitantly, the hesitation would be caused partly by a tripod head not constructed to accommodate such movement properly. It is possible also that he thought the odd angle and movement regrettable deviations from prevailing propriety rather than positive assets.

To us, if not to Porter, the conventionally painted canvas interiors mix poorly with the fine outdoor settings; they seem part of another and less innovative film. Looking back over the history of cinema we can find many valuable additions to technique forced on film makers by the requirements of nonstudio shooting. In the studio everything can be constructed and adjusted for the convenience of the camera; outside, the film maker must adapt to the world as is. With *The Great Train Robbery* it is the exteriors that are inventive in composition, depth, and movement; the interiors are conventionally horizontal and unimaginative. Learning comes from the kind of improvisation demanded by the unanticipated.

This simplified account of the evolution of narrative film technique of necessity excludes other Porter films as well as hundreds of film makers and thousands of films that contained some of the same accidents and discoveries. These early films seem to evince a conscious pursuit of what would become standard narrative technique, but the motivation of the film makers at the time and what audiences were responding to may have been something quite different. Film historians are going back to the evidence of the films that still exist to try to better understand those original purposes. It seems evi-

The Great Train Robbery (U.S., 1903, Edwin S. Porter). Museum of Modern Art/Film Stills Archive.

dent, however, that Porter did not carry his remarkable discoveries much further than in the two seminal films discussed above; in fact, he seems not to have been altogether clear what it was he had achieved. In the time between them he made a most uninspired bit of recorded theater in *Uncle Tom's Cabin.* After *The Great Train Robbery* he frequently lapsed into earlier and less interesting modes, and never surpassed that 1903 achievement. Even the seductively entitled and brilliantly ingenious *The Dream of a Rarebit Fiend* (1906) was a frank imitation of Méliès.

It was a group of English film makers, the "Brighton School" (subsequently rediscovered by the French film historian Georges Sadoul), who first refined Porter's discoveries. It could even be that they had provided inspiration for some of his most impressive achievements, most notably through the films of George Albert Smith and James A. Williamson. Robert Paul's *Plucked from the Burning* (c. 1898) and Williamson's *Fire!* (1901) may have been precedents for *Life of an American Fireman,* as *The Robbery of the Mail Coach* (1903) may have been for *The Great Train Robbery.* Of the Brighton School work succeeding Porter's two landmark films, Cecil Hepworth's *Rescued by Rover* (1905) was perhaps the most successful example. The care in the editing and the inventiveness of the exterior camera work, with movement angled toward and away from the camera, evidence full understanding of the new film principles involved. The use of a low angle and the presence of smooth panning are quite unprecedented. An improbable and not very interesting story, however, together with tedious repetition of the dog Rover's journeys, make it seem more of a thorough exercise in screen direction (lateral movement within the frame) and matching action (from shot to shot) than a signpost to the future.

The man who would most effectively take over leadership from Porter, and whom Porter himself regarded with deference, was another American, David Wark Griffith. Griffith's introduction to film was in Porter's *Rescued from an Eagle's Nest* (1907); he played the father hero, calling himself Lawrence Griffith to keep his real name unsullied for anticipated fame as a playwright. Lack of success in the theater (as a dramatist he had only one play produced, and that unsuccessfully) kept Griffith tied to the movies. While acting in them for five dollars a day he learned that he could earn an

Rescued by Rover (U.K., 1905, Cecil Hepworth). Museum of Modern Art/Film Stills Archive.

additional ten to fifteen dollars apiece for story ideas. In 1908 he directed his first film, *The Adventures of Dollie.*

In a remarkably short time Griffith mastered what there was to know about the new medium and progressed beyond his contemporaries. Working with characteristically prodigious energy, his output of short films, the prevailing form, advanced virtually all aspects of technique. The one- and two-reelers contained experiments or refinements that carried forward the rudiments established by Porter; and by the time of Griffith's monumental feature *The Birth of a Nation* in 1915, the whole syntax of silent film had been laid out for use. The essential nature of Griffith's contributions can best be appreciated by comparing his work with the film making that preceded him. The extent to which Porter, the Brighton School, and others were able to develop the narrative aspects of cinematic expression was severely limited. Every development since Griffith had its origins in him, that most modern of film makers Jean-Luc Godard once said. Whether Godard's statement is hyperbolic or not, it is unquestionable that Griffith contributed more to the evolution of film as an art form than any other individual in its history to date.

THE LANGUAGE OF FILM

Perhaps Griffith's single most important insight was that the shot rather than the scene should be the basic unit of film language. With that discovery came the possibility of varying the standard, stationary, head-on long shot. Gradually Griffith moved his

David Wark Griffith directing. Culver Pictures, Inc.

camera to setups closer to the action or farther away, altered its angle for the most effective view, let it follow a moving subject when appropriate or traverse a stationary scene for certain kinds of kinetic emphasis. These varied shots were then edited together to create the appearance of a continuous scene selectively viewed. Once understood, these options gave the film maker immeasurably greater control over the audience's emotional response, adding powerful connotations to the action itself. Méliès's framing, in unvaried long shot, had been emotionally neutral. Though Porter had begun to break away from fixed convention (and the deliberateness of his intentions is less than certain), the exceptions did not upset established rules even in his own films.

It was Griffith more than anyone who came to understand the separate psychological-aesthetic functions of the long shot, the medium shot, and the closeup, and who used this awareness consistently. In Griffith's work, and in that of his successors, the *long shot* usually begins a scene, establishing the action and its setting. It might be used to "reestablish," after closer and partial views, so that the parts could be kept related to the whole. Full of information—one could go on and on describing all the things seen in it—it is emotionally cool: We are literally distanced from the action. As the camera is placed closer, or a longer lens is used to achieve much the same effect, there are fewer things included within the frame, but we tend to be more interested in them, are closer to them emotionally as well as perceptually. The *medium shot* rather than the long shot became the standard framing from which the director departs for special purposes, just as we usually deal with life around us from middle distance. In it we are close enough to see and comprehend what is happening and what it means. Generally the stress of the medium shot is on relationships, on interaction: a person in conversation with another, or petting an animal, or cooking at a stove. When the camera is moved closer still, to a *closeup,* the visual information becomes quite limited—perhaps to one face, a hand stroking fur, a pot boiling over—but the emotional weight becomes very heavy. Our attention is directed to what we might not have noticed otherwise or might not have been able to discern at a distance. The closeup can also be used to draw us into strong identification with a character, and to suggest through facial expression what is being thought and felt. It is a freed visual statement that permits directors to show us exactly—and only—what they want us to know in the way they want us to perceive it.

Griffith called closeups "inserts," and he shot them after the scene had been filmed in long and medium shots. This frequently shifting point of view, especially to the closeup, offered a means of expression comparable to the use of spoken words in the theater. Though the stage director can block and light action in a way designed to lead our eye, we are still free to regard the whole proscenium—no more, no less—from one fixed position. Broad gestures and conspicuous props and symbolic settings may be employed, but most of what we learn comes from what the characters say to each other. Lacking the power of spoken words, Griffith substituted a kind of visual language with its own conventions and limitations. Though never as intellectually precise as words, the affective use of images can cause us to feel directly and deeply in a manner both unique and compelling.

Alternation of tempo through the editing of detached shots is something that Griffith came to understand from intuition and experiment, and that Porter understood not at all. Though Porter shifted from one scene to another, he did not break up the run of the camera within scenes. The pursuit of the bandits by the posse in *The Great Train Robbery* remains one of the slowest chases in memory as the first party of horsemen, and then the second, enters and passes through the frame. Griffith might extend actual time, as he would cut back and forth from shots of bandits to shots of a posse, building to a rhythmic climax; yet his chases (honored as "the Griffith last-minute rescue") seem incredibly more tense—and even faster. What he discovered, other film makers have learned and used since: Rapid cutting, or a succession of short shots, can create excitement; slow cutting, or shots held longer on the screen, will aid calm contemplation. Both the shifting spatial framing and the temporal alternation of shots give the film maker artistic resources extending well beyond the bare meaning of the action being recorded.

For transitions between shots, Griffith used a larger range of optical effects than is generally employed today, and gave each effect a consistently specific function. The *cut* is basic within scenes; virtually unnoticed in itself, it is necessary for the variable ordering and pacing of the action. The *dissolve* is a more noticeable transition in which one image is gradually superimposed over, and then replaces, the other. As in early Méliès, it is usually used between scenes rather than within them, and signals a change of place and/or time. When one image *fades out* to darkness and a new image *fades in* to full exposure, a different place and lapse in time are usually being signaled also. (Griffith tended to favor fades over dissolves.) As the "heaviest" screen "punctuation," the only one in which the audience is given nothing to look at for a few seconds, fade-outs frequently indicate a larger break in the dramatic action as well, marking off groups of scenes that are called *sequences* by some critics. (Other writers and many film makers use *shot* and *scene* synonymously and *sequence* for what is here being called *scene,* leaving no term for a larger dramatic/narrative unit short of the entire film.)

Griffith also liked *irises* as connective devices. An iris begins with a black screen containing only a small circle (or square or other shaped portion) of the total image: a girl's bowed head, for example. Then as the iris opens up it reveals the whole action and setting: a family standing over the girl at the dinner table in a farm kitchen. When the scene has run its course, with the girl explaining how she had been orphaned and had come in desperation to these old friends of her parents, the final shot might iris out; within the contracting circle of black we see the girl's smiling, upturned face as she learns that the family will let her stay.

Griffith employed *masking* in several different ways: the sides of the frame darkened to emphasize the height of a tower in the center; tops and bottoms darkened to form a CinemaScope-proportioned strip across the middle, stressing the horizontal movement and length of a column of galloping cavalry; or a cameo masking of the corners, to enhance the oval loveliness of Lillian Gish's face. He also experimented with *superimposition* and *split screen* for special effects—for the longing daydream in *Enoch Arden* (1911), or to make the awareness of burning Atlanta hang over the foreground of people fleeing in *The Birth of a Nation* (1915).

Griffith did not by any means confine his attention to the "grammatical" elements of screen language. Though of the theater, as Porter was not, Griffith soon began to sense that performance in film required a style quite different from that in fashion on the stage. If spoken words were lacking, the eloquence of body movement and gesture was magnified; in the new medium the camera registered and the projector projected. Actors on the screen appeared large, their every movement easily discernible from the back rows; as the camera came closer to them, its photographic authenticity rendered as false the prevailing theatrical histrionics. Griffith began to confine movement, dress, and makeup to an approximation of life; any exaggeration was kept small in scale and justified by character. Pantomime became more and more expressly tailored for the camera—the sad smile with only the face visible, the upper part of a body with hands plucking and fluttering in nervous excitement, the eyes revealing remorse or anger or frustrated passion. Richer and subtler characterizations began to replace the broad and simple performances of the first dramatic films. Faces and bodies, cut up and reassembled in edited sequence, were made to achieve a new precision of expression. Griffith commanded a thoughtfulness and invention from the actors in his developing stock company; with camera and cutting shears he shaped their performances into a dramatic entity that had existed initially only in his mind.

As for physical background to the action, Griffith's exterior locales were always carefully selected for their appropriateness to the events depicted and for their capacity to reinforce the mood of the story. Constructed sets in his films strike us as the real thing even when they're not; the style is invariably naturalistic in solidity and detail. What he couldn't find on location he had carefully and fully re-created on the back lot or in the studio. He worked within the tradition of Belasco—for whom, as much as he sought it, the stage could never offer quite the same verisimilitude. Griffith, too, was able to achieve a scale that had no theatrical precedents: real trains rushing across a wide prairie, enemy hordes encircling a besieged city. His lighting initially advanced along existing stage lines and then, as brighter lights and more sensitive emulsions became available, finally surpassed theatrical possibility. At first he and cameraman G. W. "Billy" Bitzer were content to light the scenes with sharp, even clarity, using controlled sunlight for interiors as well as exteriors—standard practice at the time; yet photographically the earliest Griffith/Bitzer films stand out from those of most of their peers, as they somehow manage to look fresh and sharp even today. In addition to exact exposure and focus, this quality must have something to do with choice of emulsion and care in processing. In later work Griffith began to experiment with the effective possibilities of modulated and directional artificial light, breaking some taboos in the process. An interior night scene might be lit as if suffused by the flickering softness of the firelight, underexposed by standards then current, or what is called "low-key lighting" today. In another scene the heroine's head might be lit from behind by simulated morning light streaming in through a window so that it bounced off her blonde hair to form a halo of overexposure, "halation" in photographic terms. Some of these experiments would be expanded and refined by the Germans in the twenties, just as the Russians would further develop Griffith's editing.

Finally, Griffith was one of the leaders in the movement against the short length of films imposed by the American industry of the day. With few exceptions, the dominant companies were conservative in their adherence to established practice and their unwillingness to risk the capital that longer films would have required. At first Griffith was confined to the one-reel (ten to fifteen minutes) standard that Méliès and Porter had achieved. As film makers became more aware of the potential of the medium, they became increasingly ambitious in terms of subject matter. Larger subjects demanded more running time. In 1910 Griffith made a two-reeler entitled *His Trust,* which the studio released as two separate one-reel films. The same thing happened to his next two-reeler, *Enoch Arden,* but Griffith and others persisted until two reels became accepted as standard length. He continued to strive for more time and larger scale, and by the end of this first period of film history, he had reached a length of four reels, with *Judith of Bethulia* (1914). It was his last important film before *The Birth of a Nation,* and in narrative structure and historical spectacle it foreshadowed his even larger feature, *Intolerance.*

INCREASING FILMS TO FEATURE LENGTH

In reaching feature length, Griffith had been passed by the French and the Italians. Free from the stringent limitation on running time imposed by the American industry, the Europeans had begun to exploit subjects that led them naturally to films of an hour and more. Available to French film makers was a long and uniquely distinguished theatrical tradition. From as early as 1908 they began to turn out film versions of successful plays starring well-known players. A company called Film d'Art was the first in the field, bestowing its name on the entire shortlived subgenre. In most respects the idea was retrogressive, extending backward to Méliès, who had wanted to "push the cinema toward the theatrical way," and even to Edison, who had earlier recorded bits of popular theater. The principal difference of the *films d'art* was that the extreme deference paid to the older medium, however perverse, meant that whole plays rather than fragments were recorded exactly as performed. Titles were abridged substitutions for the unheard dialogue the actors mouthed. Except for the new length required, it was back to the camera in twelfth row center, the scene recorded in one shot, the theatrical sets and gestures. These films did attract a certain following, however, especially among the middle class who knew or thought they ought to know the theater; and the somewhat snobbish appeal and contemporary prestige helped to drag films as a whole toward greater length.

The most consequential of the series was *Queen Elizabeth* (1912), directed by

Queen Elizabeth (France, 1912, Louis Mercanton and Henri Desfontaines). National Film Archive/Stills Library.

Louis Mercanton and starring Sarah Bernhardt and Lou Tellegen (her leading man off-stage as well as on). The divine Sarah, though sixty-eight at the time, still commanded an international audience. Unlike many theatrical artists, she seems to have been extremely interested in film. She is supposed to have said, ''I rely on these films to make me immortal.'' Alas, for Bernhardt and for us, much of her divinity must have resided in her reputedly remarkable voice and oral interpretation. What remains in *Queen Elizabeth* now seems more nearly a cruel travesty of a great talent and an exhumation of dead theatrical convention. Such problems only vaguely troubled contemporary observers however. The film was acquired for distribution in the United States by the young Adolph Zukor and played with substantial and prophetic success in converted ''legitimate'' theaters at the unheard of price of one dollar a ticket. It provided the first capital as well as the precedent for Zukor's Famous Players Company, which eventually became Paramount Pictures.

Though *Queen Elizabeth* opened up the possibility for successful American distribution and exhibition of feature films, it was the Italians who contributed more importantly to the form that features would take—along lines close to those Griffith had begun to explore in miniature. The inclination of the Italians was toward historical and religious spectacle set in their own glorious past. The first of these, *The Last Days of Pompeii,* was produced in 1908, the same year as the first of the films d'art, *The Assassination of the*

Cabiria (Italy, 1914, Giovanni Pastrone). Museum of Modern Art/Film Stills Archive.

Duc de Guise. The Fall of Troy (1910) and *Dante's Inferno* (1911), at five reels in length, continued the trend. A static and dully literal illustration of the epic poem, the *Inferno* was followed by *Quo Vadis?* (1912), at nine reels. Both were road-shown in the U.S., the latter even more successfully than *Queen Elizabeth*. Noteworthy among the like films were another *Last Days of Pompeii* (1913) and *Cabiria* (1914). Of the early Italian spectacles perhaps only *Cabiria* (twelve reels), a worldwide success at the time, is of more than historical interest today. From a script credited to Gabriele D'Annunzio and directed by Giovanni Pastrone, it is placed in the Punic Wars. The plot centers around Hannibal's crossing of the Alps and the siege of Syracuse. Vast sets were employed as well as plaster models. The action is directed and shot with an unusual amount of energy and movement, and an appropriate symphonic score was specially composed. Like its predecessor *Quo Vadis?, Cabiria* had a definite influence on American production.

    Massive in all respects, these extravaganzas not only established feature length, but they demonstrated film's superior claim over the theater to this kind of spectacle and laid down patterns that would be followed by Griffith, De Mille, and all those who have subsequently worked in the genre. They also for the first time moved the movies out of the nickelodeons and converted stores into large theaters and auditoriums, where they were often accompanied by full orchestra. The Italian lead was lost only with the outbreak of World War I.

    During its first two decades the motion picture had advanced from vaudeville turns and brief cinematographic records of life on the street to short film narratives using the rudimentary grammar of the medium. By the end of this period the length of films had increased until precedent had been established for the feature's running over an hour, which would become the staple form around which the art and the industry further developed. The subsequent consolidation of these early advances and the move towards an expanded future initially occurred mainly in the United States.

FILMS OF THE PERIOD

1894
Fun in a Chinese Laundry
  (U.S., Edison Company)

1895
The Arrival of a Train at the Station
  (France, Louis Lumière)
L'Arroseur arrosé (France, Lumière)
The Execution of Mary, Queen of Scots
  (U.S., Edison)
Feeding the Baby (France, Lumiére)
Workers Leaving the Factory
  (France, Lumière)

1896
A Game of Cards (France, Lumière)
The Kiss (U.S., Edison, starring
  May Irwin and John C. Rice)
The Vanishing Lady (France,
  Georges Méliès)

1899
The Dreyfus Affair (France, Méliès)

1900
Attack on a China Mission (U.K.,
  James A. Williamson)
Cinderella (France, Méliès)
Grandma's Reading Glass (U.K.,
  George Albert Smith)

1901
Story of a Crime (France, Ferdinand
  Zecca)

1902
A Trip to the Moon (France, Méliès)

1903
The Great Train Robbery (U.S.,
  Edwin S. Porter)
Life of an American Fireman
  (U.S., Porter)

1904

An Impossible Voyage
    (France, Méliès)

1905

Rescued by Rover   (U.K.,
    Cecil Hepworth)

1906

The Dream of a Rarebit Fiend   (U.S.,
    Porter)

1907

Ben-Hur   (U.S., Sidney Olcott)
Rescued from an Eagle's Nest   (U.S.,
    Porter)

1908

The Adventures of Dollie
    (U.S., David Wark Griffith)
The Assassination of the Duc de Guise
    (France, Charles de Bargy)
The Last Days of Pompeii
    (Italy, Luigi Maggi)

1909

The Joyous Microbes
    (France, Emile Cohl)
The Lonely Villa   (U.S., Griffith)

1911

The Lonedale Operator
    (U.S., Griffith)

1912

The Conquest of the Pole
    (France, Méliès)
The Musketeers of Pig Alley
    (U.S., Griffith)
The New York Hat   (U.S., Griffith)
Queen Elizabeth   (France, Louis
    Mercanton)
Quo Vadis?   (Italy, Enrico Guazzoni)

1914

Antony and Cleopatra   (Italy, Guazzoni)
Cabiria   (Italy, Giovanni Pastrone)

BOOKS ON THE PERIOD

France

ARMES, ROY,   *French Film.* New York: E. P. Dutton & Company, Inc., 1970. 160 pp.
SADOUL, GEORGES,   *French Film.* New York: Arno Press, 1972. 130 pp. (originally published in
    1953)

Great Britain

ARMES, ROY,   *A Critical History of British Cinema.* New York: Oxford University Press, 1978.
    374 pp.
BARNES, JOHN,   *The Beginnings of the Cinema in England.* New York: Barnes & Noble Books, 1976.
BETTS, ERNEST,   *The Film Business: A History of British Cinema, 1896–1972.* London: George Allen
    and Unwin Ltd., 1973. 349 pp.
BUTLER, IVAN,   *Cinema in Britain: An Illustrated Survey.* South Brunswick, N. J.: A. S. Barnes,
    1973. 307 pp.
CHANAN, MICHAEL,   *The Dream that Kicks: The Prehistory and Early Years of Cinema in Britain.* Lon-
    don: Routledge & Kegan Paul, Ltd., 1980.
CURRAN, JAMES, and VINCENT PORTER, eds.,   *British Cinema History.* Totowa, N. J.: Barnes &
    Noble Books, 1983. 320 pp.
LOW, RACHAEL, and ROGER MANVELL,   *The History of the British Film, 1896–1906.* London:
    George Allen and Unwin, Ltd., 1948. 136 pp.
LOW, RACHAEL.   *The History of the British Film, 1906–1914.* London: George Allen and Unwin,
    Ltd., 1949. 309 pp.

OAKLEY, C. A., *Where We Came In: Seventy Years of the British Film Industry.* London: George Allen and Unwin, Ltd., 1964. 245 pp.

PERRY, GEORGE, *The Great British Picture Show from the 90s to the 70s.* New York: Hill & Wang, Inc., 1974. 367 pp.

Italy

JARRATT, VERNON, *The Italian Cinema.* New York: Arno Press, 1972. 115 pp. (originally published in 1951)

MALERBA, LUIGI, and CARMINE SINISCALO, eds., *Fifty Years of Italian Cinema.* Rome: Carlo Bestetti, Edizioni d'Arte, 1954. 208 pp.

LEPROHON, PIERRE, *The Italian Cinema.* New York: Praeger Publishers, 1972. 256 pp.

United States

BALIO, TINO, ed., *The American Film Industry.* Madison: University of Wisconsin Press, 1976. 499 pp.

BLUM, DANIEL, *A Pictorial History of the Silent Screen.* New York: G. P. Putnam's Sons, 1982.

EVERSON, WILLIAM K., *The American Movie.* New York: Atheneum Publishers, 1963. 149 pp.

EVERSON, WILLIAM K., *American Silent Film.* New York; Oxford University Press, 1978. 387 pp.

FELL, JOHN, *Film Before Griffith.* Berkeley: University of California Press, 1983. 352 pp.

GRIFFITH, RICHARD, ARTHUR MAYER, and EILEEN BOWSER, *The Movies.* New York: Simon and Schuster, Inc., 1981.

HAMPTON, BENJAMIN B., *A History of the American Film Industry from its Beginnings to 1931.* New York: Dover Publications, Inc., 1970. 456 pp. (originally published in 1931 as *A History of the Movies*)

HENDRICKS, GORDON, *Origins of the American Film.* New York: Arno Press, 1972. 592 pp.

HIGHAM, CHARLES, *The Art of the American Film, 1900–1971.* Garden City, N. Y.: Doubleday & Co., Inc., 1973. 322 pp.

JACOBS, LEWIS, *The Rise of the American Film: A Critical History.* New York: Teachers College Press, Columbia University, 1968. 631 pp. (originally published in 1939)

JOBES, GERTRUDE, *Motion Picture Empire.* Hamden, Conn.: Archon Books, 1966. 398 pp.

KINDEM, GORHAM, ed., *The American Movie Industry: The Business of Motion Pictures.* Carbondale and Edwardsville: Southern Illinois University Press, 1982. 448 pp.

NORTH, JOSEPH H., *The Early Development of the Motion Picture, 1887–1909.* New York: Arno Press, 1973. 313 pp.

RAMSAYE, TERRY, *A Million and One Nights: A History of the Motion Picture.* New York: Simon and Schuster, Inc., 1964. 868 pp. (originally published in 1926)

SKLAR, ROBERT, *Movie-made America: A Social History of American Movies.* New York: Random House, Inc., 1975. 340 pp.

SLIDE, ANTHONY, *Early American Cinema.* Cranbury, N. J.: A. S. Barnes & Co., Inc., 1970. 192 pp.

SPEHR, PAUL C., *The Movies Begin: Making Movies in New Jersey, 1887–1920.* Newark, N.J.: Newark Museum and Morgan Press, 1977.

STANLEY, ROBERT H., *The Celluloid Empire: A History of the American Movie Industry.* New York: Hastings House Publishers, 1978. 328 pp.

TAYLOR, DEEMS, MARCELENE PETERSON, and BRYANT HALE, *A Pictorial History of the Movies.* New York: Simon & Schuster, Inc., 1949. 375 pp.

WAGENKNECHT, EDWARD, *The Movies in the Age of Innocence.* Norman: University of Oklahoma Press, 1962. 280 pp.

3

Rise of the American Film, 1914–1919

World War I involved from its outbreak all the major film-producing nations, except the United States: France, Germany, Great Britain, and Italy. The U.S. did not enter the war until 1917, and then our participation was far less than total. Since some of the materials required for the manufacture of high explosives are the same as those for photographic film (cotton, and nitric and sulfuric acids), film stock was in short supply abroad. A much more serious effect of war on European film producers was the curtailment of international distribution of completed films. Countries were separated from each other by battle lines; transportation was unavailable for many nonmilitary purposes; and the large American audience lay three thousand miles across a submarine-infested ocean.

Though the French and Italians had been the first to arrive at feature-length films, the U.S. was now in a position to pursue that development as no other country could. With its sizeable moviegoing public, an economy stimulated rather than drained by war, a tradition of business expertise, and film makers of considerable inventiveness and occasional genius, America had a crucial advantage at this important stage. The Americans made full use of their resources, and that is to their credit. If there had not been that four-year lead at exactly that historical moment, however, the subsequent domination of the world's screens by the United States might never have occurred, at least not to the extent that it has.

As it happened, during the second half of the teens, the Americans were the ones who expanded the art to a fuller expression, discovered the sorts of ingredients that would make the entertainment universally popular, and devised systems of manufacture, wholesaling, and retailing that could support the new expensiveness of feature production. In the U.S. during those years were three parallel developments that deserve particular attention. First, was the culmination of Griffith's earlier experimentation in film form, his first features. Second, there began the quite special tradition of American screen comedy in the output of Mack Sennett and his co-workers, most notably Charles Chaplin. Finally, the new and prototypical systems of mass production, distribution, and exhibition evolved—with Thomas H. Ince among the leaders in organizing production—laying the groundwork for all subsequent economic expansion.

THE FIRST MASTERPIECES

We tend to think of "masterpiece" as applying to artistic works of large size—to *War and Peace* first, and only then to *Pride and Prejudice,* which may even be qualified as a "small masterpiece." Griffith worked on both the large and the small scales. Many of his films that have aged well, or his scenes remembered with greatest pleasure, are close, intimate studies of character and feeling (for example, *Broken Blossoms,* 1919) or selective and heightened observations of everyday life in small-town America (*True Heart Susie,* 1919). Still, what was first needed to shake film completely free from the stage, in a way so conspicuous that no one could fail to understand, was probably the kind of spectacular grandeur represented by Griffith's *The Birth of a Nation* (1915) and *Intolerance* (1916). Except for their length and expensiveness, any other single element of these two films could no doubt be found in one or more of the over four hundred shorter Griffith films preceding them, especially in those produced from 1912 on. To bring together all these contributions, however, under complete control and on such a gigantic scale, was a truly staggering accomplishment. Not only had there been nothing like these two films before—in their size and intricacy of conception and in their mingling of history with passionate argument—but there has been nothing comparable since—with the possible exception of Abel Gance's *Napoléon* (1927). Today *The Birth of a Nation* may not be quite the fresh revelation of the breath-taking power of the screen that it was for its first audiences; still, it is an overwhelming experience, particularly when properly presented at silent rather than sound speed with a good print and the original music. It can come alive for those who can free themselves from unjustified feelings of superiority to any film not in a current idiom, those who can accept Griffith's artistic postulates and understand that his racial attitudes are embedded in the myths and memories that formed such a dominant part of his life.

After completing *Judith of Bethulia* in 1913 (four reels, twice as long as any film he had previously made), Griffith left his first employer, the Biograph Company. Apparently he was restive under commercial restraints that had prevented him from proceeding to even larger projects. It is not clear to what extent Griffith was influenced by the Italian features; internal evidence suggests that *Intolerance* may owe more to them than does *Birth.* Griffith claimed that he was not influenced, and associates like Lillian Gish have testified that he had been so busy making films that he rarely took time to see any. He was working along similar lines as the Italians, however, and their successes must have acted as competitive stimuli, if not as models, demonstrating that the kind of thing he was trying to do could be done. In any case, after joining the small independent firm called Mutual, where he directed some routine productions to meet the payroll, he began to plan the huge film on the Civil War and Reconstruction that became *The Birth of a Nation*. Most of the latter part of the film was based on Thomas Dixon's novel *The Clansman* and the successful play made from it; there are lesser borrowings from Dixon's *The Leopard's Spots* and other sources.

The Birth of a Nation broke all sorts of precedents. Even in production, its cost, approximately $110,000, was five times greater than the next largest sum spent on an American film up to that time. (*Judith of Bethulia* had cost $23,000—the most spent on a film prior to *Birth*, according to Seymour Stern, one of Griffith's biographers.) Having run through his backers' money, Griffith invested what he could raise and borrow on his own to finish it. There were six weeks of rehearsal; shooting extended from July into October of 1914; editing took another three months. This overall production time contrasted with the average in those days of six weeks or less. When completed, *Birth*'s length was an unprecedented three hours. It was accompanied throughout by a symphonic score specially composed by Joseph Carl Briel, and was the first American film to be so treated.

In 1915 it opened as *The Clansman* in Los Angeles, and then as *The Birth of a Nation* in New York. The title change was suggested by Dixon, the author of the novel, who felt something was needed to suggest the epic scope of Griffith's achievement. The new title also referred to the end of the sovereignty of the states, achieved by the victory over secession. Though it played in "legitimate" theaters for as much as two dollars per ticket, it has been estimated that the first six months of its national run drew more people than had attended all the performances of all the stage plays in the U.S. during any given five-year period. More than merely a motion picture, it was a cultural phenomenon that everyone felt obliged to witness. Because of its evident racial biases, it created enormous controversy, even riots, and the notoriety attracted still more customers.

Since it was distributed on a "states' rights" basis, with lump sums paid for regional distribution franchises, there are no accurate figures of what *Birth* earned at the box office. *Variety* estimates that it has grossed as much as $50 million, and until recent years it was acknowledged as the top money-maker of all time. It continues in active circulation among film societies and in nontheatrical series and academic courses, and receives occasional theatrical revivals. No doubt it is playing somewhere on the globe at this moment, and it is still capable of provoking picketing and threats of worse by civil rights groups who want to protect audiences from its depiction of black people.

Aside from the racial content (to be dealt with later), what may strike you most strongly about the film is the sheer massiveness of its subject. Part I deals with the North and South in the days before the War Between the States (as Griffith would have called it) and with the war itself; Part II covers the Reconstruction period in the South. The whole is much more than an "epic" in the vulgarized entertainment sense of a film loaded with extras; instead, it is a genuine effort to treat a national epoch in the fullest possible way.

Griffith's strategy included the portrayal of invented personalities who touch upon the salient aspects of national events. Partly through the social positions and vocations of the characters—who help shape the historical forces at work as well as representing those persons affected by the forces—a structural pattern was created which allowed for the large canvas to be colored and infused with personal drama. Historical tableaux frame and punctuate the fictional plot: the first slaves landing in Virginia, Lincoln brooding at night in the White House, Grant and Lee at Appomattox. (Griffith would use this sort of organization again in *Intolerance, Orphans of the Storm* [1921], and other historical works.) The fusing of fiction with history dates at least from Homer and was standard practice with Sir Walter Scott and other historical novelists; Griffith drew more or less consciously on nineteenth-century literary precedents for the shaping of his stories.

The dramatic parallels Griffith employed among his characters don't seem excessively schematic, given the full and lifelike detail of the incidents surrounding them. There are the two families, one northern and one southern, whose children become acquainted at a northern school—as they might well have done, given the southern aristocracy's practice of educating their sons in the North. The northern father, The Honorable Austin Stoneman, Leader of the House, is a powerful abolitionist politician (clearly modeled on Thaddeus Stevens, leader in the House of Representatives and a prime factor in the passing of Reconstruction legislation). He is a widower whose dead wife has been succeeded by a scheming, mulatto housekeeper/mistress. The southern father, Dr. Cameron, is an aging, wealthy planter with a gentle wife, thoroughly part of a chivalric tradition. Each family thus represents one of the strong causative elements in the impending conflict.

Because of their acquaintanceship, the invented characters can cross back and forth into each others' lives and surroundings: a friendly visit before the war, a fatal meeting on the battlefield, an encounter in a prisoner-of-war hospital, or the final merging through the postwar northern "occupation" of the South. They come in contact with actual personages at historical moments: when the Confederate mother approaches the Union president to plead for clemency for her captured son, or when a brother and sister attend the play at the Ford Theatre on the night the president is assassinated, and so on. The fictional characters' lives are lived within the events and re-created conditions of those times. Griffith's structuring is also strangely persuasive, drawing us into an understanding and sympathy, if we will allow it. President Woodrow Wilson, historian and southerner, is said to have exclaimed after seeing the film that it was "like writing history in lightning." After controversy arose over the film, the White House disavowed any approval on the part of the President.

It is the quality of passion that made *The Birth of a Nation* not only a *succès d'estime* but a *succès de scandale*. Though based in part on Dixon's novel, Griffith re-created the narrative world according to his own viewpoint. Born in Kentucky in 1875, he absorbed an understanding of the war and Reconstruction from his father—Colonel ''Roaring Jake'' Griffith of the Confederate Cavalry. The attitudes about blacks in *Birth* are so much part of the total view of life which the film encompasses that Griffith was apparently shocked when he was accused of racism. Incidents like those in the film had in fact occurred, he argued (and had even footnoted some of the scenes in titles). He no doubt felt that many of the emancipated slaves had indeed been ignorant and shiftless by anyone's standards, and that it would be false to present them otherwise. On the other hand, his position was that he understood and loved black people better than did his attackers; some of his best friends were "colored," he seemed to be saying.

Thoroughly embodied in the film, however, is an assumption of innate inferiority of black people. The bad, usually those of mixed blood, are led by evil or misguided white men, are vicious and greedy for power, and line up with the northerners. The good are dependent and childlike, and support the white South. Bad or good, these blacks are given few individual attributes apart from caste role and function, and viewers today feel more uneasy with Griffith's approving patronization of "the faithful souls" than with his treatment of the villains.

Whatever documentation and evidence he might offer, it is the very unconsciousness of his assumption of black inferiority, that "that was how it was," which is most disturbing. The way in which this strand becomes an integral part of a credible whole makes it particularly effective "propaganda." The conviction of the film carries viewers along, and it is impossible to put aside one aspect of it as an aberration. Because the biases are so uncalculated and rawly emotional in their appeal, they may even get past our intellectual defenses. Given the film's enormous popularity, Griffith's assumptions must have been shared by a substantial number of his white contemporaries.

The nastiest aspect of Griffith's protrayal of black-white relationships is also the one closest to the national nerve—his obsession with possible sexual intermingling of the races. Would you want your sister to be molested by or married to a Negro? Griffith asks. For him the two possible fates exert an equally morbid fascination: Marriage to a black man is presented as unthinkable except as equivalent to rape. The much more significant, consequential, and frequent forced submission of black women to white men is dealt with by Griffith only through the congressman's weakness for his housekeeper. This is presented as close to a pathological failing on his part, with the woman exercising what is clearly a sexually based power over him. Stoneman's horrified reaction to his black political protégé's asking for his daughter's hand is of a piece with the rest. Perhaps more than any other white character in the film, the congressman seems to exist solely for rhetorical purposes.

On the other hand, ambiguities are present in the attempted attack on Flora Cameron (Mae Marsh) by the renegade black, Gus, and in the behavior of mulatto politician Silas Lynch with Elsie Stoneman (Lillian Gish), as Lynch tries to force her into a marriage. Gus sets out to make advances of some sort to Flora; in fact, he has told her that he is interested in marriage. But his behavior seems to change gradually until it could be argued, from the evidence on the screen, that he ends by trying to calm her so that she won't cause harm to herself: "Wait, missie, I won't hurt yeh," Gus says. She answers, "Stay away or I'll jump!" He doesn't come any nearer, but she jumps. As presented, it is her hysterical fear, rather than anything Gus does, that motivates her fatal leap.

As for Elsie Stoneman's plight, her reactions seem so exaggerated that the hyperbolic irrationality of her response makes one aware of the obsessions underlying her fears (though Griffith surely didn't intend this implication). A false marriage could be annulled, you might well think, at least outside the spell of the film; it is the prospect of consummation that Griffith expects us to sweat over. Silas's behavior appears in part pathetic, as does Gus's, instead of seeming fixed as evil and cruel. In contrast, the climax of the film is entirely unambiguous: The white men prepare to bash in the skulls of their women if the black troops should break into the cabin. Here, it can only be conceded that if the action proposed seems tacitly approved by Griffith, it might also have been consistent with the feelings of the people upon whom the characters were based and those of the audience.

There are many who cannot accept the content of Griffith's films—not just the racial bias in *Birth*, but the sentimentality and melodramatics that color so much of his presentation and possibly his view of life. Even in his own time, his conception—rooted in nineteenth-century Victorianism—apparently came to seem increasingly old-fashioned and irrelevant to his audiences. Some critics—unable to allow for what is essentially a style, a set of conventions, a way of thinking about people and events—have tended to deplore the content while praising the form. Though other artists are infrequently subjected to this sort of dichotomy (such a separation is generally regarded as an aesthetic impossibility), perhaps a similar situation existed with the dramatists immediately preceding Shakespeare, those who fashioned the framework on which the great Elizabethan plays would be created.

In Griffith's case, it is evidently felt by some that so many unknown techniques had to be discovered and mastered in the early days of this new art form that little could be expected from what was being said. This position seems to imply, on the one hand, that any old material lying about could be pressed into service for purposes of formal experimentation; and, on the other, that Griffith was a generally silly and sometimes innocently vicious man with an innate and intuitive feeling for the language of the new medium. Perhaps a contrary proposition deserves more study: the possibility that Griffith develped the tools and materials of film precisely in order to deal, in the most effective manner possible, with what interested him. In either case, those who regard him as an artistically inspired child, and those who can see through the conventional artistic trappings of an earlier literature and theater to a validity and dignity in his view of humankind agree that in *The Birth of a Nation* his formal control over the medium achieved an unprecedented power.

From his overall conception of before, during, and after the war to his sequences that make up those parts, the scenes within the sequences, and the shots which comprise the scenes, the selection and balance are clearly and brilliantly thought out. The camera is positioned so that each shot is sure and precise in its meaning. The editing together of these shots leads an audience's perception; it tightens or loosens the emotional intensity with complete assurance and understanding of the aesthetic-psychological factors involved. Take, for instance, the scene at the Ford Theatre, which culminates with Lincoln's assassination. It begins with an iris of Elsie and her brother Phil taking their seats and speaking to acquaintances; the image opens up to a full screen of the front of the theater, taken from above and the side, showing stage, orchestra, boxes, gallery (18 seconds). Then there is a semicloseup of Phil and Elsie as she looks through opera glasses (3 seconds). A title announces, "The play: 'Our American Cousin,' starring Laura Keene" (4 seconds).

After this economical exposition, Griffith proceeds with the start of the performance, leaving Elsie and Phil momentarily; he continues to vary the angle, distance, and duration of the shots to give us a heightened sense of the mood and tempo of the public event. A title states, "Time, 8:30. The Arrival of the President, Mrs. Lincoln, and party." With this, Griffith cross-cuts from the slightly ominous, dark and shadowy stairs in back of the boxes, as Lincoln and his party ascend, to the presidential box as seen from the theater auditorium, with the first of the party entering. As Lincoln comes forward there is a medium shot of the box (4.5 seconds). Then Griffith returns to a semicloseup of Phil and Elsie, who evidently see the President, applaud and rise (6 seconds). This intimate framing is followed by a reestablishing long shot of the theater, with the audience now standing and cheering (2.5 seconds). And so it continues on through the tragic denouement.[1]

---

[1] This and the following shot lists are taken from Theodore Huff, *A Shot Analysis of D. W. Griffith's The Birth of a Nation* (New York: The Museum of Modern Art, 1961).

The Birth of a Nation (U.S., 1915, D. W. Griffith). Museum of Modern Art/Film Stills Archive.

Consider, too, the shorter, simpler, but extraordinarily moving scene of Ben Cameron's return from the war. (Ben, the Little Colonel, is played by Henry B. Walthall.) After a title, "The homecoming" (less than 1 second), there is a long shot of the street and the Cameron front yard: Everything is in need of repair; the columns are scorched, the fence is falling apart, the street and sidewalks are littered. Ben enters left background, shattered and weary; he pauses, leans against the fence, and looks about at the marks of war. Limping, he walks slowly and weakly forward along the fence (34.5 seconds). In semicloseup in the living room, his younger sister, Flora, is by a mirror admiring the effect of "southern ermine" (strips of raw cotton and soot) decorating her dress. Ben's older sister, Margaret, and his mother hurry in, indicating that they have seen Ben coming; Margaret runs to the door and back; all run out of the room (18 seconds). Medium shot of the hall: The three rush forward, excited, joined by the father (6 seconds). Three-quarter shot of Ben pausing by the gate, opening it, supporting himself against it a moment and then going in (11 seconds). Three-quarter shot of the family, waiting in the hall breathlessly, smiling at Flora's excitement (3.5 seconds). Three-quarter shot of the front yard as Ben comes to the porch (7.5 seconds). Three-quarter shot of the family in the hall; Flora rushes forward (4.5 seconds). Semicloseup of the porch as Ben climbs the steps; Flora comes out the door and meets him, smiling. They gaze at each other; she points to his worn and dirty uniform; he pulls off a piece of her "ermine." She explains, giggles, points to a hole in his hat. They both pause and gaze off into space, thinking of all that has happened. Suddenly they stop pretending. Flora starts to cry, and embraces Ben; he looks into the distance, kisses her hair, pats her.

They start into the house arm in arm (57 seconds). Semicloseup from side angle of the front door: Ben and Flora start in; a woman's arm comes from inside and encircles Ben's shoulders, gently drawing him and Flora in (17.5 seconds). Fade-out.

The shots in this latter example have a much longer average duration than those in the opening scene in the Ford Theatre. Here much more emotional content is conveyed by each shot, especially by the first two and last two. Only against Griffith's usual practice of presenting a scene from varying points of view in a rapid succession of shots did the tension of the Little Colonel's slow movement within that static frame (and the arm of the unseen mother appearing to encircle him) achieve the kind of eloquence it possesses. In the pre-Griffith years such a shot was the invariable standard in which all action took place, and thus it was not useful for special emphasis. An analogy might be made to silence, which had no dramatic meaning until the coming of sound: There had to be sound, and the cessation of sound, before silence had significance. Not until the camera was freed to interrupt the action, which would then be synthesized through editing, could a long-running wide-angle shot be used for contrasting emphasis.

As a final example, there is a famous single shot into which Griffith compresses a maximum amount of symbolic meaning. It opens with the screen dark except for an iris in the lower left-hand corner—in which we see a woman and three children huddled next to the ruins of a destroyed home on a hilltop. They look bedraggled and anguished. Then we are shown the cause—in a slow pan to the right, while the iris gradually opens to reveal a column of troops stretching off into the distance, with burning and pillaging

The Birth of a Nation (U.S., 1915, D. W. Griffith). Museum of Modern Art/Film Stills Archive.

evident in the valley below. The shot lasts 34 seconds. In this complex and changing composition Griffith tellingly presents and protests the calculated ruthlessness of Sherman's march to the sea, giving individual human meaning to the large scale by starting with the poignant detail of the effects of this destruction on an innocent family. The shot ends with a pan back from the troops to the mother and children.

Performances in *The Birth of a Nation* are advanced well beyond the conventions of stage pantomime, and clearly grow out of a sense of real persons moving through the surroundings and incidents of life. Though simplified and heightened for dramatic communication without spoken words, the gestures and expressions are generally toned down in comparison with other contemporary films and Griffith's own earlier work. For example, the contrast with *The Battle* (1911—a sort of sketch for *The Birth*) is quite marked. There is some exaggeration in the young people's high jinks, which Griffith associates with youthful good spirits; Mae Marsh is fluttery—painfully so if projected at twenty-four frames per second; and the villainies or buffooneries of the blacks appear caricatured to modern eyes. But by and large, the acting style seems quite consciously created for the silent camera, rather than being a theatrical performance recorded by it. Henry B. Walthall and Lillian Gish rise considerably above minimum expectations to

The Birth of a Nation (U.S., 1915, D. W. Griffith). George Eastman House).

create characterizations unrivaled on the screen up to that time, comparable to the best that the mature silent film would offer. The subtlety and intensity of their playing do much to imbue the whole with its sense of loss and sadness, of feelings warped and impoverished by the cruel demands of the historic time.

The care in selection and design of interiors and exteriors surpasses historical re-creation to achieve a semblance of documentary veracity that makes the past seem present. So vividly real and particularized are the interior settings that the rooms look lived in. The huge, period tableaux grow out of a vision that makes them come alive: the ball on the eve of battle, the gigantic battlefield scenes, the gathering and ride of the Klan, the rioting and fighting in the streets. These are staggering sequences, not only in their size but in their lifelike energy and the way their parts fit into the whole. Above all, we are impressed by the control Griffith exerts, even on this scale, to make the scenes function exactly as he wants them to, full of human meaning as well as historical spectacle.

Before *The Birth of a Nation* was released, Griffith had completed a feature to be called *The Mother and the Law,* its opening sequences based on an actual incident of conflict and violence in a contemporary labor dispute. After the grandeur of *The Birth,* however, particularly after its enormous success on the one hand and the angry criticism it provoked on the other, *The Mother and the Law* must have seemed an inadequate successor. As part of *The Birth* controversy, Griffith had published a pamphlet entitled *The Rise and Fall of Free Speech in America.* Then, apparently wanting to align himself clearly on the side of unquestionable social and moral rectitude to show his detractors how they had misunderstood him, and perhaps to castigate those he felt had been intolerant toward him, he conceived an even more elaborate scheme than that of *The Birth.* Added to *The Mother and the Law* were three other stories, set in widely separate historical periods and cultures. These four stories, according to a title prefacing the multilayered whole, would show "how hatred and intolerance, through the ages, have battled against love and charity." This undertaking—perhaps the most ambitious in conception and

Intolerance (U.S., 1916, D. W. Griffith). Museum of Modern Art/Film Stills Archive.

largest in size of any film ever produced in this country—became *Intolerance*, released in 1916.

The three stories added to the modern story were a re-creation of the fall of Babylon to the Persians (539 B.C.); vignettes from the life of Christ (27 A.D.), culminating in the crucifixion; and an account of the massacre of protestant Huguenots in France on St. Bartholomew's Eve, 1572. If the stories had been told consecutively (as in later anthology collections of filmed short stories from Wilde, Maugham, or O'Henry), the task would have been difficult enough. But Griffith's design went even further, using intercutting so that narratives and characters would become subservient to the overriding theme. He began with the modern story up to a certain point of development; then he moved to Jerusalem and an episode from the life of Christ; then to the introduction of the plotting at court in sixteenth-century France; back to the modern story; on to the beginning of the Babylonian sequences; then to the modern story again; and so on.

These parts are announced, separated, and connected with an image of "The Woman Who Rocks the Cradle" (Lillian Gish) accompanied by Whitmanesque titles: "Endlessly rocks the cradle—Uniter of Here and Hereafter—Chanter of Sorrows," or "Out of the cradle endlessly rocking . . ." Later, as the tension in each of the stories increases, Griffith cuts ever more rapidly from one to the other without interruption. Of

Intolerance (U.S., 1916, D. W. Griffith). Museum of Modern Art/Film Stills Archive.

Intolerance (U.S., 1916, D. W. Griffith). Museum of Modern Art/Film Stills Archive.

this complex polyphonic form, with the separate parts all progressing simultaneously, he said:

> [the] stories will begin like four currents looked at from a hilltop. At first the four currents will flow apart, slowly and quietly. But as they flow, they grow nearer and nearer together, and faster and faster, until in the end, in the last act, they mingle in one mighty river of expressed emotion.[2]

In order to finance this colossal spectacle Griffith used all of his profits from *The Birth of a Nation,* finally buying out the other backers when they lost their nerve. The total cost of the picture is said to have been $1.9 million; it has been estimated that it would cost $40 million to achieve the same results today. The sets of French streets, houses, and castle are all full scale, solid, and practicable. Babylon, constructed on a 254-acre site along Sunset Boulevard, is the most overwhelming: Its towers rise 200 feet; its walls are wide enough at their tops to allow two chariots to pass; and it took hundreds of extras to fill the courtyard and balconies in the film's victory celebration. *Intolerance* originally ran close to four hours, longer than *Birth,* and again Joseph Carl Briel composed a special score arranged to Griffith's specifications.

As he had done with *Birth,* Griffith followed *Intolerance* on its openings in Los Angeles and New York. Not satisfied with audience reactions, he continued to edit, rearranging and cutting the positive print being used for projection. Though some critics praised the film lavishly, the public seemed to find the disjunctive organization and unprecedented length confusing and exhausting. The final climactic passages became almost an assault on optical nerves as well as on emotions, as the cutting tempo increases to many shots no longer than five frames. Also, the thematic material was out of keeping

[2] Quoted by Lewis Jacobs, *The Rise of the American Film* (New York: Harcourt, Brace and Company, 1939), p. 189.

Intolerance (U.S., 1916, D. W. Griffith). National Film Archive/Stills Library.

with the national mood by the time the film was released. Brotherly love was going out of fashion. President Wilson, who had been reelected on an isolationist peace platform, asserting that America was too proud to fight, was soon moving with the country itself towards entry into World War I. Who could be tolerant of the loathesome "Hun" who was bayoneting Belgian women and children and was seemingly about to sweep over the whole face of Europe? The sentimental idealism of *Intolerance* carried nothing of the direct conviction of *The Birth of a Nation,* and was as dismal a financial failure as the preceding film had been an unrivaled success.

Griffith's career was deflected and probably permanently damaged by the necessity of paying off the debts incurred with *Intolerance.* In a desperate effort to recoup some of the losses, he cut into the original negative, without printing a copy, to make versions of *The Mother and the Law* and *The Fall of Babylon,* which were subsequently released separately. As a result of these mutilations, copies of *Intolerance* which exist to-day are reduced approximations of the original. Even so, the overall effect is undeniably impressive. In many ways it is an advance on *The Birth of a Nation.* What it lacks in coherence and genuine passion it makes up in the sweeping imaginativeness of conception and increased perfection of technique.

Intolerance was to have an influence on film history quite disproportionate to its lack of popular appeal. After the war, Lenin arranged for it to tour the Soviet Union, where it ran continuously for ten years. Very likely, Lenin was most interested in the portrayal of exploitative and repressive managerial classes in the modern story—Griffith's viewpoint being strongly anti-capital and pro-labor. But two future giants of Soviet cinema, Sergei Eisenstein and V. I. Pudovkin, saw much more in it than that. (Indeed, the strike in Pudovkin's *Mother* has some direct borrowings from *Intolerance*.) Griffith had shown them how argument (education and propaganda) could be conveyed through dramatic incident, and how its effectiveness could be heightened by the dynamics of editing. Most of what the Soviet masters formalized and articulated in theories of *montage,* Griffith had understood intuitively. In *Intolerance* the evolving unity rests on generalized idea and emotion—rather than solely on characters' decisions which forward a plot—and depends upon the unique resources of the film medium. Through skillful juxtaposition of images, disjunctive in physical place-time but related by each phase of the developing theme, the effect of the whole becomes greater than the sum of its parts.

In other respects *Intolerance* represents Griffith's growing mastery over the medium. The alternation between large vista and small human detail (the page boy sleeping in the throne room of Charles V, or the fat woman throttling her dance partner when he steps on her toes) is even more assured. Performances are completely nonstage-like and are carefully broken into shots, with especially forceful use of closeups (for example, the often cited shot of Mae Marsh's twisting hands in the courtroom, or Little Brown Eyes's face, enormous and haunting in the St. Bartholomew's Eve massacre). Griffith and Bitzer carried their experimentation with framing and lighting further than ever. Considerable camera movement was introduced: the long, crane-like dolly into Belshazzar's palace courtyard; the pan across the seated women in the marriage market, not to follow action but to compel our close attention to the women. There is some exterior night shooting in the Babylonian battle scenes, which seems almost impossible at that time. The full range of irises, fades, superimpositions, and masking (a CinemaScope shape to present the sun court of Cyrus) are employed throughout—all done in the camera. In total, *Intolerance* is felt by many to represent Griffith's fullest achievement; for all it must stand as one of the great landmarks in the history of film.

A TRADITION OF SCREEN COMEDY IS ESTABLISHED

At about the time that Griffith was contributing a new flexibility and power to screen language, a distinctive line of American film comedy was founded which would produce its own geniuses and masterworks. Although contrasting strongly with Griffith's high seriousness and Victorian sentimentality (in fact, sometimes subjecting these to parody), the early film comics nonetheless contributed importantly to solving some of the art form's basic problems that preoccupied Griffith. Given funny-looking people behaving oddly in situations filled with humor, the amount of laughter obtained could still vary considerably, depending on how it was presented. The requirements of pictorial narrative, the selection and arrangement of shots, were as important to the effectiveness of the comedians as they were to Griffith. It was one of Griffith's former co-workers and informal students, Mack Sennett, who came to best understand this newly evolved technique and to put it into practice for comic purposes. Like Griffith, Sennett didn't invent so much as he applied the insights gained from his own and others' experiments. His essential contribution was to fashion a kind of systematic, though unarticulated, comic aesthetic that would become a basic standard others would continue to develop.

As with most film genres, screen comedy was present in embryonic form from the very beginning—in fact, before the screen (for instance, *Fred Ott's Sneeze,* 1893, one of Edison's Kinetoscope fragments). Other early Edisons included visual records of comic vaudeville skits: *Fun in a Chinese Laundry* (1894) involved a chase, a policeman, and a thrown prop (not yet a pie), foreshadowing the later Keystone comedies—as did, even more clearly, the brief but fully developed *A Wringing Good Joke* (1899). Then there were the French "trick films" begun by Méliès and added to, most notably, by Ferdinand Zecca and Emile Cohl. In these the "trickery" was usually designed for humorous as well as fantastic effect; for example, pumpkins roll off a wagon and bounce around town creating all sorts of havoc (*The Pumpkin Race,* Cohl, 1907). Méliès's *An Adventurous Automobile Trip* (1905) in many ways foreshadows Sennett's later fun with Model-Ts.

It was another Frenchman, Max Linder, who from 1905 on established most clearly a pattern for the kinds of visual incongruities and surprises that were to screen comedy what verbal gags were to stage vaudeville and burlesque. The comic figure he created was a dapper, controlled, elegant, upper-class man-about-town involved with a hard-hearted lady love. Sennett admitted to having studied Linder closely, and Sennett's most brilliant discovery, Charles Chaplin, was even more obviously in Linder's debt. In Chaplin's first films for Sennett, before he had fully developed his own unique style, his costume and mannerisms not only suggest his own English music-hall background, but also bear a resemblance to the smoothly maladroit and somewhat effete dandy that Linder had created. Sennett's work, however, which would start a main line of film comedy that lasted from 1912 (the year the Keystone Company was founded) on through the twenties and into the first years of sound, was vigorously and indigenously American. It was he who earned the broad popularity for the style known as slapstick, upon which Chaplin was to ring his own, subtler changes.

Whatever other influences there were, the precedents offered by Porter and Griffith would serve Sennett as a way of structuring his films. The chase, characteristic of the filmed action-melodramas, could be used for comedy as well as for pure suspense. With exciting action situations as backbone, comic muscle and flesh were added. Perhaps the essentials of the method can best be demonstrated by suggesting a composite Keystone comedy made up of remembered scenes from several of the actual comedies. It opens in a bungalow bedroom, with two seedy-looking robbers climbing through the window. They waken the rotund homeowner at gun point, gag him, tie him to a conveniently available hot water heater which they set at "HOT" (insert of gauge); they rifle his bureau, scoop up valuables, and leave. A freckle-faced, gaptoothed urchin peers in the window, sees the trouble, and sets off, presumably to summon help. (Note the similarity so far with Porter and Griffith.)

Cut to the interior of a police station, where an out-sized sergeant sporting a large brush of mustache (Mack Swain) is snoozing at the desk. He bounces awake, answers the phone, then shouts off screen. A gaggle of policemen stumble over each other through a door and line up in front of the desk. An odder collection of physical types would be hard to imagine. There's a tall skinny one (Slim Summerville), a fat one (Roscoe "Fatty" Arbuckle), a wildly cross-eyed one (Chester Conklin), and so on. A number of them are decorated with bizarre mustaches, beards, and sideburns. Uniforms are too large or too small, and parts are as apt to be on backwards as not. They twitch and weave in an irregular line as the sergeant shouts at them, then they rush towards a door leading outside. Emerging onto the sidewalk, they jump into a couple of open jalopies at the curb. The floor on the rear car gives way under the impact. Its occupants then leap in with the others in the front car, though one can scarcely believe it is holding them all. Starting up rapidly in reverse, they crash into the rear car, which then totally collapses. Roaring out into the street, they barely slip in front of an oncoming truck; zigzagging from one side to the other, they obliviously scatter pedestrians and opposing traffic in their wake. An undercranked camera speeds up the movement to a surreal tempo.

Back in the bedroom, the nightgowned captive is still spread-eagled on a now swelling boiler. The needle of the gauge moves from ''HOT'' to ''BOILING'' and towards ''DANGER'' and ''EXPLOSION.'' Return to the police car, now careening along a highway at an improbable speed; the cops are all standing, overflowing the sides, peering ahead, gesticulating frenetically with their elbows in each others' faces.

Cut to a single file of laborers walking along a country road; the shovel on the shoulder of the last man catches a detour sign and turns it to point to a road other than the one it had been indicating. The police arrive in the patrol car, pause, zip backward and forward, and then drive off on the route we know is not the detour. Coming down a hill at breakneck speed, they fail to stop as the road dead-ends into a lake; instead, they go straight off the end of a pier, and submerge. On the other side of the lake, they emerge unfazed, still going full tilt towards their destination; and so on, with other impediments, other crosscuts to the bulging boiler distending the fat man's stomach, until the final rescue.

Keystone Kops in unidentified film (U.S., 1914–1919, Mack Sennett). National Film Archive/ Stills Library.

Several things are noteworthy about this kind of comic invention. For instance, it is clear that the same Porter/Griffith excitement and suspense of crime, chase, and rescue or capture are here turned into comedy by visual and emotional exaggeration. Also, a recognizably real world (unlike that of Méliès) is madly distorted as if certain physical laws (of gravity, acceleration, solidity of objects, and the like) operate eccentrically or not at all. The incongruity between what is expected in the real world and what happens in Sennett's universe extends throughout the films. The pleasure we get from this sportive tampering with the expected is the same as would later be offered in animated cartoons. We know that floorboards usually remain in cars, that boilers have no rubbery elasticity, that humans and machines move at predictable speeds, and that no one can drive along the bottom of a lake and come up on the other side; still, it's fun to have the unlikely made manifest. As for the people in Sennett's films, they are incredibly incompetent; also it is highly improbable that a random sample of beings would include the widely variant physical types and appearances of his cast. Further, they are always inhumanly unflappable: They cope with the irregularities of nature with a maniacal seriousness, only dimly aware that anything is amiss.

These funny-looking, oddball characters could be expected to send a less sophisticated, or perhaps only less inhibited, audience into gales of laughter merely by their cross-eyedness or fatness. This suggests that a certain sadistic pleasure in others' misfortunes underlies the jokes of physical discomfort that are such an integral part of silent screen comedy, including the pratfalls and the pies in the face. We enjoy the robbery victim being grilled and splayed on the water heater; the car going off the end of the pier looks like a multiple drowning, and we howl with glee. An emotional catharsis of some sort is provided by this controlled display of aggression and violence. The magical power of the characters to survive annihilation is probably also an important cathartic element. There is no death; Sennett's people are invulnerable, and we are free to indulge in comic-hysterical relief and reaction to normally destructive actions. Our laughter no doubt arises from a feeling of comfortable superiority—we are not the ones afflicted.

In Sennett's films the powerful and socially exalted characters are comic butts, helpless in the face of an onslaught by nature or one of its minions. The choice of policemen is significant in this respect. Though he would turn in his grave at any suggestion of Freudian notions about authority figures as resented parental surrogates, Sennett evidently did realize that the incongruous and the uncomfortable were a lot more humorous when inflicted on types of people who were taken seriously by society and themselves. The indignities to which the grotesque and incompetent policemen are subjected are funnier because they *are* policemen. And if soup spilled down a back is amusing, it is at least twice as funny if the back belongs to a plump dowager in evening gown at a formal function.

By puncturing pomposity and pretension, by making the important and respected his victims, Sennett heightened our enjoyment. To this extent there is a social edge to his comedy. It is usually on the side of the little guy in the audience and directed against institutions and conventions outside his sympathies. This general satirical intention was even more pointed in the Sennett parodies of certain popular films he felt suffered from pretentiousness. *Barney Oldfield's Race for Life* (1913), for example, was an early kidding of the Griffith last-minute rescue. In the 1920s the first of the epic westerns, *The Covered Wagon,* became Sennett's *The Uncovered Wagon;* Erich von Stroheim's *Foolish Wives* was lampooned in *Three Foolish Weeks;* and there was nothing quite like Ben Turpin playing a Rudolph Valentino in *The Shriek of Araby* to put passion and heroics in proper perspective.

Slapstick was as natural to the silent screen as were the action-melodramas and spectacles, and for the same reasons: It utilized those aspects of the world best communicated through the moving image, those not requiring the supplement of language. Most of us who didn't grow up in the tradition of silent comedy have trouble getting back to its essence except through the works of the later and greater clowns—Buster Keaton, Harold Lloyd, Harry Langdon, Stan Laurel and Oliver Hardy, and post-Keystone Chaplin. One difficulty in our appreciation of early silent comedies is that we too frequently see them in excerpted and anthologized snippets, projected at a speed faster than intended (which undercuts Sennett's use of fast motion for precise effect). Exaggerated music and sound effects, and perhaps a commentator's condescending asides, act as further distractions.

The essential point to be understood is that the best of Sennett had a disciplined lunacy. His work is not merely a succession of unrelated inanities; though not intellectual, it is not mindless either. When properly constructed and executed, the rules of silent comic geometry are consistent, and a coherence is built from gag to gag to entire film. A great deal of skill and control was involved. Today's film students and amateur movie makers who try to burlesque that style without understanding it, let alone loving it, end with films that are silly rather than funny—films with the comic logic missing. Frequently it is only these modern-day comic film makers themselves who think their work hilarious. Sennett's humor was for the audience, who rolled in the aisles.

Sennett and his colleagues were very serious about the business of being funny. Comedy is often hard work indeed, and some of the greatest comedians are known to lack a common garden-variety sense of humor, and to be anything but the life of the party off screen. Sennett's special genius lay in understanding the construction and timing of sight gags. Careful manipulation of the standard ingredients, plus a sure feeling for what each shot includes, at what point it appears, and how long it is held on the screen, make all the difference. Start with the basic comic situation of a man falling down; make that man a ridiculously pompous, rotund, middle-aged suitor on the way to his lady love's, carrying a dainty corsage, dressed in top hat, cutaway, and striped trousers; then select, quite properly, a small boy to deflate this dignity by placing a banana peel in the man's path. The comic effectiveness of character and incident may still be profoundly altered by whether we first see the man walking and falling in long shot, then the banana peel in closeup, then the boy peering around the fence in medium shot, or whether the order of these shots is reversed so we can share the boy's anticipation and sense of achievement. Of course, the film maker must judge when the audience will have gotten the full impact of a shot, and thus cut on the rising laugh—not before and not after.

In silent comedy the gag construction could advance unimpeded: No pause was needed for lines to be heard and laughs registered. The silent film maker could build steadily, milking the visual joke for all of the variations it offered. Roars of laughter crescendoed until the comic climax was reached; only then was there a slowing of pace, a transition, and a hooking into the beginning of the next gag—which started building all over again. Ideally, the audience was left weak and helpless, weeping with laughter. It was this kind of robust creation, one uniquely suited to silent film, that Sennett mastered. His work is directly related to the cinematic technique that concerned Griffith.

The early generation of American film makers who did not get their training from Griffith got it from Sennett. His transcendently brilliant protégé was, of course, Charles Chaplin, whom George Bernard Shaw called the only genius at work in film (as he thought himself the only genius at work in theater). Sennett and his partner Adam Kessel had seen Chaplin in the Fred Karno English music hall company, which had been touring the U.S. extensively between 1910 and 1913. Though Kessel didn't get the name quite right, he wired off for "Charlie Chapman" at a time when Keystone's then reigning star, Ford Sterling, was being difficult about salary. Charlie's first film—entitled *Making a Living* (1914), with prophetic understatement—was pure Sennett. *Tillie's Punctured Romance,* directed by Sennett in the same year, and featuring Chaplin, Marie Dressler, Mabel Normand, Mack Swain, and Charles Bennett, is generally considered the first feature-length comedy (six reels). It too represents Sennett's slapstick humor rather than the tragicomic elaboration of Chaplin's finest work.

From later accounts by Chaplin, and from the evidence of his early films compared to his subsequent successes, it is clear that he was not altogether comfortable in Sennett's broad, knockabout style. Gradually, especially after leaving Keystone, Chaplin would develop a comedy character of richness and subtlety beyond anything Sennett had conceived. Chaplin made that character into one of the great comic figures (along with Falstaff, Til Eulenspiegel, Don Quixote and Sancho Panza, and the creatures of the *commedia del'arte*). The personality and costume of the little tramp, assembled through dozens of one- and two-reelers, evolved full-blown by the end of the teens. The little fellow, ingenuously and ingeniously triumphant while maintaining his cheerfulness and dignity in an adverse world, was quickly taken to the hearts of audiences everywhere.

In addition to the creation of this persona, rounded and complex enough to encompass strains of pathos, from *The Tramp* (1915) on Chaplin developed his unique pantomimic grace, early evident in *The Rink* (1916) and *The Cure* (1917). He handled his body as a dancer would, and there is an exuberant joy in merely watching him skip through the world, pirouetting to offer himself to the blondly beautiful Edna Purviance, bounding into and out of an open utility hole without apparent hurt, or running and gliding around a table, just out of reach of the giant Eric Campbell. From large movements to small (the dissection of a clock in *The Pawnshop,* 1916), there was a constant flow of invention. Charlie turned what could be done with arms, hands, legs, feet, and stiff backbones into unexpected and sometimes unimaginable physical potential, a playful and precise bodily commentary on the human condition. And this is not to mention his uses of a Murphy bed (*One A.M.,* 1916), a lamp shade (*The Adventurer,* 1917), and other props.

The social dimension implicit in Sennett was expanded by Chaplin, and tended to preoccupy him increasingly as his career progressed. Even in this early period his films generally included some pointed observations about people in relation to society. *Easy Street* (1917) is a veritable catalogue: The main theme of law and order includes a delightful reversal of police brutality; revivalist religion, slums, poverty, welfare, anarchists, and drug addition are all touched upon along the way. *The Immigrant* (1917) is frequently quite sardonic as well as broadly amusing in its depiction of the experiences of new arrivals in the "Land of the Free." For example, as the ship passes the Statue of Liberty, the passengers are shoved and roped in like cattle; Charlie takes a quizzical second look at the statue. The satirical treatment of military life and the basic antiwar

The Cure (U.S., 1917, Charles Chaplin). Museum of Modern Art/Film Stills Archive.

stance of *Shoulder Arms* are all the more remarkable when you realize it was released before the armistice of 1918.

Chaplin's enormous popular success and shrewd handling of the income he earned from it allowed him, throughout his career, freedom for social-political comment and a degree of artistic autonomy (which Griffith lost after the failure of *Intolerance*). Chaplin's control over his films would become unique within the art-industry. From the early twenties on, he was his own producer; his artistic virtuosity permitted him to write the scripts for, direct, star in, compose the music for, and supervise all of the other creative functions of his films. To make fully certain that his works would reach the screen exactly as he intended, in 1919 he joined Griffith, Mary Pickford, and Douglas Fairbanks to form a distribution company called United Artists. Thus Chaplin not only succeeded in preserving his independence, but was able to proceed in a way quite opposite from the centrifugal, collective forces generally at work in the industry.

EMERGING PATTERNS OF INDUSTRY

The feature length of *Tillie's Punctured Romance* proved something of an exception as far as comedies were concerned. Chaplin continued at two reels until 1918, when he left Mutual and joined First National. He then began a Griffith-like extension of running time (to three reels in 1918–1919) that would lead him to intermingle features and shorts in the early twenties. Though the short comedies held their own against features in popularity, the standard program by the late teens was organized around the feature attraction, with the preceding shorts providing variety.

It was the independent producers who introduced and rose with the features. The Motion Picture Patents Company, the fixedly conservative combine that had included all of the principal early producers—most notably Edison, Biograph, and Vitagraph—finally failed in its efforts to exert monopoly through its patent claims and its attempts to control the manufacture of equipment and film stock. Founded in 1908, the Trust, as it came to be known, consistently resisted longer films and stuck to the outright sale of prints—through its distribution arm, General Film Company, established in 1910. With the increasing acceptance of the more expensive features, a rental system evolved whereby after they had made the rounds of the theaters, the prints would return to the producers. By 1914–1915 the Trust was clearly being beaten by the amount and quality of its competition: The independents were too numerous, aggressive, and ingenious; there simply was no way to keep them from producing and distributing films. By 1917, through court decisions in a series of antitrust suits, the Motion Picture Patents Company was declared legally dead.

During those same years, partly as a result of the attempt by the independents to escape the legal harrassment and goon squads of the trust, the center of production shifted from New York to Southern California. (From about 1907 to 1917 Chicago was also a production center, with three large Trust firms, Essanay, Selig, and Kalem located there.) With the feature film as the staple commodity, with the former independents becoming the newly dominant powers as the old trust companies faded away or were absorbed, with Hollywood the production center, and with distribution controlled out of New York, the model was established for industrial expansion for the next decade and beyond.

The general lines followed were already standard in the manufacturing, wholesaling, and retailing of other products. The movie industry had exactly the same requirements as any industry in which the annual costs of production were enormous—as in its close contemporary, the automobile industry, for example. As far as manufacture was concerned, the motion picture and automobile industries were both geographically centered near raw materials and sources of power, with specialized labor pools developed around them (the workers often being imported from abroad). Detroit was within reach of coal, oil, iron ore, and the steel mills. Hollywood's distance from New York and proximity to asylum across the Mexican border were initially among its chief attractions to the independents who settled there. Later Hollywood proved to have attributes similar to the raw materials and sources of power sought in other industries. The extraordinary variety of California scenery meant that virtually any sort of locale—mountain, desert, ocean, forest, rolling fields—could be duplicated within a few hundred miles of Los Angeles. In those days when sunshine was still the principal source of illumination for movie making—even for interiors—Southern California had more of it each year than did the Eastern centers.

Gigantic Hollywood studios became the equivalent of Detroit's River Rouge plant; enormously expensive facilities and equipment were constructed and assembled in both. Motion picture projection, incidentally, was standarized throughout the world; any change which required retooling involved vast sums, and only economic crisis would induce it (the later arrival of sound, color, and wide-screen will offer examples). The assembly-line method devised by Henry Ford eventually would have its equivalent in the Hollywood production process; tendencies in that direction were already manifest in the late teens.

It was Thomas H. Ince who first functioned as a studio head/production supervisor, planning and overseeing an entire production program. He supervised the making of hundreds of films, developing especially the western genre (and its early star, William S. Hart) into a popularity that rivaled the melodramas of Griffith and the comedies of Sennett. In 1915 Ince joined with Griffith and Sennett in the newly formed Triangle Film Corporation, named in honor of the three of them. When Ince left Triangle to form his own company, he built a big new studio at Culver City, which later became the M-G-M Studios.

The production methods that began with Ince would become standard Hollywood practice in the twenties. This piecemeal assembly—especially the practice of shooting out of sequence—however efficient and economical, tended to make the creative process disjointed and strained. The notion of separate specialists in charge of each of the many aspects of production seemed a bitter paradox to those who thought a work of art demanded, by definition, the absolute domination of a single personality. But there just wasn't enough individual genius around to keep the screens lighted with a steady and frequent change of bill. What generally resulted from this ''art by committee''—as with American automobile manufacture—was a high level of standardized technical excellence.

The mass-produced films inevitably came to look pretty much alike, especially to the critical eye. A crucial problem for the motion picture industry thus became how to create the illusion of variety without fundamental differences involving wasteful experimentation and expense. One of the solutions was not unlike the development of automobile types—the sport roadster, the family sedan—and the offering of (slightly) newer models each year. There evolved types of formula pictures (the western, the ''woman's

Thomas H. Ince, center with cigar, probably producing and perhaps directing. Museum of Modern Art/Film Stills Archive.

picture,'' the comedy, the action-adventure) and cycles within each type (the rural comedy, the vamp, the war drama). Technicians could become expert at a particular kind of film making; one western, for example, could effortlessly follow the pattern of another. Audiences always had the choice of going to one of the popular genres one week and to another the next, keeping their entertainment sufficiently varied to obscure the similarities within the limited spectrum. Then too, the familiar had its own attractions. Repetition with variation is pleasurable: Nobody wanted a western so different as to seem unlike a western.

Another device that kept audiences coming back for more was the cultivation of the star personality. People would go again and again to see Mary Pickford or Mabel Normand, Charlie Chaplin or Doug Fairbanks, just to be in their screen presence for an hour and a half on a Friday night. In this case, too, the fans didn't want radical innovation any more than did the producers; they enjoyed their favorites in vehicles rigidly constructed to exploit their appeal. The stars commanded an automatic audience. As long as the range extended from femme fatale Theda Bara to melodramatic heroine Pauline Frederick, from robust comic John Bunny to matinee idol Francis X. Bushman, what more could be asked? Aspiring performers patterned themselves, or were patterned, along the lines of the already established, so that even the individuality of personality could be moved along existing grooves.

Finally, the whole enterprise was enveloped in an unprecedented amount of promotion and advertising designed to whip up audience expectations. Each film, even if essentially indistinguishable from others preceding it, was presented as the most spectacular, the most action-packed, the funniest, the most heartwarming—in short, as something not to be missed. Press agentry soon encompassed the stars' lives off screen as well as on, and made them into demigods whose mythological existence commanded constant attendance and unswerving devotion. That was how the system came to work.

By the end of the first quarter-century of film, production—which had begun in a tar-paper shack or out on the street—had moved into large, permanent studios, clustered for the most part around Los Angeles. Distribution initially was a simple and direct affair: The producers sold prints of films outright to those showing them—at so much per foot, like cordwood; ten cents per foot, or one hundred dollars per reel, was common, regardless of the quality of the entertainment. When audiences became tired of seeing the same films from one exhibitor, it occurred to somebody to set up an ''exchange'' whereby exhibitors could trade in their prints and—for a small fee for the service—receive used prints of different films from other exhibitors. With increased competition among producers and discrimination on the part of the public, the practice of rental instead of sale gradually evolved; producers then received a share of the actual box-office drawing power of their films, greater for the more attractive and expensive, less for the others. This practice made for one of the singularities of the industry: The product is not bought or sold; customers merely pay to spend some time looking at it. The retailers (exhibitors) return a share of that income to the wholesalers (distributors), who in turn subtract their expenses and profits and pass the remainder on to the manufacturers (producers).

Exhibition, which had started as part of vaudeville programs, began to take place in nickelodeons from 1905 on, when films became longer and more of them narrative. Named for the price of admission, these first movie houses characteristically were converted store fronts, perhaps with chairs rented from a local funeral parlor. The nickelodeons showed continuous programs of assorted short films; the enormously successful *The Great Train Robbery* opened many of them. With the arrival of features and the increasing popularity of film, former stage theaters were converted to motion picture exhibition. The big era of showing movies in the town's ''opera house'' and competing with stage road shows was from 1913 through 1916. At that time, there were perhaps as many as 28,000 movie theaters of all types in the U.S. A new and more pretentious type of screen theater was initiated in 1914 with the opening of the Strand on Broadway, soon to be followed by others with equal ambitions. Widespread construction of theaters designed especially for movies did not occur, however, until the 1920s.

By the end of World War I in late 1918, the American film had arrived at its enduring essentials as an art-industry: a steady flow of features accompanied by shorts, especially by popular comedies; a national distribution in which prints circulated out of regional exchanges, within a rental system that permitted the income to flow back through exhibitors and distributors to producers; and theaters gradually being formed into chains by enterprising exhibitors, accommodating larger and more demanding audiences paying higher prices. It was these fundamentals extended to an international scale that gave the United States its lead in the conquest of the world's screens once the war was over. Growth of the medium could then be resumed unimpeded by national boundaries.

FILMS OF THE PERIOD

1914
A Fool There Was (Frank Powell)
Judith of Bethulia
  (David Wark Griffith)
Making a Living (Charles Chaplin)
The Squaw Man (Cecil B. De Mille)
Tillie's Punctured Romance
  (Mack Sennett)

1915
The Birth of a Nation (Griffith)
The Tramp (Chaplin)

1916
Civilization (Thomas H. Ince)
Intolerance (Griffith)
The Pawnshop (Chaplin)
The Rink (Chaplin)

1917
Easy Street (Chaplin)
The Immigrant (Chaplin)
Teddy at the Throttle (Sennett)

1918
Blind Husbands (Erich von Stroheim)
Hearts of the World (Griffith)
Shoulder Arms (Chaplin)

1919
Broken Blossoms (Griffith)

BOOKS ON THE PERIOD

BALIO, TINO, ed., *The American Film Industry.* Madison: University of Wisconsin Press, 1976. 499 pp.

BAXTER, JOHN, *Sixty Years of Hollywood.* Cranbury, N.J.: A. S. Barnes & Co., Inc., 1973. 284 pp.

BLUM, DANIEL, *A Pictorial History of the Silent Screen.* New York: The Putnam Publishing Group, 1982.

BROWNLOW, KEVIN, *The Parade's Gone By.* New York: Alfred A. Knopf, Inc., 1968. 590 pp.

CASSADY, RALPH, JR., *Monopoly in Motion Picture Production and Distribution: 1908–1915.* Los Angeles: Bureau of Business and Economic Research, University of California, 1959. 66 pp.

EVERSON, WILLIAM K., *The American Movie.* New York: Atheneum Publishers, 1963. 149 pp.

EVERSON, WILLIAM K., *American Silent Film.* New York: Oxford University Press, 1978. 387 pp.

GRIFFITH, RICHARD, ARTHUR MAYER, and EILEEN BOWSER, *The Movies.* New York: Simon & Schuster, Inc., 1981.

HAMPTON, BENJAMIN B., *A History of the American Film Industry from its Beginnings to 1931.* New York: Dover Publications, Inc., 1970. 456 pp. (originally published in 1931 as *A History of the Movies*)

HIGHAM, CHARLES, *The Art of the American Film, 1900–1971.* Garden City, N.Y.: Doubleday & Co., Inc., 1973. 322 pp.

JACOBS, LEWIS, *The Rise of the American Film: A Critical History.* New York: Teachers College Press, Columbia University, 1968. 631 pp. (originally published in 1939)

JOBES, GERTRUDE, *Motion Picture Empire.* Hamden, Conn.: Archon Books, 1966. 398 pp.

KINDEM, GORHAM, ed., *The American Movie Industry: The Business of Motion Pictures.* Carbondale and Edwardsville: Southern Illinois University Press, 1982. 448 pp.

RAMSAYE, TERRY, *A Million and One Nights: A History of the Motion Picture.* New York: Simon and Schuster, Inc., 1964. 868 pp. (originally published in 1926)

SKLAR, ROBERT, *Movie-made America: A Social History of American Movies.* New York: Random House, Inc., 1975. 340 pp.

SLIDE, ANTHONY, *Aspects of American Film History Prior to 1920.* Metuchen, N. J.: The Scarecrow Press, Inc., 1978. 161 pp.

SPEHR, PAUL C., *The Movies Begin: Making Movies in New Jersey 1887–1920.* Newark, N.J.: Newark Museum and Morgan Press, 1977.

STANLEY, ROBERT H., *The Celluloid Empire: A History of the American Movie Industry.* New York: Hastings House Publishers, 1978. 328 pp.

TAYLOR, DEEMS, MARCELENE PETERSON, and BRYANT HALE, *A Pictorial History of the Movies.* New York: Simon & Schuster, Inc., 1949. 375 pp.

WAGENKNECHT, EDWARD, *The Movies in the Age of Innocence.* Norman: University of Oklahoma Press, 1962. 280 pp.

4

Scandinavian Film, 1917–1924

Like the Americans, whose initial noninvolvement and later brief participation in World War I had given them such an advantage at a crucial time in film history, the neutral Swedes and Danes were free to pursue evolving screen trends. Denmark was in the best position to take advantage of the opportunity, having a well-established industry that had competed successfully throughout the world in the years before 1914. Nordisk Films Kompagni, founded in Copenhagen in 1906, made hundreds of films during the first years of the war—though by war's end its market had contracted to Scandinavia and Germany. Sweden's ascendancy began somewhat later—its major firm, Svensk Filmindustri, grew out of a merger in 1919—and carried over into the immediate postwar years.

DENMARK

Those who have seen a considerable sampling of the early Danish films have found them generally equal in quality to American efforts at the time, and sometimes startlingly advanced. In certain ways Denmark provided a transition from the forms and styles being developed by Griffith, Sennett, Ince, and the others, to the distinctive Swedish cinema arising during the war—which in turn was succeeded by the high period of German silent film. As had the Americans, the Danes made important use of the out-of-doors, rendered in clear and crisp photography; and Scandinavian films have continued to be marked by the beauty and moodiness of their landscapes.

The Danish stories, however, began to take advantage of the darker and more mystical tradition of Scandinavian folklore and literature. Predominantly psychological rather than sociological in their concerns, the narratives were often subjective (from a character's point of view) as well as objective (from the film maker's). In these latter respects they foreshadowed the Swedes as well as the German film of the 1920s. Given their themes, the acting style was required to be more subtle and introspective than the broad, emphatic performances generally employed in the American historical spectacles, action-melodramas, and comedies.

The pioneer Benjamin Christensen, contemporaneous with Griffith in his use of closeups, pans, and cross-cutting, made a strong directorial beginning with *The Mysterious X* (1913), in which he also starred. In it he introduced the themes of mystery and the supernatural that would become his specialty. His work reached its fullest development in *Witchcraft Through the Ages* (1922). With Christensen playing the devil, the film deals with diabolism from the Middle Ages to the twentieth century. It is still a disturbing, even curiously "modern" work with a singular tension among diverse elements, which include documentary and psychoanalytic aspects as well as the nudity and sexual perversion that caused it to be banned in many countries. Following its suc-

Witchcraft Through the Ages (Sweden, 1922, Benjamin Christensen). Museum of Modern Art/Film Stills Archive.

cess he made films in Germany and then in the United States (where he was known as Christiansen)—a route followed by many other Scandinavian film makers—before returning to Denmark in the early thirties.

The giant directorial figure Carl Theodor Dreyer links Denmark's early contributions most directly to the near present, and links Danish cinema to the screens of the world. Dreyer transcends national and temporal boundaries of film history such as those that mark this text. Working over a long period in a number of countries, he was his own "movement." The distinctiveness of his mature preoccupations and style finally had much more to do with Dreyer himself than with Denmark, where he was often less well appreciated than elsewhere.

Dreyer began in film as a writer of titles for Nordisk, in 1912. He then took on various jobs, including editing and script writing, until directing his first film—*The President* (1919). Adapted from a novel by Karl Emil Franzos, the film is said to be neither particularly distinguished in itself nor representative of his later work. His second film, *Leaves from Satan's Book* (1920), though also based on a novel (by Marie Corelli), was clearly influenced by Griffith's *Intolerance.* It would also seem to have some connection with Christensen's *Witchcraft Through the Ages.*

Leaves from Satan's Book has four sections, set in the Holy Land at the time of Christ, the Inquisition in Spain, the French Revolution, and finally the 1918 civil war between the Reds and the Whites in Finland. The use of the French Revolution and the Finnish war are merely coincidental; Dreyer's concern is more spiritual and moral than political. Throughout the film Satan is disguised as different characters tempting people to betray their friends and family. In spite of the apparent conceptual similarities to *Intolerance,* the *Leaves* stories are not intercut, and the film contains many of the elements that would consistently characterize Dreyer's later work. There is the emphasis on religious and supernatural themes, the use of non-actors for aptness in appearance and character, and the use of settings in which structural design is prominent and realism is combined with a simplification of detail. In addition to Griffith-like rapid cutting and large closeups, there are some long-running takes with the camera in movement, to include a maximum of uninterrupted expressive action.

As *Leaves from Satan's Book* owes something to Griffith, Dreyer's third film (which premiered six months before *Leaves*) gives evidence of homage to Victor Sjöström, the great Swedish pioneer who had started his own major work a few years earlier. Entitled *The Parson's Widow,* Dreyer's film was adapted from a Norwegian short story based on an event that occurred about 1600. The film was produced for Nordisk's Swedish rival, Svensk Filmindustri, and shot entirely on location in Norway. Against this authentic background, Norwegian peasants played themselves. The imposing title role which dominates the film was created by a seventy-seven-year-old woman who knew herself to be near death, as did the character at the end of the film.

Dreyer's work continued in Berlin and Copenhagen, with a steady succession of features during the first half of the twenties. Beyond that period stand his scattered masterpieces: *The Passion of Joan of Arc* (1928), *Vampyr* (1932), *Day of Wrath* (1943), *Ordet* (1954), and *Gertrud* (1964). It is this latter body of work—sparse because of Dreyer's rigid integrity, the difficulty of his themes, and the absolute control he demanded over every phase of production—that has assured Dreyer his place in film history. He moved increasingly away from dependence on editing as a primary means of creative control, and toward lengthy wide-angled shots with almost imperceptible camera movement,

The Parson's Widow (Denmark, 1920, Carl Theodor Dreyer). Museum of Modern Art/Film Stills Archive.

framing a succession of painterly compositions. His contributions to the evolution of film form are not of a kind that lends itself easily to use by other film makers. They are subtle, locked into a personal style, and kept subservient to the problems with which he deals.

Dreyer's obsessive concerns for the effects of organized religion in relation to individual belief—effects that he sees as usually repressive, but capable of being transcended by the human spirit—characterize *Joan of Arc, Day of Wrath,* and *Ordet.* The ambiguous malignity of what would have been a much more mechanical horror story in other hands gives *Vampyr* metaphysical dimensions; in *Gertrud* human love is expressed in terms of a creed. Only the Swede Ingmar Bergman (who owes much to Dreyer), Robert Bresson in France, and the Spaniard Luis Buñuel (in his own way) have devoted themselves in such a consistent manner to themes that are religious in a broad sense and sometimes theological in their bases. Of course the differences among the work of these four film makers, even thematically, are greater than the similarities; but to some extent they are cultural and religious differences. Dreyer and Bergman are the dark Northern Lutherans; Bresson the austere, even ascetic, French Catholic, Buñuel the angry Spanish apostate obsessed with the Church.

As for Dreyer, no film maker in the brief history of the art has dealt more directly or persistently with the fundamental questions surrounding goodness and evil, belief and meaninglessness, the forces that give life and those that lead to death. He uses his troubled, totally credible characters as evidence—the proper study of mankind being man, and with Dreyer especially, woman—and argues out of anguish and compassion for them. The positive half of his antitheses always stems from the individual human being; the negative from institutions and conventions, irrelevant if not antipathetic to the needs of the person.

SWEDEN

In the same year Dreyer began work for Nordisk, 1912, two men entered the Swedish film industry, ready to transform it. Victor Sjöström and Mauritz Stiller had both trained as theatrical actors, and each appeared in the first film that he directed—*Mother and Daughter* and *The Gardener,* respectively. Sjöström's film-acting career later extended to his performance as the old doctor in Bergman's *Wild Strawberries* (1958); but he died in 1960, after a lengthy illness, without having seen his final contribution to Swedish cinema.

Of the two, Stiller now seems the lesser artist. Absorbed with technique and somewhat lacking in depth, he turned out a steady succession of what appear to have been unmemorable films—excepting some delightful comedies such as *Love and Journalism* (1916) or *Thomas Graal's Best Film* (1917), the latter about movie making, with Sjöström playing the title role. *Erotikon* (1920) was a sophisticated, risqué comedy rather like those Cecil B. De Mille was turning out in America at that time. Ernst Lubitsch, who would become master of this genre, credited *Erotikon* as having led him to it.

But it was when Stiller turned to the novels of Selma Lagerlöf, often drawn from legend, that he acquired full stature. *Sir Arne's Treasure* (1919) is regarded by many as his masterwork. The grim foreboding of this morality tale of violence and punishment, the prominence of the rural Swedish landscape, and the use of the supernatural (in a dream sequence) set forth qualities of Swedish cinema that would become typical, and point forward to Bergman's *The Virgin Spring* (1960). *Gunnar Hede's Saga* (1922) was another of Stiller's Lagerlöf adaptations.

The last film made by Stiller in Sweden may be taken as marking the end of this briefly fruitful period. Also based on Selma Lagerlöf's writing, *The Story of Gösta Berling* (1924) is today probably the best known of Stiller's works, at least in this country, which may be because it features a young Greta Garbo in her first major role. The version remaining is about half the length of the four-hour original. We can sense, however, that the whole may have had a power not unlike the long and complicated novel on which it is based, and can admire some of the scenes for their individual worth. Along with his meticulous skill with camera and editing, Stiller seems to have been an accomplished director of actors: Garbo's performance—she was then only seventeen—is remarkable; Lars Hanson (who would also emigrate to America) is forceful and convincing as the protagonist, a clergyman with a rebellious temperament.

Stiller and Garbo went to Berlin for the premiere of *Gösta Berling* and remained there to work. As they left Sweden, the Swedish film was starting into a general decline, to which their absence contributed. After being involved in an abortive German production, and after Garbo's star-making appearance there in G. W. Pabst's *The Joyless Street* (1925), Stiller was invited to go to America. He arranged for his protégée to accompany him. As they departed from Germany, the greatest days of the German silent film were

The Story of Gösta Berling
(Sweden, 1924, Mauritz Stiller).
Museum of Modern Art/Film
Stills Archive.

coming to an end, occasioned in part by the emigration of German film makers to the U.S. Unhappily, like many another European, Stiller found himself unable to work effectively within the American studio system. He left Hollywood in 1928, and died shortly after his return to Stockholm.

Sjöström, who became Seastrom when he arrived in America two years before Stiller, was considerably more successful in making the change. His best Hollywood work retains some of the characteristics prominent in Scandinavian films. The moral and religious conflict of *The Scarlet Letter* (1926) is, of course, very like the kinds of thematic materials that attracted Dreyer and Stiller as well as Sjöström. The lonely countryside and hostile elements of *The Wind* (1928) have their counterparts in many Swedish films.

As early as 1913 Sjöström had commanded attention with *Ingeborg Holm,* an analysis of madness in a workhouse setting, with powerful performances under his direction. *Terje Vigen* (1917), from a poem by Henrik Ibsen, marked the beginning of the best years of Swedish silent cinema. In it Sjöström directed himself as the bitter old sailor who lives alone on an island. The natural setting of ocean, cliffs, and sea birds strongly reinforces the mood. *The Outlaw and His Wife* (1917) again has Sjöström in the role of an outsider—a thief hiding in isolation, attempting to escape his fate, who finally meets death in the snow and cold of a northern winter. Of the several Selma Lagerlöf works that he directed, *The Phantom Chariot* (1920) is surely the most exceptional.

Lagerlöf's contribution to Swedish silent film was profound and seems unique in the history of the motion picture. Though Dreyer insisted on using literary texts as a basis for his films (a practice by no means universal in America), I can think of no other instance in which the output of a *single* literary figure served to such an extent to inspire a national film movement. Her influence began in 1917, when Sjöström directed *The Girl from the Marsh Croft* from one of her stories, and it extended throughout this high period of Swedish film. It was as if the films at their best were extensions into a new medium of Lagerlöf's vision. Given their exceptional visual beauty, they could scarcely be called "literary" in the usual sense; that is, noncinematic. Yet the films based on her works were infused with the writer's understanding of the shared Swedish tradition and heritage.

Lagerlöf's *Körklaren,* which Sjöström made into *The Phantom Chariot,* was not altogether typical of her work. Contemporary in setting, the subject matter suggests a deadly serious *Major Barbara*—replete with Salvation Army, dedicated heroine, and the chap who doesn't want to be saved—but with the theme reversed. Shaw maintains that economics is the underlying cause of drunkenness and brutality, that faith is of no use in helping to eradicate them. Lagerlöf and Sjöström say drink is the cause that effects brutality, that the problem can be solved only through religious salvation. That alcoholism has been a serious social problem in Sweden is clear from the way it is dealt with—as an absolute, motivating force and a highly contagious, lethal disease.

The stylistic line from *The Phantom Chariot* to the films of Ingmar Bergman seems clear and direct. Bergman must have been thinking of this film particularly while making *Wild Strawberries* (1957). Not only does Sjöström play the principal role in both films, nearly forty years apart, but Bergman opens with a scene involving a horse-drawn hearse, the central symbol of the Sjöström film. Intricate flashback construction under-pins both films as each shifts from a crucial moment in the protagonist's story (New Year's Eve, a university convocation) to let us discover how life has gone wrong for him. The character in each film faces his past as he nears death. In Bergman's *The Seventh Seal* (1956), Death is remarkably close to the servant of death in *The Phantom Chariot;* close in function—as he moves about the earth collecting the dead; and close in visual treatment—the cowl. This is not to suspect Bergman of facile copying, but rather to sug-gest that Sjöström, himself stemming from a firm tradition of Swedish drama and literature, had established a main line for the Swedish film.

Certainly *The Phantom Chariot* is remarkably different from the American films preceding and contemporary with it. Unlike much of Griffith's work, it is deliberately small in scale, intimate, with essentially only four characters. More significant, it con-centrates on internal conflict and struggle rather than on the external. There are no bat-tles or chases; very little action, in fact, in comparison with the American films. Perfor-mances, too, are more subtle and restrained; more lifelike, perhaps, or maybe just closer to Strindberg and Ibsen than to Belasco and MacKaye. The expressive range of the faces is quite remarkable: slower, more simplified and controlled; capable of suggesting, with great economy and precision, subjects of thought and topics of conversation.

The sets and costuming are in a line of naturalism we associate with Zola, whose *L'Assommoir* also dealt with alcoholism among the poor. The slum apartment and rooms, the saloon and prison cell, are considerably more sordid and depressing than Griffith's tenement scenes in *The Musketeers of Pig Alley* (1913) or *The Mother and the Law* (1916). Unlike the American films, and preceding the Germans', there are a great number of night interiors and "exteriors" shot in the studio. In many technical ways the film is similar to the great German silents of a few years later, and quite superior to anything achieved before. The superimposition of the ghostly carriage as it makes its rounds is very skillfully managed. The supernatural element, incidentally, was much more characteristic of the Scandinavian and German films than of the American.

David Holm, the Sjöström protagonist, remains a curious antihero. Griffith's characters were either good or bad, or they were like Congressman Stoneman in *The Birth of a Nation*—good, but causing evil through a lack of understanding of the true situation. David Holm is a bit more complex: We know that he has good stuff in him; but after his fall from grace he remains willfully selfish and brutish. Finally, and perhaps most important, Sjöström's view of humanity and of human corruptibility is clearly much darker than Griffith's—and some would say more mature or realistic. In *The Phantom Chariot* despair becomes so great that the ending is unconvincing when it stops short of the complete destruction of husband and wife. It is scarcely a happy ending, however: As in the conclusion of Bergman's *The Naked Night* (1953), the characters have been stripped of all pride and dignity and have nothing left but the slight comfort of a shared misery and a will to survive.

In addition to the great loss represented by Stiller's and Sjöström's departure for America, the Swedish film suffered from postwar competition and a limited, largely domestic audience. During the war years the Swedish industry, like the Danish, had helped to fill the vacuum resulting from the virtual closing down of production in Europe. After the war the large popular audiences turned to the stars, adventure, spectacle, and comedy offered by American films. In an effort to regain this lost audience, the Swedes tended to reduce the distinctive qualities that had made their films appealing

The Phantom Chariot (Sweden, 1921, Victor Sjöström). National Film Archive/Stills Library.

in the first place. Instead they pursued a kind of ersatz internationalism designed to compete with Hollywood in the world market—an attempted solution to an apparently insoluble problem that we will see repeated by other countries later on.

While the larger public was lost to Hollywood, the smaller, serious audience was being attracted to the artistry of the newly ascendant German film industry. Admittedly learning more than a little from the Scandinavian films during and immediately after the war, the Germans set about with characteristic resourcefulness and thoroughness to make for themselves a place in the cinematic sun. Though they built on Scandinavian foundations, the films they made could only have appeared in Germany in the twenties; they are firmly locked into and brilliantly reflect a very special time and place.

FILMS OF THE PERIOD

1917
The Girl from the Marsh Croft
   (Victor Sjöström)
The Outlaw and His Wife
   (Sjöström)
Terje Vigen   (Sjöström)

1918
Thomas Graal's First Child
   (Mauritz Stiller)

1919
The President
   (Carl Theodor Dreyer)
Sir Arne's Treasure (Stiller)

1920
Erotikon (Stiller)
Leaves from Satan's Book (Dreyer)
The Parson's Widow (Dreyer)
The Phantom Chariot (Sjöström)

1922
Gunnar Hede's Saga (Stiller)
Witchcraft Through the Ages
   (Benjamin Christensen)

1924
The Story of Gösta Berling (Stiller)

BOOKS ON THE PERIOD

BERGSTEN, BEBE, *The Great Dane and The Great Northern Film Company.* Los Angeles: Locare Research Group, 1973. 116 pp.
COWIE, PETER, *Sweden I and II.* 2 vols. New York: A. S. Barnes & Co., Inc., 1970.
HARDY, FORSYTH, *Scandinavian Film.* New York: Arno Press, 1972. 94 pp. (originally published in 1952)
LAURITZEN, EINAR, *Swedish Films.* New York: Museum of Modern Art, 1962. 32 pp.

5

Great German Silents, 1919–1925

Following the end of World War I, while America moved towards domination of the world motion picture industry, Germany led the art into newly urbane subject matter and refinement of technique. This brief period of cinematic ascendancy occurred at a time when the country itself was desperately unstable in its political, economic, and social life. The loss of the war and the humiliation of the Versailles Treaty peace terms were damaging to national pride. The shaky and directionless Weimar Republic faced rioting and anarchy. Inflation, unemployment, and food shortages crippled the economy and brought great hardship to the German people. Morale was lower than it had ever been during the war. The highest point of German silent film (1922–1924) was precisely the lowest point for the nation. French troops occupied the Ruhr industrial heartland; the Deutschmark was utterly worthless; revolt was incipient in Bavaria.

With the stabilization of the mark in 1924 and the election of war hero Field Marshal Paul von Hindenburg to the presidency in 1925, a kind of order was restored. Within German society, however, the amorality and decadence portrayed in the American musical *Cabaret* (based on stories by Christopher Isherwood) and reflected in Bertolt Brecht's and Kurt Weill's *The Threepenny Opera* (first produced in Germany in the late twenties) succeeded the immediate postwar years and formed the setting for the triumph of Naziism. At the same time, the German film began to lose its particular excellence, a loss caused in considerable measure by American infiltration and dominance within the German film industry.

During the first half of the twenties, however, there was a vitality in all the German arts, as if the national disease had caused a feverish counteractivity. Literature and, especially, drama and the visual arts, were released from the rigidities of a Hohenzollern monarchy and Prussian militarism. Prompted by the disillusionment of the war and the radically changed values that followed its end, newly expressive forms and styles were sought. At this time the plays of Brecht, Ernst Toller, and Georg Kaiser were first produced; Max Reinhardt, in his more conventional historical-romantic stagings, added elements of lighting and handling of crowds that would be translated directly into film. Lyonel Feininger, Vasily Kandinsky, and Paul Klee were among the many active painters. Others affiliated with the Berlin *Sturm* group became stage and then film designers. The general aesthetic impulses would feed into film and in some ways find their ultimate expression in the collective and composite film art.

In America, the West Coast center of film production was separated by a continent (some would say culturally and spiritually as well) from the East Coast center of the other arts and communications media. In Germany, Berlin was not only the national capital, but the center for all the arts, including film. Those working in the traditional arts were free from feelings of condescension toward the movies that characterized many Americans; on the contrary, German artists expressed a lively curiosity about the new art form and demonstrated their interest by trying a hand at it. It was possible for them to do so without changing their place of residence or style of life, and German films owed much of their sophistication to those trained in the older arts.

Whereas American films had been populated by good guys, bad guys, funny guys, and pretty women, the Germans started probing complex and frequently disturbed characters along loosely Freudian lines, which stimulated the additions to technique noteworthy in their work. While the Americans had concentrated on action and melodrama, the Germans explored the psychological and pictorial. In their quest for means to objectify inner consciousness, they created a world on film that represents not so much a physical reality, as most of us perceive it, as a state of mind: the universe distorted and stylized to express what we might feel about it. Expressionism, as opposed to American realism and naturalism, was the prevalent mode. First appearing in extreme and sustained form in *The Cabinet of Dr. Caligari* (1919), it is also manifest in subtle ways in much of the German production of the twenties, as will be noted.

PREDOMINANT TYPES AND THEMES

Looking at these German films of 1919–1925 as a body, film historians have identified three prominent types and themes that make evident most of the major German contributions. First were the historical/mythological films in which architectural settings, careful costuming, and romantic lighting, as well as the handling of massed crowds, reflect Max Reinhardt's theories and experiments in stage production. In these films, history is treated psychologically and spectacularly, rather than realistically; they might be called historical fantasies. Ernst Lubitsch, who had acted in Reinhardt's stage company, was one master of this genre. His accounts of the Bourbons (*Passion/Madame du Barry*, 1919) or the Tudors (*Deception/Anna Boleyn*, 1920) center around a bedroom-keyhole view of the past, which suggests that great historical events can be seen as extensions of sexual intrigue. Someone once observed that Cecil B. De Mille, much indebted to Lubitsch, presented the Crusades as if they were fought for the sole benefit of Loretta

Madame du Barry/Passion (Germany, 1919, Ernst Lubitsch). Museum of Modern Art/Film Stills Archive.

Young; the same might be said about Lubitsch, the French Revolution, and Pola Negri. Onto gossipy biographies Lubitsch overlaid massive spectacles of the Bastille and the Tower of London, using hundreds of extras.

Allied to the Lubitsch pageants were Fritz Lang's less popular but more innovative and significant mythological/historical evocations. *Destiny* (1921), part legend, part fairy tale, includes three episodes placed in earlier times: one in a Moslem city, another in Venice during the Renaissance, and the final one in a charmingly fantastic China. Much of the pleasure in Lang's film is derived from the stylized settings. The dominant image is the enormous blank wall—in the connective story—which fills the whole screen and dwarfs the humans. Trained as an architect, Lang went on to even fuller expression of his themes in gigantic re-creations of the German saga *Die Nibelungen* (1924)—a film that became so vast it had to be released in two parts: *Siegfried,* and *Kriemhild's Revenge.* (*Metropolis,* 1926, though set in the future, is like the films about the past in that it re-creates another time and place through predominantly architectural means.) Much more serious in intent than Lubitsch's, Lang's spectacles are nonetheless offered as feasts for the eyes. The careful visual patterns and breathtaking scale are designed to be enjoyed in their own right as well as to be the expression of what seems an especially Germanic imagination about a prehistoric or fantasied past. Static they may be; but monumental too.

Also set in the past, though frequently even less specific as to time, were the second group: the sinister, fantastic, macabre films in which expressionistic decor plays an

Siegfried (Germany, 1924, Fritz Lang). National Film Archive/Stills Library.

important part and the subjects are often derived from old legends and ballads. *The Cabinet of Dr. Caligari* is the most famous of these. It could also be considered a precedent for the avant-garde film, predating the movement that would start in Berlin with Hans Richter's *Rhythmus 21* and Viking Eggeling's *Symphonie diagonale* (both of 1921) and would then headquarter in Paris.

Originally Fritz Lang was to direct *Caligari*. When he withdrew to complete another film, Robert Wiene was appointed in his place. It wasn't the direction, however, so much as the eerily frightening story (by Carl Mayer and Hans Janowitz) and, particularly, the expressionistic settings, that made this film both seminal and enduring in its fascination. The names of the three painters who designed the sets—Hermann Warm, Walter Röhrig, and Walter Reimann—appear in various collaborations on the credits of many of the finest of the German films of this period. *Caligari* remains the purest and fullest use of the expressionist credo in film: "Films must be drawings brought to life," said Warm. The "exteriors" as well as the interiors were all constructed from wood, plaster, and canvas. The world created is that of a madman, a paranoid whose fears derive not only from the people and events around him, but also from the shapes of nature, the town, a fairground, and an insane asylum. Jagged irregularity dominates: trees like barbed spears; pools of black shadow cast by no discernible light (shadows and light were in fact painted in order to better control them); a maze

The Cabinet of Dr. Caligari (Germany, 1919, Robert Wiene). National Film Archive/Stills Library.

of crooked streets; ramps and stairways foreshortened; and houses like clusters of strange geometrical blocks balanced precariously.

Scarcely the sort of film to inspire popular imitation (it was moderately successful), there were nonetheless a small group of films which reflected its influence. Perhaps best remembered are Paul Wegener's *The Golem* (1920) and F. W. Murnau's *Nosferatu* (1922). *The Golem* was based on an ancient Jewish legend about a practitioner of black magic—a rabbi of great erudition—who brings to life a clay monster to aid the Jews against their governing Christian oppressors. As Baron Frankenstein also discovered, such monsters often attack those who create them, punishing us for our presumption. The abstractly fashioned medieval town, with its skyline of sharply angled roofs and tilted chimney pots, looks like twisted gingerbread; there isn't a straight line visible. A gigantic gate dwarfs the human beings. Irregular arches and inverted Vs predominate. The camera frequently shoots through the archways, imposing their strange shapes on the frame itself. The citizens—in tall conical hats, filing in silhouette along the top of a wall—are again part of a nightmarish world like that of *Caligari*.

In Murnau's *Nosferatu,* the themes of somnambulism, a man under another's diabolical power, mass murder, madness, all recur, and the agent of death is destroyed while attacking the young female loved one in her bedroom. Count Orlock, who is

The Golem (Germany, 1920, Paul Wegener). Museum of Modern Art/Film Stills Archive.

Nosferatu-the-Vampire by night, strongly suggests Cesare of *Caligari* in appearance, bodily movement, and facial contortions. Tall, thin, grotesquely made up and costumed, he moves in a trance (not unlike Cesare) when under the curse of his vampirism. From real exteriors Murnau has selected the sorts of buildings (the deserted castle, the town with its steep pointed roofs, the narrow twisting streets) and landscapes (rocky roads with abrupt inclines and turns, a deformed tree) that look as if they could have served as models for the abstractions created in the studio for *Caligari*. Going beyond the prototype, the expressionistic influence appears in specifically cinematic devices: fast motion, negative images, superimposition, and stop motion—which permits a tarpulin to remove itself and a ship hatch to open of its own accord. The huge black shadow of Nosferatu, now created by light, moves horrifyingly toward and over his victims, unlike the painted theatrical shadows in *Caligari*. Unreal, irrational, and hauntingly disturbing, these expressionist works offered a totally new kind of film.

The third group of German films from this period, marked least obviously by expressionistic tendencies, and most important in advancing film technique, began with the *Kammerspielfilm* (literally "chamber play film"), which derived from the Reinhardt theater. This style was marked by unity of time, place, and action, with virtually no titles; few characters, usually lower middle class; sparse decor, with objects given extraordinary importance; and intimate psychological content. Its characteristics are further described, lovingly and sensitively, by Lotte Eisner in *The Haunted Screen: Expressionism in the German Cinema and the Influence of Max Reinhardt.* Key films were Paul Leni's *Backstairs* (1921), Lupu Pick's *Shattered* (1921), and Murnau's *The Last Laugh* (1924). Scripts for all three were written by Carl Mayer.

Finest of the Kammerspielfilms, and arguably of all German silent cinema, is

Nosferatu (Germany, 1922, F. W. Murnau). Museum of Modern Art/Film Stills Archive.

The Last Laugh. It chronicles the pathos of a proud and majestic doorman at an elegant hotel, who, having become too old to handle heavy baggage and perform his other functions adequately, is demoted to washroom attendant. Seemingly loved and respected by his family and neighbors in his earlier status, he is reviled and ridiculed when they learn of his demotion. In the epilogue, an eccentric American millionaire dies in the men's room, with a will in his wallet leaving his fortune to whomever is with him at his death. This whimsical conclusion, while lifting us out of the despair of the poor old man (played by Emil Jannings), by its very improbability reinforces the sense that real life is unhappy and that only stories have happy endings.

A genre related to the Kammerspielfilm is the ''street film,'' a term used by Siegfried Kracauer in his *From Caligari to Hitler: A Psychological History of the German Film*. Beginning with Karl Grune's prototypal *The Street* (1923), street films include G. W. Pabst's *The Joyless Street* (1925) and Bruno Rahn's *Tragedy of a Street* (1927). In these films, most typically, the male protagonists are drawn away from home, family, and bourgeois life by the lure of the city, the seductive promise of excitement and sensual pleasures. These were individualized studies of lower middle-class life, often set within or alongside entertainment, and sometimes vaguely underworld, milieus. If extracted from the frequently superb skill of their realizations, the plot themes might appear melodramatic or morbidly sentimental. Though rooted in contemporary reality, these films were concerned primarily with character study—frequently with the personality disintegration of an individual or group of individuals.

The Joyless Street, featuring Scandinavians Asta Nielsen, Greta Garbo, and Einar Hanson, deals more directly with economic and political problems in postwar

The Last Laugh (Germany, 1924, F. W. Murnau). National Film Archive/Stills Library.

The Joyless Street (Germany, 1925, G. W. Pabst). Museum of Modern Art/Film Stills Archive.

Variety (Germany, 1925, E. A. Dupont). Museum of Modern Art/Film Stills Archive.

Vienna (inflation, black market, stock manipulation, ineffectuality of government) than do other street films. Its realistic visual style is also quite different from the other street films; it was said at the time to be an example of *die Neue Sachlichkeit* (the new realism). Showing how these national problems lead to general corruption and dislocation of moral and spiritual values, Pabst concentrated on the pressures exerted on a bourgeois father: The man faces old age and poverty, and his beautiful daughter is about to be forced into prostitution; they are saved by a *deus ex machina* in the form of a U.S. aid commission.

   Variety (1925), directed by E. A. Dupont, though not exactly a Kammerspielfilm or a street film, embodies some of the characteristics of both. It concerns a trio of trapeze artists involved in a romantic triangle; the cuckolded husband (played by Emil Jannings) murders the partner who has betrayed him. The film proper is presented as a long flashback within the framework of Jannings in prison, telling his story to the warden. It was a great international success, especially popular in the United States.

PRINCIPAL TECHNICAL AND STYLISTIC ADVANCES

An underlying psychological function of all three major types of the German silent film is posited by Siegfried Kracauer in his book *From Caligari to Hitler.* According to him, they offered escape from contemporary social reality—into the past (historical or mythological), into fantasy (expressionist), or into the recesses of individual psyches (Kammerspiel and street films). Certainly it is true that German film makers were preoccupied with the psychological rather than the sociological, and that their new intentions brought innovations of technique to camera, lighting, set design, acting, and script construction.

To some extent the Germans, like the Soviets who would follow in the international spotlight, organized their industry as a vehicle of state. In 1917, when Germany's last great offensive in the West had failed, the giant firm Universum Film A. G. (Ufa) was founded by General Erich Ludendorff; over a third of its initial capital was supplied by the Reich. Mergers and affiliations with other large production firms and control of the biggest chain of first-run theaters led to its dominance. Unlike the Soviets, who used film directly for purposes of education and propaganda, the German cinema was designed primarily to add to Germany's prestige through artistic accomplishment and to project Germany's image before the eyes of the world.

For these purposes, the huge Ufa studios at Neubabelsberg were constructed. The facilities were unrivaled, and the craftspeople working there were the finest known. Many of their names later appeared on screen credits outside Germany, especially in America, decades after this original brilliant period of experiment and training.

Probably the single most striking contribution by the Germans was their fuller use of the moving camera. The Kammerspiel and street films in particular developed this possibility in order to probe character, to follow and bore into protagonists, and to let the world be seen from subjective points of view. In this latter respect the moving camera became part of the general expressionist tendency.

As far back as Porter's *The Great Train Robbery,* the camera had panned and tilted; Griffith had used trucking and dollying as well; but moving the camera while shooting was relatively rare, and usually (not always) confined to the simple function of keeping a moving subject within frame. The standard Griffith method was to rehearse performances with actors, shoot them from the most effective angles and distances from a stationary tripod, then select and arrange the images, adjust the tempo of the action, and heighten the conflict through editing. Griffith thus transcended the spatial and temporal limitations of the stage, offering the varied filmic view rather than the fixed and continuous one available to the playgoer; but the viewpoint remained essentially objective, a recording of *dramatic* action.

The Germans made their camera part of the story in a more profound way. The camera became a *narrative* tool in addition to being a means of recording dramatic action. This potential was employed in two ways, both appearing together in many of the German silent films. First, the camera could become a narrator, like Joseph Conrad's Marlow, leading viewers into and through the story. *The Last Laugh,* for example, opens with the camera descending on an elevator, peering out through its wrought-iron grillwork at the passing floors of the hotel. In one continuous take it moves down to the lobby and across to the revolving door, where it offers a view of the street and of the doorman whistling up cabs, greeting guests, and unloading luggage. It is all the world like a novelist writing "Evening was approaching at the fashionable Hotel Atlantic. On the upper floors the maids scurried back and forth with fresh linen while the guests moved toward the elevator and down into the lobby. There a string ensemble played to seated guests sipping aperitifs. If one crossed the lobby to the tall revolving door awhirl . . . ," and so on. Later, the camera follows at the shoulder of the little night watchman as he makes his rounds, permitting us to see what the light from his electric torch reveals as it bounces along the walls and floors of the corridors.

In the earlier sequences the doorman is viewed from a low camera angle, which exaggerates his size and importance in his splendid uniform and flowing mustache.

When he is reduced to washroom attendant he not only moves lower in social status (and physically below the street level), but the camera is frequently placed at a high angle, further emphasizing the crushed spirit which makes the now stooped body seem small and terribly vulnerable. Again, this kind of film making seems more analogous to a novelist's descriptive capabilities than to anything that can be achieved on a stage.

The other special use of the moving camera fully exploited by the Germans was the possibility of its taking on a character's point of view and even state of mind—what is called "subjective camera." In *The Last Laugh,* after a wedding party at his flat, the doorman is sitting alone amidst post-party debris, amiably bemused by drink. First he is seen to spin in the room as the camera moves around him (the "narrator's" viewpoint); then the room itself revolves as the camera takes on his own tipsy vision. In *Variety,* the camera is mounted on a swinging trapeze to let us experience the vertigo of the disturbed catcher as the audience below seems to approach and then recede. In the same Wintergarten scenes, specially constructed lenses fragment and distort images to suggest psychological states, those of the excited members of the audience as well as those of the principals.

Karl Freund was the cinematographer for both *The Last Laugh* and *Variety,* and it was the German camera work that most strongly impressed Hollywood. Freed entirely from a fixed base on a tripod and from a strictly objective view, the camera now ran or stumbled, got dizzy or suffered from hallucinations, and "saw" the sounds of a reveler's horn blown at midnight or of a woman's footsteps going down a corridor. In the less important films this use of narrative/subjective camera placement and movement was a mere trapping, a "special effect." In the best work this subtly profound innovation opened a whole new range of screen technique, not only affecting the way subjects could be dealt with, but making accessible themes and kinds of characters never before treated.

The other vital component of the cinematographer's craft, lighting, was important to all three major types of German silent film. In the historical-costume films, it followed rather closely the stage lighting developed earlier by Reinhardt. The tableaux were bathed in pools of light and shadow, which enhanced the mood and fit into the total composition of set design, massed extras, and featured players. In the expressionist films the lighting was one of the most evocative means of conveying the bizarre and the threatening as seen and felt by the characters. In the Kammerspiel and street films, often expressionistic in their subtler ways, lighting augmented camera movement to direct the viewer's eye where the film maker wanted it. Frequently the lighting was what most strongly evoked the feelings desired. Modeled lighting exposed a character's face (and soul) for examination. The essential significance of places and objects was rendered through the way they were lit. In these silent films things often seem to take on a life of their own, surrounding and commenting on the lives being led by the protagonists.

In all three types of German films the lighting was thought out and arranged specially to set the overall mood, and in the latter two types, to reflect the emotional states of the characters as well. Often eerie or sombre, at the same time romantic (softening) and decorative, it was vastly different from the consistent brightness and clarity of the American films (up until mid-Griffith, at least). At its most basic level, of course, film, the medium, is simply film, the material: the response to illumination by a coating of light-sensitive emulsion on a cellulose base. The title of cameraman John Alton's book, *Painting with Light,* suggests the way the Germans learned to conceive of and use this primary factor.

Two specific lighting contributions can be noted as well. First was the new prevalence of *low-key* lighting. Suddenly the screen went dark, with candlelit rooms, gloomy stairways, streets at night, cabarets, and all of the other environments that would be natural to the many "night people" of the German film. Sufficiently sensitive emulsions and expertness in laboratory processing had not been available before; nor, more important, had an understanding of the precise control that might be exercised over the cinematographic process. Second was the Germans' use of *key light* (not to be confused with low key, but often occurring in conjunction with it). The key light is the brightest light on the set, usually appearing to come from a source within the scene—a light fixture, a window, a street lamp. Griffith experimented with this possibility (notably in *Broken Blossoms*), but usually he led the eye and created emotional overtones by limiting the amount of area in the frame—cutting from long shot, to medium, to closeup—with the scene generally well and evenly lit.

The Germans came to realize that within a shot, if there is one brighter area amidst less brightly lit surroundings, it becomes the center of attention. They also sensed that it is much more satisfying aesthetically to have a variety of lighting intensities balanced around the frame—a monochromatic equivalent to the painter's placement of pigments. In short, they learned to lead the eye over the screen and to gratify it with the arrangement of the illumination, fitted into a total, ordered composition in which the main elements stand out and are reinforced by the lesser.

The importance of set design to the special effectiveness and unique qualities of the German silent film has already been noted, but can scarcely be exaggerated. Virtually all of the films were shot inside the studio; the painstaking "exteriors" were frequently constructed on a mammoth scale. In *The Last Laugh,* for example, the huge exterior of the Hotel Atlantic and the busy intersection in front of it, with autos, buses, and pedestrians flowing by, are studio creations. Even an exception like Arthur von Gerlach's *The Chronicle of the Gray House* (1923), shot in part out-of-doors, uses the East Prussian moors as Thomas Hardy used those of Dorsetshire. Nature is bent to human purposes and given an anthropomorphic coding to reinforce human conflicts. Most of the crucial action, however, takes place within large, ornate, and calculatedly oppressive, baroque rooms and castle courtyards.

Two prevalent impulses in German set design were rarely separate from each other. The pictorial beauty and grandeur of the historical films had psychological dimensions as well, especially in the work of Fritz Lang. The expressionist tendency offered visual design that was striking in its own right (*The Cabinet of Dr. Caligari*) and large in scale (*The Golem*) as well as being expressive of overall moods and subjective states. Even in the Kammerspiel and street films, which embodied a modified expressionism, the pictorial and psychological functions of the sets were commingled. The Wintergarten scenes in *Variety* dazzle us by their size and opulence, besides serving as the public setting for the private tensions of star performers.

In Lang's *Nibelungen* the huge re-creation of a forest is breathtaking, with its Klieg-light sunshine streaming through the branches of trees as big as sequoias. The blond Siegfried riding slowly into frame on a white horse approaches a sizeable, and palpably real, waterfall. Even the smoke-breathing dragon carries a rare conviction. In a wide-angle long shot of a huge castle courtyard, human figures are placed on the checkerboard tiles to form part of a total visual pattern; Lang evidently intended that we study its vastness and ingenuity as the shot holds on the screen. The costumes, too, are geometrically patterned. This sense of persons being part of a decorative whole is con-

The Chronicle of the Gray House (Germany, 1923, Arthur von Gerlach). Museum of Modern Art/Film Stills Archive.

firmed by a scene in a treasure cave: a large round table piled with ornaments and jewelry is supported by carved dwarfs in chains; when one of them moves slightly, we have an ultimate statement about person being interchangeable with object in a screen world remarkable for its nonhuman use of human beings. Lang seemed to like the idea of humans as statuary; he used it again in *Metropolis,* even more pointedly and ingeniously. The futuristic city of the latter film may have been Ufa's *magnum opus* as far as set construction was concerned. It also marks the last great burst of expressionism.

As for the acting, the monumental and mythological strands in German film did not call for any great change in the pantomimic tradition inherited from the theater; but the Kammerspiel and street films did, in their search for new psychological dimensions. Obviously there was no performance style except the theatrical when film came into being, and the evolution of screen acting included breaking away from a stage tradition—a progress to which Griffith and the Scandinavian film makers had contributed substantially. Griffith's intentions were to make his actors behave more nearly as their characters would in life, and the Scandinavians continued and advanced that approach. The more realistic style of film acting would in turn influence the theater.

In trying to delineate internal states without the help of dialogue, the Germans went beyond realism to a deliberate expressiveness. The actors began working out their characterizations by "becoming" as completely as possible the persons they were play-

Metropolis (Germany, 1927, Fritz Lang). Museum of Modern Art/Film Stills Archive.

ing. Immersing themselves sufficiently in the roles, they would inevitably reveal the characters' feelings through small gestures, the slope of a back, the movement of a head, the eyes—especially the eyes. But to these intuitive physical responses was added an intellectual refinement to make fullest use of silent film limitations (in this sense, its strengths). Through closely observed facial expression and bodily movement, the camera can capture what is eloquent and seems true in the actors' understanding of the characters. This understanding is then ''projected'' effortlessly, to every seat in the house, by the projector shining a large likeness onto the screen. Gestures and expressions formed and shaped for the screen can reveal more than can actors on a relatively distant stage, or even people across a room.

The great German silent film actors—Emil Jannings, Werner Kraus, Conrad Veidt, Lil Dagover, Asta Nielsen, Pola Negri, Greta Garbo—learned to retard and simplify their gestures to make precise psychological points. In *The Joyless Street* the neurotic intensity of Asta Nielsen and the radiant inward beauty of Greta Garbo are conveyed without any of the stage-like busyness of Mae Marsh or Lillian Gish (fine as she was) in the earlier Griffith films. Nielsen, who appeared in Danish films (beginning with *The Abyss,* 1910) before moving to Germany after the war, remains one of the great artists of the silent screen. Perhaps she was the first to suggest a dimension and complexity of feeling beneath the surface of the screen presence. Her style of passionate intensity would be developed to even greater expressiveness by Greta Garbo, who began in Sweden and worked in Germany before coming to the United States. Jannings created remarkable portrayals through a kind of stylization that called for an absolute comprehension of the psychological makeup of his characters and an abstraction and heightening of the physical expression of feeling—an artfulness that did not so much conceal art as transcend life. Jannings lived a great number of screen lives in the studio world, and all of them consistent with the stylistic level of the carefully designed sets and lighting. The total creation evoked the essence of a reality filtered through the strong feelings of a character.

Given the complex interaction of the various elements of technique, the Germans needed more-detailed scripts than did the simpler, more open-air and improvised American films. (Neither Sennett nor Griffith used scripts at all.) If the camera was going to move in a sustained take down a studio street, lights had to be arranged along a predetermined path, sets built to accommodate the full range of its shifting angle and distance, and actors directed and rehearsed to move in relationship to it. Thus script writing, and the production planning growing out of it, achieved new importance. The German script writers could blueprint a film on paper, and the best of them, like Carl Mayer, could go beyond the mechanics to communicate a complete sense of a film. Through written descriptions of images, Mayer defined the kinds of emotional values required and suggested how to achieve them. He also understood clearly what sorts of themes, characters, and emotions lent themselves best to visual expression. The action in his scripts was invariably sparse and simple; the plots, tight in construction, required few intertitles—and ultimately, almost none at all (for example, *Shattered,* 1921, *New Year's Eve,* 1923, and *The Last Laugh*). It seems paradoxical that Griffith, without scripts, tended toward the literary, and required screen words to connect and explain his action. Mayer, working with words, used them to evoke self-explanatory images, which were given physical form by directors, set designers, cinematographers, and performers—the extraordinary collective of German talent in the 1920s.

MIRROR OF THE CULTURE

E. W. and M. M. Robson, in their book *The Film Answers Back,* were possibly the first to note the ways in which the German silent film reflected certain aspects of a nation suffering from social-political sickness that would ultimately lead to a cure worse than the disease. Siegfried Kracauer, in *From Caligari to Hitler,* systematized, elaborated, and extended their insights. His book is both a film history with a thesis and a provocative demonstration of the kinds of things that can be learned about a society by analyzing the content and style of a popular art form. Because of their collective creation and appeal to an anonymous multitude, Kracauer argues, the films of a nation reflect its "mentality," the "inner dispositions" of a culture, more directly than do other arts. In examining German films from the end of World War I to Hitler's accession to power, Kracauer finds revealed a steady succession of attitudes conducive to authoritarianism.

First, he observes that no alternative between tyranny and anarchic chaos is offered: Freedom is not depicted as a possibility. In *The Cabinet of Dr. Caligari,* the options are the asylum (tyranny) or the fair (chaos). This is by no means the only film example assessed by Kracauer. According to him, none of the major German films of this period suggests possible human control over destiny through rational, democratic action. He notes as well the studio construction of unreal worlds and the penchant for organization, which requires submission. Instinct and fate are shown to rule. This is as true of the strangely driven burgher of the street film, led down into corruption by his own vague lusts and longings, as it is of the haunted worlds of the expressionist films in which an unknowable and malevolent destiny shapes the lives of the characters. The extent to which this particular world view was held by the German people and could be invoked in a propaganda program was well understood by Hitler. Finally, Kracauer asserts that fantasy and retrogression were ubiquitous: the escaping of real problems in an unreal world, as in the expressionist films; the recurring image of a man's head on a woman's breast, as in the street films. He reads these symbolic signs as indicating political paralysis and pointing ahead to the passive acceptance of Naziism.[1]

Some have accused Kracauer of bending the films to fit the theory and of ignoring those that don't fall neatly into one of his categories. There is, of course, a danger inherent in the application of any thesis to as diverse a body of data as a nation's films, and a summary condensation of Kracauer's inferences such as the above paragraph must make him seem especially vulnerable to the charge. But those who have pointed to some of his errors and hinted at other discrepancies have failed to offer an alternative understanding to replace his. George Huaco, in *The Sociology of Film Art,* and Paul Monaco, in *Cinema and Society,* deal with the same national period of film making as Kracauer. Though they use somewhat different methodologies and arrive at slightly different conclusions, their findings do not decrease the value or even fundamentally alter Kracauer's contribution. The three authors more or less agree on the very special and remarkably coherent qualities of this cinema. The more we look at the German films from the twenties, the more they seem to offer the kinds of social-psychological meanings Kracauer and others have discovered and to correspond with the findings of historians of the period.

INFLUENCE ON HOLLYWOOD

An old Hollywood saw advises: "If you can't beat 'em, join 'em." Historically this has also meant, "If you can't beat 'em, buy 'em up." There began in the twenties an emigration of German film makers to Hollywood, which would impoverish their native industry and further enrich the dominant American one. The entire principal cast and crew of *Variety* were imported—Erich Pommer (producer), E. A. Dupont (director), Karl Freund (cameraman), Leo Birinski (scenarist), and Emil Jannings and Lya de Putti (stars). Pommer, the production head of Ufa and arguably the man most directly responsible for the German "Golden Era" just surveyed, was lured by Paramount in 1927. Among other directors who emigrated were Ernst Lubitsch, Paul Leni, F. W. Murnau, and Fritz Lang. Cameramen Kurt Courant and Theodore Sparkuhl, along with Freund, brought German cinematography to American films. Actor emigrés also included Pola Negri and Conrad Veidt.

German influence on American films was persistent, lasting decades after the first invasion. The imitation of German successes and the presence of German creative personnel combined to alter earlier American style in regard to moving camera, lighting, and the use of visual narrative transitions rather than titles. Often this "Germanization" was somewhat arbitrary, being applied to native plots and themes without the aesthetic logic that had made form and content so interdependent in the best of the German silent films. Certain film types that developed later in America had their roots in the earlier Ufa and became sturdy hybrids. The horror series of Universal Studios,

[1] See *From Caligari to Hitler,* Chapters 5–10, pp. 61–130, for Kracauer's development of his thesis.

which began with *Dracula* and *Frankenstein* (both 1931), is one example, depending as it did upon sinister and fantastic subjects; expressionistic lighting, makeup and costuming; and special-effects cinematography. A later instance is the cluster of *films noirs,* as the French called them. Reminiscent of the street films, these dark crime melodramas of the middle forties also involve the probing of disordered psyches in a predominantly nighttime studio world. *The Woman in the Window* (1944) and *Scarlet Street* (1945) by Fritz Lang, *Phantom Lady* (1944) and *The Spiral Staircase* (1945) by Robert Siodmak, and *Double Indemnity* (1944) by Billy Wilder, were all made by directors who had worked in Germany.

Aside from losing a large number of their most talented creators, technicians, and performers, a kind of "internationalization" of German films began after the middle of the 1920s, which vitiated the very distinctiveness that had made them popular as well as important. Along with a similar tendency in the Swedish film, this marked the first appearance of one recurring problem of commerce affecting art (which will also be noted in the later production of Italy and Britain). Once a country earns an international prominence through a special national contribution, it attempts to compete with Hollywood on its terms; that is to say, it employs the ingredients that are thought to make American films so successful, seeking an even larger slice of the global box office (which includes the formerly huge American audience). At the same time, American studios set about to coproduce within countries that have demonstrated a successful competitiveness, contributing further to a blurring of national distinctions. In 1925 both Paramount and M-G-M negotiated with Ufa regarding joint production on the continent, using American-German casts and technicians. What Kracauer calls a "synthesis of Hollywood and Neubabelsberg" resulted in a further dilution of German themes and styles.

This is not to say that the German industry suddenly ceased to produce films of enduring value: With the arrival of sound, and before the Nazi government absorbed film into its total state, there was a flurry of innovative and valuable work. But the exceptions to a general decline have to be weighed against the dozens of uniquely fascinating films of the first half of the twenties. From about 1925 onwards the eyes of the film world shifted from Germany to a star rising in the east, a red star. Made for the new government in Russia, another remarkable body of work began to appear—films that could scarcely be more different from the German films in form, content, and purpose.

FILMS OF THE PERIOD

1919
The Cabinet of Dr. Caligari
  (Robert Wiene)
Passion (Ernst Lubitsch)

1920
Deception (Lubitsch)
Genuine (Wiene)
The Golem (Paul Wegener)

1921
Destiny (Fritz Lang)

1922
Dr. Mabuse, the Gambler (Lang)
Nosferatu (F. W. Murnau)
Vanina (Arthur von Gerlach)
Warning Shadows (Arthur Robison)

1923
The Chronicle of the Gray House
   (Gerlach)
The Street (Karl Grune)

1924
The Last Laugh (Murnau)

Die Nibelungen (Lang)
The Treasure (G. W. Pabst)
Waxworks (Paul Leni)

1925
The Joyless Street (Pabst)
Variety (E. A. Dupont)

BOOKS ON THE PERIOD

BARLOW, JOHN D., *German Expressionist Film.* Boston: Twayne Publishers, 1982. 229 pp.

EISNER, LOTTE, *The Haunted Screen: Expressionism in the German Cinema and the Influence of Max Reinhardt.* Berkeley: University of California Press, 1969. 360 pp.

HUACO, GEORGE A., *The Sociology of Film Art.* New York: Basic Books, Inc., 1965. 229 pp.

KRACAUER, SIEGFRIED, *From Caligari to Hitler: A Psychological History of the German Film.* Princeton, N.J.: Princeton University Press, 1947. 361 pp.

MANVELL, ROGER, and HEINRICH FRAENKEL, *The German Cinema.* New York: Praeger Publishers, 1971. 159 pp.

MONACO, PAUL, *Cinema and Society: France and Germany during the Twenties.* New York: Elsevier-North Holland Pub. Co., 1976. 194 pp.

WOLLENBERG, H. H., *Fifty Years of German Film.* New York: Arno Press, 1972. 80 pp. (originally published in 1948)

6

Art and Dialectic in the Soviet Film, 1925–1929

The Russians were even more profoundly affected by World War I than were the Germans. While there had been no fighting within the borders of Germany, Russia had been a vast battlefield. It had suffered defeat at the hands of the Central Powers, and the peace treaty signed at Brest-Litovsk was even more vindictive than that of Versailles. While in Germany an abortive rebellion in 1919 was quickly suppressed, the Bolshevik Revolution of 1917 succeeded. At least five years elapsed, however, before it was clear that the new government of Russia, a communist government, would survive, and that a beginning stability would be achieved.

Not until 1925 did the Soviets fully launch into the final, and some would say most brilliant, phase of the silent film before the introduction of sound. The contrast between the Soviet and German silent film, in both subject matter and technique, was even greater than that between the German film of the early twenties and the American film preceding it. Though the German effort had been state-supported in part, it was directed toward the prestige of art. It can be valued precisely because of its extreme artificiality, but a prevailing aestheticism cannot be denied. There was an anarchic indifference to the social-political implications of content—which Kracauer interprets as reflecting a kind of national neurosis. The introspection and morbidity of their major themes led to a slowness of tempo. As the veteran British director Anthony Asquith observed of German contributions, ''while the film was gaining in its ability to convey mood, emotion, and character, it was gradually losing touch with its life-source—the movement.''[1]

Soviet film, completely state-supported, was socially purposeful above all else: intended primarily to educate and indoctrinate the Russian people in the events and causes of the Revolution. Vigorous and optimistic, the films came out of the east like a blast of cold Siberian air, blowing away the hothouse atmosphere of the German studios. Objective in approach (as opposed to German subjectivism) and epic in form (as opposed to the personal dramas of the Germans), they brought rapid pace and physical action back to the moving picture and resumed the line that emphasized editing inaugurated by Porter and advanced by Griffith.

The German film makers' intellectual sources included Sigmund Freud. Their concern with the psychological led to expressionism and the subjective camera as means of portraying internal states. As used by the Germans, the moving camera became a kind of visual equivalent to the psychoanalyst's probing of the patient; the expressionistic design conveyed dreams, nightmares, and hallucinations.

In the Soviet Union the ideological basis was provided by Karl Marx and V. I. Lenin, and the film makers' concerns were social, political, and economic. The predominant aesthetic mode was futurism, which attempted to depict vividly the energetic and dynamic quality of contemporary life influenced by the motion and force of modern machinery. In film, pictorial realism rather than expressionism was the visual style required to portray the actual, external world. Cutting—paralleling the conflict and resolution of opposites in Hegelian/Marxian dialectic—was the principal formative method. A neat symbolic point is made by G. W. Pabst's having directed *Secrets of a Soul,* a popularization of Freudian psychology, in the same year, 1926, that V. I. Pudovkin made *Mechanics of the Brain,* explaining the Pavlovian scientific dialectic of stimulus-response. Even a comparison of the titles of the German and Soviet films is revealing: *secrets* versus *mechanics, a* versus *the, soul* versus *brain.*

HISTORICAL SETTING

The first films to be seen in Russia were those sent in by the brothers Lumière in 1896, the year following the initial Paris screening, and shortly after the coronation of Czar Nicholas II—an event recorded by film makers from Europe and America. In the successful exploitation method the Lumières had developed around their ''scenic views,'' a projectionist-cinematographer would visit a country and show short films of such sights as the Eiffel Tower, sidewalk cafés, the Zouaves in review, and other foreign attractions. In Russia, a troika ride, peasant dances, and the Kremlin domes would be filmed. These subjects would appeal to the national pride of the Russians and could be shown elsewhere throughout the world as scenes of exotic customs and faraway places.

It wasn't until considerably later that Russian film production commenced, pioneered by another French firm, however: Pathé, with *Cossacks of the Don* in 1908. In that same year the first Russian studio began operation in Moscow, but all film supplies and equipment continued to be imported from France and Germany. By 1917 and the

---

[1] Anthony Asquith, ''The Tenth Muse Climbs Parnasus,'' *The Penguin Film Review,* No. 1 (August, 1946), pp. 10–26.

end of pre-Communist Russia, there were over twenty producers, with Moscow the main production center. Even so, more foreign than domestic films were shown.

In czarist Russia movies were not a popular art as they were elsewhere. There were few theaters, tickets were expensive, and the working classes couldn't afford to attend regularly. The high illiteracy rate made printed intertitles a general burden, and the literary-theatrical bent of the Russian silent films further helped confine their patronage to the educated middle classes. Somewhat equivalent to *films d'art* and Adolph Zukor's famous players in famous plays, the highly theatrical tradition of the Russian film (as opposed to the later Soviet film) is generally agreed upon and is borne out by the few examples existing in archives in the United States. With rare exceptions, the Russian films seem to have been mediocre imitations of other European productions. After the Bolshevik Revolution, most of the film producers and actors emigrated, taking with them all the equipment and film they could carry.

Those producers who chose to remain were at first allowed to continue along lines of private enterprise. Though they lacked revolutionary understanding, let alone zeal, not much attention was given to their output by a government preoccupied with more pressing matters. A Cinema Committee was set up, however, under playwright A. V. Lunacharsky, Minister of Education. With truly remarkable foresight, given the uses of film generally up to that time and the negligible Russian production, Lenin had said, "Of all the arts, the cinema is the most important for us." His statement contrasts as strongly as could be expected with one from the deposed Nicholas II, who had written: "I consider cinematography an empty, useless, and even pernicious diversion. Only an abnormal person could place this sideshow business on a level with art. It is all nonsense and no importance should be lent to such trash."[2] At the same time it is known that this last of the czars was an ardent movie-goer who spent many evenings at private screenings in the palace basement.

The national conditions which prevented Lenin and the other communist leaders from promptly turning film into the voice for the Revolution that it eventually became were not unlike those of postwar Germany, and considerably more severe. In the first year of the new government famine was widespread. During one of the cruelest Russian winters on record there was no fuel. Typhus raged in epidemic proportions. After participation in the war dragged to a halt, the Soviets faced Allied armies within their borders and continuing civil warfare with the counter-revolutionaries. One curious instance of the general instability was an episode in which some 50,000 escaped Czech prisoners of war ravaged the countryside unresisted along the route of the Trans-Siberian railway.

It took some five years (1918–1922) to fully establish the new political regime and two more years before the film industry was functioning with anything approaching productivity. (Even by the end of 1923 only 13 percent of the films shown in the country were Soviet.) In 1919 the industry had been completely nationalized when it became clear that the old capitalist economics and mentality would not serve the needs of a socialist state. In the same year the Moscow Institute of Cinematography was established to train new Soviet film makers; it is thus the oldest, as well as one of the largest and best, film schools in the world. In 1925 the Sovkino Trust was formed to try to bring some order into all aspects of the domestic industry and to reestablish distribution abroad.

[2] Quoted by Jay Leyda in *Kino* (New York: Macmillan Co., 1960), p. 69.

The new Soviet cinema, which began its formative period about 1919, was thought of at the time as being divided into two creative camps. Though called the right and left wings, the labels weren't essentially political. At first the right wing carried on in the old theatrical tradition, using conventional methods and styles but substituting commisars, peasants, and Red Army soldiers for the upper-class cast of characters of traditional theater. Romance, humor, and heroics persisted. The concerns of the new state motivate the action initially and appear as background but scarcely replace standard dramaturgical elements: boy-girl, comic sidekicks, obstacles to be overcome, obstructing villains, and so on. *Kombrig Ivanov* (1923) is an example of this creative tendency; it was retitled *The Beauty and the Bolshevik* in America. Subsequently the work of the right wing achieved greater sophistication and addressed itself to sociological problems. Abram Room's *Bed and Sofa* (1927), for example, dealt with a romantic triangle, but the shifting allegiance of the woman towards the two men involves the housing shortage and her attitude and theirs toward the role of women in the new society. The general methods of the right wing became the only officially sanctioned approach after "socialist realism" was imposed in the 1930s, and continue to be predominant in Soviet cinema. *The Cranes Are Flying* (1957) and *Ballad of a Soldier* (1959) are later popular examples.

The left wing was much more radical in its innovation, which involved form as well as subject. When we think of the Soviet silent cinema, it is usually of the films growing out of the theories and experiments of two left wing pioneers. One of these was Dziga Vertov, who followed Lenin's advice that the first work of Soviet film makers be with newsreels and documentaries. This seemed advisable partly because of the drain on resources that feature film production would have represented, but especially because of the urgency of communicating the history and spirit of the Revolution to the still largely apathetic and uninformed Russian public. In 1919 Vertov founded his Kino Eye Group and began publishing manifestos.[3] "Life caught unawares" was Vertov's credo. What he meant by this was not exactly candid camera (since the subjects usually knew they were being filmed), but that nothing be staged or directed. Life in front of the camera was permitted to run its natural course; the only creative control the film maker exerted was through choosing what and how to shoot, and the placement of one shot in relation to another during the editing. In 1922 Vertov began to produce *Kino-Pravda,* a series of monthly newsfilms that lasted for twenty-three issues. The title, incidentally, is synonymous with *cinéma vérité* (film truth), a term French anthropologist–film maker Jean Rouch coined in 1961 to apply to a new kind of documentary. What *cinéma vérité* added to *kino pravda* was essentially the lightweight, synchronous sound equipment that permitted the film maker to shoot and record virtually anything without interrupting or altering it for the benefit of camera or microphone.

Unlike a director of fiction films, Vertov had no control over the action he was filming; thus editing took on a peculiarly central role in his work. Moreover, the shortage of raw stock in the Soviet Union in the early twenties (before the Soviets began to manufacture their own) meant that Vertov had to use pieces of film as he found them, frequently short ends left over from other projects. In an impulse not unlike Porter's in *Life of an American Fireman,* Vertov learned that by juxtaposing shots from old czarist newsreels with newly shot materials he could create new meanings. Russian tanks crossing a no man's land in the war could be followed by Soviet tractors breaking ground for

---

[3] Vertov's theories of film are summarized and interpreted by Vlada Petric, "Dziga Vertov as Theorist," *Cinema Journal,* XVIII, No. 1 (Fall 1978), pp. 29–44.

Kino Pravda (USSR, 1922–25, Dziga Vertov). Museum of Modern Art/Film Stills Archive.

cultivation. Juxtaposing a shot of the formal and elegant Nicholas stiffly reviewing his palace guard with a shot of a shirt-sleeved Lenin energetically addressing the workers added a significance not inherent in either shot alone. In embryonic form this was precisely the kind of editing that Sergei Eisenstein would develop into montage; the title of his film *The Old and the New* (1929) concisely sums up a principal propaganda device of Vertov's. Beyond that, one can say of *Kino-Pravda* that all the subjects were socially purposeful: There are no beauty parades, no animals at the zoo. Inspirational in tone, the films seem to be urging that there's a job to be done. In general they show one region or aspect of national life to the rest of the country (a major mission of the documentary film later to be picked up in Britain, with proper credit always given to the Soviets). Vertov's reports are not all sweetness and light by any means; hard-hitting exposés are included. "Save the starving children" one title proclaims, as we see the pitiful young victims of famine. The directness of communication with the people is further revealed in end titles which encourage the audience to mail its "inquiries regarding traveling film shows" and "all film and photo work" to Kino-Pravda.

Another left wing pioneer was Lev Kuleshov, film director, theorist, lecturer (from 1920 on), and later head of the Moscow Institute of Cinematography.[4] As Sergei Eisenstein came out of the Vertov line, another great Soviet film maker, V. I.

[4] His theories are available in Lev Kuleshov, *Kuleshov on Film* (Berkeley: University of California Press, 1974).

By the Law (USSR, 1926, Lev Kuleshov). Museum of Modern Art/Film Stills Archive.

Pudovkin, was Kuleshov's star pupil. Eisenstein's impressively talented cameraman, Eduard Tissé, had worked for Vertov, as Pudovkin's cameraman, Anatoli Golovnya, had for Kuleshov. Kuleshov coped with the shortage of raw stock by conducting a series of acting experiments performed for an empty camera. Also, he and his students spent much time analyzing and recutting existing motion pictures to learn filmic construction. When Kuleshov gained access to film stock he came to emphasize editing as heavily as did Vertov, but for different purposes. He discovered how, through cutting, to make nonactors appear to give skillful performances and how to give the acting of professionals meaning of which they were unaware at the time of performance. Following Vertov and Kuleshov, Eisenstein and Pudovkin made editing for the Soviet silent film makers virtually synonymous with the creative process itself.

A third early creative and theoretical group contributed to the scope of Soviet cinema. In 1922 a youthful Grigori Kozintsev (age 17) joined Leonid Trauberg (17), and Sergei Yutkevitch (18) to form the Factory of the Eccentric Actor: FEX. The virtually unlimited freedom for experimentation in the arts during the hectic years of revolution and civil war unleashed the progressive spirit among the young. (In 1922 Vertov was 26, Kuleshov 23, Eisenstein 24, and Pudovkin 29.) This generation of

Soviet artists, seeking new methods of expression, turned toward minor genres, "the kind of popular art which the aristocracy and bourgeoisie had scorned. To be precise: the music hall, the circus and the cinema."[5] Eisenstein's first film, *Strike* (1925), is very closely related to these aesthetic impulses. After seeing it, Kozintsev told the FEX group, "All that we're doing is childish nonsense, we must all see *Strike* again and again, until we can understand it and adopt its power for our own."[6]

THREE SILENT MASTERS

Ranked alongside Eisenstein and Pudovkin among the great Soviet silent film makers would be Alexander Dovzhenko. Because he stands somewhat apart from the principal thrust of Soviet film making, his work will be discussed first. A Ukrainian from a family of uneducated farmers, Dovzhenko includes in his films strange ethnic and mystical elements which color his Marxism and make his silent work quite distinct from that of the other Soviet film makers. He was a painter before he became a film maker, and montage was not as important for him as it was for the others; at least his use of it is quite different.

In Dovzhenko's three major silent films—*Zvenigora* (1928), *Arsenal* (1929), *Earth* (1930)—the larger sequences seem separate from each other, circular in construction, and strangely complete in themselves. He emphasizes the relationships of scenes to scenes, within the sequences, rather than of shots to each other within scenes. The numerous and varied scenes tend to be brief, but the shots (or even a single shot) that they comprise are often sustained. Contrasting and elliptical combinations involve quite extraordinary shifts of mood and statement. The connections of the parts to each other are often unclear or ambiguous on first viewing. In *Earth,* in a scene of the kulaks weeping and wailing, which follows the scene of the grandfather dying, we assume initially that they are mourning his death. When we learn that it is the threatened loss of possessions that has provoked their grief, the comment about them becomes a negative one. Ambiguity of this sort is rarely allowed to occur in the more didactic main body of Soviet work. It is as if Dovzhenko were serenely indifferent to conventional continuity in his pursuit of evocative, many-layered imagery.

Marking Dovzhenko's visual style are extremely wide-angled long shots in which a complexity of action and composition builds up within a single frame like an evolving painting. Also there are the painterly "still" shots—the striking silhouettes of *Arsenal,* the trees heavy-laden with fruit in *Earth*—which convey a sense of timelessness, of fixity. In thinking of Dovzhenko's work we remember its many images of the Ukrainian countryside composed of low horizons and small human figures moving under an enormous open sky. The shocking and beautiful balletic death of Vasily in *Earth,* as he moves down a curving moonlit road toward the camera, to be cut down almost casually by a murderer's bullet, is not likely to be forgotten. Throughout his early films Dovzhenko's intentions are clearly poetic rather than narrative, as with Pudovkin, or dramatic, as with Eisenstein.

His symbols and metaphors are not forced or belletristic, however; they grow

[5] Sergei Yutkevich in *Cinema in Revolution,* eds. Luda and Jean Schnitzer and Marcel Martin (New York: Hill & Wang, Inc., 1973), p. 16.
[6] Quoted in Leyda, *Kino,* p. 201.

out of a conception of the closeness of the people to the soil. They also contain dialectical contradictions that advance the revolutionary argument; but because Dovzhenko sees life whole, there is nothing of the agitprop about his work. In *Earth* he is saying that it is right for an old man to die (at peace) but wrong (against nature) for a young man to die (by violence). Yet death is followed by life in both cases. As the old man munches one apple, a child munches another, completing the cycle of generations. A woman gives birth during Vasily's funeral, and his comrades are clearly fulfilling the potential of his abbreviated life in building for the future. The autumn rain in the epilogue appears at first to be like tears, but it is also life-giving as it falls on the fullness of harvest. The tractor is regarded by the old as a replacement of themselves and their animals, and by the young as an extension of the people's productivity.

Though working in the service of the state, Dovzhenko's humanism causes him to extend sympathy to the old as well as the new. One can imagine that a Joseph Stalin might have regarded the ambivalence uneasily, and ultimately as subversive. To a modern American viewer, *Earth* carries a very optimistic tone and presents a remarkable argument for revolutionary change. But when it premiered in Moscow, it was attacked at length in *Izvestia* for being "defeatist" and "counter-revolutionary." Given its slowness of pace, ambiguities, obscurities, and dependence on the pictorial, it

Earth (USSR, 1930, Alexander Dovzhenko). Museum of Modern Art/Film Stills Archive.

seems unlikely that it could have had the requisite popularity in Russia to do the indoctrinational-educational job required of it by the sponsoring government. At any rate, after the brilliant experimental period of the twenties, when the hard line of "socialist realism" appeared, Dovzhenko never again achieved anything equal to the unique visual lyricism of his silent films. Even in the earlier time he seemed out of step with his colleagues. What attracted him most strongly was clearly the human and natural beauty that could be captured by the camera, rather than the arguments that could be fashioned by an editor's shears.

V. I. Pudovkin was educated as a physicist and chemist. (Dovzhenko's education, too, had been scientific and technological). He became interested in acting for films, he said, as a result of seeing *Intolerance,* which had finally arrived in Russia in 1919. Though Pudovkin would appear as an actor in many of his own films as well as those of others, while studying under Kuleshov he came to see that the real creative fulfillment in motion pictures was for the director rather than the actor. Kuleshov, for his part, fully understood that Griffith had been working out of some of the same concepts that had begun to preoccupy him. A prominent concern of Kuleshov's was the difference between the actor's contributions to stage and to screen.

On the stage, once the curtain rises the performer is in complete control of his or her performance. All the direction and rehearsal are merely preparation to be used, or ignored for that matter, in interpreting a character in the presence of an audience. In film, the director is the principal "audience" of the live performance. The screen performance is constructed after the actor has finished his or her work, out of the selection made available by the camera: a long shot of the actor in a room full of people, a closeup of just the actor's profile, a reaction shot of someone else's face, and so on. It is no longer the actor's total performance that finally appears, no longer her or his rhythm or even whole body, but bits and pieces integrated into a synthetic whole. With systematic thoroughness Kuleshov began to test the implications of this basic cinematic technique.

His influence on Pudovkin was profound, and the latter participated in a series of Kuleshov experiments that explored the potential of editing to create a time and space existing (or seeming to exist) only on film. For one of these experiments Kuleshov assembled five separate shots. In the first, a young man walks from left to right. In the second, a young woman walks from right to left. In a third, they meet and shake hands, and the young man points to something off screen. The fourth shot shows a large white building with a broad flight of steps. In the fifth, the couple ascend steps. A viewer would accept this scene as one uninterrupted action, but in actuality the five pieces had been shot in completely different times and places—the man and woman (shots one and two) in separate parts of Moscow, and the handshake (shot three) in yet another. The white building (four) was in fact the White House, snipped from an American film, and the steps (five) were those of a cathedral.[7] Rudimentary and obvious as such experiments may seem, they nonetheless isolated and held up for examination the most basic aesthetic underpinning of the medium.

Returning from their practical experiments to a further study of *Intolerance,* Kuleshov and Pudovkin began to see how to apply their discoveries to the requirements of a new Soviet cinema. Though as far from being a Marxist as is conceivable, in *Intolerance* Griffith had carried on a moral and ethical argument through his separate historical episodes, and in the modern story, economic and social ones as well. (Not only

---

[7] V. I. Pudovkin, *Film Technique* (New York: Lear Publishers, Inc., 1949), pp. 60–61.

the strike in Pudovkin's *Mother,* 1926, but Eisenstein's *Strike,* 1925, contain unmistakable borrowings from the Griffith film.) In a succession of masterworks paralleling those of Eisenstein—warmer and more moving, if not as breathtakingly experimental and brilliant—Pudovkin gave full form to his learning. Unlike the highly intellectual appeal of Eisenstein's work, Pudovkin's films reach the emotions directly. They received instant acclaim and their power seems undiminished by the years. As with Dovzhenko, Pudovkin's major silent films—*Mother, The End of St. Petersburg* (1927), and *Storm over Asia* (1928)—stand as his finest and most personal achievements, though he too continued to work for several decades in the sound film. While he became a greater director than Kuleshov, Pudovkin also wrote theoretical works—*Film Technique* and *Film Acting*—which explained and showed the applications of his former teacher's insights. After more than half a century they remain among the best texts for beginning directors, especially for those interested in documentary film and work with nonactors.

Sergei Eisenstein also had a technical education (as a civil engineer), and—like Dovzhenko and Pudovkin—he defected to the arts, first to the theater in his case. Before beginning stage work, however, Eisenstein had developed an intense interest in Japanese language and culture, which would feed into his later profound and erudite theorizing about film. He was fascinated by the Japanese hieroglyphic writing, in which the word *weeping* is formed by combining the pictograph for *eye* with that for *water; singing* is composed of *mouth* and *bird;* listening, of *ear* plus *door;* and so on. He came to feel that the two drawn symbols combined like film shots to provide a third, different meaning. Also, he noted a Japanese technique for teaching drawing, which limits the student to the composition of segments of a cherry tree branch within a frame. This attention to frame area and composition within it Eisenstein would find useful preparation for his own painstaking composing of images. Finally, Kabuki theater seemed to him to bring various artistic elements into combination in a balance not unlike that of film. In Kabuki, and in the Nō plays, spoken language is not the almost exclusive carrier of content that it is in Western drama. Japanese theater is visual as much as verbal. Words are

Mother (USSR, 1926, V. I. Pudovkin). Museum of Modern Art/Film Stills Archive.

part of an ensemble effect in which formalized gesture, choreographed body movement, music, even costumes, carry equal weight and add nuances and qualifications to a complex whole.

Eisenstein's theatrical beginning was as a scene designer for the Proletkult Theatre. From childhood on he had been a prodigious sketcher and painter; the Proletkult, dedicated to the development of proletarian artists and the education of the working class, accommodated his sympathies for the revolution. From the Proletkult he learned to distrust the character-centered theater of the nineteenth century and to seek out ways to make the masses the hero and to present social problems in place of bourgeois romantic triangles. Moving on to work with Vsevolod Meyerhold, the radically innovative theatrical producer and director, Eisenstein finally completed the theoretical education and practical experience that would propel him into film.

Meyerhold's theories of acting were in polar opposition to those of Konstantin Stanislavsky, the other great contemporary force in Russian theater. Whereas Stanislavsky started from within, in a psychological approach, instructing his actors to seek out the emotions of their characters, Meyerhold began from without, in a theory he called biomechanics. Related to Pavlov's experiments in conditioned reflexes and consistent with the scientific spirit of the new Russia, Meyerhold's method was based on the idea that emotions could be stimulated in the actor (and conveyed to the spectator) through analysis of the emotive connotations of movement, and by developing the actor's body into a precise machine capable of producing the exact effects desired. This approach pulled the Meyerhold theater closer to the *commedia del'arte* tradition and even to the technique of circus performers. It may have helped lay the groundwork for fellow-revolutionary Bertolt Brecht's aesthetic stance; certainly it had a profound effect on Eisenstein.

Returning to the Proletkult, Eisenstein arrived at his own eclectic fusion of all he had come to understand up to that point. What he sought was a "montage of attractions"—a series of sensory experiences that would involve the spectators and carry them along a predetermined path of emotional response. Perhaps his most successful realization of these theories on the stage was a parody production of Alexander Ostrovsky's *The Wise Man*. In it he combined acrobats, a tightrope walker, and satirical asides directed at foreign political figures with a caricatured religious procession bearing candles, chanting litany, and carrying placards inscribed "Religion is the opium of the people." A short comic film was specially produced for incorporation into the performance.

Eisenstein's final attempt to transform theatrical art and get closer to the emotional needs of contemporary audiences led him in a direction opposite from the circus and the music hall, toward the reality outside the theater. His production of *Gas Masks,* a play by Sergei Tretyakov, was played by workers and staged in the actual Moscow Gas Factory. Eisenstein regarded this experiment as a failure. Rather than eliminating "art" and replacing it with "life," as he had intended by using the real setting and nonactors, he had succeeded only in exposing the artificiality of conventions that would have seemed perfectly at home in the theater. Seeking a means of capturing the reality of factory and workers that so fascinated him, he arrived at film as the medium that could make art out of materials much closer to life than could theatrical drama. As he put it, "The cart fell to pieces and the driver dropped into the cinema."

Strike (1925), his first film, also used a factory setting, with the workers as the collective protagonists. The "montage of attractions" now became the rapid and rhythmic cutting together of shots that are startling in their visual contrasts, physical in

Strike (USSR, 1925, Sergei Eisenstein). Museum of Modern Art/Film Stills Archive.

their impact. Though all of the elements of Eisenstein's mature work are present, traces of the kind of theater in which he had been working account for some excesses and discordances. The "circus" elements—caricatures, gross symbolism, and exaggerated action—though striking in themselves, fit rather strangely into the prevailing naturalism. On the other hand, there is a documentary-like looseness of structure that makes the film more successful within its sequences than it is as a whole. *Potemkin* (1925) advanced upon the first work by stripping away some of the flamboyance and disciplining the fertility of imagination. Built upon a tight and firm dramatic line, its five sequences proceed with the cumulative power of the acts of classical tragedy.

Both films make essentially the same ideological points. Though *Potemkin* deals with the mutiny of the crew of an armored cruiser in the abortive 1905 Revolution, its officers are equivalent to the capitalists of *Strike;* its White Guards and Cossacks, who cut down the populace on the Odessa Steps, are like the army and police of the preceding film. In both films, the methods of the ruling class are deceitful and lead to slaughter. The sailors and workers are simple and loyal to each other; except for their proletarian leaders, they are naive in the ways of the world. Incapable of evil unless duped into it by the authorities, they resort to violence only to counter unendurable oppression. The working classes are portrayed as the most productive resource of the nation and its only democratic force. A version of the desired dictatorship of the proletariat is offered in these two films. A recurrent image shows the revolutionary leaders haranguing the sailors or workers who then move together in a single group decision: "All for one, one for all!" the *Potemkin* titles shout.

Potemkin (USSR, 1925, Sergei Eisenstein). Museum of Modern Art/Film Stills Archive.

The ''hero'' of both films is the masses—played by people who would have lived through situations much like those portrayed. In both cases, an epic scale of action is based on real or composite events. The viewpoint is broadly social-political and there is little delineation of characters except as types. Both films were shot on location rather than in studios; in the case of *Potemkin,* Odessa was the actual place of some of the incidents portrayed. Eisenstein seized upon and made full use of the accidents of setting: in *Strike,* the stairway tier of the workers' tenements; in *Potemkin,* the architectural characteristics of Odessa, a morning mist on the water, the stone lions, and the like. His play with mass, line, and movement is that of a dynamic painter; his handling of crowds is quite without peer. Always Eisenstein works through the kinetic. But, given the amount of movement within the frame and the rapidity of cutting, there is little moving camera. Instead there are an extraordinary number and variety of camera setups, as would be required by his kind of editing. At moments of climactic action some of the shots are as short as two frames, and their content is frequently horrifying: a Cossack's saber slashing downward, a woman's spectacles broken and her face bloodied. Through an intended physiological response, Eisenstein aimed to bring his viewers to a political attitude. Closeups abound and there is a prominent use of what in literature would be called synecdoche, the parts representing a larger whole. In *Potemkin,* the maggoty meat, the doctor's pince-nez which eventually dangle in the ropes, the pounding pistons of the ship's engines, and the final magnificent shot from below of its hull slicing the water, all serve this function.

Though containing some of his most extraordinary achievements, the height of his "intellectual montage," *October,* or *Ten Days that Shook the World* (1928), lacks the passion and coherence of *Potemkin* (at least the versions that appear in the West). Like Griffith's *Intolerance* in comparison to *The Birth of a Nation, October,* though in some respects Eisenstein's ultimate achievement, is on a canvas so large that the monumental conception remains only partially realized. *The General Line/Old and the New* (1929) was his final silent film. In it, though his aesthetic sensibility and intelligence are as evident as ever, they seem essentially of the wrong kind for this account of Soviet farm life and collectivization.

Dovzhenko and Pudovkin adjusted to the conventions of socialist realism and continued a steady if scarcely distinguished output into the first decades of sound. Eisenstein could not adjust, and was frequently the target of criticism from bureaucrats, critics, and other film makers. The problem was not that he was unwilling to serve the state in ways deemed socially useful, but that he was innately and supremely what he was accused of being—a formalist. His released sound films—*Alexander Nevsky* (1938), *Ivan the Terrible,* Part I (1944), Part II (1958)—great though they are, are few. He spent much of the last fifteen years of his life teaching and writing. It may be that his theoretical writings, like George Bernard Shaw's prefaces, will retain a value beyond some of the creative work which grew out of them. In any event, Eisenstein's films and theories marked an enormous advance in a conscious and articulated understanding of how the cinema works fundamentally as a means of communication, as a kind of language, and as an art form. Montage was the key term.

MONTAGE: THEORY AND PRACTICE

The word montage was borrowed from the French; *monter* simply means to mount or assemble. For the Soviet film makers, however, this assembling and mounting through editing became the ultimate creative act. Though they had learned from Griffith and were nudged into the most economic use of the shot by the shortage of raw stock, their practical experiments, published theories, and finally the great works of the Soviet silent film, led them to a kind and level of accomplishment that has served to instruct film creators and critics ever since. Eisenstein and Pudovkin, friendly rivals as film makers, were also principal spokesmen in a running debate about the proper uses of montage. They both agreed on the fundamental importance of editing, but for Pudovkin the cut was linkage, a joining of shots for the gradual accumulation of narrative meaning—the unfolding of a story. For Eisenstein its function was to achieve shock, the banging together of two contrasting shots in a way that would force the audience into a concept that was greater than the sum and different from any one of its parts. Eisenstein took particular satisfaction in what he regarded as the similarity of this process to the thesis-antithesis-synthesis of Hegelian dialectic. The argument is important as well as interesting, and worth pursuing through the words of the adversaries.

In *Film Technique,* Pudovkin, after acknowledging his indebtedness to Kuleshov and the importance of the concept of montage to the Soviet film makers, writes:

> Kuleshov maintained that the material in film-work consists of pieces of film, and that the composition method is their joining together in a particular, creatively discovered order. He maintained that film-art does not begin when the artists act and the various

scenes are shot—this is only the preparation of the material. Film-art begins from the moment when the director begins to combine and join together the various pieces of film. By joining them in various combinations, in different orders, he obtains differing results.[8]

Pudovkin continues by describing two more of the sorts of practical experiments (like the one with the couple, the steps, and the White House) that Kuleshov and his students were carrying out to test their theories.

The first involves three short strips of film. On one is the image of a smiling face, on another a hand pointing a revolver, on the third a frightened face. Pudovkin observes that if the shots are assembled in that order the impression we get is that the second man is facing the revolver and that he is a coward. If the order is reversed—frightened face, revolver, smiling face—the impression we get is that the man facing the revolver is very brave. Thus the meaning of precisely the same images is altered, even reversed, by changing their order.

In the second experiment recalled by Pudovkin, he and Kuleshov selected some closeups of the Russian actor Ivan Mozhukhin. They were static, neutral shots of Mozhukhin's face expressing no particular emotion. Those shots were then intercut with closeups of other material. First was a bowl of soup standing on a table; it seemed quite obvious that Mozhukhin was looking at the soup. Then the actor's face was followed by shots showing a coffin in which lay a dead woman. In the third instance the face was followed by a shot of a little girl playing with a funny toy bear. When the three combinations were shown without explanation to an audience what was the result? The audience raved about Mozhukhin's acting! They pointed out the heavy pensiveness of the mood created as he regarded the forgotten bowl of soup, the deep grief expressed as he looked at the dead woman, the light, happy smile that played across his features as he gazed at the little girl. In all three cases, of course, Mozhukhin's facial expression had been virtually the same, and expressing very little at that.

Pudovkin concludes his recounting of these experiments with an additional observation that:

> the combination of various pieces in one or another order is not sufficient. It is necessary to be able to control and manipulate the length of these pieces, because the combination of pieces of varying length is effective in the same way as the combination of sounds of various length in music, by creating the rhythm of the film and by means of their varying effect on the audience. Quick, short pieces rouse excitement, while long pieces have a soothing effect.[9]

In other words, Pudovkin offers a sort of formula: film creation equals (1) what is in the shots, (2) the order in which they appear, and (3) how long each is held on the screen. "To be able to find the requisite order of shots or pieces and the rhythm necessary for their combination," he summarizes, "that is the chief task of the director's art. This art we call *montage*—or constructive editing. It is only with the help of *montage* that I am able to solve problems of such complexity as the work on the artists' acting."[10]

---

[8] Pudovkin, *Film Technique,* pp. 138–39.

[9] Pudovkin, *Film Technique,* pp. 139–41.

[10] Pudovkin, *Film Technique,* p. 141.

Note the final emphasis on performance. Unlike Eisenstein's silent films, Pudovkin's make heavy use of professional actors and contain some superb characterizations. He portrays the awakening of revolutionary consciousness through the microcosm of individual experience more than through the action of the masses; for example, Vera Baranovskaya as the title character in *Mother,* Ivan Chuvelyov as the peasant lad in *The End of St. Petersburg.* Still, Pudovkin regards actors as "plastic material" not unlike any objects that might be photographed. They move and gesture, stare and weep, but for Pudovkin the film "performance" is created by the director cutting together strips of celluloid registering these actions. Pudovkin began the "Introduction to the German Edition" of *Film Technique* with: "The foundation of film art is *editing.*" As might be expected, this is a position that horrifies and infuriates actors.

Eisenstein, in an essay in *Film Form,* echoes Pudovkin: "To determine the nature of montage is to solve the specific problem of cinema." He goes on to explain that

> The earliest conscious film makers, and our first film theoreticians, regarded montage as a means of description by placing single shots one after the other like building-blocks. The movement within these building-block shots, and the consequent length of the component pieces, was then considered as rhythm.[11]

That was precisely what Pudovkin had written, as Eisenstein acknowledges with what is perhaps a feigned superiority of disbelief and an implied distinction between the theorist and the artist: "According to this definition, shared even by Pudovkin as a theoretician, montage is the means of *unrolling* an idea with the help of single shots: the 'epic' principle." (*Epic* is here used in the classical sense—narrative as opposed to dramatic.) In Eisenstein's opinion, however, "montage is an idea that arises from the collision of independent shots—shots even opposite to one another: the 'dramatic' principle."[12]

Elsewhere, in an essay in the companion volume, *The Film Sense,* Eisenstein continues the argument and expands upon his own position. As he sees the Soviet films, they are "faced with the task of presenting not only a narrative that is *logically connected,* but one that contains a *maximum of emotion and stimulating power.* Montage is a mighty aid to the resolution of this task," he concludes. Eisenstein goes on to ask rhetorically, "Why do we use montage at all?"

> Even the most fanatical opponent of montage will agree that it is not merely because the film strip at our disposal is not of infinite length, and consequently, being condemned to working with pieces of restricted lengths, we have to stick one piece of it on to another occasionally.
>
> The 'leftists' of montage saw it from the opposite extreme. While playing with pieces of film, they discovered a certain property in the toy which kept them astonished for a number of years. This property consisted in the fact *that two film pieces of any kind, placed together, inevitably combine into a new concept, a new quality, arising out of that juxtaposition.*
>
> This is not in the least a circumstance peculiar to the cinema, but is a phenomenon invariably met with in all cases where we have to deal with juxtaposition of two facts, two phenomena, two objects. We are accustomed to make, almost automatically, a definite and obvious deductive generalization when any separate objects are placed before us side by side. For example, take a grave, juxtaposed with a woman in mourning weeping

---

[11] Sergei M. Eisenstein, *Film Form* (New York: Harcourt Brace & Co., 1949), p. 48.

[12] Eisenstein, *Film Form,* p. 49.

beside it, and scarcely anybody will fail to jump to the conclusion: *a widow*. It is precisely on this feature of our perception that the following miniature story by Ambrose Bierce bases its effect. It is from his *Fantastic Fables* and is entitled ''The Inconsolable Widow'':

''A Woman in widow's weeds was weeping upon a grave.

'Console yourself, madame,' said a Sympathetic Stranger. 'Heaven's mercies are infinite. There is another man somewhere, besides your husband, with whom you can still be happy.'

'There was,' she sobbed—'there was, but this is his grave.' ''[13]

It is neatly coincidental that Pudovkin referred to a coffin in the experiment with the actor Mozhukhin. Both Eisenstein and Pudovkin are suggesting how the meaning of an action can be changed into something other than the actual or original through associative montage. But Pudovkin's addition of a coffin merely makes the actor's face seem sad where it was not necessarily. The attraction of Bierce's anecdote for Eisenstein is clearly that the normal additive principle is replaced by a combination of the unexpected, opposites in a sense, and the ''widow'' becomes an adulteress.

Eisenstein's use of an obscure piece of American literature to illustrate his conception, rather than a practical experiment with several pieces of film, represents fairly the great difference between his critical method and that of Pudovkin. Eisenstein ranged widely through the arts and across languages and cultures to show that montage as he understood it existed quite separately from film and had existed long before film appeared. His analyses of passages from the poems of Pushkin and the novels of Dickens for their shooting-script-like ordering of images offers a contribution to literary criticism as well as provocative analogues for those studying film. For Eisenstein the form and sense of film aesthetic extended into a total philosophical view of the world. For Pudovkin the insights which montage provided were carefully restricted to film technique and film acting.

In practice the argument between the two is happily muddled by some of the best examples of Eisensteinian shock montage appearing in films of Pudovkin and by Eisenstein necessarily having to resort to Pudovkinian narrative to hold together the brief pyrotechnic bursts of collision. Whether as linkage or juxtaposition, one result of this extreme fragmentation of the scene was that both film makers could use nonactors to a degree that more sustained takes would not allow. Any embarrassing self-consciousness could be stripped away and the usable moments selected and combined with other visual materials—like the actor Mozhukhin with soup, coffin, and child—to give the illusion of a performance that in fact never existed. This new possibility led to theories of *typage*, of choosing people who looked the part regardless of their thespian skills.

Another characteristic of Soviet film technique was that the naturalistic materials of ''real people'' (as opposed to actors) and ''actual locations'' (in contrast to studio interiors or back lots) were subjected to an extreme degree of highly conscious manipulation through editing. Though the style is extremely different from the Germans', in their own ways the Soviet films are just as stylized. Finally, in order to construct their intricate mosaics from small pieces of the total action, the Soviets, like the Germans and unlike Griffith, relied on highly detailed scripts and on preplanning. Eisenstein sketched virtually all of his shots in advance; a substantial portion of Pudovkin's *Film Technique* is devoted to a method of precise script construction.

[13] Sergei M. Eisenstein, *The Film Sense* (New York: Harcourt Brace & Co., 1942), pp. 4–5.

Unlike the films of any nation that had preceded them, however, all the Soviet films had social-political purposes and government sponsorship. Most of them interpreted the revolution in ways designed to improve the understanding and win the loyalty of the Russian people. When *Potemkin* first went out into the world as a revolutionary emissary—feared and hated by the reactionaries and philistines, elaborately praised by the liberals and aesthetes—its success was as much a surprise to the Russians as to anyone. That many of the Soviet silent films are universal and enduring works of art as well as being educating and indoctrinating is a tribute to the sincere enthusiasm the film makers felt for the gigantic social experiment of which they were part.

Though the significance of this body of work in the history of film is enormous, specific applications of its themes and techniques, unlike those of the Germans, were limited in the capitalist countries. Soon the formal concerns and innovations of the left wing would become unacceptable in the Soviet Union itself. Perhaps the one clear and direct link between Soviet silents and films elsewhere is with the British social documentaries of the thirties, which were state-supported for purposes of broad citizenship education and which indulged in their own experimentation with form—especially the joining of sound and image.

In the fictional film the arrival of sound largely reduced the use of montage to brief transitional sequences—of spinning locomotive wheels superimposed over a succession of billboards as the young opera star progresses toward fame and heartbreak, or of crowded beaches, golfers, and children eating watermelon, to signal summer. To be sure, and for better or worse, every television commercial builds upon the kinds of persuasiveness that the Soviets discovered lay in the combination of short strips of film. But the body of the Soviet silent cinema stands with an integrity, eloquence, and beauty that require nothing more of it than continued availability. New audiences invariably marvel at the heights achieved during this final national flowering of the silent film.

FILMS OF THE PERIOD

1925
Potemkin (Sergei Eisenstein)
Strike (Eisenstein)

1926
The Cloak
    (Grigori Kozintsev
    and Leonid Trauberg)
Mother (V. I. Pudovkin)

1927
Bed and Sofa (Abram Room)
The End of St. Petersburg (Pudovkin)
The Fall of the Romanov Dynasty
    (Esfir Shub)

1928
The Man with a Movie Camera
    (Dziga Vertov)

October/Ten Days that Shook the World
    (Eisenstein)
Storm over Asia (Pudovkin)
Zvenigora (Alexander Dovzhenko)

1929
Arsenal (Dovzhenko)
Fragment of an Empire
    (Friedrich Ermler)
The General Line/Old and the New
    (Eisenstein)
The New Babylon
    (Kozintsev and Trauberg)
Turksib (Victor Turin)

1930
Earth (Dovzhenko)

BOOKS ON THE PERIOD

BABITSKY, PAUL, and JOHN RIMBERG, *The Soviet Film Industry.* New York: Praeger Publishers, 1955. 377 pp.

BEREST, BORIS, *History of the Ukrainian Cinema.* New York: Shevchenko Scientific Society, 1962. 272 pp.

CARTER, HUNTLY, *The New Spirit in the Russian Theatre, 1917-1928; and a Sketch of the Russian Cinema and Radio 1919-1928, Showing the New Communal Relationship between the Three.* New York: Benjamin Blom, Inc., 1970. 348 pp. (originally published in 1929)

CARTER, HUNTLY, *The New Theatre and Cinema of Soviet Russia.* New York: Arno Press, 1970. 277 pp. (originally published in 1924)

COHEN, LOUIS HARRIS, *The Cultural-Political Traditions and Developments of the Soviet Cinema, 1917-1972.* New York: Arno Press, 1974. 724 pp.

CONSTANTINE, MILDRED, and ALAN FERN, *Revolutionary Soviet Film Posters.* Baltimore: Johns Hopkins University Press, 1974. 112 pp.

DICKINSON, THOROLD, and CATHERINE DE LA ROCHE, *Soviet Cinema.* New York: Arno Press, 1972. 136 pp. (originally published in 1948)

HUACO, GEORGE A., *The Sociology of Film Art.* New York: Basic Books, Inc., 1965. 229 pp.

LEYDA, JAY, *Kino: A History of the Russian and Soviet Film.* New York: Macmillan Co., 1983. 513 pp.

RIMBERG, JOHN, *The Motion Picture in the Soviet Union, 1918-1952: A Sociological Analysis.* New York: Arno Press, 1973. 238 pp.

SCHNITZER, LUDA and JEAN, and MARCEL MARTIN, eds., *Cinema in Revolution; The Heroic Era of the Soviet Film.* New York: Hill & Wang, Inc., 1973. 208 pp.

STOIL, MICHAEL JON, *Cinema Beyond the Danube: The Camera and Politics.* Metuchen, N. J.: Scarecrow Press, Inc., 1974. 208 pp.

TAYLOR, RICHARD, *The Politics of the Soviet Cinema: 1917-1929.* New York: Cambridge University Press, 1979.

VORONTSOV, YURI, and IGOR RACHUK, *The Phenomenon of the Soviet Cinema.* Moscow: Progress Publishers, 1980. 423 pp.

7

French Impressionists and the Avant-Garde, 1919–1929

The contribution of France to the maturing art of the silent cinema was much more limited in appeal than that of either Germany or Russia, yet it followed some of the same lines and in particular instances even antedated achievements in the other two countries. Its strengths, like its limitations, came from the fact that it was rooted firmly in the aesthetic ferment that marked Paris in the 1920s and made it the artistic capital of the world. The outpouring of creation in the many arts was accompanied by ongoing argument and polemic about the nature of art itself. Theory fed into practice, practice back into theory—from the ateliers and garrets to the cafés and salons. A premium was placed on the new and the experimental, the daring and the shocking, in the search for artistic styles, for forms and functions that would speak for and to the modern age.

IMPRESSIONISTS

Louis Delluc—theorist, practitioner, crusader—set out not only to link film with the other arts and aesthetic movements of the time, but also to find in what ways it was special and how it could be superior to the traditional modes of music, literature, and theater. He and other French intellectuals and artists had an especial appreciation for the popular American film genres. As they had earlier done with the mystery stories of Edgar Allen Poe, the French pointed out the formal and aesthetic beauties encased in the western, for example, and insisted that those responsible for them were genuine artistic talents.

While editing a succession of film journals, Delluc wrote prolific criticism applauding the work of the Americans—especially Ince, Griffith, and Chaplin—as well as the Swedes Sjöström and Stiller. He also attacked the French tendency to revert to the theatrical tradition of *films d'art* or to blandly imitate the commercial successes of other nations. What Delluc wanted was a cinema that was distinctively cinematic, with emphasis on the rhythmical and lyrical possibilities of the medium, and one that was distinctively French, with indigenous themes and images. In his theoretical writings and in his films, Delluc was in search of the basic quality of the motion picture, what he termed the *photogenic*. *Fièvre* (1921) and *La Femme de nulle part* (1922) are most often cited as the films directed by him which best exemplify his theories. But it was through his intellectual leadership, his organization of the *ciné-club* movement to build support for the kinds of films he valued, and his influence on other film makers that he made his greatest impact.

Around Delluc there gathered a group of film makers who have been labeled the Impressionists: Germaine Dulac (for whom Delluc wrote his first scenario, *La Fête espagnole*, 1919), Marcel L'Herbier, Jean Epstein, and Abel Gance. Their films were feature-length narratives shown in the cinemas, but they contained elements of stylization and experimentation that set them apart from the bulk of French commercial production of the time. Few of the Impressionists' films are available for viewing in the U.S., however, and we must piece together a sense of their special qualities from descriptions.

Dulac, after making a considerable body of commercial features, gravitated towards the more specialized avant-garde, which will be dealt with later. L'Herbier, a former symbolist poet, was closest to Delluc personally and is said to be most representative of the Impressionists. His work raises problems of definition from which the group itself seemed to suffer. What is accessible for viewing in the U.S. might be thought nearer to the German expressionist film makers than to the French painters from whom the Impressionist label was derived. In any case, L'Herbier seems to have concentrated heavily on the expressive use of the visual content of film through carefully contrived and subjective use of the camera and set construction. Soft focus, superimposition, and extreme camera angles are said to abound in his films. *Eldorado* (1921; a melodrama about the struggles of a barroom dancer, culminating in her suicide) and *L'Inhumaine* (1923; with Darius Milhaud and Fernand Léger among the production collaborators) are among L'Herbier's works most frequently singled out for comment.

Another is *The Late Matthew Pascal* (1925). From a novel by Luigi Pirandello, it proceeds on curiously mixed and alternating levels of reality. Farce and humor mingle with pathos and heartache. Coincidence abounds, and characters achieve outcomes different from, even contrary to, those sought. Accidents and the actions of others control their lives. Even more striking are the ways in which this is a film about film, with quotations from and anticipation of other films. There are borrowings from Keaton and Chaplin—Matthew rocking the baby's cradle with strings; a view from an apartment down onto action in the street foreshadows a scene in *Un chien Andalou* (1928); then Fritz Lang's *Dr. Mabuse, the Gambler* (1922) is evoked, (or maybe it's Louis Feuillade's *Fantomas* [1913–14]); and in a scene in a library, replete with dust, rats, and disorderly stacks of books, the librarian-in-chief is very like Dr. Caligari in the famous *Cabinet of* (1919). The sets by Alberto Cavalcanti, who designed settings for several of L'Herbier's films before making his own *Rien que les heures* (1926), play a rich part in the action; some

The Late Matthew Pascal (France, 1925, Marcel L'Herbier). Museum of Modern Art/ Film Stills Archive.

of them are breathtakingly imaginative. The performances, including those of Russian emigré Ivan Mozhukhin as Matthew and a young Michel Simon as his friend, are stylized almost to the point of burlesque. Sophisticated and modern, the very eclecticism of L'Herbier's *The Late Matthew Pascal*—with something for everyone—is, ultimately, quite original.

Jean Epstein, like Louis Delluc, was a film theorist as well as a film maker. He entered production as Delluc's assistant on *Le Tonnere* (1921). *Coeur fidèle* (1923) is thought by many to be his most successful film; it embodied some of his theoretical ideas about filmic style and established his reputation among the Impressionists. *The Fall of the House of Usher* (1928, on which Luis Buñuel worked as an assistant), even more experimental, brought him closer to the camp of the later avant-garde. With *Finis Terrae* (1929) Epstein moved on to a cycle of realist films set in Brittany.

Of those associated with the Impressionists, Abel Gance is the most special case, too large and long-lasting a creator to be contained within a single school. As the one gigantic figure of the presound French film (he began to direct in 1911), he not only rivaled Griffith during the silent years but continued on ahead of his time up to the seventies. Though his work was enormously influential, the vastness of Gance's conceptions and the originality of his technique finally made him unique in the history of film. The subjectivity and distortion in his *La Folie du Docteur Tube* (1915), achieved through the camera, preceded the later experiments of the Impressionists; but its innovations so alarmed the producer that it wasn't released at the time. The impressionism and his complex rapid cutting in *La Roue* (1922) antedated the Soviet films and strongly influenced the French avant-garde just then developing.

In his enormous *Napoléon* (1927) Gance first employed a triptych screen process called Polyvision, which preceded Cinerama by a quarter century. Unlike the film makers of Cinerama, Gance used his separate panels to carry contrasting and complementary images as well as to extend one image to panoramic proportions. The film's

Napoléon (France, 1927, Abel Gance). National Film Archive/Stills Library.

force, however, did not depend solely on the novelty of those scenes projected in multiscreen (only four out of the whole). The eighty-minute single-screen version released originally in this country by M-G-M is, as a historical-dramatic work, as powerful as the best of Griffith or Eisenstein.

Numerous subsequent efforts have been made to reconstruct the film as close to the six-hour definitive version as possible. The most popular of these, in fact notably so, was sponsored by Francis Coppola. Shown initially at Radio City Music Hall in New York City in 1981 (the year Gance died), this four-hour version, with original live orchestral score composed by Coppola's father, Carmine, then toured the U.S. Many people who had never seen silent films, or even thought about them, were overwhelmed by this one. Its amazing power remains intact.

AVANT-GARDE

Working alongside the Impressionists in the 1920s, carrying their technical and stylistic experimentation even further, were the French avant-garde film makers. The production of Impressionist films was virtually ended by 1924; the avant-garde waxed most strongly from about 1925 to the end of the decade, and in deference to the work of the Impressionists is sometimes called the second avant-garde. It emerged, however, quite directly from a nonfilmic historic line—one that began with the Impressionist painters of the late nineteenth century and departed from the film Impressionists' reliance on literary material. The usually short, silent, avant-garde films are like visual poems, jokes, or dreams—more akin to modern poetry or to abstract or surrealist painting than to novels, plays, or feature films. In most important respects they were an extension of the static visual arts into motion.

Avant-garde film making was practiced in France more than elsewhere primarily because the right kind of personnel were there. French intellectuals and artists were among the most enthusiastic admirers of "the seventh art," as critic Ricciotto Canudo called film at the time. Even more than the Germans, many French artists were demonstrating an eagerness to try their hands at more than one medium. That jack-of-all-arts Jean Cocteau—poet, novelist, playwright, painter, film maker—was one extreme case.

The avant-garde film movement in France was bolstered by the comparatively easy access to the tools and materials of the medium and by an audience receptive to experiment. In this period, the French film industry was so loosely organized and lightly financed as to be almost amateurish by standards prevailing elsewhere. Rather than an oligopoly of a few large studios, there were many small companies and individual entrepreneurs. Given the relative inexpensiveness of the silent film, it was quite possible for a painter to raise a little money from the owner of an art gallery (to pay for raw stock and processing), to have a friend borrow a camera from the studio where he or she worked, to arrange for the use of an aristocratic art-lover's chateau, to invite friends (other artists) there, and then to shoot a short, improvised experimental film in which they appeared. When completed it could be shown in one of the small cinemas on the left bank and among the *ciné-clubs* founded by Delluc and Canudo that were beginning to show specialized programs. If the painter's reputation was sufficient, general public interest in the arts, including film, could assure enough of an audience to pay back the modest costs. Man Ray's *Les Mystères du Château du Dé* (1929), for instance, was produced and exhibited that way.

Paris was the place, the 1920s the time. By then the intellectual advance that had started in the sciences shortly after the turn of the century had begun to filter through into the arts. Some of the important constructs to come out of the physical sciences gave a new understanding to the relationship between space and time. Implicit in Max Planck's quantum mechanics, Albert Einstein's theory of relativity, and the mathematics and philosophical speculation of Alfred North Whitehead was a view of the world as being one vast interconnected state of flux. This concept was matched by equivalents of artistic expression. Marcel Duchamp rendered a "Nude Descending a Staircase" in a way that attempted to evoke temporal and spatial seriality. Georges Braque painted with multiple views overlaid to suggest seeing "Le Pipe," for example, from all sides at once. Marcel Proust superimposed other places and past times onto the present in *Remembrance of Things Past;* and James Joyce, in *Ulysses,* showed the interrelatedness of simultaneous events occurring in different parts of Dublin on a day in June.

To many, film seemed the perfect medium for dealing with temporal-spatial relationships—the duration of movement, the space of picture. The French philosopher Henri Bergson, whose ideas about time as space were profoundly influential, had written in *Creative Evolution* that the *"mechanism of our ordinary knowledge is of a cinematographical kind."*[1] Art historian Elie Faure, in his seminal essay "The Art of Cineplastics" (1920), in which he nodded to L'Herbier and Delluc, wrote, "The cinema incorporates time in space. More than this, through the cinema, time really becomes a dimension of space."[2] With their new creative impulses the young poets and, especially, painters simply wrote themselves off their pages and painted beyond their canvases into the cinema. This particular intellectual, aesthetic force gave rise to the abstract and nonobjective line of the avant-garde—films that are like Mondrian paintings set in motion. It began in Berlin about 1921 with the films of Viking Eggeling (*Symphonie diagonale*) and Hans Richter (*Rhythmus 21*) and quickly moved to Paris, where it was continued by Fernand Léger (*Ballet mécanique,* 1924), Marcel Duchamp (*Anemic Cinema,* 1928), and others.

The second main line of the avant-garde came out of the new psychological sciences pioneered by Sigmund Freud, whose equivalence in literature was again offered by Proust (in his obsession with early memories) and Joyce (in his stream of con-

---

[1] Henri Bergson, *Creative Evolution* (New York: Henry Holt & Company, 1911), p. 306. The emphasis is Bergson's.

[2] Elie Faure, "The Art of Cineplastics" in *Film: An Anthology,* edited by Daniel Talbot (Berkeley: University of California Press, 1959), p. 11.

Ballet mécanique (France, 1924, Fernand Léger). Museum of Modern Art/
Film Stills Archive.

sciousness and dream episodes). In painting, the surrealists informed their canvases
with Freudian symbols and insights. Some thought the motion picture might be the art
best able to capture and reveal the dream state so significant for Freud. Film's capacity
for representing the fantasy world of dreams was almost as great as its ability to record
the objective reality of the physical world; and so, Antonin Artaud and Germaine Dulac
created *The Seashell and the Clergyman* (1928), Salvador Dali and Luis Buñuel produced
Un chien Andalou (1928) and *L'Age d'or* (1930), and others made other films within the
movement known as surrealism.

The final mode of the avant-garde was impressionism—not to be confused with
the previous feature-length narratives of the Impressionists gathered around Louis
Delluc. Objective and realistic, unlike the other two lines of the avant-garde, the impressionist impulse stemmed from the earlier painters. It was concerned essentially with
rendering the surfaces of objects, persons, or views with the strongest impressions made
by lights and darks, shapes and movements—like looking at the world from a fast-
moving railway carriage someone had said of the impressionist paintings. Impressionism in the avant-garde film largely took the form of the "city symphonies"—a clear
enough derivation from *Ulysses,* the 1922 publication of which in Paris preceded the first

Un chien Andalou (France, 1929, Luis Buñuel and Salvador Dali). National Film Archive/Stills Library.

of these films. As in Joyce's novel, there was the time-space emphasis on simultaneity of action by various people in different parts of a city, the whole organized chronologically. In the films, however, form predominated over meaning. Some excellent early examples are Alberto Cavalcanti's *Rien que les heures* (1926), about Paris, Walther Ruttmann's *Berlin: Symphony of a Great City* (1927), and Joris Ivens's *Rain* (1928), about Amsterdam. Though the concern of these films is more with visual and rhythmical patterns than with social content, they served as a transition from the avant-garde of the twenties to the documentaries of the thirties.

The avant-garde movement ended principally because of the expensiveness of sound production and the inaccessibility and complexity of sound equipment and technique. In the new technology, there was no place for the inspired amateur. A second cause was the changing attitudes of the thirties: Whereas art for the sake of art seemed worthy of artists' full attention in the twenties, the thirties became the years of art for society's sake. The Depression and rising fascism prompted new artistic intentions. The avant-garde film was replaced by the documentary as the artistic form most attractive to the artists and intellectuals of the thirties. It is no coincidence that the three "symphonic" avant-garde film makers mentioned above (Cavalcanti, Ruttmann, Ivens) became socially committed documentary film makers in the thirties.

The avant-garde film did not resume as anything resembling a movement until some fifteen years later, and then in the United States rather than in France. Its resumption was made possible by the widespread availability and comparatively low cost of 16mm nontheatrical equipment (as opposed to the 35mm theatrical standard). It began with the first film of Maya Deren, *Meshes of the Afternoon* (1943, coproduced with her then husband Alexander Hammid), which was black and white, silent (even though sound was conventional), and could have fitted comfortably within the earlier avant-garde alongside Dulac's *Seashell and the Clergyman* and Buñuel-Dali's *Chien Andalou.* Largely as a result of Deren's films and crusading activity, a new avant-garde evolved which has variously been called the experimental, the underground, or the independent film. It continues vigorously as a distinctive mode of creative expression, alongside narrative fiction and documentary, especially in the United States, Canada, Great Britain, and Japan.

In France at the end of the 1920s many of the principal avant-garde film makers returned to the less expensive and more accessible traditional métiers: Fernand Léger, Salvador Dali, Marcel Duchamp, and Man Ray (who had made *Emak Bakia* in 1926, and *L'Étoile de mer* in 1928) went back to painting and still photography. Others, however, found their way into commercial feature films. For example, René Clair (who had made the avant-garde *Entr'acte* and *Paris qui dort* in 1924), Luis Buñuel, and to an extent Jean Renoir (with *La Fille de l'eau,* 1924, and *The Little Match Girl,* 1928) and Jean Vigo (with *À propos de Nice,* 1930), had started in the avant-garde tradition. Jean Cocteau was the only one to bring avant-garde styles fully into sound features—in *The Blood of a Poet* (1930), *Beauty and the Beast* (1946), *Orpheus* (1950), and *The Testament of Orpheus* (1960). But the influence of the avant-garde, along with that of the earlier Impressionists, would extend down into the sound film and into a rich period of French cinema in the thirties.

FILMS OF THE PERIOD

1919
La Fête espagnole (Germaine Dulac)
J'accuse (Abel Gance)

1921
Eldorado (Marcel L'Herbier)
Fièvre (Louis Delluc)

1922
La Femme de nulle part (Delluc)
La Roue (Gance)

1923
Coeur fidèle (Jean Epstein)
L'Inhumaine (L'Herbier)
The Smiling Madame Beudet (Dulac)

1924
Ballet mécanique (Fernand Léger)
Entr'acte (René Clair)
Paris qui dort (Clair)

1925
The Late Matthew Pascal (L'Herbier)

1926
Rien que les heures (Alberto Cavalcanti)

1927
Napoléon (Gance)

1928
Un chien Andalou
  (Luis Buñuel and Salvador Dali)
The Fall of the House of Usher
  (Jean Epstein)
The Little Match Girl (Jean Renoir)
The Seashell and the Clergyman (Dulac)

1929
Finis Terrae (Epstein)

1930
L'Age d'or (Buñuel)
The Blood of a Poet (Jean Cocteau)

BOOKS ON THE PERIOD

ARMES, ROY,   *French Film.* New York: E. P. Dutton & Co., Inc., 1970. 160 pp.

CURTIS, DAVID,   *Experimental Cinema.* New York: Universe Books, Inc., 1971. 168 pp.

KOVACS, STEPHEN,   *From Enchantment to Rage: The Story of Surrealist Cinema.* East Brunswick, N. J.: Fairleigh Dickinson University Press, 1980. 304 pp.

LAWDER, STANDISH B.,   *The Cubist Cinema.* New York: New York University Press, 1974. 208 pp.

MANVELL, ROGER, ed.,   *Experiment in the Film.* New York: Arno Press, 1970. 285 pp. (originally published in 1949)

MATTHEWS, J. H.,   *Surrealism and Film.* Ann Arbor: University of Michigan Press, 1971. 198 pp.

MONACO, PAUL,   *Cinema and Society: France and Germany during the Twenties.* New York: Elsevier-North Holland Pub. Co., 1976. 194 pp.

RENAN, SHELDON,   *An Introduction to the American Underground Film.* New York: E. P. Dutton & Co., Inc., 1967. 318 pp.

SADOUL, GEORGES,   *French Film.* New York: Arno Press, 1972. 130 pp. (originally published in 1953)

STAUFFACHER, FRANK, ed.,   *Art in Cinema: A Symposium on the Avant-Garde Film.* New York: Arno Press, 1968. 104 pp. (originally published in 1947)

TYLER, PARKER,   *Underground Film: A Critical History.* New York: Grove Press, Inc., 1969. 249 pp.

8

Hollywood
in the Twenties,
1919–1929

While the Swedish, German, Russian, and French films of the twenties commanded much of the early serious critical consideration, the American film began its domination of the international box office, a domination that has lasted until the present. Between the signing of the Versailles Treaty and the crash of the stock market, there began in the United States forms of cultural expression and economic expansion that signaled a new kind of empire. Though in its political and military stance the country became resolutely isolationist, its business and industry extended their sphere of influence. American automobiles, refrigerators, and countless other technological products were exported around the globe. At home, while a succession of extremely conservative presidents were elected to power, there occurred an effusion in the arts that increased Americans' sense of national identity at the same time it attracted attention from abroad. It was in the twenties that modern American drama may be said to have begun—with the plays of Eugene O'Neill and Elmer Rice; that American literature achieved a new resonance—in the novels and stories of Sinclair Lewis, F. Scott Fitzgerald, John Dos Passos, William Faulkner, and Ernest Hemingway. Among America's contributions to the arts during that time, jazz is no doubt the most distinctive. But it was the American movies, which connected art most firmly with commerce, that became the pervasive centurions in the new cultural conquest.

This is not to say that no fine films were made by important American film makers; but rather, that the American flair for mass production, promotion, and selling created and supplied a worldwide market for a particular kind of entertainment. From the outset, producing for a polyglot immigrant population, American film makers had been learning to make films satisfying to many nationalities. It is possible to state without chauvinism that "the movies" are more closely identified with the United States than with any other country, and that "Hollywood" holds a fascination for the entire globe. So, it is now proper to return from the rarefied atmosphere of European "art films" to the workaday Hollywood of gold bathtub spigots, tame leopards, and white Stutz Bearcats. Since the basis for the success of the American film is industrial, the business of its art once again deserves attention.

MOVIES BECOME BIG BUSINESS

During the 1920s there was limited, but nonetheless intense, competition among the former independent companies that had become the new major studios. Old firms merged and disappeared, and not one member of the Motion Picture Patents Company, with which the independents had competed between 1908 and 1915, survived.

In 1924 a hyphenated Metro-Goldwyn-Mayer was put together by Marcus Loew—president of Loew's, Inc., which owned large theater holdings. Added to Metro Pictures Corporation (Loew's small production company) were the Goldwyn Picture Corporation and the Louis B. Mayer Pictures Corporation. Samuel Goldwyn had already left the Goldwyn Picture Corporation to become an independent producer; Mayer joined the newly created firm as studio head, beginning a reign that would last nearly thirty years. Also active were Universal (Carl Laemmle's outfit), Warner Brothers (Harry, Jack, Sam, and Albert), Paramount (which Adolph Zukor had brought along out of Famous Players-[Jesse] Lasky), Columbia (Jack and Harry Cohn), United Artists (Chaplin, Fairbanks, Pickford, Griffith), and the (William) Fox Film Corporation. Competition among these firms led to the need for increased capital—which was used to sign up stars, expand distribution and exhibition outlets, and buy out rivals. Public stock was issued, giving Wall Street a voice that would grow louder over the years.

The earlier economic battles had been fought largely in the field of production as the Motion Picture Patents Company trust attempted to stem the competition of the independents. During the first years after World War I, control of distribution was the major goal. National distribution became increasingly centralized and dominated by the major producing companies. The old "states' rights" franchise system, under which *The Birth of a Nation* and many of the first features had been distributed, faded away. For ultimate domination of the screen and long-term revenues, the struggle extended inevitably to ownership of the theaters themselves. There finally developed a pattern known as "vertical control," which lasted until it was outlawed by the federal courts in 1948. Under vertical control a few huge firms (eventually the roster became fixed at eight) produced, distributed, and exhibited their own films.

By the mid-twenties the fight for control of exhibition was being waged by three giants, which looked as if they might divide the whole pie, either forcing the other companies out or making them sit at table according to strict rules of etiquette. In 1919 Paramount had floated a $10 million issue of preferred stock, marking the beginning of the new phase. By 1921 that company was in virtual control of five hundred key theaters in the U.S. and first-run theaters in major cities around the world. By the end of the twenties Adolph Zukor had built up the most formidable combination in the industry: Paramount had the stars, the production outfit, the distribution channels, and control of two thousand theaters.

First National, the next largest production-distribution firm, had been formed by a group of theater chains to get access to the product on their own terms. The third contestant was Loew's, Inc., the vast firm of which Metro-Goldwyn-Mayer, the production-distribution arm, was only one part. Within a few years nearly all the major and first-run houses in the United States and Canada had been acquired by Paramount, Loew's, or the large circuits affiliated with the First National group. Fox and Universal also had theater outlets, but on a lesser scale.

By 1927 some four-hundred to five hundred feature films a year were being produced. Ideally, each of the large companies would release no fewer than fifty-two a year, permitting a weekly change of program for its own theaters. Distribution involved close to six hundred exchanges (that is, regional offices that handled the prints of the films) in forty-six key American cities. Approximately twenty thousand theaters in the country were attended by some 80 million customers a week. A few huge firms, the former independents, were near monopoly again. Unlike the old Trust, they minimized the role of production in favor of exhibition. The center of return on investment and of ultimate control was where distribution and exhibition were headquartered: New York City, not Hollywood. Any would-be new independents were effectively kept out of this closed system. If they wanted to produce, the screens weren't available to them; if they wanted to exhibit, they couldn't get access to films.

The emphasis on exhibition made the twenties the great decade of motion picture theater construction. Most of the "movie palaces," many of which have since been torn down or converted to other uses, stem from that era. The Capitol Theatre in New York City, for example, was built in 1919 and seated 5,300. *Photoplay* magazine wrote of it: "The mezzanine floor looks as if it had been designed for eight-day bicycle races."[1] Grauman's Egyptian and Chinese Theatres in Hollywood along with large and ornate New York City theaters, including the fabled Roxy, were all part of this extraordinary architectural tradition.

My own recollections extend back to a "million-dollar theatre," the Rialto, in Joliet, Illinois. Architecturally it was a melange of imitation Byzantine, Venetian, classical Greek, and authentic midwestern Balaban & Katz (the chain of which it was part, affiliated in turn with Paramount Pictures). The Rialto offered more than movies: It provided a total cultural experience. On the weekends there were stage shows and a pit orchestra in addition to the films. The mighty Wurlitzer organ, with a console the size of a double bed and stops capable of producing every sound from canary peep to cannon roar, sufficed for weekdays. Objets d'art—sculpture, paintings, furniture, and even fountains—circulated around the Balaban & Katz chain so that varied offerings of elegance were placed before the devotees at each temple. Perhaps most memorable of all was the scented Greco-Italian garden visitors passed through on the way to the street: Suffused in pink light, landscape murals lined the walls, and a simulated blue sky with fluffy white clouds moved overhead.

If the appeal of the films didn't always measure up to their surroundings, at least the increasing expensiveness of production kept pace with the new lavishness of

---

[1] Quoted by Lewis Jacobs, *The Rise of the American Film* (New York: Harcourt, Brace, Inc., 1939), p. 292.

Rialto Theatre, Joliet, Illinois. Theatre Historical Society.

presentation. Extravagance reigned, and the notion of spending money to make money was unquestioningly accepted. Salaries soared for directors, writers, and especially stars. While the epic *Birth of a Nation* had cost around $100,000 in 1915, *Ben-Hur* cost $6 million a decade later. By the end of the 1920s the *average* production expenditure on features was up to $200,000. The studios' steady incomes, however, came from the "program" or "B" pictures—unlike today, when television has taken over that kind of production, and theatrical features must offer something that seems special in order to attract an audience.

With such expenditures, and attendant financial concern, by the mid-twenties the director had been replaced by the production supervisor as the person in charge of film making. The production supervisor made many of the artistic decisions as well as all of the business ones. Developing out of the pattern first established by Thomas Ince, this function was most brilliantly exercised by the legendary boy wonder at M-G-M, Irving Thalberg, model for the hero of F. Scott Fitzgerald's uncompleted novel *The Last Tycoon*. Sometimes called production chief, head of studio, or vice-president in charge of production, this executive oversaw a whole program of pictures, deciding which ideas or literary and dramatic "properties" were to be developed into scripts, then casting players and assigning directors. With the cost and complexity of sound, the power of this position would become even more complete than in silent days. Film makers like D. W. Griffith and Erich von Stroheim were temperamentally incapable of working within this system and eventually were discarded by it. Griffith directed two sound films; von Stroheim one. Directors became "glorified foremen" and, with assembly-line specialization, were as much type-cast as were the players. There were directors of westerns, of comedies, of romances, and so on, with second-rank directors hired to imitate the work of first-rank ones.

The easiest way to produce pictures rapidly, and to "sell" them in advance to exhibitors, was to imitate recent successes; thus the "cycle" was born, with the "formula picture" as the unit. Movies, once novelties, were now referred to as "products." In the early days it had been possible to experiment more freely, because there was no fixed idea of exactly what a film should be; there was no way of knowing for sure what would be appealing, except by trying and finding out. Now the conception of what was good film—that is, likely to be financially successful—had hardened.

Lewis Jacobs, in *The Rise of the American Film* (the most comprehensive and best history of the subject up to 1939), says that all films had come to be assessed in terms of certain fixed criteria. The first things looked for were *names*—stars with drawing power; second, *production values*—elaborate sets, crowds of extras, and other evidence of great expense; third, *story value,* which tended to mean the huge price paid for the original, and its popularity as a novel or play. The next criterion was *picture sense*—a sort of conglomeration of the above elements plus any specific filmic qualities. Finally, there was *box office appeal*—plenty of the standardized values that had proved successful in years past.

The industrial system described above would be in effect for the next thirty years. It has not yet been fully replaced.

SOME MAJOR DIRECTORS AND THEIR FILMS

Big business interests, then, took over in the twenties and have remained dominant since. But a number of talented film makers have always managed to create important, and even great, films working within (or briefly defying) the system. In sum total the American film stands unmatched in artistic quality as well as in quantity and commercial success (which is only to say popularity). Given that fact, perhaps there is something to be said for the system, which is rarely praised in critical circles.

With a chapter heading in *The Rise of the American Film,* Jacobs acknowledges that the decade of the twenties offered "A Throng of Directors." He chose to deal with Cecil B. De Mille, Erich von Stroheim, Ernst Lubitsch, F. W. Murnau, Victor Seastrom (né Sjöström), Robert Flaherty, John Stuart Robinson (now mostly forgotten), Henry King, James Cruze, Rex Ingram, and "others." Among the others held in particular esteem today are King Vidor, Josef von Sternberg (emerging late in the period), and Frank Borzage. Jacobs does not discuss the silent films of John Ford, Howard Hawks, Buster Keaton, or Raoul Walsh, all of whom worked in the twenties and have come to be valued highly.

The first three men on Jacobs's list not only made films of intrinsic worth; their collective output, radically dissimilar though the three bodies of work are, represents some general aspects of the American film of the twenties. De Mille's values were most clearly the system's values; von Stroheim was the rebel; Lubitsch, the whimsical subversive. Incidentally, the two who continued to work in the industry beyond the twenties—De Mille and Lubitsch—became producers in order to control their directorial efforts.

In the past De Mille was often disregarded or disapproved of by critics and historians on the grounds that his films are generally superficial and frequently meretricious, and that they add nothing to film art. In recent years, a reevaluation has occurred in some quarters, based on the visual (as opposed to intellectual) merits of his films. In either case, no one can deny their enormous success. Unparalleled as a showman, publicist, and businessman, De Mille also had a unique ability to move with the times. Though the artist in him may have been uncertain, the social psychologist was uncannily accurate in his intuitions. Today's social historians can infer much about the cultural climate of the American twenties by an examination of De Mille's invariably successful pictures.

De Mille's father and mother were of the theater; his brother was the playwright William C. De Mille. Cecil himself had been associated with David Belasco, the "Dean of the American Stage." De Mille's initial film effort, *The Squaw Man* (1914), was one of the earliest features and among the first films to be made in Hollywood; it established at the outset his ability to anticipate trends in the industry. From 1919 to 1924 he turned out a rapid succession of widely popular films aimed at middle-class audiences and reflecting postwar changes in manners and morals. As the titles themselves suggest, this was indeed the *roaring* twenties: *Don't Change Your Husband, For Better or Worse, Male and Female* (all 1919); *Why Change Your Wife? Something to Think About* (both 1920); *Forbidden Fruit, The Affairs of Anatol* (both 1921); *Fool's Paradise, Saturday Night, Manslaughter* (all 1922); and *Adam's Rib* (1923). These were advertised as "typical De Mille productions—audacious, glittering, intriguing, superlatively elegant and quite without heart." Following these essays on contemporary mores, a shift began to occur in De Mille's preoccupations. *The Ten Commandments* (1923) had a long Biblical prologue to a modern story, and *The King of Kings* (1927) was the first full work of the kind with which his name would subsequently become associated: religiosity cum sex and spectacle.

Except for the latter two mentioned, De Mille's films of the twenties were trivial in content. However, they had considerable influence on the craft of motion picture making, and on the popular culture of the country at large. While he made movies that were "production-conscious" (he was painstaking with details—clothes, makeup, lighting, properties, and sets—in the manner of Belasco), he also offered styles of interior decoration and clothing fashions for imitation. He is often given credit for inaugurating the tendency of American bathrooms to aspire to the elegance of throne rooms. Theatrical in his direction, he rarely used camera or cutting obtrusively, except for "special effects." His historical spectacles are like a series of separate illustrations brought to life. The performances tend to be stiff, broad, and simple.

It must be conceded, however, that De Mille is one of a very few directors who have gotten their names onto marquees. People went to see a "De Mille picture." He achieved this star status partly from the size and dazzle of his productions, but also from a vigorous publicizing of his own personality. It is to De Mille that we owe the assumption that you can tell a motion picture director by his open-neck shirt, riding breeches, puttees, and megaphone. Also, people went partly out of curiosity to see what all the other people were seeing. The consistency of De Mille's box-office record remains remarkable: Not one of his films lost money. Appropriately (that is, supposedly very

King of Kings (U.S., 1927, Cecil B. De Mille). Museum of Modern Art/Film Stills Archive.

much to his taste), after De Mille's death the prop Ten Commandments tablet used in his second film of that title was placed on a kind of altar under his lighted portrait in the Paramount commissary. The tablet was painted gold.

Erich von Stroheim was not unlike De Mille, in that he had the same flamboyance, meticulousness with details, and extravagance. But he could never put those qualities to consistent commercial use. The iron will, artistic integrity, and rebelliousness for which he is respected by those who admire his films kept him from seeking out what the public wanted. Instead, he gave audiences the world as he saw it—in a style notable for its scathing naturalism laced with irony—in place of the usual coating of reality with a sentimental center.

Of the eight films von Stroheim made between 1918 and the end of his directorial career in 1928, *Greed* (1925) is unquestionably the masterpiece. It remains one of the most impressive films in the total history of the screen. The legend surrounding it contains omens pointing toward the end of his career as a director and his subsequent canonization: its staggering cost; its length of forty-five reels (over seven hours) cut to a conventional ten; von Stroheim's disavowal of the released version; and the power that remains in spite of the mutilation. Controversy over the film can still be heard, and there are still unshakable hopes and occasional rumors that a copy of the complete version may somehow have survived. There are those who defend von Stroheim (see biographies by Peter Noble, Joel W. Finler, Thomas Quinn Curtiss, and Richard Koszarski) and those who defend Hollywood (on the grounds that no industry, however benevolent, could be expected to tolerate such presumption and profligacy). The particular qualities of his art also raise arguments. At the time, critics faulted him for his decadence and cynicism or his slavish, plodding realism and lack of cinematic flair. Some argued that the fanatical literalness of his translation of Frank Norris's novel *McTeague* into the film *Greed* was not creation at all.

Today most would agree that a handful of his films (*Foolish Wives,* 1922, *The Merry Widow,* 1925, *The Wedding March,* 1928, and *Greed*) are original and extraordinary, powerful in a way and to a degree unlike anyone else's work. His camera-editing style rested on the long take/long shot not much in vogue during the ascendancy of montage, with its stress on fast cutting and closeups. (Others who followed von Stroheim's creative impulse would be the silent comedians, who wanted to show that their comic stunts really happened, and documentarian Robert Flaherty, who had a similar desire for different reasons to establish the authenticity of what was on the screen.) The sort of spatial-temporal coherence and realism that von Stroheim's style represented would later become a dominant aesthetic tendency. The resistance von Stroheim met from producers, critics, and public was caused not so much by his cinematic technique as by the awareness that his was an angry art. The mirror he held up to nature not only reflected warts and all, but it emphasized the warts—the venality, selfishness, and perversity present in all of us.

Jacobs observes that all of von Stroheim's films are melodramas of lust; we could add, of obsession—fixed on sexual or material acquisitiveness. Sexuality is usually interwoven with money, station, or power in an uncompromisingly unpalatable view of life. Decadence and depravity are ubiquitous. In *Foolish Wives,* "Count" Wladislas Karamzin, played by von Stroheim—"the man you love to hate"—evidently makes his way in the world through sexual enterprises based on seduction, blackmail, and the like. Enormously attractive, he obviously enjoys his work, which is accompanied by a fatal bit of recreational lechery with an idiot girl. Though he seems to be involved with five women, there is no suggestion of love in any of these relationships. This character, whom von Stroheim had created in his first film, *Blind Husbands* (1919), appears in intermittent variation throughout his work—including his last released film, *Queen Kelly* (1928). Though he doesn't appear in *Greed,* the consistent point is made most explicit as a romantic attachment gradually deteriorates into a single-minded pursuit of gold.

For the audacity of his themes, as well as for his arrogance and financial disinterest, von Stroheim was denied access to the tools of his art. His directorial career ended about the same time as that of D. W. Griffith, for whom he had first worked. The last decades of von Stroheim's life, like Griffith's, were spent in semiretirement outside the film industry.

Ernst Lubitsch's German films made within the romantic-historical tradition (*Passion/Madame du Barry* and *Deception/Anna Boleyn*) have already been discussed. They were very popular in the United States and Lubitsch followed them here in 1922. But neither those films nor his earlier training as an actor in Max Reinhardt's company foreshadowed the kind of film Lubitsch would turn to and make peculiarly his own. After studying contemporary American production, Lubitsch moved into comedy and light drama of the sort De Mille was making so successfully. Before the end of the decade he had outstripped De Mille, in quality at least, while De Mille had moved to spectacles not unlike those Lubitsch had made earlier. But he is most amazing for his command of

Greed (U.S., 1925, Erich von Stroheim). Museum of Modern Art/Film Stills Archive.

The Marriage Circle (U.S., 1924, Ernst Lubitsch). Museum of Modern Art/Film Stills Archive.

the medium: the subtlety and flexibility with which he was able to use silent film to communicate the nuances of a situation, and later his experimental leadership in sound.

Though differences of style and outlook mask the similarities, the films of Lubitsch are like those of von Stroheim in one important respect: They are about sex and money. To increase his freedom for comment, and to add a bit of glamor and suavity, Lubitsch, like von Stroheim, tended to set his plots against European backgrounds. But in Lubitsch's films, sexual intrigue is merely frivolity engaged in by the wealthy to occupy their leisure time. With few exceptions his pictures were comedies of manners, peopled entirely with the well-bred, urbane upper classes. He delineated their fads and foibles with a Viennese charm and worldliness that made them seem novel, fascinating, and a bit naughty to American audiences. His sophisticated humor came to be well known as "the Lubitsch touch." Of his American silent films, *The Marriage Circle, Forbidden Paradise* (both 1924), and *Lady Windermere's Fan* (1925) have best retained their charm.

POPULAR GENRES

Perhaps more than the business acumen of the moguls or the technical resources of the big studios, more than the attractiveness of the stars and the skills of the directors, it is the popular genres that have most typified American film and given it its greatest strength and vitality. (The only other country in which genre possibilities have developed with comparably clear identities and persistence is Japan, whose industry is also large, and whose product is very popular with a huge domestic audience.)

During the 1920s all the major types of the American film were present except, of course, the musical, which required sound. The western was our most exclusive national contribution (though the Japanese have an equivalent in their samurai films) until the Italian, and even German, "westerns" began to appear in more recent years. They started at least with *The Great Train Robbery* (1903), and matured most notably in the films produced by Thomas Ince and starring William S. Hart (for example, *The Gun Fighter* and *The Aryan,* both 1916). Paramount (Famous Players-Lasky) in the twenties added the epic western to the line: *The Covered Wagon* (1923), directed by James Cruze, and *The Iron Horse* (1924), directed by John Ford. Hart continued to work until 1925 (*Tumbleweeds* was his last and probably finest film) and was succeeded in popularity by Tom Mix, Buck Jones, Tim McCoy, Hoot Gibson, Ken Maynard, and some lesser stars.

As for the meaning and function of this genre, French critic Jean-Louis Rieupeyrout puts it this way:

> Far from being glamorized fiction, the Western is rather a faithful representation of a too often unrecognized reality. It is the expression of a typically American mythology. Its heroes and its gods offer us a thousand epic pictures and unfold on the screens of the universe a new, gigantic, and vivid Bayeux tapestry.[2]

When the comedy genre moved from one- and two-reelers to include features, the 1920s became "Comedy's Greatest Era," as James Agee calls it in his famous essay

[2] Jean-Louis Rieupeyrout, "The Western: A Historical Genre," *The Quarterly of Film, Radio, and Television,* VII (Winter 1952), p. 128.

The Covered Wagon (U.S., 1923, James Cruze). Museum of Modern Art/Film Stills Archive.

on the subject. The wonderful clowns—Charles Chaplin, Buster Keaton, Harold Lloyd, and Harry Langdon—created their masterworks during that decade. They confirmed and advanced the early discoveries and pioneering insights of Mack Sennett, making of silent film comedy a timeless and universal art form.

The features included Chaplin's *The Kid* (1921) and *The Gold Rush* (1925), Keaton's *The Navigator* (1924) and *The General* (1927), Lloyd's *Safety Last* (1923) and *The Freshman* (1925), and Langdon's *The Strong Man* and *Tramp, Tramp, Tramp* (both 1926). Along with the continuing shorts of Stan Laurel and Oliver Hardy, and others, these films gave American screen comedy an impetus that carried it through the 1940s and perhaps beyond.

If we include the work of Danny Kaye, Red Skelton, Jerry Lewis, and Woody Allen within that tradition, the influence of the comedies of the twenties has extended to the present. Though the introduction of sound required extreme modifications of style and introduced a new group of comics, the comedy, along with the western, the gangster film, and the musical, remains among the most distinctive, indigenous, and important American contributions to film forms.

The "problem picture," dealing with social and moral concerns, had appeared among the first story films shortly after the turn of the century (for example, *The Ex-Convict*, 1905, *The Eviction*, 1907). This has always been an important genre and includes some of this nation's most substantial work. Often the problem pictures look at society from the vantage point of a new generation and deal with the alarms and discomforts caused by social change. From the attempts of De Mille and others to treat the "jazz age," postwar morality and the "modern generation" of the twenties, there runs a more or less straight line to the Depression films of the thirties. In the twenties, however, the loosening of sexual morality, on the screens as in life, was accompanied by political and economic conservatism.

The General (U.S., 1927, Buster Keaton). Museum of Modern Art/Film Stills Archive.

A number of films attacked Bolshevism at home and abroad, revealing American uneasiness over the successful Russian revolution. Other films dealt with strikes, usually portraying them as resulting from misunderstanding between management and labor, rarely acknowledging that they had any real economic causes. The overwhelming preponderance of "problems" considered in the other films of this genre had to do with morals and mores: the changing conception of marriage (*Wine of Youth*, 1924, *Trial Marriage*, 1929); women's increased independence (*Daring Youth*, *For Ladies Only*, both 1927); youthful rebellion (*Flaming Youth*, 1923, *Our Dancing Daughters*, 1928); promiscuity (*Husbands for Rent*, 1927, *Breakfast at Sunrise*, 1927); bootleg debauchery (*The House of Youth*, 1924, *The Mad Whirl*, 1925), and like subjects.

In spite of a remark attributed to Samuel Goldwyn—"If you got a message, send it by Western Union"—the problem picture has been remarkably persistent in an industry presumably devoted to "escapist entertainment." This means, of course, that the problem picture has been good box office. Self-criticism and exposé form a strong thread that extends through American history beginning before Tom Paine and continuing past the "yellow journalism" of the twenties to Sunday night's *60 Minutes* on CBS. Films in this tradition—even if frequently exploiting as well as examining problems—have remained significant in reflecting and changing an awareness of our culture.

The Crowd (U.S., 1928, King Vidor). Museum of Modern Art/Film Stills Archive.

    The love stories, vehicles for glamorous stars, were called ''women's pictures'' by the trade. Though they also go back to the beginning (*The Kiss,* 1896), they reached a romantic peak in the twenties. Since by then women constituted a majority of the audience, female as well as male stars were tailored to their expectations. Rudolph Valentino, Ronald Colman, and John Gilbert presented idealized characters in situations notably distant from the lives of those watching. Gloria Swanson, Pola Negri, and Greta Garbo offered models of allure that might help the female audience attract those male

Flesh and the Devil (U.S., 1927, Clarence Brown). Museum of Modern Art/Film Stills Archive.

ideals—or more modest realities closer to home. Romance has persisted on the screen, of course, but the changes of time have made it almost unrecognizable. Nowadays there isn't anything quite like the lives lived for love by Garbo and Gilbert in *Flesh and the Devil* (1926), *Love* (1927), or *A Woman of Affairs* (1928). We can't help but agree with Gloria Swanson in *Sunset Boulevard* (1950), when she stands in the beam of the projector shining her own youthful image onto the screen and growls, "They don't make faces like that any more."

War dramas were also common before the twenties, but had only the old-fashioned wars for subjects and treated those from a historical perspective. Moviegoers of the twenties had recently been through a world war, and the experience was both personal and significant to most of them. Though films about the war had been made during it, the "war is hell" prototypes were first offered in King Vidor's *The Big Parade* (1925) and Raoul Walsh's *What Price Glory?* (1926). A subspecies of the war dramas of the twenties was the air-war cycle, including *The Lone Eagle* (1927), *The Legion of the Condemned* (1928), *Lilac Time* (1928), and *Wings* (1929). The latter group suggest the impossibility of making an *anti*-war film—at least along standard lines. The ultimate drama of war cannot be denied: life and death, bravery and fear, selflessness and leader-

The Big Parade (U.S., 1925, King Vidor). Museum of Modern Art/Film Stills Archive.

ship, comradeship and love; they are present even within the impersonal slaughter of modern warfare. War may be hell; but on film, war has always been highly dramatic.

Action and adventure—a category, if not exactly a genre—takes various forms, most of which appeared in the twenties. Often the action-adventure films deal with a chase and pursuit, or with survival in some distant and colorful locale. There are adventures on the sea, under water, in the jungle (*Tarzan of the Apes* began the Tarzan series in 1918), in the mountains, the desert, and in polar regions. Documentaries and semi-documentaries of the period appealed more factually to the same sort of interest— *Nanook of the North* (1922), *Grass* (1925), *Moana* (1926), *Chang* (1927). Another kind of action-adventure of the twenties (and thirties) was the animal picture, with animal stars; Rin-Tin-Tin and Rex, ''King of the Wild Horses,'' were successful enough to have their imitators.

When you think of action-adventure films of the twenties, you think first of the kind in which Douglas Fairbanks excelled. A star of considerable magnitude, his obvious attractions were a marvelous body, dazzling smile, acrobatic grace, and an ingeniously intricate way of moving about the world by scaling walls, sliding down draperies, leaping from roof to balcony and balcony to roof, and swinging on chandeliers. Those qualities and abilities, together with his enormous good cheer and easy superiority to the normal nagging concerns of the modern world, guaranteed the popular success of his films— *The Mark of Zorro* (1920), *The Three Musketeers* (1921), *Robin Hood* (1922), *The Thief of Bagdad* (1924), *The Black Pirate* (1926), and others. As the titles of the Fairbanks films suggest, their action and adventure were usually set in a past time as well as a distant place; the improbable could be given freest reign in exotic settings.

Another kind of historical film featured more spectacle than derring-do. *The Execution of Mary Queen of Scots* (1895) was the first, and it was most certainly Griffith who

Robin Hood (U.S., 1922, Alan Dwan). Museum of Modern Art/Film Stills Archive.

reached a level of spectacle—in *Intolerance* (1916)—that in many respects has never been equalled. De Mille, admitting his indebtedness to Griffith, took over the historical/ Biblical extravaganza with *The Ten Commandments* (1923) and *The King of Kings* (1927), and pursued his own special form of it until his last film, the second *Ten Commandments* (1956). Other especially noteworthy historical/religious spectacles of the 1920s were Griffith's *Orphans of the Storm* (1921), about the French Revolution, and Fred Niblo's *Ben-Hur* (1926). This genre is currently less prevalent than it sometimes is, but the lull is surely temporary; the form has been too popular in American film, and in theater before it, to be doing more than pausing for breath. *Variety's* annual listing of all-time box-office champions has a preponderance of the spectacular in its upper echelons. Probably at this very moment someone is trying to put together another *Gone with the Wind.*

Until fairly recently, critics tended to discount or ignore the importance of genres to the history of the American film. A case could be made, however, that the conventions of genre—fixed yet capable of infinite variation—have supported and given strength to the work of many of the finest script writers and directors (as Shakespeare had built upon the conventional revenge tragedy introduced by Thomas Kyd). Though genres came about because of the requirements of mass production and popular appeal, they have nonetheless been consistently developed by major American film makers. Howard Hawks's films, though they vary widely, all fit within conventional genres: war drama (including flying pictures), gangster, comedy, private eye, the western, sea and jungle action-adventure, historical spectacle (*Land of the Pharaohs,* 1955), even the musical (*Gentlemen Prefer Blondes,* 1953), and science-fiction (*The Thing,* 1951). We tend to identify John Ford with westerns, D. W. Griffith with historical spectacles, Alfred

Ben-Hur (U.S., 1926, Fred Niblo). Museum of Modern Art/Film Stills Archive.

Hitchcock with mystery and suspense. The latter genre, because of plot intricacies requiring dialogue, did not develop fully until sound arrived. Though his silent *The Lodger* (1927) and early sound *Blackmail* (1929) are memorable, Hitchcock didn't hit full (British) stride until the mid-thirties, when the inadequacies of early sound technology and technique had been largely overcome.

The convulsions brought on by sound would shake up and modify much about Hollywood of the twenties. Even so, the more things changed the more they remained the same. New corporate combines emerged, rather than altered business practices. Older silent film makers were sometimes replaced, but more often they were joined by new film makers. The popular forms and content carried on into sound, with some losses (silent comedies) and some gains (musicals). The patterns established in the twenties, in fact, seem to have become more fixed and rigid during the thirties and forties. But the breathtaking rapidity with which the almost entirely silent film of 1927 became the almost entirely sound film of 1929, a profound technological transmutation, was a particularly harrowing but exciting experience for all involved, including audiences and critics.

FILMS OF THE PERIOD

1919
Blind Husbands
   (Erich von Stroheim)
Male and Female (Cecil B. De Mille)

1920
The Last of the Mohicans
   (Maurice Tourneur
   and Clarence Brown)
The Mark of Zorro (Fred Niblo)
Way Down East (David Wark Griffith)

1921
The Four Horsemen of the Apocalypse
   (Rex Ingram)
The Kid (Charles Chaplin)
Orphans of the Storm (Griffith)
Tol'able David (Henry King)

1922
Foolish Wives (von Stroheim)
Nanook of the North (Robert Flaherty)
Robin Hood (Allan Dwan)

1923
The Covered Wagon (James Cruze)
Safety Last (Harold Lloyd)
The Ten Commandments (De Mille)
A Woman of Paris (Chaplin)

1924
The Iron Horse (John Ford)
The Marriage Circle (Ernst Lubitsch)

The Navigator (Buster Keaton)
Sherlock Junior (Keaton)
The Thief of Bagdad (Raoul Walsh)

1925
The Big Parade (King Vidor)
The Freshman (Lloyd)
The Gold Rush (Chaplin)
Greed (von Stroheim)
Lady Windermere's Fan (Lubitsch)
The Phantom of the Opera (Rupert Julian)

1926
Ben-Hur (Niblo)
Moana (Flaherty)
The Scarlet Letter
   (Victor Sjöström/Seastrom)
What Price Glory? (Walsh)

1927
The General (Keaton)
Hotel Imperial (Mauritz Stiller)
The King of Kings (De Mille)
Seventh Heaven (Frank Borzage)
Sunrise (F. W. Murnau)
Underworld (Josef von Sternberg)

1928
The Crowd (Vidor)
The Docks of New York (von Sternberg)
The Last Command (von Sternberg)
The Wind (Sjöström/Seastrom)

BOOKS ON THE PERIOD

Balio, Tino, ed., *The American Film Industry*. Madison: University of Wisconsin Press, 1976. 499 pp.

Baxter, John, *Sixty Years of Hollywood*. New York: A. S. Barnes & Co., Inc., 1973. 284 pp.

Blum, Daniel, *A Pictorial History of the Silent Screen*. New York: The Putnam Publishing Group, 1982.

Brownlow, Kevin, *The Parade's Gone By*. New York: Alfred A. Knopf, Inc., 1968. 590 pp.

Everson, William K., *The American Movie*. New York: Atheneum Publishers, 1963. 149 pp.

Everson, William K., *American Silent Film*. New York: Oxford University Press, 1978. 387 pp.

Griffith, Richard, Arthur Mayer, and Eileen Bowser, *The Movies*. New York: Simon & Schuster, Inc., 1981.

Hampton, Benjamin B., *A History of the American Film Industry from its Beginnings to 1931*. New York: Dover Publications, Inc., 1970. 456 pp. (originally published in 1931 as *A History of the Movies*)

Higham, Charles, *The Art of the American Film, 1900–1971*. Garden City, N.Y.: Doubleday & Co., Inc., 1973. 322 pp.

Jacobs, Lewis, *The Rise of the American Film: A Critical History*. New York: Teachers College Press, Columbia University, 1968. 631 pp. (originally published in 1939)

Jobes, Gertrude, *Motion Picture Empire*. Hamden, Conn.: Archon Books, 1966. 398 pp.

Kindem, Gorham, ed., *The American Movie Industry: The Business of Motion Pictures*. Carbondale and Edwardsville: Southern Illinois University Press, 1982. 448 pp.

Ramsaye, Terry, *A Million and One Nights: A History of the Motion Picture*. New York: Simon & Schuster, Inc., 1964. 868 pp. (originally published in 1926)

Robinson, David, *Hollywood in the Twenties*. Cranbury, N.J.: A. S. Barnes & Co., Inc., 1968. 176 pp.

Sklar, Robert, *Movie-made America: A Social History of American Movies*. New York: Random House, Inc., 1975. 340 pp.

Spears, Jack, *Hollywood: The Golden Era*. Cranbury, N.J.: A. S. Barnes & Co., Inc., 1971. 440 pp.

Stanley, Robert H., *The Celluloid Empire: A History of the American Movie Industry*. New York: Hastings House Publishers, 1978. 328 pp.

Taylor, Deems, Marcelene Peterson, and Bryant Hale, *A Pictorial History of the Movies*. New York: Simon and Schuster, Inc., 1949. 375 pp.

Wagenknecht, Edward, *The Movies in the Age of Innocence*. Norman: University of Oklahoma Press, 1962. 280 pp.

9

Sound Comes to America, 1927–1935

In the United States, France, Great Britain, Italy, and elsewhere between 1895 and 1914, film makers had learned to tell a story with images in movement, and their films had become sufficiently long to tell a significant one. The consolidation and advance of techniques that established film as an art form, and the founding of an industry that enabled it to become popular entertainment, were achieved in the U.S. between 1914 and 1918. Refinements of visual expression in Swedish films between 1917 and 1924 and, especially, in German films from 1919 to 1925 made possible a new intensity and unity of mood, emotion, and characterization. From 1925 to 1929 the Russians further explored the dynamic shot-to-shot relationship Griffith had begun, and developed a systematic theory of editing which allowed for an unprecedented eloquence and complexity of idea, feeling, and kinetic rhythm. The French Impressionists (1919–1924) and avant-garde (1925–1929) made films for art's sake and brought the motion picture into the stream of modernism in the arts. Each of these national contributions marked an important addition to some aspect of the expressive possibilities of silent film. The end of this evolutionary stage was signaled on October 6, 1927, in New York City, when Warner Brothers presented *The Jazz Singer*, the first feature film with synchronized speech as well as music and other sound.

As with most technological innovations in film, sound was experimented with from the beginning. In fact, Edison seems initially to have conceived of the motion picture as illustration to go with his highly successful cylindrical phonograph—so that those purchasing the sound machines would have something to look at while they listened. W. K. L. Dickson, Edison's talented assistant (and the man most responsible for the development of motion picture equipment at the West Orange, N.J., laboratory), had joined sound to image prior to the first Lumière showings. A film made by Dickson (available from the Museum of Modern Art) shows a pair of Edison technicians dancing in eerie slow motion to a violinist, supposedly Dickson himself, playing into a huge phonograph horn. The further problem of amplifying sound adequately to fill a theater had been solved by 1914: primarily by Lee de Forest's invention of the silenium, or vacuum, tube which permitted a "loud speaker" (audio amplifier).

TECHNOLOGICAL AND ECONOMIC PROBLEMS

Like the later additions of color, wide screen, and 3-D, it took strong economic motivation to bring on sound. In 1924 and 1925 the comparatively small production firm of Warner Brothers, which owned no theater chains, was competing against the large companies that controlled distribution and exhibition. According to the Warners' account, accepted by many film historians, they decided in desperation to try the novelty of sound to see if it would help them out of their financial difficulties. Another, more credible and thoroughly documented explanation has been advanced by Douglas Gomery in his Ph. D. dissertation, "The Coming of Sound to the American Cinema: A History of the Transformation of an Industry" (University of Wisconsin, 1975). According to this version, Wall Street interests looking for a source of investment in the motion picture industry chose Warner Brothers. Though a small firm, it was tightly managed and well run financially. The infusion of new capital permitted competitive expansion along a number of lines, one of them being experimentation with sound.

Whatever the reason, Warner Brothers added a sound track to a silent feature entitled *Don Juan,* starring John Barrymore, and released it in August 1926. Their Vitaphone system, as they called it, having acquired the Vitagraph company in 1925, used disc recordings mechanically synchronized with the projector. In the case of *Don Juan* the track consisted of a symphonic score plus some sound effects—especially the clanging of swords in the dueling scenes. To the feature they attached a few shorts of distinguished musicians in performance, including violinist Mischa Elman and Metropolitan Opera stars Giovanni Martinelli and Marion Talley.

Leading off this program, incidentally, was a short in which Will Hays appeared. Former Postmaster General and national chairman of the Republican Party, Hays had become president of the Motion Picture Producers and Distributors of America. This trade organization of the major studios (today called the Motion Picture Association of America) had come into being mainly as an attempt by the industry to protect itself—through public relations—from threats of censorship being provoked by the new frankness of the postwar films. Mr. Hays welcomed the public to the epochal event presented by the brothers Warner and predicted a glorious future for the motion picture accompanied by recorded sound.

Though the opening night audience was enthusiastic enough, the success of Vitaphone was limited because of the few theaters equipped for it. It wasn't altogether clear whether *Don Juan* with Vitaphone was making any more money than it would have without recorded sound. Two other programs of shorts and features with synchronized musical scores released in the following year met with only moderate success. The

Warners had gambled so much on the experiment, however, that they couldn't stop or back out.

With the exception of William Fox, who had begun experimenting with his own sound system, the rest of the producers were annoyed with the Warners for rocking the industrial boat. Box office was down slightly and competition from the new sound entertainment of radio seemed one possible cause, but it was by no means certain that the addition of recorded sound to movies would bring larger audiences into the theaters.

The other studios held back because of general uncertainty and for several specific reasons. First, the expense of changing equipment and facilities for production and, especially, for projection (in the eighty thousand theaters throughout the world) loomed as ominous as the national debt. Second, the studios didn't relish paying royalties to Warner Brothers or Fox for use of their patented sound systems, and losing face to a competitor. Third, it was possible that sound might change production technique radically, and no one was yet trained to make sound features. Fourth, there was the backlog of silent films and others in production that might have to be written off as complete losses if they didn't conform to the new technology. Fifth, if the movies ever began to talk (a prospect only vaguely foreseen), the long-term contracts with silent stars, foreign stars, and directors might prove frozen assets if those individuals couldn't adapt themselves to the altered medium or the English language. Finally, if the marvelous esperanto of the silent film were sacrificed, audiences abroad would be curtailed: whereas titles could easily and inexpensively be translated and re-shot, what could the Hungarians, for example, make out of conversations in English? The industry continued to watch and wait.

For their fourth Vitaphone feature the Warners chose a popular musical play, *The Jazz Singer,* which had starred George Jessel on the Broadway stage. When they approached Jessel to repeat his performance for the film, negotiations broke down over the amount of money he asked. As it turned out, Al Jolson was hired for twice as much and insisted that his salary be in cash. Though the film's sound was thought of principally in terms of Jolson's six numbers (including his theme song, "Mammy"), two of his four sound scenes contain a little dialogue that seems scarcely to have been planned. In one scene, after finishing a song in a nightclub, Jolson utters the words that had become his trademark on Broadway: "Wait a minute, wait a minute, I tell ya. You ain't heard nothing." In this context the expression became unexpectedly prophetic. In the second scene, a bit of dialogue leading up to and intervening between two renditions of "Blue Skies" is certainly unscripted. It consists of Jolson joshing his little old screen mother, who is obviously embarrassed and can't think of a thing to say. It's almost as if the conversation had been recorded accidentally, or as a kind of test, and only afterwards did the Warners decide to include it. Whatever the intent, the response of the movie-going public was emphatic.

Though someone once took the trouble to determine that there are something like 309 words of dialogue in *The Jazz Singer,* it was clearly those spoken words more than the songs that had audiences queuing up four-deep around the block of the Warner Theatre. The comparative indifference to the sound in *Don Juan* had apparently occurred because it consisted solely of recorded music in place of the usual live orchestra, organ, or piano to which audiences were accustomed. With the ensuing success of *The Jazz Singer,* the "talkie" was born, and the suggestion of a new dramatic dimension in the spoken word was made. Except for songs and fragments of dialogue, however, *The Jazz Singer* looks and sounds like the standard silent film of the time, with a recorded or-

The Jazz Singer (U.S., 1927, Alan Crosland). National Film Archive/ Stills Library.

chestral score (which makes heavy use of Tschaikowsky's overture to *Romeo and Juliet*) and with printed titles carrying the bulk of the verbal communication.

On the basis of *The Jazz Singer's* success, the Warners extended what looks as if it had been intended as a two-reel short into a seven-reel feature. Entitled *The Lights of New York* and released in July 1928, it became the first "100 percent talkie." It begins with a prologue, which gets the young hero from "Main Street" to "Broadway." There he and his sidekick get mixed up with a couple of con men, and with a gang of bootleggers who use their barbershop as a front. The film contains what is surely the longest exposition in history; in fact, it is all exposition. The characters talk about what has happened, will happen, should happen, and might happen; very little except conversation does happen on the screen.

One of the subsidiary pleasures that *The Lights of New York* now affords is in detecting where the stationary microphone is hidden—in a telephone, for instance, as Hawk orders his henchmen to "Take him for a ride." There is the marvelous moment in which the barber hero finishes a phone call and has to stride clear across the room—to another microphone (probably in the lamp overhead)—before he can tell his partner that the call was from Kitty. An intriguing nightclub scene, including a bizarre master of ceremonies and a chorus line of dancing pirates, was obviously shot from a glassed-in booth to keep the noise of the camera from reaching the microphone. Because the camera was immobilized, the illusion of moving closer could be obtained only by changing lenses; a long shot (wide-angle lens), a medium shot (standard lens), and a closeup (telephoto lens) are all along an axis from a slightly right angle. Then, evidently, the action was stopped and the booth moved over to the center for the same progression of shots. Since there was no air conditioning, the camera operator probably had to be hauled out and revived after each take.

We can feel a kind of morbid fascination in watching the limitations that sound imposed at first on the former brilliance of the best silent films. Everything is static, all is talk. The fluid camera work of the Germans is gone, along with Soviet montage. The flexible fluency of the mature silent film is reduced to a jabbering infancy. (The M-G-M musical *Singin' in the Rain,* 1952, provides a marvelously enjoyable account of the pains of this transition; it is funny because so true.) Though we can relish *The Lights of New York*'s authentic "roaring twenties" flavor, it is impossible not to notice how much more dated it seems than many of its silent contemporaries (such as *The Crowd, The Wind,* or *The Last Command*). Speech is more firmly rooted in the particularities of time and place than is image.

At first, some observers thought that sound was merely a fad, one that would pass away once audiences got over their fascination with lips moving and voices seeming to come from them. Others felt that the talkies might coexist with the silents, the one appealing to the rubes who liked the yackety novelty, while the other remained for the more sensitive and intelligent. Whatever view was taken, the lines at the box office clearly indicated that the rest of the industry could no longer afford to ignore the Warners' unsettling contribution.

By the close of the twenties there was no doubt that the synchronous sound film would be the universal form of the future. At the end of 1928 Hollywood had only 16 recording machines in use; by the end of 1929 there were 116, and almost half the more than twenty thousand theaters in the country were equipped for sound reproduction. The consensus was that a sound system using optical patterns along the edge of the film

Lights of New York (U.S., 1928, Bryan Foy). Museum of Modern Art/Film Stills Archive.

(Fox Movietone), rather than discs (Warner Vitaphone), would provide more reliable synchronization. In 1931, in order to achieve standardization, the patents on the various sound systems held by most of the major studios and others were pooled and divided between Western Electric and RCA. From then on, the sound systems of those two firms became the only ones in use.

As the industry borrowed money to retool, the financial center of gravity, which had gradually moved eastward with the expansion of exhibition and the mergers, now rested firmly in the big banks of New York City and Boston. Among the major studios, there were shifts in power (Warner up, having absorbed First National; Paramount down) and new alignments (RKO and Twentieth Century-Fox). Incidentally, the *R* in RKO stands for Radio Corporation of America, which had become involved in motion pictures because of sound; the *K* and *O,* for the Keith-Orpheum theater circuit, which stemmed from the days when vaudeville was still competing with film for popular audiences. As for the Fox (William) in Twentieth Century-Fox, he was forced out of his firm by the new large financial interests. He then commissioned a socialist author to expose the evils of capitalism, as he had experienced them, in the book *Upton Sinclair Presents William Fox.*

But during the first years of confusion and adjustment, as Hollywood learned to work in the augmented medium, the money kept rolling in. For awhile on the stock exchange, the movies were regarded as a Depression-proof industry. The public, attracted by sound, continued to enjoy Friday nights at the movies throughout hard times. Food for the spirit and escape from the daily realities of a painfully constricted economy were apparently as important as meat and vegetables to a large proportion of the country's millions.

AESTHETIC DIFFERENCES

Sound was a somewhat mixed blessing for the art as well as for the industry. In a book entitled *Heraclitus; or The Future of Films* (1928) the young English author, Ernest Betts, went to the trouble and expense of adding, after publication, a special footnote:

> Since the above was written, speaking films have been launched as a commercial proposition, as the general pattern of the film of the future. As a matter of fact, their acceptance marks the most spectacular act of self-destruction that has yet come out of Hollywood, and violates the film's proper function at its source. The soul of the film—its eloquent and vital silence—is destroyed. The film now returns to the circus whence it came, among the freaks and the fat ladies.[1]

Betts was not alone among the critics in mourning the death of a great visual art. Exacerbated by the crudities of the early technology, certain basic aesthetic problems were raised when the spoken word was joined to the moving image. Rudolf Arnheim, writing a foreword in 1957 to a new edition of his *Film as Art,* first published in 1932, saw no reason to change his mind about dialogue as corruption rather than addition. Some of the finest creators, too, resented and resisted the imposition and didn't

[1] Ernest Betts, *Heraclitus; or The Future of Films* (New York: E. P. Dutton & Co., 1928), unpaginated insert.

know what to do with sound once they had it. Chaplin is the extreme case: He did not make a sound film (in the sense of using dialogue) until *The Great Dictator* (1940).

While the addition of sound brought film closer to a full rendition of physical reality, it also returned it into the sort of recorded theater it had been attempting to escape from its earliest days. All the efforts of the great film makers up to this point had been directed toward advancing the medium beyond mere photographic record, to make of it an expressive and distinctive art form. "Canned theater," as the early sound films were called by some, represented a mixed, reproductive art at best. Talkies slowed the editing pace and tended to restrict the use of closeup of anything but the faces of actors. In filmed conversation the words dictate what will be seen, and the choice of images becomes limited to the person speaking, the person(s) listening, or both together. This spatial limitation is accompanied by a temporal one: Words require natural time in which to be spoken, and they communicate much less in that amount of time than could images. To those who regarded editing and the closeup as the bases of film technique, sound seemed to bring losses rather than gains. With sound, emphasis shifted from the images and action—with which film was uniquely qualified to deal—to plot and performance, elements shared with theater.

As for the new realism added by sound, this too presented a kind of aesthetic danger. As art draws closer to life, it loses some of its value as art. The artist's function is to select from reality and arrange in significant form: to reduce and clarify the "blooming, buzzing confusion" that surrounds us. Art demands limitations and thrives upon them; to a degree, the more limited, the more pure and expressive. Music, that art to which all other arts are said to aspire, can say much more about the human spirit with its purely abstract tones than can the detailed accuracy of wax figures, for all their simulated lifelikeness.

Another loss was the universality of silent film art. Chaplin was well known not only as "Charlie," but also as "Charlot," "Carlino," "Carlos," or "Carlitos," and could be enjoyed equally by all. With sound, there is no really satisfactory means of presenting film dialogue to audiences who don't understand the language. Initially, multiple-language versions were produced with separate and/or multilingual casts. For example, *The Blue Angel* (1930), directed by Josef von Sternberg, with Emil Jannings and Marlene Dietrich, had an English as well as a German version; *Don Quixote* (1933), directed by G. W. Pabst and starring the renowned Russian basso Fyodor Chaliapin, was produced in French and English. But this practice proved cumbersome and expensive. Usually, only one version, the original, had a dynamic life of its own, the others being merely dutiful copies. Subtitles, superimposed on the images themselves rather than being placed between them on separate intertitle cards as in silent film, restrict and inevitably distort the meaning of the dialogue and distract attention from the visual. The "dubbing" of native voices for foreign ones became the accepted European practice; in Italy, for example, there developed a regular subindustry employing actors to supply Italian voices for James Cagney, Gary Cooper, Bette Davis, and the rest. But the personalities expressed through the original quality of voice and style of delivery could be only faintly approximated, as technically skillful as some of the dubbing became.

Finally, the much greater expense and technological complexity of the sound film limited artistic experimentation and increased the pressure to play it safe. The introduction of sound, more than anything else, ended the individual and small-group film making of the French avant-garde of the twenties. In Hollywood the standard-size crew increased to about sixty persons, and production by committee, with the producer as chair, prevailed.

But after all, we're glad to have sound; only a few FOOFs, as they're called (Friends of Old Films), cherish silence as golden anymore. In actuality, there never were silent films; there was always music and frequently sound effects—of horses' hooves and thunder claps, for instance. By the late twenties the titles, too, had pretty much abandoned the earlier narrative and expository functions to substitute for dialogue; it was as if the film makers, perhaps unconsciously, had already started to feel a need for "lip-sync" sound recording. In these silent films that weren't really silent, the means of providing sound was clumsy and approximate, an aspect over which film makers could have little control. Unless a complete score was provided, which was rarely done, the film maker was at the mercy of the theater musicians. Inappropriate or clichéd music can go a long way towards destroying the most effective scenes.

With the arrival of sound, the music, noises, and words were added by the people who made the film, and became an integral part of their work. Sound also reduced the awkwardness of silent narrative and permitted films to flow more freely without interruption of titles or the tortuous circumlocutions of visual exposition. In the final shoot-out in von Sternberg's silent *Underworld* (1927) we are constantly being shown bits of wood chipping off and bottles breaking as reminders that a gunfight is being waged. Presenting a simple point—like a couple's intention to meet next day under the big oak—often challenged the ingenuity of silent film makers in ways that now seem wasteful of creative effort. In one of F. W. Murnau's last great silent films, *Sunrise* (released with a synchronized musical score in 1927), scriptwriter Carl Mayer and he characteristically minimized titles. But following the film's climax it is necessary for an old fisherman to explain how he had rescued the young wife washed overboard during a storm; this is accomplished through a redundant flashback that slows and diverts the main narrative thrust.

There is no doubt that sound has permitted the tackling of more complex ideas and emotions. This is particularly evident in a greater depth of characterization and increased precision in communicating it. With sound, actors can reveal more nuance and ambivalence, even contradiction, through saying what they think and feel as well as showing it. Though dialogue didn't necessarily add emotional intensity (the moments of highest drama in the sound film tend very often to be without dialogue), it certainly contributed a new intellectual weight.

Sound—noises and music as well as speech—offered an artistic resource in itself, and in support or counterpoint to the images. Rather than the single line of shot to shot, like unison Gregorian chants, there was a polyphonic blending of four separate lines—image, word, music, noise. This meant that films had to be created and understood in a totally different way: The sound film is not simply a silent film with sound added. Vertical montage, as Eisenstein called the relationships between sight and sound, offered a new source of expressiveness.

EVOLUTION OF TECHNIQUE

The principal understanding that film makers had to arrive at was that movement and rhythm were as much the basis of the sound film as they had been of the silent. In silent film, composition depended upon the movement of people or objects within the limits of the shot, and on the rhythmical relationship of one shot to another. The rhythm of the whole, however complicated in structure and detail, was simple in that it appealed to one sense only; it was purely visual. In the sound film, with its visual and aural streams, the movement of images had to be related to the movement of sound—whether music, dialogue, or incidental noises. Until these movements were related (not merely synchronized) in more than a casual, haphazard way, there were no true sound films.

These new problems attracted new people to aid in their solution, and some of the veterans did not make the transfer into sound. The turnover was especially marked among performers. Foreign film actors who had not mastered English sailed back to Europe—Emil Jannings, Pola Negri, and Vilma Banky among them. Greta Garbo, on the other hand, made a brilliant debut in the altered medium in *Anna Christie* (1930) under the triumphant slogan "GARBO TALKS!" The addition of her low, husky voice and accented speech complemented her extraordinarily attractive screen presence in *Grand Hotel* (1932), *Queen Christina* (1933), *Camille* (1937), *Ninotchka* (1939), and her other successes of the thirties. Some of the silent American stars couldn't or didn't choose to work in sound: Colleen Moore, Norma Talmadge, Corinne Griffith, and Mary Pickford all dropped out of pictures after a few early talkies. John Gilbert, a talented and popular star whose high voice didn't record well in the crude technology, is often cited as an especially sad case: Heavy drinking and an early death followed the failure of his few sound films. (There is evidence suggesting that Louis B. Mayer, head of M-G-M, used sound as an excuse to end Gilbert's career.)

The silent comedians had a particularly difficult time. Their techniques bound them closely to pantomime. Not only had they no need for words (they used few titles), but dialogue had no place in their kind of comedy. Chaplin used only music, sound effects, and amusingly unintelligible gibberish in *City Lights* (1931) and *Modern Times* (1936). Keaton, Lloyd, and Langdon never quite succeeded in finding a style that would suit the new form. Among the top silent clowns, only Laurel and Hardy were able successfully to add their wryly inane dialogue to the earlier sight gags. Some who had been only modestly successful in the silents achieved a new eminence when verbal humor could be added. Most of these had had stage as well as screen experience. W. C. Fields was preeminent, of course, but there were also Will Rogers, Marie Dressler, and Wallace Beery. Their distinctive voices and delivery of lines were crucial to their kinds of comedy. Coming to films directly from the theater were the Marx Brothers, whose surrealist patter combined with plenty of zany action, and Mae West, of the superb sexual innuendo. Joe E. Brown, with siren wail, and Jimmy Durante, with his Brooklynese and raucous songs, also entered film from the stage.

In general, Hollywood turned to Broadway for people who had had experience with spoken words. Every day the Twentieth-Century Limited pulled out of New York City, heading west with a load of actors, writers, and voice coaches. The silent directors were joined by a new crop who would carve their careers out of the possibilities opened up by sound: George Cukor, Leo McCarey, Rouben Mamoulian, Busby Berkeley, John Cromwell, Tay Garnett, all began to direct films in the first years of sound.

Three technical problems were solved during the early thirties, allowing the sound film to return to the movement of the silent film, reducing the dependence on dialogue, and regaining the visual richness. The first of these problems was to find a means of removing the camera from its sound-proof booth. For that purpose a "blimp" was constructed: a metal cover filled with acoustic insulation that encased the camera. As heavy and large as the blimped cameras were, they still could be moved about quite freely on dolly and crane.

The second problem was to free the actors so that they could move about without regard to the stationary microphones. Lionel Barrymore, who directed as well as acted in those days, claimed credit for solving this difficulty. As an actor he no doubt felt the performer's frustration in being rooted to one spot; he insisted, against technicians' protests, that a mike be swung overhead from a fishpole and moved around to follow the actors. The directional boom microphone, able to capture sounds from overhead while remaining out of frame, completely replaced the nondirectional fixed microphones that had been hidden about the set.

The blimped camera and boom microphone permitted more dynamic studio shooting, but they did not help the camera get outside the sound stages into the world of unwanted noises, bad acoustic conditions, and wind creating a roar in the microphone. *In Old Arizona* (1929), codirected by Raoul Walsh, was the first sound feature known to be recorded principally out-of-doors. "Location shooting" was made fully possible when sound technology advanced sufficiently so that sight and sound did not have to be recorded at the same time: Footage could be shot silent; sound could be recorded separately, then added to the images. Noteworthy early experiments included King Vidor's *Hallelujah!* (1929). In a frightening chase scene at night in a swamp, snapping twigs, splashing water, and the heavy breathing of the actors are the principal sounds. The battle scenes of Lewis Milestone's *All Quiet on the Western Front* (1930) were shot with the sort of tracking camera movement and rapid cutting that marked the best silent work. The addition of rattling machine gun fire, the detonation of high explosives, and the screams of dying men made the images even more horrifying.

By 1932 sound effects, and even dialogue, could be added in "post-sync" recording and mixing. By 1935 the fidelity of optical sound recording was quite acceptable. In fact, the frequency range fixed then (100 to 8,000 cycles per second) remained standard until the addition of the 35mm stereophonic optical tracks with the Dolby noise-reduction system in the late 1970s. As late as 1984, only 70mm magnetic striped tracks with the Dolby system used for science-fiction spectacles like *Return of the Jedi* (1983) could compare with the high fidelity available even in amateur tape decks for home use.

During the early sound years numerous American film makers added to conception and technique so that by the mid-thirties sound film had reached a level of artistic maturity at least comparable to its technological adequacy. The script writer, working in collaboration with the director, now made a much larger creative contribution. Dialogue, of course, was conceived, memorized, and rehearsed in advance of filming. Script writing became an absolutely essential, and in some ways dominant, part of the Hollywood sound film of the 1930s. Accordingly, certain writer-director teams emerged, like Jules Furthman with Josef von Sternberg, Robert Riskin with Frank Capra, Dudley Nichols with John Ford.

A look at two passages from a Nichols script based on a Liam O'Flaherty novel, *The Informer,* directed by Ford in 1935, will show how the power of an essentially visual conception could be increased by using sound to reinforce images and editing rhythm. Though there is virtually no speech in the excerpts following, the sorts of coordinated effects of sound in relation to sight that Nichols calls for could scarcely be trusted to improvisation. Some of the symbolic sight-sound linkages do not appear in the completed film, but its conception and style are essentially as called for in the script. As presented below, the scenes are in play-script form, with no reference to camera distance, angle, or movement.

The Informer takes place at the height of the Irish rebellion against the British in 1922, "The Troubles." The protagonist, Gypo Nolan (played by Victor McLaglen), is planning to betray his I.R.A. friend Frankie McPhillips to the British troops (Black-and-Tans) for £20 reward. The scene below is one in which Frankie is slipping into his mother's house. Italics have been added to the directions relating to sound to make them stand out.

> we see a doorway close to the lodging house steps and, looking out across the steps towards a lamppost in the fog, is FRANKIE in silhouette against the lamplight. As his dark figure starts furtively up the steps, *he hears footsteps tramping up the street,* and immediately he backs down the steps and glides around to the shelter of the doorway, so that he is in very close silhouette. . . . *Now the steps are loud* and through the fog in background, a patrol of eight BLACK AND TANS comes swinging along briskly.[2]

Note that sound motivates Frankie's action. In silent film an effect of this sort would most likely have required cutting to the soldiers, or having Frankie cup his ear with his hand, or inserting a title; in any case, weaker and clumsier. As it is, we hear and see just as he does, increasing our sense of identification with him and fear for his safety. Also, there is a kind of aesthetic tension created by the sound coming from an unseen source offscreen while we see a silent Frankie close up. In film, as in life, we more often see what we hear—and the closer it is, the louder it is.

Shortly thereafter Gypo enters Black-and-Tan headquarters to betray Frankie. But instead of letting us watch and listen to the betrayal, which we know is going to occur, Nichols calls for a cut from the sound of the door closing behind Gypo to a shot of those same loud, swinging marchers of the scene above. From that shot, there is then a cut to—

> THE INNER OFFICE:
> *As the sound of the tramping continues* . . . we see GYPO sitting hunched up beside a desk . . . at the desk beside GYPO, sits the officer; and two TANS, both officers, are standing beside him, their heads close together as they ignore GYPO. GYPO faces a big clock and he stares at it numbly *as he listens to the tramping feet outside. Presently the tramping stops and the sound of two lorry engines starting across the street can be heard.* GYPO never moves. *The engines are raced and we hear voices;* then the beams of light from the lorries come in through the windows as they start, and the beams sweep across GYPO's face. . . . *And now there is neither tramping nor any other sound, only a deathly stillness in which the sound of the* [clock's] *ticking grows loud. The three officers are whispering in undertones we cannot hear,* and nod to each other. GYPO stares at the clock and the slow swinging pendulum, which catches a flash of light on each swing and shoots it into his eyes with a hypnotic gleam. . . . *Tick tock, tick tock goes the clock.* . . . GYPO stares at the clock. Sweat comes out on his face and unconsciously he wipes it off with the sleeve of his coat.[3]

Here the sounds of the swinging door, the marching soldiers, the lorry engines, the silence and unheard whispering, and the clock ticking, all complement beautifully the movement of the headlights, the nodding heads, the swinging pendulum. To express Gypo's growing tension and fear, the clock's tick is made increasingly louder than life.

There is a kind of sensory and symbolic richness here that couldn't be achieved in a silent film, even with the help of musical accompaniment. Note as well how powerfully the silence and the absence of speech are used. It was toward this full and signifi-

---

[2] "*The Informer:* A Screenplay by Dudley Nichols," *Theatre Arts,* XXXV (August 1951), p. 61.
[3] "*The Informer,*" *Theatre Arts,* pp. 62–63.

The Informer (U.S., 1935, John Ford). Museum of Modern Art/Film Stills Archive.

cant use of sound in relation to image that film makers had to make their way. Only gradually, and after considerable experimentation, were the essential differences between silent and sound films clearly seen.

Since it was to America that sound first came, the Americans were the first and the most prolific (given their output of four hundred to five hundred feature films per year) in their successes and mistakes. Of course they were neither alone nor necessarily the most inspired in their contributions to the evolving form. The inventive and playful use of sound in Frenchman René Clair's delightful bits of proletarian whimsy laced with music—*Sous les toits de Paris* (1930), *Le Million,* and *À nous la liberté* (both 1931)—deserves special praise. Alfred Hitchcock, at work in England, provided what would become standard textbook examples: *knife* being the only word intelligible in a conversation as heard by a young woman who has murdered someone (*Blackmail,* 1929); a woman's mouth opening to scream, but seeming to emit a screeching whistle as a cut is made to a rushing train (*The Thirty-Nine Steps,* 1935). In Germany the American Josef von Sternberg made what many would regard his masterpiece—*The Blue Angel* (1930)—and Fritz Lang, a German about to become an American, made what could be argued to be his—*M* (1931). G. W. Pabst, another of the great German film makers about to emigrate, did some of his best work during the early thirties—*Westfront 1918* (1930), *The Threepenny Opera* (1931), *Kameradschaft* (1931). By mid-decade the "100 percent all talking," "canned theater" had been largely transcended and the mature sound film achieved. Once this point had been reached, France in the latter half of the thirties made particularly full use of the new opportunities sound film offered.

FILMS OF THE PERIOD

1927
The Jazz Singer (Alan Crosland)

1928
The Lights of New York (Bryan Foy)
Steamboat Willie (Walt Disney)

1929
Applause (Rouben Mamoulian)
Hallelujah! (King Vidor)
The Love Parade (Ernst Lubitsch)

1930
All Quiet on the Western Front
    (Louis Milestone)

Monte Carlo (Lubitsch)

1931
Dr. Jekyll and Mr. Hyde (Mamoulian)
The Smiling Lieutenant (Lubitsch)

1932
Love Me Tonight (Mamoulian)

1934
Our Daily Bread (Vidor)

1935
The Informer (John Ford)

BOOKS ON THE PERIOD

BALIO, TINO, ed.,   *The American Film Industry.* Madison: University of Wisconsin Press, 1976. 499 pp.

BAXTER, JOHN,   *Hollywood in the Thirties.* New York: A. S. Barnes & Co., Inc., 1968. 160 pp.

BAXTER, JOHN,   *Sixty Years of Hollywood.* New York: A. S. Barnes & Co., Inc., 1973. 284 pp.

BLUM, DANIEL,   *A New Pictorial History of the Talkies,* rev. and enlarged by John Kobal. New York: G. P. Putnam's Sons, 1982.

CAMERON, EVAN WILLIAM, ed.,   *Sound and the Cinema: The Coming of Sound to American Film.* Pleasantville, N.Y.: Redgrave Publishing Co., 1979.

COE, BRIAN,   *The History of Movie Photography.* Westfield, N.J.: Eastview Editions, 1981. 176 pp.

EVERSON, WILLIAM K.,   *The American Movie.* New York: Atheneum Publishers, 1963. 149 pp.

GEDULD, HARRY M.,   *The Birth of the Talkies: From Edison to Jolson.* Bloomington: Indiana University Press, 1975. 352 pp.

GRIFFITH, RICHARD, ARTHUR MAYER, and EILEEN BOWSER,   *The Movies.* New York: Simon & Schuster, Inc., 1981.

GRIFFITH, RICHARD, comp., *The Talkies: Articles and Illustrations from Photoplay Magazine 1928-1940.* New York: Dover Publications, Inc., 1972. 360 pp.

HIGHAM, CHARLES,   *The Art of the American Film, 1900-1971.* Garden City, N.Y.: Doubleday & Co., Inc., 1973. 322 pp.

JACOBS, LEWIS,   *The Rise of the American Film: A Critical History.* New York: Teachers College Press, Columbia University, 1968. 631 pp. (originally published in 1939)

JOBES, GERTRUDE,   *Motion Picture Empire.* Hamden, Conn.: Archon Books, 1966. 398 pp.

KINDEM, GORHAM, ed.,   *The American Movie Industry: The Business of Motion Pictures.* Carbondale and Edwardsville: Southern Illinois University Press, 1982. 448 pp.

SKLAR, ROBERT,   *Movie-made America: A Social History of American Movies.* New York: Random House, Inc., 1975. 340 pp.

STANLEY, ROBERT H.,   *The Celluloid Empire: A History of the Hollywood Movie Industry.* New York: Hastings House Publishers, 1978. 328 pp.

TAYLOR, DEEMS, MARCELENE PETERSON, and BRYANT HALE,   *A Pictorial History of the Movies.* New York: Simon & Schuster, Inc., 1949. 375 pp.

THRASHER, FREDERICK, *Okay for Sound: How the Screen Found Its Voice.* New York: Duell, Sloan, & Pearce, 1946. 303 pp.

TIBBETTS, JOHN C., ed., *Introduction to the Photoplay—1929: A Contemporary Account of the Transition to Sound in Film.* Shawnee Mission, Kans.: National Film Society, 1977. 382 pp.

WALKER, ALEXANDER, *The Shattered Silents: How the Talkies Came to Stay.* London: Elm Tree Books, 1978.

10

Golden Age of French Cinema, 1935-1939

The economic history of the French film has so persistently tended toward anarchy and chaos that it's easy to imagine its trade press keeping headline type standing to prophesy and then report "TOTAL COLLAPSE OF INDUSTRY." Made up of numerous small firms and individual impresarios, rather than a few huge studios, production companies have been born and laid to rest with a single film. Individual successes and fitful bursts of popularity have been supplemented by various forms of government protection and subsidy in efforts to achieve sustained good health. Since American movies as mass entertainment have dominated in France, as elsewhere, the French have felt no need to produce large numbers of films each year. Instead, their relatively small output has included a high proportion of carefully crafted works that could compete with those of the Americans by virtue of artistic quality and distinctive national personality. During certain periods of rapid change the lack of economic ballast, which has otherwise been a liability, has given the French a peculiar advantage.

This was the case at the time sound was introduced. At first the greatly increased expense meant that only the two largest firms, Gaumont and Pathé, were capable of exploiting the new medium. When both collapsed from overextension of their resources, the situation returned to French-normal. In part because they didn't have the heavy investments the American industry did, the French moved more readily into the experimental stage with sound, and hence exerted considerable leadership in the development of the altered art. In France the individual film maker frequently enjoyed a freedom of and control over expression seldom granted in Hollywood's major studios, or, for that matter, in the Ufa of Germany or the state-financed cinema of the U.S.S.R. A French film maker who could find a backer—wealthy lover, moribund aunt, reckless stock broker—could hope to make a film. With sound, French production returned to an international prominence it had relinquished after the first decade of the century.

First there was the delightful series of René Clair successes already mentioned—*Sous les toits de Paris* (1930), *À nous la liberté* (1931), *Le Million* (1931). Enchanting though these films are, Clair, coming from silence into sound, was a little like Méliès who left the stage for the screen. Méliès gave us theater on film; Clair gave us silent film trimmed with delightful audio embellishments. He understood music and noises well and used them charmingly, often fantastically (a flower in the field bursting into song) or satirically (assembly-line work performed to the same music and monotonous sounds in the factory as in the prison). Dialogue had little place in his first sound works.

In those same early sound years Marcel Pagnol began his memorable trilogy of *Marius* (1931), *Fanny* (1932), and *César* (1936). In these a warmly human story about simple people is enacted in definitive performances against a Marseilles setting. For Pagnol dialogue was perhaps too important and the overall style remained "theatrical." Sharing Pagnol's predilection for the everyday, Julien Duvivier, in *Poil de carotte* (1932), and Jean Benoit-Levy, in *La Maternelle* (1933), treated their subjects in a manner closer to documentary than to theater. Both films involve extraordinarily sensitive performances on the part of children. Both were also quite early and quite remarkable in

Le Million (France, 1931, René Clair). Museum of Modern Art/Film Stills Archive.

breaking out of the sound stages to give a full sense of social and cultural particularities—of a country town in *Poil de carotte,* of a Paris suburb in *La Maternelle.*

Only a little later, Jean Vigo, the supreme poet of the French cinema, made his two enduring and influential features before his tragically premature death. *Zéro de conduite* (1933), also concerning children, deals with life in a strangely surreal boys' school—a film to which Lindsay Anderson paid obvious and respectful homage in his own film *If . . .* (1968). *L'Atalante* (1934) is the tender and somewhat haunted, as well as haunting, love story of young newlyweds and a bizarre, elderly Caliban—set in a barge on the Seine. Both films are models for sparse and assured use of sound in support of images. The poetry is primarily visual rather than verbal, and the words, noises, and music coming from the loudspeakers add reverberations to what is already clear and rich on the screen.

Also before mid-decade, Jean Renoir's *Boudu Saved from Drowning* (1932) established the main elements of his later sound features. Already in *Boudu* there is the celebration of human life (of freedom and diversity) and the affectionate attention to the people who comprise it, loveable in spite of, and maybe even because of, their eccentricities and weaknesses. Renoir's *Toni* (1934), on the other hand, is a dark account of rural passion and crime among Italian migrant workers in Southern France. Brilliantly made, it seems to foreshadow Italian neorealism more than Renoir's own future development. Quite specifically it suggests *Ossessione* (1942), that harbinger of neorealism—whose director, Luchino Visconti, began in film in 1936 as Renoir's assistant on *A Day in the Country* and *The Lower Depths.* But *Toni,* as well as *Boudu* and other pre-1935 Renoir sound films, showed an almost unique ease with the new medium. There is no sense of restraint or constriction imposed by the microphone, nor any self-conscious experimentation. Players and camera move freely in relation to each other, and the life portrayed is that of the world outside the sound stages, replete with its sounds.

In 1934, however, the year of *L'Atalante* and *Toni,* it looked to many as if the

Zéro de conduite (France, 1933, Jean Vigo). Museum of Modern Art/Film Stills Archive.

French industry *was* finally at an end, that it had reached that state of total collapse frequently predicted. Major cause of the catastrophe was the worldwide Depression that had by then hit France. Now no investment money was available for production, no films were being made, and film artists and technicians joined the millions of unemployed. The year 1934 was also one of grave political unrest, not unlike 1919 in Germany. Demonstrations and riots preceded the formation of the Popular Front, a short-lived effort by the parties of the left to keep France from succumbing to fascism, as had Italy and Germany, and as Spain soon would. Perhaps this is yet another instance of periods of great national film expression growing out of troubled times. In any case, out of the ashes of 1934—and for reasons that aren't altogether clear in the general quirkiness of French film economics—a phoenix rose, becoming what is still referred to as the Golden Age of French Cinema.

One of the causes of revival seems more evident to the historian of today than it would have been to investors at the time. France was specially blessed with a cultural tradition that, though not fully accessible to the silent film, offered the stuff of which the best sound films are made. Whereas action-melodrama, spectacle, and slapstick comedy were ideal forms for the strictly visual requirements of the silent medium, the addition of dialogue demanded a new thoughtfulness, subtlety, and refinement of dramatic values. From 1935 until the end of the decade, French film makers utilized the resources of the new technology to emphasize intellectual content, to explore philosophical and psychological themes. Intelligent screenplays and superior screen acting were France's chief additions to the maturation of the sound film, contributed by some of its distinguished literary and theatrical talents. Those qualities, all of prime importance in the new medium, were often achieved without loss of visual brilliance—owing in no small measure to the well-known French affinity for the graphic arts. As tangible evidence of their excellence, it can be noted that French films of the late thirties became the first substantial body of foreign-language pictures to interest American audiences. In major American cities a few little ''art theaters'' sprang up to show them, somewhat as *The Great Train Robbery* had opened the nickleodeons in the earliest days. The first five annual New York Film Critics' Awards for the Best Foreign Film, which began in 1936, went to France: *Carnival in Flanders, Mayerling, The Grand Illusion, Harvest,* and *The Baker's Wife,* successively.

LITERARY, THEATRICAL, AND PAINTING TRADITIONS

Direct influence of the silent avant-garde tradition of the twenties on French sound features of the thirties is evident in a few instances. Jean Vigo's *Zéro de conduite* and *L'Atalante* have strongly surrealistic overtones, which become quite explicit in the schoolboys' pillow fight of *Zéro* and in the hallucinatory underwater interlude of *L'Atalante.* Traces of the avant-garde also remain in the largely realistic and ''theatrical'' style of other fiction features. There is, for instance, the epileptic sequence in Julien Duvivier's *Carnet de bal* (1937), with its canted camera and exaggerated noises; also, there are the bizarre chase scenes (with echoes of Mack Sennett) in Jean Renoir's *The Rules of the Game* (1939).

In general, because of the avant-garde inheritance, the best of French cinema of the thirties was saved from the ''staginess'' that often marred the Hollywood studio film. The avant-garde's attention to *cinéma pur,* and the fact that some of France's major directors came out of that informal school, kept the French aware that motion and picture was still the best two-word aesthetic of the motion picture, even when accompanied by sound.

But the French sound feature film, while showing the influence of a painterly tradition and of silent avant-garde film making, drew even more heavily upon literary and theatrical sources available to it. Historically, the French novel has been noteworthy for a kind of realism closely akin to the dominant style of the sound film. The works of Stendhal, Balzac, Flaubert, Zola, and de Maupassant represent a main line in French literature; much of the French cinema of the latter half of the thirties can usefully be seen as a continuation of that tradition. Often the films are set firmly within the provinces (*Carnet de bal,* 1937, *The Baker's Wife,* 1938), or amongst the urban working classes (*La Belle Équipe,* 1936, *Le Jour se lève,* 1939). Violence and crime frequently occur, but in French fashion, more out of passion than hatred or greed. Robust, sexually based humor alternates with worldly *tristesse.* The earthiness and honesty strike the viewer at once. Small important details of a scene are searched out; nearly tangible contact between characters and audience is established. Principal script writers were Jacques Prévert, Charles Spaak, and Henri Jeanson—all of whom had literary as well as filmic reputations—and they can claim a heavy share of the creative credit for the films bearing their names. Most of the finest films of the period had scripts by one or another of them.

Excelling in psychological depth and intimate characterization, these films also depended to considerable extent upon the skill of French acting. Sound film was obviously more attractive than silent to actors trained in the theater. France had its great heritage of private and state-supported theatrical companies which for decades, even centuries, had provided one of the finest cadres of performers in the world. French cinema owes much of its luster and subtlety to the contributions of such actors as Arletty, Jean-Louis Barrault, Harry Baur, Pierre Blanchar, Pierre Brasseur, Jean Gabin, Louis Jouvet, Michèle Morgan, Raimu, Michel Simon, and Françoise Rosay. They approached the new medium with enthusiasm and quickly learned to adapt their talents and techniques to its special requirements.

FIVE MAJOR DIRECTORS

The quality of French films of the late thirties depended heavily upon the contributions of scriptwriters and performers. The directors who did the most important work in France from 1935 through 1939 came to film out of essentially theatrical or literary careers. Jacques Feyder began by acting in the theater; Julien Duvivier started as an actor as well; Marcel Pagnol had achieved distinction as a playwright and theatrical producer; Marcel Carné had been a journalist and film critic. Only Jean Renoir, younger son of the great Impressionist painter Pierre Auguste, had begun his artistic career with an interest in the visual/plastic arts (ceramics).

Jacques Feyder was a veteran commercial director, his career beginning far back in the silents with *Thérèse Raquin* (1928) the most enduring. After the coming of sound Feyder established the style of "poetic realism" that would become predominant in the late thirties. *Pension Mimosas* (1935), especially, became a prototype for later work, and Feyder's principal collaborators—Charles Spaak as scriptwriter and Marcel Carné as assistant director—would carry forward and elaborate on the themes, characterizations, and moody visual surface of that film.

Feyder's next effort, *Carnival in Flanders* (1935), was his greatest success. Essentially a richly amusing comedy about the battle between the sexes, it had certain political implications that gave it another kind of interest as well. Set in the Spanish Netherlands of the seventeenth century, it deals with the threat to a small Flemish town posed by an approaching military expedition led by the duc d'Olivarès. Pusillanimous and fearful of bloodshed, the men of Boom go into hiding, leaving the stalwart women to greet the conquerors. What develops between the women and the gallant dashing Spaniards, with the Flemish men looking jealously on from their hiding place, is the main line of comic invention. Note, however, that Feyder (and the writer of the script and the novel from which it was taken, Charles Spaak) has the Flemish undergoing an invasion and occupation and, as it happens, indulging in fraternization and collaboration with the occupying power. (The ironic French title, *La Kermesse héroique,* means, "the heroic village festival.") At the time, Feyder and Spaak, both Belgians, were attacked by the Flemish nationalists among their fellow citizens for their unflattering portrayal. Subsequently, in World War II, the Flemish became notorious collaborators under German occupation, whereas Feyder and others who worked on the film were persecuted by the Nazis.

In *Carnival in Flanders* the arrival of the Spanish messengers in town—galloping horsemen shot from low angle with fluid camera movement and cutting to the music—is

Carnival in Flanders (France, 1935, Jacques Feyder). Museum of Modern Art/Film Stills Archive.

as splendid a piece of cinema of that sort as can be found. Françoise Rosay gives a striking performance as the mayor's spirited wife, who takes command (''Femmes!'' she shouts authoritatively from a balcony as she begins a speech to the assembled women below) and perhaps yields softly to the elegant duc. Louis Jouvet, in a lesser part as the cadaverous and worldly priest, is an equal delight; this is the first in a long series of such roles for him. The re-creation of the town and of the burghers themselves is a succession of Dutch paintings brought to life, reminiscent of Rembrandt, Vermeer, and particularly of Breughel in shots of the town square from an upper window in the burgomaster's house. The wit and sophistication, however, strike us as distinctly Gallic.

Julien Duvivier, who also began directing in silent films, reached the height of his achievement between 1935 and 1939. He worked even more consistently and successfully within the style of poetic realism. Among his successes of the latter half of the thirties, most memorable (or perhaps merely most likely to be remembered in the U.S.) are *La Belle Équipe* (1936), *Pépé le Moko* (1936), and *Carnet de bal* (1937). The first two, starring Jean Gabin, explore the theme of escape; the third, in a way, deals with escape from self, escape to the past. *La Belle Équipe,* which means something like ''the good gang,'' concerns a group of urban working-class buddies who win a lottery and attempt to establish a restaurant in the country. *Pépé le Moko* is set in Algiers, with Gabin as the fugitive who desperately wants to return to his native Paris but is safe only so long as he

Carnet de bal (France, 1937, Julien Duvivier). Museum of Modern Art/Film Stills Archive.

hides from the authorities in the Casbah. *Carnet de bal* began Duvivier's experimentation with the anthology film, which he continued in *La Fin du jour* (1939). (In Hollywood during the war he made *Tales of Manhattan,* 1942, and *Flesh and Fantasy,* 1943; and back in France, *Under the Paris Sky,* 1950; all employing a similar form.) A ''carnet de bal'' is a dance program, and the film revolves around a lonely widow who tracks down—some twenty years later—her partners from her very first dance. This scheme allowed for the stringing together of seven varied vignettes and a chance to display a galaxy of some of the most popular stars in French cinema: Françoise Rosay plays the demented mother of one of the old beaux who has committed suicide; Harry Baur is a disillusioned musician turned monk; Pierre-Richard Willm is an Alpine guide; Raimu, the hen-pecked mayor of a little town; Louis Jouvet, a master criminal and night club proprietor; Pierre Blanchar, a one-eyed abortionist beset by a harridan mistress and epilepsy; Fernandel, a philosophical beautician.

Marcel Pagnol's *Marius* trilogy of the early sound years has already been mentioned. Before it was completed he produced *Joffroy* (1933), a charming anecdote about an old Provençal peasant who sells his orchard land but claims that the fruitless old peach trees on it still belong to him. Perennial in its charm, it appeared in the United States nearly two decades later as one of the three short films that formed *The Ways of Love.* (Renoir's *A Day in the Country* and Rossellini's *The Miracle* were the other two.) *Regain* (or *Harvest,* 1937) was also set in Provence and concerns an abandoned village. It has a back-to-the-earth theme and stars the popular comedian Fernandel in a role embodying a certain plaintiveness.

Pagnol's culminating achievement of the late thirties was *The Baker's Wife* (1938). Like *Regain* it is adapted from a Jean Giono story. In its title role is the marvelously drole Raimu, one of the world's great comic actors, who has a distinctively French provincial quality. When his attractive young wife runs off with a handsome shepherd, he refuses to bake any more bread, thus involving the whole village in a search for the adulteress and in efforts towards reconciliation. Though Raimu's style is in total contrast to Chaplin's, he has the same ability to edge comic situations with pathos.

Pagnol was resolutely a man of the theater who saw film as ''a printing press for drama.'' If the pleasures he offers aren't essentially cinematic, they are very good theater indeed. His main preoccupations are with rural France—the simple and enduring way of life in the villages. His themes provide fascinating, if broad, understandings of traditional modes of Gallic thought and behavior. With Raimu at their center, both the theatrical aspects of fine performance and the earthy wisdom and humor of provincial France are at their best.

Marcel Carné, a superb craftsman, did his best work in collaboration with the poet/screenwriter Jacques Prévert; in fact, it seems quite possible that Prévert was the auteur in the filmic as well as the literary sense. Together they achieved an epitome of the poetic realism most characteristic of French film in the late thirties. The themes of doomed love, the tight dramatic structures, and the careful, evocative, and symbolic studio reconstructions of the real world mark their special aesthetic and give their work a sad beauty of lasting value. Their two greatest films of the period—*Quai des brumes (Port of Shadows),* 1938, and *Le Jour se lève (Daybreak),* 1939—are also remarkably consistent in the dark and despairing view they present of society. In them Carné and Prévert follow the ubiquitous Jean Gabin through urban lowlife on the fringes of the criminal world. Forced and led into a crime of passion that causes his own destruction, Gabin meets his

The Baker's Wife (France, 1938, Marcel Pagnol). Museum of Modern Art/Film Stills Archive.

end with the special sort of stoicism that he carried with him from film to film. Even individual scenes seem almost interchangeable: The lighting and wallpaper in the lonely hotel rooms look alike; a woman (Michèle Morgan or Arletty), with a kind of tired sensuousness, peels off a silk stocking; the same little bistro reappears, as do the same unadorned and cheerless flights of stairs. It's as if a bleak vision of the society had been frozen on the screen and Carné-Prévert insist that we see it over and over again with them. The social implications of this vision will be dealt with in the following section.

Then there was Jean Renoir, the giant figure among French film makers of that time. In fact, Renoir stands astride nations and periods in his long and fruitful career. His total corpus places him among the foremost film makers in the history of cinema to date; he is protean, experimenting in many forms and styles, yet usually saying essentially the same things. For Renoir life is fundamentally good—the life of the heart and of the senses. Sexual love and natural countrysides are to be celebrated along with food and wine. In Renoir's world there are no bores and few villains. (In *The Rules of the Game* one of his characters, played by Renoir himself, remarks, "Everyone has his own good reasons.") His people may cause themselves and others difficulties, but they are never less than human; always they are interesting, and ultimately verifiable in what we can recognize as one of humanity's possible aspects. Clearly enough, this celebratory view of life was inherited by Jean from his father.

As observed earlier, Renoir's world view had already been formed in his sound films preceding the high years of French cinema. *La Chienne* (1931), *Boudu Saved from Drowning* (1932), *Madame Bovary* (1934), and *Toni* (1934) can stand alongside his later work without apology. This is particularly true of *Boudu*. In it Renoir developed the notion of the social group, with the "outsider" (in one sense or another) serving as catalyst. This protagonist stirs up the group, unhinges it a bit; when he or she leaves, the group re-forms, changed by the experience. But the cohesiveness of the social unit, the need of people for each other, is one of the *idées fixes* in Renoir's universe.

In *The Crime of Monsieur Lange,* made in the landmark year 1935, Renoir restates these thematic materials in even fuller detail and more controlled form. Around the courtyard and within the offices of the publishing firm, a virtual microcosm of society at large is created, with basic human needs and weaknesses motivating the action. Yet, with Renoir, these social themes never seem schematic: They are made manifest through close observation of particular, often mildly eccentric, human beings rather than through reliance on types. His use of the camera (shots of considerable duration, wide-angled, composed in depth, and often inconspicuously panning) seems designed to capture what is happening to his characters without intruding upon them. The performances are so fresh and spontaneous that they surpass an impression of improvisation to convey a sense of authenticity, of real persons at their core. Though the films are not life itself, they are definitive comments upon life as seen by one wise and humane artist.

Even the Gorky drama *The Lower Depths* is turned into a film (1936) that becomes part of Renoir's cosmos, and the viewer can't quite be sure how the alteration has taken place. *The Grand Illusion,* a year later, is unquestionably one of the director's masterworks. The script, which he wrote with Charles Spaak, is based on his own experiences and those recounted to him by others. Here the group is that of French prisoners of war in German prison camps during World War I, of two of the prisoners who have escaped, and of a German woman and her child with whom they stay. To be sure, this is an antiwar film; but as is usual with Renoir, the negative cannot contain him. It is even more profoundly a prohuman film, against all of those restrictions placed on the human potential—nationality, class, military rank, religious prejudice—that keep us all from solidarity.

The Rules of the Game
(France, 1939, Jean Renoir).
Museum of Modern Art/Film
Stills Archive.

After *La Marseillaise* and *The Human Beast* in 1938, there came the final master-piece of the thirties, *The Rules of the Game* (1939). It was completed just before French liberty was extinguished by the nation's collapse in the face of German onslaught. In the film the illnesses of the society are diagnosed with such uncanny accuracy that it was banned during the Occupation. It is one of Renoir's very few dark films, and is exceptional in that his characters seem trapped—in their individual lives and in the social "game" they play. The "rules" are fixed, and under them there is very little freedom of action and even less joy and human dignity. *Rules of the Game,* though funny as well as sad, is essentially a requiem marking the end of an era.

REFLECTIONS OF A TROUBLED NATION

Just as Siegfried Kracauer saw evidence in the German films of the twenties that that nation was ready to accept a Hitler, so it seems possible to infer from the French films of the thirties certain attitudes that would contribute to the rapid and ignominious fall of France—signs of fatigue and demoralization. Examining the French cinema of the late thirties against a backdrop of contemporary French politics and popular culture, Rod Whitaker found that the films of Carné-Prévert expressed most consistently and eloquently certain recurrent motifs. He analyzed them in especially great detail as they appear in *Quai des brumes*. Whitaker identified three major and two minor themes prominent in that film and reiterated, not only in additional Carné-Prévert works, but in a significant number of other films from that time and place.

First and strongest theme in *Quai des brumes* is the need for escape. This is also a major theme in *La Belle Équipe, Le Jour se lève, The Grand Illusion,* and *Pépé le Moko*—to name just a few of the other distinguished films of the period. All starred Jean Gabin, by the way, who most closely among the French stars personified the average guy, the working-class man. Second is the important role of a malignant fate. Whitaker found that the events and actions of *Quai des brumes* occur in a climate of fatalism, that the characters react as though they anticipated and accepted a certain malevolency in their destinies. The same can be said of Renoir's *Toni* and *The Human Beast,* in addition to the other films mentioned above. The third major theme is the ineffectiveness of action: Any attempts to achieve a goal by taking the initiative are either ineffectual or expose the characters to danger. Whitaker points out that this places the hero in a dilemma: on the one hand is the need to escape, on the other, to remain inactive. This situation may reflect what many of the French felt more or less consciously in the months leading up to and immediately following the outbreak of World War II. Perhaps crawling down underground and waiting in the Maginot Line seemed a way to embrace both horns of the dilemma.

The two minor themes may not extend so widely throughout the French films of the late thirties, but are offered here so the reader can conduct a personal investigation in subsequent viewings. *Quai des brumes,* Whitaker observes, "presents fear as a constant condition of human existence." "One of the trademarks of the villain," he adds, "is to surrender to it, while one of the salient features of the hero is a victory over it."[1] Finally, Whitaker notes the pervasiveness of solitude in *Quai des brumes:*

[1] Rodney Whitaker "The Content Analysis of Film: a Survey of the Field, an Exhaustive Study of *Quai des brumes,* and a Functional Description of the Elements of the Film Language" (Ph.D. dissertation, Northwestern University, 1966), p. 238.

The cosmos within which the events of the film take place is one in which man is essentially alone, but not independent in the sense that he controls his fate (as the cowboy prototype is alone and independent in the classic western). Nor can the hero depend upon friends; indeed, he cannot even rely on the mass as a cover under which to hide from avenging fate.

One last observation of Whitaker's does seem to apply to many of the French films of the late thirties mentioned in this chapter, and to others: "In the world of *Quai des brumes* there are . . . no children, no future, there is no joy, there are no homes, there are no great causes. There is, however, an innate dignity of man that seems to be worth preserving at all costs; but the final test and proof of this dignity lies not in the life of the man, but in his death."[2] It was Jean Gabin who most consistently (and satisfyingly) embodied that particular kind of tragic dignity. Romantic, anarchic, predestined, and with

Quai des brumes (France, 1938, Marcel Carné). Museum of Modern Art/Film Stills Archive.

[2] Whitaker, "The Content Analysis of Film," p. 228. Elizabeth Grottle Strebel, *French Social Cinema of the Nineteen Thirties: A Cinematographic Expression of Popular Front Consciousness* (New York: Arno Press, 1980), identifies similar themes.

pathos written on his face, he believes in nothing but love and comradeship. The unhappy ending tended to be as typical of the French films of the late thirties as the happy one was of the American; Gabin might be thought of as Bogart's equivalent in developing a character of great and special meaning for his own culture.

At first glance, many of Renoir's films of the thirties may seem to be the great exceptions in any attempt to extend Whitaker's observations. Renoir was committed to the Popular Front, which came into power in 1936, when Léon Blum of the Socialist Party was elected president, and lasted until 1938. In fact his films of that brief, hopeful period are among those most clearly reflecting its liberal, egalitarian values. And in general, we would expect Renoir's humanism and *joie de vivre* to be at war with the fatalism and defeatism so pervasive in the other films—particularly in those of Carné-Prévert. But Renoir is an exception only in his treatment of the themes; the themes themselves remain as prominent in his work as in that of others. The need for escape is just as prevalent (*Boudu Saved from Drowning, The Crime of Monsieur Lange, The Lower Depths, The Grand Illusion*), but in Renoir's case the emphasis falls on an escape *to* as well as *from* something, and the escapes are apt to succeed.

Fate functions through coincidence in Renoir's films, as in those of others; but in his case fate tends to be benign rather than malignant. For example, in *The Lower Depths*—a version that has as much to do with Renoir as with Gorky, and is definitely French rather than imitatively Russian—the plot frequently turns on chance, but the outcomes are favorable. The thief and the baron are brought together by accident; Pepel (Jean Gabin assuming his archetypal role for the first time) happens to be at the outdoor restaurant to save the girl from dishonor; the death of the old landlord staves off catastrophe and offers escape to the tenants. Then too, with Renoir action *is* effective. In *The Crime of Monsieur Lange* the title character helps create a cooperative and then saves it by killing the former owner and escaping across a border. As for fear, Renoir's films are

Grand Illusion (France, 1937, Jean Renoir). Museum of Modern Art/Film Stills Archive.

as remarkable for its absence—even in situations that would seem to call for it (the prisons of *Grand Illusion*)—as those of Carné-Prévert are for its presence. Finally, Renoir's *oeuvre* is consistently and conspicuously redolent with solidarity and friendship; solitude or aloneness are almost entirely excluded from his screen world. Carné-Prévert and Renoir are equally concerned with the need for human warmth and companionship. But whereas Carné-Prévert present a world in which these qualities exist tenuously if at all, Renoir cannot conceive of existence without them.

If Renoir had the greatness and individuality of vision to withstand a common attitude, he still chose to look at the same things other French film makers did in the late thirties. He simply saw them in the positive light that permeates all of his major work rather than in the darkness and despair that was descending on his country and the rest of the world. If France had done no more than give tools and working space to this great film maker in the thirties, we would be grateful.

Renoir seems to many a supreme talent of that time and place—but first among equals. The group of creative film artists and cluster of brilliant films produced during that national flowering were influential and remain memorable. In retrospect they seem to have been the first to put the sound film to its full mature use. Though some of the work would be later criticized by the New Wave critics—the young removing the old to make way for themselves—it would be criticized as the "tradition of quality," which seems fair enough.

FILMS OF THE PERIOD

1935
La Bandera (Julien Duvivier)
Carnival in Flanders (Jacques Feyder)
The Golem (Duvivier)
Pension Mimosas (Feyder)

1936
La Belle Équipe (Duvivier)
César (Marcel Pagnol)
The Cheat (Sacha Guitry)
The Crime of Monsieur Lange
   (Jean Renoir)
A Day in the Country (Renoir)
The Lower Depths (Renoir)
Pépé le Moko (Duvivier)

1937
Carnet de bal (Duvivier)
The Grand Illusion (Renoir)
J'accuse (Abel Gance)

1938
The Baker's Wife (Pagnol)
The Human Beast (Renoir)
La Marseillaise (Renoir)
Quai des brumes (Marcel Carné)

1939
Le Jour se lève (Carné)
The Rules of the Game (Renoir)

BOOKS ON THE PERIOD

ARMES, ROY,   *French Film.* New York: E. P. Dutton & Co., Inc., 1970. 160 pp.
SADOUL, GEORGES,   *French Film.* New York: Arno Press, 1972. 130 pp. (originally published in 1953)

11

Hollywood in the Thirties, 1929–1939

The 1930s in America were the years of the Depression and of the New Deal; of business collapse and bank failure, and of the WPA, the CCC, and the NRA (Works Progress Administration, Civilian Conservation Corps, and National Recovery Administration). They were years of economic stagnancy, industrial strife, and individual frustration. At the same time, they were years of rediscovery of American tradition, of affirmation of an American character, of the unearthing and preservation of folklore and folk music, and of attempts at the restoration and conservation of our land and water through federal government efforts after decades of neglect and despoilation.

During these years the movies continued as a vital form of popular culture. Usually they seemed to avoid direct confrontation with the problems of the time, but inevitably they carried along its themes and concerns—even into seemingly escapist entertainment. Sometimes social stance was implicit in what was omitted or disguised. In other instances the movies spoke more or less directly to national fears and aspirations. The populist rhetoric and symbols of the first government documentaries, Pare Lorentz's *The Plow that Broke the Plains* (1936) and *The River* (1937), had their analogues in the fiction films of Frank Capra, *Mr. Deeds Goes to Town* (1936) and *Mr. Smith Goes to Washington* (1939).

The American entertainment films of the 1930s were designed to function in a way quite different from theatrical feature films of today—at which attendance becomes something of a special occasion. Those earlier movies were more like current television series, and with similar audience expectations. Admission prices were much lower then; theaters were more easily accessible; and they were attended with greater casualness, more frequently—by 80 million customers a week. The men and women who created the films for that mass audience conceived of themselves as making entertainment. They didn't think of their work as art.

A standard technique for screen narrative became fixed—what is now sometimes called classic Hollywood cinema. It involves a master long shot covering the whole scene, which introduces it and is returned to from time to time to reestablish spatial orientation. Within it are inserted medium shots and closeups in shot/reverse shot order, back and forth between action and reaction to it, speaker and listener(s). Screen direction and screen action are matched perfectly from shot to shot, and sight lines are carefully observed: When an actor looks, we see what he or she is looking at from approximately the same angle and distance. Those earlier American film makers working within that style aspired toward the well-made film, and the best of them had very high standards for their craft. But to regard the motion picture as a means for personal expression would generally have been considered a somewhat peculiar idea. Art existed in them of course; but in comparison to other more self-conscious artistic efforts it was arrived at surreptitiously, sometimes unconsciously. We can tell this from the evidence of the five thousand or so features produced during the decade, and from an understanding of the industrial system within which they were made and marketed.

The thirties were the years of the giant studios having nearly complete control over the careers of their employees, more absolute than that of today's professional football teams over their players. The studios assembled their rosters of creators, performers, and technicians who, as they worked together over the years, became very expert indeed. Because of this continuity of personnel, which extended from top management to lowliest grip, each studio had its own "look." In some ways we can deal with the American films of the thirties more adequately by identifying them with their studios rather than with individual film makers.

As much as we have come in recent years to think of the director as principal creator of a film, we must remember that in Hollywood in the thirties the producers and the stars would generally have been considered the more important controlling agents. Producers, with a stable of script writers at their disposal, put together vehicles for the stars. Producers like Irving Thalberg, Hal Wallis, and Darryl F. Zanuck left strong imprints on the films they produced. The director was sometimes merely a supervisor who oversaw the recording of images and sound. It makes sense, then, to look first at the industrial system before considering its product and the work of a few powerful creative figures who emerged.

THE INDUSTRY

Rising out of the twenties, after seismic upheavals and shifts during the transition from silence to sound, the Hollywood economic terrain hardened into a pattern that would remain virtually unchanged for two decades. In fact, vestiges of the modus operandi of the thirties still characterize what is left of the once mighty feature film industry.

The system was built around eight major companies—five more major than the other three—and around the *vertical control* exerted by those firms over distribution and exhibition as well as production. Chains of theaters were owned by the five largest studios: Metro-Goldwyn-Mayer (the production arm of Loew's, Inc.), Twentieth Century-Fox, Paramount Pictures, Warner Brothers, Radio-Keith-Orpheum (RKO). Each studio produced upward of fifty features a year for its theaters and for those of the others. "Program," or "B," pictures might play only within their producing company's chain as weekly or semiweekly filler between hits. The more popular films were sought by all the exhibitors, regardless of which studio produced them. Whatever part of the country you are from, chances are that names of local theaters still pay tribute to these former owners: the RKO Grand, the Paramount, Loew's, and so on. The three smaller studios—Universal, Columbia Pictures, United Artists—produced and distributed, but to survive had to have their films shown in the theaters owned and controlled by the big five. Besides the eight major studios there were also those producers called independents. Some of them were reasonably large and well established (Samuel Goldwyn Productions, Walt Disney Studio, Republic, Monogram [now Allied Artists]); others were individual entrepreneurs working out of one of the major studios (David Selznick at M-G-M, Walter Wanger at Paramount).

In 1939 the eight majors were responsible for 76 percent of the feature films released, and took in 86 percent of the total rental income. These studios were the members of the Motion Picture Producers and Distributors of America—the trade organization that self-censored the content of the films produced, bargained with foreign governments regarding export abroad, and performed other functions on behalf of the industry as a whole. Through the MPPDA (now the MPAA—Motion Picture Association of America) the majors dominated the industry. Control of distribution was perhaps the one factor most crucial to their power.

The distribution branches of the majors undertook to "sell" the films to the exhibitors and to physically handle and circulate prints to the theaters. Selling involved advertising and promotion, which took two forms. First, each film was presented to "the trade" through advertisements and reviews in the trade press, and by sales representatives and advance screenings at the regional offices. Second, the distributor developed a promotional campaign to attract general public attention to the new release—through the national press, radio, billboards, sky writing, and any other means available or imaginable. The budget allocated for the promotion of each film was a key factor in determining the rental the exhibitor would pay for it. The more important the studio thought the picture, the more money it spent on the campaign, and the more the exhibitor might expect to take in at the box office.

The distributor worked out the kinds of appeals thought to be best suited and most effective for selling each picture. There was a staff to design the graphics, write advertising copy, even prepare canned "reviews" for those newspapers that didn't choose to hire their own reviewers. Often the approaches to the public and to the trade were strikingly different. We are all aware that sex and violence are not only staples of popular entertainment but of the advertising for it. It may be less obvious that novelty is stressed almost as often: "For the first time on the screen . . . ," "At last it can be told . . . ," "Never before in the history of the motion picture. . . ." Usually pains were taken to disguise the probability that the film would be rather like the ones shown last week and a month ago, and to promise a unique experience no one could conceivably miss. To the exhibitor, however, the exact opposite (and a bit more honest) appeal was more often used: "The studio, the director, and the star who gave you *Dark Victory,*" "Judy and Mickey together again in the kind of story that made *Babes in Arms* a smash."

The exhibitor could think only in terms of known quantities in relation to the audience's tastes as demonstrated by their purchase of tickets in the past.

Some two hundred to four hundred prints of each film, costing around $250 apiece, were shipped from the laboratories to the regional film "exchanges." There were roughly thirty distribution centers in the country—Chicago, Dallas, Spokane, Atlanta, and so on, the same cities used as wholesale outlets by the garment manufacturers, meat packers, and other industries. Each distributor had an exchange along "film row." Prints were delivered from the exchanges to the theaters in time to open; prints of the closing program were returned for inspection and repair, then made available to other theaters in the region. In the eighteen- to twenty-thousand theaters across the country (estimates vary) nine thousand bookings were considered a good average for individual pictures. The first thirty-five hundred to four thousand bookings were critical to the success of a film. Box office returns were scrutinized carefully to determine likelihood for success. If the projected income looked hopeful, more money might be spent on promotion. If not, the film was allowed to die quietly; prints would be kept in the exchanges, but no more money would be spent on promotion. Many fine films, particularly some small ones with quiet tone and subtle appeal, met this fate without being given a chance to reach the audience that might have existed for them.

The flow of money that started at the box office moved from the exhibitor to the distributor and finally back to the producer. Each took his cut to cover costs and make a profit, if any. With a looseness of accounting that flabbergasted people in other businesses, the distributor had to trust the exhibitor's report, and the producer the distributor's. Everyone cheated, it was said, and yet there was usually enough income to go around.

Helping to ensure the profits of distribution and production were certain characteristic trade practices. *Block booking,* for example, meant the exhibitor had to rent films in packages that included the "dogs" along with the "hits." This assured some return on even the weakest items in a studio's annual program. *Blind buying* occurred when an exhibitor was forced to book films unseen—sometimes even before they were made—to guarantee an advance market that would cover at least some of the considerable production and distribution costs. Block booking and blind buying led to *overbuying.* In those days of surplus product, the exhibitor might have to book more films than could be shown in order to get those that would attract the largest audiences. In return for what might be regarded as economic harassment (in 1940 the federal courts ruled the practices illegal) the exhibitor got *clearance* and *zoning.* If the theater was a downtown first-run theater in a city, the exhibitor was assured that the film booked would not be shown in any other theater downtown or in the neighborhoods or suburbs until after a certain lapse of time—six months, say; or, if the theater was in a small town, the exhibitor knew that the film would not be shown in a town closer than perhaps twenty miles away.

In the days of vertical control this set of ungentlemanly agreements successfully kept out independents in any of the three phases—production, distribution, and exhibition—except by tolerance of the major studios. Since profits could be made at any of the three levels, competition was largely internal within a single company: among its production, distribution, and exhibition branches. As for competition among the eight firms, since the members of the MPPDA parceled out their spheres of influence (kinds of production, regions in which theaters were owned), they competed with one another only in somewhat the manner of the several divisions of the General Motors Corporation. Vertical control also meant that the industry could thoroughly police itself in terms of the kinds of screen content it felt would be acceptable to the public. By self-censoring it was able to forestall outcries of moral indignation that might hurt at the box office and invite government intervention.

CENSORSHIP, SELF-REGULATION, PRESSURE GROUPS

To some creators, the system of self-regulation that developed was an even more onerous feature of the industrial organization than was the single-minded pursuit of profits by front office and stockholders. Certainly it had substantial effect on what would appear on the screen or, more accurately, what would not. This "production code" remained in operation with only minor revisions until 1968, when the industry adopted the practice, common abroad, of regulating attendance (the G/PG/R/X ratings) rather than content. The United States is almost unique among nations in never having had federal censorship of motion pictures.

As noted earlier, the move toward self-regulation began in the years immediately following World War I. It came in response to public criticism and the industry's fear of increased state and municipal censorship, and perhaps even federal government involvement. Eight states and a number of cities had passed film censorship laws by the early twenties. Public indignation was provoked by films reflecting (exacerbating, some argued) a new, freer morality that featured hip flasks, knee-length skirts, and petting in the rumble seats of roadsters. Rocked by scandals surrounding the death of a starlet after an orgy (comedian Roscoe "Fatty" Arbuckle was accused of having caused her death), and by the unsolved murder of director William Desmond Taylor, Hollywood was the subject of particularly violent criticism.

In 1922 the Motion Picture Producers and Distributors of America hired Will H. Hays, Postmaster General and former national chairman of the Republican Party, to become its head at $100,000 a year. The choice was a shrewd one in several ways. Given his political clout, Hays could be expected to fend off government censorship. As an elder in the Presbyterian Church, he was known to be a pillar of morality; his photograph alone, with high starched collar and ascetic features, was enough to attest to his virtue. The public relaxed, certain that Mr. Hays (dubbed the "Czar" of motion pictures) would launder the dirt out of the movies and prevent members of the industry from flouting conventional morality in their private lives.

This public-relations effort succeeded well enough for a number of years, until the public began to notice that the content of films had changed little. By the late twenties the tide of moral outrage was again rising. The response of the "Hays Office" to new threats of economic boycott and government intervention was the Motion Picture Production Code. Adopted in 1930, this curious document was drafted by Father Daniel Lord, S. J. (professor of dramatics at St. Louis University), assisted by Martin Quigley (publisher of the *Motion Picture Herald* and prominent Catholic layman).

Like the Ten Commandments, the Code's language was largely negative. Restrictions on what could be dealt with and how, appeared under twelve main headings: crimes against the law, sex, vulgarity, obscenity, profanity, costume, dances, religion, locations (that is, bedrooms), national feelings, titles ("salacious, indecent, or obscene''), and repellent subjects (actual hangings or electrocutions, third degree, brutality, branding of people or animals, apparent cruelty to children or animals, the sale of women, surgical operations). Totally forbidden were presentations of drug traffic or the use of drugs, sexual perversion, ''white slavery,'' sexual relationships between the white and black races, and nudity. The authors' detailed knowledge of human peccadilloes was at its most impressive under the heading profanity, the potential for which was now expanded with the talkie. Proscribed were ''alley cat,'' ''bat'' or ''broad (applied to a woman).'' Also prohibited were: ''Bronx cheer (the sound); . . . cripes; fanny; fairy (in the vulgar sense); finger (the).'' A cryptic ''in your hat'' was banned from the screen, as were ''nance; nerts; nuts (except when meaning crazy [one wonders about when meaning almonds]) . . . tom cat (applied to a man),'' and so on, and on.

Once again everyone settled down, feeling that the Hays Office had a firm grip on Hollywood's transgressions—until, once again, the more observant observed that what was seen on the screen and heard from the speakers had changed little as a result of the Code. In 1932 a resolution was introduced into the U.S. Senate to investigate the motion picture industry. In 1933 the first large-scale social-scientific studies of the effects of mass media on the social attitudes and behavior of audiences were published: the twelve-volume *Motion Pictures and Youth,* sponsored by the Payne Fund. (The results of this research were popularized in Henry James Forman's *Our Movie-Made Children,* published in 1935, which emphasized and even exaggerated potential harmful effects.) In 1934 Catholic forces, particularly unhappy about Hollywood flouting a Code drafted by one of their own, formed the Legion of Decency.

Since the Legion's program rested on boycotting films that violated the Code (their titles to be read out from pulpits across the country), the industry finally became sufficiently alarmed to institute a mechanism to enforce adherence: the Code seal, to be applied by the Production Code Administration. Joseph I. Breen, a young Catholic newspaperman, was appointed director. The members of the MPPDA agreed not to release or distribute films unless they carried the seal. A $25,000 penalty was instituted for producing, distributing, or exhibiting any picture which had not received it. Given vertical and nearly complete control of the industry by the major studio members of the association, not a single important feature was released without the seal in the next two decades.

This enforced, official morality imposed on the creative personnel by the business leaders resulted in a screen world which many found more than a little removed from life. Though it was argued to be ''self-regulation,'' the Code was embraced much more warmly by studio heads than by those who actually made the pictures. Writers, directors, and actors—who often came out of theater and the other less financially encumbered traditional arts whose audiences were smaller and more select—felt particularly inhibited by it. One principal problem was that the Code sapped creative energy at its source. Staying within the Code's standards of conventional, conservative middle-class morality became at least as important as creating a fine work. Another problem was the patent hypocrisy involved. The real reasons for the Code and the seal were financial rather than moral. If organized pressure groups succeeded in keeping audiences away from theaters, this would mean a substantial loss of income. If local and state censorship bodies increased in number and were joined by a threatened federal agency, this might entail the considerable expense of providing several versions of a film to meet the varying standards.

Naturally film makers working within the Code tried to suggest what they could not show; the leer replaced a frank look at many of life's realities. Since restrictions were greatest on sexual matters, sexuality was replaced by violence (regarded with more equanimity by the society as well as by the Production Code Administration), which came to be one of the noteworthy characteristics of the American film. Our popular genres contain more crime and violence than the films of any other nation; as Robert Warshow pointed out in two brilliant essays reprinted in *The Immediate Experience,* the gun is the central symbol of both the western and the gangster film. It is possible that we are the most criminal and violent nation on earth; but even if that much of the image were accurate, it became distorted by the Code's overall insistence that virtue be rewarded and vice punished.

On the other hand, the synthetic morality may have been appropriate, even aesthetically, to the world of the studio films of the thirties, created as they were out of imagination, plaster, lath, and klieg lights. From this distance in time, at least, considering what those films are generally about and the characters who usually inhabit them, it seems that reality is not so much excluded (as was argued by the social critics of the thirties) as dealt with obliquely and within the fixed rubrics of the popular forms. In *Trouble in Paradise* (1932), for example, after Gaston and Lily embrace passionately on a couch, the culmination of that embrace is expressed by a dissolve to the same couch, now empty, followed by a cut to Gaston's hand hanging a "Do Not Disturb" sign on the bedroom door. The indirection of content, like the stylization of technique, frequently adds to rather than detracts from the charms and resonant effectiveness of the best of the films of the thirties.

EMERGENT GENRES

Of the popular genres that had formed into recognizable patterns during the twenties, silent comedy was affected most radically by the introduction of sound. While lamenting the loss of comic pantomime and the great clowns who made it the universal and timeless form it is, we would still want to welcome the new kinds of comedies and the creators who entered with sound. The westerns, of course, could only be hampered by the sound stages; during the thirties they were largely relegated to "B" and "C" production budgets and comparable prestige. They became the "oaters" beloved by rural adult populations and small boys everywhere on Saturday afternoons, but had little to do with the advance of the motion picture generally. With only a few exceptions (for instance, *Cimarron,* 1931), not until the mid-thirties was there a return to the earlier epic western: *The Texas Rangers* (1936), *The Plainsman* (1936), *Wells Fargo* (1937). Not until the end of the decade did *Stagecoach* (1939) establish a model for the "modern" western that has survived to this day.

Of the narrative forms emerging with the new sound medium, the most vigorous and characteristic of the thirties were the musical, the gangster film, the horror film, the sound comedy, and the animated cartoon.

The musical, of course, was dependent on sound for its existence. Though there had been harbingers, such as von Stroheim's most popular film, *The Merry Widow* (1925), audiences had to be content with a live pit orchestra or organist providing a potpourri of Lehar melodies to accompany the pantomimed action and printed titles. Fittingly, the film that caused the revolution, *The Jazz Singer* (1927), foreshadowed the backstage musical, an important early subgenre. What it lacked most essentially was dancing, for the appeal of the musical came to depend as much on choreography as on music. From *The Hollywood Revue of 1929* through *Saturday Night Fever* (1978), and *All That Jazz* (1979), and *Flashdance* (1982), the creators of musicals have been men and women of dance as well as of song.

The Hollywood Revue of 1929 was a prototype for one line of musical, the revue, which flourished in the thirties and first half of the forties. It disappeared after World War II, with only a few exceptions (*Ziegfeld Follies,* 1946, *New Faces,* 1952). Consisting of separate ''acts'' unconnected by narrative linkage, like its stage counterpart, the screen revue let audiences throughout the world see the great entertainers whose performances had formerly been confined to Broadway and infrequent tours. Generally presented very much as they might have been on a superstage (by the impresario Florenz Ziegfeld, let's say), the film revues substituted the possibility of perfection—ideal performers in their best performances—for the special excitements of live theater.

Another early film musical form deriving from theater was the filmed operetta. It began with the romantic comedies-cum-music of Ernst Lubitsch (starting with *The Love Parade,* 1929) and Rouben Mamoulian (*Love Me Tonight,* 1932). These operetta-like screen originals were made at Paramount and starred Maurice Chevalier and/or Jeanette MacDonald. Moving to M-G-M, in 1934 Lubitsch directed the same stars in his version of *The Merry Widow.* It was at M-G-M that the operetta continued, in a series of standard stage favorites beginning with *Naughty Marietta* in 1935. In them Chevalier was replaced by Nelson Eddy; he and MacDonald helped make a great deal of money for everyone concerned.

If the filmed operetta came out of Paramount and M-G-M, the backstage musical began at Warner Brothers. In 1930 Warner imported Broadway veteran Busby Berkeley, who became master of the production number. His ranks and clusters of chorines moving with military precision through elaborate patterns are understandably the subject of ''camp'' appreciation today. Those extravagant creations nonetheless contain an authentic if frequently exotic charm. Early in the period Berkeley's spectacular staging and bravura use of camera, cutting, and special effects were brought together in the narrative musical.

First of the stories with music and dance (which the term *musical* now generally means) was *42nd Street* (1933). Directed by Lloyd Bacon (with ''Dances and ensembles created and staged by Busby Berkeley''), the story revolved around the production of a Broadway musical, *Pretty Lady.* The tough director of the show (Warner Baxter) is dependent on an ''angel'' (Guy Kibbee) who has put up $70,000 because of his infatuation with its star (Bebe Daniels). The night before opening she breaks her ankle, permitting the young unknown (Ruby Keeler) to take her place. As a result of the crisis, the established star realizes her love for her former vaudeville partner (George Brent), and the newcomer hers for the junior lead (Dick Powell). Una Merkel and Ginger Rogers play seasoned chorines—Rogers as Anytime Annie (''She only said no once—and then she didn't hear the question'').

The prototypical content elements work largely because of the pace and dazzle of the film. The lines are witty and delivered in rapid-fire staccato. Characterizations are deftly etched, stereotypical as they should be. The performers take themselves only seriously enough to blend in with what would become the conventional hard-boiled-exterior, soft-on-the-inside view of show biz. Climaxing the film, and what it's all building toward, are the three production numbers: ''Shuffle Off to Buffalo,'' ''I'm Young and Healthy,'' and the title song, ''42nd Street.'' After the numbing exhaustion of rehearsals and the nervous tension of the young heroine, we are given an enormous release in the polished extravaganza, which goes considerably beyond what could be created on any stage. Each of the three numbers exceeds the last in terms of spectacle, and each pulls farther away from the possibilities of live theater into strictly cinematic manipulations of space and time, of image and movement.

In *42nd Street,* Berkeley started full scale on that special kind of creation we associate with his name. The massed lovelies of the chorus are viewed by the camera from almost any position except a stationary one in front of a theater stage. They are seen from overhead as they form floral patterns or strange concentric rings suggesting interconnecting gears. Or the camera gets down on the floor and moves right through their spread legs in as slyly elegant a bit of erotica—funny in a way, but lovely too—as one could imagine. Costumes and settings are designed to support and underscore the extravagant fantasy of the total choreographic conception; or, to put it the other way around, the dances grow out of and take full advantage of every suggestion provided by the visual decor. The chorus line performs a jerky, syncopated march up stairs; they turn toward the camera and raise cardboard profiles of skyscrapers, covering themselves and becoming a miniature Manhattan. Berkeley would later sustain and elaborate on delights of this sort at their most breathtaking (and bizarre) in the *Gold Diggers* series (*of 1933, 1935, 1937*).

If on one level *42nd Street* can be seen as the most purely escapist kind of entertainment, on another it seems to be dealing with the fear and paralysis of the Depres-

42nd Street (U.S., 1933, Lloyd Bacon). National Film Archive/Stills Library.

sion. It's not just the apple vendor, that symbol of the unemployed, in the "42nd Street" number; in a way the whole film is about lack of money and joblessness. The director insists that the only reason he's doing the show is for the money. Portrayed as a driving entrepreneurial type, he says he's been called a machine, producing a steady succession of hits. Sure he's made a lot of money in the past, but he's spent and lost it all on friends and high living and the stock market. As he delivers these lines he is standing against a window high above the street, suggesting the many suicidal leaps of those who had lost their money in the crash. This time, he says, he's going to sock away his earnings so hard they can never be taken from him. The control exerted by the unattractive and stupid, but wealthy, angel over all of the members of the production—and on the quality of the show itself, when he insists that Anytime Annie replace the injured star—is made pointedly clear. There is reiteration that two hundred jobs depend on the success of the show. Keeping cast and crew from falling back into the ranks of the unemployed is the strongest point made in the pep talk the director gives the young replacement for the star just before she goes on. There was surely a special poignance to that plea in 1933.

In this same narrative line, a series of films starring Fred Astaire and Ginger Rogers were the first to drop the theatrical setting as excuse for music and dancing. Though they play professional dancers, thus making their terpsichorean skill plausible, they move from the theater out into the world, breaking into song and dance whenever the emotional charge is sufficient. This observation covers all ten of their costarring films to one degree or another. In *Shall We Dance* (1937), for example, Astaire (as the great Petrov, a Russian Ballet dancer) is first seen tap dancing in his room to a jazz record. (Really he's Peter Peters from Philadelphia, PA.) Returning from Paris on board the *Queen Anne,* he wanders down into the (extraordinarily stylized) engine room, and sings and dances with the black crew and the rhythmically pumping, eccentrically designed machinery. That number suggests a benign and jazzy *Metropolis,* with the ebullient individual replacing the deadened mass, and the machines beating it out in swingtime. Another number on board ship has Rogers and Astaire walking their dogs to the Gershwin music. In New York they are seen roller skating with a group of extras in a soundstage Central Park. Soon they wander off to sing a song, and traject themselves into an energetic and skillful dance on skates. Astaire and Rogers, whose films together extend from 1933 to 1949, served to link the backstage musical inaugurated by *42nd Street* (same year as *Flying Down to Rio,* the first Rogers and Astaire) and the vintage cluster of M-G-M musicals beginning with *On the Town* (the same year as the last Rogers and Astaire, *The Barkleys of Broadway*), which offered song and dance as the normal response to life. But of course the grace and charm, the subtle and sophisticated virtuosity of Fred and Ginger gives its own lasting pleasure, which transcends their place in the history of the Hollywood musicals. Their appeal remains as inimitable as it is irresistible.

Of the popular American genres, the musical remains one of the most indigenous and enduring. Surely it is the loveliest, offering aesthetic pleasures that by comparison cause many of the more "serious" films valued contemporaneously to fall behind in lumbering earnestness. As long as the simple and sensible Aristotelian notion is accepted—that art offers beauty and beauty is a good in itself—the musical is assured its deservedly important place in the history of the American film. Long may it talk, and sing, and dance.

Though there were many films about gangsters in the twenties (von

Swing Time (U.S., 1936, George Stevens). Museum of Modern Art/ Film Stills Archive.

Sternberg's *Underworld,* 1927, is one example), the gangster film was really a product of the thirties. To make it viable, perhaps, it needed the growling of limousines in low gear, the squealing of tires and the screeching of brakes, the ratchet noise of tommy guns, the explosions and tinkling glass. In its conventional form it was born, brought up, and buried within that decade. *Little Caesar* (1930) began the cycle.

In film generally, and in the form, style, and subject-matter cycles of the popular American genres in particular, it frequently happens that the prototypical films remain the strongest and best of type. It's as if Elizabethan drama started with *Hamlet* and *Much Ado About Nothing* rather than building to them. In film, documentary commenced with *Nanook of the North; Potemkin* and *Mother* led off the high period of Soviet silent film, as *Open City* and *Shoeshine* did that of postwar Italian neorealism. In the American film, *On the Town* (1949) began the vibrant cluster of M-G-M musicals of the early fifties; *Destination Moon* (1950), the futuristic science-fiction genre; *Rebel Without a Cause* (1955), a succession of problem pictures dealing with misunderstood teenagers. So it was with the gangster film of the thirties. The three prototypical films—*Little Caesar* (1930), *The Public Enemy* (1931), and *Scarface* (1932)—so richly explored the potential of the genre that there was little left for other film makers to do immediately except repeat and vary. One study, *The Gangster Film,* by Stephen Karpf, makes this point in its subtitle: *Emer-*

gence, Variation and Decay of a Genre, 1930–1940. It is true that the thirties-type gangster film disappeared during the years of World War II. The genre itself, however, like the western, has remained sufficiently strong and healthy to give us a succession of important works such as *White Heat* (1949), *Bonnie and Clyde* (1967), and *The Godfather* (1972/74), to name but a few.

If the musical sometimes offered masked representations of the Depression society of the thirties, the gangster film seems to present a metaphorical explanation of what had gone wrong with the country. The attitudes in them are quite amoral. The goals of the gangster protagonists are confined to acquiring wealth and power. They are the ones who understand the system and how to succeed within it. Others, those who believe in honest work, loyalty, affection, and decency are ineffectual dupes. In these films gangsterism can be seen as supercapitalism, just as war was seen by military strategist Karl von Clausewitz as an extension of diplomacy. If gangsters are businessmen as well as criminals, might it not be equally true that businessmen are gangsters? Couldn't utilities magnate Samuel Insull be seen as a legitimized Al Capone? In any case, the ordinary citizen was caught in a corrupt system controlled by the greedy and ruthless. How come the banks couldn't pay back their investors? Why was it that profits made on the stock market suddenly became losses? In a later example of a related subgenre, *The Asphalt Jungle* (1950), the outwardly respectable lawyer secretly involved in criminal activity remarks to his wife, "Crime, my dear, is merely a left-handed form of human endeavor." In the initial gangster films the police are no better nor worse than the gangsters, and the methods of both are more or less interchangeable. When the first tough phases of the cycle came under severe public criticism and the studios were pressured by the Production Code Administration, the producers simply changed their gangsters into G-men, Treasury agents, and other law enforcement officers.

Though perhaps not the best aesthetically of the first three prototypical films, *Little Caesar,* directed by Mervyn LeRoy, contains the essential thesis of the gangster film in its simplest and clearest form. Rico (Edward G. Robinson), the hero, or antihero if you prefer, begins as a gun-toting thug with ambition—the toughest, most ruthless of the lot. What motivates him is the exercise of power. The film's makers don't feel obliged to justify their dramatic premise: It is presented as a given. Those on top are enviable because they are rich and powerful. But as you climb upward there's a danger of becoming soft. Refinement and sentiment make people vulnerable and lead to destruction through "loss of nerve." The film begins with Rico murdering a robbery victim and ends with Rico being gunned down by the police after he fails to shoot his friend, Joe Massara (Douglas Fairbanks, Jr.), who becomes indirectly responsible for his death.

In *Little Caesar* there are no "good guys." The detective Flaherty is simply on the other side, a nasty character with his own strong-arm men, who carries on a personal vendetta with Rico. McLure, the crime commissioner, is an unrealistic and ineffectual snob. The Big Boy represents a corrupt and criminal high society. But Rico, for all his viciousness, is not a sadist. He doesn't torture, doesn't get pleasure from killing. His view is presented as pragmatic, up to a point. Like Hitler in *Mein Kampf,* he pronounces on human behavior and values, and acts effectively as long as he follows his own cynical understanding. The world is a jungle, and the most effective predator kills fast and without compunction. When he fails to kill, he himself is killed.

Given the nature of artistic experience, something more than the relevance of these thematic statements to contemporary attitudes must have accounted for the wide and continuing appeal of the gangster films. As with the musical, in the gangster genre

Little Caesar (U.S., 1931, Mervyn LeRoy). Museum of Modern Art/Film Stills Archive.

formal elements and creative personalities command our attention. At a time when films generally were bound to the theater by the confines of the sound stage, the gangster films seemed to break out into the real life of the headlines, to be situated within recognizable slums, penthouses, streets, and speakeasies of big-city America during the Prohibition era. Indeed, they were full of life, driven forward by action, violence, and competition for the highest stakes. They were also frenetic in their pace, clipped and colorful in their dialogue. With their usual tightness of construction, economy of means, and the fact that they deal with matters of life and death, at their best they provide satisfactions that are classic, that make us think of the Greek dramas—though the film makers themselves apparently had no self-conscious pretensions. More fascinating and credible than anything else, perhaps, were the conceptions of their roles and the dynamic performances by Edward G. Robinson, James Cagney, and Paul Muni as the first protagonists. Though painfully limited in education and outlook, these characters have stature. Within their small and evil world they are the tragic kings doomed by flaws, ambition and pride usually the dominant ones. Their inevitable deaths provoke pity and fear, as they should.

While the musical and gangster genres flourished at Warner's, horror films were the specialty of Universal. The appearance of these successors to *The Golem* and *Nosferatu* seems to have had less to do with the advent of sound technology than with American mastery of the lighting techniques originated earlier in Germany. Chiaroscuro lighting was crucial to the evocation of terror, and the names of German emigrés dot the technical credits of this series. Also, as in Germany, it may be that audiences respond especially to horror on the screen during times of national depression. At any rate, as with the gangster films, the two prototypical American horror films set forth fully the traits of their progeny. *Frankenstein* and *Dracula*, both released in 1931, are still in active circulation on television, in theater revivals, and in college series and courses. Of the two, *Frankenstein* is the more satisfying aesthetically, and remains a very fine film aside from generic considerations.

The opening graveyard scene, with its low-angled shots among the tombstones, an iconic cross, and a figure of death, establishes the mood. The desolate landscapes, remote ancestral castle, forbidding stone tower in which Baron Henry Frankenstein conducts his experiments, the laboratory interior with its flashing electrodes—all would become familiar images of the Gothic horror movie. A sense of impending doom hangs over the film like a pall. Stylized Ruritanian settings and the bleak black-and-white cinematography create the visual atmosphere of shadowy gloom which dominates successive films of the genre.

Frankenstein's cast of characters includes several archetypal figures of the horror film. Frankenstein is the demonic scientist whose obsessive thirst for knowledge has misdirected the humanistic aim of his work. In his feverish search for the source of life, morality is forgotten: He desecrates both the grave and the hangman's gibbet in order to obtain specimens for his experiments. As a result, he is ostracized by his friends and colleagues. As the misfit scientist who defies the conventions of society in his quest for knowledge, he stakes his reputation on one major breakthrough which will bring him fame and power. His presumption, of course, is the original sin of Adam in seeking to know more than humans should. Frankenstein goes even beyond this in attempting to rival God as creator—an ultimate blasphemy. For his arrogance he is punished by the creature of his creation.

Other archetypal figures include the heroine whose true affection heals the ravages of Frankenstein's soul. The conflict of love and faith (feeling) with science (reason) is a popular theme in later films of this genre. The scientist's malevolent assistant is another standard figure; the same actor played a similar role in *Dracula*. The central archetype, however, is the monster himself. As played by Boris Karloff, he takes on a dimension of pathos. The scenes in which the monster raises his arms to the light and plays with the little girl contrast strongly with, and give added power to, those in which he is possessed by an inhuman fury. The terror evoked by this myth is all the more penetrating because of the sympathy aroused by the monster's dignity and by the anguish expressed in his tormented eyes. As an outcast of society, he prompts an empathic response in our own feelings of loneliness and alienation. Perhaps a Depression-ridden society, economically and culturally deprived, was particularly attuned to this appeal— and also to the suggestion that there is madness in high places, which can set loose a monstrous, impersonal, uncontrollable, destructive force.[1]

In any case, the archetypical horror film, like the gangster film, waxed in the thirties and waned after that decade, degenerating into more simplistic tales of horror, and finally even to self-parody (the series of *Abbott and Costello Meet* films: *Frankenstein,* 1948; *the Invisible Man,* 1951; and others). Though ailing, the genre didn't die with the thirties. Instead, the horror films produced by Val Lewton in the forties—such as *Cat*

---

[1] Much of this description and interpretation of *Frankenstein* is borrowed from a CinemaTexas program note written by Courtenay Beinhorn.

Frankenstein (U.S., 1931,
James Whale). Museum of
Modern Art/Film Stills Archive.

People (1942), *I Walked with a Zombie* (1943), *The Body Snatcher* (1945)—mark a sharp departure from the earlier patterns and are noteworthy for their intelligence and taste. Later the horror film was restored to something like full health by Roger Corman in his series of Edgar Allan Poe adaptations (such as *The Fall of the House of Usher,* 1960; *The Masque of the Red Death,* 1964) made in England. Though not as distinctively American as the musical or gangster film, like the other genres, the horror film has been worked at consistently by Americans including Corman, Brian De Palma, and John Carpenter. It is another lasting contribution of the American thirties.

One line of sound comedy took advantage of the new possibilities for repartee and double entendre. Though like drawing room comedies of the theater, in the best film examples (Lubitsch's *Trouble in Paradise,* 1932) visual interest was retained and sight and sound were worked into counterpoint. A second line, out of vaudeville and stage, and replacing the silent clowns, featured talking comic stars in vehicles tailored to their special talents and the verbal styles associated with them. The Marx Brothers, for example, merely transferred to film their theatrical hits *The Cocoanuts* and *Animal Crackers,* in 1929 and 1930. W. C. Fields had been a popular vaudeville performer whose most memorable film bits (for instance, the crooked cue-stick routine) had often been worked out before on stage. Mae West, long before she appeared in movies, had played her particular version of herself on stage. The point is that the great comic movie stars of the thirties were experienced with sound, especially with their own distinctive voices, as supplement to pantomime. In fact, they required sound for full comic effect.

Take as illustration a Fields short, *The Barber Shop*. In addition to his gin-honed voice and throwaway delivery, there are sound gags accompanying verbal and sight gags. The poor unfortunate customer being shaved accounts for some droll lines. Fields: "I didn't recognize your face when you first came in." Man: "No, it's all healed up since I was in here last." At the same time, Fields wields the razor as if it were some sort of harvesting tool. While the man's back arches in discomfort we are able to share his feelings along our own spines because of the sandpapering noise that accompanies each stroke. Fields's solo work with his bass fiddle, Lena, is funny to look at; his comments about his ability are amusing; but the whole is bound together by our hearing that he is merely banging the bow against the strings in toneless percussionistic thumping.

The Marx Brothers used sounds in much the same way, and combined them with rapid-fire dialogue full of non sequiturs and malapropisms. The delivery of the lines augments their humorous content: the timing, Groucho's Lower East Side accent, and Chico's phoney Italian one. Harpo's feigned muteness, his honking of horns, banging on pans, and the like would make sense only in a sound medium. Obviously, the same is true for his harp and Chico's piano playing.

Mae West confined herself almost entirely to verbal humor, except for the ribald leer and undulating walk. Though Fields and the Marxes expanded the scope of their comic jousts with society to take advantage of the variety of backgrounds and situations that could be encompassed within a single film, West used film mostly to record

A Night at the Opera (U.S., 1935, Sam Wood). Museum of Modern Art/Film Stills Archive.

My Little Chickadee (U.S., 1940, Edward Cline). Museum of Modern Art/Film Stills Archive.

her great self in a room talking to a man. Given her marvelous way with talk and men, this seems quite enough.

In the star vehicles individual personalities dominated the plot. A third kind of comedy developed in the thirties in which, rather than being a projection of a single or team comic persona, the plot dictated the personalities of the actors (who, to some extent, became interchangeable). It was like the first line mentioned above except less genteel and more energetic, and it originated in film rather than in theater. Called the "screwball" comedy, this style combined intellectual sophistication with slapstick behavior. It depended on fast, witty dialogue and a battle of the sexes in which male and female roles were often reversed (in terms of traditional expectations of male strength and dominance). The performers most frequently inhabiting the screwball world were Claudette Colbert, Gary Cooper, Irene Dunne, Cary Grant, Jean Harlow, Katharine Hepburn, Carole Lombard, Rosalind Russell, Barbara Stanwyck, and James Stewart.

Frank Capra's enormously successful *It Happened One Night* (1934) may have been the first of the screwball comedies. Howard Hawks also directed effectively in this subgenre (*Twentieth Century,* 1934; *Bringing Up Baby,* 1938; *His Girl Friday,* 1940; *Ball of Fire,* 1941). Other directors who did memorable work in this style were Gregory La Cava (*My Man Godfrey,* 1936), William Wellman (*Nothing Sacred,* 1937), and Leo McCarey (*The Awful Truth,* 1937). The distinctive series of comedies written as well as directed by Preston Sturges are also of this type (*The Lady Eve,* 1941; *The Palm Beach Story,* 1942; *The Miracle of Morgan's Creek,* 1944; and more).

Scripts, even more than direction or performance, seem to provide the basis for the screwball cycle; the writers (especially Ben Hecht, Robert Riskin, Charles Brackett, Billy Wilder, and Sturges) worked out the typical patterns of theme, plot, and dialogue. Ludicrously improbable situations were devised and then dealt with as if they were everyday occurrences. In *Bringing Up Baby,* screenplay by Dudley Nichols and Hagar

Bringing up Baby (U.S., 1938, Howard Hawks). National Film Archive/Stills Library.

Wilde, the plot is furthered as Katharine Hepburn, playing an heiress, has her dress torn off while in an elegant dining room—much to the embarrassment of Cary Grant, a paleontologist. Subsequently: (1) they collide with a truck full of chickens; (2) Grant chases her aunt's dog around a country estate, to find a brontosaurus bone; and (3) a wild leopard is mistaken for a tame one (Baby of the title). The dialogue has speed and sparkle, is filled with unmistakably American exuberance. Language plays an important part in the screwball style, and these films all evidence a close and sensitive attention to the native idiom—wisecracks, slang, and wrenched clichés are rapped out with uproarious effect. *Ball of Fire* points up this aspect neatly. It is about a group of professors compiling a dictionary of American slang who become involved with gangsters and a tough-talking burlesque queen.

The live-action comedies and other features of the thirties were often preceded on the program by the newly emergent and enormously popular cartoon shorts. Animated cartoons, which had appeared intermittently from Winsor McCay's *Gertie the Dinosaur* (1914), seemed also to need sound, perhaps color, and evidently Walt Disney to propel them into the popularity they achieved during the 1930s. Disney's first big hit, *Steamboat Willie* (1928), was also the first animated film with synchronized sound. Soon cartoon shorts, provided by Disney and his imitators, became almost obligatory in theater programs, and Disney's ambitions carried him on to animated features.

The animated cartoon is not a genre, of course, even in the loosest sense of that term. It is a special film technique having as much to do with painting as with the motion picture. Yet, as developed at the Walt Disney Studio during the thirties it did contain standard genre-like elements, the anticipation of which set off delighted screams and whistles whenever the titles and familiar music announced Mickey and Minnie, Donald, Pluto, Goofy, and the rest. It was the mouse upon whom the empire was founded. Among twentieth-century comic figures only Charlie's Tramp could rival the universal affection in which Walt's Mickey was held.

Disney's talking animals, like Aesop's, were caricatured human beings. They inhabited a world recognizable as an extension of Mack Sennett's, with the comic violence and destruction, the fanciful manipulation of time and space now given free reign in artists' drawings. Not only did the animals behave like humans, distinct personalities were developed for each. Mickey, jaunty and optimistic, afflicted with less able companions for whom he assumed responsibility, performed heroic feats through a combination of pragmatism and ingenuity. Minnie was naive and coy, trusting and appreciative, with some resourcefulness and more than a little spunk of her own. Pluto, plagued by conscience, almost suffocating in his canine loyalty and affection, remained rambunctiously good humored as he committed one blunder after another. Goofy, the country bumpkin protected by his own innocence, was given to hiccups and half-witted ruminations. Donald, the irascible Duck, sputtered a steady stream of nearly unintelligible expletives.

Even more than the live-action sound comedies the Disney creations relied heavily on sound. The voices were almost as important as the drawings in establishing characterizations (Mickey's was provided by Walt himself initially). Sound effects were given a new status and freedom of invention, detached from realistic sources. A whole range of crashes, bangs and screeches accompanied the bumps and thumps of the frantic action. As for the music, in Disney animation the score was recorded first and the pictures drawn to it, unlike live-action production where the score is the last element to be added. Music provided the audible continuity, punctuation and commentary. "Mickey Mousing" is a term still applied to a style in which music sounds like and is exactly synchronized to the action on the screen.

The importance of music to Disney's conception led him to alternate the Mickey shorts with the ambitious and innovative *Silly Symphonies*. They began in 1929 with *Skeleton Dance,* set to Saint-Saëns's *Danse Macabre.* In that series the experimentation of Disney's technicians was allowed to develop most fully. In the best examples the animation is richly complex and breathtakingly inventive. The multiplane cel animation technique designed to give a greater sense of dimensionality and depth remained infused with flowing, rhythmical movement. Particularly lovely in this writer's recollection were *Flowers and Trees* (1932) and *The Old Mill* (1937). Most popular was *Three Little Pigs* (1933), whose cheery song "Who's Afraid of the Big Bad Wolf?" was interpreted as a defiance of the Depression. Perhaps it was linked in popular consciousness with the new President Franklin Delano Roosevelt's famous aphorism, "The only thing we have to fear is fear itself."

Though the *Silly Symphonies* ended in 1939 the impulse to illustrate music imaginatively, which they made manifest, carried over into other and later work. *Snow White and the Seven Dwarfs* (1937), Disney's first feature-length cartoon, is virtually an animated musical. Its human characters sing, and the animals and the rest of nature join in what can only be called dances. *Fantasia* (1940), also feature-length, is the apogee of the *Silly Symphonies*. Its seven separate episodes are animated ballets set to classical music. In visual style *Fantasia* ranges from total abstraction (for Bach's *Toccata and Fugue in D Minor*) through more typical Disney romanticization and prettification (for Tschaikowsky's *Nutcracker Suite* and Beethoven's *Pastoral Symphony*) to horrification (for Moussorgsky's *Night on Bald Mountain*). Even Mickey appears, as the bedeviled servant in Dukas's *The Sorcerer's Apprentice*.

Accompanying Disney's stylistic experimentation was the constant employment of new technological means as they became available. His quickness to seize upon sound and his unparalleled exploitation of its untried and limitless relationships with images place his films among those most fully using the newly augmented medium. *Flowers and Trees* was the first film to employ the three-color Technicolor process, and color throughout the Disney animation, particularly in the *Silly Symphonies,* is handled in highly stylized and controlled ways for emotional effect impossible in live-action color cinematography. *Fantasia* introduced stereophonic sound, an addition not picked up by other film makers until more than a decade later. *Toot, Whistle, Plunk, and Boom* (1953), an amusing conjecture about the origins of the instruments of the orchestra, was an apt exploration of the recently arrived CinemaScope screen.

What Disney started others continued. Ub Iwerks seems to have become the principal creative force at the Disney Studio as Walt concerned himself more and more with administration. In the forties Chuck Jones, who had worked with Iwerks and Disney, moved to Warner Brothers and created a rival menagerie in Bugs Bunny, Tweetie Pie, Daffy Duck, Speedy Gonzalez, Road Runner, and Wily Coyote. Others who left Disney about the same time, following the studio strike of 1941, later established United Productions of America. UPA offered the first radical departure from Disney in the extreme simplification and stylization of its drawings, much in the manner of modern French painting, and in the use of the human characters Mr. Magoo and Gerald McBoing Boing.

Animation for the theaters lost its reason for being when its cost, especially the laborious process perfected by Disney, and the disappearance of short subjects in movie programs made it financially unfeasible. Creative leadership passed from the Disney Studio to UPA, and to government film making like that of the National Film Board of Canada, with Norman McLaren, and especially to animation units in Poland, Czechoslovakia, and Yugoslavia (with the studio in Zagreb particularly noteworthy). In this country Ralph Bakshi has tried to create an audience for adult animated features, which have included *Fritz the Cat* (1972), *Heavy Traffic* (1973), and *American Pop* (1980). In 1979, Don Bluth, who had exerted animation leadership at the Disney Studio, left it to try independently to bring animation back to the sort of exquisitely detailed style that Disney earlier pursued. *The Secret of Nimh* was the first feature of his group. Whether or not he succeeds, his effort is testimony to the enormous innovative contributions the early Disney and his collaborators made to every aspect of animated film production. For bet-

Steamboat Willie (U.S., 1928, Walt Disney). National Film Archive/Stills Library.

ter or worse the standard techniques and predominant styles and content of animation were established at the Disney Studio during the 1930s. Everything that has happened in animation since has either grown out of that work or been a conscious reaction against it.

In the live-action features of the thirties, what wasn't genre and originally conceived for the screen was taken from literature, drama, history, or a combination of those sources, and included the most expensive and prestigious productions of the decade. In 1935 alone there were the spectacular *Mutiny on the Bounty;* Max Reinhardt's production of Shakespeare's *A Midsummer Night's Dream; Becky Sharp,* the first feature in three-color Technicolor; *Captain Blood,* with some marvelously conceived and executed sea battles; *David Copperfield;* and *Lives of a Bengal Lancer.* All manifested the kind of scale and skill that we associate with the big-studio Hollywood film of the thirties. They cost a lot of money and made a lot. They were created by experts at that special sort of elegant illusion and were enjoyed by audiences who responded to it unselfconsciously and in large numbers. The kinds of pleasures offered by *Captains Courageous* (1937), say, or *The Adventures of Robin Hood* (1938), once regular if not routine, are no longer available except as those films and others of the thirties may still be replayed in reduced form on television. By now the resources needed for that sort of film making—the carefully assembled and developed character players, along with the stars, the museum-like collections of props, the set construction and special effects departments—have all passed away with the older big-studio system itself. They don't make pictures like that the way they used to; or, when they do, the exceptions only prove the rule.

Mutiny on the Bounty (U.S., 1935, Frank Lloyd). Museum of Modern Art/Film Stills Archive.

MAJOR DIRECTORS

Given five hundred feature films a year, the conventions of genre and hybridism of adaptation, and the emphatic collectivity of Hollywood production in the thirties, it is not altogether easy to distinguish the work of particular directors most worthy of study. Within recent years, thanks at first to a few critics writing for *Cahiers du Cinéma* in France, the young English groups associated with *Movie* magazine, and especially to Andrew Sarris in this country (his *The American Cinema: Directors and Directions 1929–1968* is discussed later), substantial progress has been made on this huge task. We have begun to identify those directors who were able to impose their own personalities on the assembly-line output in spite of the system and all of the forces that would seem to have militated against that possibility. The phenomenon may represent a unique tribute to human irreducible individuality and unquenchable desire to create. At any rate, out of those walled-fortress-like factories, with their guards and huge cement blocks of sound-proof stages (thought by the literati of the time to be idea-proof as well), there came some works of wit and beauty, of effervescent charm and lasting power.

The process of sifting continues, but to date, and partly with the aid of hindsight, certain major figures seem to stand tall. If the number of names were arbitrarily limited to four, Josef von Sternberg, Howard Hawks, Frank Capra, and John Ford would appear on the lists of many historians as preeminent. Each is very much his own man, with an identifiable personal style evident in both the themes he is drawn toward and the visual treatment of those themes, in his direction of the camera and of what's in front of it. Though all four men started in silent film in the twenties and continued to work fruitfully for decades after the thirties (Hawks and Ford more so than von Sternberg and Capra), they all reached creative maturity in the thirties.

Von Sternberg is the supreme visual stylist. With him the shadow is the substance. In a series of films starring Marlene Dietrich—*Morocco,* 1930; *Dishonored,* 1931; *Shanghai Express,* 1932; *The Scarlet Empress,* 1934; *The Devil Is a Woman,* 1935—he fashioned and perfected his own unique, exotic screen world. To have true value, von Sternberg felt, a film ought to be capable of offering an aesthetic experience when projected upside down and backwards. He had a thorough background as an editor and cameraman, and there is evidence to indicate that he did much of the cinematography on the films he directed. Certainly he understood lighting and used it for extraordinarily intricate and consistent effect. During the last few years of his life, on a campus tour, von Sternberg was asked by a beginning film production class at the University of Iowa to show them how he would light a set. What was intended as a courteous gesture to this old

The Scarlet Empress (U.S., 1934, Josef von Sternberg). Museum of Modern Art/Film Stills Archive.

man provoked gasps of astonishment as, with limited and simple portable lights, von Sternberg began to create his chiaroscuro. It was as if at any moment Dietrich would enter, the lights falling precisely to model those famous features and flare the blonde hair.

It may be a mixed compliment to remark that a still from a von Sternberg film gives a fuller sense of its essence than would a still from any other director's work. John Grierson, leader of the British documentary movement, wrote of him: "When a director dies, he becomes a photographer." What von Sternberg's films may lack in reality or even in drama, they make up in the sort of transcendent vision associated with certain very special painters—those who seem to create worlds to inhabit rather than art objects to be contemplated—like a Paul Delvaux, perhaps. von Sternberg's work is obsessive and strange and perhaps stiff, but it is also beautiful and, above all, haunting.

Hawks is a quite different sort of artist. His is the art that conceals art. Working within the genre conventions he nonetheless managed to state and restate what evidently were for him persistent preoccupations: professionalism, individual courage (and cowardice, its complement), loyalty to the group, friendship among men, and battle between the sexes. He began and ended the thirties with films dealing with flying (*The Dawn Patrol*, 1930; *Only Angels Have Wings*, 1939) and he himself had been a flyer in World War I. In both films Hawks is obviously admiring and loving in his treatment of the aviators. Dangerous flying can be senseless and frightening, but the camaraderie,

Only Angels Have Wings (U.S., 1939, Howard Hawks). Museum of Modern Art/Film Stills Archive.

pride, and bravery it allows for are to be honored. In *Dawn Patrol* there are no women (not even a mention of them, except the mothers of dead aviators), and their absence is filled by a "female" tenderness among the flyers towards each other. *Only Angels Have Wings* sets Jean Arthur off in pursuit of Cary Grant; but, since she is a woman, she can't really understand why the men behave as they do, and she represents a tacit threat to the group. These are some of the consistent thematic materials of Hawks the action director, the director of men's pictures.

Visually there is the notable kinetic energy of his films. *Scarface,* arguably one of the finest of the gangster cycle, moves with a controlled power evident in all aspects, from the details of the actors' performances to the cutting. *Twentieth Century* and *Bringing Up Baby,* two of his screwball comedies, are also explosive with frenetic activity. In the former an egomaniacal Broadway producer (John Barrymore) and his star/mistress (Carole Lombard) batter and rant at each other as the famous train of the title carries the producer from disastrous failure in Chicago to an ingeniously fraudulent attempt at comeback in New York. Money and jealousy are the two motivating factors in this cockeyed love story of sorts. In *Bringing Up Baby* a domineering, scatterbrained Katharine Hepburn has her way finally with scientist Cary Grant through unstoppable energy and wacky charm.

Peter Wollen, in *Signs and Meaning in the Cinema,* acknowledges the dynamism and tension prevalent in all of Hawks's work, its force. He also sees what he calls the crazy comedies as the inverse of the adventure dramas. "They are the agonised exposure of the underlying tensions of the heroic dramas," he writes. "Whereas the dramas show the mastery of man over nature, over woman, over the animal and childish; the comedies show his humiliation, his regression. The heroes become victims; society instead of being excluded and despised, breaks in with irruptions of monstrous farce."[2] The two strata must be taken together, Wollen argues, if we are to get a full sense of the meanings Hawks offers in the recurrent motifs of his films.

Though *It Happened One Night* is of the screwball type, and though others share stylistic similarities, Frank Capra's comedies are essentially social. They present an explicit view of American society, its economy and its politics—a view that is uniquely Capraesque. In *Mr. Deeds Goes to Town* (1936), *You Can't Take It with You* (1938), and *Mr. Smith Goes to Washington* (1939), he celebrates the "little guy" (Gary Cooper/James Stewart)—not as dumb as he seems and certainly once aroused, able to defeat the city slickers and the power figures. His victories are achieved through pluck, persistence, Jean Arthur, and his overwhelming decency, which is matched by the decency of the American people when they see the true situation. Frequently even the villains are redeemed in Capra's films, since at heart they too are usually well intentioned.

Capra country is essentially an idealized small town America (no matter that *You Can't Take It with You* ostensibly takes place in New York City and *Mr. Smith* is set in Washington). He celebrates lovable eccentricities and homely virtues. Even in the thirties his view was clearly nostalgic. Perhaps it would be more accurate to say that the society Capra depicts never existed at all except in his imaginings which, through great artistry, he was able to share with the movie-going public. Similarly, his notion of economics and political action rests on a kind of folksy populism: If the little people would get together and help each other in cooperative endeavors, they could defeat the Depression and unemployment and live in peace and harmony. Richard Griffith, in *The*

---

[2] Peter Wollen, *Signs and Meaning in the Cinema* (London: Secker & Warburg, 1972), p. 91.

Mr. Smith Goes to Washington (U.S., 1939, Frank Capra). Museum of Modern Art/Film Stills Archive.

Film Till Now, labels Capra's conception the "fantasy of goodwill." The huge popular success of his pictures attests to the appeal his vision had in those troubled times. The corollary box office failure of *It's a Wonderful Life* (1946), made with exactly the same ingredients and as finely crafted as any of his films (it's Capra's favorite), suggests that the country in the mid-forties was a radically different place after the experience of World War II. In spite of his own contribution to the war effort in the *Why We Fight* series of documentaries made for the Armed Forces, Capra's own thinking and feeling seem to have remained in the earlier time. Be that as it may, the warmth and affection, the whimsical and engaging charm of his films of the thirties are readily available to anyone who approaches them with sympathy. His mastery as a director should be evident to all.

Finally, John Ford, who, like Hawks and unlike von Sternberg and Capra, continued to do some of his finest work after the thirties, nevertheless shaped his art into personal and full expression during those precedent-setting years. *The Informer* (1935), dealt with earlier in regard to its use of sound, though a very fine film indeed, relates chiefly, among Ford's preoccupations, to his Irishness. It is not one of his favorites, and the strongest creative forces in it seem to have come from the script by Dudley Nichols and the overlay of studio expressionism. It was the cycle that began with *Steamboat 'Round the Bend* (1935) and continued with *The Prisoner of Shark Island* (1936), *Stagecoach* (1939), and *Young Mr. Lincoln* (1939) that showed Ford most clearly as the chronicler of American history, the reworker of American folklore, especially of its frontier West, that he became. *Stagecoach* lifted the non-epic western up to a kind of dignity and mythic evocation that has made it a viable form ever since. Classic in its proportions (the script by Nichols again), it is set in the West of the 1870s, when the frontier was disappearing. It picks up those elements of the gunfighter and his gun, of the moral and ethical decisions, of the kind of courage and code of honor that Robert Warshow wrote about so eloquently in his essay "The Westerner" (in *The Immediate Experience*). From that powerful progenitor stemmed Ford's later *My Darling Clementine* (1946), Hawks's *Red River* (1948), Henry King's *The Gunfighter* (1950), Fred Zinnemann's *High Noon* (1952), George Stevens's *Shane* (1953), Sam Peckinpah's *Ride the High Country* (1961), the westerns of Anthony Mann and Budd Boetticher, and many other important works within this most vigorous and indigenous tradition.

In his own westerns that followed *Stagecoach,* Ford was always concerned with the antithetical forces represented by the human desire to tame the wilderness. In *Signs and Meaning in the Cinema,* again, Wollen ticks off the "pairs of opposites" that run throughout Ford's work: ". . . ploughshare versus sabre, settler versus nomad, European versus Indian, civilised versus savage, book versus gun, married versus unmarried, East versus West."[3] "The master antinomy in Ford's films," Wollen suggests, "is that between the wilderness and the garden."[4]

Ford offers no Rousseau-type arguments for a return to nature, but it is clear in his films that he feels something is lost once the first stages of civilization have been achieved. Though he has dealt with the horse soldier of the U.S. Cavalry even more sympathetically than with the more conventional figure of the gunfighter, it is the same story. Ford's past is a brief epoch that is forever ending and yet stands for us in much the same way that the time and events of the Trojan War did for the ancient Greeks. Looking to our past frontier Ford reminds us of what is best (and also worst) in our society,

Stagecoach (U.S., 1939, John Ford). Museum of Modern Art/ Film Stills Archive.

[3] Wollen, *Signs and Meaning,* p. 94.
[4] Wollen, *Signs and Meaning,* p. 96.

sings the praises of the heroes, and tries to help us understand the villains. The lessons Ford draws from American history are mythical and poetic rather than didactic, however; taken together they tell a very large story from a viewpoint that is more than a little Homeric. This is so not out of academic imitation but because he shares some of the same simple and enduring concerns about the survival of a culture. Ford is more romantic than Homer, of course, but the romance is of strong people and a big country.

In addition to the pleasures they may offer individually, the paradoxes of the American films of the thirties taken as a whole can fascinate endlessly. There is the studio system with its big bosses and front office, mass production and distribution. It allowed for and surely in some ways must have encouraged the scattering of masterpieces among those thousands of films. There is the repressive self-regulation that attempted to bleach art into the palest imitation of life. In the face of this, with ingenuity and energy, the creators managed to retain their robustness and abide only by the letter of the law, sometimes playing with the prim conventions in ways that became fresh and inventive. There are the genres, cycles, and formula pictures with their fixed patterns which at the same time permitted some of the finest directors in all cinema to create some of their best work. Though most of us wouldn't want a return to that kind of film making if it were possible, the films produced out of that special conjunction of system and circumstance continue to provide enjoyment for audiences and inspiration for film makers. One can ask no more of a national period.

FILMS OF THE PERIOD

1929
The Cocoanuts (Joseph Santley and Robert Florey)
The Virginian (Victor Fleming)

1930
Little Caesar (Mervyn LeRoy)
Morocco (Josef von Sternberg)

1931
City Lights (Charles Chaplin)
Frankenstein (James Whale)
The Public Enemy (William Wellman)
Tabu (F.W. Murnau and Robert Flaherty)

1932
I Am a Fugitive from a Chain Gang (LeRoy)
Scarface (Howard Hawks)
Shanghai Express (von Sternberg)
Trouble in Paradise (Ernst Lubitsch)

1933
Duck Soup (Leo McCarey)
42nd Street (Lloyd Bacon)
Gold Diggers of 1933 (LeRoy)

King Kong (Merian C. Cooper and Ernest B. Schoedsack)

1934
It Happened One Night (Frank Capra)
The Scarlet Empress (von Sternberg)
Twentieth Century (Hawks)

1935
A Night at the Opera (Sam Woods)

1936
Fury (Fritz Lang)
The Green Pastures (Marc Connelly and William Keighley)
Mr. Deeds Goes to Town (Capra)
Modern Times (Chaplin)
Swing Time (George Stevens)

1937
Snow White and the Seven Dwarfs (Walt Disney)
A Star Is Born (Wellman)
You Only Live Once (Lang)

1938
Bringing Up Baby (Hawks)

1939
Gone with the Wind (Fleming)
Mr. Smith Goes to Washington (Capra)
Ninotchka (Lubitsch)

Only Angels Have Wings (Hawks)
Stagecoach (John Ford)
Young Mr. Lincoln (Ford)

BOOKS ON THE PERIOD

BALIO, TINO, ed., *The American Film Industry.* Madison: University of Wisconsin Press, 1976. 499 pp.

BAXTER, JOHN, *Hollywood in the Thirties.* Cranbury, N.J.: A. S. Barnes & Co., Inc., 1968. 160 pp.

BAXTER, JOHN, *Sixty Years of Hollywood.* Cranbury, N.J.: A. S. Barnes & Co., Inc., 1973. 284 pp.

BERGMAN, ANDREW, *We're in the Money: Depression America and Its Films.* New York: New York University Press, 1971. 200 pp.

BLUM, DANIEL, *A New Pictorial History of the Talkies,* rev. and enlarged by John Kobal. New York: G. P. Putnam's Sons, 1982.

DAY, BETH, *This Was Hollywood: An Affectionate History of Filmland's Golden Years.* Garden City, N.Y.: Doubleday & Co., Inc., 1960. 287 pp.

DOOLEY, ROGER, *From Scarface to Scarlett: American Film in the 1930s.* New York: Harcourt Brace Jovanovich, Inc., 1981. 704 pp.

EVERSON, WILLIAM K., *The American Movie.* New York: Atheneum Publishers, 1963. 149 pp.

GRIFFITH, RICHARD, ARTHUR MAYER, and EILEEN BOWSER, *The Movies.* New York: Simon & Schuster, Inc., 1981.

GRIFFITH, RICHARD, comp., *The Talkies: Articles and Illustrations from Photoplay Magazine 1928– 1940.* New York: Dover Publications, Inc., 1972. 360 pp.

HIGHAM, CHARLES, *The Art of the American Film, 1900-1971.* Garden City, N.Y.: Doubleday & Co., Inc., 1973. 322 pp.

HUETTIG, MAE D., *Economic Control of the Motion Picture Industry.* Philadelphia: University of Pennsylvania Press, 1944. 163 pp.

JACOBS, LEWIS, *The Rise of the American Film: A Critical History.* New York: Teachers College Press, Columbia University, 1968. 631 pp. (originally published in 1939)

JOBES, GERTRUDE, *Motion Picture Empire.* Hamden, Conn.: Archon Books, 1966. 398 pp.

KINDEM, GORHAM, ed., *The American Movie Industry: The Business of Motion Pictures.* Carbondale and Edwardsville: Southern Illinois University Press, 1982. 448 pp.

SKLAR, ROBERT, *Movie-made America: A Social History of American Movies.* New York: Random House, Inc., 1975. 340 pp.

STANLEY, ROBERT H., *The Celluloid Empire: A History of the American Movie Industry.* New York: Hastings House Publishers, 1978. 328 pp.

TAYLOR, DEEMS, MARCELENE PETERSON, and BRYANT HALE, *A Pictorial History of the Movies.* New York: Simon & Schuster, Inc., 1949. 375 pp.

THORP, MARGARET FARRAND, *America at the Movies.* New York: Arno Press, 1970. 313 pp. (originally published in 1939)

TRENT, PAUL, *Those Fabulous Movie Years: The 30's.* New York: Crown Publishers, Inc., 1975. 192 pp.

WALKER, ALEXANDER, *The Shattered Silents: How the Talkies Came to Stay.* London: Elm Tree Books, 1978.

12

British Wartime Semi-Documentaries and Postwar Comedies, 1939–1955

Along with other social and economic abrasions the 1930s contained the beginnings of World War II in military conquest and imperialist expansion. Japan gobbled up chunks of a China weakened by internal factionalism. Italy overran a defenseless Ethiopia. Germany joined Italy in testing weapons and tactics and helping to defeat the Republicans in Spain. The Germans continued to bluff their way through a series of territorial acquisitions culminating in the notorious Munich agreement concluded between Reichskanzler Adolph Hitler and Prime Minister Neville Chamberlain. On September 1, 1939, German dive bombers took to the skies, and tanks and trucks rolled across the Polish border, causing England and France to declare war on Germany. By some ten months later, not only Poland but France (along with Denmark, Norway, the Netherlands and Belgium) had been ignominiously defeated. Germany's occupation of virtually all of Western Europe was complete, and England was left to fight on alone against that massed power.

Britain's ability to withstand the German onslaught, to endure, with "blood, toil, tears and sweat," made this that nation's "finest hour." Not only did the achievement justify the Churchillian rhetoric, it provided a national mood and spirit that seemed to infuse British life totally. Class tensions that had so preoccupied Britain before the war eased; a new sense of common cause developed. Industrial and agricultural productivity increased; even public health improved, in spite of wartime food shortages and the nightly huddling together of Londoners in the Underground. There was also a considerable revival in the arts, particularly those that best expressed national pride and tradition, such as theater and music.

At the outbreak of war the situation in British film was as usual: The industry was dominated by the Americans. While we call our film industry "Hollywood," where films are made, the English call theirs "Wardour Street," where distribution is head-quartered in London. The entertainment films being distributed and exhibited were mostly American; Gary Cooper, Greta Garbo, James Cagney, Bette Davis commanded the popular audiences. French, and, to a lesser extent, Soviet films attracted the dis-criminating movie-goer in London.

British features lacked distinction and a specific national tradition like French poetic realism or American genres of western, gangster, or musical. Isolated exceptions were the work of Alfred Hitchcock (such as *The Lady Vanishes,* 1938), Anthony Asquith (*Pygmalion,* 1938), or the young Carol Reed (*Bank Holiday,* 1938). But in general, the public regarded British features as second best to Hollywood; the intellectuals were com-pletely indifferent to them.

The British nonfiction film, on the other hand, had achieved a special sort of distinction: The documentary film as we know it developed in Britain in the thirties. Founder and leader of the British documentary movement was John Grierson; the films made under him were sponsored by government and, later, by private industry. These short films of fact established film as an instrument of social and scientific enquiry. Documentary had prestige among the intellectuals and fitted into the thirties' ideas of social utility of the arts. It was a movement with trained and skilled workers, a distinct style, and lasting contributions to film form and technique.

British documentary of the 1930s produced films related to many aspects of public need and national interest. Of primary concern to the film makers was the effect of their films upon the ideas and actions of audiences. Aesthetic and entertainment con-siderations were subordinated to the requirements of communication and informal education. For Grierson, documentary art was the byproduct of a job of work done, as he himself said. British documentaries were designed chiefly to increase general aware-ness of existing social problems and to suggest attitudes that might lead to their solution. Eventually the documentarians came to think of their kind of film making as "a method of approach to public information," its function "to be in the forefront of policy," as Basil Wright, one of Grierson's colleagues, put it.

WARTIME SEMI-DOCUMENTARIES

Growing out of the documentary tradition and fired by the drama of war, a new film form—new in degree if not in kind—appeared. It communicated the concerns of the wartime years with special eloquence, first to the British themselves, then to the rest of the English-speaking peoples. Feature-length, narrative in structure, these films were called semi-documentary. The term was intended to indicate a chronicle of authentic wartime events: part fiction, part fact; part acted, part lived; but always starting from the stuff of actuality rather than from the imagination of a script writer. Produced by both government units and the commercial studios, they not only truly embodied the ethos of the time and place, they exerted considerable influence on postwar film making at home and abroad.

The semi-documentaries took the war itself for their subject matter. Inherent in military engagements are the beginning, middle, and end of Aristotle's dramaturgy, as well as the ultimate dramatic conflict between victory and defeat, life and death. Reenactment of composite and representative incidents constituted the action. Real servicemen played themselves in real bombers and ships and tanks. They simulated a nighttime air raid over Germany, the cruise of a single destroyer, a patrol lost in the desert fighting of North Africa. In those years the facts were much more exciting than any fiction a script writer could conceive. The audience brought great empathy to the global saga that was unfolding around them and on the screens. They were all involved in the war one way or another—were either in service or had friends and loved ones who were, worked in war industries, queued up with ration books to buy groceries, or stood in chow lines, mess kits in hand. If World War II was the first film war, as was said, it was because the documentary, and especially the semi-documentary, achieved a kind of expressiveness and power that affected audiences widely and deeply in a way unequalled in film history.

Target for Tonight (1941), produced by the government Crown Film Unit and directed by Harry Watt, veteran of British documentary, was the prototype. It concerned a bombing raid over Germany. *In Which We Serve* (1942), co-directed by David Lean and Noël Coward, about a destroyer and its crew, was the first of the semi-documentaries to come out of the commercial studios. These two were followed by some twenty or more semi-documentary features from both the government units and the studios, including: *Coastal Command, The Foreman Went to France, One of Our Aircraft is Missing, Next of Kin* (all 1942); *Close Quarters, San Demetrio London, Nine Men, We Dive at Dawn, Millions Like Us* (all 1943); *The Way Ahead* (1944). *The Overlanders* (1946), directed by Watt, produced by Ealing Studios, based on a harrowing wartime cattle drive across the Australian outback, might be thought of as the final film in the cycle. To give a fuller sense of how these films worked at their best, let's examine three particularly successful examples from Crown, which had a wartime record of extraordinary distinction: *Target for Tonight, Fires Were Started,* and *Western Approaches.*

The action of *Target for Tonight* (1941) is representative rather than actual, though enacted entirely by Royal Air Force flyers. It concerns a raid directed against an oil refinery and storage and distribution center at Freihausen. Made early in the war, it was something like whistling in the dark, since most of the bomber traffic was moving in the opposite direction. Its propaganda intent was to show the British and their friends that Britain had not only survived the massive German air raids but now was commencing to strike back.

Roll titles at the beginning explain the RAF table of organization, and the scenes that follow move from Bomber Command down to a particular air field, then to one squadron, and finally concentrate on the crew of a single aircraft, "*F*" (for Freddie). Watt's considerable achievement here was to draw credible and unselfconscious performances from his nonactors. With dialogue added the challenge was even greater than that faced by earlier documentarians. It is much easier to get nonprofessionals to do what they do naturally than to get them to talk about it, especially if they have to speak words or even express ideas that are given to them. There is a consistently nice understatement throughout and some engaging humor. (Someone says of the young Scottish navigator that he wouldn't know whether he was over Hanover or Hampton Court and he, humorless, explains indignantly to the others, "That's a joke.") We get to know the men just well enough to care about their chances of getting back, without losing sight of the larger stakes and of this group as representative of the

Target for Tonight (U.K., 1941, Harry Watt). National Film Archive/Stills Library.

total British effort. It was Watt who initially succeeded in successfully fusing the heightened emotion and characterization of fiction with the authenticity of documentary.

Perhaps the most beautiful and affective of all the wartime semi-documentaries is Humphrey Jennings's *Fires Were Started* (1943). While Jennings had worked in the Grierson group from the mid-thirties on, it was the war that seemed to focus his very special sensibility and intense feelings for England, to supply him an objective correlative as T. S. Eliot would have said. Jennings became without question the wartime film laureate. His other two masterpieces, *Listen to Britain* (1942) and *A Diary for Timothy* (1945), though the first contains vignettes and the latter has five slight stories interwoven, are essentially impressionistic in form, closer to the earlier city symphonies than to the narrative of the semi-documentary. They are also shorts (twenty and forty minutes) rather than features.

Fires Were Started is even more impressive than *Target for Tonight* in the way it informs, persuades, and moves us, all at the same time. It, too, is based on the microcosm group (of the Auxiliary Fire Service) in one engagement (a twenty-four hour shift during one of the great fire raids on London). Jennings went beyond Watt in differentiating and developing the characters of his nonactor real firemen. (Admittedly he has more time: sixty-two minutes to Watt's forty-five). To Watt's great narrative skill Jennings added a touch of the poet—a visual-aural poet who could capture the precise image for a feeling that has symbolic reverberations of both English tradition and wartime exigencies; who could find the exact words men and women might speak, and even the songs they might sing in the circumstances, that would register in the memory of the audience.

By using the device of a new recruit to the unit, Jennings lets us see through the recruit's eyes and learn not only of the functioning of this fire-fighting service but of the diverse and likable personalities brought together in it. When the raid begins we are able to follow the tactics of the firefighters without aid of commentary, through their actions and conversations, the phone calls from headquarters, the maps with pins stuck in them, the chalked lists of equipment. Among other things, *Fires Were Started* is a model of teaching without didacticism.

But where the true greatness of *Fires Were Started* lies is in the depiction of feeling. Take, for example, the marvelous scene in the evening as the men gather their gear and assemble in the recreation room to wait for the raid and their first assignment. Barrett, the new man, is improvising at the piano (he's very good). He picks up the traditional "One Man Went to Mow," adapting the style, with the assistance of one of the veterans in the group, to fit the personality of each man entering—swinging for one of them, ponderous for the chief, and so on.

Later, when the calls have started coming in and most of the units have left, Barrett and his group remain, belting out the old pop American tune "Please Don't Talk About Me When I'm Gone." As the sirens wail, a bomb hits close, shaking the room. After a slight pause the men pick themselves up and with renewed vigor continue their jocular rendition as a chant of defiance into the night skies overhead. It's a moment impossible to describe because it carries with it all of the overtones of meaning of the war to the English people and of their will to survive, in a way that is funny/sad, commonplace/heroic.

Fires Were Started (U.K., 1943, Humphrey Jennings). National Film Archive/Stills Library.

Feelings like these are interlaced throughout much of the film. When the unit winds up the hoses in the gray and grimy morning after a long and exhausting night in which one of their members has been killed, we have a heightened sense of the historical moment not unlike that offered by Shakespeare in scenes of the Battle of Agincourt in *Henry V* (Act IV, scene 3):

> We few, we happy few, we band of brothers;
> For he to-day that sheds his blood with me
> Shall be my brother . . .

And, incidentally, Laurence Olivier's fine film of that play was made during those war years, inspired by and infused with much the same tradition and feeling that is evident in Jennings's work.

Late in the war (1944) *Western Approaches* appeared (called *The Raider* in the U.S. and not released here until 1946). Extremely popular, it was easily the most ambitious of the semi-documentaries in its scale and technical challenges. It deals with the British Merchant Navy and the great convoys that crossed the North Atlantic from America under constant threat of submarine attack to supply Britain and the Allied Forces. To film on the rolling sea at all takes some doing, but to employ the huge and complex Technicolor camera must have added to the difficulties enormously. Also, here the nonactors are made to enact a very tight and demanding script. They are required not only to be believable as the real seamen they are, but to draw from us feelings of extreme tension, of pathos and ironic humor, in ways that are closer to the straight fiction film than the other two semi-documentaries here discussed. It was directed and cowritten by Pat Jackson, another of the documentarians who, like Watt, would continue in the semi-documentary feature after the war. (Jennings was killed in 1950, in a fall while on location in Greece.)

The considerable suspense of *Western Approaches* is built around a three-part configuration of a lifeboat of survivors from a torpedoed freighter, the German U-boat which follows them, using them as bait, and an approaching convoy with a straggling freighter that sights the lifeboat. The men in the lifeboat, adrift for fourteen days, are near the end of their endurance. The evidence that a U-boat is hovering about is far from conclusive, and when the chance to be rescued appears it takes considerable courage (and the stemming of a near mutiny) for the men to choose to warn off the freighter.

The very skill with which the plot and performances were handled carries *Western Approaches* beyond the usual confines of the semi-documentary over into the action melodrama. A curious thing had come about which may indicate that the semi-documentary form has a kind of boomerang built into it; as film makers get better and better at shaping the materials of actuality into artistic form, the point in using them rather than creating pure fiction, with sets and actors, may become lost. If art is usually thought to imitate life, much in *Western Approaches* suggests life imitating art. Though suspense is strong in *Target for Tonight,* less so but present in *Fires Were Started,* here it becomes excruciating in the cat and mouse game we have come to know so well in films about submarine warfare. Jackson's very effectiveness with this aspect led him away from a basic documentary strength maintained in the Watt and Jennings films: appreciation of the nature as well as the danger of the work involved. By giving us the German point of view as well as that from the lifeboat and the convoy, Jackson crossed over most clearly into the fictional mode. The men in the lifeboat not only couldn't see into the submarine, as we are permitted to do, we know that the ''Germans'' are of necessity not Germans.

Western Approaches/The Raider (U.K., 1944, Pat Jackson). National Film Archive/
Stills Library.

Finally, there is the casting of the nonactors. As sure as anything there is a
"James Robertson Justice" (the captain), a "Robert Newton," and a "Donald
Crisp." This convenience of type to help trigger known responses is not as satisfying as
the men in *Fires Were Started,* who seem to communicate something closer to their actual
personalities, with less predictable, fresher, and more varied responses. Though enormously impressive, what Jackson did finally manage to do with his nonactors seems
even less desirable, somehow, than the low-key, comparatively unshaped performances
of *Target for Tonight.*

The extent to which Jackson converted the purpose, subject matter, production
methods, and resultant style of documentary into fiction may raise the question, Where
will it all end? At the same time it shows the flexibility and wide range that exist, and the
many ways within this realistic kind of film making in which fact and fiction can be combined. It also looks ahead to the postwar developments in the American semi-
documentary and problem picture, to the great period of Italian neorealism, and to the
British comedy series that came out of Ealing Studios.

POSTWAR COMEDIES

If the British semi-documentary became as rare soon after the war as it had been
prevalent during wartime, it might be argued that it didn't so much cease as go underground and come up looking and sounding like the Ealing comedy. Michael Balcon,

head of Ealing Studios, had always been a friend of the documentary movement and favored fiction films that were distinctively British rather than imitatively American. When the documentarians began to cross over into feature film making via the wartime semi-documentary it was to Ealing that they came. Alberto Cavalcanti, former production head of the Crown Film Unit, as well as Harry Watt, one of its star directors, were among these. Two of the principal directors of the Ealing comedies, Charles Crichton and Alexander Mackendrick, had had considerable documentary experience. The result of these biases and this personnel, plus the fine writing talents Balcon acquired, especially T. E. B. Clarke, gave the string of comedies their distinctive flavor.

The first of the series was *Hue and Cry,* directed by Crichton in 1947. The lower- and middle-class milieu, location shooting, bumbling crooks and police, and fast pace all typify the Ealing manner. There followed, in fairly rapid succession, *Whiskey Galore* (1949, Mackendrick, *Tight Little Island* in the U.S.), *Passport to Pimlico* (1949, Henry Cornelius), *A Run for Your Money* (1949, Charles Frend), *The Lavender Hill Mob* (1951, Crichton), *The Man in the White Suit* (1951, Mackendrick), *Genevieve* (1953, Cornelius), *The Titfield Thunderbolt* (1953, Crichton), *The Maggie* (1954, Mackendrick, *High and Dry* in the U.S.), *The Ladykillers* (1955, Mackendrick). In 1952 financial problems caused Ealing to sell its studios to BBC-TV; in 1955 the company itself was dissolved. Between 1951 and 1955 similar kinds of comedies were being made at Group 3, a government-financed experiment in feature production headed by John Grierson, former leader of the documentary movement.

These British comedies have much in common with the documentary tradition as well as with each other. They simply turn documentary seriousness on its ear. The themes of the Ealing films are notably social, economic, political, or at least cultural (in the anthropologist's sense), designed to bring out a particular facet of national life. They deal with the Scots' fondness for a wee drop, strict Calvinism, dislike of the English *(Tight Little Island),* the bureaucratic entanglements in which the British found themselves after the war *(Passport to Pimlico),* the expected honesty and trustworthiness of the English middle class *(The Lavender Hill Mob),* the collusion among management and labor, government and opposition within the English system *(The Man in the White Suit).* Laughter is provoked only through the incongruity and exaggeration with which these subjects are treated; even so, the comic style is noteworthy for its deadpan seriousness, underplaying, and throwaway delivery of lines.

Casting called on nonglamorous, quintessentially British actors (rather than stars)—Alistair Sim *(Hue and Cry),* Stanley Holloway *(Passport to Pimlico),* Alec Guinness *(The Lavender Hill Mob, The Man in the White Suit, The Ladykillers)*—and used local citizens as extras. The humor in every case is heightened by realistic background and detail—of cockney London as well as of the Hebrides. The films were shot largely on location, and for *Tight Little Island* Mackendrick even set up processing equipment there so he could look at the rushes without undue delay, just as Robert Flaherty had done for his famous documentary feature *Man of Aran,* shot on an island off the coast of Ireland some fifteen years earlier. *Tight Little Island,* in fact, seems to be rather pointedly kidding the British documentary style in its opening post-card shots of the Hebrides (almost identical with those of the General Post Office Film Unit's *The Islanders*) and voice-over commentary.

This gentle kind of spoofing is well within an old and honorable British tradition, enjoyed abroad as well as at home. If we would not expect the British to kill the thing they love, their famous sense of humor could be aimed at it. From their documentary of the thirties has come a lot that is finest and most British in British cinema, and the

Whiskey Galore/Tight Little Island (U.K., 1949, Alexander Mackendrick). National Film Archive/Stills Library.

rest of the world has shared in their achievement. Documentary has become a respected and enduring mode of film art and communication; the social content and realist style related to it have spread widely into fiction films of many countries.

FILMS OF THE PERIOD

1941
Forty-Ninth Parallel (Michael Powell)
Target for Tonight (Harry Watt)

1942
Coastal Command (J. B. Holmes)
The Foreman Went to France
    (Charles Frend)
In Which We Serve (David Lean and
    Noël Coward)
Next of Kin (Thorold Dickinson)
One of Our Aircraft is Missing (Powell)

1943
Close Quarters (Jack Lee)
Fires Were Started
    (Humphrey Jennings)

Millions Like Us (Frank Launder and
    Sidney Gilliat)
Nine Men (Watt)
San Demetrio, London (Frend)
We Dive at Dawn (Anthony Asquith)

1944
The Way Ahead (Carol Reed)
Western Approaches (Pat Jackson)

1945
The Way to the Stars (Asquith)

1946
The Overlanders (Watt)

1947
Hue and Cry (Charles Crichton)

1949

Passport to Pimlico (Henry Cornelius)
A Run for Your Money (Frend)
Whiskey Galore/Tight Little Island
    (Alexander Mackendrick)

1951

The Lavender Hill Mob (Crichton)
The Man in the White Suit
    (Mackendrick)

1953

Genevieve (Cornelius)
The Titfield Thunderbolt (Crichton)

1954

The Maggie/High and Dry
    (Mackendrick)

1955

The Ladykillers (Mackendrick)

BOOKS ON THE PERIOD

ARMES, ROY, *A Critical History of British Cinema*. New York: Oxford University Press, 1978. 374 pp.

ARTS ENQUIRY, THE, *The Factual Film*. London: Oxford University Press, 1947. 260 pp.

BALCON, MICHAEL, et al., *Twenty Years of British Film: 1925–1945*. New York: Arno Press, 1972. 116 pp. (originally published in 1947)

BARR, CHARLES, *Ealing Studios*. London: Cameron & Tayleur Ltd. in association with David & Charles Ltd., 1977. 198 pp.

BETTS, ERNEST, *The Film Business: A History of British Cinema 1896–1972*. London: George Allen & Unwin Ltd., 1973. 349 pp.

BUTLER, IVAN, *Cinema in Britain: An Illustrated Survey*. South Brunswick, N. J.: A. S. Barnes, 1973.

CURRAN, JAMES, and VINCENT PORTER, eds., *British Cinema History*. Totowa, N. J.: Barnes & Noble Books, 1983. 320 pp.

DURGNAT, RAYMOND, *A Mirror for England: British Movies From Austerity to Affluence*. New York: Praeger, 1971.

OAKLEY, C. A., *Where We Came In: Seventy Years of the British Film Industry*. London: George Allen & Unwin Ltd., 1964. 245 pp.

PERRY, GEORGE, *Forever Ealing: A Celebration of the Great British Film Studio*. London: Pavilion, 1982. 200 pp.

PERRY, GEORGE, *The Great British Picture Show from the 90's to the 70's*. New York: Hill & Wang, 1974. 367 pp.

POWELL, DILYS, *Films Since 1939*. London: Longmans Green & Co., 1947. 40 pp.

13

Hollywood in the Forties, 1940-1952

If the notion of history by the decades is an arbitrary one, it becomes particularly so in regard to the forties in America. Though the preceding decade ended with the outbreak of World War II in Europe, for the United States 1940 and 1941 were really a continuation of the thirties. We had been backing into the war, pushed by the commitment President Franklin D. Roosevelt and other opinion leaders felt to Great Britain and its struggle against Nazi Germany. But the majority of the American public continued isolationist, preoccupied with continuing domestic difficulties. When the Depression finally ended, it didn't die of natural causes; it was merely replaced by the artificial boom of a wartime economy after the Japanese attack on Pearl Harbor pulled us into the war in December, 1941.

America would continue to provide the Allied and neutral countries with the bulk of their screen entertainment. Diversion was required in those stressful years in a way that it hadn't been in other times. The Hollywood films of wartime, for the most part, were more an extension of those of the thirties—appropriately trimmed with references to the war—than a prelude to those of the second half of the forties. The memorable *Casablanca* (1943) is one prominent example, its bittersweet romance tinged with antifascist idealism. To be sure, Orson Welles's exceptional *Citizen Kane* (1941) and *The Magnificent Ambersons* (1942) looked even beyond the forties in their seminal contributions to the evolution of film language and art. The remarkable social satires of Preston Sturges—including *Sullivan's Travels* (1941), *Hail the Conquering Hero*, and *The Miracle of*

Morgan's Creek (both 1944)—would have been astonishing at any time for their ir-reverent wit and were especially so in wartime. Some of the films dealing directly with the war, derived from popular genres and toughened by wartime realities, antedated the realist postwar tendency to be discussed. Among the most popular were *Wake Island* (1942), *Air Force, Bataan, The Moon is Down* (all 1943), *Lifeboat, Thirty Seconds Over Tokyo* (both 1944), and *The Story of G.I. Joe* (1945). But it has been estimated that fewer than a third of the wartime films dealt with the war. More characteristic was the continuation, with home-front themes or military ruffles and flourishes added, of the comedies, the light romantic or family dramas, and the musicals, now increased in number and vital-ity.

Still, the bulk of American films of World War II undoubtedly contributed to the war effort. When not inspirational and hortatory, they were wholesomely entertain-ing and supportive of the culture the war was being fought to preserve. The top box of-fice hits of the war years (films that grossed more than $4 million in rentals in the United States and Canada, according to *Variety*), which also won major awards, were *Mrs. Miniver* and *Yankee Doodle Dandy* (in 1942); *The Song of Bernadette* (in 1943); *Going My Way, Meet Me in St. Louis,* and *Thirty Seconds Over Tokyo* (in 1944); *The Bells of St. Mary's, Lost Weekend,* and *Spellbound* (in 1945). Of these nine films only one directly treated American involvement in the war, *Thirty Seconds Over Tokyo;* another concerned Britain's home front before the U.S. entered the war, *Mrs. Miniver.* Of the rest, four were musicals and/or comedies; one was a biography of a French Catholic religious figure; two of the comedies, *Going My Way* and *The Bells of St. Mary's,* were about Catholic priests and nuns in this country (there were no atheists in the foxholes, a phrase of the time asserted); one was about an alcoholic and alcoholism; one was a suspense-mystery with psychoanalytical trappings.

FILM NOIR

The last two films in the list above, especially *Lost Weekend,* offer evidence of a sort of substratum, or a kind of counterforce, that existed amidst wartime patriotism and wholesomeness. The subgenre or style subsequently identified by French critics as *film noir* was referred to in the close of the chapter on German silent cinema. These dark melodramas of crime and corruption, of psychological dislocation and aberration, reveal a Germanic influence (curious that they should appear during a war with Ger-many) in their intricate and artificial visual style and their preoccupation with dis-ordered psyches. Austrian-born Billy Wilder, who coscripted as well as directed *Lost Weekend,* was one of the masters of the black film. His *Double Indemnity* (1944), which he coscripted with Raymond Chandler, is about a murderous pair of adulterers (Barbara Stanwyck and Fred MacMurray), and preceded *Lost Weekend.* His *Sunset Boulevard* (1950) and *Ace in the Hole/The Big Carnival* (1951) followed it. *Sunset Boulevard* deals with a decaying part of contemporary Hollywood peopled by a megalomaniac silent star (Gloria Swanson), her present butler and former director and husband (Erich von Stroheim), and an opportunistic young screen writer (William Holden). *Ace in the Hole* concerns a cynical and ruthless newspaper reporter (Kirk Douglas) who exploits human tragedy in an effort to regain his lost professional status. The latter was the only Wilder film up to that point that was not successful commercially, and it came near the end of the noir impulse, Wilder himself turning to comedies in which the black touches could be made more palatable.

Noir, an attitude as well as a style, descended not only from German expressionism of the 1920s but from French poetic realism of the 1930s, especially the films of Carné-Prévert. In Hollywood in the mid-forties it emerged in the work of a few German and Austrian expatriates. Along with Wilder there were Robert Siodmak (*Phantom Lady,* 1944; *The Spiral Staircase,* 1945; *The Killers,* 1946), Otto Preminger (*Laura,* 1944; *Fallen Angel,* 1945), and Fritz Lang (*The Woman in the Window,* 1944; *Scarlet Street,* 1945). It spread to include films of a number of other distinguished Hollywood professionals, among them Alfred Hitchcock *(Shadow of a Doubt,* 1943; *Rope,* 1948; *The Paradine Case,* 1948) and Michael Curtiz (*Mildred Pierce,* 1945; *The Unsuspected,* 1947). And it cut across genres: private eye (*The Maltese Falcon,* John Huston, 1941; *Murder, My Sweet,* Edward Dmytryk, 1944; *The Big Sleep,* Howard Hawks, 1946), gangster (*Kiss of Death,* Henry Hathaway, 1947; *Cry of the City,* Siodmak, 1948; *White Heat,* Raoul Walsh, 1949), and even the fight picture (*The Set-Up,* Robert Wise, 1949).

The fantasies the noir films offered were wrought with intelligence, cynicism, and considerable skill. Theirs is a nightmare hallucination full of indecipherable complications, a pervasive sense of threat, of fear and helplessness in the face of enigmatic human malevolence. The protagonists are typically trying to comprehend the incomprehensible motives that exist within their subterranean world; they are trapped, seeking to find their way out of a tortuous labyrinth of unpleasantness, violence, and evil. It's Dick Powell, as Raymond Chandler's Philip Marlowe in *Murder, My Sweet,* who is drugged and beaten, endlessly it seems, as he tries to trace the whereabouts of a missing woman someone doesn't want him to find. He encounters a dim-witted amorous giant, an aging drink-sodden floozy, an ailing millionaire and his lecherous and lethal young wife, as well as other denizens of this shadowy netherworld in a succession of late-night bars and sleazy apartments. Or, it's the weak, lonely, middle-aged Edward G. Robinson in *The Woman in the Window* (quite literally a nightmare of lust, crime, and entrapment) and *Scarlet Street* as he reaches out for the unobtainable and deceptive appearance of young loveliness in a corrupt and predatory Joan Bennett. Or it's Ella Raines of the hollow cheeks and shoulder-length hair, more wraith than actress, in *Phantom Lady,* trying to find the persons and the reasons behind the frameup of her lover. The scenes with the hopped-up jazz drummer (Elisha Cook, Jr.), with the swirling cigarette smoke, the glaring lights and harsh shadows, the oblique camera angles, the tension of the editing, and the brittleness and vulnerability of the human figure, are characteristic of noir.

As opposed to the idealism of the society fighting together to combat the political evil of fascism, film noir dealt with individuals conspicuously antisocial in their greed and selfishness, driven to betrayal, violence, and crime (usually including murder) out of an incurable sickness (often ending in death or incarceration). Their malaise was presented as endemic to the human species, and the world they inhabited was a dark one literally as well as morally. The films seem to take place mostly at night, in seedy furnished apartments and on rain-washed streets of big cities. A jungle atmosphere was created in those studio sets (a human jungle, an asphalt jungle, a neon jungle), with predators stalking prey and danger lurking in the shadows, intermittently revealed by flashing electric signs.

The noir films eschewed the direct social meanings of the gangster films of the thirties, just as they remained in opposition to the liberal films of good causes of the late

Murder, My Sweet (U.S., 1944, Edward Dmytryk). Museum of Modern Art/Film Stills Archive.

forties though they shared realist aspects with both. They were clearly popular, perhaps appealing to something in audiences that distrusted the official rhetoric and optimism espoused by the dominant political forces. If not among the big hits, for the most part, the noir films continued as a steady stream.

REALISM

The prestigious pictures of the postwar forties were not the noir films, however. Among those that were part of that tradition only *The Killers* (1946), *Kiss of Death* (1947), and *Sunset Boulevard* (1950) received major awards for their years. On the other hand, films with a heightened realism and/or dealing with social problems appeared frequently among those honored by the New York Film Critics, the National Board of Review, and *Film Daily,* or were nominated for Academy Awards as best picture of the year. The 1946 award winners included *The Best Years of Our Lives* (readjustment to civilian life by returning servicemen) and *A Walk in the Sun* (authentic portrayal of an infantry combat mission). In 1947 there were *Boomerang* (justice for the individual under the law), *Crossfire* and *Gentleman's Agreement* (both dealing with anti-Semitism in the U.S.). Among the award winners of 1948, *Call Northside 777* was a re-creation of an actual criminal investigation, and *The Naked City* offered a detailed, on-location account of the work of a New York City police homicide squad. *The Snake Pit* dealt with treatment of the insane; *State of the Union* with the functioning of American national party politics. In 1949 *All the King's*

Men was about a Southern political demagogue unmistakably modeled on former Louisiana governor Huey Long; *Home of the Brave, Intruder in the Dust,* and *Pinky* were about prejudice and discrimination directed against blacks. In 1950 there were *No Way Out,* also about racial discord, *The Men,* a painfully realistic drama of the rehabilitation of war casualties, and *Panic in the Streets,* concerning the responsibility of government officials for protecting the citizenry from epidemic disease, much of it shot on location in New Orleans. In 1951, *Fourteen Hours* was based on actuality, in which a disturbed young man on a window ledge high above Manhattan threatens to jump while friends and police try to dissuade him. *Death of a Salesman,* a transcription of Arthur Miller's play, indicted the ways in which America's economic system and values cramped and warped the lives of some of its citizens.

If the British were able to hang onto some of the aspects of documentary within their comedies, the Americans were drawn toward a tradition of exposé which had special need for a kind of fiction film making that stayed close to actuality. The American postwar equivalent to the British wartime semi-documentary began with *The House on 92nd Street* (1945), produced by Louis de Rochemont, former creative chief of *The March of Time* series.

Of three more or less distinct subspecies of the American fictional film with documentary tendencies, *The House on 92nd Street* fits into the one of films based on fact, on real persons or incidents. It re-created an actual FBI investigation that had uncovered a German espionage ring centered in New York City. It also contained many documentary-like stylistic characteristics, and even some blown-up 16mm footage of the

The House on 92nd Street (U.S., 1945, Henry Hathaway). Museum of Modern Art/Film Stills Archive.

German agents taken surreptitiously by the FBI. *House on 92nd Street* was followed by *Boomerang* (1947, also produced by de Rochemont), based on events in the life of Homer Cummings, who had become Attorney General of the United States under Franklin Roosevelt. *Call Northside 777* (1948) is another example. It recounted the efforts of a crusading Chicago newspaperman that led to the exoneration of a prisoner who had already served ten years of a life sentence for the murder of a policeman.

Closely allied to the based-on-fact picture was "the inside story": how a police department works, for example. In *The Naked City* (1948, produced by former newspaperman Mark Hellinger) the emphasis and most of the running time are given to the dogged, dull, day-to-day routine of trying to track down a murderer living somewhere among New York's millions. *The Frogmen* (1951) devotes at least two-thirds of its footage to clear and interesting exposition of how Navy underwater demolition teams are trained. Only the final scenes of a mission into a Japanese-held harbor seem within the more familiar mode of screen heroics. The same documentary emphasis on how a thing is done pervades the opening passages of *13 Rue Madeleine* (1946, de Rochemont again producer), which deals with the training and a mission of Office of Strategic Services personnel.

Finally there were the "problem pictures," which sometimes didn't look as real as the above two categories but which did attempt to come to some sort of grips with real problems. It was in this line that the exposé tendency was strongest—films dealing with alcoholism (*The Lost Weekend,* 1945), prisons (*Brute Force,* 1947, Hellinger producer), and mental health (*The Snake Pit,* 1948), for example. A whole cycle concerning race relations began in 1947 with *Crossfire* and *Gentleman's Agreement,* both concerning anti-Semitism, and quickly moved to relations between blacks and whites. In 1949 alone there were *Home of the Brave* (produced by Stanley Kramer, who specialized in the problem picture), *Lost Boundaries* (de Rochemont once more), *Pinky, Intruder in the Dust* (the finest of the cycle), and others.

The trend toward realism of treatment, and social problems as subjects in American film lasted from the immediate postwar years to the early 1950s. It ceased in an outbreak of political paranoia that came to be known as McCarthyism.

LIBERALISM, COMMUNISM, AND ANTICOMMUNISM; THE HOUSE UN-AMERICAN ACTIVITIES COMMITTEE AND BLACKLISTING

Though in some ways World War II was a cataclysmic event in the history of this nation, in other ways it proved to be only an interruption of some of the tensions of the thirties, especially the political ones. In the decade before the war, left-wing activities in the United States had achieved an unprecedented vigor and popularity. While the forces of conservatism and reaction feared the "communist influence" at home and abroad, and attempted to check it through the power of capitalist business and government, they were ultimately ineffectual in halting a leftward swing. Some felt the New Deal itself represented a kind of totalitarian communism, with its powerful presidential leader and its sweeping program of social change. Even more unsettling, during the war the pre-eminent communist state, the Soviet Union, became our ally in the fight against fascism.

In the U.S. following the war, after a brief period of optimism about a new

United Nations and attempts to ameliorate racial and ethnic discrimination and class and partisan differences, a new climate, or return to an older climate, developed. By the late forties we were locked into a fierce struggle with the U.S.S.R. and international communism, and had become prey to fears of communist subversion in our midst. Now the reactionaries, supported by great numbers of unthinking conservatives and some frightened liberals, led us into a period of military belligerence abroad and political repression at home that would climax in the early fifties in the Korean War and congressional investigating committees instigated most conspicuously by Senator Joseph McCarthy, Republican of Wisconsin.

The films of the time reflected the prevailing shift in political sentiment. When Russia had been our ally during World War II, Hollywood had made some pro-Soviet films, most notably *Mission to Moscow* (1943), *The North Star* (1943), and *Song of Russia* (1944). By 1951, one of the increasing number of anticommunist films, *I Was a Communist for the FBI,* was nominated by the Academy of Motion Picture Arts and Sciences as best feature-length documentary. In 1952 another anticommunist film, *The Hoaxters,* more properly categorized as documentary, received a nomination for the same award, and the anticommunist fiction feature *My Son John* was named by the National Board of Review among its ten best for the year. The rest of the films receiving major awards in 1952 were noticeably removed from contemporary domestic reality and its problems.

The appearance of the first anticommunist films after the war occurred following an investigation in 1947 by the House Un-American Activities Committee (HUAC) into alleged communist influence in Hollywood. Initially, the industry united to oppose such an inquiry as unnecessary, punitive, and itself un-American in infringing civil liberties. In Hollywood a Committee for the First Amendment (which guarantees freedom of speech and opinion) was organized by film directors William Wyler and John Huston, and screenwriter Philip Dunne. A sizeable delegation from the industry, headed by Eric Johnston, president of the Motion Picture Association of America, and including such celebrities as Lauren Bacall, Humphrey Bogart, John Huston, Gene Kelly, Danny Kaye, and Jane Wyatt, appeared before the HUAC in Washington to protest its activities.

They weren't called upon immediately, however. Instead, the committee called on a series of witnesses whose ties or sympathies with the Communist Party had been suggested by its earlier investigations. John Howard Lawson, screenwriter and leader in Hollywood guild and union organizing, was first to be heard. He angrily denounced the committee and refused to answer its questions. His prepared statement, which he was not allowed to read, began: "For a week this committee has conducted an illegal and indecent trial of American citizens, whom the committee has selected to be publicly pilloried and smeared." Lawson was followed by nine other "unfriendly" witnesses, who also refused to answer the committee's questions about their political beliefs and associations and invoked the First Amendment to the Constitution. The "Hollywood Ten," as they came to be known, comprised, in addition to Lawson, screenwriters Alvah Bessie, Lester Cole, Ring Lardner, Jr., Albert Maltz, Samuel Ornitz, and Dalton Trumbo; directors Herbert Biberman and Edward Dmytryk; and producer Adrian Scott. All were cited for contempt of Congress.

In the face of the unfavorable publicity occasioned by the truculent defiance of these ten witnesses and the allegations of communist infiltration made by "friendly" ones (including actors Adolphe Menjou, Robert Taylor, Robert Montgomery, George Murphy, Ronald Reagan, and Gary Cooper; producer-directors Sam Wood, Leo Mc-

Carey, and Walt Disney; and executives Jack Warner and Louis B. Mayer), the Committee for the First Amendment collapsed, and the studio heads and principal independent producers hastily met at the Waldorf-Astoria Hotel in New York City. The Waldorf statement, which resulted, deplored the action of the ten Hollywood men who had refused to testify. Its key concession, a complete reversal from the producers' earlier opposition to the intentions and procedures of HUAC, read as follows: ''We will not knowingly employ a Communist or a member of any party or group which advocates the overthrow of the Government of the United States by force or by any illegal or unconstitutional methods'' (aims alleged to be those of the Communist Party U.S.A.).

That sentence was followed by a paragraph which, ironically, while arguing for reasonableness and humanitarianism, described what already had happened and predicted precisely the situation that would arise as a result of the industry's changed stance.

> In pursuing this policy, we are not going to be swayed by hysteria or intimidation from any source. We are frank to recognize that such a policy involves dangers and risks. There is the danger of hurting innocent people. There is the risk of creating an atmosphere of fear. Creative work at its best cannot be carried on in an atmosphere of fear. We will guard against this danger, this risk, this fear.[1]

The Hollywood Ten were sent to jail, and the industry moved into the era of blacklisting, in which people who were suspected of opinions and activities on the political left were denied employment. Failing to establish the presence of communist propaganda in the Hollywood film, HUAC sought to remove from the industry those who might have been able to support communism through their incomes and prestige. The studio heads were not primarily concerned either with possible communist subversion or with violation of democratic principles. What rendered them compliant with the committee's wishes was the fear of boycott and picketing of theaters by indignant citizens. Such picketing did actually occur and numerous pressure groups joined HUAC in the attack on the industry. The largest, most energetic, and most powerful of these was the American Legion, which insistently demanded that Hollywood ''clean house.''

In 1951 and following, in the Hollywood ''mass hearings,'' over two hundred motion picture workers were named as suspected communists or supporters by HUAC. These congressional investigations into communism became, in fact, trials of the witnesses called. Those appearing before the committee who claimed protection under the Fifth Amendment to the Constitution (designed to protect witnesses from incriminating themselves) were automatically assumed to be ''guilty.'' A bizarre extralegal system of ''clearances'' was set up by the industry and representatives of the pressure groups to ''rehabilitate'' those accused individuals who were willing to meet the requirements made of them. Public confession and recantation, including the naming of former political associates, was required from the admitted communists. Noncommunists with suspicious liberal tendencies had to repudiate their past political attitudes and behavior and promise to sin no more in a letter to the studio executive employing them. Those who were named by HUAC or one of the anticommunist organizations and were un-

---

[1] Quoted in John Cogley, *Report on Blacklisting I. Movies* (Santa Barbara, Calif.: The Fund for the Republic, 1956), p. 22.

willing to take such steps could no longer find employment in the Hollywood industry. Some screen writers were able to sell their work under assumed names, at greatly reduced rates; some directors worked under pseudonyms on low-budget productions abroad. The blacklisted actors and actresses, whose presence on the screen could not be concealed, had no recourse.

The blacklisting continued even after HUAC's final Hollywood hearing in 1954. The economic damage suffered by hundreds of individuals and their families—with accompanying anger and fear, bitterness and humiliation—was matched by the corrosive effect on the morale of the industry as a whole. The inhibiting and vitiating influence of the political climate became evident in the films as Hollywood headed into the fifties. The documentary residue of World War II was washed away, replaced by glossy wrappings and bland content. Meaningful statements about contemporary American society were sometimes made within modest genre pictures or might appear in cryptic form in more ambitious productions; but, in general, the integrity, assurance, and purposefulness that had begun to mark the work of a few of the American film makers coming out of the war years was missing in the decade that began with the election of Dwight Eisenhower as president in 1952 and will be dealt with in Chapter 16.

SIX DIRECTORS

I have chosen to focus on these film makers: Alfred Hitchcock, William Wyler, Preston Sturges, Orson Welles, Michael Curtiz, and John Huston. My choice is somewhat arbitrary, because all continued to direct after the 1940s, several doing especially noteworthy work later. In addition, the directors we will deal with in Chapter 16, on the American fifties, directed in the forties as well. And the forenamed directors are only some of those who were important during this period, and only some of their films are discussed here. At the time these six were regarded generally—by the Hollywood community, by critical and box office responses—as worthy of attention.

Alfred Hitchcock begins the list partly because his American career (following his British one) began in 1940, when he was imported by producer David O. Selznick to direct *Rebecca.* That film was followed by the much more characteristic *Foreign Correspondent* (1940), produced by Walter Wanger. As an espionage thriller, it connects back to Hitchcock's British successes (*The Man Who Knew Too Much,* 1934; *The Thirty-Nine Steps,* 1935; *The Lady Vanishes,* 1938); and ahead to later American ones, such as *Saboteur* (1942) and *Notorious* (1946). The latter film, invoking recent memories of German espionage (Claude Rains as master spy), American counterespionage (Ingrid Bergman and Cary Grant, the agents), and atomic secrets, is a most expert blend of sex, suspense, and humor, with Hitchcock in full control of the medium.

A second line, which also had British precedents (*The Lodger,* 1926; *Blackmail,* 1929), combined murder mystery (or mystery of suspected murderous intent) with psychological probing. It includes *Suspicion* (1941), *Shadow of a Doubt* (1943), *Spellbound* (1945), and *Strangers on a Train* (1951). Of these, *Shadow of a Doubt* and *Strangers on a Train* seem darkest and most disturbing. The first involves a multiple murderer (Joseph Cotton); his namesake niece (Teresa Wright), who has incestuous feelings for him; and a very real small California town. In the second, an exchange of killings—of a wife by one stranger for a father by the other—is engineered by an equally evil, charming, and psychotic villain (played by Robert Walker).

Shadow of a Doubt (U.S., 1943, Alfred Hitchcock). Museum of Modern Art/Film Stills Archive.

Not only do Hitchcock's films contain ambiguities, they have provoked still-continuing arguments over whether they are merely conventional, rather mechanical entertainments contrived by a cynical manipulator of audience expectations, or whether they are, beneath their cleverness and skill, moral meditations stemming from their maker's strict Catholic upbringing and emotionally repressed adulthood. In either case, they are about life and death, guilt and punishment, the temptations to innocence and tortured pleasures of sin, the omnipresence and commonplaceness of evil. In either case, also, they reveal their creator's considerable experience and careful study of movie making (or "pure cinema," as he would prefer it).

Whatever their maker's true creative intentions, Hitchcock's films have been extraordinarily attractive to both pit and gallery. Huge audiences have gone to see each film because it was a Hitchcock film. As much serious critical writing has been published about the Hitchcock films—also because they are Hitchcock films—as about those of any other film maker. As both popular and critical successes, he and his films stand out prominently in the history of cinema.

When Hitchcock helped prepare a script for *Rebecca,* Selznick complained that he had turned Daphne du Maurier into Alfred Hitchcock. Selznick would not have been troubled in this way by William Wyler, whose tendency would have been to turn Wyler into du Maurier. If Wyler is faulted in any way by the critics, it is usually only as lacking his own identity as an artist; he is universally praised as being among the finest of interpreters and most expert of directors.

Wyler's directorial career began in the 1920s with westerns. In the 1930s he directed a number of noteworthy films, frequently based on dramatic or literary works (*Dead End,* 1937; *Jezebel,* 1938; *Wuthering Heights,* 1939). He began the 1940s as his career had begun, with a western called *The Westerner.* It is his only film of this period that was not an adaptation of an already successful play or novel. The plays are: Somerset Maugham's *The Letter* (1940); Lillian Hellman's *The Little Foxes* (1941); the play made from Henry James's novel, *Washington Square, The Heiress* (1949); Sidney Kingsley's *Detective Story* (1951). The novels are: Jan Struther's *Mrs. Miniver* (1942); MacKinlay Kantor's *Glory for Me,* which became *The Best Years of Our Lives* (1946); Theodore Dreiser's *Carrie* (1952).

Of these films, the much-awarded *The Best Years of Our Lives* would seem most to embody Wyler's personal response to life in addition to his response to another artist's art. It followed wartime service in the Air Force and the making of the documentary *Memphis Belle* (1944), which provided Wyler an opportunity to know bombardiers like the one played by Dana Andrews. The script, by Robert E. Sherwood, centers on three servicemen returning to civilian life at the end of the war (the other two played by Fredric March and nonactor amputee Harold Russell). It examines the varied and representative problems faced by each with honesty and compassion. The details of time and place, situation and attitude, are exact. In terms of visual style, many of the scenes involve complex compositions in great depth, including multiple planes of action. One that sticks in mind takes place in a bar. A group at the piano, including two of the protagonists, is in the right foreground; several persons at the bar are in left middle ground reacting to the piano playing; the third protagonist is telephoning in center background. The cinematography is by Gregg Toland, who was important to a number of Wyler's finest films. *Best Years* was produced by Samuel Goldwyn, for whom Wyler did much of his best work.

Like Hitchcock, Wyler was admired by the Hollywood community for his professionalism. His direction was also admired by many distinguished foreign film makers—some whose approaches seem quite different from his (Akira Kurosawa and Satyajit Ray, for example)—who recognized his great skill and learned from it. Audiences went in large numbers to films directed by William Wyler, but they went to see a movie of a play they had heard about or a book they had read, or to see stars they liked, rather than to a Wyler film. No harm in that if the movie was an expert and moving rendition and the stars' performances were fully rounded, rich, and satisfying. Wyler frequently met these requirements.

Preston Sturges was not dependent on others for his material; he wrote his own. In fact, he began as a writer (of plays before films), directing his first film, *The Great McGinty,* in 1940. It is the writing—the idiosyncratic, not to say "wacky," behavior and dialogue of his characters—that provides the special charm of his films. The behaving and talking were done by character actors assembled by Sturges at Paramount. They appear again and again—for instance, William Demarest and Franklin Pangborn. If the technique of his films is not as "cinematic" as that of Hitchcock or Wyler, the content has a consistency and coherence that mark him as a distinctive film maker. Within his frames are enclosed representations of the United States of America in the early 1940s as it looked to him.

The Lady Eve (1941) and *The Palm Beach Story* (1942) cover the upper classes. In the former, Barbara Stanwyck plays a professional gambler (who becomes Lady Eve), in feigned then real amorous pursuit of Henry Fonda, as Charles "Hopsy" Pike, heir to an ale fortune, but almost exclusively interested in snakes. The latter film offers a satirical commentary on success and marital tension, exposing the unrivaled effectiveness of sexual manipulation in a supposedly puritanical society, and the American ideal of luxurious ease as it is lived by the jovially senile members of the Ale and Quail Club.

The Miracle of Morgan's Creek and *Hail the Conquering Hero* (both 1944) take care of the middle class, the American small town, parenthood, marriage, and patriotism, in one fell (or should it be fallen) swoop. The "miracle" is the birth of sextuplets; the comic problem is that the father/husband seems to be a GI who had met and married the wife/mother on his last night before going overseas and whose name she has forgotten. The "hero" is Woodrow Lafayette Pershing Truesmith (Eddie Bracken), discharged from the Marines for chronic hay fever, who is presented to his home town as a genuine Marine hero by a bunch of genuine Marine heroes.

Sullivan's Travels (1941) surveys the whole social scene from the posh elegance of a (perhaps Beverly Hills) mansion to the deprivation and brutality of a (perhaps Georgia) chain gang, including movie makers and the making of movies about the social scene. The conclusion reached by Sullivan, and presumably by Sturges, is that the most socially useful thing a film maker can do is to make the audience laugh. Sturges makes us laugh a lot; but if we laugh with him, it is always at ourselves.

Orson Welles came to Hollywood following a phenomenal burst of creative leadership and experimentation in theater and radio. He was twenty-six when his first film, *Citizen Kane* (1941), was released. It became a landmark in the history of film, like *The Birth of a Nation* or *Potemkin* before it. What *Kane* did was to move film into the

The Best Years of Our Lives (U.S., 1946, William Wyler). Museum of Modern Art/Film Stills Archive.

Hail the Conquering Hero (U.S., 1944, Preston Sturges). Museum of Modern Art/Film Stills Archive.

modernism present in the other arts. With its unconventional approach to theme, character, and narrative, as well as its range of cinematic technique, it would become a source book for future film makers. If, as Rick Altman has observed, modernist narrative "is usually associated with the foregrounding of filmic language, multiple levels of narration, and estrangement of the spectator,"[2] *Citizen Kane* might be said to be fully if not overly qualified for modernity.

The fictional Charles Foster Kane, played by Welles, was modeled closely enough on the real William Randolph Hearst to make him furious and vengeful. At the time of Kane's death, with which the film begins, Kane is a lonely and egocentric man of vast wealth and failed political ambition. He had built a newspaper empire, and his life is now investigated by a reporter for a new form of the press, a *March-of-Time*-like screen magazine. The edited work print of an issue of *News on the March* gives us our first account of Kane.

Using investigative journalism as a device, script writers Herman J. Mankiewicz and Welles track back through Kane's life with interview and flashback recollection from his banker-guardian, his business manager, his best friend, his second wife, and his butler. From their divergent points of view, we are presented with different Kanes. Though we learn about the complexity of his activities, neither we nor the reporter get at Kane's essence. We do find out what "rosebud," his final word, referred to, as the reporter does not, but we are left standing at just as much a distance from him—the sort of distancing or estrangement of the spectator employed by Bertolt Brecht.

[2] Rick Altman, ed., *Genre: The Musical* (London: Routledge & Kegan Paul, 1981), p. 159

   As for filmic language, it is pushed very much into the foreground, obviously and brilliantly used to dazzling effect. The great depth of field of the images was provided by cinematographer Gregg Toland and made possible by improvements in film stock, light sources, and optics. It introduces a kind of intricacy in the relationship of characters to setting and to each other. It permits, in fact demands, a fuller "reading" than the selectivity and emphasis of image practiced by Griffith and Eisenstein, which had been developed into the standard technique of filmed narrative. Ceilings are present in *Kane's* rooms, as they usually are not in film rooms; low angles and chiaroscuro lighting abound. The soundtrack takes on the acoustical character of the surroundings. Sound montage, growing out of Welles's radio work, includes a character beginning a sentence in one scene and completing it later in a different location; or, in a famous sequence, wittily and concisely suggesting through breakfast conversation and then lack of it the deterioration over a period of time of Kane's first marriage.

   Many of the characteristics of *Kane*—deep-focus cinematography, innovative uses of sound, exceptional performances from members of Welles's Mercury Theatre troupe (Joseph Cotton, Agnes Moorehead, Roy Collins, with Welles as narrator)—

Citizen Kane (U.S., 1941, Orson Welles). Freelance.

were present in Welles's second film, *The Magnificent Ambersons* (1942), but RKO terminated his contract before he finished it and he exerted no control over the editing of the final version. *The Lady from Shanghai* and *Macbeth* (both 1948) are both accomplished and both very Wellesian, each in its own way.

Welles's career has continued. As a film maker, he has had some inspired flashes and some partially realized creations. There has also been his exploitation of a highly theatrical personality and impressive girth, as performer and celebrity; and much discussion with interviewers and by critics, especially French ones, about his film making. But of his work to date, it is for *Citizen Kane* that he will be most remembered. If Charles Foster Kane's fortune came out of a silver lode, the film that contains him has yielded its own kind of riches to generations of viewers.

Welles has been the darling of critics who regard the director as "author" of the work; Michael Curtiz confounds them. His films offer no evident signature, as do those of Hitchcock, Sturges, and Welles, nor even consistent professional expertise, like Wyler's. Most of the extraordinary number of films Curtiz directed—beginning in Hungary (1912–19), continuing in Austria (1919–26), then in the United States (from 1926 until his death in 1962)—seem unmemorable. His American films, some forty-five in the 1930s alone, range as widely across genres as one could conceive, the misses more or less balanced by the hits, with some particularly effective and lasting historical action-adventures starring Errol Flynn: *Captain Blood* (1935), *The Charge of the Light Brigade* (1936), *The Adventures of Robin Hood* (1938, codirected by William Keighley), *The Sea Hawk* (1940).

But in the 1940s he directed three films that are quite special, markedly different from each other, and very much of their time and place. Although the extent of Curtiz's contribution to their creation can't be determined, their commercial and critical success are unquestionable.

Yankee Doodle Dandy (1943) is a biography of that most popular and most American of theater people, playwright, producer-director, and performer George M. Cohan. James Cagney plays the title role, Walter Huston his father. This is as satisfying a bit of nostalgia, as charming and cheering a tribute to American vaudeville and musical theater, as has been created. Was it Michael Curtiz (*ne* Mihály Kertész) who was responsible for this very native accomplishment? Who is/are saying all of those splendid things about the Cohans, about an earlier period in this country, about its popular musical forms?

Yankee Doodle Dandy was followed by that ultimate romantic Hollywood delight, *Casablanca* (1943). In it Dooley Wilson tinkling away at the piano and growling "As Time Goes By" leads us all to believe in and care what happens to Rick, aka Humphrey Bogart, and Ilsa, aka Ingrid Bergman, as much as we've cared for any screen lovers, and maybe to confuse them with ourselves. In this instance the themes and settings are European and North African; its charm is thoroughly contemporary, topical even, and thoroughly cosmopolitan.

But if we were to think that Curtiz had finally settled into his own true sensibilities, *Mildred Pierce* (1945) put the thought to rest. That film, from the novel by James M. Cain, is at one and the same time a masterful example of film noir, a vehicle for presenting its star Joan Crawford's persona as directly and forcefully as it has ever appeared, and a dark, complicated, devastating commentary on American materialism, sexuality, and parenthood. These ingredients, plus the great style and control evident, have ensured its survival, and account for its power with audiences today.

Casablanca (U.S., 1943, Michael Curtiz). Freelance.

Each of these three films of Curtiz is a singular achievement; taken together—and one could add other fine films he directed—they seem to represent as well the studio system within which they were made (Warner Brothers in Curtiz's case). A system instead of, or at least as well as, artistic genius would seem to be required for varied excellence of this sort.

John Huston worked both inside and outside that system, and many observers feel that his best work was done inside. Certainly the films he made between 1940 and 1952 represent him at his best and virtually bracket the period we've been dealing with. All of them have to do with groups of people undertaking dangerous enterprises at great risk, even involving death; all but one of them end in failure. In them Huston demonstrates special talent for a kind of sentimental realism and observation of the particularities of human behavior that seem to have literary analogues in the writing of Ernest Hemingway.

The Maltese Falcon (1941) was Huston's first direction—he had been a screenwriter before that—and its success established a private-eye formula and the beginning of film noir. The performances of the cast—Humphrey Bogart, Mary Astor, Peter Lorre, Sydney Greenstreet—are definitive, for the genre and for each of them, and would often be repeated.

Huston's documentary work during World War II seemed to strengthen his qualities as an American realist. *The Battle of San Pietro* (1945) is a close and sensitive study of infantry combat, accurate in fact and feeling, a film of permanent value. Following the war, Huston directed a succession of what are his most representative features.

The Treasure of the Sierra Madre (1948), from a novel by B. Traven, is about three men (played by Humphrey Bogart, Tim Holt, and Huston's father, Walter Huston) prospecting for gold in Mexico in the 1920s. They find it and then lose it. *The Asphalt Jungle* (1950) is similar in many ways, though set in the contemporary urban United States. In it a group of men come together to commit a big jewel robbery. They obtain the jewels, but suspicion and treachery and their own psychological weaknesses lead each to his death or capture. *The Red Badge of Courage* (1951), an adaptation of the Stephen Crane novel of the Civil War, deals with a young man's initiation into the terrors of warfare, its stupidities, brutalities, and pointlessness.[3]

In *The African Queen* (1952) the group consists of two (Katharine Hepburn as the missionary's prim sister and Humphrey Bogart as the hard-bitten riverboat captain), unless one counts the rickety, quirky steam launch of the title on which they escape down river from German East Africa at the outbreak of World War I. This is the adventure, from the C. S. Forester novel, with a script by James Agee and Huston, that ends in success: They do escape, their lives have been changed for the better as a result of their enforced intimacy under perilous conditions over a period of weeks. But perhaps

Treasure of the Sierra Madre (U.S., 1948, John Huston). Museum of Modern Art/Film Stills Archive.

[3] The making of this film and the reasons and ways in which it was not completed as Huston had intended are chronicled by Lillian Ross in *Picture* (New York: Rinehart, 1952), the most perceptive and illuminating diary of Hollywood feature film making at the end of the big studio era.

the success is qualified. Though it seems churlish to ask it, given the satisfaction of the ending, a question remains: What will become of them and their love for each other?

In 1952, the year *The African Queen* was released, Huston moved from Hollywood to Ireland, because he could not abide McCarthyism, he has said. His subsequent films were made mostly abroad. As a matter of fact, *The African Queen,* shot in Africa and London, was a British picture in spite of its American creative personnel and its producer, Sam Spiegel. Increased internationalization was only one of the new tendencies that started to become apparent in the American film beginning about 1952.

If "the thirties" in Hollywood had extended into the early forties, "the forties" extended into the early fifties, 1952 a key transitional year that will be returned to. By 1952 the wave of realist/problem pictures of the late forties had virtually ceased, as had film noir. It is probable that both cycles ended partly as a result of the House Un-American Activities Committee investigations and the pressure being applied by militant anticommunist groups then at their height. Perhaps the realist/problem pictures were too explicitly liberal in their portrayal of the inadequacies and inequities that exist in this society. The noir films, on the other hand, may have been too dark and pessimistic in their view of humanity and too critical, implicitly, of American society to be popular or even safe in the American fifties. Individual film makers of talent, such as Hitchcock, Wyler, Sturges, Welles, Curtiz, and Huston, had to, one way or another, adjust themselves and the styles and content of their films to the demands of the period. Though not many persons could have foreseen it at the time, the forties turned out to be the last decade of what would come to be called the old Hollywood.

In 1940 David Selznick had brought Alfred Hitchcock from London to Hollywood to direct *Rebecca,* which is set in England; by 1953 Selznick went to Italy to have Vittorio de Sica direct *Indiscretion of an American Wife.* In the late forties and early fifties it was Italy in the spotlight, stage center of the realist tendency so prominent in the postwar years. Neorealism it was called there.

FILMS OF THE PERIOD

1940
Fantasia (Walt Disney)
Foreign Correspondent (Alfred Hitchcock)
The Grapes of Wrath (John Ford)
The Great Dictator (Charles Chaplin)
The Great McGinty (Preston Sturges)
The Letter (William Wyler)
The Long Voyage Home (Ford)
Of Mice and Men (Lewis Milestone)
The Philadelphia Story (George Cukor)
Rebecca (Hitchcock)
The Westerner (Wyler)

1941
Citizen Kane (Orson Welles)
High Sierra (Raoul Walsh)

How Green Was My Valley (Ford)
The Lady Eve (Sturges)
The Little Foxes (Wyler)
The Maltese Falcon (John Huston)
Sergeant York (Howard Hawks)
Sullivan's Travels (Sturges)
Suspicion (Hitchcock)
Tom, Dick and Harry (Garson Kanin)

1942
The Magnificent Ambersons (Welles)
The Major and the Minor (Billy Wilder)
Mrs. Miniver (Wyler)
The Palm Beach Story (Sturges)
Wake Island (John Farrow)

1943
Air Force (Hawks)
Bataan (Tay Garnett)

Casablanca (Michael Curtiz)
The Moon is Down (Irving Pichel)
The More the Merrier (George Stevens)
Ox-Bow Incident (William Wellman)
Shadow of a Doubt (Hitchcock)
The Song of Bernadette (Henry King)
Yankee Doodle Dandy (Michael Curtiz)

1944
Gaslight (Cukor)
Going My Way (Leo McCarey)
Hail the Conquering Hero (Sturges)
Lifeboat (Hitchcock)
Meet Me in St. Louis
  (Vincente Minnelli)
The Miracle of Morgan's Creek (Sturges)
Thirty Seconds Over Tokyo
  (Mervyn LeRoy)
Wilson (King)

1945
The Bells of St. Mary's (McCarey)
The Clock (Minnelli)
The House on 92nd Street
  (Henry Hathaway)
Lost Weekend (Wilder)
Mildred Pierce (Curtiz)
The Southerner (Jean Renoir)
Spellbound (Hitchcock)
Story of G.I. Joe (Wellman)
A Tree Grows in Brooklyn (Elia Kazan)

1946
Anna and the King of Siam
  (John Cromwell)
The Best Years of Our Lives (Wyler)
Diary of a Chambermaid (Renoir)
The Killers (Robert Siodmak)
My Darling Clementine (Ford)
Notorious (Hitchcock)
A Walk in the Sun (Milestone)

1947
Boomerang (Kazan)
Brute Force (Jules Dassin)
Crossfire (Edward Dmytryk)
A Double Life (Cukor)
Gentleman's Agreement (Kazan)
It's a Wonderful Life (Frank Capra)
Life with Father (Curtiz)

Miracle on 34th Street (George Seaton)
Monsieur Verdoux (Chaplin)

1948
Call Northside 777 (Hathaway)
I Remember Mama (Stevens)
Johnny Belinda (Jean Negulesco)
The Naked City (Dassin)
The Quiet One (Sidney Meyers)
The Search (Fred Zinnemann)
Sitting Pretty (Walter Lang)
The Snake Pit (Anatole Litvak)
State of the Union (Capra)
The Treasure of the Sierra Madre (Huston)

1949
All the King's Men (Robert Rossen)
Battleground (Wellman)
The Champion (Mark Robson)
The Heiress (Wyler)
Home of the Brave (Robson)
Intruder in the Dust (Clarence Brown)
A Letter to Three Wives (Joseph
  Mankiewicz)
Pinky (Kazan)

1950
All About Eve (Mankiewicz)
The Asphalt Jungle (Huston)
Born Yesterday (Cukor)
Father of the Bride (Minnelli)
The Men (Zinnemann)
No Way Out (Mankiewicz)
Panic in the Streets (Kazan)
Stage Fright (Hitchcock)
Sunset Boulevard (Wilder)
Twelve O'Clock High (King)

1951
An American in Paris (Minnelli)
Decision Before Dawn (Litvak)
Detective Story (Wyler)
Fourteen Hours (Hathaway)
A Place in the Sun (Stevens)
Quo Vadis (LeRoy)
The Red Badge of Courage (Huston)
Strangers on a Train (Hitchcock)
A Streetcar Named Desire (Kazan)

1952
The African Queen (Huston)
My Son John (McCarey)
Carrie (Wyler)

BOOKS ON THE PERIOD

BALIO, TINO, ed., *The American Film Industry.* Madison: University of Wisconsin Press, 1976. 499 pp.

BAXTER, JOHN, *Sixty Years of Hollywood.* Cranbury, N.J.: A. S. Barnes & Co., Inc., 1973. 284 pp.

BLUM, DANIEL, *A New Pictorial History of the Talkies,* rev. and enlarged by John Kobal. New York: G. P. Putnam's Sons, 1982.

CEPLAIR, LARRY and STEVEN ENGLAND, *The Inquisition in Hollywood: Politics in the Film Community, 1930-1960.* Garden City, N.Y.: Doubleday & Co., Inc., c. 1980. 530 pp.

COGLEY, JOHN, *Report on Blacklisting I. Movies.* Santa Barbara, Calif.: The Fund for the Republic, 1956. 312 pp.

DAY, BETH, *This Was Hollywood: An Affectionate History of Filmland's Golden Years.* Garden City, N.Y.: Doubleday & Co., Inc., 1960. 287 pp.

DEMING, BARBARA, *Running Away from Myself: A Dream Portrait of America Drawn from Films of the Forties.* New York: Viking Press, Inc., 1969. 212 pp.

EDITORS OF *Look, Movie Lot to Beachhead: The Motion Picture Goes to War and Prepares for the Future.* Garden City, N.Y.: Doubleday, Doran & Company, Inc., 1945. 292 pp.

EVERSON, WILLIAM K., *The American Movie.* New York: Atheneum Publishers, 1963. 149 pp.

GRIFFITH, RICHARD, ARTHUR MAYER, and EILEEN BOWSER, *The Movies.* New York: Simon & Schuster, Inc., 1981.

HIGHAM, CHARLES, *The Art of the American Film, 1900-1971.* Garden City, N.Y.: Doubleday & Co., Inc., 1973. 287 pp.

HIGHAM, CHARLES and JOEL GREENBERG, *Hollywood in the Forties.* Cranbury, N.J.: A. S. Barnes & Co., Inc., 1968. 192 pp.

JONES, KEN D., and ARTHUR F. McCLURE, *Hollywood at War: The American Motion Picture and World War II.* Cranbury, N.J.: A. S. Barnes & Co., Inc., 1973. 320 pp.

KINDEM, GORHAM, ed., *The American Movie Industry: The Business of Motion Pictures.* Carbondale and Edwardsville: Southern Illinois University Press, 1982. 448 pp.

MANVELL, ROGER, *New Cinema in the USA: The Feature Film Since 1946.* New York: E. P. Dutton & Co., Inc., 1968. 160 pp.

NAVASKY, VICTOR S., *Naming Names.* New York: The Viking Press, Inc., 1980. 468 pp.

SAYRE, NORA, *Running Time: Films of the Cold War.* New York: Dial Press, 1982. 256 pp.

SHINDLER, COLIN, *Hollywood Goes to War: Films and American Society, 1939-52.* London: Routledge & Kegan Paul, Ltd., 1979.

SKLAR, ROBERT, *Movie-made America: A Social History of American Movies.* New York: Random House, Inc., 1975. 340 pp.

STANLEY, ROBERT H., *The Celluloid Empire: A History of the American Movie Industry.* New York: Hastings House Publishers, 1978. 328 pp.

TAYLOR, DEEMS, MARCELENE PETERSON, and BRYANT HALE, *A Pictorial History of the Movies.* New York: Simon & Schuster, Inc., 1949. 375 pp.

THOMAS, TONY, *The Films of the Forties.* Secaucus, N.J.: Citadel Press, 1975. 278 pp.

WOLFENSTEIN, MARTHA, and NATHAN LEITES, *Movies: A Psychological Study.* Glencoe, Ill.: Free Press, 1950. 316 pp.

WOOD, MICHAEL, *America in the Movies.* New York: Basic Books, Inc., 1975. 206 pp.

14

Italian Neorealism, 1945–1952

The eruption of a brilliant cluster of films that began with Roberto Rossellini's *Open City* (1945) was stimulated by the removal of Fascist power after nearly a quarter of a century and the release of the bottled up feelings of frustration and humiliation generated by Italy's ambiguous and shifting position in the war. Beginning as a nominal equal to the other two Axis powers, Germany and Japan, Italy subsequently was reduced to a subservient role. When Mussolini was overthrown, a separate peace was signed with the Allies. The Germans in Italy then turned into an occupying force, retreating slowly as the Allies advanced up the peninsula to replace Germany as the new occupier. It is against this background that *Open City* is set, at the point when the Allied forces were approaching Rome and had already begun bombing its outskirts. An agreement was then reached whereby the Germans would not attempt to hold the Eternal City, thus averting its destruction.

THREE MAJOR DIRECTORS

In *Open City* Rossellini chronicles in cross section the activities of the partisans, the raids and reprisals of the German military and the Italian police, the painful tensions among collaborators, resisters, and the great majority of people who simply wanted enough bread and wine, and an end to the killing and misery of war.

The film begins with German soldiers arriving outside the building lived in by Manfredi (Marcello Pagliero), a partisan activist. After he flees, his former lover (Maria Michi), now dependent on the Gestapo to supply her with drugs, tries to reach him by phone. Manfredi goes to the apartment of a friend and fellow partisan, whose financée (Anna Magnani) takes him in and sends for a Catholic priest who is aiding the resistance. The friend returns from work and the action proceeds with the Gestapo net closing in on Manfredi and the priest. But equal attention is given to the daily lives of the Roman people under the stress of a foreign presence, from child resistance-fighters to an irritable old man who scarcely comprehends what is happening but attempts to supply his needs nonetheless.

Script writers Sergio Amidei and Federico Fellini, and director Rossellini, make as good a case as they can for the instances of courage, heroism and martyrdom that occurred in a generally demoralized Italy. *Open City* seems in part an attempt to ease the national conscience in regard to the immediate past and, for the grim postwar problems yet to be solved, to provide models of behavior. The Catholic priest and professional communist revolutionary unite in their efforts and sacrifice their lives in the fight to free their country from fascist rule. The film is a passionate requiem, like Verdi's for his novelist friend Manzoni, and its rough beauty and emotional intensity carry all before it.

No tyro, Rossellini had been working in films since 1934. The Italian industry was heavily controlled and subsidized by the government, and Mussolini used it as a relatively harmless field in which to place some of his less able relatives. After a few unsuccessful attempts to use the fiction film for direct propaganda—invoking the glories of ancient Rome and associating them with the contemporary Italy of the black shirts, for example—the Fascists had to accept the evidence that audiences would simply stay away. Instead, the authorities became content to keep the films from making any significant statement whatever about modern reality; the filmed opera, costume melodrama, and romance built around a box office idol became ubiquitous. The latter type were known as the "white telephone films," since an ultimate in luxurious dalliance was frequently portrayed as a langorous heroine lounging in negligee on an elaborate bed cooing to her lover on the phone. Knowing Rossellini's political and humanitarian convictions we can imagine his private rebellion at the restraints placed on him.

That *Open City* was made at all is something of a marvel; Vernon Jarratt, who lived in Italy at the time, recalls the travail in his excellent *The Italian Cinema*. Rossellini filmed secretly between 1943 and 1945, scraping together funds from various sources. The money kept running out and at one point Rossellini and Anna Magnani, who plays her first great screen role in the film, sold all their clothes to obtain enough to carry on for a few more days. Production conditions were incredibly primitive. The shooting was done on odds and ends of raw stock of various manufacturers. Studios weren't available to them, and nearly all the scenes were enacted on the actual locations they represent in the film. Even the electrical power in wartime was so erratic that maintaining consistent exposure was a constant problem. In spite of the technical and financial difficulties (dead broke, Rossellini is said to have sold the rights for $28,000; *Open City* grossed $5 million in the U.S. alone), the film emerged as a towering achievement that would inspire other Italian film makers to emulate its concepts and its method of dealing with contemporary reality.

Of the three major directors of the neorealistic period—Rossellini, Vittorio de Sica, Luchino Visconti—the first two better represent the characteristics of the move-

Open City (Italy, 1945, Roberto Rossellini). Museum of Modern Art/Film Stills Archive.

ment as a whole in its techniques and commitments. At the same time it must be acknowledged that Visconti's *Ossessione* (1942), an unauthorized version of James M. Cain's novel *The Postman Always Rings Twice,* can be seen as a harbinger of neorealism even before the appearance of *Open City.* This is true more because of its naturalistic style, purposefully drab and unlovely, than its thematic content—passion, jealousy, and greed. With *La Terra Trema* (1948) Visconti offered one of the accepted masterpieces of neorealism but, curiously, in that case it is largely the thematic materials and method of production that qualify it rather than the style. It is about a family of Sicilian fishermen being ground down into poverty by the dealers who exert a monopolistic control over the prices and conditions under which the fish can be marketed. Sponsored initially by the Communist Party, shot entirely on location, the film uses nonactors exclusively. But having said that, I must add that the realistic and ideological elements are molded into a kind of operatic form. Visconti was a Marxist, and in many ways his work reminds us of Eisenstein's silent films, especially, in this instance, in the extreme stylization imposed on the materials of actuality. The fishermen are grouped carefully, decoratively, their movements choreographed; the lighting is exquisite in its rich contrasts and as carefully controlled and patterned as if the film were made in a studio. There are also the emotionally surcharged scenes of passion and drunkenness that would fit better into classical Greek drama, perhaps, than into the films of the other neorealists. In *Rocco and his Brothers* (1960), in some ways a sequel to *La Terra Trema,* Visconti returned briefly to his own version of the neorealist canon. But as his subsequent work confirms, he was really more at home with what Walter Korte called "the scenographic baroque."[1]

[1] Walter F. Korte, Jr., "Marxism and the Scenographic Baroque in the Films of Luchino Visconti" (Ph.D. dissertation, Northwestern University, 1970).

La Terra Trema (Italy, 1948, Luchino Visconti). Museum of Modern Art/Film Stills Archive.

Rossellini, on the other hand, quickly followed *Open City* with his other major film fully within the general terms of the neorealist style and intention, *Paisan* (1946). In six separate episodes it traces the Allied campaign up the long boot of Italy, exploring the relationships between the conquerors (principally American) and the conquered. Maps and newsreel footage connect the parts, suggesting that the dramatic vignettes are incidents happening within the larger historical context. Each episode sketches one aspect of the complex and changing American-Italian relationships, which move from an initial distrust to a growing closeness.

The first episode, the invasion of Sicily, takes place during the initial phase of the campaign. In it mutual suspicion and fear of treachery between a patrol of GIs and a group of peasants lead to the death of two likable young people who were trying to get to know each other—a Sicilian Carmela and a Joe from Jersey. The second episode, set in Naples, is concerned with the black market; thieving, homeless children; poverty; and a military government—all characteristics of that devastated port city. It centers around a black MP who, while dead drunk, has his boots stolen by one of the thousands of urchins who kept alive on the streets of Italian cities during the war. The third story takes place in Rome and deals with prostitution and disillusionment in the wake of liberation. Hundreds and hundreds of girls separated from their families by the war gravitated to Rome. There was little work for which they were qualified, and what there was didn't pay enough to live on; so, for a fee they slept with the troops coming into Rome on rest leave. Nice young girls and lonely boys were forced by the situation into unfulfilling and sometimes hurtful relationships, as the Rome episode indicates.

The Florentine sequence suggests the prewar ties between America and Italy through an American Army nurse who tries to find her former lover, a painter, now leader of the partisans fighting to free Florence from the retreating Germans. Next, in a monastery near Bologna three U.S. Army chaplains gain understanding and respect for a cloistered order of monks as they try to establish a relationship through their common

Paisan (Italy, 1946, Roberto Rossellini). Museum of Modern Art/Film Stills Archive.

service to God. In the final episode, members of American OSS and British Intelligence fight beside courageous Italian partisans in the Po valley in the last days of the war. But courage, shared trust, and growing comradeship are incidental concomitants; the whole meaning of war is suffering and death, Rossellini is clearly saying. This last episode, the finest, is the most documentary-like; it is also the most grim and tragic.

Rossellini worked the stories out as he went along, with the aid of a group of writers that included Federico Fellini. Each incident is particularly representative of that phase of the campaign. Taken together they treat, with extraordinary comprehensiveness as well as precision, the significance of the American presence in Italy. The camera and editing techniques are as sparse and unprettified as the stories. Of *Paisan's* large cast only four members had had previous acting experience (the GI and the prostitute in Rome, the nurse in Florence, the Catholic chaplain in Bologna); the others were picked up by Rossellini as he found them on location. The whole achieves a directness and power through its spontaneity. Rossellini's style is in perfect keeping with the material and his attitude toward it.

Vittorio de Sica and his script writer, Cesare Zavattini, picked up this national saga with an examination of the immediate postwar years. Before directing, de Sica had been a well known screen actor in the thirties. His first important film as a director, *The Children Are Watching Us* (1943), was also his first collaboration with Zavattini. Roughly contemporary with Visconti's *Ossessione,* it was somewhat comparable in its realistic tendencies. In the main line of postwar neorealism, de Sica's *Shoeshine* (1946) is concerned with the Roman *ragazzi* who eked out a living shining GIs' shoes, pimping, and dealing in black market American cigarettes, candy bars, and, in this instance, blankets. Two boys are apprehended, tried, convicted, and sent to a reformatory, where their affection for each other is turned into hatred, resulting in the death of one of the boys. There are no villains, however, simply a bad system. We are not sure why there aren't enough staff and money to run the institution properly, except that there never are in institutions of this sort. Nor are we told what steps might be taken to obtain adequate resources. Though the neorealist films dealt with social problems, they tended to hold them up for examination in terms of their effects on individual lives rather than explain causes or propose solutions.

Zavattini's and de Sica's most successful collaboration, and among those films

Shoeshine (Italy, 1946, Vittorio de Sica). Museum of Modern Art/Film Stills Archive.

The Bicycle Thief (Italy, 1948, Vittorio de Sica). National Film Archive/Stills Library.

closest to the neorealist ideal, was *The Bicycle Thief* (1948). It deals with the simplest possible situation. An unemployed laborer with his first chance to work for some time has the bicycle stolen that he must have in order to keep his job. The events leading up to the theft and the attempt to recover the bicycle provide sufficient "plot" for a complete and significant work of art, even including implied social and political criticism. In following the man's and his young son's search for the bicycle, various aspects of Italian society are sketched, with apparent casualness it may seem at first; on reflection the highest degree of economy and skill become evident. *The Bicycle Thief* was shot almost entirely outside the studio, in the streets and apartments and offices of Rome. The father in the film was in real life a machinist in the big Breda steelworks. The boy who played his son was a Roman newsboy. The performances elicited from the pair can only be described as miraculous. De Sica's work with nonactors, especially children, is always sensitive and sure; here he surpassed himself. Though methods formerly found only in documentary are basic to its conception, the emotional richness of *Bicycle Thief* depends to considerable extent upon the portrayals of its Everyman and his small son.

THEORY

The working principles of the neorealist films which Rossellini had first improvised partly by necessity and accident, partly out of conviction, in turn became loosely codified into a theory of cinema. The premises underpinning neorealism were most forcefully articulated by scriptwriter Zavattini, who became spokesman for, as well as one of the principal creators in, the movement. Perhaps the only other scriptwriter to have achieved a comparable intellectual-aesthetic dominance in a period of national excellence is Carl Mayer, in relation to the German-expressionist films of the twenties.

In a famous interview, Zavattini had the following things to say about the content and purposes of neorealism:

> The most important characteristic, and the most important innovation, of what is called neorealism, it seems to me, is to have realised that the necessity of the "story" was only an unconscious way of disguising a human defeat, and that the kind of imagination it involved was simply a technique of superimposing dead formulas over living social facts. Now it has been perceived that reality is hugely rich, that to be able to look directly at it is enough; and that the artist's task is not to make people moved or indignant at metaphorical situations, but to make them reflect (and, if you like, to be moved and indignant too) on what they and others are doing, on the real things, exactly as they are.[2]

Asking himself what effects on narrative the neorealist style had, Zavattini answered:

> To begin with, while the cinema used to make one situation produce another situation, and another, and another, again and again, and each scene was thought out and immediately related to the next (the natural result of a mistrust of reality), today, when we have thought out a scene, we feel the need to "remain" in it, because the single scene itself can contain so many echoes and reverberations, can even contain all the situations we may need. Today, in fact, we can quietly say: Give us whatever "fact" you like [a stolen bicycle], and we will disembowel it, make it something worth watching.

[2] Cesare Zavattini, "Some Ideas on the Cinema," *Sight and Sound,* XXIII (October-December 1953), pp. 64, 65.

Frequently Zavattini sounds exactly like a documentarian rather than a fiction film maker, and many of his statements could fit quite comfortably into the polemical writings of John Grierson, founder and leader of British documentary. In the same interview Zavattini said:

> Substantially, then, the question today is, instead of turning imaginary situations into "reality" and trying to make them look "true," to make things as they are, almost by themselves, create their own special significance. Life is not what is invented in "stories"; life is another matter. To understand it involves a minute, unrelenting, and patient search.

Grierson had written about his efforts in the 1930s as attempts to find "drama on the doorstep."

PRACTICE

Like the British and American semi-documentaries and problem pictures dealt with in Chapters 12 and 13, the newly realistic Italian films were based on a real incident, a composite of several, or a representative event; they had factual rather than fictional bases. For example, a film might be based on an actual situation of a staircase collapsing under the weight of hundreds of unemployed young women applying for a job as a typist (*Rome, Eleven O'Clock,* 1952), or on a typical one like that of an old man finding it difficult to live on his pension (*Umberto D,* 1952). The problems treated by these films had some degree of immediacy and broad concern. Their themes were not necessarily universal and timeless, as those of the arts tend to be; they were more tied to the here and now, like documentary: sociological as much as psychological in their approach. Among the prevalent concerns were poverty (*Miracle in Milan,* 1951; *Two Cents Worth of Hope,* 1952), prostitution (*Without Pity,* 1948), collaboration with and resistance to occupying military forces (*Outcry* and *To Live in Peace,* both 1947), exploitative agricultural conditions (*The Tragic Hunt,* 1947; *Bitter Rice,* 1949).

Works of this sort were split in the attention they gave to the social problem and to individual character and conflict. An effort was made to fuse the characters and the problem. Roles were created not so much for what the persons were like as for what they did (a resistance leader in *Open City,* 1945) or did not do (an unemployed worker in *The Bicycle Thief,* 1948). The personality of the protagonist could be of any sort—grouchy, or an unfaithful spouse (since the film was not about exclusively personal qualities), as long as the public function was performed. Various aspects of the problem were represented by individuals, but its social (anonymous) nature was kept to the fore.

To put much the same thing another way, in these semi-documentary-like films there *is* a plot and there *are* characters, but they are less fully developed than in pure fiction, and are used quite directly to embody the theme and ideas. The conflict and resolution are apt to be drawn out of the larger situation rather than out of interpersonal relationships. A poor fishing family is in contention with the boat owners; when the owners win, the fishermen are forced to work the boats on the owners' terms. The family that had been resisting is broken (*La Terra Trema,* 1948). In other words, in films of this sort the characters and their lives (plot incidents) are used deliberately to express an ideology.

Finally, in these films the film-making methods are drawn from both fiction

Umberto D (Italy, 1952, Vittorio de Sica). Museum of Modern Art/Film Stills Archive.

and documentary. They tend to depend less on performance and dialogue than do conventional fiction films. Actors may appear in principal roles, but frequently nonactors are used in lesser roles and as extras (*Open City,* 1945; *The Tragic Hunt,* 1947), and even as leads (*Shoeshine,* 1946; *The Bicycle Thief,* 1948; *Umberto D,* 1952). In any event there is usually an avoidance of stars. Considerable location shooting (exteriors) is combined with studio (interiors). Sometimes candid or newsreel footage is used. Frequently commentary, montage, even maps, suggest a broader scope and help bridge a less-tight plot. Lighting, costumes, makeup, sets are actual, or naturalistic in style. The editing is less "smooth" than in the usual story picture, being dictated by the subject-matter requirements. The cutting pace is frequently more rapid, too, as it tends to be when ideas more than emotions are being dealt with, and when film makers (as in documentary) are working with people (nonactors) who cannot sustain performances. There tends to be a stress on source sounds and an avoidance of heavy musical scoring.

AFTERWARDS

It must be admitted that universal meaning given to the ordinary was not always, and seldom completely, attained in neorealist films. Melodrama superimposed upon reality was still the rule. But films of the neorealist style attracted Italy's most talented directors, writers, and performers; received the widest foreign distribution; and exerted the strongest influence on the film production of other countries during the immediate postwar years. Incidentally, this seems to be another instance of a film movement growing out of troubled times, like the post-World War I German and Russian cinemas. The neorealist films began in a defeated and occupied country, with a badly disorganized economy and political life, widespread poverty and unemployment, and uncontrolled inflation.

Problems of national identity, political turmoil, economic misery, and social dislocation continued, but by 1949 neorealism had begun to wane as the predominant force in Italian film making. Pressure from the Roman Catholic Church and the Italian government in the early 1950s resulted in a decline of the export of "social problem" films to the United States, the chief source of economic support for neorealism. A realization by the film makers themselves that the neorealist conception of reality, with its externalized nonpsychological approach, was limiting, led to an enlargement or alteration of their scope of concern. An often quoted comment by Michelangelo Antonioni about *The Bicycle Thief* is revealing. He said that if he had directed the film, he would have told more about the people and less about the bicycle.

If neorealism began with Rossellini's *Open City* in 1945, it ceased, or changed direction anyway, after the de Sica-Zavattini *Umberto D* (1952), about an old man whose fixed income had become insufficient to support life with any dignity let alone pleasure. After that last great neorealist film, Italian film makers began shifting their attention from the lower classes and poverty to the upper classes and the unsatisfying and corrosive values of much of modern life that are most evident among them. Most of Rossellini's films of the middle and late fifties look ahead to a later kind of cinema, and some of them exerted great influence on the upcoming generation of French as well as Italian film makers. His *Voyage to Italy* (1953) is startlingly predictive; Antonioni's *L'Avventura* (1960) seems to grow directly out of it.

Fellini also can be considered a transitional figure who moved from the essentially materialistic concerns of the neorealist films to the, for want of a better word, spiritual concerns of the next generation of Italian film makers. "For me," he said, "neorealism means looking at reality with an honest eye—but at any kind of reality: not just social reality, but also spiritual reality, metaphysical reality, anything man has inside of him." His *La Strada* (1954) might in many ways be regarded as a pivotal film. Though set among the lower classes, it is not concerned with poverty but with inadequacies in human relationships, the inability to communicate and most of all to love.

De Sica attempted to return to neorealism with *The Roof* (1955), but this tale of a young couple trying to obtain their own place to live seemed strangely old fashioned and inessential in the newly prosperous Italy. Rossellini's *General della Rovere* (1959) and de Sica's *Two Women* (1960) are also efforts to recapture some of the earlier themes of the immediate postwar films. In spite of the professional polish, in part because of it of course, and some excellent things in each, both seem anachronistic. It may be fitting that in the former film Rosellini is directing de Sica, playing the lead as the General's impersonator who dies a hero. Those two films were a kind of final reprise, not so much for the two directors—because by then even those stalwarts of neorealism were making other kinds of films—but for the original movement.

The practice and the theory of neorealism did not cease to exist, however, and its influence has been discernible ever since the initial period. In Italy the films of Ermanno Olmi (*Il Posto*, 1961, *The Fiancés,* 1962) embodied it most directly. Also the works of Vittorio de Seta (*The Bandits of Orgosolo*, 1961) and Pier Paolo Pasolini (*Accatone,* 1961), in their methods and explicitly Marxist ideologies, recalled the earlier films, as did the films of Francesco Rosi (*Salvatore Giuliano,* 1961, and *Hands Over the City,* 1963). The French New Wave, Eastern European cinema, and the British social-realist features, to be dealt with later, all owed something to the kind of film making practiced in Italy between 1945 and 1952.

Before that national period ended, and fittingly, at the Venice International Film Festival, another country stepped into the spotlight. The year was 1951, the country Japan. The film was *Rashomon,* and its director, Akira Kurosawa, would soon be recognized among the world's great film makers, along with a number of his compatriots. But even across the globe there were connections with the earlier Italian films: Kurosawa's *Ikiru* (1952) and Kaneto Shindo's *The Island* (1961) showed the strong marks of neorealism. In India, Satyajit Ray acknowledged that he could not conceive how to make *Pather Panchali* (1955), the first of his celebrated Apu trilogy, until he saw *The Bicycle Thief.*

FILMS OF THE PERIOD

1945
Open City (Roberto Rossellini)

1946
Paisan (Rosselini)
Shoeshine (Vittorio de Sica)

1947
Germany Year Zero (Rossellini)
Outcry (Aldo Vergano)
To Live in Peace (Luigi Zampa)
The Tragic Hunt (Giuseppe de Santis)

1948
The Bicycle Thief (de Sica)
La Terra Trema (Luchino Visconti)
Under the Sun of Rome (Renato Castellani)
Without Pity (Alberto Lattuada)

1949
Bitter Rice (de Santis)
In the Name of the Law (Pietro Germi)

1950
The Mill on the Po (Lattuada)
The Road of Hope (Germi)

1951
Bellissima (Visconti)
The Forbidden Christ (Curzio Malaparte)
Miracle in Milan (de Sica)

1952
The Overcoat (Lattuada)
Rome, Eleven O'Clock (de Santis)
Two Cents Worth of Hope (Castellani)
Umberto D (de Sica)

BOOKS ON THE PERIOD

ARMES, ROY, *Patterns of Realism: A Study of Italian Neo-Realist Cinema.* Cranbury, N. J.: A. S. Barnes & Co., Inc., 1971. 226 pp.

BONDANELLA, PETER, *Italian Cinema: From Neorealism to the Present.* New York: Frederick Ungar Publishing Co., Inc., 1983. 440 pp.

HUACO, GEORGE A., *The Sociology of Film Art.* New York: Basic Books, Inc., 1965. 229 pp.

JARRATT, VERNON, *The Italian Cinema.* New York: Arno Press, 1972. 115 pp. (originally published in 1951)

LEPROHON, PIERRE, *The Italian Cinema.* New York: Praeger Publishers, 1972. 256 pp.

MALERBA, LUIGI, ed., *Italian Cinema 1945–1951.* Rome: Carlo Bestetti, Edizioni d'Arte, 1951. 99 pp.

MALERBA, LUIGI, and CARMINE SINISCALCO, eds., *Fifty Years of Italian Cinema.* Rome: Carlo Bestetti, Edizioni d'Arte, 1954. 208 pp.

OVERBEY, DAVID, *Springtime in Italy: A Reader on Neo-Realism.* Hamden, Conn.: The Shoe String Press, 1979. 242 pp.

WLASCHIN, KEN, *Italian Cinema Since the War.* Cranbury, N.J.: A. S. Barnes & Co., Inc., 1971. 224 pp.

15

Asian Film, 1951–

We in the West have been slow in becoming familiar with eastern cinema. Our acquaintance has usually begun at international film festivals—especially those held at Cannes, Venice, Berlin, and Edinburgh. On these occasions the work of different countries and of new film makers is seen, reported in the press, and sometimes acquired for distribution. At the time of *Rashomon*'s appearance, we knew little about film in Asia except that reputedly large and heavily commercial industries seemed to be turning out entertainment aimed mainly at huge domestic audiences, at other countries in Asia, and at Asian populations living elsewhere in the world. Along with Japan, eventually India, Hong Kong, and China also caught our attention at European festivals, with world-class films that subsequently received some distribution internationally.

By the fifties Japan was producing over five hundred films a year, more than any other nation. *Rashomon* was particularly astonishing in that, not only was it clearly the work of an impressive individual talent, it suggested a whole industry and film culture able to support the sophistication of its conception and technique. This indeed proved to be the case. Subsequently we learned that *Rashomon* was by no means the only important Japanese film nor Kurosawa the sole great film maker; on the contrary, Japan had a distinguished cinematic history and many other film artists of considerable eminence.

In number of films produced annually Japan was followed by India—by the fifties the United States had become third. The Indian industry, even less known abroad than the Japanese, was apparently even more commercial and parochial in its outlook, with only a very occasional film of interest to anyone outside its own vast population. Indian cinema gained western consideration through another single entry in an international film festival. In 1956 at Cannes, *Pather Panchali* was voted the "best human document." It was the first film of a young director named Satyajit Ray. Appropriately, its screening followed right after a Kurosawa film, *I Live in Fear.* Unlike Kurosawa's works, however, Ray's film was created completely apart from the Indian industry and was not representative of it. Whereas *Pather Panchali* made viewers think of the Italian neorealist films, in its deep social concern as well as in its use of nonactors and location shooting, in the rest of Indian film it seemed that the big studios turned out the most resolutely escapist entertainment in the world.

At Cannes in 1975 one of Hong Kong's myriad kung fu films, *A Touch of Zen,* won the Grand Prix. Large in scale, three hours in length, it added Buddhism to martial arts. It was directed by King Hu. Evidently his *Legend of the Mountain* and *Raining in the Mountain,* shown at Edinburgh in 1979, also evoke the legends of ancient China and contain much visual elegance and a philosophical dimension along with their balletic fight scenes. Also admired at international festivals were Ann Hui's first three features: *The Secret* (1980, reportedly a homage to the American *The Exorcist*), *The Spooky Bunch* (1981, with ghosts loose amongst a Chinese opera touring company), and *The Story of Woo Viet* (1982). For her next film, *The Foreign Friend,* an account of the communist takeover of South Vietnam after U.S. withdrawal in 1975, Ann Hui shot on location in China. Though quite a number of Hong Kong films have been shot in China since the 1950s, this huge neighbor remains a less well known and apparently less active film producer than the small British crown colony perched on its southern coast.

The People's Republic of China, established in 1949, had at first produced many films for revolutionary indoctrination and education, much as had its communist predecessor, Soviet Russia. An exceptional fiction feature made later was *Two Stage Sisters* (1964), directed by Xie Jin. It chronicles the parallel lives of two actresses during the political turmoil of 1935–1950, intermingling melodramatic and dialectic treatment, bravura camera style, and fine performances. But during the "cultural revolution," 1966–1976, very few films were made and those were mostly confined to themes of the "revolutionary operas" approved by the authorities. Studios were closed; writers, directors, actors, producers, technicians (and millions of others) were sent off to the countryside to be "reeducated." Since 1977 Chinese film production has resumed on a larger scale with a more sophisticated approach to the needs of the nation and its vast population. In 1982 the People's Republic was represented for the first time in the official competition at Cannes with *The True Story of Ah Q.* The first movie from mainland China to receive widespread distribution in the U.S. was *Rickshaw Boy* (1983).

But among the Asian nations it is the films from Japan and India that have predominated at the international festivals and deserve fuller attention here. In 1952, the year after *Rashomon,* the American military occupation of Japan ended. The Japanese were now free to pursue their film destiny without foreign supervision.

JAPAN

The structure of the Japanese industry was curiously like the "classic" American one of the thirties and forties (which was breaking up in the fifties): six major production companies controlled distribution and the theater circuits as well. Japanese film also had popular genres, some with close American counterparts. In a general way Japanese films were divided into main categories: *jidai-geki,* or historical films, and *gendai-geki,* or contemporary films. The division between "historical" and "contemporary" times was marked by the year 1868, when the Emperor Meiji acceded to the throne and first opened Japan to commercial and cultural exchange with the West. It was during his reign that the country passed from feudalism to a modern way of life. Because the change was both sudden and radical, Japanese society in the contemporary period offered a striking contrast to that of the historical period. The two categories of films were also in sharp contrast to each other because each faithfully depicted the mores, thought, and feeling of the two periods. Each category had its own conventions, not only in regard to sets and costumes, but also production style and even acting. Studios, directors, and actors tended to specialize in one or the other of the two modes. The *jidai-geki* (historical) accounted for only 40 percent of Japanese production, but it enjoyed constant popularity with the domestic audience and achieved the first successes abroad.

After its victory at Venice, *Rashomon* was distributed internationally. Daie Motion Picture Company, which had produced it, was Japan's most prestigious studio, like an earlier M-G-M. Daie followed *Rashomon* with other films sent out into (and perhaps in part produced for) world distribution. Masaichi Nagata, the Irving Thalberg of Daie, to pursue the analogy, was producer of many of these. *Ugetsu* (1953) came next, directed by the veteran Kenji Mizoguchi. *Gate of Hell* (1953), the first Japanese film in the new Eastman Color, was directed by Teinosuke Kinugasa. Kurosawa's *Seven Samurai* (1954) reached the United States in a truncated version: two-and-a-half rather than three-and-a-half hours long. His *Ikiru,* though produced earlier (1952), followed. The latter was the first of the *gendai-geki* (contemporary films) to be seen here. The lovely Machiko Kyo, who appeared in the first three Japanese films to be imported, was much appreciated abroad, and Toshiro Mifune, whose finest work has been done with Kurosawa, established an international reputation with *Rashomon* and *Seven Samurai.*

Yet when the Japanese films began to arrive they seemed considerably more foreign than the films of other, western nations; perhaps they still do. It was not clear whether the Japanese had invented a separate cinematic language (whether they were operating out of distinct forms of representation is still being argued; see Noël Burch, *To the Distant Observer*); their films were as intelligible to American audiences as any others requiring subtitles. If the world hadn't seen Japanese films until the early 1950s, the Japanese had been seeing the world's films since the late 1890s, and their use of the medium had developed along lines parallel to those of other countries. The differences appeared to be more cultural, or in any case stylistic, than grammatical or syntactical.

Even when the themes were universal in significance, they received an interpretation and emphasis embodying unfamiliar assumptions and artistic conventions. In treatment there often seemed to American audiences a sentimentality, different in kind, no doubt, more than in degree from our own. This sentimentality was not so evident in the first, carefully selected exports and occurs more in the modern than in the period films. A didactic quality also seemed common (and presumably generally accepted) in Japanese cinema.

A final major difference was the pacing, which appeared generally slower than that of the West, Kurosawa usually an exception. Shots and scenes were allowed to extend beyond the requirements of the narrative point being made, seemingly to let audiences savor the feelings just expressed. If American film makers most frequently concerned themselves with action and Europeans with the psychology of character, as was sometimes said, the Japanese seemed to be more interested in overall mood and atmosphere.

Other, more precise formal characteristics were equally noteworthy, especially in contrast to the immediately preceding Italian neorealism. Many of the Japanese films are very beautiful, visually elegant. If one of them were stopped at random during projection, any frame held on the screen would probably be perfect in terms of composition and lighting. Long passages without dialogue give emphasis to the image. With a cultural tradition that places great importance on the visual arts, Japanese directors and cinematographers thought as painters. Their frame lines always serve as organizational matrices for graphic design as well as for enclosing chunks of content. Planes of action seem constantly to be considered and shots painstakingly composed in depth—foreground in relation to middle ground in relation to background.

These visual characteristics are especially striking in *Ugetsu* (and in Mizoguchi's work generally, we later discovered). In it images were designed not only to create feelings of unease or of calm security, but also to offer aesthetic pleasure in the very arrangement and balance of the blacks, whites, and grays. The full-color palette of *Gate of Hell* allowed for the most dynamic and dramatic use of color film anyone had seen up to that point—especially in its first glowing orange-red scenes of violent action in a civil war. Camera movements, too—for these films are full of kinetic energy along with their careful pictorial qualities—had a calculation and control in relation to subject movement that frequently results in a kind of cinematic dance. In *Rashomon* the shots of the woodsman moving through the forest, the camera tracking with him and tilting up into the sunlight glinting down through the tall trees, are a breathtaking example. *Rashomon* suggested what would be confirmed by *Seven Samurai:* that Kurosawa was a special master of camera movement. Another even more extraordinary instance in *Rashomon* occurs when Machiko Kyo weaves about after yielding to the bandit, confronting her husband's accusing stare as the camera swoops, backs, and glides with her. Reviewers resorted to phrases like "painting in motion" to describe the visual riches the Japanese films offered, and after the deliberate austerities and rough irregularities of the Italian neorealists, this was heady stuff indeed.

Stylistically still, but in terms of performance, the Japanese films drew on another ancient artistic tradition—that of the theater. Classical Nō plays, which go back for centuries, and the popular Kabuki have both reflected and influenced Japanese culture generally. They seem to represent a true expression of national sentiment and belief, at least of the older Japan, which evidently was giving way more slowly and less fundamentally than appeared on the surface. Donald Richie, American authority on Japanese cinema, has insisted that Kabuki hasn't really affected the Japanese film to any great extent. Kurosawa has said much the same thing in regard to his own work, with an obvious exception in a film like *The Men Who Tread on the Tiger's Tail* (1952). That may be, and yet there is something very different from western performance styles in the Japanese historical (not the contemporary) films. A composite outline of the conventional samurai films (of which *Gate of Hell* is one example; *Samurai,* 1954, directed by Hiroshi Inagaki, another) may suggest some of the differences.

A young warrior is in love with his lord's wife. Out of loyalty to his master he does not show that love. The acting in the first two-thirds of the picture would be not only restrained but extremely formalized. We can infer that each gesture and every movement (as well as costumes, makeup, and hairdos) have some sort of fixed and known meaning. An enormous tension is built up through this constraint of powerful feeling expressed in behavior limited by rigid, social/aesthetic convention. Then, when the young warrior can bear it no longer and his passion overleaps those self- and societally-imposed bounds, he pursues the lady, fights the lord, and gives vent to his charged-up store of emotion. There never had been seen such full-blown representation of lust and anger, such lunging and sweating, crawling and panting. The cold, inscrutable Oriental indeed! *Rashomon* first showed us these two extremes of performance—theatrical stylization in the trial scene, earthy naturalism in the bandit's behavior—within a single film. How important the Japanese theatrical tradition is to the themes and characters and style of the historical films is impossible for an uninitiated westerner to say. That the elements described above add to their exotic charm in the West is undeniable.

That exotic charm is part of the problem in evaluating these films that come out of a culture and tradition so vastly different from the Greco-Judeo-Christian one. We cannot always be certain to what extent they are offering new filmic possibilities which might be incorporated into international cinema at large, or to what extent we are merely responding to things Japanese seen for the first time through their films. Perhaps the distinction is unimportant, yet I am intrigued by reports that the Japanese films most valued in the West are frequently not those that have found high favor with Japanese audiences and critics. Evidently there is a greater difference in this regard than between, say, Italian and American response to Italian films. We are told that the historical films usually are based on ancient legends, kept alive by a still-popular oral narrative tradition and well known to the Japanese audience. The stories about The Forty-Seven Ronin (masterless samurai), for example, have been the source for a good many films, those of Inagaki among the most popular. What can seem a lack of plausibility or of character motivation to us—a difficulty in *Gate of Hell*, for example—may be attributable to the film makers' assumption that viewers will be familiar with the source material or at least the attitudes of an earlier time. Japanese film makers may feel they can jump over certain connecting incidents, or omit supporting ideas and emotions, and that their audience will still be with them at the next juncture. Classical Greek dramatists did something of the sort in their segmentation and interpretation of Greek history and legend. But in addition, and much more basic, isn't it inevitable that Japanese literary and dramatic conventions and even life itself would operate by different rules and psychological understandings than they do in the West? Joseph Anderson, in comparing "Japanese Swordfighters and American Gunfighters," states that "The Japanese unities are not those of plot, time and place, character, viewpoint, or thesis but are rather those of mood, tone, rhythm, effect."[1] From the period films we learn that the Japanese historical experience has had certain similarities to that of western nations, feudalism for instance, as well as certain differences, such as religion. It is the differences which fascinate most.

A philosophical stance, growing out of the Japanese historical experience, appears in the modern as well as the period films. It is distinctively and characteristically Japanese and is identified by one of those terms for which translators offer a sensible-enough English explanation but add that the concept remains essentially untranslatable. The phrase in this case is *mono no aware*. According to Richie, in *Japanese Cinema*, it means something like "that awareness of the transience of all earthy things, the

---

[1] J. L. Anderson, "Japanese Swordfighters and American Gunfighters," *Cinema Journal*, XII (Spring 1973), p. 21.

knowledge that it is, perhaps fortunately, impossible to do anything about it: that celebration of resignation in the face of things as they are."[2] Mizoguchi's films have this attitude in abundance, and the opening and closing shots of *Ugetsu* are its visual expression. The original title, *Ugetsu Monogatari,* translates as "Tales of the Pale and Mysterious Moon after the Rain." Set in the sixteenth century, the film begins with a slow overhead pan across the countryside, then a tilt down and dolly-like movement towards two couples. They are frantically loading a cart with pottery, while the noises of war are heard in the background. This is exceptionally economical exposition, to be sure. The shot also manages to suggest that the lives and events with which we will be concerned are embedded in a universal and timeless whole—the land and the people which go on—made up of ephemeral human existences and changing historical conditions. *Ugetsu* ends with the camera moving up and away from the potter's small son (while his dead mother's voice is heard on the sound track), back across the landscape. (Mizoguchi's *Sansho Dayu/The Bailiff,* 1954, employs much the same device.)

That initial cluster of five films opening the world's screens to Japanese cinema introduced us to two of Japan's greatest film makers: Akira Kurosawa and Kenji Mizoguchi. Both carry their personal concerns from film to film whether the setting is modern or feudal. The work of the third, Yasujiro Ozu, is even more resolutely fixed on certain themes and is always set in contemporary Japan. Of the three, in terms of content and style, Kurosawa is the most easily appreciated by westerners.

Rashomon, for example, seems to require no special sense of Japanese culture or sympathy for a foreign point of view. It is based on two stories by the popular author Ryunosuke Akutagawa, who was much influenced by western culture. Though set in the Heian period (794 to 1184), its four-times-told tale of a rape (or seduction), murder (or suicide), and robbery (or disappearance) is indebted to Robert Browning's novel-length poem *The Ring and the Book,* while the musical score is a close imitation of Maurice Ravel's *Bolero.* This acknowledgement is not meant to detract from the originality and power of Kurosawa's film; but rather, simply to point out that it was made in a cinematic *lingua franca* available to all. According to reports it was at first more fully appreciated in the West than in Japan. *Rashomon* was later redone in America by Martin Ritt as *The Outrage* (1964).

Seven Samurai brings out even more remarkable, because pervasive, parallels between the American western and the samurai films. This is especially true in films of Kurosawa, and quite directly in relation to the westerns of John Ford, which Kurosawa is known to admire. Substitute swords for six-guns and samurai warriors for professional gunslingers, and much else remains the same. In 1960 *Seven Samurai* was remade into a western by John Sturges, *The Magnificent Seven.* Kurosawa's *Yojimbo* (1961) and *Sanjuro* (1962), along with their other meanings, are obviously deliberate parodies of the western, although Joseph Anderson, in the fascinating article referred to earlier, is no doubt more accurate in stating that what is being parodied are the conventions most common to both the *jidai-geki* and the American western.

Seven Samurai is set in the sixteenth century at a transitional time when the ancient and honorable profession of the samurai was coming to an end as gun powder and new military tactics appeared. The samurai we see have fallen on hard times, and in their unemployment a group of them accept a proposal by a committee of peasants to

---

[2] Donald Richie, *Japanese Cinema: Film Style and National Character* (Garden City, N. Y.: Doubleday & Co., Inc., 1971), p. 77.

Rashomon (Japan, 1950, Akira Kurosawa). Museum of Modern Art/Film Stills Archive.

protect their village from bandit raids. The film combines precise psychological observation with stunningly choreographed action and violence. Each of the seven warriors is
carefully delineated. The leader and eldest (Takashi Shimura, who also plays the wood-
cutter in *Rashomon* and the lead in *Ikiru*) is a compelling personality. He eschews wasteful
bloodshed, advocates strategy over force, is wise, calm, and compassionate, with a sad
acceptance of his destiny for leadership. Of the others, one samurai is tired of fighting,
another is cool and skillful, a third bloodthirsty, a fourth a frightened youth, and so on.
Crammed with action, the larger scenes of the bandits attacking the village are shot and
cut with immense dynamism. The film is meant to be enjoyed for the kind of empathic
release such material can provide when formally controlled; the separate shots are intricate and precise in their composition, movement, and rhythm. The insistently used
telephoto lens compressed the images in a way that gives them a strange muted power.
Kurosawa has no superior at this kind of film making. His *Throne of Blood* (1957), a version of *Macbeth,* offers us more of the same.

In *Seven Samurai* the action of the smaller, more intimate scenes carries with it
fuller emotional meaning. But even then Kurosawa worked through physical movement, and camera and cutting in relation to it. For example, there is the scene in which
the preeminent swordsman is introduced. He is challenged by another samurai to a test
of skill, using staffs in place of swords. The result is contested: The challenger says that
their blows landed at the same time; the master says that the other would be dead. The
former foolishly insists that they fight again, with swords. When the great swordsman

cuts his adversary down, he shows little emotion, simply having proved what he already knew. His interest is solely in further perfecting his awesome skill. The two seduction scenes between the youngest samurai and a peasant girl—one on a sunny flower-covered hillside, the other in the dark interior of a hut dappled by light—are also played largely with their bodies. His intense shyness and uneasy attraction and her almost wild abandonment to awakened sensuality are portrayed wordlessly, with beautifully exact gesture and movement. A final instance of Kurosawa's exceptional ability to transmute the physical into the emotional occurs in the scene of the raid on the bandits' fort. In the eerie early morning light amidst a surrealist, Dantesque inferno of fire, torn bodies, and steaming pool, there is a haunting exchange between a husband and wife. She has come out of the burning fort after having been kept there as a concubine since the last raid. As she stands at the door, he runs to her; they look at each other for a full minute; nothing is said; then she turns and runs back into the flames.

In Kurosawa's films set in contemporary times, he tends to subdue this kind of direct sensory appeal. Instead he keeps us focused on the subtler, more complex characters and on the sorts of social problems that more clearly show his dimension as a humanist. *Ikiru,* made in the same year as de Sica's and Zavattini's *Umberto D,* bears some resemblance to the Italian film. It concerns an inconsequential petty official who, after learning that he has cancer, tries to instill some meaning into his life as he faces death. His final positive act of helping create a playground in a poor section allows him to die satisfied, but it sets off social and political reverberations that are reviewed and discussed in a crazy drunken Joycian wake. In its complicated and experimental structure *Ikiru* descends in personal tragedy during the first two-thirds and then ascends back over the same material throughout the last third, with wry social comment and a sort of

Seven Samurai (Japan, 1954, Akira Kurosawa). Museum of Modern Art/Film Stills Archive.

bitter comedy reinterpreting on a broader scale what we have seen. *Red Beard* (1965) is regarded by Richie as Kurosawa's masterpiece. At the same time he concedes that we must be able to look through and beyond a sentimental surface to get at the greatness of the film. The title character (played by Toshiro Mifune) is a crotchety, selfless, driven doctor who devotes his whole life to treating the poor. His qualities are revealed to us as they are discovered by a young intern who comes to study under him. The film follows the young man's maturation and final success in finding his true self—his vocation, almost in the religious as well as practical sense. The kind of spiritual journey and discovery at the core of these two contemporary films appears frequently in Kurosawa's work. Even in his historical pieces he is always commenting on contemporary life, and the concerns are profoundly social and moral.

From 1974 to 1984 Kurosawa made only two films. *Dersu Uzala* (1975), a Soviet-Japanese coproduction, is visually stunning in wide-screen color. Its title character and protagonist is a native hunter living in the wilds of Siberia. In *Kagemusha* (*The Shadow Warrior,* 1981) Kurosawa returned to the period of change in the last quarter of the sixteenth century, when Japan was beset by ceaseless internal wars. A poor thief is chosen for his resemblance to the dying leader of the Takeda clan to take the latter's place—to become a ''kagemusha'' (shadow warrior). At first frightened, the thief gradually becomes the man he is impersonating. Replete with large-scale period re-creation and battling armies, the film moves from history to myth. It may prove to be Kurosawa's final statement.

A similar use of historical material containing lasting cultural values and psychological truths typifies the films of Kenji Mizoguchi, though the ratio of historical to contemporary in his work is much higher than in Kurosawa's. Also, Mizoguchi's attitudes, themes, and style are more traditionally Japanese, and therefore his films have been less widely appreciated in America and Europe. *Ugetsu* tackles the big themes with disarming simplicity—a kind of elementariness. Also set in the sixteenth century, it deals with war and peace in relation to work and love; or perhaps, even more simply and broadly, war as it affects the total human condition. It centers around two brothers, a potter and a farmer, and their wives. The profiteering that wartime makes possible goads both men into an inordinate desire for gain. The potter wants money to buy extravagant presents for his wife and child, the farmer to equip himself as a samurai in order to impress his wife. While in the city selling his pots, the potter is seduced (partly through flattery about the aesthetic qualities of his pottery) by a mysterious and finally sinister Lady Wakasa. She causes him to abandon his wife for the sensuality and luxury she seems to offer. During the same time the farmer comes to be regarded as a military commander through a faked heroic exploit. But the potter is no more an artist (nor should be) than the farmer is a warrior, Mizoguchi seems to be saying. Work ought to be for its own sake, not for money (or false praise for creativity), nor for glory (based on feigned valor). Also, it should be part of the family, not done away from home with the results brought back.

In *Ugetsu* both work and war have for goals material wealth and women's love. But false ambitions are suggested and made possible by war, leading men away from true satisfactions. They are carried away from their wives and proper married love to erotic refinement (Lady Wakasa) on the one hand or animal lust (raping and whoring) on the other. The wives are destroyed by wartime conditions of hunger and rapine and by the husbands' desertion. The end of the film marks a return to the original state: work in peace, and conjugal and parental love.

Stylistically Mizoguchi's films are even more "painterly" than Kurosawa's. His shaping of the visual-dramatic content takes place within the shot more than through juxtaposition of shots. Composition is always conceived in depth, often with objects at the side of the frame in foreground to accentuate the perspective. Also, he uses the long shot quite deliberately to frame action at a distance; for example, there are the repeated views across the courtyard of Lady Wakasa's house, the scenes of the soldiers pillaging the village, the shot of the farmer shopping for armor seen at a distance and from behind the armorer. Mizoguchi's frequent pans, too, are used pointedly as a compostional device rather than merely to follow action. One particularly memorable usage of the sort is the high-angled pan across the refugees from the village as they are camping for the night. In constructing his scenes he typically allows the camera to pick up action and then follow it remorselessly to its conclusion. But unlike the films of the German silent film makers who worked this way, there is an enormous amount of action within Mizoguchi's shots, and sharp contrasts—calm to frenetic, lyrical to horrifying—from scene to scene. He likes to have action explode into frame. Looting soldiers move around a corner and emerge in the middle of the frame, the potter's wife rushes directly toward the camera (shot from low angle with short focal-length lens) and scoops up her child right under our noses. Entrances are frequently from behind the camera—from right or left and sometimes from below—which creates a startling, disruptive effect.

Mizoguchi seems to be equally concerned with the sound track. In *Ugetsu* the music is extremely important. More of it is oriental than western, the opposite of Kurosawa's usual practice, and it is fully integrated with the visuals. It complements and frequently takes precedence over the dialogue. In part it is used in place of natural sounds; elsewhere as *leit motif,* evocative and symbolic. The bright piercing bell of Lady Wakasa's theme is matched by a gently melodic ensemble of bells in the return of the potter's wife. On the other hand, cries in the background sometimes supply an almost musical accompaniment to the action. When the two men and the farmer's wife leave the potter's wife and child on the shore of the lake, the farewells become a melancholy round. The ghost of Lady Wakasa's father groans in eerie and wordless recitative accompanied by strange and discordant instrumentation.

Ugetsu (Japan, 1953, Kenji Mizoguchi). Museum of Modern Art/Film Stills Archive.

Thematically rich as they are, Mizoguchi's films may finally be most valuable for their total, combined use of sensory resources. He can create a mood, an atmosphere that encapsulates characters and ideas, making them seem truly and fully representative of the culture and its history. Inevitably, therefore, his films must at first appear somewhat exotic to us. At the same time they can be seen as both universal in the significance of their artistic statements and uniquely beautiful in themselves.

In contrast not only to the work of Mizoguchi and Kurosawa but to that of any other film maker of any country you can think of, the style of Yasujiro Ozu is marked by the most rigorous austerity. Frequently he appears to be indifferent to Hollywood codes of matching continuity. In later films he rarely moved the camera, and then slightly and slowly solely to accommodate the action. Interiors predominate in his films and the action consists almost entirely of conversation among a few people. He worked exclusively in the formerly standard three-by-four screen ratio; though he used color when it became available to him for his last pictures, it was always muted and unemphatic, as if he were trying to keep the full palette from distracting. Characteristically, his camera sits at seated eye level, as if part of a formal tea ceremony, unblinkingly observing two of his characters reacting to each other. Very often the pair is made up of one old person and one young adult—an old man and a young woman perhaps most frequently in the final films. For above all Ozu was concerned with the relationships between the traditional ways and the newer ones in a changing Japan. Implicit in all of his films is an awareness of the extraordinary cultural dislocations that began to occur when Japan was opened to the West in the late nineteenth century and have increased in geometric progression with each passing decade. Ozu observed these changes and tensions not on a broad social scale but within the intimacy of the family unit—parents and children, husband and wife—where they finally have their deepest effect. His view is a calm and balanced one. Though sad to see the old go, he has to acknowledge its passing, with sympathy but without complaint—*mono no aware*. Of the three giants of the Japanese cinema, Ozu is unquestionably the most "Japanese."

What Ozu's films are incalculably rich in is the observation of human behavior in the most ordinary and universal of situations. In *Late Autumn* (1960), for example, he is concerned with a widow, her twenty-four-year-old daughter, and the deceased husband's three old college friends who involve themselves with trying to find suitable mates for both mother and daughter. At the emotional center of the film is the mother's reluctance to lose her daughter, which she tries to check, and the daughter's growing desire to marry, stubbornly denied even to herself out of loyalty and affection for her mother. The so subtly changing situation is observed most discreetly—we learn no more about the characters than they know about each other—but for all of the quietness and control of Ozu's people, they possess a wonderful amount of robustness. Practical and realistic, they are willing to restrain their desires when necessary; at the same time they know that the pleasures to be found in this world are those of the senses and feelings—eating, drinking, sex, and most of all, love and companionship.

Abundant humor is interlaced throughout with tenderness and sadness; bawdy talk can exist within the confines of good manners. Ozu's narratives are like those of a kindly and merry old grandfather who doesn't need the large and exceptional events and characters conventionally required by storytellers. With astounding clarity and economy, through a few words, a tentative gesture, a partial smile, he makes a listener feel that yes, I know that person, or that yes, something like that has surely happened countless times in many cultures. Ozu's genius was very special: an ability to put life

Late Autumn (Japan, 1960, Yasujiro Ozu). National Film Archive/Stills Library.

back together whole out of closely observed bits and pieces. His films, in total, form an extraordinary tapestry, depicting the everyday, the intimate, the habitual, the lived-in world of unglamorous work and a few enduring relationships that compose life for most of us. How many tapestries can there be that so celebrate the ordinary?

Accompanying and succeeding the work of Kurosawa, Mizoguchi, and Ozu are the films of a small host of other noteworthy directors. In *Japanese Cinema,* Richie devotes considerable space to over twenty who worked from the 1950s on. Three prolific veterans who began to direct in the 1920s were still active. Teinosuke Kinugasa made *Gate of Hell* in 1953, the only one of his more than a hundred films to be seen in this country until recently. Subsequently his extraordinary surrealist *A Page of Madness* (1926) was rediscovered and made available. Heinosuke Gosho made one of his most important films, *Four Chimneys,* in 1953. Mikio Naruse continued to direct almost up to his death in 1969, but the only films of his that are known here are *Kimiko* (1936), *Sounds from the Mountains* (1954), and *Floating Clouds* (1955).

Among the generation which began work in the 1930s, Kimisaburo Yoshimura has not been seen in the U.S. at all. Several of Tadashi Imai's films have been shown here: *Muddy Waters* (1953), *Rice* (1957), *Night Drum* (1958). All three films attack exploitation and repression that are part of the "modern feudalism" of the traditional Japanese society.

Keisuke Kinoshita and Kon Ichikawa began to direct in the 1940s. In this country the best known of Kinoshita's films is the comic-satire *Carmen Comes Home* (1951), about a Tokyo stripper who returns to the country town where she was born. Other of his films from the fifties are equally important and quite varied in style: *A*

Japanese Tragedy (1953), melodrama of generation conflict ending in a mother's suicide; *Twenty-four Eyes* (1954), using what might be called a neorealist approach to deal with the lives of a teacher and her pupils through two decades; and *The Ballad of Narayama* (1958), a legend about a remote mountain community whose custom it is to allow the old to die through exposure to the elements, done in the style of Kabuki drama. Ichikawa will be discussed later.

Among the important film makers who directed their first features in the 1950s are Kaneto Shindo, Masaki Kobayashi, and Nagisa Oshima. The films of Shindo that have been seen widely abroad are *Children of Hiroshima* (1952), concerning the aftermath of the atomic destruction; *The Island* (1961), a Flaherty-like account of a peasant family eking out a terribly difficult existence on a small island; and *Onibaba* (1964), a horrifying tale of sexual passion and jealousy involving a mother, daughter-in-law, and lover, set in the sixteenth century. Kobayashi and Oshima will be considered below.

This confined roster might be completed with two of the newest directors, who began their significant work in the 1960s. Hiroshi Teshigahara commenced feature direction in 1961 and is best known for his *Woman of the Dunes* (1964), extremely popular in this country. It is a modern allegory concerning a young man who chooses, rather than return to his city life, to share the fate of a woman confined in a pit lined by cascading sand, which must be ceaselessly shoveled out. Masahiro Shinoda's *Pale Flower* (1964) is said to be his first important film. Though it was not shown in this country, his *With Beauty and Sorrow* (1965), *Punishment Island* (1966), and *The Scandalous Adventures of Buraikan* (1970) were. It was *Double Suicide* (1969), however, which swept the festivals and earned him international notice. Based on a classical play about the conflict between love and duty, the stylistic devices of the traditional puppet theater from which the story was taken are fused with a fluid moving-camera style. The black-garbed puppeteers from the opening scenes in the theater remain hovering about the human characters throughout as a strange chorus heightening the sense of destiny and impending doom.

Those Japanese directors after Mizoguchi, Ozu, and Kurosawa whose films have elicited the most sympathetic and sustained appreciation abroad are Ichikawa, Kobayashi, and Oshima. The major works of all three contain elements of social criticism that is one of the characteristics of modern Japanese cinema.

In the films of Ichikawa which have been shown in this country, he seems consistently concerned with dramatizing the conflict within people under peculiar stress. His films combine visual refinement—many of the images are memorable for their extraordinary beauty—with philosophical, even political statement; they tend toward allegory, or at least metaphor. *The Burmese Harp* (1956), his first international success, takes place at the end of World War II. The protagonist, a Japanese soldier separated from his unit, becomes converted to Buddhism. The values that had sustained him during the war are now meaningless to him, and he remains on alone in Burma to bury his fallen comrades. *Enjo* (1958) is about a young monk who, tortured by the hypocrisy and evil he sees around him, sets fire to and destroys a temple that he loved more than anything else in the world. *Odd Obsession* (1959), a dark comedy, is an even more convoluted psychological study, centering on the hypereroticism, bizarre sexuality, and voyeurism of a kind of *ménage à quatre* made up of a middle-aged husband, younger wife, and daughter and her fiancé. *Fires on the Plain* (1959) returns to the Japanese army in defeat. Suffering the horrors of starvation while straggling across a hostile and alien landscape, some of the soldiers are finally driven to cannibalism. *Alone on the Pacific* (1963) deals with the obsession of a single man who attempts to cross the Pacific in a

The Burmese Harp (Japan, 1956, Kon Ichikawa). Museum of Modern Art/Film Stills Archive.

small sailboat. *An Actor's Revenge* (1963) is the story of a female impersonator in Kabuki theater. The subject of *Tokyo Olympiad* (1965), a gigantic documentary tribute to that athletic event, permitted Ichikawa to continue the themes of obsession and unusual stress. In it he humanized the competition with emphasis on the athletes and individuals in the crowds rather than on the events; Ichikawa's splendid visual flare and superb imagery of human bodies being pushed to their utmost raise sports to the level of poetry.

Of Masaki Kobayashi's films, *Kwaidan* (1964), an elegantly beautiful anthology of three period ghost stories, has been most popular in the U.S. It does not represent the main thrust of his work, however. He is especially noted for the consistent criticism his films have leveled at aspects of Japanese social tradition, especially as it extends into political and military systems. *Black River* (1957) exposed the crime and corruption surrounding American military bases in occupied Japan. His massive trilogy, *The Human Condition* (comprising *No Greater Love, Road to Eternity,* and *A Soldier's Prayer*), was made between 1958 and 1961. The action takes place in Japanese-occupied Manchuria from 1943 to 1945. It chronicles the fate of a young pacifist intellectual forced into military service. He survives combat and, after the Japanese collapse, is captured by the Russians. Escaping from prison, he dies on his way to rejoin his wife. Antimilitary as well as antiwar, the trilogy aroused enormous controversy in Japan. Though *Harakiri* (1962) is a *jidai-geki* samurai film, it presents the traditional code of honor as senseless and destructive, a system ruled by a corporate class that wreaks the cruelest of punishments on the individual (an impoverished young samurai is forced to disembowel himself with a bamboo sword blade) in their efforts to keep themselves in power and the feudal system intact. The message is clearly directed toward contemporary Japan.

Of the Japanese film makers discussed in this chapter, Nagisa Oshima is the most "modern." Using narrative structures and techniques comparable to those of the French Jean-Luc Godard, Oshima is yet profoundly Japanese in his sensibility, at least so it seems from the limited evidence available from his prolific output. The gentle, humanist criticism implicit in Ichikawa, the direct social-realist confrontation apparent in Kobayashi, become radical and revolutionary statements in Oshima. He challenges the moral assumptions underpinning Japanese society as well as its institutions. The values of the older generation are seen as neither valid nor relevant to the problems faced by youth, with whom he identifies.

Death by Hanging (1968) not only attacks capital punishment but goes further to suggest that the very concept of crime (and punishment) is a conception of the police, at considerable variance with actual human conduct and the motives behind it. It is the police rather than the criminal who are obsessed with crime. *Diary of a Shinjuku Thief* was

Harakiri (Japan, 1962, Masaki Kobayashi). Museum of Modern Art/Film Stills Archive.

made in the same year. Within an extremely fragmented structure and a mixture of modes, from the actuality of student riots to the artificiality of a ghost play, it links themes of sex as performance with theft as a revolutionary act. The film is dense and difficult; the actions of its individuals are intended to be read as symbolic statements about Japan. *Boy* (1969), based on a real incident, as was *Death By Hanging,* is about a child trained by his parents to run in front of moving autos to be hit and injured slightly so they can collect damages. It is about that particular situation, but the indictment, as Oshima has said, is not of the parents, but of a society which makes it necesary for them to live in that manner. In *The Ceremony* (1971), the plot revolves around a family over a period of twenty-five years since the end of the war. As they come together for weddings and funerals their traditional attitudes become increasingly divorced from the realities of modern life, their behavior ever more ritualistic, abstract, and finally bizarre.

Oshima received his greatest international attention, not to say notoriety, with *In the Realm of the Senses* (1976). It centers exclusively on a couple obsessed with each other and with sensual experience; sexual activity, varied and sustained, is its content. It ends in death (for him) and madness (for her). *Realm of Passion* (1979), dealing with a pair of rural lovers, is a companion piece, though more restrained emotionally, less explicit sexually, and more social in its content. *Merry Christmas, Mr. Lawrence* (1983), with dialogue half in Japanese, half in English, is about life in a Japanese prisoner of war camp in Java in 1942.

Though these last three Oshima films contain much sex and violence—especially sexual violence—individual passions are set within political contexts, sometimes clearly evident, sometimes seeming to be more in Oshima's mind than on the

In the Realm of the Senses (Japan, 1976, Nagisa Oshima). Museum of Modern Art/ Film Stills Archive.

screen. However particular films of his may be interpreted, it can be said in general that, like other modern political film makers, Oshima has fashioned new forms to express new ideas. Disjunctive narrative, diverse styles within a given film, reality mingled with surrealist fantasy, formalized patterns achieving the effect of ritual—all are present in his work. His vision is frequently uniquely personal and difficult to comprehend in its complexity. As a Japanese film maker Oshima also offers images of exquisite beauty, especially unnerving (and thus suitable for his purposes) when they are of events horrifying in their human meanings.

Today, except for occasional science-fiction and monster movies, Japanese films don't move as freely about the globe as American or even French. They do appear frequently at international festivals, however, and some play with modest success in the cities of the West. Each new work of Kurosawa is regarded as required viewing by those who care seriously about the cinema. He has been followed by several generations of valuable and varied film makers since *Rashomon* surfaced in Venice almost thirty-five years ago. Whereas before the fifties Japan was barely mentioned, if at all, in world film histories (written by Europeans and Americans), since that time we have come to realize that respectful attention is due. But in that other large Asian film-making nation, India, there still seem to western eyes to be few major artists, Satyajit Ray, going his own deliberate way, being the most prominent. Averaging a film a year, he has successively explored aspects of his own culture with something of the same kind of preoccupation and concentration that has marked the greatest of the Japanese directors. Within recent years he has been joined by other Indian film makers of unusual talent.

INDIA

Indian film production is headquartered in Bombay, Madras, and Calcutta. The first two centers are the largest, making films mostly in the Hindi language; the Calcutta films are in Bengali. A huge industry, as has been noted—currently it produces more films than any other nation—by the 1950s it was second only to Japan's in the number of films produced each year.

Its commercial entertainment conventions and limitations are more restrictive than anywhere in the world. Purely escapist fare, for the most part the films are based on traditional myths and stereotypical romances. Set in an imagined past, or a timeless fantasy land, they are peopled by handsome princes, beautiful princesses, and mustachioed villians. In their history, *Indian Film,* Erik Barnouw and S. Krishnaswamy observe that every film requires "a star, six songs, three dances." The songs and dances have little bearing on the subject matter and are interspersed more or less at random: The story merely comes to a halt to accommodate them, then resumes when the number is finished. Running times are extremely long—four hours preferably—to give as full an evening's entertainment as possible. These conditions have to be met in order for the public to feel it is getting its rupees' worth. The Indian film audience is huge but the fixed low admission price and conventional greed of the big studios keep film makers in petty competition with each other and their unadventurous films within the fixed mold. The standard approach is more of the same instead of something different.

From the outset Satyajit Ray was a maverick. He first became seriously interested and active in film as one of the founders of the Calcutta Film Society. A commercial artist by profession, he was a passionate student of film in his free time. He saw as many movies as he could and paid particular attention to the work of such American directors as John Ford, William Wyler, Frank Capra, John Huston, and Billy Wilder. He was influenced strongly, he has said, by Flaherty's *Nanook of the North,* Jean Renoir's *The Southerner,* and "of course, all the Chaplins."[3]

In 1950 Ray met Renoir, who was in Calcutta shooting *The River.* Renoir encouraged him and permitted him to observe production. Later that year Ray was sent by his advertising agency employers to their headquarters in London for six months. While there he talked with leading British film critics and theorists and attended movies daily. He was especially inspired, he said, by de Sica's-Zavattini's *The Bicycle Thief.*

On the boat going home he wrote the first draft of the script for *Pather Panchali,* adapted from a popular novel. The film was almost an amateur production—in personnel as well as scale. Only two of the cast and only one of the crew of eight—the art director—were professionals. The cinematographer was an amateur still photographer. To show him what he wanted, Ray, who had never directed a film before, drew pen-and-ink sketches from the camera's viewpoint. Shot on weekends over a period of almost four years, production was frequently halted for lack of funds. Eventually the money ran out. Ray was about to give up when the West Bengal government agreed to back him in return for ownership of *Pather Panchali* (1955).

First of a trilogy (followed by *Aparajito,* 1956, and *The World of Apu,* 1958), *Pather Panchali* begins the account of a Bengali family of five during the 1920s, which extends from the time the boy Apu is about twelve, until he himself has a son about that age. In spite of its total three-feature length (each of the films can stand by itself, of course), the trilogy is not an epic in conception; or, at least, it is epic only by implication. When social, religious, and economic themes and problems appear it is within the detailed texture of the family's daily life. Out of the microcosm a true and accurate picture of one kind of India, at least, seems to emerge—from the inside out as it were. Yet Ray also achieves a rare degree of universal validity and timelessness because these people, as most people, are concerned primarily with the conflicts and loyalties of generations, familial and marital love, the necessity of maintaining existence (frequently at odds with the pursuit of an ideal), and fulfillment through satisfying work. He speaks for humankind as well as for Bengalis.

Pather Panchali, and *Aparajito* even more, is made up solely of diverse incidents from the life of the family. It has no story in the usual sense, nor is it documentary either, obviously. If (maybe because) it lacks beginning, middle, and end, it flows as life itself to a degree I can't remember equalled elsewhere, even in the greatest of the Italian neorealist films. It ends when the father, who has been away trying to earn enough money to support them, returns home. In his absence the aged aunt has died, and more recently and cruelly, his older child, a lovely adolescent girl, died of pneumonia caught while playing in the first of the rains. Father, mother, and Apu—their grim and intractable economic situation unresolved—load their few belongings onto an ox cart and depart for Benares.

Early in *Aparajito* the father dies, and the remainder of the film, with its sustained note of moving sadness, concerns the gentle and loving tension created by Apu's ambition for an education (which also means westernization) and his mother's conflicting need for his affection and the traditional ways. *The World of Apu* deals with Apu's

---

[3] Paul Grimes, "Indian Moviemaker Who Flees Escape," *The New York Times Magazine,* June 26, 1960, pp. 42–43.

Pather Panchali (India, 1955, Satyajit Ray). National Film Archive/Stills Library.

early manhood—his life in Calcutta, his marriage—and concludes with his relationship to his young son after his wife dies in childbirth.

Following the trilogy, Ray moved toward more strictly Indian and personal concerns. Somewhat like the Italian film makers, he shifted from the poorer to the middle and upper-middle classes of which he is a member and away from material to spiritual (even religious) and psychological themes. In *Devi* (*The Goddess,* 1960), a deeply religious feudal landlord becomes obsessed with the notion that his daughter-in-law is a goddess. *Kanchanjungha* (1962), *Charulata* (1964), and *Days and Nights in the Forest* (1970) are all concerned with complicated and shifting family, marital, and sexual relationships among the well-to-do and well educated. Frequently, like Ozu in Japan, Ray treated the old in a changing India, and the peculiar and fascinating mixture of East and West left as a legacy of British colonialism. *The Music Room* (1958), for example, deals with a vanishing feudal culture, the protagonist being the last in a line of landed aristocrats in British India. *The Chess Players* (1977) is set amidst nineteenth-century expansion of British colonial power. Ray was also consistently concerned with the role of women. *Mahanagar* (*The Big City,* 1963), addressing attitudes about women and work and independence from male-dominated households and traditional roles, is one example.

In the totality of his work to date, Ray has been neither the "Indian neorealist" nor the "Flaherty of Bengal" that he has been called. Instead, he is a strong, highly individualistic film maker who has achieved a position from which he can pursue his own artistic preoccupations. While his films have become less easily universal, demanding more understanding of Indian cultural and social traditions and problems, they have also become more polished and theatrical, noteworthy for their brilliant acting. (This tendency first became evident in *The World of Apu.*) The post-trilogy films offer both less and more than the trilogy, but to date Ray has remained an Indian film maker who has continued to command our attention.

Following the success of *Pather Panchali,* there developed what is called, in reference to the commercial mainstream of Indian film making, New Indian Cinema, or Parallel Cinema. Along with Ray, Mrinal Sen and Ritwik Ghatak are considered its founding fathers. Except for Ray's work, New Indian Cinema has scarcely reached the West; the films discussed below were shown in a series under that heading which toured museums in the United States in 1982–1983.

Mrinal Sen's features, some twenty-five or more in number, are quite different from those of either Ray or Ghatak, though all three are Bengalis. A Marxist, Sen experimented for awhile with form as well as content, in the manner of Frenchman Jean-Luc Godard, in an effort to create a revolutionary cinema. *Bhuvan Shome (Mister Shome,* 1969), Sen's biggest success, was the first low-budget feature financed by the Indian government. Its title character is a stuffy senior officer of the Indian railways. During a holiday in rural India he is transformed by his experience of country people and country ways, especially those of the cheeky young wife of a lowly railway clerk. It is both funny and lyrical. *In Search of Famine* (1980) is about film makers visiting a rural settlement in order to get the villagers to reenact the terrible famine of 1943 (also the subject of Ray's *Distant Thunder,* 1973). The interaction between the urban film crew and their rural subjects generates tension and ultimately forces the crew to abandon the actual and retreat to the security of the make-believe world of the studio. Biting irony is the prevailing tone.

Ritwik Ghatak, who died in 1976, directed only seven feature films, though he made a good many documentaries and wrote scripts for others' features. It is said that practically all of his films are about the social tensions and turmoil in Bengal. *Ajantrik (Pathetic Fallacy,* 1958) is about a taxi driver in a small provincial town and his ancient and decrepit Ford. The taxi is his only, and highly valued, companion, except for his brief encounters with the varied fares who join him in it. The film ends with the death and dismemberment of his faithful friend, the taxi; his sense of loss is shared by the audience, thanks to the special blend of enchantment and realism that Ghatak managed to create.

Among the other directors of New Indian Cinema, Shyam Benegal, who lives and works in Bombay, is perhaps best known abroad. *Ankur (The Seedling,* 1974), his first feature, was a considerable success. Evidently it is a strong, tragic protest against the feudal society that has persisted in rural South India. *Manthan (The Churning,* 1976) seems to be the only film of the New Indian Cinema available on 16mm in the U.S. It was financed by individual contributions from the farmers of Gujarat State and deals with the attempts of a westernized Indian government official to set up a milk cooperative in a little village. The official becomes ensnared in caste and hierarchical entanglements that arise to thwart his efforts. The film seems extraordinarily honest in its portrayal of the difficulties, misunderstandings, and cross purposes that surely would face an outsider attempting to bring about change in a tradition-bound society. *Bhumika (The Role,* 1977), another considerable success, is based on the biography of an actual female star of theater and film in the 1940s, dubbed the "Joan Crawford of India." It reveals much about the world of popular entertainment and the constrictions placed on the life of even a successful woman in Indian culture. Benegal's concerns seem to embody feminism and Marxism; his style is more extravagant and sensuous than that of other directors of the New Indian Cinema. He seems to have kept steadily at work and continues to attract attention at international film festivals.

Perhaps best thought of as adjunct to Indian film are the collaborations of

Ismail Merchant (producer), James Ivory (director), and Ruth Prawer Jhabvala (writer). Though made for the international market, with dialogue in English, their features are mostly about India—particularly about Anglo-Indian relationships. *Shakespeare-Wallah* (1965), centered on a resolutely English family of touring actors in postcolonial India, was their first success. It was followed by *The Guru* (1969), *Bombay Talkie* (1970), *Autobiography of a Princess* (1975), *Hullabaloo Over Georgie and Bonnie's Pictures* (1978), *Heat and Dust* (1982), among others. These films all have a kind of close and subtle observation of surface manners and cultural strains reminiscent of E. M. Forster's *A Passage to India,* or of Henry James (to whom they devoted one of their films, *The Europeans,* 1979), an author who dealt with other cross-cultural exchanges. These concerns are not surprising since the three film makers themselves comprise a striking cultural mix: Merchant is Indian, Ivory is American, and Jhabvala is German-born of Polish-Jewish descent who became an Indian by marriage.

Because it reaches international audiences, Merchant Ivory Productions falls within the orbit of the American film industry. Though what we call Hollywood changed radically in many ways during the fifties, when the Japanese and Indian film first began attracting world attention, one way in which it did not change so much as become more so was its dependence on and domination of world distribution. The next chapter is a return to America and what happened here during the decade following 1952, the year we left it at the end of Chapter 13.

FILMS OF THE PERIOD

India

1955
Pather Panchali (Satyajit Ray)

1956
Aparajito (Ray)

1958
Ajantrik/Pathetic Fallacy (Ritwik Ghatak)
The Music Room (Ray)
The World of Apu (Ray)

1960
Devi/The Goddess (Ray)

1962
Kanchanjungha (Ray)

1963
Mahanagar/The Big City (Ray)

1964
Charulata/The Lonely Wife (Ray)

1969
Bhuvan Shome/Mister Shome (Mrinal Sen)
Sara Akash/The Whole Sky (Basu Chatterji)

1970
Days and Nights in the Forest (Ray)
Samskara/Last Rites
   (Pattabhi Rama Reddy)
Uski Roti/Daily Bread (Mani Kaul)

1972
Maya Darpan/Magic Mirror
   (Kumar Shahami)

1973
Distant Thunder (Ray)
Kaadu/The Forest (Girish Karnad)
27 Down (Awtar Kaul)

1975
Garm Hava/Scorching Wind
   (M. S. Sathyu)

1976
Manthan/The Churning (Shyam Benegal)

1977
Bhumika/The Role (Benegal)
The Chess Players (Ray)

Ghatashraddha/The Ritual
  (Girish Kasaravalli)
Kanchana Sita/Golden Sita (G. Aravindan)
Kodiyettam/Ascent
  (Adoor Gopalakrishnan)

1978
Ondanondu Kaladalli/Once Upon a Time
  (Karnad)

1980
Aakaler Sandhaney/In Search of Famine (Sen)
Aakrosh/Cry of the Wounded
  (Govind Nihalani)
*Albert Pinto Ko Gussa Kyon Aata Hai/What
Makes Albert Pinto Angry*
  (Saeed Mirza)
Bhavni Bhavai/A Folk Tale (Ketan Mehta)
Chakra/Vicious Circle
  (Rabindra Dharmaraj)

Japan

1950
Rashomon (Akira Kurosawa)

1952
Ikiru (Kurosawa)
The Life of O'Haru (Kenji Mizoguchi)

1953
Gate of Hell (Teinosuke Kinugasa)
Tokyo Story (Yasujiro Ozu)
Ugetsu (Mizoguchi)

1954
Chikamatsu Monogatari (Mizoguchi)
Sansho Dayu/The Bailiff (Mizoguchi)
Seven Samurai (Kurosawa)

1955
Princess Yang Kwei Fei (Mizoguchi)

1956
The Burmese Harp (Kon Ichikawa)

1957
The Lower Depths (Kurosawa)
The Throne of Blood (Kurosawa)

1958
Enjo (Ichikawa)

1959
Fires on the Plain (Ichikawa)

1961
An Autumn Afternoon (Ozu)
The Human Condition
  (1958–61, Masaki Kobayashi)
The Island (Kaneto Shindo)

1962
Harakiri (Kobayashi)

1964
Kwaidan (Kobayashi)
Onibaba (Shindo)
Woman of the Dunes
  (Hiroshi Teshigahara)

1965
Red Beard (Kurosawa)

1968
Death by Hanging (Nagisa Oshima)
Diary of a Shinjuku Thief (Oshima)

1969
Boy (Oshima)
Double Suicide (Masahiro Shinoda)

1970
Dodeska-den (Kurosawa)

1971
The Ceremony (Oshima)

1975
Dersu Uzala (Kurosawa)
Kaseki (Kobayashi)

1976
In the Realm of the Senses (Oshima)

1979
Realm of Passion (Oshima)

1981
Kagemusha/The Shadow Warrior
  (Kurosawa)

BOOKS ON THE PERIOD

China

LEYDA, JAY,   *Dianying: Electric Shadows: An Account of Films and the Film Audience in China.* Cambridge, Mass.: The MIT Press, 1972. 272 pp.

Hong Kong

MO-LING, LEONG, ed.,   *A Study of the Hong Kong Swordplay Film (1945–1980).* Hong Kong: Fifth International Film Festival, 1981.

Study of the Hong Kong Martial Arts Film, A. Program book for the Fourth International Hong Kong Film Festival, April 1980.

India

BARNOUW, ERIK, and S. KRISHNASWAMY,   *Indian Film.* New York: Oxford University Press, 1980. 327 pp.

CUNHA, UMADA, ed.,   *Film India: The New Generation, 1960–1980.* New Delhi: The Directorate of Film Festivals, 1981. 184 pp.

Japan

ANDERSON, JOSEPH L., and DONALD RICHIE,   *The Japanese Film: Art and Industry (Expanded Edition).* Princeton, N.J.: Princeton University Press, 1982. 500 pp.

BOCK, AUDIE,   *Japanese Film Directors.* New York: Kodansha International USA, Ltd., 1978.

BURCH, NOËL,   *To the Distant Observer: Form and Meaning in the Japanese Cinema.* Berkeley: University of California Press, 1979. 387 pp.

MELLEN, JOAN,   *Voices from the Japanese Cinema.* New York: Liveright, 1975. 295 pp.

MELLEN, JOAN,   *The Waves at Genji's Door: Japan through its Cinema.* New York: Pantheon Books, 1977. 463 pp.

RICHIE, DONALD,   *Japanese Cinema: Film Style and National Character.* Garden City, N.J.: Doubleday & Co., Inc., 1971. 261 pp.

RICHIE, DONALD,   *The Japanese Movie: An Illustrated History.* New York: Kodansha International USA, Ltd., 1982. 216 pp.

SATO, TADAO,   *Currents in Japanese Cinema.* New York: Kodansha International USA, Ltd., 1982. 352 pp.

TUCKER, RICHARD N.,   *Japan—Film Image.* London: Studio Vista Publishers, 1973. 144 pp.

16

Hollywood in Transition, 1952–1962

In the history of motion pictures, 1952 marked the beginning of a transition that would lead the American film industry from the hardened confines of a production-distribution-exhibition pattern that had lasted for over two decades into uncertainty and changing forms and functions. In film history, what affects the industry affects the art; what happens in America influences the world.

Richard Dyer MacCann, in his perceptive book from which the title for this chapter has been borrowed, refers to the major changes that began in Hollywood about 1952 as "expanded freedoms." He lists freedom from censorship, from centralized studio production, from domination by the domestic box office, and from the tyranny of the assembly line. In what follows, much the same matters will be organized and dealt with in a somewhat different way, but 1952 remains the key year. That was the first full year in which the whole nation was blanketed by network television. It was also the year that brought wide screens and stereophonic sound, and more practicable and less expensive (Eastman) color. About that time, too, cracks began to show in the major studios and a new growth of independent production sprouted. Concurrently, the making of American films abroad and the dependence of Hollywood on foreign revenue increased. Finally, 1952 was the year of a Supreme Court decision that marked the beginning of a loosening of the social controls on film content.

Central factors accounting for and accompanying these changes were the decline in theater attendance from the booming war and postwar years and the breakup

271

of the single, mass audience into separate specialized audiences—youths, intellectuals, blacks, and so on. The former "family audience" was now a minority audience, administered to mainly by Walt Disney Productions. Going to the movies, once the staple form of entertainment, became more of a special occasion somewhere between staying home to watch TV and attending live theater or a concert. With increased public affluence, motion pictures were competing for leisure time with spectator sports, bowling, motorboating, hi-fi sets, and a whole range of new activities. Whereas in 1946, as *Variety* noted, almost $1.7 billion (or almost 20 percent of all U.S. recreation expenditures) were paid in movie admissions, by 1962 that figure had plummeted to $930 million (or about 4.5 percent)—in spite of inflating ticket prices.

By 1952, the major studios had had to divest themselves of their theater holdings. After a decade of litigation, from 1938 to 1948, the Supreme Court had finally ruled, in *U.S.* v. *Paramount Pictures Inc. et al.,* that the practice of "vertical control" was in restraint of trade and tended toward monopoly. The majors might continue to produce and distribute but not exhibit. In the mid-forties about 400 features had been produced annually—300 by the major studios, 100 by the independents. Every week between 80 million and 100 million persons had paid admission to see them in 18,719 "hard-top" theaters and 300 drive-ins. By 1960 the average weekly attendance—in 13,200 indoor and 4,600 outdoor theaters—had dropped to an estimated 46 million weekly. Of the 136 features produced in that year, only 70 came from the major studios while 66 were from the independents. Those trends—fewer pictures, more of which were by independents; smaller audiences; and a decrease in the total number of theaters, with the proportion of drive-in theaters increasing—would continue throughout the sixties and into the seventies.

TELEVISION

It was TV, of course, that occupied most of the leisure time of the public who formerly would have gone to the movies. The shifting relationship between motion pictures and broadcasting is one of the main chapters in the history of those two industries during the fifties and sixties. Television had begun on an experimental basis just before World War II, but wartime priorities and shortages had frozen its development until the postwar years. From five stations and a few hundred sets in 1946 it expanded rapidly to the first year of big-time television in 1948, when Milton Berle and Ed Sullivan were seen and heard in the large urban centers. By 1950 there were one hundred stations and 4 million sets. From there the next step was to cover the nation; in 1951 coaxial cable and microwave relay connected coast to coast and most of the land in between. From the early fifties on the audience has continued to expand. Today there are more television sets than persons in the country. An especially popular program (*Dallas*), sporting event (all-star football) or government activity (Congressional investigating committee) might draw viewers in excess of 40 million.

Until 1948 the motion picture industry's reaction to the TV threat was ostrich-like. At one studio it was reported to be forbidden even to use the word *television* in executive conversation. Then the stance shifted to passive resistance through deliberate withholding of the enormous resources of talent and reservoir of product. No actors, writers, or directors under contract were permitted to work for television. No feature films produced by the major studios were offered for airing. Films playing in theaters were not advertised on television. Revenues from the box office continued to decline, of course, and complaints from stockholders about dwindling dividends, steadily to increase.

The critical problem was finding access to an audience. Since the production companies no longer owned the theaters, which anyway were being converted into supermarkets or razed to make way for parking lots, their loyalty to the theater owners and resolve to try to protect them from even greater television competition was weakened. When the pressures finally became too great, the studios followed the old industry saw about joining 'em if you can't beat 'em. They began by making available to TV the vast libraries of feature films that had accumulated over the past decades.

The unloading of the vaults, if it set the motion picture industry in competition with itself, was also designed to cause some damage to the enemy. The leasing and outright sale of the hundreds of old feature films was directed toward the independent stations, either directly or through packaging agencies, so as to constitute maximum competition to network programming. The number of features totaled in the thousands and were all disposed of within a couple of years. RKO, after Howard Hughes's withdrawal, and tottering on the brink of financial collapse, was the first major to sell: 740 of its features went to General Teleradio in December 1955. This sale was followed in rapid succession by Columbia, Warner, M-G-M, United Artists, and the others. Paramount was last to dispose of its great backlog of 750 features, in February 1958.

By 1961 the networks joined the local stations to provide prime-time airing of past major films, which could now be seen in color by an ever-increasing number of viewers. The popularity of theatrical feature films with television audiences has, of course, been enormous. When *The Bridge on the River Kwai* was aired by ABC-TV on Sunday night prime time in 1966, the audience was estimated at 60 million. *The New York Times,* sounding like *Variety* in its excitement, offered to explain "Why 'Kwai' KO'd 'Bonanza' and Ed Sullivan." By the early seventies not only had the backlog of old features been used up, but the supply of recent theatrical film releases was far below the television demand.

The ultimate response of Hollywood to television was to undertake production directly for the tube. It began in 1952 when Columbia Pictures formed the first of the television subsidiaries among the major studios—Screen Gems. This television film making started with the half-hour entertainment series, which became hour-long and, in some cases, even ninety minutes in length, resembling more and more the old "B" pictures that were no longer a profitable kind of production for the more specialized audiences of the theaters. The production for television exerted a gravitational pull towards the West Coast. Soon virtually all nighttime television entertainment was being produced in the Los Angeles area. Only news, documentary and public affairs, and some daytime game shows and soap operas continued to come out of New York. By the mid-sixties Hollywood began to make feature films directly for TV rather than for initial theatrical showing.

As television became established people and product began to flow from it into film. Out of the so-called Golden Age of live TV drama in the early fifties, theatrical feature films were created from the writings of Paddy Chayefsky, Rod Serling, Robert Alan Aurthur, Reginald Rose, Merle Miller, and others. *Marty* (1955), *The Catered Affair* (1956), *Patterns* (1956), *Edge of the City* (1957), *Twelve Angry Men* (1957), *The Bachelor Party* (1957), *The Goddess* (1959), and *Requiem for a Heavyweight* (1962) had all appeared live on the tube. Directors as well as writers came to features from television: Delbert Mann,

Marty (U.S., 1955, Delbert Mann). Museum of Modern Art/Film Stills Archive.

Sidney Lumet, John Frankenheimer, Robert Mulligan, Sam Peckinpah, Norman Jewison, Ralph Nelson among them. Some of the new stars—Dick Van Dyke, Steve McQueen, James Garner, Rod Taylor—male only, it seems, had also gotten their start in television.

Financial control, studio facilities, story material, production personnel and performers have continued to move back and forth between film and television. This is a situation that doesn't seem likely to change.

NEW SCREEN PROCESSES

All three major technological additions to the silent black-and-white film—sound, color, wide screen—were around from the very beginning. Their introduction was in every case dependent more upon economic considerations than upon technical feasibility. Whenever the industry is in trouble somebody will say, "There's nothing wrong with the movies that a few good pictures can't cure." But if the producers knew how to make consistently profitable films, there wouldn't have been any trouble in the first place. If popular success can't be guaranteed, technical novelty can be tried. Sound came in 1927 because of the competition radio then offered for the audiences of silent films, and because Warner Brothers was attempting corporate expansion. Technicolor was added to feature film production in 1935 in an attempt to remedy the continuing Depression slump. In 1952 the failing box office and television competition once again goaded the industry into introducing a number of "new screen processes." All were designed to offer sights and sounds that the competitive medium could not duplicate, and to give the screen a greater illusion of depth.

Stereoscopic, or 3-D, feature films first appeared in the fall of 1952. (In the thirties, there had been a series of M-G-M black-and-white 3-D shorts; polaroid lenses now permitted the addition of color.) Natural Vision was what veteran radio and film writer-producer-director Arch Oboler called the 3-D process when it was inaugurated with *Bwana Devil*. It seemed to the audience that a lion was charging them (promotion for *Bwana Devil* promised "A lion in your lap"), or a spear was being thrown over their heads.

The 3-D films were at first extremely successful, but their attraction wore off within less than a year. It was said that audiences didn't like the special glasses required, nor the eye strain that sometimes resulted. If they weren't as discontent with the routine quality of the films rushed out to capitalize on the novelty (such as *House of Wax,* 1952; *The Charge at Feather River* and *Devil's Canyon,* both 1953), they might well have been. By the time any substantial work was undertaken in 3-D the audience had lost interest. A few films opened in New York City in both 3-D and two-dimensional versions with no appreciable difference in the number of tickets sold. *Kiss Me Kate* (1953) and Hitchcock's *Dial M for Murder* (1954), both made for 3-D, were released in two-dimension. Introduced a couple of months after the wide screen had made its appearance with Cinerama, 3-D came and went, while the wide screen has lasted in one form or another ever since.

Though 3-D systems give a stronger illusion of depth and are in some ways more interesting in their aesthetic potential, it was the wide screens, with the grandeur they added (in the late twenties a wide-screen system called Magnascope had been referred to as the "grandeur screen"), that caught the public fancy. The first of the new wide-screen processes was the biggest and best of them in terms of spatial illusion. *This Is Cinerama* opened in New York City in September 1952. Developed by Fred Waller from 1939 on, it had been used in an earlier version by the Armed Forces during World War II for aircraft identification and mock gunnery practice. The screen, with a 2.85 to 1 ratio of width to height, was deeply curved and vast. A necessarily small audience sitting well forward had virtually everyone's whole field of vision filled by the image. Viewers felt they really were on that roller coaster or on that plane coming in over the Chicago skyline.

Accompanying the visual format of great width and depth was a hi-fidelity,

Dial M for Murder (U.S., 1954, Alfred Hitchcock). Museum of Modern Art/Film Stills Archive.

Artist's representation of an audience watching *This Is Cinerama* (U.S., 1952, Merian C. Cooper). Museum of Modern Art/Film Stills Archive.

stereophonic, magnetic sound system. Its enormously increased range of frequencies brought sound reproduction much closer to life than the woefully inadequate optical recording in standard use. Multiple microphones and speakers (up to seven tracks and eleven speakers in later Cinerama productions; twenty speakers were used for the stereoscopic *House of Wax*) caused the sound to follow the images; volume increased and decreased across the screen and around the auditorium in accord with the location of the sound-producing sources.

　　The development of Cinerama had been backed by people outside the Hollywood industry—Mike Todd, Louis de Rochemont, Lowell Thomas, and others—but the studio heads could scarcely be blind to its huge financial success. *This Is Cinerama* was soon numbered among the great moneymakers of all time, and the several features that followed it, playing in only a few specially equipped and converted "legitimate" theaters at live theater prices, consistently appeared high on *Variety*'s box office tallies. The opportunities and problems Cinerama posed for the industry were not unlike those that had accompanied *The Jazz Singer*'s success a quarter of a century earlier. The appeal of this new gadget to audiences, who had been staying away from the theaters in droves, as Sam Goldwyn is said to have remarked on another occasion, was obvious. But the expense of conversion and unfamiliarity with the techniques required by the new system were awesome obstacles.

　　Cinerama's cumbersome technology and the small audiences which could be accommodated at each showing presented too severe a wrench to existing production and exhibition practices to be contemplated without alarm. Furthermore, the Cinerama films were essentially a group of travelogue shorts anthologized to feature length. The kinds of stories that might fill that monstrous screen seemed extremely limited. An appropriate size and shape for parades down Fifth Avenue, a train speeding across the

Mojave Desert, or two boa constrictors copulating, as someone observed, it offered no clear advantage in dealing with individual human beings (who happen to stand upright), unless they were in quantities of thousands. Even more basically, the use of closeups and editing, essential to screen narrative technique as practiced, would be greatly reduced if not prohibited by what seemed acres of image. What was needed was a sort of poor man's Cinerama—one which spiced up but didn't depart too much from the existing standard.

It was Spyros Skouras, head of Twentieth Century-Fox, who performed the trick. The rabbit he pulled out of the hat was called CinemaScope (and better not forget to capitalize the middle S if you were a Fox employee). It was based on a principle worked out in the twenties by a French inventor, Henri Chretien. Its wide screen was less wide than Cinerama's and curved only enough to accommodate focus. Though wider than standard (2.55 to 1 rather than 1.33 to 1), CinemaScope did not approximate peripheral vision. It was accompanied in its premiere by hi-fidelity four-track stereophonic sound.

Unlike the inauguration of the earlier 3-D, CinemaScope was launched with a feature that probably would have made money no matter what the size and shape of the screen. As it was, *The Robe,* which opened in September 1953, proved a tremendous success with its De Mille-like blend of spectacle and religiosity. It was followed by a series of expensive and well-made features, musicals and comedies especially, equally designed to show off the attractions of the new screen process; for example, *Gentlemen Prefer Blondes* (1953), *How to Marry a Millionaire* (1953), *A Star Is Born* (1954), *Seven Brides for Seven Brothers* (1954).

Fox was to wide screen what Warner had been to sound, and again the rest of the industry soon followed along. CinemaScope proved the almost ideal compromise between Cinerama and the conventional screen ratio. It required no major change in production technology or even technique, and was simple and inexpensive to install in existing movie houses. Though it favored certain film types—historical spectacles, musicals, westerns—and was awkward for others—intimate romances, social dramas—stories could be told in it, with fewer camera setups and less editing required. Some of the purists complained that the image it offered was like looking at the world through a postal slot, and Jean Cocteau is credited with remarking that he recognized progress when he saw it and henceforward would put paper in the typewriter sideways when he wrote his poems. But who cared about the purists; the box office was registering public response in large figures. As with sound, directors learned to work with CinemaScope, many reluctantly at first. The new technological addition was incorporated into the medium, with resultant aesthetic shifts and even some gains—like all of the earlier technological additions. In *East of Eden* (1955), for example, director Elia Kazan and cinematographer Ted McCord made stunning and highly dramatic use of the new proportions for what was essentially an intimate story of family strife.

Other wide-screen systems soon appeared. VistaVision, from Paramount, was a good alternative, providing a sharper image than CinemaScope. Projection for it was never worked out adequately, however, and it was soon abandoned. Todd A-O was the first to use 70mm film; Cinerama converted from three 35mm strips to a single 70mm one beginning with *It's a Mad, Mad, Mad, Mad World* (1963); Panavision was a later 70mm system.

But the extremely wide screens didn't become the exclusive shape, as some feared they might when CinemaScope first appeared. (Full 'Scope, as it's called, is now

The Robe (U.S., 1953, Henry Koster). Museum of Modern Art/Film Stills Archive.

2.35 to 1.) Rather, they eventually became reserved for the extravaganza—the big musical (*My Fair Lady*, 1964; *The Sound of Music*, 1965), the block-busting war picture (*The Guns of Navarone*, 1961; *The Longest Day*, 1962), the historical spectacular (*Lawrence of Arabia*, 1962; *Doctor Zhivago*, 1965). For more conventional pictures what is called the "standard wide screen"—1.85 to 1 its most common ratio—has replaced the former 1.33 to 1 that has remained standard for television sets.

Wide screens with hi-fidelity stereophonic sound, and the predominant use of (better) color, have led film away from the formal aesthetics of Sergei Eisenstein, Rudolf Arnheim, and others, which dominated up through the forties. Eisenstein had taken particular satisfaction in the temporal-spatial fragmentation of filmed reality possible through montage, and Arnheim, in the limitations of the silent black-and-white two-dimensional image of conventional ratio that kept it from being a faithful recording of life. Since the writings of these early formalists, technological additions have provided a greater "redemption of physical reality," which realist Siegfried Kracauer exalted in his *Theory of Film* as the special power of the medium. The amount and fidelity of the sensory data reproduced by the newer screen processes brings film several steps closer to the "total cinema" invoked by André Bazin in *What is Cinema?*

FALL OF THE STUDIOS AND RISE
OF THE INDEPENDENTS

Another result of the pressures and changes experienced by the industry in the early fifties was a shakeup in production-distribution practices, which also affected the content and form of the films being made. Among the producing companies it was the former giants, now stripped of their theaters, that were hit hardest by the dwindling and erratic earnings of their films. The enormous overhead in real estate, sound stages, expensive equipment, and high-salaried technical and creative personnel on long-term contracts could no longer be supported by the fewer, more costly films that current audience response dictated. Whereas M-G-M had once boasted as its greatest asset ''More Stars Than There Are in Heaven,'' these expensive nonworking actors, along with the writers and directors, had become a liability. All of the major studios except one were keeping their books in red ink.

That exception was United Artists, which had never owned theaters and didn't even have a studio. Instead, it had acquired films from independent producers and distributed them to theaters owned by others. It would choose from among the projects presented to it, perhaps supervise the scripts, put up some money and go to the bank for more. What it could guarantee to its producers was major distribution, for which it took a healthy cut. Its production overhead consisted mostly of offices, secretaries, and smart lawyers good at contracts and finance. Billy Wilder, one of United Artists' top producer-directors, observed ruefully, ''We used to make pictures; now we make deals.'' A weak competitor in the old days, when the larger studios controlled exhibition, under the new conditions UA prospered and became the model others would imitate.

The rest of the studios freed themselves from employees under long-term contracts, except for skeleton technical crews. The actors, directors and former staff producers went into production for themselves, or worked for other independents, with corporate profits and shares in the income from a picture replacing salaries. The studios rented out production space and facilities to the independents, financed their productions wholly or in part, and distributed the completed films. Rather than reading simply ''Produced by,'' Paramount or Warner Brothers, opening credits now read ''A Judd Bernard–Irwin Winkler Production for Metro-Goldwyn-Mayer'' or ''A Horizon Picture, Released through Columbia Pictures Corporation,'' and the like.

The independent companies were by no means totally independent, however, and the kinds of films they produced departed very little from those that had preceded them. The domination once exercised by the heads of five studios (Metro-Goldwyn-Mayer, Paramount, Warner Brothers, Twentieth Century-Fox, and RKO) was steadily being reduced. The independents still had to play ball with the majors, however, whose remaining strongholds were their worldwide distribution organizations. This gave them power to exercise substantial control over the choice of subject matter and its presentation.

Another reason there was less change than might have been expected in the kinds of films being made with this new independence was that the smaller companies were subjected to exactly the same necessity for popular appeal as the large ones had been. In fact, in the case of the independents, the pressure was even greater. With only one picture produced at a time on borrowed money, rather than an annual production program of forty or fifty features financed out of studio reserves, each film had to be a success. Hits couldn't pay for flops. In some respects there seemed less room for experiment and risk than there had been under the old system. Many of the former studio personnel who formed their own companies stuck even closer to tested ingredients than the studios had done. Those who had cried for freedom from the repeated formulas of studio production and expressed the desire to strike out into bold new areas, to do something "really worthwhile," settled for the tried and true. To paraphrase G. B. Shaw, there's nothing as timid as several million dollars.

The little "B" programmers of the thirties and forties had sometimes proved an excellent if modest field for trial and error. They had also served as a training ground for talent and permitted the careful building of careers. Now the stakes were too high. Bidding on the open market for stories and the services of top-flight performers and directors had reached an unprecedented level. Without the major studios' vested interest in the industry as a whole, there was no one to assume responsibility for developing new creative talent.

Yet, if we have come to reevaluate the studio production of the thirties and forties, and found excellences that weren't as apparent when they were routine, few would want to go back to the old studio system even if that were possible. With picture-by-picture film making there began to be a greater chance, however high the odds, for the strong creative personality to dominate and control a work without ruinous interference from the front office. It is more than coincidental that in those years of the fifties in which the studios were declining, directors were gaining a new status. When M-G-M, once biggest and proudest of the studios, virtually went out of the motion picture business altogether in the 1970s, the film makers who would have worked for M-G-M still found their way to film making if they were smart enough and tough enough—constant prerequisites to creation in motion picture art. If film artists spent a lot of their time making deals, as Wilder quipped, they were free from the power and over-zealous supervision of production chiefs like Irving Thalberg, and from conceptions of God, country, and motherhood as revealed to Louis B. Mayer.

INTERNATIONALIZATION

Along with all of the other sweeping changes, there even seemed some danger that Los Angeles, as film capital of the world, might cease to exist and fall into ruins like Carthage or ancient Rome. American films were in increasing competition with foreign ones—especially with those of Britain, Italy and France—for audiences abroad and even in this country. Co-national productions and multinational crews and casts became commonplace. And "American" films themselves were as likely to be shot anywhere in the world as within proximity of Hollywood and Vine.

The first consideration to prompt this increased internationalization may have been in part an artistic one. Wide screens encouraged special emphasis on authentic and exotic locales. For conventional sorts of love stories that formerly would have been shot on the sound stages and back lots, film makers now journeyed to Rome (*Three Coins in a Fountain,* 1954), Hong Kong (*Love Is a Many-Splendored Thing,* 1955), or Tokyo (*Sayonara,* 1957). Audiences of the fifties began to get moving-picture postcards along with stars and stories. Some of the spectacles made for the wide screen were very much about the places and terrain where the stories took place: *The Bridge on the River Kwai* (1957), the Southeast Asian jungle; *Lawrence of Arabia* (1962), the Middle Eastern desert.

The secondary considerations were exclusively financial. First, by shooting abroad, American producers could more easily assemble a cast drawn from a number of countries to better ensure the warm reception of their films in various parts of the globe. Then too, there was the advantage, for the Americans involved, of delayed payment of U.S. corporate and income taxes on work done outside the country. Also, it was thought to be, and in many cases actually was, cheaper to make films abroad. Generally costs were less in Mexico, Spain, or Italy, for example—especially for labor. (A counter-argument was that the apparent saving was often canceled out in working with less-efficient crews who used unfamiliar methods and languages.) There was no doubt that the various schemes of subsidy offered by most foreign governments to encourage national production was a real incentive. Many essentially American films were disguised as British, say—their production set up in a way that met minimum requirements for assistance from Britain's National Film Finance Corporation. In addition, where a quota system existed for proportionate release of foreign to domestic films, as in Britain and elsewhere, a film flying the local flag would be assured immediate exhibition there rather than having to wait among the films of other nations. In some cases, India for example, American profits had become "frozen currency" and couldn't be taken out of the country. One way to make use of that money was to spend it on a production which could then be distributed worldwide and earn revenue elsewhere.

Distribution as well as production became increasingly internationalized. Not only were American companies seeking income from the distribution of foreign films in the United States; but also, as their own production expenses increased and the size of the domestic audience decreased, they needed to earn back more and more of their costs from abroad. In former years the huge American market could return a profit on a film, and what was earned elsewhere was gravy. Now over 50 per cent of the income from American films came from overseas. More than ever Hollywood courted the world audience.

Finally, the motion picture industry developed its own equivalent to the plants set up abroad and the multinational corporations that had become common practice among other industries. Not only was there a British M-G-M, as there was an English Ford, but the United States dominated and to some extent controlled foreign financing of production and international distribution. In terms of financial backing and distribution, Antonioni's *Blow-Up* (1966), made in England, was as much an American film as his *Zabriskie Point,* made in the U.S. American influence began to reach even into films that appeared to be totally French, and the work of auteurs at that. Jean-Luc Godard's *A Married Woman* and *Band of Outsiders* (both 1964) were financed by Columbia Pictures. Though the European Economic Community tried to set up an alternative financing-distribution pattern to counter American domination, little came of the effort.

Given the increased internationalization of film production-distribution-exhibition, American-controlled or not, it became possible for works that did not appeal to the large audience to earn back their costs by playing for six weeks or longer in small theaters in London, Copenhagen, Paris, Mexico City, New York, and elsewhere. This change, along with the increase in independent production, loosened the rigidities and altered the mass-product conception underlying the old industrial patterns. The new system was able, if not as easily as we would like, to adjust to a greater variety of films and to give them wider international distribution than ever before. Sometimes this increased internationalization and Americanization tended to dilute valuable national qualities. At the same time, it served to stimulate film makers and audiences by affording a greater sampling of the total range of subjects and forms than had ever before been available, even in the silent years. The international spotlight began to whirl very rapidly. It was not so much one nation's production calling for attention and influencing other nations' as it was individual film artists jumping across cultural boundaries to demonstrate to each other and introduce audiences to a wide diversity of personal concerns and styles. Together, recently arrived auteurs and newly sophisticated audiences significantly advanced the art within the industry during the late fifties and early sixties.

LOOSENED CONTROLS ON CONTENT

In America, beginning in the 1950s, the social controls placed on the content of motion pictures began to be eased. This encouraged, if not always a greater maturity, at least a new freedom and frankness in the presentation of sexual behavior, states of undress, and kinds of language. During those years, the United States Supreme Court rendered a series of decisions which curtailed the activities of state and local censoring bodies. The Motion Picture Association of America liberalized its code of self-regulation and then started to classify rather than regulate screen content. Organized pressure groups—religious, ethnic, political—turned their attention away from what was showing in the theaters to what was appearing ever more widely on the tube. Producers eagerly, some desperately, took advantage of the new freedom in order to try to attract audiences away from television and to compete with the franker European films.

In 1952, in *The Miracle* case, the Supreme Court delivered what became a historic decision. The Rossellini short, which had been packaged with Pagnol's *Joffroy* and Renoir's *A Day in the Country* to be shown as *The Ways of Love,* had aroused Catholics in the New York City area, especially a Catholic veterans' organization. A modern parable of Christ's birth, *The Miracle* starred Anna Magnani as a feeble-minded peasant "Mary"; a bearded Federico Fellini appeared as an itinerant "Joseph." After a round of contretemps, including picketing and bomb threats, the New York State Board of Regents, the censoring agency, revoked the film's license on the grounds that it was "sacrilegious." When the case eventually reached the Supreme Court, the Court seemed to reverse its own precedent. In 1915, in *Mutual Film Corporation* v. *Ohio,* it had been held that motion pictures were "business pure and simple . . . not to be regarded as part of the press of the country or as organs of public opinion," and hence not subject to the freedom from censorship guaranteed by the First Amendment to the Constitution. The 1952 Court did not rule on the constitutionality of film censorship as such, however. It simply stated that "sacrilege," particularly one faith's conception of it, was not sufficient grounds for the Board of Regents' action. Nonetheless, the decision suggested some sympathy toward affording the motion picture the same freedom from restraint prior to release as that enjoyed by the other media of communication and art.

There followed a succession of cases the decisions in which seemed to support that interpretation of the Court's position. Then, in 1954, a small distributor of foreign films, Times Film Corporation, decided to further test the Court by failing to submit to the Chicago Police Department for licensing a perfectly innocuous Italian film entitled *Don Juan.* In this case the Court appeared to take a step backward. It ruled that the City

The Miracle (Italy, 1948, Roberto Rossellini). Museum of Modern Art/Film Stills Archive.

of Chicago had the right to license films, just as it licensed automobiles, push carts, and taverns. The clear implication that those films denied licenses were being censored was ignored.

In 1965, in a case brought by an exhibitor, *Friedman* v. *Maryland* (by then one of the few states still censoring films), the Court again advanced in a liberal direction. It ruled that when films were prevented from being exhibited, the burden of proof must be assumed by the government agency, and that legal processes must be expedited so as to create as little hardship as possible for the defendant. In such a case, unlike any other in our legal system, it had been as if a film were assumed "guilty" (that is, obscene) unless proven otherwise. In 1968 the Supreme Court ruled, in *Telsen* v. *Chicago,* that the Chicago film licensing act was unconstitutional.

With a later shift in Court membership toward the conservative, however, a 1973 decision regarding obscenity cases was rendered which many, not just those within the motion picture industry, regarded with consternation. It altered and clarified the former criteria for determining what constituted obscenity. Specifically, the Court mandated that the affront need be only to local—as opposed to national—community standards, and that local standards were employable in determining appeal to prurient interest. Additionally, the Court withdrew the "utterly without redeeming social value" test and substituted for it a mere lack of "serious literary, artistic, political, or scientific value."

The way now seemed open for every interested local body to impose conceivably thousands of conflicting sets of requirements on every film released within its area of jurisdiction. That this was not an imaginary danger was made clear when, less than a month after the Supreme Court ruling, the Georgia Supreme Court confirmed a ban on *Carnal Knowledge* and the conviction of a theater owner for showing it. While the citizens of Albany, Georgia, were prevented from seeing Mike Nichols's serious dark comedy about sex, the exploitive and frankly pornographic *Deep Throat* was playing to packed houses in other communities across the land.

During the same years the Motion Picture Association of America was making its own efforts, on the one hand to allow producers greater freedom of subject and treatment, and on the other to fend off attacks from those who protested that what had resulted was license rather than freedom. Since 1934 no important picture had been distributed without the seal of the MPAA's Production Code Administration. In the fifties, when two "A" features of United Artists were denied a Code seal, UA released them anyway, without it. The MPAA, now that the theaters were no longer owned or controlled by the studios, was unable to prevent the films from playing to large audiences. The first, *The Moon Is Blue* (1953), was from a popular comedy and would appear today patently moral. It was in fact about Maggie McNamara's successfully resisting the charms of David Niven. But it did contain considerable talk about sex and the word "virgin" was used. The Code office subsequently conceded that it had been unwise in refusing that film a seal. No such option existed for the second one, *The Man with the Golden Arm* (1956). Taken from the Nelson Algren novel, it dealt directly with narcotic addiction, a subject expressly forbidden by the Code.

Both films were produced and directed by Otto Preminger, who made much of the publicity and set himself up as a champion of free speech. In a show of self-righteous indignation, United Artists withdrew from the MPAA; however, it rejoined after it had collected all of its profits from the two offending films. This defiance of the Code ad-

The Man with the Golden Arm (U.S., 1955, Otto Preminger). Museum of Modern Art/ Film Stills Archive.

ministration clearly threatened the whole system of self-regulation, and other production companies, especially the independents, were becoming restive. In 1956 the Code was revised, the main change being to permit the treatment of narcotics.

A decade later Jack Valenti succeeded Eric Johnston as president of the MPAA. Since pressures from producers for increased freedom from restraint had continued to mount, and an ever-increasing number of films were being released without the Code seal (distributors of foreign films rarely bothered to apply), one of Valenti's first acts was to further liberalize the Code. Among the concessions in the 1966 revisions were permitting the use of common profanity (*Gone with the Wind*'s famous final line, "Frankly, my dear, I don't give a damn," had required a special ruling in 1939), the treatment of abortion, and justifiable suicide. In general the Code language was softened, with phrases like "good taste" and "dramatic necessity" replacing the strict prohibitions of the earlier Code.

Still, the onrush of new explicitness continued. Inasmuch as the trend seemed irreversible and the outcries provoked were largely on behalf of impressionable children, the MPAA decided that, rather than attempt to control screen content, it would regulate audience attendance. The shocking language and sexual intensity of *Who's Afraid of Virginia Woolf?* (1966) were allowed when its advertising carried the statement "Suggested for Mature Audiences." In 1968 the MPAA adopted, not without protest from members of the industry who objected to potential earnings being limited in any way, a system of age classification like those already operating in many countries, the United Kingdom, for instance. A "G" for "general" rating meant suitable for all. "M" advised parents that the content was "mature" (subsequently this became "GP" and then "PG," "parental guidance suggested"). "R" stood for "restricted": those under seventeen had to be accompanied by a parent or adult guardian. "X" indicated that only those eighteen and older would be admitted; *Midnight Cowboy* (1969) was the first X-rated Oscar winner. What once was the Production Code Administration became the Classification and Rating Administration. Enforcement was left to the theaters.

Much dissatisfaction about classification was expressed. Producers complained when they felt their films had been given a too-restrictive rating. Theater owners resented the encroachment on their domains and the nuisance involved. Organized pressure groups, notably the National Catholic Office of Motion Pictures (which replaced the Legion of Decency), protested that the ratings were too laxly administered. All pointed to the inevitable inconsistencies in the labeling of particular films. Even so, in the face of the continuing threat of legal censorship, which the 1973 Supreme Court decision seemed to encourage, most of the industry accepted the MPAA classification system as the least of possible evils.

If the freedom of expression of American film makers was still limited (and the vast sums of money involved seemed to require that), it was much closer than ever before to that enjoyed by artists working in the traditional arts, and the American screen became among the freest in the world.

SIX DIRECTORS

In 1952 General Dwight Eisenhower, hero of World War II, was elected President of the United States and again in 1956. It is generally agreed that the Eisenhower years were prosperous, placid, and very "American." The war in Korea ended in 1953. Undercurrents of disaffection that hindsight has revealed didn't surface until the troubled six-ties.

Much the same might be said of Hollywood films of the fifties in terms of placidity and Americanism. As shown earlier in this chapter, these years were not as prosperous for the film industry as the preceding decade had been. The six directors whose work will be examined here, however, were among those who were most produc-tive and successful during the period. They are George Cukor, George Stevens, Billy Wilder, Fred Zinnemann, Vincente Minnelli, and Elia Kazan. Though all worked before and afterwards, their work at this time fairly represents the qualities of American film most valued by those within the Hollywood industry, by the major critics, and by the domestic audience.

Of the six, George Cukor was the consummate professional, his direction stylish and impeccable. He began in theater in 1919 as stage manager and then director, and his films always had qualities traceable to theater. Invariably, his films were praised for their performances, especially those of women: Katharine Hepburn, Norma Shearer, Greta Garbo, Joan Crawford, Judy Holliday, Judy Garland, and Marilyn Monroe among them. Cukor specialized in literary adaptations, sophisticated come-dies, musicals, and period pictures. In the 1930s and 1940s most of his major films, many of them produced by David O. Selznick, were based on plays or novels: *A Bill of Divorcement* (1932), *Dinner at Eight* (1933), *Little Women* (1933), *David Copperfield* (1935), *Romeo and Juliet* (1936), *Camille* (1936), *Holiday* (1938), *The Women* (1939), *The Philadelphia Story* (1940), and *Gaslight* (1944).

With *A Double Life* (1947), Cukor began a collaboration with Garson Kanin and Ruth Gordon, the husband-wife screen-writing team, which lasted through six more of their original scripts. *Adam's Rib* (1949), starring Spencer Tracy and Katharine Hep-burn, with Judy Holliday in a supporting role, was the first of a series of intelligent, witty, and urbane battle-of-the-sexes comedies. It was followed by *Born Yesterday* (1950), starring Judy Holliday. These performers—Tracy, Hepburn, Holliday—continued working with Cukor in fresh and breezy vignettes of middle-class American life, much of them shot on location, eastern seaboard rather than western. In *The Marrying Kind* (1951) and *It Should Happen to You* (1954), Holliday further developed the lovable zany she had introduced in *Adam's Rib*. In *Pat and Mike* (1952), Hepburn and Tracy, who had been adversary lawyers in *Adam's Rib,* became athlete and manager, respectively. In *The Actress* (1953) Tracy played the beleaguered father of a daughter studying acting in New York City.

With *A Star Is Born* (1954) Cukor was back to Hollywood full-scale, and then some. This CinemaScope Technicolor extravaganza musical-comedy-melodrama was not only shot on the sound stages and back lots, it was about Hollywood. Furthermore, it was a remake, by Warner Brothers, of a 1937 film produced by Selznick and directed by William Wellman. Songs and dances were added; Judy Garland played the Janet Gaynor role and James Mason, Fredric March's. Among its many delights was a superb and innovative use of the new wide-screen shape, with intricate moving camera and rapid cutting. The color, too, was quite exceptional: muted and darker hues, with lots of browns and blues, replaced the standard solid and bright primary colors.

It was also a triumph for Garland and Mason in their roles of band singer Esther Blodgett, who becomes Vicki Lester, a movie star on her way up, and Norman Maine, a movie star on his way down, through a miasma of alcohol. Their love for each other, tender and touching, ennobles Norman's losing battle with himself and the

A Star Is Born (U.S., 1954, George Cukor). Museum of Modern Art/Film Stills Archive.

Hollywood system, and permits Vicki to stand up in final dignity, after her husband's suicide, as Mrs. Norman Maine.

Some regard this film as both Garland's and Cukor's finest. Both were deeply wounded, it was said, when Warner Brothers cut it from 181 minutes to 154, deleting two musical numbers along with transitional and motivational narrative material. Almost thirty years later, film historian Ronald Haver, who also had loved *A Star Is Born,* engaged in some dogged detective work that unearthed parts of the missing film. With a complete sound track plus added bits and pieces of footage and stills for the irrecoverable scenes, it was reissued in 1983 in a form that at least indicated what had been intended. Cukor, alas, died, at the age of 83, shortly before the reconstruction's first showing.

A native Californian, George Stevens was in some ways even more firmly placed in the Hollywood aristocracy than George Cukor. Both of Stevens's parents were actors, and he made his debut on stage at the age of five, performing in his father's traveling company. He began work in the film industry in 1921, as an assistant cameraman; he became a cameraman and eventually a director of shorts. He directed his first feature in 1933.

Stevens's films of the thirties varied considerably in genre but were consistently well made. For example: *Alice Adams* (1935) offers some delightful small-town Americana; *Swing Time* (1936) is one of the best of the Astaire-Rogers musicals; *Gunga Din* (1939), based on a Kipling poem, commemorates the British in India. In the forties he made three engaging comedies in succession: *Woman of the Year* (1942), the first film costarring Hepburn and Tracy; *The Talk of the Town* (1942), a distinguished jurist and his landlady joined by a suspected arsonist; *The More the Merrier* (1943), wartime housing shortage in Washington, D.C.

Then in the 1950s Stevens's work seemed to change direction and he made three of his finest films in succession: *A Place in the Sun* (1951), an updated and softened version of Theodore Dreiser's novel *The American Tragedy; Shane* (1953), a mythic tribute to the western genre (Stevens's only western); and *Giant* (1956), from the Edna Ferber novel, a celebration and castigation of Texas. These were more serious than his earlier films, with more substantial characterizations (and excellent performances), and a fuller, more exploratory use of cinematic technique.

A Place in the Sun is especially remarkable for its experimentation with sound in relation to sight. Its sound track, rich and detailed, complements the visuals to an unusual degree. A radio, unnoticed by the lonely and pregnant Alice (Shelley Winters), softly plays dance music, adding poignancy to a scene in which she waits in vain for George (Montgomery Clift), who is being drawn away from her by his attraction to the wealthy and glamorous Angela (Elizabeth Taylor). Or again, a portable radio on a deserted lakeside dock carries a newscast of the discovery of Alice's drowning, as George and Angela roar past in the near distance in a powerful speedboat. From time to time, sirens and barking dogs are heard, as they would be in life, contributing to a sense of uneasiness. A loon's cry just before Alice's death is a foreboding.

The film has a sad, romantic glow that sticks in the memory; for example, the scene in which George and Angela dance, late at night, dreamily in love. In this scene the shots, many of them huge closeups, are joined by slow dissolves rather than cuts, holding the delicate, unrecapturable moment before us. The loveliness of Angela, the hopelessness of George's longing for her, given their class differences and his obligation to Alice, are eloquently manifest. Stevens considered *A Place in the Sun* his best film.

Westerns tend to be more closely connected to genre conventions than to the historical or geographical West, but *Shane* seems to be about westerns. Its West, filmed mostly on location in Wyoming, is a lovely valley enclosed by snow-capped mountains seen in expansive panoramic shots (VistaVision and Technicolor). A drab clapboard settlement squats along a muddy street in the middle of it. The farmers settling the valley look real enough and seem to have real problems—with the land and with the ranchers who don't want them on it. Into this community rides the mysterious title character (played by Alan Ladd in white buckskin) at the time the homesteaders need him to face up to the cattle baron's hired gun, the black-garbed Wilson (Jack Palance). The simple story is seen through the eyes of a boy (Brandon de Wilde) who idolizes Shane. Shane almost becomes part of the community, almost acknowledges the attraction he and the wife (Jean Arthur) of the farmer (Van Heflin) feel for each other. But the gunfight with Wilson is what he has to do. After Wilson's death, Shane rides off into a mountain sunset. When asked where he's headed, he replies, "Someplace I've not been." When asked what it is he wants, he says, "Nothing."

Giant involves ranchers and conflict, too: the clash of landed cattle gentry, represented by Bick and Leslie Benedict (Rock Hudson and Elizabeth Taylor), and the coming technology of the oil and gas industry, represented by Jett Rink (James Dean, who died before the film was released). Its time extends from the 1920s to the 1950s; its scale is large enough to encompass the sprawling Ferber novel. A roundup, a barbecue, the excitement of an oil strike, and myriad details are closely observed and convincing;

A Place in the Sun (U.S., 1951, George Stevens). Museum of Modern Art/Film Stills Archive.

the huge Victorian mansion on the plain is extraordinary. Like the country, the characters seem bigger, more open, and flatter than life; courtesy and graciousness mingle with hardness and meanness. The awesome size and wealth that feed the legend and the legend itself are captured—*Giant* feels a lot like Texas.

Taken together, these three Stevens films make a large statement about the United States of America. Andrew Sarris labeled them the "American Dream *Sun-Shane-Giant* trilogy." Romantic and mythic they are. Stevens seemed to acknowledge that myths and legends are necessary parts of a culture. He re-stated them in ways that help us not so much to understand as to recognize values and behaviors that are indigenous, that must nourish us in some way.

As 1951 and *A Place in the Sun* marked a turning point in George Stevens's career, so it was with Billy Wilder and *Ace in the Hole* in the same year. This was Wilder's first film after the breakup of his fruitful scriptwriting collaboration with Charles Brackett, which had begun in 1938. Among their many successful scripts were *Ninotchka* (1939), directed by Ernst Lubitsch, and *Ball of Fire* (1941), directed by Howard Hawks. The first of their scripts to be directed by Wilder was *The Major and the Minor* (1942).

With the commercial failure of *Ace in the Hole* (it was rereleased as *The Big Carnival* in an effort to attract more customers), Wilder stopped making "films noir" (discussed in Chapter 13—*Double Indemnity*, 1944; *The Lost Weekend*, 1945; *Sunset Boulevard*, 1950). Instead, he turned mostly to comedies in which dark touches and underlying cynicism were lightened or concealed by laughter.

The first of these, *Stalag 17* (1953), was based on a Broadway hit about American prisoners of war held by the Germans during World War II. (Stalag 17 is the name of the camp.) Its center of interest is an opportunistic POW (played by William Holden) who seems devoted totally to self-interest, even to the point of collaborating with the Germans. Wilder's view of the characters is scathing; the laughter generated is not comfortable. Though it was popular with audiences, some reviewers complained of the film's nihilism and tastelessness.

Sabrina (1954), by contrast, is a Cinderella story that takes place on a lavish Long Island estate. It is about a chauffeur's daughter (Audrey Hepburn) and her romances with the two wealthy brothers her father drives for, the playboy (William Holden) and the stuffy businessman (Humphrey Bogart). Elegant and charming, it is essentially a good-humored joke about class differences and romantic dreams in America. Social meaning could be read into it only with considerable, and serious effort.

The Seven Year Itch (1955), a stage-bound, quite amusing film of George Axelrod's play, chucks class differences altogether: Money is no object. The title refers to the sexual longings, fantasies, and guilts of a husband (Tom Ewell) of seven years, inspired by the luscious, kooky blonde (Marilyn Monroe) living in the Manhattan apartment directly above his.

In *Love in the Afternoon* (1957) much the same sort of material is moved to Paris, as a young woman (Audrey Hepburn) falls in love with an aging American playboy (Gary Cooper). This was Wilder's first film with the screenwriter who would become his second long-lasting collaborator, I.A.L. Diamond.

The above three romantic and/or sexual comedies are very Ernst Lubitsch-like, a comparison Wilder readily acknowledged. The next three comedies—*Some Like It Hot* (1959), *The Apartment* (1960), and *One, Two, Three* (1961)—are very Wilder-Diamond-like. In them there is a fusion of the acidic noir films with the joie de vivre of the Lubitsch comedies. Given this understanding of his work, *The Spirit of St. Louis* (1957), Charles Lindbergh's trans-Atlantic flight, and *Witness for the Prosecution* (1958), a courtroom melodrama, seem out of character, though the latter was expertly made and highly profitable.

Some Like It Hot combines elements of the gangster film (two musicians, Tony Curtis and Jack Lemmon, witness the St. Valentine's Day massacre), knockabout farce, fast-paced witty dialogue à la screwball comedy, and transvestism (to escape Spats Colombo, played by George Raft, the two male musicians become ''girls'' in an all-girl band that includes Marilyn Monroe). Perhaps it is also a critique of American capitalism (at least of organized crime and Florida retirement) and sex (whether hetero- or homo-, male or female, makes not much difference). Confused identities and sexual mismatches are forced to incredible limits. The closing line, delivered by lustful millionaire Osgood Fielding III (Joe E. Brown), is ''Nobody's perfect.''

The Apartment, its amalgam of sex and capitalism straightforward by comparison, adds a strong note of poignancy. An accountant for an insurance firm, C. C. ''Bud'' Baxter (Jack Lemmon), allows company executives to use his apartment for extramarital affairs. This arrangement presents only minor inconveniences, offset by the possibility for advancement, until Bud discovers that one of the users of his apartment, head of personnel (Fred MacMurray), is having an affair with the elevator operator, Fran Kubelik (Shirley MacLaine), whom Baxter secretly cherishes himself. The evident lack of meaning in the business of the insurance business, the manipulation of people by other people within the bureaucratic hierarchy, the coldness and joylessness of the sexual games being played, cause every laugh to bear some discomfort. Unlike the characters in other Wilder films, Bud and Fran offer the possibility of decency against which the prevailing moral corruption can be measured. Wilder's comments on the way

The Apartment (U.S., 1960, Billy Wilder). Museum of Modern Art/Film Stills Archive.

of the world are at least as misanthropic as usual, but the relationship between the principals is one of the tenderest in Wilder's films—one of a very few observed with tenderness.

Any satirical barbs not included in Wilder's work up to this point must be contained in *One, Two, Three* (1961). It is about corporate executives and sex again, and pleasing the boss, but it invades new territory: politics, on an international scale. The setting is Berlin at the time of the Cold War. (The wall between East and West Berlin was being erected during the shooting of the film; topical references abound.) The protagonist (James Cagney) runs the Berlin Coca Cola bottling plant. Americans and Russians are ridiculed evenhandedly; capitalism is shown to be only slightly less obnoxious than communism. Everybody in the film seems to be self-centered and on the make. When the East German Comrade Piffl asks "Is everyone in this world corrupt?" the Russian Perpetchikoff replies "I don't know everyone." Though very funny, *One, Two, Three* is exceedingly dark.

It is interesting and no doubt significant that these dark comedies of Wilder's were commercial successes during the Eisenhower years, as film noir crime melodramas had been earlier. They allow a side of America to be seen, and a particular view of that side to be taken, that the films of George Cukor and George Stevens do not.

Fred Zinnemann was an immigrant like Wilder. Both were Viennese, Zinnemann a year younger. Both worked in film in Berlin before coming to America. In fact, they had worked together on an unusual and interesting semi-documentary feature, *Menschen am Sontag* (*People on Sunday,* 1929), Wilder on script and Zinnemann as assistant, along with Edgar Ulmer, to director Robert Siodmak. All four of those members of the crew subsequently came to Hollywood, Zinnemann arriving in 1929, Wilder in 1934. And there the similarities may end.

Wilder became a satirist, a parodist, a caricaturist; Zinnemann remained close to the documentary impulse of *People on Sunday*. An even more profound influence on his way of thinking about film making and about life in general, he has repeatedly acknowledged, came from his brief association with Robert Flaherty, American documentary pioneer, on an abortive project. In Hollywood, Zinnemann worked in various capacities on various sorts of films, such as codirector, with Paul Strand, of the documentary *The Wave* (1935), and director of shorts at M-G-M (1937–1942), and from 1942 on, of features.

The Search (1948)—a moving, authentic study of displaced and orphaned children in post-World War II Europe and of Americans in military and relief organizations trying to help them—was the first feature to establish his distinctive qualities. His realistic bent continued in *The Men* (1950), about paraplegic veterans of World War II, and *Teresa* (1951), about conflicts that arose when returning GIs brought home foreign wives, in this case Italian. Both films involved a good deal of location shooting—at a veterans hospital in the former, in Italy and New York City's Little Italy in the latter—and the use of nonactors in supporting roles.

With *High Noon* (1952) Zinnemann achieved his first big box-office success. This western—produced by Stanley Kramer, photographed by Floyd Crosby, whose credits include most of the major documentaries of Pare Lorentz—is much more conventional than his three films just discussed. Even when directing non-documentary-like material, Zinnemann is consistently careful about the particularities of the physical

High Noon (U.S., 1952, Fred Zinnemann). Museum of Modern Art/Film Stills Archive.

settings, as well as of the psychological situations. *High Noon* is tightly scripted along generic lines and uses only professional actors. In allegorical fashion it deals with an ethical problem important to American society at the time, the political paranoia called McCarthyism (discussed in Chapter 13). Only the sheriff (Gary Cooper) will stand up against the vengeful outlaw and his gang as other members of the community think of reasons why they cannot act. Its script writer, Carl Foreman, was one of those blacklisted, following testimony before the House Un-American Activities Committee, and exiled himself in England.

From Here to Eternity (1953), from the best-selling novel by James Jones, was an even bigger box-office success than *High Noon*. It, too, examines the ethical expectations and behavior of Americans and the functioning of an institution, the peacetime army in Hawaii before the Japanese attack on Pearl Harbor. Though Zinnemann used well-known performers, he cast them against type: Montgomery Clift as a committed soldier, Deborah Kerr as the adulterous wife of the captain, Frank Sinatra, in his first straight dramatic role, as the doomed Maggio. Though the film reduces the novel's indictment of the army system to a matter of individual excess, it is about the army system and the hurt done to some men and women connected with it.

During the remainder of the period being discussed Zinnemann never succeeded in recapturing the critical and commercial success of *High Noon* and *From Here to Eternity*, but three films embodied some of the characteristic Zinnemann thematic and stylistic elements.

A Hatful of Rain (1957) is about a drug addict and the effects of his addiction not only on himself but on his family. It was the first film on the subject after the 1956 revision of the Production Code, referred to earlier, permitted it. The location shooting in New York City is noteworthy—the scene in a Lower East Side park in which a pusher is caught by the police, and the night scenes on the streets of the city.

The Nun's Story (1959) concerns the spiritual struggles of a young Belgian nun (Audrey Hepburn) whose desire to nurse the sick and learn more about medicine conflicts with the strict discipline of her order. The first half takes place in the austere convent and deals with the training of the novitiates; the second half is set in the lush Congo jungle and involves an intense and troubling relationship with a surgeon (Peter Finch).

The Sundowners (1960) is a large and sprawling comedy-drama about an Australian family of sheep herders. The exteriors were shot in Australia, and careful attention is given to things Australian—sheep herding and shearing, for example, and a rural horse race.

Though Zinnemann's direction proved expert in various kinds of films (during this period he also directed film versions of Carson McCullers's novel/play *The Member of the Wedding* [1953] and the Rodgers and Hammerstein musical *Oklahoma!* [1955]), he seems at his best when his characters are involved in individual moral dilemmas that relate to a larger social dimension—cultural or institutional. His concerns and his style have been closer to the documentary impulse than have those of other Hollywood directors.

Vincente Minnelli arrived in Hollywood in 1940 after a substantial career as a stage designer and director. Following an apprenticeship at M-G-M, his first film direction was a version of the all-black Broadway musical *Cabin in the Sky* (1943). Minnelli's most distinctive contributions in the forties were his musicals (for example, *Meet Me in St. Louis,* 1944; *The Pirate,* 1948), but he directed noteworthy films in other genres as well (*The Clock,* 1945, romantic drama; *Father of the Bride,* 1950, a domestic comedy).

In 1951 Minnelli directed what is felt by many to be his finest film, *An American in Paris*. It was one of a number of especially memorable musicals made between the mid-forties and the mid-fifties by the M-G-M team assembled by producer Arthur Freed. With seasoned talent in every department, music and lyrics of George and Ira Gershwin, choreography and dancing by Gene Kelly, with Leslie Caron as his partner in her first screen appearance, *An American in Paris* nonetheless bears the stamp of Minnelli. The complexity within the coherence of the overall visual design, the expressive use of color and lighting are characteristic of his work in general. In the elaborate twenty-minute daydream ballet sequence, set to the Gershwin music of the title, the changing settings are in the styles of various painters—Renoir, Rousseau, Toulouse-Lautrec, Dufy, Van Gogh, and Manet. Within those artistic worlds, the dancers interpret the feeling evoked by each painter with American energy and grace. It is a dazzling, breathtaking climax.

The Bad and the Beautiful (1952) followed. This movie about Hollywood moviemakers revolves around a producer, Jonathan Shields (played by Kirk Douglas). Though egotistical and ruthless, he has achieved success not only with films he has produced but with careers he has made possible. In a manner reminiscent of *Citizen Kane* (John Houseman, closely involved in the production of *Kane*, produced *The Bad and the Beautiful* and other Minnelli films), the story is told by three persons whose lives Jonathan has affected and whom he is trying to bring together for yet another production. We can relish *The Bad and the Beautiful* as exposé; many of its characters and incidents are based on actuality or rumor. It is replete with the glamor and ambition, the mistrust and vulnerability, the wealth and unhappiness associated with Hollywood success. Visually elegant—in stunning black and white with pervasive low-key and high-contrast lighting—its style is faithful to the sort of illusion-making it is about.

The Band Wagon (1953) is to the musicals of Fred Astaire what *An American in Paris* is to those of Gene Kelly: top drawer. Both films came out of the Arthur Freed group at M-G-M. In *The Band Wagon* Astaire is joined by Cyd Charisse. It is about theater people, and though rampant egos are kidded, Minnelli's view of them is much gentler and more affectionate than his view of the Hollywood crowd the year before. Yet it has the same roman à clef elements, with Astaire more or less playing himself as a former song-and-dance man of the Broadway stage who has gone to Hollywood and attained widespread popularity. In fact, the title, *The Band Wagon*, is that of a 1931 Broadway revue Astaire had starred in. The big number is "The Girl Hunt Ballet," in which Mickey Spillane and New York City private-eye toughness are burlesqued, Fred Astaire dancing a Mike Hammer surrogate.

Lust for Life (1956) is Minnelli's large dramatic achievement of this period. A biography of Vincent Van Gogh (with Kirk Douglas looking remarkably like Van Gogh of the self-portraits), it is in wide-screen color. Much of it was shot on location in Holland, Belgium, and France in the regions in which Van Gogh lived. The images, shifting from the real landscape to the famous paintings and back to the landscape, are conceived with obvious sensitivity and appreciation. It is one of the most rewarding Hollywood films about art and artists.

Gigi (1958) is Minnelli's last completely successful musical—it won nine Academy Awards. It has connections with, is in some ways a reprise of, his earlier work out of the Arthur Freed group. For example, it contains: Minnelli's attraction to things French (it is based on the novel by Collette); a script by Alan Jay Lerner (who also scripted Minnelli's *An American in Paris; Brigadoon*, 1954; and *On a Clear Day You Can See*

An American in Paris (U.S., 1951, Vincente Minnelli). Museum of Modern Art/Film Stills Archive.

Forever, 1970; the latter two from his stage originals); Leslie Caron; color; wide screen; and art, in a way, as the young Gigi in fin-de-siècle Paris is groomed by her grandmother and great aunt to become an accomplished courtesan, as they were.

Much of Minnelli's best work brought art and life together—was about life in relation to art—and was pronouncedly reflexive before the notion of film being about film had achieved currency. This letting the audience in on the spirit of creation added a playfulness to the musicals; in the serious dramas it provided an irony which amplifies and intensifies the strong emotionality. Minnelli seems an artist's artist: his conception was securely rooted in the expressiveness of art; his filmic statements about life moved lightly and gracefully or surely and dramatically along channels that artistic expression makes available. Slightly removed from life, his films nonetheless commented on it in ways that are beautiful and moving.

Elia Kazan, on the other hand, though the stylization in his films may equal that in Minnelli's, used artistic heightening to make life on the screen appear to be that taking place outside the theater. His verisimilitude and dramatic power were achieved primarily through his work with actors. A principal practitioner of "the Method," as the acting style derived from Konstantin Stanislavsky was popularly called, he directed numerous important Broadway productions before and during his work in film (for example, Thornton Wilder's *The Skin of Our Teeth* and Arthur Miller's *Death of a Salesman*). Screen performances directed by Kazan are among the most valued in cinema.

A second striking aspect of Kazan's films is the ways in which they seem to have been connected with the national life, with the political life of the time. Of the six directors discussed in this chapter, Kazan best exemplifies certain of the shifting tendencies in American film generally over several decades. After *A Tree Grows in Brooklyn* (1945) and *Sea of Grass* (1947), both based on popular novels, Kazan directed a body of work that was at the center of the realistic/problem films of liberal sentiments and good causes discussed in Chapter 13. *Boomerang* (1947) and *Panic in the Streets* (1950) were taut crime melodramas which at the same time honored the courageous work of government officials on behalf of the individual and the public in the face of misunderstanding, resistance, and lack of appreciation. *Gentleman's Agreement* (1947) and *Pinky* (1949) were prominent in the race relations cycle. In 1951 he directed the film version of Tennessee Williams's play *A Streetcar Named Desire,* which he had also directed on the stage. Then, in 1952, Kazan was called before the House Un-American Activities Committee, confessed to his own Communist Party membership between 1934 and 1936, and named those he had known as Party members. He placed an ad in *The New York Times* justifying his change of political attitude and calling upon others to join him in confessing past error and denouncing communism and communists.

Elements of self-justification can also be seen in Kazan's subsequent films. *Viva Zapata!* (1952, with a script by John Steinbeck) shows the seeds of corruption taking root within the Mexican revolutionary leader, Emiliano Zapata, and the ultimate failure of the revolution through the adoption of the same totalitarian measures as those of the dictatorial regime which had been overthrown. *Man on a Tightrope* (1953), based on a screenplay by Robert Sherwood, was one of the anticommunist films of the period which dramatized actual events of the Cold War. It recounted the escape of a Czech circus from behind the Iron Curtain.

On the Waterfront (1954), the most powerful and empathic of these social-political statements, is from a script by Budd Schulberg, who also had confessed past Party membership to the Un-American Activities Committee and named people he had known as communists. It deals with the matter of informing to a government crime commission. Longshoreman Terry Malloy (played by Marlon Brando, who had also played Zapata) comes to realize that in order to stand upright as a moral being he must expose the gangster forces controlling the waterfront labor unions and inform on his former associates. (Lee J. Cobb, who plays the union boss, and Leif Ericson, who plays one of the Waterfront Crime Commission investigators, were others involved in the production who had confessed and named names to HUAC.) The symbolism built around Terry's care and training of his flock of pigeons takes on a special significance when we remember that screenwriter John Howard Lawson, one of the "unfriendly witnesses," had charged that HUAC's "so-called 'evidence' " had come from a parade of "stool pigeons, neurotics, publicity-seeking clowns, Gestapo agents, paid informers and a few ignorant and frightened Hollywood artists."[1]

With these three films Kazan seemed to release his need for broad ideological statement, though *A Face in the Crowd* (1957, script again by Schulberg) concerns a radio-television personality who comes to savor the enormous political power inherent in his mass popularity, and *Wild River* (1960) deals with the individual in conflict with big government in the Tennessee Valley of the 1930s. Instead he confined himself to individual drama (*East of Eden,* 1955, the finest, starring James Dean; *Baby Doll,* 1956; *Splendor in the Grass,* 1961) which became increasingly personal and even autobiographical. In subsequent years his connection with the Hollywood film industry and with the movie-going public became less frequent and less direct.

---

[1] Quoted in John Cogley, *Report on Blacklisting I. Movies* (Santa Barbara, Calif.: The Fund for the Republic, 1956), p. 19.

On the Waterfront (U.S., 1954, Elia Kazan). Museum of Modern Art/Film Stills Archive.

The changes that followed in the wake of television's impact on the American motion picture were profound and pervasive—technological, economic, sociological. MacCann, in his view of *Hollywood in Transition,* suggested that they were actually expanded freedoms; but he added that "Freedom is seldom as agreeable as it looks, and never easy." It took the industry time to absorb the changes and to adjust to the newly reduced and more specialized sorts of production, distribution, and exhibition that emerged.

Changes in the actual content and form of American films during this period—except for those caused by the wide screen, stereophonic sound, and increased use of color—were not nearly so evident. As distinguished as was the work of the six directors discussed above, and of other American film makers in the fifties, it came out of firmly established tradition. Not until the middle and late sixties did American films begin to take on some of the characteristics identified with trends of modern cinema that had been germinating in Europe from the mid-fifties on.

FILMS OF THE PERIOD

1952

The Bad and the Beautiful (Vincente Minnelli)
Bwana Devil (Arch Oboler)
Five Fingers (Joseph L. Mankiewicz)
The Greatest Show on Earth (Cecil B. De Mille)

High Noon (Fred Zinnemann)
Limelight (Charles Chaplin)
The Quiet Man (John Ford)
Singin' in the Rain (Stanley Donen and Gene Kelly)
This Is Cinerama (Merian C. Cooper)
Viva Zapata! (Elia Kazan)

1953

From Here to Eternity (Zinnemann)
Julius Caesar (Mankiewicz)
Lili (Charles Walters)
Mogambo (Ford)
The Robe (Henry Koster)
Roman Holiday (William Wyler)
Shane (George Stevens)
Stalag 17 (Billy Wilder)
The Wild One (Laslo Benedek)

1954

Beat the Devil (John Huston)
The Country Girl (George Seaton)
Dial M for Murder (Alfred Hitchcock)
Executive Suite (Robert Wise)
On the Waterfront (Kazan)
Rear Window (Hitchcock)
Sabrina (Wilder)
Seven Brides for Seven Brothers (Donen)
A Star Is Born (George Cukor)

1955

Bad Day at Black Rock (John Sturges)
East of Eden (Kazan)
Marty (Delbert Mann)
Mister Roberts
    (Mervyn LeRoy and Ford)
Picnic (Joshua Logan)
Rebel Without a Cause (Nicholas Ray)
Summertime (David Lean)

1956

Bus Stop (Logan)
The Catered Affair (Richard Brooks)
Friendly Persuasion (Wyler)
Giant (Stevens)
Lust for Life (Minnelli)
Somebody Up There Likes Me (Wise)

1957

The Bachelor Party (Mann)
Bridge on the River Kwai (Lean)
Funny Face (Donen)
A Hatful of Rain (Zinnemann)
Heaven Knows, Mr. Allison (Huston)
Paths of Glory (Stanley Kubrick)
Twelve Angry Men (Sidney Lumet)

1958

The Brothers Karamazov (Brooks)
Cat on a Hot Tin Roof (Brooks)
The Defiant Ones (Stanley Kramer)
Gigi (Minnelli)
The Goddess (John Cromwell)
I Want to Live (Wise)
The Last Hurrah (Ford)
Separate Tables (Mann)
Touch of Evil (Orson Welles)
Vertigo (Hitchcock)

1959

Anatomy of a Murder (Otto Preminger)
Ben-Hur (Wyler)
The Diary of Anne Frank (Stevens)
Middle of the Night (Mann)
North by Northwest (Hitchcock)
The Nun's Story (Zinnemann)
On the Beach (Kramer)
Some Like It Hot (Wilder)
Suddenly Last Summer (Mankiewicz)

1960

The Alamo (John Wayne)
The Apartment (Wilder)
Elmer Gantry (Brooks)
Home from the Hill (Minnelli)
Psycho (Hitchcock)
The Sundowners (Zinnemann)
Wild River (Kazan)

1961

The Hoodlum Priest (Irving Kershner)
The Hustler (Robert Rossen)
Judgment at Nuremberg (Kramer)
The Misfits (Huston)
One, Two, Three (Wilder)
Shadows (John Cassavetes)
West Side Story
    (Jerome Robbins and Wise)

1962

Billy Budd (Peter Ustinov)
Lawrence of Arabia (Lean)
Long Day's Journey Into Night (Lumet)
The Miracle Worker (Arthur Penn)
To Kill a Mockingbird
    (Robert Mulligan)
War Hunt (Denis Sanders)

BOOKS ON THE PERIOD

BALIO, TINO, ed., *The American Film Industry.* Madison: University of Wisconsin Press, 1976. 499 pp.

BAXTER, JOHN, *Sixty Years of Hollywood.* Cranbury, N.J.: A. S. Barnes & Co., Inc., 1973. 284 pp.

BLUM, DANIEL, *A New Pictorial History of the Talkies,* rev. and enlarged by John Kobal. New York: G. P. Putnam's Sons, 1982.

COE, BRIAN, *The History of Movie Photography.* Westfield, N.J.: Eastview Editions, 1981. 176 pp.

DOWDY, ANDREW, *"Movies Are Better Than Ever": Wide-Screen Memories of the Fifties.* New York: William Morrow & Co., Inc., 1973. 242 pp.

EVERSON, WILLIAM K., *The American Movie.* New York: Atheneum Publishers, 1963. 149 pp.

GOW, GORDON, *Hollywood in the Fifties.* London: The Tantivy Press, 1971. 192 pp.

GRIFFITH, RICHARD, ARTHUR MAYER, and EILEEN BOWSER, *The Movies.* New York: Simon & Schuster, Inc., 1981.

HIGHAM, CHARLES, *The Art of the American Film, 1900–1971.* Garden City, N.Y.: Doubleday & Co., Inc., 1973. 322 pp.

KINDEM, GORHAM, ed., *The American Movie Industry: The Business of Motion Pictures.* Carbondale and Edwardsville: Southern Illinois University Press, 1982. 448 pp.

MacCANN, RICHARD DYER, *Hollywood in Transition.* Boston: Houghton Mifflin Co., 1962. 208 pp.

MANVELL, ROGER, *New Cinema in the USA: The Feature Film Since 1946.* New York: E. P. Dutton & Co., Inc., 1968. 160 pp.

SAYRE, NORA, *Running Time: Films of the Cold War.* New York: Dial Press, 1982. 256 pp.

SKLAR, ROBERT, *Movie-made America: A Social History of American Movies.* New York: Random House, Inc., 1975. 340 pp.

STANLEY, ROBERT H., *The Celluloid Empire: A History of the American Movie Industry.* New York: Hastings House Publishers, 1978. 328 pp.

STUART, FREDERIC, *The Effects of Television on the Motion Picture and Radio Industries.* New York: Arno Press, 1976. 213 pp.

WOOD, MICHAEL, *America in the Movies.* New York: Basic Books, Inc., 1975. 206 pp.

17

The Film of the Auteur and the French New Wave, 1954–

AUTEURISM

It was an article by a young critic named François Truffaut, published in *Cahiers du Cinéma* in January 1954, that established the designation and first premise for a critical position that would gain increasing strength both in France and elsewhere in the years to come. Quietly entitled "A Certain Tendency in the French Cinema," Truffaut's piece was against the writer's film—the well-wrought "literary" scenario executed by expert technicians. This "tradition of quality," as he called it, began with the prewar "poetic realism" best represented by the writing-directing team of Jacques Prévert and Marcel Carné; their *Quai des brumes* (*Port of Shadows,* 1938) remained the masterpiece of the method and style, according to Truffaut. During the postwar years emphasis shifted to "psychological realism," and within that style the writing team of Jean Aurenche and Pierre Bost adapted for the screen literary works like *Symphonie Pastorale* (1946), *Devil in the Flesh* (1947), *God Needs Men* (1950), and *Forbidden Games* (1952), which were "illustrated" by such directors as Claude Autant-Lara, Jean Delannoy, and René Clement. Works in this main line were essentially "scenarists' films," Truffaut insisted. At the time of writing, he felt that the French cinema had degenerated into films made to win prizes at festivals rather than because anyone had anything urgent or personal to say.

In place of the creations of script writers, Truffaut called for films that would reflect as totally as possible the creative personality of their directors. He argued that only in this way could French cinema overcome literary stasis and utilize the dynamic filmic potential available. A handful of French directors were capable of this sort of creation, he wrote, and they were the "authors" of their films; that is, in control of, or at least fully involved in, conception as well as execution. He cited Jean Renoir, Robert Bresson, Jean Cocteau, Jacques Becker, Abel Gance, Max Ophüls, Jacques Tati, and Roger Leenhardt as *auteurs* who often wrote their dialogue and some of whom invented the stories they directed. In asking for the elimination of the old psychological realism and dominance by script writers, to be replaced by strongly original directors in creative control, Truffaut declared that he could not believe in the peaceful coexistence of the *tradition of quality* and a *cinema of auteurs*. What his criticism pointed toward was the French New Wave, which would break a few years later and carry him along with it.

The background for Truffaut's manifesto extends at least to Alexandre Astruc's call, as early as 1948, for a *camera-stylo*—a similar notion of "writing with the camera"; that is, creating the film in its making rather than merely supplying images and sounds for a fully realized and pre-fixed conception. Also, by those early postwar years, the French national film archive and screening center, the Cinémathèque Française, had been thoroughly reestablished, making available a systematic viewing of great amounts of the international history of the motion picture. It became possible to see that the moments of aesthetic excitement among the hours upon hours of films were provided by directorial vision, like that of Griffith or Eisenstein, Murnau or Gance.

Perhaps of even greater consequence was the arrival of the backlog of American films which had been kept from France by the German Occupation. Seeing in rapid succession films produced over a period of years permitted comparisons that provoked new insights. Even among the popular generic entertainments turned out by the big Hollywood studios there were differences, not only of artistic quality but, more important, of artistic personality attributable to certain directors. Both Hawks and Ford made excellent westerns, and yet a Ford western was subtly but nonetheless surely and consistently advancing different themes and offering a different visual style than one by Hawks. The same was true of the musicals of Minnelli compared to those of Donen and Kelly. Further, directors who had been thought of only as having been involved with a few good pictures along with some less good ones could be seen to carry with them a certain special vision; among these were Orson Welles, Fritz Lang, and Alfred Hitchcock. For the young French critics, films by the latter kind of director were much more interesting and rewarding than those of others, however prestigious and expert, whose direction was impersonal. Especially was this so when they regarded all of a director's films together; that is, the director in relation to the total body of work. Even—sometimes especially—the humble action directors working on "B" budgets were able to maintain and articulate their own particular visions: Raoul Walsh in gangster films, Anthony Mann in westerns, Samuel Fuller in war pictures, for example.

It was the application of *la politique des auteurs* to the popular American movie that created the most excitement and controversy. Reevaluations of the total corpus of the American sound film were prompted by the young writers of *Cahiers*, who announced and defended newly discovered masters and masterpieces with enthusiastic rhetoric. Auteurism was attacked by the more conventional critics for ignoring the collective nature of film making, especially Hollywood's, and for turning critical standards upside down by insisting that bad films were good merely because they were made by favored directors.

Whatever the merits of the arguments, the French word *politique* translated badly as *theory;* what it means more nearly is *position* or *policy.* As with Truffaut initially, the auteur critics' positions were partisan and polemical. What they were insisting was simply that, after looking at hundreds of films in relation to who directed them, there were certain directors they valued and others they did not. The judgments were not based on the importance of the films' statements in humanist terms, or on their beauty in aesthetic ones. Rather the criterion was the consistency with which a uniquely personal point of view was expressed through recurring themes, characters, situations, imagery. Pushed to its extreme, the position was that any film directed by Otto Preminger or Nicholas Ray, or Douglas Sirk (among the auteurists' favorites) was of more value than any film directed by William Wellman, or William Wyler, or Robert Wise, just because the former were auteurs and the latter merely interpreters, realizers of someone else's conception. What's more, auteurists seemed often to value most auteur films in which the script was weakest or the content slightest precisely because they allowed the director's creative personality to be disclosed most nakedly, without the cloak of satisfying form.

Quite appropriately, since he had been cofounder of *Cahiers* and patron of Truffaut, critic André Bazin provided the best reasoned analysis of the contributions and pitfalls "De La Politique des Auteurs," in the April 1957 *Cahiers.* In general sympathy with auteurism—largely because it brought cinema into a kind of criticism and onto a level of seriousness longstanding in the other arts—Bazin at the same time pointed out the dangers of excessive zeal. First, film was an industrial and commercial art and did not permit anything like the individual control over the work exerted by a Picasso or a Matisse. This should be taken into account, argued Bazin. The ability of the Hollywood production system to provide on occasion fine works within its popular genres, by directors who were not consistent personal film makers (auteurs) should be applauded rather than denigrated. Second, there was the matter of the auteurists' characteristically preferring, for instance, Welles's *Mr. Arkadin* (1953) over his *Citizen Kane* (1941). Since, they insisted, Welles was older when he made *Arkadin,* he must have matured as an artist. And because it was much less a collaborative endeavor than *Kane,* it contained more of Welles's unique artistic sensibility and understanding. Bazin could see that this evaluation followed logically from the auteur position, but maintained that, for himself, though he admired *Mr. Arkadin* and found in it the same gifts as in *Citizen Kane,* the latter opened up a new age of American cinema and *Arkadin* remained a second-rate film.

Elaborating on that example of the *politique* at work, Bazin added:

> In other terms, they want to retain of the equation, auteur + subject = work, only the auteur, the subject being reduced to 0. Some of these auteur adherents would feign to grant me that, all other things being equal, a good subject is obviously worth more than a bad one, but the most frank or the most insolent will admit to me that anything goes, as if their preference were on the contrary for little B films in which the acknowledged banality of the scenario leaves that much more room for the personal contribution of the auteur.[1]

Writing as a friend throughout, Bazin finally embraced *la politique,* not only because it had the merit of treating the cinema with an approach traditional in the other

---

[1] André Bazin, "On The Politique des Auteurs," *Cahiers du Cinéma in English,* No. 1 (January 1966), p. 14.

arts, but also because it represented a reaction against the impressionistic relativism which was the basis for most film criticism. There were, wrote Bazin, two symmetrical heresies inherent in criticism generally: on the one hand that of applying a critical grid or overlay to all films; on the other, that of considering it sufficient to express pleasure or distaste with individual films. The first position tended to deny the role of taste (auteurs are auteurs are auteurs); the second set up the critic's taste a priori as superior to that of the auteur (by pronouncing judgment on each work as good or bad). Presenting himself with the inescapable choice, Bazin opted for the more systematic *politique,* a position which honored the film maker over the critic.

THREE AUTEURS

Certain film makers have stood outside the national tendencies at given periods that have served as an organizing basis for this text. In transcending the concerns of their time and place, to the extent that any artist can, they offer analogues to the great creators in the more traditional arts. Three contemporary film artists who cannot conveniently be fitted into a broad historical plan, but whose individual distinction demands recognition, are Robert Bresson, Ingmar Bergman, and Luis Buñuel. Though their creative personalities are markedly different from each other, all three share a preoccupation with basic metaphysical problems, and have developed increasingly precise and unelaborated cinematic styles through which to articulate their attitudes. These qualities make their work seem at once old-fashioned and uniquely modern—timeless perhaps.

Bresson was among the French directors Truffaut first cited as auteurs. His important films began shortly after those of the great French film makers of the 1930s and extend to the present. Throughout his career Bresson has remained an isolated figure, among the most personal of film makers. The austerity of his subject matter, concerned more with moral and theological questions than with psychological analysis, and his insistence on rigorous control over every aspect of production have kept him removed from critical and creative fashion and have limited his output to thirteen films, which stand as monuments to his intellectual and aesthetic integrity. Though Bresson is part of the Catholic humanist tradition, his views take on a particular severity which has caused him to be called the Jansenist of French cinema.

In *Les Anges du péché* (1943), Bresson's first feature as director, the setting is a convent and the protagonist, a young novitiate. Its closed world and struggle for spiritual release into something approximating a state of grace are narrative components present in many of Bresson's films. *Les Dames du bois de Boulogne* (1945), a dark study of passion and revenge is drawn from Diderot's *Jacques le fataliste.* Less typical in its complete secularism and also in its theatricality (dialogue by Jean Cocteau), it has earned a lasting reputation on its own terms.

With *Diary of a Country Priest* (1950), adapted from a novel by Georges Bernanos, Bresson moved into the main themes and mature style of his subsequent work. Set firmly in the midst of French provincial Catholicism, it is concerned not so much with religion as with faith, with the preservation and sharing of belief in God. Further, it is about the misunderstanding and misinterpretation of motives to which the truly saintly are subjected in a world of petty selfishness, rivalry, ambition, and smallness of spirit. Shot on location in the Artois region in bleak fall and early winter weather, the cast comprises nonactors in many of the roles including the principal one of the young curé.

The next film, *A Man Escaped* (1956), was based on a real incident involving the imprisonment of a member of the resistance and his escape from a Gestapo prison in France in 1943. The film is only indirectly about the war and occupation, however; directly, as with so many of Bresson's works, it is about a human being in isolation, physical as well as spiritual in this case. The inner experience of the protagonist (as in *Diary of a Country Priest*) is refined to a pure, concentrated, intense expression. Again nonactors were used—here the entire cast—directed by Bresson as if they were professionals, with extremely precise and detailed performances obtained through endless repetition.

Pickpocket (1959), a present day paraphrase of Dostoevski's *Crime and Punishment,* concerns a petty thief locked inside his inchoate and unarticulated feelings. Drawn to his type of crime through obsessive compulsion, he lives emotionally only through the alternating sensations of fear and release accompanying his repeated thefts. The customary nonactors and location shooting were employed, and as in *A Man Escaped,* Bresson closely observed the physical processes in which the subject is involved and emphasized the objects and sounds which are part of his milieu: documentary means to arrive at nondocumentary ends—spirit through matter.

In *The Trial of Joan of Arc* (1962) Bresson dealt with the same material as had Carl Dreyer, a director with whom Bresson is often compared, in his *The Passion of Joan of Arc* (1928). Like Dreyer's film, Bresson's is based on the actual court records; in his case the dialogue of Joan and her accusers is confined to those words spoken at the trial. This interrogation, this spiritual drama stripped bare, is presented with remarkable austerity even within the context of Bresson's work.

Au hasard, Balthasar and *Mouchette,* both made in 1966, are linked in their examination of the casual, gratuitous inhumanity to which the meek of this earth are subjected: a donkey in the former, a fourteen-year-old girl in the latter. Both films end in the death of their protagonists, as do so many of Bresson's. *A Gentle Creature* (1969) and *Four Nights of a Dreamer* (1971) are based on Dostoevski stories transposed to modern Paris. *Lancelot of the Lake* (1974) was the realization of a long-held ambition to film the Arthurian legend. Knightly idealism is set against the clash and clangor of arms on muddy battlefields, and Lancelot emerges as a troubled, tragic hero torn between his love for Guinevere, his religious dedication, and his loyalty to Arthur.

Bresson's *L'Argent* (1983), made at the age of seventy-six, concerns the role of chance and predestination so prominent in his work. Based loosely on a story by Tolstoy, it follows a fuel-oil deliveryman who, after unsuspectingly receiving some counterfeit money, loses his job, participates in a holdup, is imprisoned, is abandoned by his wife after the death of their child, and finally commits multiple murders. Remorseless and disturbing, spare and yet almost sensuous in its physicality, it is quintessential Bresson.

While his films have never been widely popular with audiences nor noticeably influential on the work of other film makers, Bresson has emerged as one of the rare examples of a consummate individual stylist. His search for ever-greater clarity and simplicity of visual-aural statement, his concentration on only those themes that most deeply concern him, place him among the very select company with which he is being considered.

Almost exactly coincidental with Bresson's major work in France was that of

Diary of a Country Priest (France, 1951, Robert Bresson). National Film Archive/Stills Library.

another, even more isolated film artist, Ingmar Bergman in Sweden. The uniqueness of his work, as well as that of Bresson's, was noted by those advancing the *politique des auteurs.* Of Bergman, young critic and film-maker-to-be Jean-Luc Godard wrote, in the July 1958 *Cahiers du Cinéma,* that he was "the most original auteur of the modern European cinema." Today Bergman stands unchallenged as Sweden's preeminent film maker.

From its high achievements in the late teens and early twenties, Swedish film had descended to a kind of accomplishment appreciated mainly by Scandinavian audiences. The one major director at work in the years between Sjöström/Stiller and the rise of Bergman was Alf Sjöberg. It was with Sjöberg that Bergman began his film career, as script writer of *Torment,* the first postwar Swedish international success (produced in 1944). Coming out of the theater, as playwright and director, Bergman continued his theatrical work alongside the cinematic, directing plays in the winter and making films in the summer. He has said that the theater is his wife, the cinema his mistress.

Bergman's initial film direction was *Crisis* (1945), from his own script, interesting now chiefly as a harbinger of things to come. The first works of stature were *Three Strange Loves* (1949), *Summer Interlude* (1951), *Secrets of Women* and *Monika* (both 1952). All were shown abroad. *The Naked Night* (1953, also called *Sawdust and Tinsel*) marked a turning point; it is a small masterpiece. But it was *Smiles of a Summer Night* (1955), *The Seventh Seal* (1957) and *Wild Strawberries* (1957) that confirmed the earlier promise and set forth fully the thematic preoccupations we associate with the mature Bergman.

For it is what his films are about that becomes the ultimate measure of Bergman's worth. Stylistically he is conservative, somewhat theatrical in manner, with emphasis placed on script and performance. This is not to say that the form of his films doesn't match his intentions perfectly, nor that he is not in absolute command of the medium for his own purposes. His films originate totally with him, from first story idea through the framing of images to the emphasis given a noise laid in on the audio track. We can get at his artistic statements only through the cinematic sights and sounds in which they are embedded. Given the nature of the film medium, of course, he must work in collaboration with others. But in addition to providing script and direction, Bergman commands a devoted stock company of some of the finest performers in film and a crew of technicians who after years of working together have grown accustomed to making tangible his every inclination.

Like Bresson, Bergman deals solely with the questions that obsess him and that he attempts to answer through the creation of his films. They have been seen much more widely than Bresson's and have attracted audiences who have become capable of recognizing and appreciating the essential differences between Bergman and other film makers. To a quite remarkable extent, he (and to lesser degree Federico Fellini) was responsible for inspiring the widespread serious intellectual consideration of film, in the U.S. at least. Bergman's great appeal to the new kind of audience that began to appear at the end of the fifties was that his films dealt with matters of transcendent importance, and the manner in which he addressed himself to those issues resonated powerfully in modern consciousness.

The familiar image of the game of chess between the Knight and Death in *The Seventh Seal* suggests a visual metaphor for the fifty some films of Bergman. Taken collectively, his work is like a huge chessboard on which a single game is being played. Parts of the game—the characters and themes—may receive his concentration in a particular film, with the rest of the board receding into the background, but most or all are present in each film. This was true at least up through his trilogy—*Through a Glass Darkly* (1961), *Winter Light* (1962), *The Silence* (1963)—in which he claimed to have exorcised his religious preoccupations. In subsequent films he has not so much changed his concerns as moved in ever more closely and insistently on those that have come to seem most important to him. He conforms to Jean Renoir's observation that a great film maker spends his whole life making a single film.

In *The Seventh Seal* we could see clearly what Bergman felt to be the essential problems confronting humanity, or at least himself. First of all was the human need for God, and His apparent absence, or was it merely silence? Then there was death, the inevitable, unknown and unknowable end. What lay beyond life, if anything; if something, how could we find our way to it? Salvation, for Bergman, had to come through faith rather than knowledge or good works—the young couple Jof and Mia, and their baby, apparently have it and are saved; the Knight and his companions do not and are not (though the Knight, in his one meaningful deed, does distract Death so that Jof's family can escape). If in Bergman's world you can't learn or earn your way to faith, it is occasionally granted to the elect, who are saved. Invariably the faith is simple and unquestioning.

On the other hand, we might see human love, though largely unattainable, as the key to salvation: the love of the young couple for each other and their child in *The*

Seventh Seal, and the beginning love of the old doctor for his daughter-in-law in *Wild Strawberries,* which brings him an almost paradisiacal dream. Through love between human beings, faith may come, and from faith, salvation. Bergman's salvation may be merely meaningfulness: answers to the Knight's desperate questions about God and death. If the Knight has to ask them though, of course they can't be answered.

Sex in Bergman's films is not to be confused with love; on the contrary, it is frequently presented as a compulsive and destructive itch (*The Silence*), the scratching of which can sometimes quite literally draw blood (*Cries and Whispers,* 1972). Sex is the field of conflict rather than the source of fulfillment between the sexes (*Smiles of a Summer Night,* 1955, and *The Passion of Anna,* 1970, each in its own different way). Marriages evidently contain their own heaven and hell, but we see much more of the latter (*Scenes from a Marriage,* 1973).

Finally, Bergman is consistently absorbed with the role and function of the artist in society, and even in the cosmos, because, after all, he is a creator, if only with a small *c.* Bergman sees the artist as a charlatan, a kind of fake who may *almost* achieve understanding of the inscrutable mysteries of the universe and the mysterious ways of humankind. Artists may come closer to this understanding than other people, but thereby suffer more for their ultimate failure and the exposure of their pretensions and pretenses. The artist is invariably subjected to humiliation. *The Magician* (1958) is one of the serious films in which this concern is the center of attention; *Now About These Women* (1964) is one of the comedies. It is hard to say whether Bergman is sincere in this view or whether it is merely an engaging conceit. But in *Persona* (1966), which some regard as the most profound statement of all of his recurrent philosophical/psychological probings, he takes pains to remind us that we are seeing a movie. A projector shines its beam directly at us; a break in the film is simulated; and so on. He has expressed his delight with the basic technology and perceptual illusion on which his medium is based: that about half the time while one is watching a film the screen is in darkness. In a figurative sense, it's "all done with mirrors," as is said scornfully about certain kinds of magic performances.

In some quarters Bergman is faulted for the narrow range and frequent morbidity of his themes. Increasingly he became vulnerable to this sort of criticism after he abandoned God altogether and concentrated on the ways in which human beings can torture each other out of impulses that may have started as (may still contain something recognizable as) love. It is true that in his pictures there isn't room for the pleasures and positive aspects of human existence celebrated by Jean Renoir, say. Though Bergman's people are mostly physically attractive, intelligent, successful in their vocations, well-to-do, living in pleasant surroundings, they are generally miserable—the thinking ones anyway. Part of their suffering seems to be caused by their not understanding why they are miserable. In Bergman's films misery seems to come from a lack (an absence of meaning, significance, or fullness) rather than from an active cause. "Ripeness is all," said Lear, but there is a forbidding amount of spoilage and decay in Bergman's universe.

Fanny and Alexander (1983), which he said would be his last film (as he said of others), at last offers ripeness. It is like a huge old-fashioned novel. Or, to return to a simile suggested earlier, Bergman here attempts to include most of the chessboard in his view. The well-worked themes are present, but this time Bergman's regard is mellow and, yes, valedictory. Beginning on Christmas Eve in 1907 in a Swedish town that might be Uppsala, where Bergman was born, it is about a large, influential family, a

Wild Strawberries (Sweden, 1957, Ingmar Bergman). National Film Archive/Stills Library.

dynasty almost. There are many sharply differentiated characters and varied relationships among those living and visiting in the seemingly vast apartment presided over by the grandmother of the twelve-year-old Alexander and his younger sister, Fanny. It has elements traceable to what we know of Bergman's own growing up, and Alexander serves as the observer. What Bergman seems to be saying finally, if this is finally, is that, though a lot of curious and awful things may happen in this world, and people may torment themselves and each other in strange and pitiable ways, life is colorful and full, rich in its stimulations, tender and tranquil in old age—well worth living.

As a film artist Bergman tends to appeal most directly and strongly to those who aren't interested primarily in film art but regard film from the vantage point of the other arts, especially literature and drama. He has been the first enthusiasm of many people attracted to film who have then gone on to put him aside in favor of more ''filmic'' directors. But when Bergman has worked his conception completely into cinematic language—when he has created fully and deeply in terms of sights and sounds as well as characters and situations—his films become among the finest and most profoundly moving in all of cinema. Although he has not quite lost himself in the medium, he has transcended its frequent limitations—in regard to what Aristotle in the *Poetics* called Character and Thought—in a way that must be acknowledged. If Judgment Day were tomorrow (a prospect Bergman's films sometimes seem to entertain), his total body of work, granting the criteria appropriate to it, would entitle him to a place in the company of major artists from all the arts. This can be said of few other film makers in the history of the young art. Bergman is indeed an auteur.

Luis Buñuel was not only a truly independent and therefore isolated artist, like Bresson and Bergman, but his work stands outside a particular national culture. Perhaps one might better say that he carried his Spanish inheritance and later adoption of surrealism with him in films made in a number of countries over a period of fifty-five years.

Buñuel's first work in cinema was in France in the 1920s, as an assistant to Jean Epstein and other Impressionists, culminating in his turn to surrealism and collaboration with Salvador Dali on *Un chien Andalou* (1928) and *L'Age d'or* (1930). After a long fallow period spent mostly in the United States—except for *Land Without Bread* (1932), a seering documentary about the impoverished Las Hurdes region of Spain—Buñuel settled in Mexico in 1946. There his production became steady and commercially successful, for the most part, within the popular Latin American genres of melodrama and comedy.

The first exceptional film in the Mexican period was *Los Olvidados* (1950). It extends out of the naturalism of *Land Without Bread*, examining the violence and squalor in a shantytown on the edge of Mexico City as experienced by a gang of juvenile delinquents. An introductory title asserts that the film is "entirely based on actual incidents and all characters are authentic." But, as with *Land Without Bread*, Buñuel's unsparing and unsentimental observation of the horrors created by poverty and the inadequacies or callousness of social institutions in the face of human need moves beyond the usual ways of presenting social problems. As in the earlier Spanish film, reality in *Los Olvidados* becomes *sur*real because we are not used to being forced to contemplate a situation as hopeless as this, or its implications about the structure of society and perhaps the nature of humankind. More conventionally surreal is the beautiful dream sequence in slow motion. Dreams and hallucinations appear throughout Buñuel's work as part of his efforts to capture the irrational drives and fears underlying human behavior.

Other noteworthy films among Buñuel's Mexican work include *Subida al Cielo* (*Mexican Bus Ride*, 1951). As a comedy set in rural Mexico it contrasts strongly with *Los Olvidados*, and a collection of amiable caricatures and bizarre incidents dot its picaresque narrative. In *The Adventures of Robinson Crusoe* (1952) Buñuel turns Defoe's account of individual resourcefulness into a study of the effect of total solitude upon the human psyche, which includes a feverish nightmare mingling Christian symbolism with the sadistic cruelty of Crusoe's father, who will not give his son water to quench his thirst. *El* (1952) deals with the madness of possessive love and the perversions of emotional and sexual expression engendered by the repressiveness of the Catholic Church.

In 1955 Buñuel returned to France and began a body of films, some of them cofinanced by Italian, Mexican, and Spanish sources and shot outside France, which constitute his latter-day career and confirm his position among the great auteurs of international cinema. Among these is *Viridiana* (1961), which though made in Spain, was denounced and banned in that and other Catholic countries after its completion. *Viridiana* represents Buñuel's most unambiguous attack on what he views as the unhealthy sentimentality and restrictive and warped morality of institutionalized Christianity. The film climaxes as the filthy and deformed, cynical and misanthropic collection of beggars—whom Viridiana has assembled in order to save their souls through prayer—enter into a drunken orgy that includes an outrageous parody of da Vinci's *The Last Supper*. In his own way Buñuel seems to have been as preoccupied with religion—"Thank God I am still an atheist," he would say—as Bresson the believer or Bergman the agnostic have been.

The Exterminating Angel (1962) concerns a group of guests mysteriously (miraculously?) unable to leave a sumptuous dinner party for days, maybe even weeks, and the ways in which their enforced proximity to each other brings out the idiosyncracies and destructiveness lurking beneath their conventionally elegant exteriors. In *Diary of a Chambermaid* (1964), based on the novel about the French upper classes by Octave Mirbeau (from which Renoir also made a film, in Hollywood, almost twenty years earlier), Buñuel examines the pervasive evil and moral decadence of an updated, crypto-fascist society. The heroine/protagonist of *Belle de jour* (1967), frigid and sexually unfulfilled with her husband, whom she nonetheless loves, attempts to bring alive her masochistic fantasies of sexual debasement by volunteering her services to a chic brothel. *The Discreet Charm of the Bourgeoisie* (1972) is a loosely structured, amusing and anecdotal attack on the values of polite society. It reverses the situation of *The Exterminating Angel,* with six persons attempting to hold a dinner party which is constantly interrupted. *The Phantom of Liberty* (1974) is a darker companion piece to *The Discreet Charm of the Bourgeoisie.* It turns on a series of chance encounters that expose the illogic at the core of modern society.

That Obscure Object of Desire* (1978) was Buñuel's last film before his death in 1983. Inspired by Pierre Louÿs's novel *The Woman and the Puppet,* also the basis for Josef von Sternberg's *The Devil is a Woman* (1935), it deals with a womanizer's pursuit of a woman who constantly eludes him. It contains Buñuelian themes of obsessive and frustrated desires, fetishism, and the blurring of the distinction between reality and dream.

Throughout Buñuel's work his unflinching contemplation of human cruelty reminds us that he comes from the land of the Inquisition and the bullfight. Some of his films seem clearly to follow the tradition of Goya's horrifying documentation of the human's capacity for inhumanity in his series of etchings entitled *The Disasters of War.* (A live reenactment of a Goya painting opens *The Phantom of Liberty.*) On the other hand,

Viridiana (Spain, 1961, Luis Buñuel). National Film Archive/Stills Library.

Buñuel's surrealism led him to explore the subconscious and powerful forces of sexuality, dangerous and destructive when suppressed, rendering any view of life incomplete and invalid when unacknowledged. His attacks on bourgeois institutions (religion and state, class distinctions, and conventional morality) carry the political charge of the surrealists' revolt. Closer to the anarchist's goal of individual freedom than to the Marxist's credo of cooperative endeavor, yet we can infer from *The Phantom of Liberty* that for Buñuel the concept of individual freedom remained a ghostly one. Buñuel's vision stands as his own, full of endless surprises in its forms of expression while he continually readdresses the themes that concern him most. Along with Bresson's and Bergman's, Buñuel's stature depends on the weight of his moral observations, the way in which his style was refined over the years in order to state his views with increasing economy of means, and his integrity and his steadfastness to his own understanding of human nature. Alongside the mature work of these three masters, and out of the critical movement which had placed preeminent value on the director as creative artist, as author of the films, there appeared in France a new national outpouring by new young film makers of very different sorts of talents and preoccupations.

NEW WAVE

Having constructed a critical system which exalted the director, it is little wonder that the young *Cahiers* critics soon left criticism to become directors themselves. Most of them had from the outset considered criticism only a stepping stone to creation. Still, the ensuing development of a creative movement out of a critical movement is unique in the history of film and seems, to Anglo-Saxons at least, peculiarly Gallic. In America to date, only Peter Bogdanovich and Paul Schrader have come to film directing from writing about film; in England, only Lindsay Anderson and Karel Reisz. In France, however, many of the leading film makers of the New Wave, which began at the end of the fifties, were *Cahiers* alumni and auteurists. Aside from Alexandre Astruc and Roger Leenhardt, already established directors at the time they were writing for *Cahiers,* there were among the younger generation of critics-turned-film-makers François Truffaut, Jean-Luc Godard, Claude Chabrol, Jacques Rivette, Jacques Doniol-Valcroze, and Eric Rohmer.

While the critical context of auteurism was being constructed, conditions in the French film industry also came to favor a new kind of film maker. The glut of Hollywood film released during the late forties—a backlog from the Occupation years plus current releases—not only gave rise to its reevaluation by the *Cahiers* critics but also provoked an important series of responses from French producers and government attempting to meet the competition.

Immediately after the war, in 1946, a rather half-hearted quota system was established. Known as the Blum-Byrnes agreement (Léon Blum, President of France, and James F. Byrnes, U.S. Secretary of State), it required French cinemas to show French films at least sixteen weeks out of the year. All that this did was to establish modest limits on importation. It did not encourage French production, which dwindled in the years immediately following the agreement. In short, it scarcely checked the Americans and further contributed to the stagnation of French film about which Truffaut would complain.

In 1948 a new agreement was reached that stretched the period for exclusive showing of French films to twenty weeks and offered what was intended as temporary government subsidy to the French industry. The aid was financed through a tax on admissions. Money was refunded to the producers, in addition to their regular profits, as a rebate in proportion to the amount taken in at the box office. It was a system that favored the established and already successful: the rich got richer while the poor remained poor. Because producers were afraid to risk a share of future admissions, the norm became the repetition of tested ingredients. Kinds of films that had made money in the past were repeated; script writers who had solid success to their credit were hired again; stars who were in public favor had vehicles created for them. But audiences became restive with the standard programming, and the industry soon had yet another crisis on its hands as it became more and more difficult to anticipate public reaction on the basis of the old formulas.

In 1953 André Malraux, Minister of Culture, put forth a new variation on the "temporary" assistance offered to producers. Feature films were given an *avance sur recettes,* a method of funding before the film was finished if the project looked worthwhile to the government advisers. Bresson's *A Man Escaped* (1956) was financed in that manner when he had difficulty finding private backing. Shorts as well as features were covered under the new system, being awarded money in relation to their artistic quality. *Primes de qualité* for the production of short films encouraged directors like Georges Franju, Alain Resnais, and Chris Marker.

Taken together, the developments in France by the mid-fifties—an industry that began to support talented individual film makers, the critical climate created by the *Cahiers* group, the beginning rise of European auteurs such as Bergman plus new works by Max Ophüls, Jacques Becker, Jean-Pierre Melville, and Bresson—prepared an audience to accept innovation and a more personal kind of film making. The dominating script writer's cinema of standard dramaturgy based upon psychological realism began to give way to the director's cinema of eccentric artistic vision and varied style.

At the same time, what would prove to be the precursors of the New Wave began to appear: Alexandre Astruc's *Les Mauvaises rencontres* and Agnes Varda's *La Pointe courte* (both 1955), and Roger Vadim's *And God Created Woman* (1956). The latter, enormously successful and creating a new sex goddess in Brigitte Bardot, also bore—superficially at least—many of the thematic and stylistic marks of the later body of New Wave work. Louis Malle's *The Lovers* and Claude Chabrol's *Le Beau Serge* were so close to the main upswing, in their year of release (1958) and in their artistic character, as to be part of the larger whole. But 1959 was the decisive year and the Cannes Film Festival the appropriate occasion on which three French features signaled to the world the beginning of the first new period of heightened national creativity since Italian neorealism of the late forties and early fifties.

Of the three the most popular was *Black Orpheus,* the second feature of Marcel Camus, who had worked for many years as an assistant director. Based on the Greek legend of Orpheus and Eurydice, shot on location in Rio among Brazilian blacks at carnival time, it became an international success, winning an Academy Award as best foreign picture of the year. However, with its exoticism on the one hand and derivative narrative technique on the other, it belonged to the New Wave only by virtue of its year of release. Camus, in his mid-forties at the time, was part of an earlier generation; he made no other important film after *Black Orpheus.*

The 400 Blows, by François Truffaut, former critic, maker of a few shorts including the delightful *The Mischief Makers* (1957), was a semiautobiographical account of a young boy estranged from his parents, who is caught up in the juvenile judicial and penal system. It began the Antoine Doinel series with the twelve-year-old Jean-Pierre Léaud playing his first role. The subject matter if not the style of *The 400 Blows* also seemed closer to what had gone before than other of the New Wave films. If its warmth and humanity owed something to Renoir, one of Truffaut's heroes, it bore resemblances to Italian neorealism as well, specifically to de Sica's-Zavattini's *Shoeshine*. There were, however, the bravura flourishes—the tracking shots in wide screen and the famous final freeze-frame closeup of the young Léaud—which marked the personal stylist and looked ahead to Truffaut's later work.

Last, there was *Hiroshima, mon amour,* directed by Alain Resnais, whose background was in editing and documentary film making. Among the most distinguished of his shorts were *Van Gogh* (1948), *Gauguin* (1950), *Guernica* (1950, on the Picasso painting), *Night and Fog* (1955, about the German concentration camps of World War II), and *Toute la memoire du monde* (1956, dealing with the great French library La Bibliothèque Nationale). The script for *Hiroshima,* by the eminent *nouveau roman* novelist Marguerite Duras, concerned a transient and strained love afsair between a French actress and Japanese architect. The personal relationship was embedded in painful memories of the German occupation of France and the atomic holocaust in Japan. It was *Hiroshima, mon amour* that seemed to many in 1959 the most successfully and profoundly revolutionary of those three films at Cannes. Its transcendence of temporal-spatial unities, Proustian emphasis on memory, linkage of sexual love and global war were all strange and absorbing—and typically Resnais, as it would turn out.

Also in 1959 were Chabrol's second feature, *The Cousins,* which continued the subtle character studies and preoccupation with moral corruption begun in *Le Beau Serge. The Cousins* set forth fully what would become standard traits of Chabrol's work—the dark fascination with dominance and dependence between characters set among the modish upper classes, and the elegant, austere visual imagery. Though it examined the contemporary ambience of disenchanted young Parisian intellectuals, as did so many of the New Wave films, *The Cousins,* too, seemed a departure from what had preceded it in degree more than in kind.

Eric Rohmer, another of the *Cahiers* critics, finished his first feature, *Le Signe du lion* (*The Sign of Leo*), in 1959 but it had to wait three years for release. It was his later series of *six contes moraux*—especially *My Night at Maud's* (1969), *Claire's Knee* (1970), and *Chloe in the Afternoon* (1972)—which established him alongside the other major figures to emerge from the Wave.

Released in 1960 were Jean-Luc Godard's first feature, *Breathless,* an idiosyncratic tribute to the American gangster film; Truffaut's second, *Shoot the Piano Player,* with similar generic connections; and Chabrol's *Les Bonnes Femmes,* among his most important films. *Breathless,* though filled with verve and originality in its fragmented storytelling and iconoclastic camera and editing style, seemed somewhat slight at the time. It scarcely predicted the radical experimentation with content along with form that would characterize Godard's subsequent output. Jacques Rivette's difficult and puzzling *Paris nous appartient* (*Paris Belong to Us*), begun in 1958, was completed in 1960. Least popular, most eccentric and obscure of the first of the Wave, it was the subject of admiration by other film makers and thereby influential. Like the other films in Rivette's oeuvre, it remained a special case.

If no one of the seminal films contained all of the most striking or representative characteristics of the New Wave, as a group they outlined its chief concerns and formal innovations. These first films marked the beginning of what was not so much a movement as an explosion. Between 1959 and 1963 something like 170 directors in France made their first feature films, 67 during 1959 and 1960. Naturally the majority of these young and new film makers were less than geniuses and the bulk of their films scarcely masterpieces. When the novelty and excitement began to wear off, self-indulgence and ineptitude became a kind of commercial undertow. Audiences grew increasingly resistant and producers wary. But before the Wave receded an extraordinary number of valuable and/or interesting films were produced which left a permanent mark on the international history of film and established a whole new generation of French film makers.

The term *nouvelle vague* was said to have been coined by a journalist. Used for promotional purposes, it covered a diversity of film makers many of whom had little in common with each other. If the New Wave was not as cohesive a movement as, say, German expressionism in the twenties or post-War II Italian neorealism, still there were certain characteristics that were either shared or that received a new and strong emphasis beginning about 1959 in France.

First was a base in the existentialist philosophy of Jean-Paul Sartre and Albert Camus, especially the latter. Camus's short novel *The Stranger* seems in many ways prototypical of the attitudes and approaches of the New Wave. There is, arguably, a direct line between it and *Breathless*. A distanced, antisentimental stance on the part of their creators typifies both works and much of the New Wave (Truffaut being generally a notable exception). Within those films it was as if no preexisting, external moral codes operated, even to be rebelled against. Events happened that were unprepared for and unexplained in the usual manner, like the seemingly gratuitous death of the heroine at the end of Godard's *My Life to Live* (1962), and the suicide-murder of two of the three principals climaxing Truffaut's *Jules and Jim* (1961). Characters made decisions that appeared arbitrary or lacking in motivation, of a conventional sort at least (Resnais's *Last Year at Marienbad,* 1961, is an encyclopedia of such behavior). They conceived of themselves as responsible only to themselves (Charles Aznavour in Truffaut's *Shoot the Piano Player* was one instance) in a world devoid of logic, justice, or even order.

Then there was the looseness and openness of narrative construction—the picaresque quality that dominated so many of the films (Godard's *Pierrot le fou,* 1965, a prime example of the general tendency). At the least they were narrative rather than dramatic, more allied to the New Novel than the well-made play. The ascending climaxes of traditional dramaturgy were abandoned, even the ends of narrative threads were no longer neatly tucked in. Randomness replaced the mechanisms of omnipresent fate at work in the French films of the thirties noted earlier. Audiences were left to put together the disjointed experience after they left the theater. Godard, when asked by an exasperated interviewer if a film shouldn't have a beginning, middle, and end, thought a moment and replied, ''Yes, but not necessarily in that order.''

Accompanying the freedom from strict narrative confines was a tendency to organize time and space according to the dictates of feeling (the film maker's and the characters') rather than the requirements of chronology or contiguity. The intricacies of memory was so dealt with in Resnais's work. *Last Year at Marienbad* seemed to contain three tenses—past, present, and future conditional—and jumbled the real and the imagined as the protagonist tried to persuade the heroine and perhaps himself of what had happened between them during the previous summer. The jump cuts, abrupt transitions, and asides of Godard and Truffaut in *Breathless* and *Shoot the Piano Player* similarly defied orderly linear perception.

Finally, many of the New Wave films were about films and film making. Because these young film makers, many of them former critics, felt so at home in their medium, they played with it in uninhibited ways. These included encouraging improvisation by actors (Jeanne Moreau, Jean Paul Belmondo, Charles Aznavour rose to stardom in their films), taking advantage of the accidents of location shooting, and using new lightweight equipment to attach onto the unfolding action without making it conform to the restraints imposed by the studio method. (*Breathless* was shot in four weeks in indoor and outdoor locations, night as well as day, using "fast" still-photographic stock, a hand-held camera and postrecorded sound.) There were allusions to other film makers and films, a use of the full range of cinematic conventions, some of them stemming from the silent years (irises, intertitles, masking to change the size and shape of the images), and in-jokes (film friends appearing in apt and amusing bit parts: the director Jean-Pierre Melville as a novelist in *Breathless,* two critics from *Cahiers* as blind men in *A Woman Is a Woman,* 1961). Truffaut's *Day for Night* (1973) is, of course, a summation of this tendency: Its subject *is* film making. Often the films were created as objects for contemplation in their own right rather than as commentaries on the world outside the darkened confines of the theater. These were "movie movies," dedicated to the proposition that if not more real than life, film was a good deal more interesting. In general the New Wave seemed not so much art imitating life, as life, at least as it was portrayed in those films, imitating art.

One way of thinking about these aesthetic and stylistic innovations is that the modernism percolating in the other arts since the turn of the century had at last seeped into narrative fiction film. The modernism of the French avant-garde films discussed in Chapter 7 was allied to and mostly came out of painting and painters. The New Wave modernism was literary in origins, sometimes bearing striking resemblances to what James Joyce had explored in *Ulysses,* published in Paris in 1922. What we now generally think of in relation to the feature film as contemporary cinema or modern film can be said to have begun in France at the end of the fifties.

SOME CONTEMPORARY FRENCH DIRECTORS

As the New Wave began to roll in the sixties it was Truffaut, Resnais, and Godard who first emerged as the major figures. Like Eisenstein, Pudovkin, and Dovzhenko in the Russian twenties, the French triumvirate maintained their preeminence. Parallel to their work is that of Chabrol, Rivette, Rohmer, and others.

After *The 400 Blows,* Truffaut made *Shoot the Piano Player* (1960), *Jules and Jim* (1961), and the other films (see Films of the Period) which have earned for him the appelation of auteur that he first coined to apply to others. He has written or cowritten all of his films. Generally they are imbued with the sort of romantic realism we would expect from a spiritual godson of Bazin and Renoir. But they also, especially the earlier ones, contain amusing and astute references to the conventions of the medium within which he was working. Throughout there are signs of the well-informed former *cinéphile* and critic, and *hommages* to particular films and favorite film makers, most pointedly to Hitchcock in *The Bride Wore Black* (1967).

Among his recent films the most effective and commercially successful was *The Last Metro* (1981). It deals with the theater in affectionate and knowledgeable detail (as *Day for Night* does with film making) but as a means of getting at the strange, muted, complicated, unnerving human tensions in German-occupied Paris of 1942. A wife (Catherine Deneuve) continues to run the Théâtre Montmartre in place of her Jewish husband. But the husband did not flee the country, as was assumed; he hides in the cellar of the theater and observes its continuation, including the addition of a young actor (Gérard Depardieu) with whom his wife has an affair.

Aside from the undervalued *Shoot the Piano Player,* and *Jules and Jim,* which many regard as his masterwork, the Antoine Doinel series (*The 400 Blows;* the episode in *Love at Twenty,* 1962; *Stolen Kisses,* 1968; *Bed and Board,* 1970) may be Truffaut's most distinctive contribution to date to the history of film. In addition to their worth as separate art works, they represent the closest theatrical films have come to the sustained use of autobiographical material, except perhaps those of Fellini. In *Day for Night* (1973) Truffaut added his own performance to Léaud's to infuse his art with his life. This sort of creation is recognized as the basis for much of the world's great literature, from Cervantes to Faulkner. The idea of a director's life, at least his personal vision, being reflected in his films was inherent in *la politique des auteurs.* Truffaut has brought his own experiences more directly to the screen through the evolving Doinel character than any other director has so far done. He has said that *L'Amour en fuite* (*Love on the Run,* 1979) is his farewell to Antoine Doinel.

Jules and Jim (France, 1961, François Truffaut). Museum of Modern Art/Film Stills Archive.

Resnais's qualifications as an auteur are of a different sort. A skilled film maker, his films display a dazzling technical virtuosity and formal elegance that separate them from other New Wave works. Also, his concern with older characters and the past contrasts with the youthful protagonists and present attitudes dominant in the films of Truffaut and Godard. With noteworthy consistency Resnais has pursued his absorption with the processes of memory; his features (*Hiroshima, mon amour; Last Year at Marienbad; Muriel,* 1963; *La Guerre est finie,* 1966; *Je t'aime, je t'aime,* 1968; *Stavisky,* 1974; *Providence,* 1977; *Mon Oncle d'Amérique,* 1981; *La Vie est un roman,* 1983) all reveal and insist upon the presence of times past in every present moment. This was true even of the earlier shorts, especially the greatest of them, *Night and Fog.* In *Mon Oncle d'Amérique* the real-life biologist Dr. Henri Laborit, on whose theories the film is based, says "A living creature is a memory that acts." This might be a description of the protagonists of Resnais's films.

The problem Resnais presents in his candidacy for authorship is that on his features he has usually collaborated with strong literary figures such as Marguerite Duras and Alain Robbe-Grillet (who subsequently directed their own scripts), or Jean Cayrol. He has always been generous (perhaps more than) in acknowledging his indebtedness to others, and self-effacing in regard to his own contributions to the conceptions. According to published statements from some of those collaborators, Resnais was almost insistent that the scripts be conceived quite apart from his personal style as a film maker and without special deference to the medium of film. "Give me an original 'literary' work," he seemed to be saying, "and I will make it into cinema."

In *Je t'aime, je t'aime,* a science fiction involving a time machine, Resnais worked with Jacques Sternberg, a Belgian writer of less stature than Duras or Robbe-Grillet. Though his standard preoccupations were in their purest form, *Je t'aime, je t'aime* is less commanding than those films preceding it. With *Stavisky,* about the legendary entrepreneur-swindler of the thirties, Resnais returned to form. The script was by political novelist/screenwriter Jorge Semprun, who also scripted *La Guerre est finie.* Resnais's first English-language film, *Providence* (1977), is *about* literary creation. The script was by playwright David Mercer. Its protagonist, a famous novelist, draws from his relationships with his children and dead wife to shape and re-shape scenes intended for his final novel. His characters are at variance with what we are permitted to see of the "real" persons who exist outside his imagination, and the whole, of course, is presented to us in a filmic illusion which is, ultimately, Resnais's interpretation and creation.

His last two films, *Mon Oncle d'Amérique* and *La Vie est un roman,* were both scripted by Jean Gruault. A screenwriter rather than a literary figure (his credits include Truffaut's *Jules and Jim, The Wild Child, Two English Girls, The Story of Adele H.,* and *The Green Room;* Rivette's *Paris nous appartient* and *La Religieuse;* Godard's *Les Carabiniers;* and Rossellini's *The Rise of Louis XIV*), his contributions to these two films must have been central. (The original screenplay for *Mon Oncle d'Amérique,* Resnais's first major commercial success, was nominated for an Oscar.) Both are complex three-part narratives: the former telling the stories of three quite different modern characters whose lives interact; the latter consisting of three stories set in different times and filmed in different styles which yet connect thematically. Both are based on philosophical propositions: the first relating to the aggression innate in humans and human responses to it; the second to utopias, education and imagination, adulthood and childhood. The intellectual content of Resnais's films is high, and the ideas appear always to be ones that interest him, that he believes.

Hiroshima, mon amour (France, 1959, Alain Resnais). National Film Archive/Stills Library.

While the level of achievement may vary, it nonetheless seems clear that as a body of work Resnais's films remain notably coherent regardless of who is credited with the script. We can assume that, whatever the creative relationship between writer and director during production, Resnais is not altogether part of the tradition of writer's cinema about which Truffaut complained.

Perhaps it is Godard who represents better than any other single film maker the sort of experimental stretching of the medium that the New Wave provided. In fact, it may be only Griffith and Eisenstein who have contributed as much formal innovation—additions to the ''language'' of the medium—as Godard. His early work included variations on the melodrama and chase conventions of popular American movies. It is amusing but not surprising that his first feature, *Breathless,* was dedicated to Monogram Pictures, a defunct Hollywood studio of ''B'' production. *Band of Outsiders* (1964), another ''gangster film,'' has ''musical numbers'' as well, with Anna Karina singing on the Metro and dancing with two of the petty crooks; in *A Woman Is a Woman* (1961), Karina says she wants to be in a musical choreographed by Bob Fosse.

On the other hand, Godard employed the sort of ''distancing'' associated with avant-garde theater, or with Bertolt Brecht, whom Godard frequently invoked in interviews. In the famous opening scene of *My Life to Live* (1962) the camera remains mostly on the backs of Nana and Paul, preventing us from seeing their facial expressions as they converse. Its twelve episodes are punctuated by titles, pulling us further out of the narrative, which is already deliberately disjunctive, and suggesting a series of moral lessons (Montaigne furnishes the text for one of the tableaux).

But a new kind of realism was also present in Godard's mixed style. In *Sympathy for the Devil* (1968) and elsewhere, *cinéma vérité* actuality mingled with fictive elements. Godard has said that there are two kinds of cinema, Flaherty and Eisenstein: There is documentary and there is theater; but that ultimately, at the highest level, they are one and the same. Through documentary realism we arrive at the structure of theater, and through theatrical imagination and fiction we arrive at the reality of life.[2] Even when working with actors, as he generally did, Godard observed aspects of their actual personalities as much as the created roles they played. In *Breathless,* Belmondo's energy and toughness, coiled-spring tension and handsome-ugliness were first revealed. Jean Seberg, who had failed badly as Joan of Arc in Preminger's film, succeeded completely in playing a young American in Paris whom we suspect might be rather like herself. The series of films with Anna Karina, Godard's wife for a time, were, among other things, poems to her loveliness and essays on the difficulties of understanding and communicating with her (*Le Petit Soldat,* 1960; *A Woman Is a Woman; My Life to Live; Band of Outsiders; Pierrot le fou,* and *Alphaville,* 1965). In *Contempt* (1963) Fritz Lang played himself as a renowned film director.

As Godard's work progressed, his philosophical observations came increasingly to obtrude, extending from the moral and ethical to the political. Later films (*Made in USA,* 1966; *La Chinoise,* 1967; *Weekend,* 1967) became defiantly expository and didactic. In *Le Gai Savoir* (1969), his first film after the May 1968 uprising in France, he abolished narrative altogether (and alienated much of his audience) in an effort to find a revolutionary form suitable to revolutionary content. Concomitant with this move towards philosophical abstraction, the dialogue became denser and was assigned a more significant share of the total communication. In *My Life to Live,* Brice Parain, a philosopher in real life, carried on a long dialectical near-monologue that was only tangentially related to the slight plot. Later in the same film Godard's voice on the sound track reads an Edgar Allan Poe story to the heroine. In *See You at Mao* (also called *British Sounds,* 1969) there is so much speech over the images that the words become incomprehensible.

Godard's absorption with politics and formal rarefactions meant that with the exception of *Tout va bien* (1972) and *Numéro deux* (1975)—both of which received limited commercial distribution—his work disappeared from public view after 1968. More recently, however, *Sauve qui peut . . . La Vie* (*Every Man for Himself,* 1980) seemed to connect back to *Weekend* (1967) and the films that preceded it. The narrative structure and character psychology offer difficulty to be sure—like Resnais's *Mon Oncle d'Amérique* it is built around three characters whose lives become intertwined—but there is a story and there are characters. Formal experimentation is present—video techniques and stop motion, for example—along with Godard's abiding concern for "the politics of the image," and there is much visual beauty.

If *Sauve qui peut* might be thought of as being about the nature of cinema, as was said at the time, *Passion* (1982) most certainly can be. At its center are two East European film makers making a film called *Passion.* However, their film-within-the-film, and therefore Godard's film, is full of famous paintings (by Rembrandt, Goya, Delacroix, El Greco) brought to life in *tableaux vivant* accompanied by famous music (extracts from Mozart, Fauré, Ravel). Although art and politics are linked in *Passion,* as they are in Godard's thinking, the political problems don't seem to receive as much of his attention as the aesthetic ones. It is then a familiar Godardian jumble of elements treated with philosophical engagement and emotional detachment—a truly "modern" film, we might say.

The fecund originality of Godard's conception, the inventiveness and freedom

---

[2] Tom Milne (trans. and ed.), *Godard on Godard* (London: Martin Secker & Warburg Limited, 1972), p. 181.

My Life to Live (France, 1962, Jean-Luc Godard). Museum of Modern Art/Film Stills Archive.

with which he employs all of the technical and stylistic resources available to the film maker, has not been equalled. He makes one think of the painter Marcel Duchamp, who outlined so many of the forms of modern art. Godard is like Duchamp, too, in his intellectualism and coolness. If, ultimately, he withholds, or is unable to provide, kinds of aesthetic experience that may be valued most, within the humanist tradition at any rate, the importance of his contributions to an evolving art form and his influence on the work of others is unquestionable.

Claude Chabrol has continued—with increasing strength and control in later years—a succession of cohesive works. Narrow in vision (usually they involve an ill-fated triangle which often ends in death), they nonetheless gain power from their concentration. Overtaking Godard as the most prolific of the New Wave directors, Chabrol has consistently pictured a dark underside of bourgeois morality. Among the most carefully wrought, intense, and disturbing of his films are *Les Biches* (1968), *La Femme infidèle* (1969), *Le Boucher* (1970), and *Just Before Nightfall* (1971). His work would seem to be the most conventional of the New Wave directors—frequently following lines laid out by Lang and Hitchcock, whose films Chabrol admires—steadily produced and commercially successful.

Jacques Rivette made only two films in the 1960s, following *Paris nous appartient*, when Truffaut, Godard, and Chabrol were prolific: *La Religieuse* (1965) and

Les Bonnes Femmes (France, 1960, Claude Chabrol). National Film Archive London.

L'Amour fou (1968). In 1971 he completed *Out One* (running 12 hours and 40 minutes and never released), which became *Out One: Spectre* (1974), re-edited from the same footage. *Celine and Julie Go Boating* (1974) is his most "accessible" film, whimsical and amusing; *Le Pont du Nord* (1981), perhaps closest to it in style, has menacing overtones. All of his films maintain the enigmatic qualities of his first feature, either attacking or toying with the whole notion of illusionistic storytelling. In most of them the characters are in some ways involved in the production of plays from classical drama which are intricately interwoven with the modern stories. Rivette has said that his films "are about theater, about truth and lies." He continues to be the most cinematically radical of the New Wave directors, questioning the nature of the film making process even more constantly and openly than Godard. Generally controversial, fascinating for those attuned to his particular obsessions and the demands he places upon audiences, his films in most ways remain independent and even isolated from the main lines of French production.

    Not so Eric Rohmer's. Though Rohmer was a late bloomer, *My Night at Maud's* (1969), first feature of his "Six Moral Tales" to be released, achieved commercial suc-

Celine and Julie Go Boating (France, 1974, Jacques Rivette). Museum of Modern Art/Film Stills Archive.

cess and established his international reputation. The "literary" is even more conspicuous in Rohmer's work than in Resnais's. Whereas Resnais has collaborated with authors, Rohmer is one. His *Six Moral Tales* (published in translation under that title by Viking in 1979) were written as stories before he made them into films between 1962 and 1972. *The Marquise of O . . .* (1976) and *Perceval* (1978) are films of world literary classics. Consistent with this literary quality, the settings within which his characters are placed are observed with a particularity that suggests the term *described;* and his characters talk a lot. The way Rohmer thinks of his films is that they deal "less with what people do than with what is going on in their minds while they are doing it." His intricate explorations of what are essentially conservative moral positions—supported by a perfection of performance, intelligent and witty dialogue, subtle and exact psychological observation—continue to intrigue. *The Aviator's Wife* (1981) began a new series which Rohmer has entitled "Comedies and Proverbs," and continued with *A Good Marriage* (1982) and *Pauline at the Beach* (1983). Truffaut, interviewed twenty years after the New Wave began, when asked about "the new directors in France," said: "The one I like best is Eric Rohmer, but of course he is of my generation . . ."[3]

Not all contemporary French directors were part of the New Wave. On its edges, Louis Malle, already mentioned, after a career of varied and always interesting

---

[3] Don Allen, "Truffaut: Twenty Years After," *Sight and Sound,* XLVIII, (Autumn 1979), pp. 225–26.

My Night at Maud's (France, 1969, Eric Rohmer). Museum of Modern Art/Film Stills Archive.

fiction features (such as *Murmer of the Heart*, 1971; *Lacombe, Lucien*, 1973) and documentaries (*Phantom India* series, 1969; *Human, Too Human*, 1972), worked in America (*Pretty Baby*, 1979; *Atlantic City*, 1980; *My Dinner with André*, 1982). Jacques Demy, whose *Lola* (1961) might be considered a New Wave film, went on to make *The Umbrellas of Cherbourg* (1964), a charming and freshly experimental musical. In 1982 he tried a much heavier operatic form with *A Room in Town*, a tragic love story set against a background of violent labor conflict in the shipyard of Nantes. Working quite apart from New Wave influence was Jacques Tati, who nonetheless in his last two films before his death in 1982, *Playtime* (1968) and *Traffic* (1971), created intricate modernist comedies of contemporary life. Claude Goretta (*The Lacemaker*, 1977; *Roads of Exile*, 1979; *A Girl from Lorraine*, 1981) and Alain Tanner (*Jonah Who Will Be 25 in the Year 2000*, 1976; *Messidor*, 1979) are Swiss French. Recently Bertrand Tavernier (*The Clockmaker*, 1974; *Death Watch*, 1980), who has no connection with the New Wave, has been attracting critical attention abroad. *Diva* (1982), directed by Jean-Jacques Beineix, was the big French commercial success of the 1980s, especially popular in the U.S.

Though the New Wave as something resembling a movement lasted only a few years, roughly 1959 to 1962, its effects have extended down to the present. It completely revitalized French cinema and spawned most of the major directors currently at work. Together with the critical reevaluation of *la politique des auteurs* which preceded it, it gave more emphasis than had previously been the rule to a personal cinema under individual artistic control. Thinking of film as an art, and of the director as the controlling artist, became a predominant view in France and extended widely abroad. To some degree at least, personal cinema underlies what we mean when we talk about "contemporary cinema" or "modern film."

At the end of the fifties, first in France and then elsewhere, the kind of authority with which Bresson, Bergman, and Buñuel had been able to make their filmic statements began to be acquired by a growing number of film makers. Since then an ever-increasing range of distinctive personal styles has enriched the medium and our contemplation of it. What had been thought of largely as commercial entertainment, collectively produced and mass consumed, now appeared, under the right conditions, to be capable of the complexities and subtleties of the traditional arts. Though rarely challenging the box office dominance of the more popular forms, this new kind of creation opened up a modest but viable system of distribution and exhibition of "difficult" films for selective audiences. The "art cinema," as it is misleadingly called (as if there hadn't always been art in popular cinema), has been with us since the early sixties, and the French film makers can claim a large share of credit for its emergence.

Further, the influence of the New Wave extended not only to other countries but even into the popular cinema. We can point to "new wave" elements in Tony Richardson's *Tom Jones* (1963), Arthur Penn's *Mickey One* (1964, shot by one of the New Wave cameramen, Ghislain Cloquet), the Beatles films of Richard Lester (*A Hard Day's Night,* 1964, and *Help!,* 1965) and his American *Petulia* (1968), John Schlesinger's *Darling* (1965), and Stanley Donen's *Two for the Road* (1967, set appropriately in France). These are only a few among the many films made subsequently elsewhere that have used styles and themes which first came to the fore during the New Wave. But it was Italy that advanced most immediately and solidly into the breach France had opened in established convention. A dimension and weight were added as well, making modern Italian cinema uniquely contributive to the whole, a rival to the French in competition for creative leadership.

FILMS OF THE PERIOD

1956
And God Created Woman (Roger Vadim)
A Man Escaped (Robert Bresson)

1958
Le Beau Serge (Claude Chabrol)
Black Orpheus (Marcel Camus)
The Lovers (Louis Malle)
Mon Oncle (Jacques Tati)

1959
The Cousins (Chabrol)
The 400 Blows (François Truffaut)
Hiroshima, mon amour (Alain Resnais)
Pickpocket (Bresson)

1960
Les Bonnes Femmes (Chabrol)
Breathless (Jean-Luc Godard)
Paris nous appartient
    (Jacques Rivette)
Shoot the Piano Player (Truffaut)
Zazie dans le Métro (Malle)

1961
Cleo from 5 to 7 (Agnes Varda)
Jules and Jim (Truffaut)
Last Year at Marienbad (Resnais)
Lola (Jacques Demy)
Viridiana (Luis Buñuel)

1962

The Exterminating Angel (Buñuel)
My Life to Live (Godard)
The Trial of Joan of Arc (Bresson)

1963

Contempt (Godard)
Muriel (Resnais)

1964

Band of Outsiders (Godard)
Diary of a Chambermaid (Buñuel)
A Married Woman (Godard)
The Umbrellas of Cherbourg (Demy)

1965

Alphaville (Godard)
Le Bonheur (Varda)
Pierrot le fou (Godard)

1966

Au hasard, Balthasar (Bresson)
La Guerre est finie (Resnais)
A Man and a Woman (Claude Lelouch)
Masculine-Feminine (Godard)

1967

Belle de jour (Buñuel)
La Collectioneuse (Eric Rohmer)
Mouchette (Bresson)
Weekend (Godard)

1968

Les Biches (Chabrol)
Playtime (Tati)

1969

Charles—Dead or Alive (Alain Tanner)
La Femme infidèle (Chabrol)
My Night at Maud's (Rohmer)

1970

Le Boucher (Chabrol)
Claire's Knee (Rohmer)
Tristana (Buñuel)
The Wild Child (Truffaut)

1971

Just Before Nightfall (Chabrol)
Murmer of the Heart (Malle)
The Salamander (Tanner)
Traffic (Tati)

1972

Chloe in the Afternoon (Rohmer)
The Discreet Charm of the Bourgeoisie (Buñuel)
Return from Africa (Tanner)
Tout va bien (Godard)
Two English Girls (Truffaut)

1973

Day for Night (Truffaut)
Lacombe, Lucien (Malle)
The Mother and the Whore (Jean Eustache)

1974

Celine and Julie Go Boating (Rivette)
The Clockmaker (Bertrand Tavernier)
Lancelot of the Lake (Bresson)
The Middle of the World (Tanner)
Nada (Chabrol)
The Phantom of Liberty (Buñuel)
Stavisky (Resnais)

1975

Numéro deux (Godard)
The Story of Adele H. (Truffaut)

1976

Jonah Who Will Be 25 in the Year 2000 (Tanner)
The Marquise of O . . . (Rohmer)

1977

The Devil Probably (Bresson)
The Lacemaker (Claude Goretta)
The Man Who Loved Women (Truffaut)
Providence (Resnais)

1978

Mon Oncle d'Amérique (Resnais)
That Obscure Object of Desire (Buñuel)
Violette (Chabrol)

1979

Love on the Run (Truffaut)
Messidor (Tanner)
Roads of Exile (Goretta)

1980

Death Watch (Tavernier)
Sauve qui peut . . . La Vie (Godard)

1981
The Aviator's Wife (Rohmer)
A Girl from Lorraine (Goretta)
The Last Metro (Truffaut)
Le Pont du Nord (Rivette)

1982
A Good Marriage (Rohmer)

Passion (Godard)
A Room in Town (Demy)

1983
L'Argent (Bresson)
Pauline at the Beach (Rohmer)
La Vie est un roman (Resnais)

BOOKS ON THE PERIOD

ARMES, ROY, *French Cinema Since 1946,* 2 vols. Cranbury, N.J.: A. S. Barnes & Co., Inc., 1966, 1970.

ARMES, ROY, *French Film.* New York: E. P. Dutton & Co., Inc., 1970. 160 pp.

DURGNAT, RAYMOND, *Nouvelle Vague: The First Decade.* Loughton, England: Motion Publications, 1963. 90 pp.

GRAHAM, PETER, *The New Wave.* Garden City, N.Y.: Doubleday & Co., Inc., 1968. 184 pp.

MONACO, JAMES, *The New Wave.* New York: Oxford University Press, 1976. 364 pp.

18

The New Italians, 1960–

Like the French New Wave which broke at Cannes in 1959, a new kind of Italian cinema emerged at the Venice International Film Festival the following year. Unlike the French, however, the Italian films were by experienced directors whose landmark works of 1960 were set within careers that extended back into immediate postwar neorealism. The films also pointed ahead to the subsequent development of their directors and to a younger generation that would quickly grow up around them. The films were *Rocco and his Brothers, La Dolce Vita,* and *L'Avventura;* their directors were, respectively, Luchino Visconti, Federico Fellini, and Michelangelo Antonioni.

RELATIONSHIPS TO THE NEW WAVE

The Italians shared some of the thematic and stylistic innovations of the French—a reaction against the classical Hollywood narrative; a basic orientation that might be called modernist—Visconti being the exception. *Rocco and his Brothers* looked back to neorealism even if, like the bulk of Visconti's work, it departed from accepted neorealist tenets in its melodramatic emotionality, its heightening of character and incident. *La Dolce Vita* and *L'Avventura,* on the other hand, contained much identifiable as new in both subject and form.

There was the shared existentialist base, deriving out of the novels of Cesare

Pavese, whom Antonioni much admired, as well as the writings of Sartre and Camus: the sense that life was merely the sum of actions lived, the emphasis on alienation and the failure of communication. There was also a similarity with Bergman, acknowledged by both Antonioni and Fellini, in picturing a world in which divine faith has been lost and human love seems unattainable.

Then too, the narrative structure of the new Italian films had the same sort of looseness as the French. Both *L'Avventura* and *La Dolce Vita* were episodic rather than tightly woven, and picaresque. The first was organized around a journey and search for a missing person; the second around a sort of spiritual quest for values amidst various physical settings and social groups in and near contemporary Rome. Much of Fellini's work gives us the sense of being on the road; *La Strada* (1954) is the extreme case, the emphasis acknowledged in the title. Antonioni's films, too, set people in motion through countrysides and across cities. He is resolutely narrative rather than dramatic, and that in a low key of slight action and sparse, inconclusive dialogue. Of all film makers perhaps he is closest to certain tendencies in the modern novel in his attempts to deal with the interior lives of his characters. Since little is accidental in an Antonioni film, significance can be attached to a copy of F. Scott Fitzgerald's *Tender is the Night* lying open on a footstool in *La Notte* (1961). The characters and themes of his "trilogy" (*L'Avventura, La Notte, The Eclipse,* 1962) make us think of Fitzgerald. Perhaps he is closer still to the French *nouveau roman* and a novel like Alain Robbe-Grillet's *Jalousie* in his efforts to convey feeling states through description of the particularities of physical surroundings. *The Eclipse* ends with a seven-minute montage of images devoid of people: places and objects that had appeared earlier, now stripped of anthropomorphic meaning.

Unlike the French, though, new Italian film makers as a whole have shown little interest in manipulating time and space in extra-real, purely filmic ways. Fellini, of course, does make use of fantasy (in *8½*, 1963, and *Juliet of the Spirits,* 1965, for example), in which he plays with the physical laws of the universe as well as subjective and hallucinatory emotional states, but he clearly sets the imagined and remembered apart from the ongoing present reality. In *La Dolce Vita* and elsewhere, in his approach to the "real world," time and space are dealt with in a perfectly straightforward manner—that is, within the conventions employed in realistic films generally. Antonioni, on the other hand, gets even closer than the conventional to the felt passage of time and experienced movement across space. After seeing *L'Avventura* the filmgoer could make out a complete itinerary, with a journal and a map. Antonioni's long-held shots, with slow panning and trucking, are as far removed as possible from the ellipses and staccato jump-cutting of early Godard and Truffaut. Nor do Antonioni's films ever retreat to the past, let alone advance into the future, as do those of Resnais. Fantasy scenes occur only rarely in his work—for example, in *Zabriskie Point* (1969), in the ghostly desert love-in, and the conclusion in which the heroine imagines the destruction of her boss's modern mansion.

Last, the Italians did not indulge in the self-conscious playfulness with the medium enjoyed by the French. Fellini is somewhat an exception to that generalization, but his fun and games are more likely to be drawn from the circus and music hall than from the characteristics of the film medium or the work of other film makers. Antonioni and Visconti, of course, are notably unplayful in every respect, though the former in later work undertaken abroad—*Blow-Up* (Britain, 1966), *Zabriskie Point* (U.S.), *The Passenger* (Italy/U.S., 1975, shot in Algeria, Spain, England, and Germany)—departed sharply from the austerity of his Italian films. *Blow-Up* offers a rich aesthetic, even ontological commentary on the very nature of the photographic image (upon which motion as well as still pictures depend) and its relationship to reality. *The Passenger* so emphasizes the shifting frame area and perspective of a moving camera that it too forces the viewer to consider the cinematic process that adds to the cryptic nature of the events observed.

ROOTS IN NEOREALISM: THREE FILM MAKERS

What the new Italian cinema was moving away from and what toward was consolidated at the Venice Festival of 1960. In an Italy that had recovered with astonishing rapidity from the social-political-economic upheaval and aftermath of World War II, the concerns were with the beliefs one might live by now that life itself and the living of it were more assured and comfortable. One indication of the change was that the new Italian film makers turned their attention from the lower to the upper classes. With their capacity to spend life more or less as they chose, the wealthy made most clearly manifest the moral vacuum, the angst, the idle pursuit of meaningless pleasures that had accompanied the "economic miracle." In the Italy of the sixties, gone or seriously eroded were, on the one hand, the support of traditional Catholic morality and faith in God and His church, and on the other, the solidarity and militancy of the Left that had infused Italian society and political life in the immediate postwar years. Whatever the differences among their films, Visconti, Fellini, and Antonioni established a newly prominent moral, even spiritual, concern, and redirected attention to individual psyches, rather than collective conditions, in a contemporary Italy.

But it is reality of one sort or another, psychological as well as physical, that has prevailed in the Italian film and precluded the excessive whimsicality sometimes indulged in by the New Wave. Most likely that is so because of the closely preceding tradition of neorealism. As already noted, all three directors of the major Italian films of 1960 had roots in that tradition.

Visconti, in fact, along with Rossellini and de Sica, could lay claim to being one of the founders and principal practitioners of that movement. His *Ossessione* (1942) was clearly a precurser, with its harshly naturalistic approach to character, theme, and setting at a time when Italian films were either patriotic or escaping the realities of wartime Italy, optimistic or cheery in either case. *La Terra Trema* (1948) is among the great neorealist films, though its overlay of highly stylized studio-like cinematography and staged groupings onto actual fishermen and Sicilian village make us think of Eisenstein of *Old and the New* rather than of the other neorealists.

In *Rocco and his Brothers* Visconti in a sense returned to his Southern Italians of *La Terra Trema,* but now they were immigrants in Milan. Though social and economic forces are shown as contributing to the destruction of the family, the drama grows out of the personal conflicts and psychological flaws of the characters. The film employs the emotional intensity and extravagant behavior of Greek drama rather than the deliberate understatement and restraint associated with neorealism at its purest. Subsequently, of course, Visconti used various sorts of historical and literary materials—initiated in *Senso* (1954) and *White Nights* (1957) and continued in *The Leopard* (1963), *Sandra* (1965), *The Stranger* (1967), *The Damned* (1969), *Death in Venice* (1971), and *Ludwig* (1972). As a nobleman whose distinguished family had figured prominently for centuries in Italian history, Visconti had the deep concern for tradition (at odds with his Marxism) and cultivated taste you would expect. His penultimate film before his death in 1976, *Conver-*

The Leopard (Italy, 1963, Luchino Visconti). Museum of Modern Art/Film Stills Archive.

sation Piece, offers an elegiac commentary on an aristocratic intellectual and art lover forced into uneasy but fascinated contact with the strident exigencies and vulgarities of modern political and social reality. We can imagine that the protagonist (played by Burt Lancaster, who also had played the prince in *The Leopard*) must have been seen by Visconti as some kind of equivalent to himself.

The Visconti who evolved out of neorealism traveled as far from it in style and subjects as could be imagined. If Marxism and the scenographic baroque combined in his earlier films, the creation of lush imagery (a joy in itself) and re-creation and examination of varied forms of decadence, usually aristocratic, seem to carry the main weight in the total body of his work. A film maker of international scope as well as stature, Visconti can be thought of as Italian primarily because of the ''operatic'' qualities of his films. As a film artist he stands in splendid isolation, his work unique and rather formidable.

Fellini had been script writer on *Open City, Paisan,* and *Europe 51* (for Rossellini), *Without Pity* and *Mill on the Po* (for Alberto Lattuada), and *In the Name of the Law* (for Pietro Germi), among other noteworthy neorealist films. The first works he directed as well as wrote—*Variety Lights* (1951, with Lattuada), *The White Sheik* (1952), and especially the autobiographical *I Vitelloni* (1953)—fell clearly within the neorealist tradition, even if they already began to reflect Fellini's predilection for the popular arts and his own personal experiences as source material. The enormously successful *La Strada* (1954) represented a turning point. Though set amidst the poverty and drabness of small-town rural Italy, its protagonists are vagabonds (a traveling strong man and his female assistant) rather than workers or peasants. And Fellini was onto new themes quite outside the persistently materialistic view of the earlier neorealism. What we care about in *La Strada* is not that times are hard and social institutions culpable, but that Zampanò and Gelsomina learn to give and receive the warmth and comfort of human love.

Fellini's films, more obviously Italian in attitude and subject than Visconti's, departed more gradually from the accepted limitations of neorealism. What attracted him, instead of the historical and literary, was the subjective and fantastic. The only films of his which have literary-historical bases are *Fellini Satyricon* (1969) and *Fellini's Casanova* (1976). In these, as their titles imply, Petronius's ancient Rome and Casanova's eighteenth-century Europe were converted into the director's fantasies of debauchery and sexuality, and into extravaganza. Fellini has remarked of his *Satyricon* that it may be even more autobiographical than his much more obviously autobiographical *8½* (1963). Even the two filmed essays, *The Clowns* (1970) and *Fellini's Roma* (1972), keep the film maker's own interests, experiences and tastes, and yes, fantasies at their center: it is *his* fascination with clowns from young boyhood on, *his* Rome. *Amarcord* (1973) was a sort of compendium of his recollections filtered through the exaggeration and imagination of adolescent perception. *City of Women* (1980) brought together and made quite explicit (as dreams) the sexual fears and desires that appear throughout his work.

From the beginning of Fellini's directorial career the autobiographical elements were present either in foreground or background, and usually both. *Variety Lights* dealt with the music hall entertainment which he had experienced first hand. *The White Sheik* satirized the comic book industry, and Fellini had been a cartoonist. *La Strada* was again about touring entertainers. *Il Bidone* (1955), though perhaps not drawn so directly from experience, contained many of the recurring themes and images, especially the religious ones. *The Nights of Cabiria* (1957) portrayed the life of Roman prostitutes as Fellini had come to understand it. A special aspect of Fellini's "personalizing" of his work is that his wife, Giulietta Masina, played in all but one of those early films, as well as in many of the later ones.

Up through *Nights of Cabiria,* however, Fellini maintained that he was still working within the neorealist tradition, that he had simply shifted his concentration from external to internal reality. Certainly his films had much the look of the earlier neorealism. If shot more carefully and intimately, with emphasis on composition and the symbolic reverberations of the images, they were still objective in point of view. *I Vitelloni* is especially remarkable in the feeling it gives that the camera just happened to be there to capture bits of lives as they were being lived. Also, those early films make significant use of actual locations and nonactors and are set among the lower classes, the outcasts and dispossessed. But the poverty that concerned Fellini most was the impoverishment of the spirit. Though in his work, as in the original neorealist films, there are things to be sad about and no solutions are outlined, the hope that is offered for the human condition lies not in working-class solidarity but in the joy and love, in an almost religious sense, that the individual soul is capable of. The ending of *Nights of Cabiria,* with the little prostitute picking herself up after a near drowning and walking down a lane encircled by playing children, is very different in its implications from that of *Bicycle Thief,* with father and son walking hand in hand off into the crowd, however similar the action. Both attest to human resiliency; but Antonio and his son, though comforted by their love for each other, merge into the masses to face another jobless day; Cabiria, through the children, recovers her own optimism and sense of self-worth.

With *La Dolce Vita,* Fellini took a long step further away from neorealism. It is concerned with the decadent idle rich of Rome and the sensational press which reports their doings to a voracious public. The journalist-protagonist (played by Marcello Mastroianni, who would become "Fellini" in *8½*) is in search of meaning in life and values to live by. His passage through the sort of cafe society life well known to Fellini is like a descent into Dante's *Inferno*. The various pursuits to which he might devote himself—wife and family, business success, sexual excitement, religious fervour, philosophical speculation—are successively shown to be corrupting or insufficient to support meaningful existence. By inference we learn that God is absent from this world, or silent as He was in Bergman's. (The pointedly ironic opening scene of a gilded statue of Christ being hauled by helicopter over the rooftops of modern Rome, and the scene of a highly publicized fake miracle flail at the hollow and superstitious religion subscribed to by the masses and tacitly approved by the Church.) Though it dealt with the upper classes and matters of the spirit, *Dolce Vita* was still in a completely realistic style. It was merely that the locations now included *palazzi* and the nonactors, actual members of the Roman aristocracy.

It wasn't until "The Temptation of Dr. Antonio" episode for *Boccacio 70* (1962) that Fellini turned to fantasy—one of his own, more than likely. Not until *8½* did he combine the autobiographical and the extravagant personal phantasmagoria that would depart from neorealism entirely and mark the remainder of his work to date. Certainly his most complex film, *8½* may also be his finest. It is a witty and revealing account of a director's harried life and the difficulties he has in conceiving his next film, that is, this one, hence the title: Fellini had directed eight films up to that point. Just to make certain there would be no mistake, Mastroianni wore a wide-brimmed western hat like the one Fellini habitually wears on the set.

8½ (Italy, 1963, Federico Fellini). Museum of Modern Art/Film Stills Archive.

Antonioni had served his apprenticeship as a critic (like the French New Wave film makers) and script writer, including work on films in the neorealist tradition such as Giuseppe de Santis's *Tragic Hunt* and Fellini's *White Sheik.* He also directed a number of documentary shorts. But his features, aside from *Il Grido* (1957), which is set in a working-class milieu in the Po Valley, treat the values and interpersonal relationships of the middle and upper classes.

In extreme contrast to Fellini's ebullience is Antonioni's austerity. Though *La Dolce Vita* and *L'Avventura* deal with the same social strata (and both are organized around protagonists on the fringes rather than part of the upper classes) and contain the same themes (loss of meaning and values replaced by promiscuity and debauchery), these two films and the subsequent work of their respective makers could scarcely be more different from each other. Whereas Fellini's films are informed with a Catholic humanist view of the world (evidently deep-rooted if informal and anticlerical), Antonioni's view is that of a post-religious Marxist and existentialist intellectual. While Fellini exposes the shoddiness of the moral values offered by "the sweet life," at the same time that he is clucking moralistically he seems to be enjoying the naughtiness and glamor.

Antonioni offers no such titillation or spectacle. In *L'Avventura* and his Italian films which follow it—*La Notte* (1961), *The Eclipse* (1962), *The Red Desert* (1964), and *Identification of a Woman* (1982)—he dissected the values that he saw operative in upper-class modern Italy with the disinterested precision and functional grace of a skilled surgeon, or perhaps of a weary but alert coroner conducting a post-mortem. For the "sweet life" in Antonioni's portrayal of it seems closer to death in that the souls have left the bodies. Not only is meaning lacking, but feeling too, except for the instinctual sexual twitching as bodies refuse to acknowledge what minds know. Eroticism is prominent in the films of Antonioni, as it is in those of Fellini, and Antonioni has described it as "a dominating factor in our civilization." But whereas the orgy at the end of *La Dolce Vita* has some prurient appeal (the strip-tease and the horsey-back ride on the bovine blonde actress), the sexual interludes in *L'Avventura* leave us cold and sad: the early scene with Anna in Sandro's apartment, Sandro with Claudia outside the deserted town and later in the hotel room after his encounter with the young architect, Sandro with the high-class prostitute in the early morning. Never has "sin" looked less inviting. The sensuality, pleasure, guilt, and remorse felt by Fellini's characters are replaced by pervasive ennui and irritability, and a sense of the inability of any person to make contact with another even in the most intimate moments. Sex in Antonioni's world may stem from a desire to communicate, but it frequently takes the form of aggression or tired surrender to habit. Among his characters a life in which the sexual act has meaning or even gives pleasure seems unavailable and perhaps unimaginable.

But it isn't that dreary human landscape alone, or the sensitivity with which certain kinds of despair are revealed, that account for the fascination Antonioni's films hold for his times. As with any considerable artist it is the enveloping form of his works that gives the themes and insights their unique significance. *L'Avventura* is the rare sort of film that sets forth a whole new range of possibilities within the art that hadn't been sensed before and that can be drawn upon ever afterward. Like *Intolerance,* or *Potemkin,* or *Citizen Kane,* it closes off one era and opens up another.

The extraordinary visual surface of *L'Avventura*, and of Antonioni's succeeding work, seems less radical now than it did when it first appeared precisely because it has been incorporated into the language of film as one of the prominent styles. Growing out of Antonioni's artistic intentions and statements, of course, it also took peculiar advantage of the attributes of the wide screen, seemed almost to require it. The camera was placed at a medium distance more often than close in, frequently moving slowly; the shots were permitted to extend uninterrupted by cutting. Thus each image is more complex, contains more information than it would in a style in which a smaller area is framed and the shots are briefer in duration. In this respect he harks back to Murnau or Dovzhenko rather than Eisenstein. In Antonioni's work we must regard his images at length; he forces our full attention by continuing the shot after others would cut away.

By demanding that we read the complex meaning of several characters in relation to each other and their surroundings, rather than selecting and emphasizing, he makes us become active observers. The action and dialogue, the settings and circumstances must be comprehended almost as life itself, without the exposition and graduated intensity that usually clue us in fiction. The positions in which the characters stand or sit, the way they walk, the irrelevancies of their conversations, the cool overcast light, the starkness and lack of movement in many of the compositions—all cohere into a total view of a kind of existence. A cold and empty world it is, degenerative not in the mode of marathon orgies but because the values are not substantial enough to sustain life at a level of human warmth and dignity. Love, pursued persistently if lethargically, can't be distinguished from lust. Work has no meaning with the impulse to create atrophied. Diversion and puzzling accidents fill in the time, and characters keep on the move or lapse fitfully into hopelessly self-indulgent self-analysis. If we, the audience, are put in the position of onlookers, what we see is a world in which the possibility of significant action has been lost.

While Antonioni offers us a view in certain respects closer to life than is usual, he is an artist of superb control which extends into and balances every aspect of his films. His method does not include the spontaneity and improvisation of Fellini, nor does it permit the rough edges that Visconti allows to go uncorrected in his impatience to outline a grand plan. Consider, for example, the much-noted island sequence in *L'Avventura*. In it the characters are continually being commented upon, linked, and separated, by their positions in relation to each other and within the frame: their movements and the camera's are choreographed with equal care. The growing awareness and desire of Sandro and Claudia for each other is initially signaled through such means. For instance, one shot begins with the camera looking down on Sandro. Then it tilts up and, on another plane above him, frames Claudia in the distance as she walks toward the camera (and Sandro's position). Or, in another shot, there is a slight, slow pan from left to right with Claudia in the background. As the shot proceeds, Sandro enters frame left, mid-foreground. Then there is the *pas de deux* in successive shots when Claudia is trying to avoid Sandro and he, somewhat unconsciously and helplessly, tries to attach himself to her. Sometimes the camera even becomes like a member of the group as it moves ahead of the actors until they catch up with it and walk into frame again.

But with Antonioni, that kind of visual calculation—the framing and movement of actors and camera, the settings (barren rocky island, eerie deserted town), the way the light falls (the cold gray of early morning in the halls of the palatial hotel)—is everywhere designed to enrich narrative. A director like Eisenstein, who planned and executed his films with equal attention to detail, for all of his visual and kinetic brilliance was saying simple things. The complexity in his films resides almost entirely in their visual artistry. Antonioni, on the other hand, has provided the sorts of ambiguity considered proper to narrative art. It is his kind of imagery and storytelling, rather than the

L'Avventura (Italy, 1960, Michelangelo Antonioni). Museum of Modern Art/Film Stills Archive.

more selective and directive method of Eisenstein, that has come to characterize the best of modern cinema and to represent a profound break with what had gone before. It also appeals most strongly to the needs and sensibilities of a new kind of audience which now looks to film rather than to the older arts for the fullest and most satisfying expression of a modern world view.

OTHER DIRECTORS AND SUBSEQUENT FILMS

Following Visconti, Fellini, and Antonioni, and building on their foundation to greater or lesser extent and in various ways, there appeared a cluster of powerfully talented younger Italian film makers. The first two to be dealt with here, rather than paralleling the then-current concerns of the three veterans, returned to some of the earlier neorealist impulses. One had had extensive documentary experience before turning to fiction; the other began his film career as assistant director on a neorealist feature.

Ermanno Olmi's first features contained socially significant themes, were shot on location, and used nonactors as in the earlier tradition. But instead of unemployment and poverty, he dealt with jobs that offered little satisfaction and the difficulties of creating fulfilling lives and relationships within the conformist demands of an industrialized society. What Olmi provided was a subtle and absorbing attention to the in-

Il Posto (Italy, 1961, Ermanno Olmi). Museum of Modern Art/Film Stills Archive.

dividual among the working classes. *Il Posto* (1961) is about a teen-age boy from a small village on his first job as messenger for a large firm in Milan. The tenderness and gentle humor with which the director regards the boy's tentative relationship with a girl, his loneliness at a dreary office party, and his feelings when he first sits at a clerk's desk are uniquely Olmi's own. *The Fiancés* (1963) concentrates on a worker who goes from the North to a new plant in Sicily. The slender story deals largely with his efforts to come to a better understanding of the fiancée he has had to leave behind and of their relationship. In later films, *One Fine Day* (1968) and *The Circumstance* (1974) for example, Olmi moved to the middle and upper classes, from workers to bosses, and fragmented his narrative, the present and recollected past sometimes intermingled with Resnais-like complexity. But in *The Tree of Wooden Clogs* (1979), about the life of a peasant community in Lombardy at the close of the nineteenth century, Olmi returned to the earlier lyrical and unadorned style.

Francesco Rosi, little known in the U.S., is much admired in Italy and in Europe generally. His first considerable achievement was *Salvatore Giuliano* (1962), shot entirely on location in Sicily with an almost exclusively nonprofessional cast. It concerns an actual Mafia leader whose banditry and guerrilla activities are seen as aimed towards achieving Sicilian independence. *Hands Over the City* (1963), in many ways similar in method and ultimate intent, examines the exploitation of capitalist power and political corruption by an unscrupulous housing developer in Naples. *The Mattei Affair* (1972) retains its basis in actuality but ascends to a national, even international, scale. Enrico Mattei was an industrial manager who created a state-controlled oil company which loomed large in Italian political-economic affairs and competed against the other national and multinational oil interests in the world market. *Christ Stopped at Eboli* (1979) is

Hands Over the City (Italy, 1963, Francesco Rosi). Museum of Modern Art/Film Stills Archive.

Rosi's version of the Carlo Levi book about the condition of rural Southern Italy in the 1930s. *Three Brothers* (1981) traces the fortunes of three sons of a peasant in the Puglia region whose lives mirror the development of post-World War II Italy. The enigma of power, the pervasiveness of political influence, and the factual source remain characteristic of Rosi's work. Perhaps of the neo-neorealist directors, Rosi has most fully made manifest the political tenets implicit in the original movement.

But even in the work of directors emerging in the 1960s who were closest to the earlier neorealists we can see signs of the changing times. And, rather than either Olmi or Rosi, perhaps another two Italian film makers, clearly influenced by the French New Wave, are more representative of the generation which followed Visconti, Fellini, and Antonioni.

Piero Paolo Pasolini and Bernardo Bertolucci had many things in common. Bertolucci even counted Pasolini as a ''father'' and was considerably influenced by his films and theoretical writings. Both were strongly committed to the political left, but the new rather than the old, Italian intellectual rather than doctrinaire Marxist. Both used their films as means of exploring the structure of society. Even when the surfaces or foregrounds seem devoted solely to the relationships among individuals, the attitudes of their characters and the kinds of dilemmas they find themselves in have political dimensions. While in France there is an active political consciousness at work among certain film makers and critics, in Italy this sort of concern is almost endemic among those involved with the cinema. Much of the critical discussion of a film there—from both right and left—will be devoted to its ideological significance and likely effects on social attitudes.

Pasolini, a novelist, poet, linguist and film theorist before he directed his first feature, *Accattone!*, in 1961, consistently dealt with the "subproletariat"—beggars and outcasts. Even *The Gospel According to St. Matthew* (1964), his best-known film, conforms to that generalization. In it Christ is portrayed as a revolutionary orator-leader from the masses of a sort common in the history of the Middle Eastern peoples. Shot as if it were reportage rather than re-creation, hand-held camera and nonactors give the Biblical story a feeling of contemporary actuality and urgency. *The Hawks and the Sparrows* (1966), an allegorical comedy, reveals and examines the relationships between Christianity and Marxism. *Teorema* (1968) and *Pigpen* (1969) include strange mythic evocations of transcendental states, perverse sexuality, and cannibalism in their attacks on capitalist society. Pasolini's ability as a writer and translator led him to attempt new interpretations of classic literary works. Following *Oedipus Rex* (1967) were *Medea* (1970), *The Decameron* (1971), *The Canterbury Tales* (1972), *The Arabian Nights* (1974). His last film, *Salò or the 120 Days of Sodom,* suggested by a work of the Marquis de Sade and full of violence, was completed just before his own violent death in 1975. Brilliant and multitalented, at the same time idiosyncratic and unpredictable, Pasolini occupied a position of leadership among the new Italians.

Bertolucci, who worked as assistant director on *Accatone!*, achieved a prodigious international success with *Before the Revolution* (1964), which he completed at the age of twenty-four. (His first feature, *The Grim Reaper,* based on a rough draft by Pasolini, had been made two years earlier.) Of the post-Visconti-Fellini-Antonioni generation, Bertolucci has made least use of the neorealist inheritance. His films more nearly resemble those of the later Visconti, in their sorting through of intertwined personal relationships and political attitudes, and in their bold painterly style (for example, *The Conformist* and

The Gospel According to St. Matthew (Italy, 1964, Pier Paolo Pasolini). Museum of Modern Art/Film Stills Archive.

The Spider's Stratagem, both 1970). His most exceptional work to date, *Last Tango in Paris* (1972), also bears some resemblance to Antonioni thematically and aroused something of the same excitement as *L'Avventura* in suggesting a new sort of film language, or personal idiom at least. In Bertolucci's case his contributions to cinematic expressiveness may lie solely in the style which is the man. Dense and unanalyzable in many respects, it is hard to know just what makes *Last Tango* work so powerfully. If it is too early to tell whether it is an enduring masterpiece, there is no question about its initial impact, the force with which Bertolucci was able to speak to his contemporaries. It was followed by the vast panorama of *1900* (1976), covering some seventy years of life and social conflict in the Emilia region of Italy; *Luna* (1979), the intimate study of an incestuous relationship between mother and son which occasioned controversy at least equal to that caused by *Last Tango;* and *Tragedy of a Ridiculous Man* (1981), involving a father-son relationship, kidnapping, and terrorism in present-day Italy.

Especially popular in the U.S. have been films by Lina Wertmüller and the Taviani brothers, Paolo and Vittorio. Wertmüller's initial film work was as assistant director to Fellini on *8½*. *The Seduction of Mimi* (1972) was her first big success, followed by *Love and Anarchy* (1973) and *Swept Away* (1974). The most ambitious and important of

Last Tango in Paris (Italy, 1972, Bernardo Bertolucci). National Film Archive/Stills Library.

her films to date is *Seven Beauties* (1976). All of them are comedies, though the latter, set in a Nazi concentration camp, contains horror and pathos. Giancarlo Giannini, who stars in all of them, has developed a comic persona of the little man whose behavior is determined by the requirements of survival. The films mingle sex and politics, dominance and dependence, in what seems a puzzling ideological mix. The Tavianis became known in this country chiefly for *Padre Padrone* (1977), an adaptation of a best-selling account of the progress of an ignorant Sardinian from shepherd to university professor. *Night of the Shooting Stars* (1982), shot in their native Tuscany, was based on their own experiences as young boys and on oral accounts of fellow Tuscans. It concerns a group of villagers who in 1944 defied the retreating Germans to welcome the advancing Americans.

Seen as a whole, the Italian film from 1960 onward represents a kind of range and maturity of statement that has earned wide admiration. Artistic innovation has been tempered by continuing awareness of the role of film in society. A common sense of national identity among the film makers has strengthened individual efforts. In spite of the obvious personal and generational differences, the Italian directors share many aesthetic and political as well as cultural assumptions. That cohesiveness has permitted artists of the stature of Visconti and Fellini and Antonioni to have long productive careers. It has also provided a background from which newcomers have emerged to command worldwide attention. The term "Italian New Wave," bandied about at the

Night of the Shooting Stars (Italy, 1982, Paolo and Vittorio Taviani). Museum of Modern Art/ Film Stills Archive.

time of the 1960 Venice Festival, wasn't really appropriate. What was being revealed in the three remarkable films shown there was merely the beginning of another evolutionary stage in an ongoing tradition that has existed in Italy at least since the end of World War II.

FILMS OF THE PERIOD

1960

L'Avventura (Michelangelo Antonioni)
La Dolce Vita (Federico Fellini)
Rocco and his Brothers (Luchino Visconti)

1961

Accatone! (Piero Paolo Pasolini)
Bandits of Orgosolo (Vittorio de Seta)
Divorce, Italian Style (Pietro Germi)
La Notte (Antonioni)
Il Posto (Ermanno Olmi)

1962

The Eclipse (Antonioni)
Salvatore Giuliano (Francesco Rosi)

1963

8½ (Fellini)
The Fiancés (Olmi)
Hands Over the City (Rosi)
The Leopard (Visconti)

1964

Before the Revolution
   (Bernardo Bertolucci)
The Gospel According to St. Matthew
   (Pasolini)
The Red Desert (Antonioni)

1965

The Battle of Algiers (Gillo Pontecorvo)
Juliet of the Spirits (Fellini)
Sandra (Visconti)

1966

Fists in the Pocket (Marco Bellochio)
The Hawks and the Sparrows (Pasolini)

1967

China Is Near (Bellochio)

1968

One Fine Day (Olmi)

1969

The Damned (Visconti)

1970

The Conformist (Bertolucci)
The Garden of the Finzi-Continis
   (Vittorio de Sica)
Investigation of a Citizen above Suspicion
   (Elio Petri)
The Spider's Stratagem (Bertolucci)

1971

In the Name of the Father (Bellochio)

1972

Last Tango in Paris (Bertolucci)
The Mattei Affair (Rosi)

1973

Amarcord (Fellini)

1975

Conversation Piece (Visconti)
The Passenger (Antonioni)

1976

Fellini's Casanova (Fellini)
The Innocent (Visconti)
1900 (Bertolucci)
Seven Beauties (Lina Wertmüller)

1977

Padre Padrone
   (Paolo and Vittorio Taviani)

1978

Orchestra Rehearsal (Fellini)

1979

Christ Stopped at Eboli (Rosi)
Luna (Bertolucci)
The Tree of the Wooden Clogs (Olmi)

1980

City of Women (Fellini)
The Mystery of Oberwald (Antonioni)

1981

Three Brothers (Rosi)
Tragedy of a Ridiculous Man (Bertolucci)

1982

Identification of a Woman (Antonioni)
Night of the Shooting Stars (Taviani)

1983

And the Ship Sails On (Fellini)
Cammina Cammina (Olmi)

BOOKS ON THE PERIOD

BONDANELLA, PETER, *Italian Cinema: From Neorealism to the Present.* New York: Frederick Ungar Publishing Co., Inc., 1982. 400 pp.

LEPROHON, PIERRE, *The Italian Cinema.* New York: Praeger Publishers, 1972. 256 pp.

RONDI, GIAN LUIGI, *Italian Cinema Today, 1952–1965.* New York: Hill and Wang, Inc., 1966. 279 pp.

WITCOMBE, R. T., *The New Italian Cinema: Studies in Dance and Despair.* New York: Oxford University Press, 1982.

WLASCHIN, KEN, *Italian Cinema Since the War.* Cranbury, N.J.: A. S. Barnes & Co., Inc., 1971. 224 pp.

19

Eastern European Cinema, 1954–

Throughout the first years of the new revolutionary government in Russia, considerable freedom and experimentation had been present in the arts as well as in other aspects of life. With Stalin's consolidation of power, permissiveness and variety gave way to enormous monolithic control. By the early thirties "socialist realism" was the official and only state aesthetic. Prescribed content was locked into straight-forward unambiguous narrative form. The seductive artistry of the Soviet silent films was replaced by the positive, wholesome, uplifting, and bland portrayal of Russian heroes whose lives might have some implication for the revolution, or with the presentation of ideologically "correct" modern peasants, workers, and professional people. *Chapayev* (1934) was the model. Since that time, with rare exceptions, Russian films have aroused little interest in the West. Conversely, when Fellini's *8½* was shown at the first Moscow Film Festival, in 1963, it was subjected to violent criticism as a decadent bourgeois work full of "vagueness and morbidity." It was awarded first prize only after considerable argument and insistence on the part of the invited western judges. Neither it nor other of the new French and Italian films were shown generally in the U.S.S.R.

In the communist countries the effect of a film on the audience's social and political attitudes is regarded as more important than the money it brings in. Given this concern, film content is carefully scrutinized and regulated to one degree or another by the state. Consequently film production in the Soviet bloc can be analyzed as a kind of barometer measuring political pressure operating within a society at any given time. A few months before the 1963 Moscow Festival, Communist Party Chairman Nikita Khrushchev had delivered an important speech regarding his attitude toward the arts in the Soviet Union. He said, in part,

> We adhere to class positions in art and resolutely oppose peaceful coexistence between socialist and capitalist ideologies. Art belongs to the sphere of ideology . . . . Abstractionism and formalism, whose right to a place in socialist art is advocated by some of their champions, are forms of capitalist ideology . . . .

One of the contemporary Soviet film makers who has managed to escape the dictates of socialist realism and express a strong personal vision through structures and styles more nearly resembling those of contemporary film makers in Western Europe is Andrei Tarkovsky. His *My Name Is Ivan* (*Ivan's Childhood,* 1962), *Andrei Rublev* (1966), and *Solaris* (1972) all won prizes at festivals abroad. *My Name Is Ivan,* with its strong and clear humanist message carrying along its unusual display of technical virtuosity, was extremely popular at home as well. *Andrei Rublev,* however, a more involuted and complex film about a monk icon painter who lived at the turn of the fifteenth century, was held up for several years and then released in a cut version. (The uncut version has only recently become available in the U.S.) Evidently it was suspect because of its religious themes, unorthodox view of history, and scenes of brutality. *Solaris,* a science-fiction film, evoked comparisons with Stanley Kubrick's *2001,* though Tarkovsky eschewed spectacular technology and psychedelic fantasy in favor of the philosophical implications of his vision of the future and its effects on human lives. *Mirror,* released in a very limited way in the Soviet Union in 1974 and not until nearly a decade later in the U.S., is autobiographical as well as experimental, mingling dream and reality, childhood memories with an ongoing marriage. In *Stalker* (1979), Tarkovsky returned to science-fiction. It is a grim odyssey of two Russian intellectuals led by the title character into

Andrei Rublev (USSR, 1966, Andrei Tarkovsky). Museum of Modern Art/Film Stills Archive.

"the Zone," a devastated postapocalyptic wasteland sealed off by the authorities. *Nostalgia* (1983), a brooding account of a journey through Italy by a Russian scholar, was shot on location in Italy for European television. Its main theme seems to be the impossibility of transcultural understanding.

Another exceptional contemporary Soviet film maker has been less successful in pursuing his own vision under the Soviet system. Sergo Paradjanov is known abroad for his *Shadows of Our Forgotten Ancestors* (1964) and *The Color of Pomegranates* (1969); the former is available in the U.S., the latter is familiar only through reports from overseas. *Shadows* is an extraordinary and unique epic blend of fact, fiction, and poetry in celebration of peasant life, lore, and mythology in a remote part of the Ukraine. Loose and elliptical in construction, "formalistic" and at the same time sensual, it is a film that would seem to stand quite outside the requirements of a modern socialist state, as did Dovzhenko's *Earth*. *The Color of Pomegranates* appears to bear certain resemblances to Tarkovsky's *Andrei Rublev*. Both films are about an artist monk who suffers in an alien society; in Paradjanov's film the hero is Sayat Nova, an eighteenth-century Armenian poet. It too was shelved after completion and re-edited by others, over the film maker's protest, before release in 1973. It was never distributed abroad and Paradjanov's subsequent projects were either not accepted for production or not permitted to be completed. In 1974 he was convicted of homosexuality (a criminal offense in the Soviet Union), illegal currency dealings, and "incitement to suicide," and sentenced to six years hard labor. Though tried as a citizen and not as an artist, considerable suspicion was expressed that his real crime may have been his ebullient and rebellious spirit and the individualistic and iconoclastic nature of his finest and most important films. By 1983 he was out of prison and working on a new film.

In the Eastern European countries within the Soviet sphere, the situation has not been as consistently restrictive. On the contrary, the idealistic aspects of communism infused with an apparently unquenchable nationalism and exposure to the new

Shadows of Our Forgotten Ancestors (USSR, 1964, Sergo Paradjanov). Museum of Modern Art/Film Stills Archive.

films from the West have accounted for fertile periods of creativity in the cinema of Poland, Hungary, Czechoslovakia, and Yugoslavia.

Prior to World War II the film production of the Eastern European countries had been negligible in quantity and quality. Few of their films found audiences beyond their own borders, and the small national populations could not be counted on to return the profits necessary to private enterprise. With the establishment of communist governments in those countries immediately after the war, there were new incentives for production, like those in the Soviet Union earlier, and a new base for economic support. It took a few years for the ground to be prepared, but once the state film schools had begun turning out graduates, and film production, distribution and exhibition had been stimulated and coordinated, the Eastern People's Republics were ready to take their places in the international spotlight. The governments wanted films that would inform and indoctrinate, that would interpret events of the immediate past to give a sense of solidarity, and that would instill attitudes contributing to future progress. Replacing the subject of the Bolshevik Revolution dealt with by the first Soviet film makers was the resistance to Nazi Germany during World War II. Communism was represented as the only force with the people's interest at heart capable of opposing fascism effectively and offering an alternative, more democratic way of life.

POLAND

Immediately after the war the communist regime in Poland rigidly followed the Stalinist line, including tight controls on the arts. During those years only a few Polish films achieved distinction. Among them were Wanda Jakubowska's *The Last Stage* (1948), a tragic account of suffering and endurance in the notorious concentration camp at Auschwitz, and the films of veteran Aleksander Ford (*Border Street,* 1948 and *Five Boys from Barska Street,* 1953), about wartime and immediate postwar problems. At the end of the forties there was established at Lodz the most famous and influential of the new national film schools of the Eastern European republics. As a result of its training and leadership a whole generation of young film makers emerged who would change the nature of Polish film and bring it to worldwide attention.

In 1953 Stalin died, and a lessening of Soviet domination, relaxation of internal controls, and growing expression of national sentiment gradually began at the rate of two steps of liberalization forward to one of repression back. In Polish film the three important events of 1954 were the criticism by Jerzy Toeplitz, head of the state film school, of Polish production as oversimplified and uninspired; the reorganization of the national industry into independent production groups; and the appearance of the first feature of Andrzej Wajda, *A Generation.* Though the latter contained remnants of the simplistic communist morality tale, it was a film full of beauty and idealism, a key transitional work, and a harbinger.

Wajda, who would become one of Poland's major directors, led the sudden upsurge of Polish production which reached a peak between 1955 and 1958. *A Generation* began an unplanned trilogy completed with *Kanal* (1956) and *Ashes and Diamonds* (1958). Together the three films explored the conflicting loyalties, confused politics, bravery, and sacrifice that had characterized Poland's sad history during the years following German invasion and occupation to the first days of peace. Though Wajda's romanticism tended to soften and mythologize, his intellectual stance was often antiheroic, probing and implicitly critical of the leadership and causes for which so many young men his age had died. In *Ashes and Diamonds,* and in his and others' subsequent films, the actor Zbigniew Cybulski frequently portrayed a young man trying to sort out values and create a life amidst the shifting and unclear postwar conditions. He resembled an existentialist antihero more than a working-class hero of orthodox socialist realism. (He and his roles occasioned comparison with his contemporary, American actor James Dean.) Many of the Polish films of the time had in common as major or minor themes the inability of the individual to discover a place for himself in his own national community.

But it is the overall mood and separate images of Wajda's films that are remembered long after their content has receded from memory. The visual style is strong and distinctive—romantic, dramatic, and symbolic all at the same time. In *Ashes and Diamonds,* for instance, there is the scene of Cybulski lighting glasses of vodka lined up along the bar in solitary salute to his dead comrades. Then there is the stately formal dance in the early morning hours, a dream-like souvenir of former pleasures now tired and faded. Finally we recall the mortally wounded Cybulski staggering through sheets hanging on a clothes-line to fall to his death on a garbage heap. These and other memorable scenes measure the extent of the director's evocative power.

Wajda's career has continued down to the eighties as he has retained his place among what is now the older generation. *Everything for Sale* (1968) was in part a tribute to Cybulski, who had been killed accidentally in 1967 as he jumped from a train. It is also Wajda's reflection on his own relationship to life and art. With a film director pro-

Ashes and Diamonds (Poland, 1958, Andrzej Wajda). Museum of Modern Art/Film Stills Archive.

tagonist and a film within a film, as in works of Fellini and Godard earlier and Truffaut later, it is one of the major examples of this reflexive tendency of modern cinema. In *Landscape After Battle* (1970) Wajda returned to the war, but now the underlying philosophy seemed truly existential and some of the action and imagery almost surreal.

Andrzej Munk directed his first feature, *Man on the Track,* in 1956. It departed from the broad historical settings of other Polish films of the time for a close observation in psychological terms of an old locomotive engineer. Not only is he no positive socialist hero, he is at odds with the new order. With *Eroica* (1958) Munk turned to the war. The first of its two complementary but separate parts is set in the Warsaw uprising of September 1944, the same futile and tragic gesture Wajda had dealt with in *Kanal.* What is amazing about the first episode of Munk's film, ''A Scherzo in the Polish Manner,'' is that it completely deprives the rebellion of sentimentality in a macabre and at times hilarious tale of a con man who becomes a hero in spite of himself. The second episode, ''Lugubrious Obstinacy,'' takes place in a German prisoner-of-war camp for resistance fighters. The false values of the Polish officers frequently compel them to join their captors in a bizarre partnership to maintain a false myth so as not to destroy their own morale. The ''heroism'' of the title is clearly intended ironically since Munk, even more than Wajda, took a skeptical view of the efficacy of Polish valor. In 1961 Munk was

Eroica (Poland, 1958, Andrzej Munk). Museum of Modern Art/Film Stills Archive.

killed in an auto accident while working on *Passenger*. To provide some inkling of its qualities, the material he had shot was pieced together and released posthumously in 1963. From the evidence it might well have been Munk's masterpiece. With a base in the present, *Passenger* reflects on the past of Auschwitz through recollections of a German woman who had been a guard there.

The national traumas of the war were returned to again and again in the films of Eastern Europe generally. Often the social and psychological insights they contained were clearly if indirectly applicable to the postwar societies. Beginning about 1959, however, the Poles began to turn away from war themes. Jerzy Kawalerowicz, for example, made two important "period pieces" dealing with non-Polish history. *Mother Joan of the Angels* (1961) was based on the incidents of demonic possession and exorcism in a seventeenth-century French convent that inspired Aldous Huxley's book *The Devils of Loudon* and Ken Russell's film *The Devils* made from it. Kawalerowicz followed *Mother Joan* with *Pharaoh* (1965), a huge historical re-creation of ancient Egypt.

More typical of the changes taking place in Polish production was the work of two younger directors, Roman Polanski and Jerzy Skolimowski. Both developed quite personal styles and were preoccupied with the kinds of themes that would shortly cause them to work abroad. After his first feature, *Knife in the Water* (1962), a tight triangle of latent sexuality and violence, Polanski moved on to England (*Repulsion*, 1965; *Cul de Sac*, 1966; *Macbeth*, 1971; *Tess*, 1979) and America (*Rosemary's Baby*, 1968; *Chinatown*, 1974). Skolimowski, after *Identification Marks: None* (1964) and *Walkover* (1965), made his last Polish film for awhile with *Barrier* (1966). The latter is especially remarkable for its abstract and symbolic qualities, a truly avant-garde experiment as well as a highly personal statement. If Skolimowski's earlier work had suggested the influence of the New Wave, his first film made in the West, *Le Départ* (Belgium, 1967), became part of it. Its stars, Jean-Pierre Léaud and Catherine Duport, and cameraman, Willy Kurant, had worked on Godard's *Masculine-Feminine* a year earlier, and other New Wave films. In what proved to be a brief return to Poland, Skolimowski made *Hands Up!* (1967), which he regarded as his best and most mature work up to that time. It was banned, and he again left. He has worked abroad since, mostly in Germany (*Deep End*, 1970; *King, Queen, Knave*, 1972) and England (*The Shout*, 1978; *Moonlighting*, 1982).

In Poland in 1968 there occurred a violent repression of students and intelligentsia. The film production groups were once again reorganized and controls on film content appeared to become tighter. Since that time Poland has not been represented as prominently on the international film scene as it had been during the heady years of the late fifties. Among the directors working in Poland in the 1970s it was Krzysztof Zanussi whose films, along with the continuing work of Wajda (*Promised Land*, 1974; *Without Anesthetic*, 1979), received the most attention abroad. Zanussi stuck to contemporary themes, often dealing with moral and existential issues of corruption, careerism, and exploitation. *Family Life* (1971), *Illumination* (1973), *Camouflage* (1977), and *The Contract* (1980) were particularly noted. Krzysztof Kieslowski was another director whose work had similarly aggressive qualities. *The Calm Before the Storm* (1976) was about then current Polish working conditions; *Camera Buff* (1979) revealed a reportedly quite accurate picture of the way the film making system functioned in Poland.

In 1980 the shipyard workers in Gdansk struck and wrested from the authorities the concessions that created Solidarity, Eastern Europe's first independent labor union. The national euphoria that followed was short-lived, but before and during

Camouflage (Poland, 1977, Krzysztof Zanussi). Museum of Modern Art/Film Stills Archive.

Man of Iron (Poland, 1981, Andrzej Wajda). Museum of Modern Art/Film Stills Archive.

it two of Wajda's films were released that expressed to Poland and the rest of the world the spirit of the times (and also the deeply embedded official distrust that might cause it to end). *Man of Marble* (1977) encompassed the events of 1970, when workers rebelling against food prices were shot down in Gdansk and elsewhere along the Baltic coast. Though it was temporarily suppressed and kept from export for several years, the film had such an impact it is said to have precipitated a government shake-up. *Man of Iron* (1981), its sequel, carried the story into the 1980 events. Its frankness about government control and manipulation of the media and its obvious commitment to Solidarity are breathtaking, particularly in light of subsequent developments. In 1981 martial law was imposed, in part to counter the threat of Russian invasion, and Solidarity was outlawed. Wajda left for France, where he made *Danton* (1983), about the struggle of that leader of the French Revolution with Robespierre for the freedom of the French people. It had obvious parallels with the struggles being waged in Poland at the time of its making.

But the Polish film did not stand alone among the films of the Eastern European countries. Even during its earlier period of ascendancy in the late fifties Poland had shared the spotlight before yielding it. An upcoming Hungary was taking advantage of some of the same new creative opportunities, with an increased expression of nationalism on the one hand and of quite individual concerns on the other.

HUNGARY

In 1956 there were uprisings in Poland and Hungary. Both occurred in populations who, having been given a small taste of increased liberty and independence, wanted more. In the case of Poland concessions were made to "the Polish road to socialism." Soviet troops were withdrawn, a new era of greater freedom and nationalism began, and the Polish film flourished. As for Hungary, the Russian army quashed the rebellion; hundreds were killed, nearly 200,000 fled the country, and the national film flowering just beginning was temporarily ended.

Most prominent among Hungarian directors at work at the time was Zoltán Fábri. His *Merry-Go-Round* (1955) and *Professor Hannibal* (1956), made just before the uprising, moved well outside the confines of prevailing socialist realism. The first dealt with contemporary youth trying to find their way to new attitudes in a changed society. Its humor and lyricism were especially original. The second went even further, taking as target for social satire the question of historical revisionism, a sensitive subject in communist countries.

It wasn't until about 1963 or 1964 that a new era began with the reorganization of the film industry and of the Academy of Film and Dramatic Art. The first works of a younger generation appeared during those same years, including films by András Kovács (it was the later *Cold Days,* 1966, which gained him international attention), István Gaál (*The Falcons,* 1970, his fourth feature, is his best known), and István Szabó (whose *25 Fireman's Street,* 1974, presented a brilliant kaleidoscope of the Hungarian historical experience).

But it was Miklós Jancsó who—from *My Way Home* (1964), his third feature, on—carried Hungary's banner most conspicuously out into the world. Dominated by an obsessive subjective vision and intricate formal design that make it unique within Eastern European cinema, his work is coherent and consistent almost to a fault. The strange world of his films has no exact counterpart anywhere, for that matter; reviewers habitually refer to it as "Jancsó country." Among his films available in this country, besides *My Way Home,* are: *Cantata* (1963), *The Round-Up* (1965), *The Red and the White* (1967), *Silence and Cry* (1968), *The Confrontation* (1969), *Winter Wind* (1969), *Agnus Dei* (1971), *Red Psalm* (1972). *The Red and the White,* seen most widely, is typical.

Like so many of Jancsó's films, *The Red and the White* takes place on a vast wind-swept plain. The historical setting is the civil war which followed the Russian Revolution. Armies battle, but the causes seem arbitrary and unavailing in relation to universal and casual inhumanity. Sides can't be told apart once uniforms are removed; nationalities aren't distinguishable except when characters speak. At one moment the Whites are winning, at the next the Reds. Everyone is subject to pursuit, capture, humiliation, and execution.

Applied to this disturbing narrative material, and informing and affecting its meaning profoundly, is an equally extraordinary visual style. Shot in wide-screen black-and-white, the takes are long in duration. Camera movement is almost continuous and exceptionally varied: pans, tilts, dollies, tracking, and helicopter shots all combined. In addition to the insistently moving camera, there is constantly shifting and complex movement within the frame—mainly of men and horses. The movement is unusually frantic, with much running and galloping, and its meaning tacitly ironic. These humans behave instinctively, like other animals; their capacity for reason and emotion merely causes unnatural self-destruction. All of the frenzied activity leads only to death in this land of the still. The highly stylized and decorative visual treatment applied to ugly human actions formalizes and distances them from us—they form part of a *danse macabre.* The choreographic quality plus the repetition of event, as each side achieves temporary victory or suffers more certain defeat, turns the action into arcane ritual.

The Red and the White (Hungary, 1967, Miklós Jancsó). National Film Archive/Stills Library.

In recent years the films of István Szabó and Károly Makk also have attracted considerable attention outside Hungary. Szabó's *Confidence* (1980), a chamber drama about two fugitives forced to live together as man and wife during the Nazi occupation, preceded his hugely successful *Mephisto* (1981). The latter is concerned with an opportunistic actor in Hitler Germany who shifts his personal allegiances (including wife and mistresses) and adjusts his principles to conform to the requirements placed on an artist in a totalitarian state. Makk's *Another Way* (1982) is about a tragic love affair between two women who work for a political journal after the 1956 uprising. It is also about Hungary.

It still seems to be Jancsó, however, who stands as Hungary's major film maker. (*Hungarian Rhapsody* and *Allegro Barbaro,* both 1979 and part of a trilogy entitled *Vitam et Sanguinem,* and *The Tyrant's Heart,* 1981, are more recent Jancsó films.) It is among the "dark artists" of the cinema, along with Bergman and Antonioni in their very different ways, that he takes his place. It seems remarkable that his bleak vision has been supported by a socialist state that generally demands of its artists positive and constructive service in the building of a new society. The existence of his work may imply a broadening view of the social function of art by the Hungarian authorities. It may also mean that Jancsó speaks with peculiar resonance to a people bearing the scars from centuries of conquest, tyranny, and rebellion. Perhaps his art provides a kind of national expression and escape valve for feelings that cannot, finally, be either ignored or suppressed.

Mephisto (Hungary, 1981, István Szabó). Museum of Modern Art/Film Stills Archive.

CZECHOSLOVAKIA

In Czechoslovakia the stirrings of 1956 were quietly quelled by the local Communist hierarchy so that the Czechs neither gained additional freedom and independence, as did the Poles, nor were they subjected to Soviet invasion, as were the Hungarians. It wasn't really until the sixties that the political and cultural climate warmed sufficiently for the Czechs to freely expand into their own equivalent of the New Wave.

In 1963 a generation of FAMU (national film school) graduates that included Miloš Forman, Jaromil Jireš, and Věra Chytilová made their feature debuts. Following these in the "Prague spring" were other features by new young film makers: Forman's *Black Peter* (1964) and *Loves of a Blonde* (1965), Jan Němec's *Diamonds of the Night* (1964), Pavel Jurácek's and Jan Schmidt's *Joseph Kilián* (1964), and Chytilová's *Daisies* (1966). But the big international success was *The Shop on Main Street* (1965), by two veterans, Ján Kadár and Elmar Klos. The first Czech film to win an Academy Award, it was made up of known ingredients skillfully and movingly blended. Set in a small town under German occupation it exposed the evils of fascist mentality and its most heinous manifestation in anti-Semitism and genocide. *Shop on Main Street* treats these large themes on an intimate scale. The horrors inflicted upon inconceivable millions are expressed through events occurring in the lives of a simple carpenter, his greedy wife and fascist brother-in-law, and an ancient Jewish shop-keeper. Their paradoxical situation, as the carpenter tries to save the old lady from extermination, becomes credible through the fully

The Shop on Main Street (Czechoslovakia, 1965, Jan Kadár and Elmar Klos). Museum of Modern Art/Film Stills Archive.

rounded performances. Warmly and delicately observed detail, and humor mingled with pathos, together characterize script and direction. Satisfying within its own terms, *The Shop on Main Street* was more conventional than the Czech films that would follow.

One of the leaders of a truly new Czech cinema was Miloš Forman, whose widely seen *Loves of a Blonde* and *The Firemen's Ball* (1967) make you think of Italian Ermanno Olmi's early work. Forman uses a similar *cinéma-vérité*-like style and draws the same remarkable performances from casts surely composed largely of nonprofessionals. His observation of average people and everyday situations is more humorous and satiric than Olmi's, however. The cross-purposes, confusions, and inarticulateness of the petit-bourgeois characters in their relationships with each other, the tensions and misunderstandings between generations, the hopeless incompetence and self-inflated importance of bureaucracy are all wryly commented on in a totally disarming way. Life goes on, it seems, with its usual bumblings and eccentricities, irrespective of ideologies, governments, and large causes. Forman's script writer, Ivan Passer, conceived and directed *Intimate Lighting* (1966) in much the same manner. In it he observes the reunion in a provincial Czech town of two old musician friends, one with wife and family, the other with a mistress.

Of Jiři Menzel's films the best known in the West is *Closely Watched Trains* (1966). (It too won an Academy Award.) Like Forman and Passer, Menzel observes with careful attention and detached amusement the actions of "the little people." Though set in World War II and including partisan sabotage of the German-controlled railway, instead of epic events *Closely Watched Trains* concentrates on the coming-of-age of a shy and ineffectual young station attendant and the peculiar sexual goings-on around him in the isolated post.

The films of Evald Schorm have not received the same wide circulation in the

The Fireman's Ball (Czechoslovakia, 1967, Miloš Forman). National Film Archive/Stills Library.

Closely Watched Trains (Czechoslovakia, 1966, Jiří Menzel). Museum of Modern Art/ Film Stills Archive.

West as those mentioned above—perhaps because he dealt seriously with significant contemporary themes. Both *Courage for Everyday* (1964) and *The Return of the Prodigal Son* (1966) ran into censorship trouble, the first withheld for many months, the second virtually banned on its release. *Courage for Everyday* concerns a politically active youth who attempts to maintain his own integrity in the face of a society which demands that he be judged by its standards. *Return of the Prodigal Son* treats sympathetically a talented and successful young artist who becomes depressed and alienated from those around him, attempts suicide, and is institutionalized. The overall thrust of Schorm's work would seem to be more like that of his Polish contemporaries than his own compatriots in its intense probing of the conflicts between individuals and society. He has been called the "conscience" of the new Czech cinema.

Finally, Jan Němec, too, makes one think of the Poles, especially of Jerzy Skolimowski. *Report on the Party and the Guests* (1966), for example, carries the surrealist impulses of *Barrier* even further. In fact, it is a sort of political allegory clothed in trappings of the avant-garde—at times it looks like Resnais's *Last Year at Marienbad*—with overtones of Kafka. The party takes place at formally set tables beside a lake in a lonely wood. The characters move and behave as if they are part of some sort of game with arcane rules, frenetic endeavor being followed by somnambulistic languor. The threat of violence and punishment hangs over the whole. Promptly banned upon completion, it was defiantly awarded the Czech Critics Prize a year later. Němec was forcibly exiled in 1974.

Even if unenthusiastic and vacillating, an official liberalization had clearly occurred within Czechoslovakia that permitted statements from film artists which were either openly or covertly critical of the society. The Czechs, like the Poles and Hungarians before them, responded by striving for still more freedom from Party conformity and for self-identification as Czechoslovaks. The years 1966 to 1968 saw the greatest ferment. Then, in the summer of 1968, an uprising was crushed by Soviet tanks, and Czechoslovakia once again became an occupied country for a time. As with the Hungarians earlier, many who weren't killed, imprisoned, or forced underground, fled. Some came to the U.S. and continued to work here; for example Kadár (*Lies My Father Told Me,* 1975), Forman (*One Flew Over the Cuckoo's Nest,* 1975; *Hair,* 1979; *Ragtime,* 1981), and Passer (*Cutter's Way,* 1981).

As far as Western audiences are concerned, those who stayed behind have remained largely silent. How curious and yet fitting that the Czechs' most distinctive filmic contribution has been in celebration and gentle criticism of individual lives lived more or less oblivious to the earthshaking events that have marked the history of Czechoslovakia along with that of its neighbors.

YUGOSLAVIA

Among the Eastern European countries Yugoslavia is special in that its communism is resolutely national. In 1948 it removed itself from the Soviet orbit and maintained its independence in spite of every Russian effort short of invasion to make it return to the fold. Stalin took out his resentment on the other ''satellite'' nations in severe repressive measures designed to make certain they did not follow the Yugoslav example. After Stalin's death the new Soviet leaders journeyed to Belgrade to offer public apologies for past Russian policies. From that time on Yugoslavia's territorial integrity, as the phrase goes, has seemed more assured.

Though the Yugoslavs, following earlier Czech example, developed an animation industry in Zagreb which today is the most imaginative if not most prolific in the world, its live-action features plodded along the path of socialist realism as doggedly as if still being guided by the Soviets. It wasn't until the late sixties that there appeared a new generation of feature film makers, including Dušan Makavejev, Aleksander Petrović, Živojin Pavlović, and a cluster of their innovative films (such as *Man Is Not a Bird,* 1965; *I Even Met Some Happy Gypsies,* 1967; *When I'm Dead and White,* 1968). Makavejev and his early works seen widely abroad—*Love Affair, or The Case of the Missing Switchboard Operator* (1967), *Innocence Unprotected* (1968), *WR: Mysteries of the Organism* (1971), *Sweet Movie* (1974)—burst on the scene like some sort of Slavic bombshell. His experimental bent went even beyond that of the Pole Skolimowski or the Czech Němec. Makavejev's work makes you think of the most stylistically mixed of Godard's features. Or perhaps a better comparison would be with the Swedish Vilgot Sjöman's *I Am Curious* (1967), with its similar combination of sex and politics, fantasy and fact, fiction and newsreel.

In subject matter *Innocence Unprotected* is quite different from Makavejev's other films; in technique it has aspects in common. An affectionate recall of the first Serbian talkie, made in 1942 during the German occupation, it is subtitled ''A New Edition of a Good Old Film.'' Interspersed with the original are interviews with its surviving creators—who talk about its production—and newsreels of military and political events of that time. *Love Affair, WR,* and *Sweet Movie,* on the other hand, all elaborate on the relationship between sexuality and the social-political restraints and expectations faced by the individual. Wildly funny, bawdy, if not obscene, and irreverent, jumbled and complex, they are finally impossible to describe, even thematically. Of the three, *Love Affair* is the most coherent, with two central characters and a slender thread of plot spun out in flashes forward as well as back, preceded by a lecture on sex and interrupted by another on murder. *WR* includes an informal television-style "profile" of psychologist Wilhelm Reich, replete with interviews of people who knew him, a fragmented account of two zany sexually preoccupied young women and their encounters with men, satirical political references, phallic jokes about Stalin, and other odds and ends including a demonstration by a markedly strange lady making a cast of a penis. Makavejev encapsulated "the message" (in an interview in *Film Quarterly,* Winter 1971–72) as: "the main thing in sexual repression or sexual freedom is actually the political content of human personal freedom." *Sweet Movie* is an even more scabrous, hilarious and at the same time darker mixture of diverse elements, scatology added to sexuality and politics. It throws haymaker punches at both the capitalist and communist mythologies, in about equal proportion, and provoked enraged responses from all sides. *Montenegro* (1981), shot in Sweden, was much more straightforward in narrative form but its content reiterated Makavejev's fascination (obsession?) with sexual homicidal mania. How extraordinary that the kind of film making that in this country would be confined to the so-called underground, with no viable economic base and seen only by a small audience with

WR: Mysteries of the Organism (Yugoslavia, 1971, Dušan Makavejev). National Film Archive/ Stills Library.

esoteric tastes, should ultimately if indirectly be paid for by the taxpayers of a socialist state.

But in some respects Makavejev's work does not stand altogether alone. In the films of Poland, Hungary, Czechoslovakia, and Yugoslavia, over the past three decades there have been intermittent periods in which critical self-examination, doubt and even despair have appeared. Often the questioning, criticism, and satire have seemed remarkably pointed and frank to Westerners whose biases and ignorances may preclude an understanding of how these nations actually function socially and politically. Also, within what we call the Soviet bloc there has been an equally surprising amount of experimentation with form and the development of personal styles that include the ambiguous and the obscure. In these societies not only has the French New Wave had an effect on film makers' creation and audiences' responsiveness, but the Eastern Europeans have themselves contributed much to the new in terms of national expression, major film artists, and enduring works of art.

Beginning in the late fifties the Eastern European countries, joining France and Italy, achieved their own versions of a New Wave. Despite prominent differences, one thing all of these countries had in common was a new emphasis on personal expression in film with the director as artist. Another was the use of new methods and techniques, defiance of former conventions, and the breaking up of traditional forms. In a general way the most interesting and important films from the countries on the continent, West or East, departed from the usual entertainment "package" as commercially conceived. Instead they attempted to offer directly the kinds of moral, ethical, and aesthetic sustenance looked for in art works. It is these qualities in total that roughly characterize the New Wave, or Contemporary Cinema, or Modern Film, as the terms have come to be understood.

Over Great Britain, however, the New Wave washed only lightly. There the Old Undertow, as someone dubbed the American financial and distribution interests still dominant in the world art-industry, exerted a stronger pull.

FILMS OF THE PERIOD

Czechoslovakia

1964

Black Peter (Miloš Forman)
Diamonds of the Night (Jan Němec)
Joseph Kilián
   (Pavel Juráček and Jan Schmidt)

1965

Intimate Lighting (Ivan Passer)
Loves of a Blonde (Forman)
The Shop on Main Street
   (Ján Kadár and Elmar Klos)

1966

Closely Watched Trains (Jiři Menzel)
Daisies (Věra Chytilová)

The Martyrs of Love (Němec)
Report on the Party and the Guests (Němec)
The Return of the Prodigal Son
   (Evald Schorm)

1967

The Firemen's Ball (Forman)

Hungary

1955

Merry-Go-Round (Zoltán Fábri)

1956

Professor Hannibal (Fábri)

1963

Cantata (Miklós Jancsó)

1964
The Age of Daydreaming (István Szabó)
My Way Home (Jancsó)

1965
The Round-Up (Jancsó)

1966
Cold Days (András Kovács)
Father (Szabó)

1967
The Red and the White (Jancsó)
Ten Thousand Suns (Ferenc Kósa)

1969
The Confrontation (Jancsó)

1970
The Falcons (István Gaál)
Lovefilm (Szabó)

1971
Agnus Dei (Jancsó)

1972
Red Psalm (Jancsó)

1974
25 Fireman's Street (Szabó)

1976
Budapest Tales (Szabó)

1980
Confidence (Szabó)

1981
Mephisto (Szabó)

1982
Another Way (Károly Makk)

Poland

1954
A Generation (Andrzej Wajda)

1956
Kanal (Wajda)
Man on the Track (Andrzej Munk)

1958
Ashes and Diamonds (Wajda)
Eroica (Munk)

1961
Mother Joan of the Angels
  (Jerzy Kawalerowicz)

1962
Knife in the Water (Roman Polanski)

1963
Passenger (Munk)

1964
Identification Marks: None
  (Jerzy Skolimowski)

1965
Walkover (Skolimowski)

1966
Barrier (Skolimowski)

1968
Everything for Sale (Wajda)

1970
Landscape After Battle (Wajda)

1971
Family Life (Krzysztof Zanussi)

1973
Illumination (Zanussi)

1974
Promised Land (Wajda)

1976
The Calm Before the Storm
  (Krzysztof Kieslowski)

1977
Camouflage (Zanussi)
Man of Marble (Wajda)

1979
Camera Buff (Kieslowski)
Without Anesthetic (Wajda)

1980
The Contract (Zanussi)

1981
Man of Iron (Wajda)

Yugoslavia
Man Is Not a Bird (Dušan Makavejev)

1967

I Even Met Some Happy Gypsies
   (Aleksander Petrović)
Love Affair (Makavejev)

1968

Innocence Unprotected (Makavejev)
When I'm Dead and White
   (Živojin Pavlović)

1971

WR: Mysteries of the Organism
   (Makavejev)

1974

Sweet Movie (Makavejev)

1981

Montenegro (Makavejev)

BOOKS ON THE PERIOD

BANASZKIEWICZ, WLADYSLAW, et al., *Contemporary Polish Cinematography*. Warsaw: Polonia Publishing House, 1962. 173 pp.

BROZ, JAROSLAV, *The Path of Fame of the Czechoslovak Film*. Prague: Film Export, 1967. 112 pp.

DEWEY, LANGDON, *Outline of Czechoslovakian Cinema*. London: Informatics, 1971. 122 pp.

HIBBIN, NINA, *Eastern Europe*. Cranbury, N.J.: A. S. Barnes & Co., Inc., 1969. 239 pp.

LIEHM, ANTONÍN J., *Closely Watched Films: The Czechoslovak Experience*. White Plains, N.Y.: International Arts & Sciences Press, Inc., 1974. 485 pp.

LIEHM, MIRA and ANTONÍN J., *The Most Important Art: Eastern European Film After 1945*. Berkeley: University of California Press, 1977. 467 pp.

NEMESKÜRTY, ISTVÁN, *Word and Image: History of the Hungarian Cinema*. New York: Frederick Ungar Publishing Co., Inc., 1982. 296 pp.

PETRIE, GRAHAM, *History Must Answer to Man: The Contemporary Hungarian Cinema*. Gyoma, Hungary: Corvina Books, 1978. 284 pp.

SKVORECKY, JOSEF, *All the Bright Young Men and Women: A Personal History of the Czech Cinema*. Toronto: Peter Martin Associates Ltd., 1971. 280 pp.

STOIL, MICHAEL J., *Balkan Cinema: Evolution after the Revolution*. Ann Arbor, Mich.: UMI Research Press, 1982. 170 pp. (The book covers Albania, Bulgaria, Romania, Yugoslavia.)

STOIL, MICHAEL JON, *Cinema Beyond the Danube: The Camera and Politics*. Metuchen, N.J.: Scarecrow Press, Inc., 1974. 198 pp.

VRONSKAYA, JEANNE, *Young Soviet Film Makers*. London: George Allen & Unwin, Ltd., 1972. 127 pp.

WHYTE, ALISTAIR, *New Cinema in Eastern Europe*. New York: E. P. Dutton & Co., Inc., 1971. 159 pp.

20

British Film, 1956–

To have kept Britain sidetracked up to this point, alongside a sort of mainline from auteurism and three continental auteurs through the French New Wave to the new Italian and Eastern European cinemas, seems characteristic of the treatment generally afforded the British film—not least by the British themselves. About their own cinema, British critics habitually complain that it lacks a distinctive tradition like that of the French or Italians (or even the Eastern Europeans) and that it is dominated and subsumed by the Americans.

American money and personnel are so inextricably interwoven with British production and distribution that it is difficult to determine where one industry leaves off and the other begins. In an article entitled "Tomorrow the World: Some Reflections on the un-Englishness of English Films" (*Sight and Sound,* Spring 1974), John Russell Taylor suggested that, with only a little simplification, the whole history of British cinema could be seen in terms of the fluctuating relations with America and the American market. If in the days of gunboat diplomacy commerce followed the flag, in modern economic imperialism culture follows the dollar.

The problem that British films present, then, is one of national identity, not of artistic quality. British technicians and the technical level of Britain's films are generally conceded to be among the best in the world; the acting talent available is unsurpassed. And there are kinds of films which the British have made with a particular excellence. Films drawn from their literary or dramatic or historical heritage, or a type of sophisticated crime or espionage thriller are examples. The David Lean versions of Noël Coward and Charles Dickens (*Blithe Spirit*, 1945; *Brief Encounter*, 1945; *Great Expectations*, 1946; *Oliver Twist*, 1948), the Laurence Olivier adaptations of William Shakespeare (*Henry V*, 1944; *Hamlet*, 1948; *Richard III*, 1955), the Carol Reed collaborations with Graham Greene (*The Fallen Idol*, 1948; *The Third Man*, 1949) distinguish its immediate postwar history.

Then there were the films about World War II growing out of the wartime semi-documentary: *The Cruel Sea* (1953, Charles Frend), *The Dam Busters* (1953, Michael Anderson), *The Battle of the River Plate* (1956, Michael Powell and Emeric Pressburger). There were many other fine individual works within a sort of "academic" tradition: significant subjects treated with self-effacing expertness. But prestigious ventures of this sort became increasingly multinational in conception, financial backing, and creative personnel. John Huston's *The African Queen* (1952), *Moulin Rouge* (1953), and *Moby Dick* (1956), and David Lean's *Summertime* (1955) and *The Bridge on the River Kwai* (1957) are prominent examples.

What was lacking in Britain, for one thing, were popular native but exportable genres like those of the Americans. (The *Carry On . . .* comedies were tricked out in eccentric and finally ersatz Englishness with an eye to American art-house audiences; the James Bond cycle, enormously successful, was backed by American money and aimed at a world market.) For another, the always conservative English film seemed to provide insufficient latitude for the truly personal film maker, the auteur who had begun to appear on the continent.

But beginning in the mid-fifties a sort of bloodless cultural revolution commenced, which affected British life generally and became manifest in film as well. With the advent of commercial television and a vitality in the political left that extended into the arts, new popular values ("vulgar" they were thought to be in some quarters) came to the fore. During these years two lines of film making started, both of which seemed very English even if in direct contrast to each other. The first attracted international critical attention; the second packed theaters abroad as well as at home. About the same time, several film makers with quite personal preoccupations and distinctive styles began work in England.

SOCIAL-REALIST FEATURES

For their one most indigenous kind of film making, which has taken various forms within an overall continuity, the British have sometimes shown a peculiar lack of pride. The line referred to, of course, is the realistic one that extended from the documentaries of the thirties, into the wartime semi-documentaries, on to the Ealing comedies and war dramas of the postwar years. The next outcropping of that tradition began in the mid-fifties with a documentary movement called Free Cinema. Combined with the work of new young playwrights and novelists, the Free Cinema spirit inspired a noteworthy series of feature films that began with *Room at the Top* (1958) and *Look Back in Anger* (1959). If not exactly a British New Wave, the dozen or so films which comprised that cycle represented a national achievement worth recognition. They grew out of the sort of social-realist impulse that the British keep rediscovering from time to time and which has inspired some of their most vital as well as most characteristic contributions to the history of film.

Early in 1956 a program of three short films was shown at the National Film Theatre under the Free Cinema banner. *O Dreamland* (1954), by Lindsay Anderson, castigated the dull and synthetic pleasures being offered the bemused masses at a seaside amusement park. *Momma Don't Allow* (1955), by Karel Reisz and Tony Richardson, celebrated a lively London jazz club patronized by working-class teen-agers. *Together* (1956), by Lorenza Mazetti and Denis Horne, described the emotionally impoverished lives led by two deaf-mute dock workers in the East End. The films' makers stated in their program notes for the occasion that Free Cinema was free from serving the sponsor's purpose (as in documentaries) and free from pandering to the demands of box office (as in fiction features). It was to be an "entirely personal cinema," socially committed but also poetic. "Implicit in our attitude," they wrote, "is a belief in freedom, in the importance of people and in the significance of the everyday."[1]

The year 1956 was a crucial one in the political and cultural life of Britain. It was the year of a last gasp of imperial arrogance in the foolish and failed invasion of Suez. As a result of that debacle the whole governmental system was discredited. To many on the Left, the Labour Party, which worked within the system, seemed as culpable as the ruling Conservatives. Nineteen fifty-six was also the year of the Khrushchev attack on the cult of personality under Stalin, and of the Soviet invasion of Hungary, which caused many Marxist intellectuals finally to become disillusioned with Stalinist communism. Partially in reaction to those events, a politically sophisticated younger generation of dissidents arose around the universities—particularly Oxford, which most of the Free Cinema group had attended. The label "New Left" was attached to them, and their publication was entitled *New Left Review* (originally *Universities and Left Review*). The New Left wanted to go beyond the old-line socialists, with their basis in dialectical materialism, trade unionism, nationalization of industry, and social welfare. They were concerned more with theory and a fundamental reorganization of society that would affect the total quality of people's lives. As an intellectual movement which also encompassed the arts, the New Left in Britain was more like the continental Left.

The artists in various media who arose out of the spirit of the time, many of them from the working classes, were dubbed the Angry Young Men for their attacks on the establishment and the rigidities and inequities of the class system. In 1956 John Osborne's play *Look Back in Anger,* directed by Tony Richardson, opened at the Royal Court Theatre. At about the same time Joan Littlewood's Theatre Workshop was started. Playwrights such as Arnold Wesker and Shelagh Delaney soon joined Osborne to create an outpouring of plays set among the lower classes that were articulate and sometimes strident in their social criticism. A new crop of actors—Albert Finney, Rita Tushingham, Rachel Roberts, Tom Courtenay, Richard Harris, Ronald Fraser—also came out of that sort of theater and later worked in film. Novels of a similar tone began to appear as well, with John Braine's *Room at the Top* in 1957 followed by Alan Sillitoe's *Saturday Night and Sunday Morning,* Stan Barstow's *A Kind of Loving,* and David Storey's *This Sporting Life,* among others.

Though Free Cinema had in fact appeared slightly before the explosions in the other arts, it wasn't until it connected with the new drama and literature that its kind of expression moved over into the feature film and became economically viable. Following

---

[1] As quoted in Elizabeth Sussex, *Lindsay Anderson* (New York: Frederick A. Praeger, Inc., Publishers, 1969), p. 31.

Nice Time (Claude Goretta and Alain Tanner) and *Every Day Except Christmas* (Anderson) in 1957, the Free Cinema movement as such virtually ceased with *We Are the Lambeth Boys* (Reisz) in 1958. Nonetheless, the attitudes and some of the rough-hewn style of Free Cinema were carried into the new social-realist features which began the same year the Free Cinema shorts ended. It was *Room at the Top,* however, much more conventional than Free Cinema in both content and form, that launched the new phase. It was directed by Jack Clayton, who had come up through the commercial industry and had no connection with Free Cinema.

Set in an industrial northern town, *Room at the Top* deals with the compulsions and confusions of a cynical young arriviste determined to climb up out of his slum origins. Its romantic conflict was class-based—to marry the daughter of a local industrialist in order to get ahead, or to stay with the mistress he loves but who would impede his chances for success—yet scarcely without precedent. It reminds us of Stendahl's *The Red and the Black* or of Dreiser's *An American Tragedy.* Audiences in the U.S. could be excused for considering it extraordinary that this sort of class thing was still bothering the British after all these years. But there it was up on the screen for the first time, and creating a huge stir.

Look Back in Anger put some of the same matters, and others, in a clearer and less ambiguous way. Through the Jimmy Porter character's brilliant and paranoiac monologues, we could begin to understand what the anger was all about. At least it was clear what he was trying to tear down (the establishment, personified by his wife's parents) and what he was trying to preserve (the working-class virtues represented by his friend Ma Tanner). It was not so clear (if at all) what the replacement society would be like, and certainly not how it might come about.

In any case, these two films, double-billed in the U.S., began the social-realist cycle that dealt with various aspects of working-class character and problems. As a body the films tended to be set in the industrial regions north of London. Thus they contrasted with British entertainment films up to that time which, according to the Free Cinema group at least, had reflected almost exclusively the outlook of metropolitan southern English culture and the middle and upper classes. Here were efforts to include "the rich diversity of tradition and personality which is the whole of Britain" called for in one of Free Cinema's manifestoes.

Of the Free Cinema trio of Anderson, Reisz, and Richardson, it was Richardson who first entered the feature field, with *Look Back in Anger.* Those three were joined by John Schlesinger, an Oxford classmate of Richardson's. Together they constituted the main directorial talent of the social-realist features of the early sixties. All of their films were based on the writings of the so-called Angry Young Men (or Women, as the case might be).

With the profits from *Look Back in Anger,* Richardson and Osborne set up Woodfall Productions, responsible for many of the social-realist features. In addition to his role as producer, Richardson directed three more of those features in rapid succession. *The Entertainer* (1960), from another Osborne play and script, was seen as offering evidence of collapse within British society. Laurence Olivier starred as the down-at-heel music hall comic in a seedy seaside town. Aging and hollow, his life lacks significance in his own eyes and those of others; his social alienation is matched by his messy and unsatisfying personal relationships. *A Taste of Honey* (1961) was from a play by Shelagh Delaney, who worked on the screenplay as well. The remarkable location cinematography in Lancashire was by Walter Lassally, one of two key technicians on the Free

Cinema shorts and social-realist features; John Fletcher was the other. *A Taste of Honey* also deals with the complex psychological relationships and unfulfilled needs of a group of individuals existing below the level of middle-class respectability. *The Loneliness of the Long Distance Runner* (1962)—from a story by Alan Sillitoe, who also did the script—portrays the life, frustrated ambitions, and resentments of a lower-class youth who wanders into crime and is sent to prison. The causes of his problems are portrayed as societal, and sympathy as well as understanding is offered for his form of rebellion. All four of Richardson's social-realist features, interesting and modestly important, are marked by especially fine performances. His *Tom Jones* (1963), while remaining more or less faithful to Fielding's eighteenth-century novel, includes some of the same themes of youthful rebelliousness, plus a playfulness with the film medium clearly owing to the French New Wave.

Karel Reisz directed only one of the social-realist features (Richardson produced it); his *Saturday Night and Sunday Morning* (1960) is in many ways the most exemplary of their tendencies as a whole. From Sillitoe's popular novel (and he again did the script), it focuses on a working-class rebel. Though hostile to the system, the young lathe operator finally lacks the resources—the imagination and understanding—to fight free from it. Proudly indigenous as the film is, we don't have to know England to sense that the rows of identically drab houses, the father glued to the telly, the job without meaning, and the inadequate release of a Saturday night drunk and a tumble in the hay

Saturday Night and Sunday Morning (U.K., 1960, Karel Reisz). National Film Archive/ Stills Library.

must be how it is for a large segment of the population (as it is elsewhere). The documentary intention dominates. It is served equally by a story that grows out of the situation rather than being imposed upon it and by convincingly natural performances. The ending, conclusive in spite of seeming inconclusive, consists simply of the protagonist (played by Albert Finney, in his first starring role) walking down into a new housing estate with his girl. It flies in the face of accepted demands of both box office and dramatic convention, as does much else in this uncompromising picture. If an epilogue were to be added to it, it could borrow from Dylan Thomas, as did the Free Cinema film makers for their first program: "This is the world/Have faith."

Lindsay Anderson, though acknowledged as leader and spokesman of the Free Cinema group, was the last to arrive at features. Curiously, his first, *This Sporting Life* (1963), if it marked a high point in the social-realist cycle, also indicated a turning away from the sources that had given that demimovement its character and strength. From a novel and script adaptation by David Storey, it has the requisite general characteristics of northern industrial town and working-class background. Where it departs from the other films is in its concentration on the tortured love affair between the miner-turned-footballer and his widowed landlady, and in its flashback sequences of surrealist exaggeration. At the time of its release Anderson was complimented by British reviewers for having broken out of the confines of the social-realist films, with their air of objectivity and use of the representative to make their criticism stick, into richer areas of individual feeling, the traditional concerns of great art. Perhaps what was by then being referred to as the "kitchen sink" school of film making was limited in certain important ways and had run its course. Whatever the reasons, *This Sporting Life* along with *Billy Liar* (directed by John Schlesinger in the same year) proved to be the last films directly connected with the line that had begun with *Room at the Top*. Of the directors who worked in it, Anderson has stuck closest to the earlier commitments (and made the fewest features). *If . . .* (1969), *O Lucky Man!* (1973), and *Britannia Hospital* (1982), though different in subjects and settings, grew out of the same impulses of social criticism as the earlier films.

It was Schlesinger who proved to be the real transitional figure leading on to the next phase of British film. His *A Kind of Loving* (1962) belongs in the social-realist line, with its young draftsman protagonist who gets a woman pregnant and enters reluctantly into marriage. *Billy Liar,* on the other hand, though set in the North and about a young man of the middle class and the thwarting of his ambitions, is more concerned with his amusing neurotic eccentricities and Walter-Mitty-like fantasies than with class-based causes. It also introduced Julie Christie, who would star in Schlesinger's next film, *Darling* (1965). It was the success of this latter film that confirmed the end of the social-realist cycle and heralded a new "swinging London." About a spoiled and charming model who sleeps around more and enjoys it less, *Darling* could have been made anywhere. To the extent that it is about the loss of values and the restlessness among the affluent, and given the modish direction, you might have thought it came from France or Italy. In the brief boom of which it was part, "British" films as often as not had American or Italian, French or Polish directors. And the subjects, well the subjects had merely become part of an undifferentiated cinematic Esperanto. The "mid-Atlantic films" (for example, *Casino Royale* and *You Only Live Twice* in 1967) which seemed to come from no culture of their own, were compounded out of American capital and diverse ingredients taken from recent international successes.

In the past the documentary influence contributed to some of the most interesting and distinctive cycles of British fiction production. In each instance, once the documentary impulse was lost much of the significance and quality seemed to disappear as well—at least the succeeding films tended to lose their national character. It might be argued that the quiet genius of British cinema has always pointed most surely in the direction of realism and what John Grierson called the documentary idea.

It is as exciting as it is rare when the cumbersome and expensive machinery of the entertainment film can be geared to problems of national concern. When this happens, as in the Soviet silent films of the late twenties or the Italian neorealist films of the late forties, the resulting aesthetic richness and experimentation is accompanied by evolving theory which opens up still other areas of this relatively unexplored medium. In Britain in the early sixties something of the sort occurred briefly on a small scale with the social-realist features. For awhile in the sixties, as the young members of Free Cinema came together with the young men and women of theater and literature who had been tackling similar themes, the veracity of documentary detail was warmed and strengthened by the addition of story and character. Perhaps those who made the social-realist features between 1958 and 1963 got some of the older documentarians' preoccupations and methods more widely and effectively before a larger public.

GOTHIC TRADITION

Paralleling the developments out of documentary that began in the mid-fifties with Free Cinema and culminated in the early sixties with the social-realist features, there appeared a completely contrasting but equally distinctive line of British cinema. The horror series from a small studio named Hammer Films followed the tradition of the Gothic horror story, every bit as indigenous as the impulses towards social-realism and self-improvement which had given rise to the documentary. In fact the Gothic tradition had its beginnings in the eighteenth- and nineteenth-century English novel, appearing full-blown in Mary Shelley's *Frankenstein* and Bram Stoker's *Dracula*. In hindsight it seems curious that the Americans rather than the British were the first to make sustained screen use of this heritage, but the Universal horror series of the thirties already discussed was rather more indebted to German expressionism than to English literary models. By the mid-fifties the Americans had virtually abandoned conventional horror movies in favor of science fiction, leaving the field open to the British.

No one seems to know exactly how Hammer happened onto the horror genre, but its entrance occurred in that year of 1956 which witnessed the Suez debacle as well as the appearance of Free Cinema and the first stage production of Osborne's *Look Back in Anger*. There is no obvious, let alone necessary, connection between the rise of the horror films and the rest of those events. Superficially, at least, the Hammer series would seem to be as far removed from contemporary reality and seriousness of purpose as one could imagine. The British critics found the films meretricious in style. In search of redeeming social value, they found none; their reviews were hostile in the extreme, especially toward what appeared to them to be gratuitous and excessive violence and gore. The public, of course, loved the horror cycle from the outset. The critics, eventually, would be faced with a series at the National Film Theatre devoted to Hammer Films.

The first of the Hammer horrors, *The Curse of Frankenstein,* produced in late 1956 and released in early 1957, became a phenomenal success, not only in Britain but abroad, including especially the United States. It was followed by *Dracula,* which also became enormously popular throughout the world. These two films staked out Hammer's claims, never seriously challenged, on the two prototypical horror stories. The immediate progeny (*The Revenge of Frankenstein,* 1957; *The Brides of Dracula,* 1960) were soon joined by many other close and distant relatives. David Pirie, in his appreciative study *A Heritage of Horror: The English Gothic Cinema, 1946–1972,* points to *The Devil Rides Out* (1967, entitled *The Devil's Bride* in America) as one of the most masterful achievements within the general field. Though not dealing with either of the prototypical stories directly, it includes many of the most significant thematic and stylistic elements of the genre as a whole.

Pirie insists that the films of Hammer and its imitators are distinctively English Gothic as opposed to European. He attributes the attraction of English audiences to the earlier Gothic literature and the later films to the repressions of Victorian morality. These forms fed a fascination with death and violence and sexuality by cloaking them in the exoticism of distant places, supernatural powers, and fanciful scientific imaginings. The English treatment of the mythic elements in these tales has a robustness and conviction, Pirie contends, devoid of the self-conscious artiness of certain European Gothic strains. He also makes the point that the horror genre, as developed by Hammer and its rivals, "remains the only staple cinematic myth which Britain can properly claim as its own, and which relates to it in the same way as the western relates to America."[2]

The principal director at work in the horror films was Terence Fisher. He inaugurated the entire cycle with *The Curse of Frankenstein* and worked almost exclusively for Hammer from that point on. Most interesting, in part because most representative, Fisher's work in the horror genre rests securely on the archetypal struggle between good and evil. The dualities of light and darkness, spirit and matter, are rigidly maintained as the trappings of ritual formulae, sacred books, crucifixes, and the like are set in opposition to the vampires, werewolves, and monsters of all kinds who populate the films. Pirie argues that Fisher more than any other British director can lay claim to a recognizable and coherent world view presented throughout his work. He was greatly aided in this by the repertory acting company at Hammer. Two male stars closely identified with the horror films contributed much to their success: Peter Cushing and Christopher Lee. Both appeared in the initial *Curse of Frankenstein* and *Dracula* and alone and together throughout much of the series.

The earlier concentration of key personnel and artistic elements in the Hammer production subsequently became diffused into other sorts of films, some of the appealing simplicity and clarity becoming lost in an increasing sophistication on the part of film makers and audiences alike. Noting this perhaps inevitable evolutionary process, Pirie concludes his study with the following observation:

> perhaps the highest compliment that can be paid to any popular form is to acknowledge its regenerative effect and, at their best, these films have reinstated and recharged some of England's most powerful and idiosyncratic myth-cycles, using the most exciting medium yet for fantasy and dream—the cinema—to rediscover crucial elements of the Romantic experience.[3]

[2] David Pirie, *A Heritage of Horror: The English Gothic Cinema, 1946–1972* (London: Gordon Fraser Gallery Ltd., 1973), p. 9.

[3] Pirie, *A Heritage of Horror,* p. 168.

The Devil Rides Out/The Devil's Bridge (U.K., 1968, Terence Fisher). Films, Inc.

One director working quite outside the horror field might still be seen as attempting to rediscover crucial elements of the Romantic experience in a way that may be essentially English, though generally it is considered pure Ken Russell. Russell's earlier films did not deal with the supernatural, and it seems unlikely that many horror fans would have been among his audiences, but his work has consistently contained flamboyant and mythopoetic characteristics surely related, at least, to the Gothic tradition. He has been strongly attracted to the past, and to characters who are mystical and visionary, obsessive and driven, who attempt to transcend their humanity, often through their art. Many of Russell's most original and forceful films have been biographies of artists, and with them he invented a sort of personal genre of British cinema.

His film work began with documentaries for BBC-TV. *The Debussy Film* (1965); *Isadora Duncan, The Biggest Dancer in the World* (1966); and *Dante's Inferno* (1967, about Dante Gabriel Rossetti) are among the best remembered. *The Dance of the Seven Veils: A Comic Strip in Seven Episodes on the Life of Richard Strauss* (1970) created a storm of controversy because of its fanciful and highly subjective interpretation of the composer's life, including his involvement with Naziism. It embodied the eclectic elements, always diverse and sometimes eccentric, that would mark Russell's subsequent theatrical features.

Women in Love, however, his first important feature, made a year earlier than the Strauss television documentary, had been a comparatively subdued and faithfully sensitive rendering of the D. H. Lawrence novel. But even it added Russell's own understanding of the implications of Lawrence's attitudes about love and friendship so that the film becomes a critical examination of the novel as well as an adaptation of it.

It was in his next feature, *The Music Lovers* (1970), on the life of Tschaikowsky, that Russell cut loose with the full range of bombast and beauty, simplification and exaggeration that have both outraged and fascinated critics and audiences. The nineteenth-century Russia he presents is lush and decadent, the characters alternating between repressed longings and passionate explosions. The famous music is broken up, moved around and fitted together to underline, and in some instances inflate, the rich sensuality of the images of nature, of carriage rides, of fireworks displays, and sexual abandon.

The Devils (1971) contains the same visual and emotional ripeness, or is it fulsomeness, centered around sexual/religious frenzy. (*The Boy Friend,* made in the same year, seemed at the time something of an aberration: a camp parody of early Hollywood musicals replete with homages to Busby Berkeley. A later counterpart was Russell's film version of the rock opera *Tommy,* 1975.) *Savage Messiah* (1972) deals with the life of the sculptor Henri Gaudier. More limited in visual scope, it nonetheless characteristically treats extravagant emotions and artistic creation erupting out of a strange and frustrated life. *Mahler* (1974), about the great late nineteenth-century Austrian composer was summed up by *Sight and Sound:*

The Music Lovers (U.K., 1971, Ken Russell). Museum of Modern Art/Film Stills Archive.

Mahler given the full Ken Russell treatment—bizarre dream sequences, death scenes galore—though less neurotic than might have been expected. Inventive in its fashion and superbly photographed; the music is heavily cut up, and the slangy dialogue should have been cut further.[4]

Lisztomania (1975) is another such film, a bit more extravagant. In *Valentino* (1977) the biography is of the legendary screen lover, played by dancer Rudolf Nureyev. The science fiction of *Altered States* (1979), though uncongenial material for Russell, placed him centrally in a Gothic-style horror story with a modern equivalent of Henry Frankenstein in search of the ultimate mystery of life.

The imagination, talent, and energy combined with the excesses, erratic taste, and mixture of styles manifest in Russell's films can be exhilarating, exasperating, or both. However one responds to them ultimately, the joyous exuberance with which their director plays the full range of the medium, all stops pulled, is evident. Here is a film maker above all else; an auteur as well if your definition emphasizes the immediate identifiability of the work. Ken Russell's signature is always writ copious and large, a refreshing rarity in the generally discreet British cinema.

AMERICANS ABROAD

Apart from the culturally distinctive qualities of the social-realist features and of the Gothic tradition, British cinema of the last thirty years seems distinguished by a cluster of sometimes brilliant directors whose films for the most part have an international rather than a national identity. They work on either side of the Atlantic and for American money in any case. Within the past two decades there has been more interchange than ever. Of the former social-realist directors, Reisz (*Who'll Stop the Rain?*, 1978; *The French Lieutenant's Woman*, 1981) has worked in America and on American projects; Richardson (*The Charge of the Light Brigade*, 1968; *The Border*, 1982) and Schlesinger (*Midnight Cowboy*, 1969; *Sunday Bloody Sunday*, 1971) have alternated between the U.K. and the U.S. John Boorman, an Englishman, has done some of his best and most striking work in America (*Point Blank*, 1967; *Deliverance*, 1972). On the other hand, three Americans, long-time residents in England, have clearly become English to the extent that Henry James and T. S. Eliot became English, and will be dealt with here.

Joseph Losey, after a modestly successful Hollywood career, exiled himself in 1951 in order to escape the blacklisting of the McCarthy era. In Britain his reputation was first established with a succession of moderately budgeted pictures within conventional idioms that are packed with political meaning and psychological, even philosophical, complexities. *Time Without Pity* (1957), a thriller in which a father attempts to save his son from execution for a murder he didn't commit, goes beyond an attack on capital punishment to examine the individual apathy, selfishness, and lack of social responsibility which support the injustice perpetrated by the judicial system. *Blind Date* (1959, *Chance Meeting* in the U.S.) is a detective story which implies that a person's understanding of reality is more likely an illusion predetermined by past experience, including especially that of class. *The Criminal* (1960, *The Concrete Jungle* in the U.S.), a

[4] "Film Guide," *Sight and Sound*, VIIL (Spring 1974), p. 126.

crime-and-prison picture on the surface, makes clear the ways in which the criminal is a natural part of a society based on power and acquisitiveness, and that the prison community is a mirror image of the one outside its walls. *The Damned* (1961, *These Are the Damned* in the U.S.), is a science-fiction forecast of the kinds of social malaise—violence and authoritarianism—that will erupt in a society which allows itself to come under the threat of nuclear warfare.

With *The Servant* (1963) Losey began his association with the playwright Harold Pinter and moved from the partially covert investigation of British society to a more direct observation less restricted by rigid and complex plotting. To be more exact, beginning with *The Servant* a group of Losey's films comment directly upon a culture which he observed with the eye of an outsider who had experienced fresh what others had absorbed from birth. *The Servant* concerns a contemporary young aristocrat who attempts to exercise the prerogatives of his class with the arrogance but without the force which once accrued naturally to rulers of an empire. He is led down into a mire of dissipation and self-indulgence by a malicious and clever servant who in fact becomes master. Though succeeding in the struggle for domination, the servant is no happier as a result and remains subject to class-based feelings of inferiority and impotence. The microcosm of this strange pair living together in a destructive relationship within a Chelsea house must be taken to represent a Britain in which an outmoded class system enervates and embitters all of its inhabitants.

King and Country (1964) is even more claustrophobic in setting than *The Servant* and direct in its socio-political comment. It concerns the trial of a deserter during World War I. A simple working-class youth, caught in a war the reasons for which he doesn't understand and that terrifies him, has simply walked back away from the front lines headed for home. Within the military code, the officers-gentlemen have no recourse but to sentence him to execution even while realizing the enormity of the punishment in relation to the crime. As the war seems to the soldier to have little to do with what is important in his life, so his death becomes a pointless irony, another corpse added to the hundreds of thousands already fallen.

In *Accident* (1967) Losey is back with Pinter and in some ways resumes the examination begun in *The Servant* of values and satisfactions inadequate to sustain meaningful, productive lives. Here the characters are middle-class and middle-aged on one side (Oxford dons and their wives) and aristocratic and youthful on the other (an English boy and Austrian girl students). While the plot moves through a complex series of sexual attractions and rivalries, the qualities of these humans at the very apex of the English social pyramid are weighed and found wanting. They are too pallid somehow and too fixed in ritual patterns. Pinter's and Losey's observation is exact; the details of the sort of lives the two dons lead are completely convincing. If very English they are yet as recognizable elsewhere as another American emigré's J. Alfred Prufrock, who measured out his life with coffee spoons.

The Go-Between (1971, script by Pinter), set in Edwardian times, is an even more muted study of class and sexuality. This tale of passion between an elegant and self-centered young lady and a robust and attractive tenant farmer is refracted through the imperfect comprehension of a thirteen-year-old middle-class summer visitor. Confused and disturbed by the unfamiliar proprieties of the wealthy household and what he can jealously sense of the relationship he becomes party to, his vacation experience proves a shattering one. As an outsider the boy serves as a perfect surrogate for Losey himself, and the tensions that lie beneath the apparent calm of polished upper-class

The Servant (U.K., 1963, Joseph Losey). National Film Archive/Stills Library.

manners are revealed obliquely, with seeming inadvertence. *The Romantic Englishwoman* (1975) continued many of the same concerns.

Losey has made other kinds of films as well in recent years, including those made while living in Paris for awhile (*Mr. Klein,* 1976; *Don Giovanni,* 1979). But that earlier body of work which surveys aspects of British society in ways that few native British film makers have done might be regarded as his most important achievement. The subtlety of his technique as well as the refinement of his sensibilities increased until they might well remind us of the mature Henry James, reflecting on the intricacies of cultural and class attitudes that must strike Americans as different from their own no matter how long they've lived abroad or how closely they empathize with the life of their adopted country.

Stanley Kubrick, who arrived in Britain ten years after Losey, had an even more substantial career before leaving the States. In his American films Kubrick seemed to be setting off in several directions at once: antiwar statement (the youthful outcry of *Fear and Desire,* 1953; the mature condemnation of *Paths of Glory,* 1957); gangster film (the experimentally expressionistic *Killer's Kiss,* 1955; the expertly professional *The Killing,* 1956); and even historical spectacle (*Spartacus,* 1960). Beginning with his first film made in Britain, *Lolita* (1962), he began gradually to settle into a consistently cynical, increasingly misanthropic view of humankind. Like Resnais, Kubrick came to depend upon strong literary figures for sources and/or collaboration: Vladimir Nabokov for *Lolita,* Terry Southern for *Dr. Strangelove, or: How I Learned to Stop Worrying and Love the Bomb* (1964), Arthur Clarke for *2001: A Space Odyssey* (1968), and Anthony Burgess for *A Clockwork Orange* (1971). Each of those films is laced with dark humor and enlivened by extraordinary set constructions.

Stanley Kubrick shooting a scene for his *A Clockwork Orange* (U.K., 1971). Museum of Modern Art/Film Stills Archive.

It is interesting and no doubt significant that Kubrick's first three British films were not set in Britain. Instead they were situated in a studio-constructed America and dealt fixedly with American themes, problems, and peculiarities—past, present, and future. If almost unprecedented in film, American artists abroad sorting through mixed feelings about their homeland have been a literary tradition extending at least from Henry James through Henry Miller. At his worst, or best, Kubrick brought a cold-blooded savagery to his analysis of the American scene; at the same time, and a mark of his consistency, it must be granted that the view *A Clockwork Orange* presents of modern English society is chilling and violent in the extreme. Its Droods exist in a kind of culture of their own, set within but at war with English culture.

When the production of *Barry Lyndon* (1975) was announced, it appeared that Kubrick had come round to an identification with the British historical tradition. Based on a Thackeray novel, the film was written, produced, and directed by Kubrick. It is, first of all, a massive, elaborate and meticulous re-creation of the look of the eighteenth century, often with references to the ways contemporary painters saw it: the verdant countrysides, the formally laid out battles, the interiors of country houses and gaming rooms, the costumes, even the candlelight (with special lenses for the purpose). There is much elegance, much beauty. But behind that pleasing exterior, the life that is depicted is largely cheerless and more than a little harried. The confines of a rigid social system are shown to imprison imagination and spontaneity, and warmth and gaiety are absent. The film ends in random and pointless disaster and desolation for virtually all of its characters.

Barry Lyndon represented no increased "Englishness" on Kubrick's part after all. In *The Shining* (1980) he returned to (a fantastical) present-day America (created in the Elstree Studios outside London). Its protagonist is a writer who becomes winter caretaker of a monstrous, deserted hotel in the Colorado Rockies. It centers around his descent into madness, including homicidal designs on his wife and young son. With these last two films the question of national coloring—American or English—remains moot. The world they portray is the world as it looks to an idiosyncratic individual film maker; and a somber spectacle it is.

Richard Lester is a much different sort of American from Losey or Kubrick, and was attracted to a much different kind of England—the rock, the mod, and the trendy in his case. Moving to London in 1955 (at the age of twenty-three) Lester worked on television commercials during his first years there, developing the technical facility—including rapid cutting, freely moving camera, and improvisational performance style—that is associated with his earlier, and some of his later, work. *The Running, Jumping, and Standing-Still Film* (1960), a short for BBC-TV's *The Goon Show,* set forth his special talents in capsule form.

A Hard Day's Night (1964) was his first noteworthy feature, an affectionate tribute to the Beatles in which they play themselves within a slight narrative. A heightened *cinéma vérité* style with breathtaking zooms and jump cuts complements their energetic and irreverent playfulness. *The Knack* (1965) also celebrated the new youthful life styles of a swinging London; and *Help!*, the same year, brought the Beatles back for a wildly assorted mixture of farcical villains in pursuit of a sacrificial ring, and musical performances high in the Alps or in the midst of military maneuvers. With *A Funny Thing Happened on the Way to the Forum* (1966), however, the directorial style Lester had developed seemed to many observers extraneous to the requirements of translating a stage musical into film.

In *How I Won the War* (1967) he brought his dazzling array of techniques to bear on a comic-bitter satire on the inevitable sameness and meaninglessness of all war which, despite the causes and objectives (in this case the immediate one is that of establishing an advanced-area cricket pitch deep in enemy-held territory), consists finally of endlessly repeated deaths. It was the first film in which he attempted to get at themes of the utmost seriousness through farcical means.

Petulia (1968) is an even further departure for Lester and stands alone in his work to date in many respects. His only feature shot in the U.S., it not only appraises the American scene through the revealing exaggerations that California manners and mores offer, but attempts a much more intense and sustained probing of character than any of his other films. *The Bed Sitting Room* (1969) returned to the same sort of satirical antiwar themes as *How I Won the War,* this time tackling the Bomb. The humor is even colder and more distancing than in the earlier film, and it was even less successful at the box office.

After a hiatus caused by the failure of *The Bed Sitting Room,* Lester returned to feature direction in the capacity of clever, intelligent, international entertainer with *The Three Musketeers* (1974). There is little specifically English, or even American-English, in that film or in the others that followed it; for example *Robin and Marian* (1976), another historical comedy; *Butch Cassidy and the Sundance Kid—The Early Days* (1979), his only western; *Superman II* (1981) and *III* (1983), comic strip adventures. It does not seem possible to predict exactly where their commercial success will lead him. It does appear likely, however, that Lester's as well as Losey's and Kubrick's contributions, if international in appeal, will continue to be made from a British base.

A Hard Day's Night (U.K., 1964, Richard Lester). National Film Archive/Stills Library.

RENAISSANCE

In 1982 there was talk of a British film renaissance. *Chariots of Fire,* produced by David Puttnam with American and Egyptian money, had become the most successful British film ever released in the U.S. and won the Oscar for best picture of 1981. It was quickly followed by *Gregory's Girl* (1981), *Gandhi* (1982), *The Draughtsman's Contract* (1982), *Local Hero* (1983), *Educating Rita* (1983), and other films well received by critics and public, at home and abroad.

Amidst this bustle of profitable activity at least two contemporary film makers have established trustworthy creative credits. Bill Forsyth, the most recent of the two to emerge, has worked within what can be described as a revival of the earlier Ealing comedy tradition. Nicolas Roeg, whose achievements extend back into the seventies, is closer to the tradition of the modernist European auteur.

Forsyth, a Scot, began film making with documentaries. His first fiction feature, *That Sinking Feeling* (1979), is a comedy about a bunch of Glasgow slum urchins who engage in an elaborate and preposterous scheme to burgle some stainless steel sinks. His second feature, *Gregory's Girl,* became one of the most profitable British films of 1981. Also a comedy, it concerns the adolescent infatuation of a gawky lad for a lovely lass who insists on playing soccer with (and plays better than) the boys' team. It also was set in Scotland, as was his third, *Local Hero* (1983), produced by David Puttnam, fresh from the success of *Chariots of Fire.* Shot on location in Fort William, *Local Hero* concerns the oil strike in the North Sea and a visiting agent for a Houston oil company. It is reminiscent of the situation in *Tight Little Island* (1949), with an American intruder replacing the earlier English one. In this case, however, the intruder succumbs to the charms of the villagers and longs to be one of them.

Local Hero (U.K., 1983, Bill Forsyth). Museum of Modern Art/Film Stills Archive.

So far, Forsyth's films have offered Scottish looks and Scottish ways with a knowing and affectionate humor. Like the work of Ealing Studios, his films manage to celebrate things British in the face of American competition.

Nicolas Roeg, who had become a topflight cinematographer (on, for example, Resnais's *Fahrenheit 451,* 1966; Schlesinger's *Far from the Madding Crowd,* 1967; and Lester's *Petulia,* 1968), turned to direction with *Performance* (1970, codirected by its script writer, Donald Cammell). It features rock star Mick Jagger and a plot that intermingles music, drugs, sex, and identity confusions. *Walkabout* (1971), filmed in Australia, is about a teen-age girl and her younger brother, who become lost in the bush. They are saved by an aboriginal youth but eventually become the occasion for his suicide, through failure in understanding and communication. *Don't Look Now* (1973), with Julie Christie and Donald Sutherland in Venice, combines murder, illusion, and perhaps the supernatural somewhat in the manner of Hitchcock's *Vertigo. The Man Who Fell to Earth* (1976) is an eerie science fiction featuring rock star David Bowie as the alien being. In *Bad Timing* (1980), Art Garfunkel and Theresa Russell play two Americans in Vienna, he a diffident college professor, she an unrestrained hedonist. They meet in an art gallery; the Gustav Klimt paintings on exhibit suggest the fragmented style adopted by Roeg in this tale of tortured erotic love. *Eureka* (1983) is about a prospector (played by Gene Hackman) in northern Canada obsessed with finding gold who, when he does, buys a Caribbean island. The plot is concerned mostly with the miner's attempts to hang onto what he has achieved in the face of others' efforts to take his island away from him.

Roeg's films present increasingly complex and dazzling mosaics of structure and style in which logic is transcended; the images, extraordinarily sensual, are cut together in pursuit of feeling, like the stories of Argentinian writer Jorge Luis Borges (who is in fact invoked in *Performance*). Roeg's ambiguities offer many readings, but the consistency of his disturbing vision—the threat of violence that we bring to each other

Bad Timing (U.K., 1980, Nicolas Roeg). Museum of Modern Art/Film Stills Archive.

through our mismatchings and misunderstandings—marks a film maker emotionally and artistically clear about what he is saying. His kind of film making, rare anywhere, is unusual indeed in Britain.

But, whatever it looks like in the atlas, Britain is no island entire of itself but part of the main. Even its specifically national film types and most distinctive creators fit into an international economic context. As has been suggested, in some ways parts of British cinema are really American bases, like those of our military abroad. It is to the still-major force in the global industry that we now return.

FILMS OF THE PERIOD

1957
The Curse of Frankenstein
  (Terence Fisher)
Time Without Pity (Joseph Losey)

1958
Dracula (Fisher)
Room at the Top (Jack Clayton)

1959
Blind Date (Losey)
Look Back in Anger
  (Tony Richardson)

1960
The Criminal (Losey)
The Entertainer (Richardson)

Saturday Night and Sunday Morning
  (Karel Reisz)

1961
The Damned (Losey)
A Taste of Honey (Richardson)

1962
A Kind of Loving (John Schlesinger)
Lolita (Stanley Kubrick)
The Loneliness of the Long Distance Runner
  (Richardson)

1963
Billy Liar (Schlesinger)
The Leather Boys (Sidney Furie)
The Servant (Losey)
This Sporting Life (Lindsay Anderson)
Tom Jones (Richardson)

1964
Dr. Strangelove (Kubrick)
A Hard Day's Night (Richard Lester)
King and Country (Losey)

1965
Darling (Schlesinger)
Help! (Lester)
The Knack (Lester)

1967
Accident (Losey)
How I Won the War (Lester)

1968
Petulia (Lester)
2001 (Kubrick)

1969
If . . . (Anderson)
Women in Love (Ken Russell)

1970
The Music Lovers (Russell)
Performance (Nicholas Roeg)

1971
A Clockwork Orange (Kubrick)
The Devils (Russell)
The Go-Between (Losey)
Sunday Bloody Sunday (Schlesinger)
Walkabout (Roeg)

1972
Savage Messiah (Russell)

1973
Don't Look Now (Roeg)
O Lucky Man! (Anderson)

1974
Mahler (Russell)
The Three Musketeers (Lester)

1975
Barry Lyndon (Kubrick)
Lisztomania (Russell)

1976
The Man Who Fell to Earth (Roeg)

1979
That Sinking Feeling (Bill Forsyth)

1980
Bad Timing (Roeg)
The Shining (Kubrick)

1981
Chariots of Fire (Hugh Hudson)
The French Lieutenant's Woman (Reisz)
Gregory's Girl (Forsyth)

1982
The Draughtsman's Contract
  (Peter Greenaway)
Gandhi (Richard Attenborough)

1983
Educating Rita (Lewis Gilbert)
Eureka (Roeg)
Local Hero (Forsyth)

BOOKS ON THE PERIOD

ARMES, ROY,   *A Critical History of the British Cinema.* New York: Oxford University Press, 1978.
  374 pp.
BETTS, ERNEST,   *The Film Business: A History of the British Cinema, 1896–1972.* New York: Pitman
  Publishing Corporation, 1973. 349 pp.

BUTLER, IVAN,   *Cinema in Britain: An Illustrated Survey.* Cranbury, N.J.: A. S. Barnes & Co., Inc., 1973. 307 pp.

CURRAN, JAMES and VINCENT PORTER, eds.,   *British Cinema History.* Totowa, N.J.: Barnes & Noble Books, 1983. 320 pp.

DURGNAT, RAYMOND,   *A Mirror for England. British Movies from Austerity to Affluence.* New York: Praeger Publishers, 1971. 336 pp.

KELLY, TERENCE, GRAHAM NORTON, and GEORGE PERRY,   *A Competitive Cinema.* London: Institute of Economic Affairs, 1966. 204 pp.

MANVELL, ROGER,   *New Cinema in Britain.* New York: E. P. Dutton & Co., Inc., 1969. 160 pp.

OAKLEY, C. A.,   *Where We Came In: Seventy Years of the British Film Industry.* London: George Allen and Unwin Ltd., 1964. 245 pp.

PERRY, GEORGE,   *The Great British Picture Show, from the 90s to the 70s.* New York: Hill & Wang, 1974. 367 pp.

PIRIE, DAVID,   *A Heritage of Horror: The English Gothic Cinema, 1946–1972.* London: Gordon Fraser Gallery Ltd., 1973. 192 pp.

POLITICAL and ECONOMIC PLANNING,   *The British Film Industry 1958.* London: P.E.P., 1958. 40 pp.

SPRAOS, JOHN,   *The Decline of the Cinema: An Economist's Report.* London: George Allen & Unwin, 1962. 168 pp.

WALKER, ALEXANDER,   *Hollywood, UK: The British Film Industry in the Sixties.* New York: Stein & Day, 1974. 493 pp.

21

American Reevaluation and Reemergence, 1963-1977

Frequently Americans have been slow, not to enjoy but to value what is most vital and characteristic among our own popular art forms. The French, on the other hand, have often responded to the pleasures offered by our entertainment with a serious appreciation which initially may have seemed inflated but later prevailed. It was Baudelaire and the symbolist poets who first exalted that writer of tales Edgar Allan Poe. It was Louis Delluc and the Impressionists who early celebrated the virtues of American movies, notably those of Douglas Fairbanks, Pearl White, Mack Sennett, Thomas Ince, and, of course, Charles Chaplin. It was the writers for *Cahiers du Cinéma* who later recognized the merits of unsung auteurs at work among the staple genres of the contemporary Hollywood film who would become principal sources of inspiration and influence for the French New Wave.

REEVALUATION

By 1957, the year of Bazin's critique of *la politique des auteurs,* it had become the principal critical approach of *Cahiers du Cinéma.* As the "auteur theory," it moved westward to the United States in 1961, as evidenced by Andrew Sarris's writing in *Film Culture* and by the appearance of *New York Film Bulletin.* The auteur theory appeared in Great Britain in 1962, upon the publication of *Movie* magazine. Sarris first fully articulated his own views in ''Notes on the Auteur Theory in 1962'' in *Film Culture,* winter 1962/63; the spring 1963 special issue of the same journal comprised the initial version of his herculean effort to organize and assess, by director, the vast output of the American sound film.

The ideas of auteurism subsequently gained ground until the founts of established criticism, which had been under attack by the auteurists, gradually came to reflect their tastes. In 1968 Sarris consolidated the auteur position in his book *The American Cinema: Directors and Directions 1929–1968.* No work since the much earlier writings of Paul Rotha (*The Film Till Now,* 1930) and Lewis Jacobs (*The Rise of the American Film,* 1939) has done as much to shape our thinking about the history of the American film. ''Re-shape'' would be the better term, since Sarris's book reduced the status of many directors whose work had formerly been most valued, and raised that of others who had attracted little critical attention up to that point.

Into his ''Pantheon'' Sarris admitted fourteen directors he felt had ''transcended their technical problems with a personal vision,'' had created ''a self-contained world with its own laws and landscapes.'' By the time *The American Cinema* was published, almost half of them were dead and others in retirement. Let's call the roll of Sarris's company to see who was present or accounted for. They are here listed in the order in which they began making films.

D. W. Griffith, film's earliest master and greatest contributor to the fashioning of an art form out of a means of communication, had died in Hollywood in 1948 after nearly two decades of inactivity, ignored by the industry he had helped found. Until his death in 1977, Charles Chaplin lived in Switzerland in self-imposed exile, emerging only occasionally to make films in England. In 1972 he was welcomed back to America by the Academy of Motion Picture Arts and Sciences for a tearful ceremony; in 1974 he was awarded a knighthood in his native Britain. Chaplin's one-time rival for the comedy throne, Buster Keaton, who had appeared as his partner in *Limelight* (1952), died in 1966. In his last years a renewed interest in Keaton's earlier great comedies had begun, and he was being offered bit parts in contemporary films as well.

John Ford died in 1973, but not before giving us memorable work in his last two decades. From the fifties, *The Quiet Man* (1952), *The Searchers* (1956), and *The Horse Soldiers* (1959) take their place among his most important films; from the sixties, *Two Rode Together* and *The Man Who Shot Liberty Valance* (both 1961), and *Cheyenne Autumn* (1964). Some of those films contain a rare depth and darkness, like the later work of another American poet, Mark Twain. It was as if Ford, too, had caught sight of the underside of the American dream he had so long and epically celebrated—the dross of the ignoble commingling with the ore of the heroic.

Among the celebrated emigrés from Germany, Ernst Lubitsch had died in 1947. Fritz Lang remained active in the fifties with films of considerable interest and occasional power. After *The Thousand Eyes of Dr. Mabuse,* made in Germany in 1960, Lang returned to retirement in California until his death in 1976. F. W. Murnau, after making only four films in this country, had been killed in a car crash in 1931. Robert Flaherty, the great pioneer documentarian, worked with him on his last, *Tabu* (1931). Flaherty died in 1951.

Jean Renoir, whose American career in the forties was set within the longer and more distinguished French one, from the fifties on lived mostly in California. He worked only occasionally, and then in France. During this latter years he gave us *The Golden Coach* (1952), *French Cancan* (1954), *Paris Does Strange Things* (1956), *Picnic on the*

Grass (1959), and *The Elusive Corporal* (1963). He died in 1979. Josef von Sternberg, who had been living in retirement in Hollywood, died in 1969. *Anatahan* (1954) had been his final film.

Howard Hawks, Ford's contemporary and fellow worker in native genres, continued to direct familiar Hawksian westerns, battle-of-the-sexes comedies, and masculine adventures: *Rio Bravo* (1959), *Hatari!* (1962), *Man's Favorite Sport?* (1964), *Red Line 7000* (1965), *El Dorado* (1967), *Rio Lobo* (1970). He died in 1977.

Alfred Hitchcock during his later years achieved a new level of intensity and heightened control. He also earned increasing respect for the metaphysical speculation lurking beneath the smooth surfaces of polished thrillers. Though his lifelong work contains enough for two careers (one-third British to two-thirds American), his films from the fifties, sixties, and seventies are among those of greatest and most lasting significance. Since Hitchcock movies have always attracted large audiences of widely ranging tastes, a listing of some of their titles from the past three decades is apt to recall viewing experiences for more readers than would those of any other director. Given his fecundity and consistently high level of achievement, the sampling offered is of necessity inadequate, but *Rear Window* (1954), *Vertigo* (1958), *North by Northwest* (1959), *Psycho* (1960), *The Birds* (1963), and *Frenzy* (1972) must certainly be noted. His last film was *Family Plot* (1975). He died in 1980.

All those in Sarris's Pantheon had begun work in the silent period except Max Ophüls and Orson Welles. The greatest achievement of each of these two directors looked ahead to the future even more than it grew out of the past.

Max Ophüls's last film, *Lola Montès* (France, 1955), has some of the same characteristics as Welles's *Citizen Kane.* These include the use of multiple flashbacks chronicling a colorful life lived in high places, a life which contains a secret unhappiness and much that is enigmatic. In *Lola Montès* Ophüls made a truly astonishing exploration of the nonnaturalistic uses to which color and wide screen could be put. His camera, moving intricately through takes of long duration, becomes the chief formative device; editing is secondary. As with *Citizen Kane, Lola Montès* seems to have more in common with Antonioni's *L'Avventura* (1960) or Resnais's *Last Year at Marienbad* (1961) than with any works that preceded it. Ophüls, who had made films in Germany before coming to America, then in France after leaving Hollywood, died in 1957.

Welles, last-born of the Sarris Pantheon, has continued his brilliant and variable career working where and when he could, mostly in Europe: *Mr. Arkadin* (Spain, 1955), *Touch of Evil* (U.S., 1958), *The Trial* (France, 1962), *Falstaff* (Spain, 1966), *The Immortal Story* (France, 1968), *F for Fake* (France, 1975). He is the only one of the Pantheon still alive.

In his second category, labeled "The Far Side of Paradise," Sarris included twenty directors who fell short of the Pantheon "either because of a fragmentation of their personal vision or because of disruptive career problems." Like his first category, most of the choices—of the older veterans, especially—were acceptable to the more traditional, nonauteur critical approaches, with only minor quibbles. A number of these men had died by the time Sarris's book was published; more have died since.

Cecil B. De Mille made *The Greatest Show on Earth* in 1952 and his second *The Ten Commandments,* his last film, in 1956. Raoul Walsh continued active into the sixties as director of he-man adventures. Frank Borzage directed *China Doll* in 1958 and *The Big Fisherman* in 1959. Erich von Stroheim's career ended much earlier; *Walking Down*

Broadway (1932–33) was the last film he directed—it was never released. King Vidor's last film was *Solomon and Sheba* (1959).

Of three directors remembered for their comedies, Gregory La Cava directed his last in 1947; Frank Capra, still alive, made *A Hole in the Head* in 1959 and *Pocketful of Miracles* in 1961; and Leo McCarey *An Affair to Remember* (1957), *Rally Round the Flag, Boys!* (1959), and *Satan Never Sleeps* (1962) as his last.

George Cukor continued his considerable output until near the end of his life; *The Blue Bird* (1976) and *Rich and Famous* (1981) were his final films. George Stevens concluded his career with *The Greatest Story Ever Told* (1965) and *The Only Game in Town* (1970). Preston Sturges ended his with *The French They Are a Funny Race* (1957).

The auteurist reappraisal raised some of those veteran directors in stature. Sarris wrote that Borzage had been undeservedly neglected because of what was assumed to be commercially motivated romanticism. Though Sturges's place seemed assured in revived appreciation of his irreverent comedies of the forties, La Cava and McCarey still needed defense for their alleged looseness of direction (which Sarris honored as improvisation) and their lapses into sentimentality. Walsh, the action director, and Cukor, the superb entertainer, were regarded by the auteurists with a new seriousness.

But it was another group of directors in Sarris's second category, mainly of a younger generation, who most clearly reflected the contention surrounding auteurism and the evaluative shifts it contributed. These were directors who had seemed to other critics to embody, even epitomize, the excesses of the Hollywood film, its formulas and superficialities, its glossy unreality on the one hand and gratuitous violence on the other. The auteurists celebrated the visions of these directors and the styles in which they were encased as being especially American and distinctively individual. These directors attempted to turn what had been regarded as trivial or meretricious into a consistent and coherent view of life, operating often below the surface or around the edges of the frequently assigned plot material on which they worked.

Heretofore these directors had not been identified with so-called serious film. Conventionally, critics had most valued content of moral substance and social significance dealt with in realistic style. The auteurists generally defended their choices more in terms of manner than matter; it was not what the script had in it so much as what the director made of the subject. In the course of their investigations the auteurists frequently offered evidence of a kind of directorial intelligence and control in operation that had not been acknowledged up to that point.

The work of one of these directors, Joseph Losey, need not be discussed further here, since all of his films during the period now under consideration were made in England. But that of an exact contemporary of his, Nicholas Ray, must be considered, for he became a cause célèbre of the auteur theory. Some of the auteurists advanced him as the greatest director who ever lived; some other critics considered him a Hollywood hack. Sarris placed him somewhere between those two extremes. As with most of the directors in his top two categories, Sarris found that Ray had "always displayed an exciting visual style." Sarris noted that Ray, unlike some of the directors of this second category, did have a consistent and important statement running through his work; namely, that "every relationship establishes its own moral code and that there is no such thing as abstract morality." Among Ray's films that transcend auteur enthusiasms and are generally considered major works are: *They Live by Night* (1949)—his first feature and a precursor to Arthur Penn's *Bonnie and Clyde* and Robert Altman's *Thieves Like Us;*

Rebel Without a Cause (U.S., 1955, Nicholas Ray). Museum of Modern Art/Film Stills Archive.

Rebel Without a Cause (1955)—which made James Dean spokesman and symbol for his generation; and *Bitter Victory* (1958)—made in France but set in the British Libyan campaign of World War II. Ray's final film, *Lightning Over Water* (1979), is an extraordinary, painful document, part fiction, mostly fact. Codirected by German film maker Wim Wenders, who finished it after Ray's death, it is about Ray as artist-film maker and about his dying.

The remaining directors in Sarris's "Far Side of Paradise" were equally crucial to the auteur theory and needed similar explication and defense. First, there were the special sort of Hollywood stylists who frequently worked with conventional melodrama, adaptations of popular novels, or sex farces, and used a screen iconography that was strong on clear-cut dramatic composition and assertive color. The thematic materials of these films were often so patently the stuff of which mass daydreams are made that most critics dismissed them as vacuous. The auteurists, however, saw in them a deliberate exaggeration and flaunting of the generic elements on which they were based; it was through this kind of hyperbolic excess, they argued, that the auteurs were able to criticize the very values to which the films seemed to be pandering. Generally this alleged sophistication on the part of the films' makers was more apparent abroad than at home.

Douglas Sirk, who received a full-scale retrospective at the 1972 Edinburgh International Film Festival, is something of an extreme case. Born in Denmark, with a career in Germany before coming to Hollywood, he took to the kind of stories we associate with broadcast daytime serials and certain women's magazines. But "even in his most dubious projects," Sarris insisted, "Sirk never shrinks away from the ridiculous, but by a full-bodied formal development, his art transcends the ridiculous, as form comments on content."[1]

Sirk was also greatly admired by Werner Rainer Fassbinder, one of the new generation of German film makers, who made frequent nods to him in his films. Fassbinder's *Ali: Fear Eats the Soul* (1974), for example, can be considered a working-class version of Sirk's *All That Heaven Allows* (1956). The Sirk film has a conventional melodrama plot—of a well-to-do widow (Jane Wyman) who is torn between maintaining a fulfilling relationship with a gardener (Rock Hudson) and abandoning it in the face of disapproval by her social peers and her two children. Yet the film is embroidered with an implicit commentary on the falseness and hollowness of the bourgeois values depicted.

For his portrayal of the glossy worlds his characters inhibit, Sirk found color and wide screen particularly well suited. If "the cinema of tomorrow is the cinema of

All that Heaven Allows (U.S., 1956, Douglas Sirk). Museum of Modern Art/Film Stills Archive.

[1] Andrew Sarris, *The American Cinema* (New York: E. P. Dutton & Co., Inc., 1968), pp. 109–10.

wide screen and color,'' observed Sarris, ''then Sirk's formal achievements will have helped lead the way into a more sensuous future.''[2] After *Imitation of Life* (1959) Sirk retired to Germany.

Austrian-born Otto Preminger is another European working in Hollywood who became adept at popular American idioms—including melodrama, but ranging widely in type and theme; in fact, as widely as any director I can think of. He too is generally faulted on grounds of content. In his case, the criticism is most often leveled at the lack of complexity and subtlety with which he handled large issues in his adaptations of best-selling novels; for example, *Exodus* (1960), Jewish fight for independence of Israel; *Advise and Consent* (1962), struggle for power on Capitol Hill; *The Cardinal* (1963), young American priest's rise to eminence; *In Harm's Way* (1964), Navy drama of World War II; and *Hurry Sundown* (1966), bigotry and greed in the South.

Preminger's defenders point to a consistent visual-dramatic style that matches his way of looking at the world, is especially appropriate to the wide-screen format, and is exemplary of one main line of contemporary film usage. V. F. Perkins argues:

> what matters is less the originality or otherwise of Preminger's theme than the freshness, economy and intelligence of the means by which the theme is presented. . . . Preminger reveals significance by a dramatic structuring of events which his camera seems only to follow—never to anticipate. Moreover, the image appears to attempt always to accommodate the entire field of action so that it is the spectator's interest which defines the area of concentration.[3]

Exodus (U.S., 1960, Otto Preminger). Museum of Modern Art/Film Stills Archive.

[2] Sarris, *The American Cinema,* p. 110.

[3] V. F. Perkins, *Film as Film* (Harmondsworth: Penguin Books Ltd., 1972), pp. 82, 129.

Continuing active into the 1970s, *The Human Factor* (1979) is Preminger's last film to date.

Vincente Minnelli can be accepted as a master stylist more easily by most people than either Sirk or Preminger. His credentials date from his series of lovely and inimitable M-G-M musicals, including *Meet Me in St. Louis* (1944), *The Pirate* (1948), *An American in Paris* (1951), and *The Bandwagon* (1953). Still, Minnelli's subsequent work raises the question of whether the kind of prettiness appropriate to the musical doesn't become a sustained mannerism rather than a functional, legitimate style in his dramatic pictures. Once again the auteurists valued style as style. The young English critics gathered around *Movie* magazine were able to make some connections between the substance and the decorous look of Minnelli's nonmusicals of the fifties and sixties. They argued that in the latter films, as in the musicals, Minnelli quite deliberately plays illusion against reality in order to set up a tension between the two and offer a reflexive commentary on the relationship of his films to life: illusion of art (*The Bad and the Beautiful*, 1952, and *Two Weeks in Another Town*, 1962, both about film making); and illusion of a kind of dream, with the dreamer at the center of it (*The Cobweb*, 1955; *Some Came Running*, 1959; *Home from the Hill*, 1960). In 1970, *On a Clear Day You Can See Forever* brought Minnelli back to the musical genre; *A Matter of Time* (1976) is his most recent film.

The last of Sarris's problem cases on "The Far Side of Paradise" who seems to fall in with the decorative talents is Blake Edwards, who directed his first feature in 1955. In Sarris's 1963 list he appears under "Esoterica," complimented for "the con-

Home from the Hills (U.S., 1960, Vincente Minnelli). Museum of Modern Art/Film Stills Archive.

The Pink Panther (U.S., 1964, Blake Edwards). Museum of Modern Art/Film Stills Archive.

viction he applies to a bright, if artificial style.'' Subsequently Edwards found his métier in farce-comedy and Sarris pointed with approval to *The Pink Panther* and *A Shot in the Dark* (both 1964), *The Great Race* (1965), and *What Did You Do in the War, Daddy?* (1966). Throughout his work he uses familiar genre materials in fresh and ingenious ways, juxtaposing scenes of apparent verisimilitude with those of wildly improbable farce and parodying the pretensions of his heroes. At odds with the Hollywood system, Edwards emigrated to England in the early 1970s. There he made three highly successful *Pink Panther* sequels before his return to America with the even more popular *''10''* (1979) and *Victor/Victoria* (1982).

Other Sarris inclusions that continued to raise critical hackles could be shorthanded as the tough guys, the directors working in the conventional action genres. They, too, had made manifest their world views and obsessions through personal styles, but the styles were frequently pared lean and fitted efficiently to the events and themes of their films, which contained a prevailing violence.

Anthony Mann is best remembered for his westerns— *Winchester 73* (1950), *The Naked Spur* (1953), *The Far Country* (1955), *The Man from Laramie* (1955), or *Man of the West* (1958). Here is another instance in which the auteurists were first impressed more by a director's manner than by his meaning. In 1963 Sarris had written ''Anthony Mann . . . is a style without a theme. His westerns are distinguished by some of the most brilliant photography of exteriors in the history of the American cinema . . .''[4]

Subsequently Jim Kitses identified the major themes running consistently throughout Mann's westerns, developed through ''the dialectic of landscape and hero,''

---

[4] Andrew Sarris, ''The American Cinema,'' *Film Culture,* No. 28 (Spring 1963), p. 25.

and leading to "the interior and finally *metaphysical* conflict of his characters." The Mann hero, Kitses observed, "is a revenge hero"; but the revenge

> is taken upon *himself,* a punishment the inner meaning of which is a denial of reason and humanity. In general all of Mann's heroes behave as if driven by a vengeance they must inflict upon themselves for having once been human, trusting and, therefore, vulnerable. Hence the schizophrenic style of the violent explosions of passion alternating with precarious moments of quiet reflection.[5]

Regardless of style or theme, Sarris concluded in 1968, "Mann, like Sirk, was overlooked by the American critical establishment until it was too late for his career to find a firmer footing than obscure cult interest."[6] He had died in 1967.

If Mann never found favor among the more cultivated critics, Samuel Fuller could be counted on to set them climbing walls. His works (he has produced and written as well as directed most of his films) not only abound in violence; they seem to exult in it. But it is violence of a special sort, psychological more than physical. There is surprisingly little blood and gore in Fuller's films, but his screen world is full of constant threat. His politics are of the Right, and pro-U.S. militarism and anticommunism mark many

Man of the West (U.S., 1958, Anthony Mann). Museum of Modern Art/Film Stills Archive.

[5] Jim Kitses, *Horizons West: Studies in Authorship in the Western* (Bloomington: Indiana University Press, 1970), p. 33.

[6] Sarris, *The American Cinema,* p. 99.

of his films. "The excitement Fuller arouses in critics sensitive to visual forms," wrote Sarris, "is equaled by the horror he arouses in critics of the Left."[7]

Loyalty and conflicts of loyalty preoccupy Fuller. Though he celebrates individualism, it is apt to be highly destructive when it comes in conflict with allegiance to the group. The protagonist torn between conflicting loyalties is common in Fuller's films; treason or treachery invariably traumatize. Stylistically Fuller frequently violates the Hollywood conventions of visual continuity, particularly in his juxtaposition of long shots and closeups without transitional medium shots, and often in a way that is completely disorienting. When a character is at a height of emotion there are apt to be a succession of probing closeups—of face, of eyes—without any reestablishing shots to orient the viewer spatially. The world is not an orderly place in the films of Sam Fuller, and things are at war with each other.

Park Row (1952), *Pickup on South Street* (1953), *House of Bamboo* (1955), *China Gate* (1957), *Run of the Arrow* (1957), *Forty Guns* (1957), *Merrill's Marauders* (1962), and *Shock Corridor* (1963) are among the Fuller films cited by Sarris as being of special interest. As with Sirk, a retrospective of Fuller's work was offered at the Edinburgh Festival, in 1969. *The Big Red One* (1979) and *White Dog* (1983) are his most recent films.

Robert Aldrich's style, wrote Sarris, "is notable for its violence even in genres that subsist on violence." He also found Aldrich to be one of the most strikingly personal directors to emerge during the fifties and sixties, "discovered by European critics long before American viewers deigned to acknowledge his existence."[8]

Most of Aldrich's work can be broken into two independent, in many ways antithetical, clusters: the male action films and the female melodramas. Some of the former have virtually no female characters (*Attack!,* 1956; *Flight of the Phoenix,* 1966; *Too*

Shock Corridor (U.S., 1963, Samuel Fuller). Museum of Modern Art/Film Stills Archive.

[7] Sarris, *The American Cinema*, p. 94.
[8] Sarris, *The American Cinema*, p. 84.

Late the Hero, 1970; *Ulzana's Raid,* 1972; *Emperor of the North Pole,* 1973). There is a hero who is reluctantly responsible for others and a villain, often charming and colorful, who is amoral and totally self-centered. Their relationship is curiously symbiotic; in fact, the character who appears initially to be a generic super-hero frequently turns out to be disturbed and destructive—the villain. The settings are predominantly out of doors and stark. In the female melodramas (*Whatever Happened to Baby Jane?,* 1962; *Hush, Hush . . . Sweet Charlotte,* 1965; *The Killing of Sister George,* 1968), the women dominate the screen. Here, too, there are two people opposed to each other, but we can't be sure which is the hero and which the villain until the end. These films take place primarily indoors; the settings are cluttered and claustrophobic.

Throughout both types of films, as well as in those in which men confront women (for example, *Autumn Leaves,* 1956; *The Legend of Lylah Clare,* 1968; *The Grissom Gang,* 1971), there is a plethora of psychologically disturbed characters. When their education and understanding are sufficient they even talk about emotional illness. Aldrich's films, Sarris noted, ''are invariably troubled by intimations of decadence and disorder.''

As for the critical evaluation of Aldrich's work, most nonauteurist critics would

Attack! (U.S., 1956, Robert Aldrich). Museum of Modern Art/Film Stills Archive.

agree with Sarris's appraisal of *Apache* (1954), *Kiss Me Deadly* (1955), *The Big Knife* (1955), and *Attack!* These are generally regarded as strong films making important statements. But Sarris was much more on his own in taking seriously the baroque horrors of *What Ever Happened to Baby Jane?* and *Hush, Hush . . . Sweet Charlotte* and the action adventures of *Flight of the Phoenix* and *The Dirty Dozen* (1967), though all four had considerable, and the last phenomenal, popular success. *The Longest Yard* (1974), involving a prison football game between convicts and guards, and *Hustle* (1975), about a Los Angeles cop undergoing some sort of existential crisis, are among Aldrich's later films. Though *Twilight's Last Gleaming* (1977) fits easily enough into Aldrich's work (a nuclear doomsday action-suspense thriller), it marked an important departure in its explicitly political statements about the tension and corruption that has wracked American government and society since the Vietnam War.

So much for the auteurists' reevaluation and contribution to our understanding of the American cinema of the recent past. About the time that Sarris's *The American Cinema* was published, a new sort of creative vitality—new kinds of films and new film makers—began to make itself felt. The emerging artistic characteristics and films of some of the principal present-day creators were at first embedded in a Hollywood response to the sociological and political phenomenon of youthful revolt.

REEMERGENCE

Spread across the sixties were the civil rights movement, with sit-ins, marches, and riots, and the Vietnam War resistance, with demonstrations, moratoriums, and student strikes. Along with these protest movements there arose a youth culture, as it was called. Young people in large numbers disassociated themselves from what they regarded as their parents' too exclusive concern with material accumulation; lack of honesty and decency in dealing with each other; complacency, apathy, and conformity within a society dominated by big business and the governmental and educational systems which seemed to be in collusion with it. They signaled their solidarity by letting their hair grow, and by donning clothes that were, by conventional fashion, either sexually indeterminate or outlandish—in either case, not like those worn by the olders and the straights. Their disaffection also took the form of refusal to assume the expected roles of wage earners, husbands, wives, or parents. Some of them "dropped out" of society into drugs, Eastern mysticism, communes. Others became active in attacking the political-economic structure that had dictated our involvement in what they regarded as an immoral war, and which tolerated poverty, injustice, and racial discrimination at home.

The spirit of these times was echoed in a film cycle called the "youth films" or the "now films," which achieved a significant popularity before tapering off—as the protest movements themselves did. The films were about youth and new lifestyles in conflict with the old. They were made for the youthful audiences who were now the principal patrons of the theaters. Sometimes they were even made by young film makers. All of them explored social, and some of them political, problems in one way or another. A few sounded strong notes of dissent. They also combined forms—documentary and experimental styles and subject matter along with those of conventional fiction—in ways that some of the recent films coming from abroad were doing (those of Godard and Makavejev, for example).

The trend started off indirectly in 1967 with three of the most popular releases of that year: *Bonnie and Clyde, The Graduate,* and *Cool Hand Luke.* Though *Bonnie and Clyde* was a sort of gangster film set in rural America of the thirties, encoded within it were themes of current youthful protest: the individual against the system; an unconventional and hedonistic lifestyle that put emphasis on kicks; and the implicit justification of violence directed against the impersonal institutions of society and against the conscientious, middle-aged, and humorless who served them. *The Graduate,* more explicit if less bold and beautiful, expressed other manifestations of contemporary youthful tension and conflict. *Cool Hand Luke* may seem a peripheral case, but it was about another resister, passive protester, who wouldn't buckle under to the demands of his (in that case prison) society.

It took Hollywood two years to contemplate those three films before producing more which incorporated some of the elements that seemed to have been responsible for their success. In 1969 the youth/now cycle proper began with *Easy Rider, Medium Cool, Zabriskie Point,* and *Alice's Restaurant. Easy Rider,* the seminal film, became an immediate favorite with the eighteen- to-twenty-five year-old audience. Those two young men riding their bikes and getting high on pot and LSD "in search of America," as pop-song lyrics of the time put it (*Easy Rider* used folk-rock throughout for its score), were adopted as youth-cult heroes. Like Bonnie and Clyde, Billy and Captain America were killed by the squares and the rednecks. *Easy Rider* spawned a profusion of features with related themes, some of them much more direct in their criticism of the dominant values of contemporary American society.

Coming up through those years of national turmoil and dissidence were a number of important film makers who maintained a strong interest in critically examining certain aspects of American culture, including the violence so prevalent during the past two decades. Some of the five to be dealt with here had established roots earlier; all have continued into the eighties as creators of individual distinction. The choices are Arthur Penn, Sam Peckinpah, Francis Ford Coppola, Robert Altman, and Martin Scorsese.

Arthur Penn seems preoccupied with the meaning of America. Every one of his films to date explicitly examines a facet of American culture. The people who interest him most, however, are the outcasts from this society. Coming out of theater and television, Penn, in his first film, *The Left-Handed Gun* (1958), reinvented the legend of Billy the Kid along speculative Freudian lines. *The Miracle Worker* (1962) considers the young Helen Keller, blind, deaf, and mute, and the teacher who helped her overcome the terrible handicaps and go on to a remarkable life and career. *Mickey One* (1965) explores the fear and threat of violence omnipresent in American cities through the eyes of a paranoid and desperate nightclub comic pursued by the Mob. *The Chase* (1966) follows that same climate of violence into a small Southern town and adds to it the general erosion of sexual morality. *Bonnie and Clyde* (1967), surely one of the most influential American films of the recent past, sets real-life bank robbers of the thirties in the light of the myth they themselves had helped create. *Alice's Restaurant* (1969), based on actuality, deals understandingly with troubled American youth of the sixties. *Little Big Man* (1970) moves backward over white responsibility and guilt for the genocide perpetrated on American Indians in the conquest of their land. *Night Moves* (1975) was of the post-Watergate moment: an existential detective story in which the culpable protagonist chases elusive criminals through a confusing society that seems to have lost its moral equilibrium.

Though Penn's preoccupation with things American evidently continues (*The*

Bonnie and Clyde (U.S., 1967, Arthur Penn). National Film Archive/Stills Library.

Missouri Breaks, 1976, and *Four Friends,* 1981, are his most recent features), of the five directors here being considered he seems to have the strongest attraction to the kind of artistic modernism in film that has been emanating from Europe since the late fifties. *Bonnie and Clyde* was originally conceived by its script writers, David Newman and Robert Benton, for direction by Truffaut or Godard. *Mickey One* and *Night Moves* are the full-scale examples—what the trade would call art movies—experimental and philosophical beneath their genre trappings. Penn may be the most "intellectual" of the five directors, noteworthy for his integrity in choice of subjects and for his articulateness in discussing his intentions in regard to them. He also has become a film maker of considerable skill and sensitivity to the medium.

Sam Peckinpah is another of the crop of directors who came to features from television. He had been a writer-director on several TV western series and has remained mostly loyal, even when working in a form that is not outwardly a western, to that most American of film genres. He has added to its basic patterns his particular attitudes and absorption with loners and losers, with outmoded responses to cultural change, and with violence. His first feature, *Deadly Companions* (1961), gives special emphasis to the way in which a hostile countryside reflects as well as conditions human motives and actions that are more confused and troubled than those of the classic western. Along with the autumnal beauty of mountain scenery and the raucous, violent humor of a mining camp, *Ride the High Country* (1962) offers an essay on the fading myth of the western itself—embodied by the aging characters played by aging western actors Joel McCrea and Randolph Scott. *Major Dundee* (1964), set in the Civil War West of cavalry and Indians, concentrates on the conflict of character between two strong, wrong men—which leads to their violent ends. One is a grim, pragmatic Union major, the other, a flamboyant Irish mercenary who had been fighting for the Confederate cause. *The Wild Bunch* (1969) brings violence to the fore—gross in quantity, refined in quality of treatment; gruesome detail combined with poetic reflection. Peckinpah's statement in that film seems at once repellent and profound. It is a highly personal, obsessive, microcosmic view of the kind of society which might emerge when the traditional values that had given frontier violence meaning no longer functioned.

The Ballad of Cable Hogue (1970), though also a western, attempts to transcend the specificity of the American myth through a curious mixture of comedy and universal, quasi-religious themes symbolically stated. In *Straw Dogs* (1971) Peckinpah moved to an English village; out of his culture altogether, except for the inclusion of an American protagonist. But its themes are not unfamiliar in westerns, especially those of Peckinpah. It concerns the nastiness and sadistic violence built into human nature, and the need for a good man with gun in hand to face the rest of society, obtain justice, and confirm his manhood. *Junior Bonner* (1972) deals with a modern rodeo rider trying to survive and maintain an anachronistic individualism. *The Getaway* (1972) is a more or less routine chase-thriller set in the contemporary Southwest, which nonetheless manages to continue some of Peckinpah's favorite themes. Some of the potential force of *Pat Garrett and Billy the Kid* (1973), a highly personal interpretation of that legend, was evidently deflected by an excess of the sort of producer interference Peckinpah seems prone to. *Bring Me the Head of Alfredo Garcia* (1974) is a present-day revenge story set in Mexico, in which a down-at-heel piano player fights a smoothly functioning capitalist-criminal system out of a need for self-redemption, a commitment to principle, and feelings for one other human being.

The Killer Elite (1975), a pot-boiler of espionage and assassination carried out for a CIA-like organization by two eccentric executioners, seems in part a self-parody of Peckinpah's own obsession with killings that have dubious motives. *Cross of Iron* (1976), about a German platoon on the Russian front in World War II, explores some of the same themes much more personally and seriously. War is seen as an occasion for the ruthless expenditure of brave men's lives for ideals that aren't worth living for.

The Wild Bunch (U.S., 1969, Sam Peckinpah). Museum of Modern Art/Film Stills Archive.

Peckinpah's view of the human animal's struggle for survival in the face of malevolent and cynical forces, with only a professional code for sustenance, is recognizably his own. Though his understanding of the world is scarcely everyone's, it is a view expressed with great technical control, considerable strength, and some beauty, and one which evidently exerts an uneasy attraction for American audiences.

Francis Ford Coppola is the first major American director to have graduated from a university film program (UCLA's). Given that academic training, with its emphasis on personal expression, it is interesting that during the first part of his career Coppola largely withheld or concealed his own personality in his work, opting instead for a ''professional'' range of subjects and styles. *Dementia 13* (1963), a low-budget horror film, was financed by Roger Corman (who has given other young talent their first chance). It was Coppola's second feature, *You're a Big Boy Now* (1967), that caught public attention. A charmingly light and unpretentious comedy, it is about a teenager's attempts to free himself from his parents' domination and find love and sex, in either order. Among its attractions are its New York location and the handling of bit-players in bizarrely eccentric roles. The next film, *Finian's Rainbow* (1968), a semiblockbuster musical, was a complete switch that offered no threat to the masters of the genre. It is an over-inflated, rather unlovely and unamusing, stage-bound version of the Broadway hit. *The Rain People* (1969) is something else. Flawed in part, and oddly unresolved, it is nonetheless a serious and quite original attempt to get at the stresses felt by a particular American woman, stresses which cause her to leave her husband, though she is several months pregnant, to try to find herself in a cross-country journey by car.

With *The Godfather* (1972) Coppola's career took off in a rocket-like trajectory. What quickly became one of the great financial successes in the history of film is also a work of enduring value. Expert in every respect, the great appeal of the film clearly comes from the warm glow of people and times remembered, when not only were men men and women women, but families were families, including especially the Mafia. While *The Godfather* satisfied the constant American appetite for the simplicities and verities that a nostalgic view can best afford, the sentiments expressed were especially close to Coppola, who was himself from an Italian-American background. As for the gangster-film tradition, he chose to heighten rather than disturb the myths and to flesh them out with convincing and moving human detail, much of which had surely been observed and felt at first hand. *The Conversation* (1974) slightly preceded Penn's *Night Moves,* and deals even more specifically with the Watergate syndrome. It concerns an electronic eavesdropper who applies his expertise impartially and amorally, gaining his only satisfactions from his considerable skill and the vicarious experiencing of fragments of other lives. *The Godfather, Part II* (1974) expanded on the themes and confirmed the mastery Coppola had demonstrated in the original.

Apocalypse Now (1979), about the Vietnam War, was a behemoth of a film, years and many millions of dollars in the making. It offers surreal experience of jungle and battle; colors and sounds overwhelm the senses, and one feels that this is the way it must have felt to American soldiers, especially if their sensations were heightened by fear and perhaps drugs.

It was followed by an entirely different, old-fashioned, romantic musical, *One from the Heart* (1981), made completely inside Coppola's own studio in San Francisco, Zoetrope, and using the advanced electronic technology with which he has become increasingly preoccupied. *The Outsiders* (1982) and *Rumble Fish* (1983) are different yet again, both from S. E. Hinton novels about troubled teenagers. If the direction Coppola

The Godfather (U.S., 1972, Francis Ford Coppola). Museum of Modern Art/Film Stills Archive.

is taking is less than clear, his need for personal expression about important aspects of American life seems constant.

Robert Altman, like Penn and Peckinpah, came to film out of directing for television series. What many of his features have in common is a dissection of the traditional American film genres, in the course of which he pokes fun at, questions, and attacks the values and shibboleths that their conventions support. He has said, and one can infer from his work, that he employs a good deal of improvisation in his direction. *M*A*S*H* (1970), his first substantial success (which spawned an even more successful long-running television series), rode the crest of the youth/now cycle and launched Altman's subsequent career. An outrageous satire of both the military and medical professions, it simultaneously desecrated our memories of *All Quiet on the Western Front* and *Young Doctor Kildare.* In the same year, *Brewster McCloud* went to work on science fiction and private-eye sleuthing. It was mainly slapstick farce, about a young man who tries to develop an apparatus and muscles that will enable him to fly like a bird.

Brewster McCloud was followed by the visually extraordinary and thematically haunting *McCabe and Mrs. Miller* (1971). Totally unlike Altman's previous work, it is a kind of antiwestern. In place of the conventional assurance, solitary strength, and fast draw with a sure shot, it introduced psychological vulnerability, the need for human companionship, and the impossibility of avoiding one's destiny. Though *McCabe and Mrs. Miller* is somber in what it says about the nature of humanity, Altman's view of the two protagonists remains warm, affectionate, and humorous.

With *The Long Goodbye* (1973), also, the parody is softer and subtler than in *M*A*S*H* or *Brewster McCloud,* and the film works in its own right, not requiring us to know how it contrasts with the Raymond Chandler novel. Altman's point seems to be that the old-fashioned nobility of a whole genealogy of screen Marlowes, however muted in tough talk, is no longer applicable to these unheroic times. Elliott Gould replaces Humphrey Bogart, with a fumbling ineptitude designed to put the legend to rest.

Thieves Like Us (1974), though related to the exploits of the Barrow gang that had been treated in a number of other films, drops parody altogether. In part ironic and distanced, it is yet a serious and sensitive, if quite different, version of the legendary material. *California Split* (1974) has its generic origins in a cycle of films that dealt with what might be described as bonding between men (that had begun with the great success of *Butch Cassidy and the Sundance Kid,* 1969). There are lots of laughs and a happy ending of sorts, but along the way the film explores compulsive gambling, the milieu in which it takes place, and a significant relationship between two contrasting characters.

From the confines of a California casino, Altman moved to *Nashville* (1975), the Middle America capital of country-and-western music, and to numerous characters caught up in that industry and in the presidential campaign of a populist demagogue. The subjects of parody and satire here are popular music and popular politics, the sorts of performance and manipulation involved in both, and the audiences to which both appeal. A big, ambitious film, some regard it as his crowning achievement to date; Altman himself has referred to it as his "metaphor for America." *Buffalo Bill and the Indians* (1976), based on the play *Indians* by Arthur Kopit, debunks the legend surrounding and exploited by William F. Cody as touring showman. *3 Women* (1977) explores the incomplete psyches and changing relationships of two southern California roommates and their landlady, a painter of mysterious and grotesque murals.

A Wedding (1978), somewhat like *Nashville* in its tangle of characters at a public event, though more comic than serious, examines life among the wealthy. Lately Altman has been pursuing his interest in experimental theater with film adaptations of plays he himself has staged; for example, *Come Back to the Five & Dime Jimmy Dean, Jimmy Dean* (1982) and *Streamers* (1983).

Of the five contemporary American film makers dealt with in this section, Altman is the most prolific, averaging over a film a year since the success of *M*A*S*H.* Through producing as well as directing, he seems able to control what he says and the way he says it. Yet, perhaps he works too fast, content to offer adroit sketches for a larger canvas that must be imaginatively completed by the viewer from assorted scenes and characters in his sprawling work. Though the potential of each individual film doesn't always seem to be fully realized, Altman has achieved a position from which he can carry his own distinctive, sardonic view of American society from one film to the next. This is a considerable achievement in an art which is first of all an industry.

Martin Scorsese is the newest and youngest (born in 1942) of the five directors; Coppola is next (born in 1939), whose career Scorsese's in some ways parallels. Both are from Italian-American backgrounds, which they have drawn upon in their films; both attended university film departments (New York University, in Scorsese's case). But there are differences, of course. Coppola has ranged more widely in his subjects and forms; Scorsese has stuck with remarkable and commendable closeness to what he

Nashville (U.S., 1975, Robert Altman). National Film Archive/Stills Library.

learned while growing up in New York's Little Italy. When Coppola tried his hand at a musical it was *Finian's Rainbow,* a bit of Irish whimsy replete with leprechaun and pot o' gold at rainbow's end; Scorsese's musical was *New York, New York,* about a self-absorbed tenor sax man obsessed with jazz.

    Who's That Knocking at My Door? (1968) was the transitional feature between Scorsese's quite brilliant student shorts and his fully professional career. It sets up the Scorsese world of young Italian-American punks, one of them troubled by yearnings for emotional freedom from the limited lives of the ethnic enclave. The time seems predominantly late at night; much of the action consists of piling into, riding in, or getting out of cars, standing around in cheerless deserted bars, or luring "broads" to a sleazy apartment.

    Boxcar Bertha (1972) was an exploitation film directed for Roger Corman (as *Dementia 13* had been by Coppola); it was Scorsese's first commercial feature. Then he returned to Little Italy with *Mean Streets* (1973), a fuller, tougher, more assured development of the same sorts of characters, themes, and milieu that had appeared in *Who's That Knocking?*. In *Mean Streets* the protagonist (Harvey Keitel) attempts to reconcile his persistent sense of decency and concern for others with his ambition to succeed in the Mafia-imbued life around him. Specifically, he wants to manage the restaurant owned by his uncle, who demands that he reject both his epileptic girlfriend and his maddeningly irresponsible buddy. The latter role is played by Robert De Niro, who has become a fully participating collaborator in the expression of Scorsese's mythos.

Alice Doesn't Live Here Anymore (1975) broke away from the earlier New York films. Set in small towns and on the road in the far Southwest, its title character, played by Ellen Burstyn, is a thirty-five-year-old housewife with a bumptious twelve-year-old son. After the death of her unsympathetic husband of fifteen years, she pursues her nostalgic illusion of returning home to Monterey and having a singing career. The film centers on Alice's efforts along the way (she never reaches Monterey) to cope with various relationships and a desultory and unrewarding life, wisecracks and humor covering loneliness and confusion. (Apart from its prevailing comedy, *Alice* resembles Coppola's *Rain People* in many respects.)

Taxi Driver (1976) returned to New York City and to what might be seen as an extreme variation on the failed saint figure who appeared as protagonist in both *Who's That Knocking?* and *Mean Streets*. Here the character, played by De Niro, is locked into near catatonia, and becomes obsessed with cleansing the world's evil through a bath of blood. The isolation of the De Niro character is truly frightening in its credibility, the homicidal violence shocking and unnerving.

New York, New York (1977) is not so much a musical as it is a drama with music, or, even more precisely, a funny-sweet-sad love story about two musicians. It salutes the city in the manner of the films of the forties and offers a loving reprise for the music being played at the end of the big band era. De Niro's performance is full of charm and pyrotechnics, from marvelous wacky humor to tight-faced pathos, and the Liza Minnelli persona is softened and warmed in this production.

Raging Bull (1980), a biography of middleweight champion Jake LaMotta, is apparently very close to the life of a violent and insensitive man. It was shot in black and white and a documentary style. De Niro plays the fighter in a remarkable performance. In *King of Comedy* (1983), again a New York City setting and characters, he is an obsessive would-be comic who threatens the life of talk-show host Jerry Lewis to get his

Taxi Driver (U.S., 1976, Martin Scorsese). National Film Archive/Stills Library.

big break. It is a venturesome (the film did not do well at the box office), seemingly personally felt, and certainly acerbic essay on show biz success and celebrity. The jagged, frenetic camera and cutting style of his earlier films is no longer present. It reasserts Scorsese's affection for and identification with his characters, however, as well as his obvious familiarity with and control of the medium, qualities that seem likely to keep his contribution to the fore in the renewed vitality of the American film.

By 1977, the end of this arbitrary period being considered, the United States had regained its place among the leading nations of film art. It had achieved that position as France, Italy, and the Eastern European countries had done, by giving working space to film makers with originality and distinction—Penn, Peckinpah, Coppola, Altman, and Scorsese among them. But if America was once more back within the international artistic spotlight, it was sharing it. If it remained dominant in world commerce, it did so partly through employing the film makers and distributing the films of other countries. Perhaps the clearly identifiable phases of national creativity up through postwar Italian neorealism have given way. In the chapters on the films of Japan, France, Italy, Eastern Europe, and Britain, no ending dates were assigned to the periods under consideration. All of these national cinemas have continued vital and restive. The emerging Third World nations, the renascent German production, and other international developments may be too recent and inconclusive to be properly assessed, but they must at least be dealt with at this point.

FILMS OF THE PERIOD

1963
The Birds (Alfred Hitchcock)
The Cardinal (Otto Preminger)
The Courtship of Eddie's Father
  (Vincente Minnelli)
Dementia 13 (Francis Ford Coppola)
Donovan's Reef (John Ford)
55 Days at Peking (Nicholas Ray)
How the West Was Won (Ford with
  Henry Hathaway and
  George Marshall)
Shock Corridor (Samuel Fuller)
Sodom and Gomorrah
  (Robert Aldrich)

1964
Cheyenne Autumn (Ford)
A Distant Trumpet (Raoul Walsh)
The Fall of the Roman Empire
  (Anthony Mann)
Four for Texas (Aldrich)
Goodbye Charlie (Minnelli)
In Harm's Way (Preminger)
Major Dundee (Sam Peckinpah)
Man's Favorite Sport?
  (Howard Hawks)

Marnie (Hitchcock)
My Fair Lady (George Cukor)
The Pink Panther (Blake Edwards)
A Shot in the Dark (Edwards)

1965
Bunny Lake Is Missing
  (Preminger)
The Great Race (Edwards)
The Greatest Story Ever Told
  (George Stevens)
The Heroes of Telemark (Mann)
Hush, Hush . . . Sweet Charlotte
  (Aldrich)
Mickey One (Arthur Penn)
The Naked Kiss (Fuller)
Red Line 7000 (Hawks)
The Sandpiper (Minnelli)
Young Cassidy
  (Ford and Jack Cardiff)

1966
The Chase (Penn)
Flight of the Phoenix (Aldrich)
Hurry Sundown (Preminger)
Seven Women (Ford)

Torn Curtain (Hitchcock)
What Did You Do in the War, Daddy?
   (Edwards)

1967
Bonnie and Clyde (Penn)
A Countess from Hong Kong
   (Charles Chaplin)
The Dirty Dozen (Aldrich)
El Dorado (Hawks)
Falstaff (Orson Welles)
Gunn (Edwards)
You're a Big Boy Now (Coppola)

1968
A Dandy in Aspic (Mann)
Finian's Rainbow (Coppola)
The Immortal Story (Welles)
The Killing of Sister George (Aldrich)
The Legend of Lylah Clare (Aldrich)
Skidoo (Preminger)
Who's That Knocking at My Door?
   (Martin Scorsese)

1969
Alice's Restaurant (Penn)
Justine (Cukor)
The Rain People (Coppola)
Shark/Caine
   (Fuller, who has disowned this film)
Topaz (Hitchcock)
The Wild Bunch (Peckinpah)

1970
The Ballad of Cable Hogue (Peckinpah)
Brewster McCloud (Robert Altman)
Little Big Man (Penn)
M*A*S*H (Altman)
On a Clear Day You Can See Forever
   (Minnelli)
Rio Lobo (Hawks)
The Only Game in Town (Stevens)
Tell Me that You Love Me Junie Moon
   (Preminger)
Too Late the Hero (Aldrich)

1971
The Grissom Gang (Aldrich)
McCabe and Mrs. Miller (Altman)
Straw Dogs (Peckinpah)
Such Good Friends (Preminger)
Wild Rovers (Edwards)

1972
Boxcar Bertha (Scorsese)
The Carey Treatment (Edwards)
Frenzy (Hitchcock)
The Getaway (Peckinpah)
The Godfather (Coppola)
Junior Bonner (Peckinpah)
Images (Altman)
Travels with my Aunt (Cukor)
Ulzana's Raid (Aldrich)

1973
Dead Pigeon on Beethoven Street   (Fuller)
Emperor of the North Pole   (Aldrich)
F for Fake   (Welles)
The Long Goodbye   (Altman)
Mean Streets   (Scorsese)
Pat Garrett and Billy the Kid   (Peckinpah)

1974
Bring Me the Head of Alfredo Garcia
   (Peckinpah)
California Split   (Altman)
The Conversation   (Coppola)
The Godfather, Part II   (Coppola)
The Longest Yard   (Aldrich)
The Tamarind Seed   (Edwards)
Thieves Like Us   (Altman)

1975
Alice Doesn't Live Here Anymore
   (Scorsese)
Family Plot   (Hitchcock)
Hustle   (Aldrich)
The Killer Elite   (Peckinpah)
Love Among the Ruins   (Cukor)
Nashville   (Altman)
Night Moves   (Penn)
Return of the Pink Panther   (Edwards)

1976
The Blue Bird   (Cukor)
Buffalo Bill and the Indians   (Altman)
Cross of Iron   (Peckinpah)
The Missouri Breaks   (Penn)
Taxi Driver   (Scorsese)

1977
New York, New York   (Scorsese)
The Pink Panther Strikes Again   (Edwards)
3 Women   (Altman)
Twilight's Last Gleaming   (Aldrich)

BOOKS ON THE PERIOD

BAXTER, JOHN,   *Hollywood in the Sixties.* Cranbury, N.J.: A. S. Barnes & Co., Inc., 1972. 172 pp.

BAXTER, JOHN,   *Sixty Years of Hollywood.* Cranbury, N.J.: A. S. Barnes & Co., Inc., 1973. 284 pp.

BLUM, DANIEL,   *A New Pictorial History of the Talkies,* rev. and enlarged by John Kobal. New York: G. P. Putnam's Sons, 1982.

GRIFFITH, RICHARD, ARTHUR MAYER, and EILEEN BOWSER,   *The Movies.* New York: Simon & Schuster, Inc., 1981.

HIGHAM, CHARLES,   *The Art of the American Film, 1900–1971.* Garden City, N.Y.: Doubleday & Co., Inc., 1973. 322 pp.

JACOBS, DIANE,   *Hollywood Renaissance.* Cranbury, N.J.: A. S. Barnes & Co., Inc., 1977. 192 pp.

KEYSER, LESTER,   *Hollywood in the Seventies.* Cranbury, N.J.: A. S. Barnes & Co., Inc., 1981.

KINDEM, GORHAM, ed.,   *The American Movie Industry: The Business of Motion Pictures.* Carbondale and Edwardsville: Southern Illinois University Press, 1982. 448 pp.

MANVELL, ROGER,   *New Cinema in the USA: The Feature Film Since 1946.* New York: E. P. Dutton & Co., Inc., 1968. 160 pp.

MONACO, JAMES,   *American Film Now: The People, The Power, The Money, The Movies.* New York: Oxford University Press, 1979. 540 pp.

PYE, MICHAEL AND LINDA MILES,   *The Movie Brats: How the Film Generation Took Over Hollywood.* New York: Holt, Rinehart, and Winston, 1979.

SKLAR, ROBERT,   *Movie-made America: A Social History of American Movies.* New York: Random House, Inc., 1975. 340 pp.

SMITH, JULIAN,   *Looking Away: Hollywood and Vietnam.* New York: Charles Scribner's Sons, 1975. 236 pp.

STANLEY, ROBERT H.,   *The Celluloid Empire: A History of the American Movie Industry.* New York: Hastings House Publishers, 1978. 328 pp.

TOEPLITZ, JERZY,   *Hollywood and After: The Changing Face of Movies in America.* Chicago: Henry Regnery Co., 1975. 288 pp.

22

Third World Cinema
and
Recent National
Movements, 1959–

LATIN AMERICA AND AFRICA

Films from the so-called developing nations which have attracted international attention have generally expressed a strong sense of nationalism, frequently accompanied by anti-imperialism (specifically anti-Americanism in many instances), and sometimes a call to revolution. Film making in some of the Latin American countries, especially, conforms to these generalizations. Among them Cuba is preeminent. With its socialist revolution achieved, it has been able to offer inspiration, encouragement, and actual assistance to the independent leftist film makers in the neighboring countries of South America.

The Cuban Revolution of 1959 (against foreign—that is, American—domination as well as the Fulgencio Batista government) brought sweeping changes in the Cuban motion picture industry. Like Russia following its revolution in 1917, or the Eastern Republics after 1945, Cuba established a government agency to organize and regulate all production, distribution, and exhibition. Called Instituto Cubano del Arte y Industria Cinematográficos (ICAIC), it created first-rate production facilities, and invited Czechoslovakian film makers in to train Cuban personnel.

Consistent with Lenin's advice to the earlier Soviet film makers, the Cubans used newsreels and documentaries to meet the needs of the people as seen by the new state. The leading figure of this nonnarrative short-film output was Santiago Alvarez, whose *L.B.J.* (1968) and *79 Springtimes* (1969, about Vietnamese leader Ho Chi Minh) have been seen on a limited basis in this country. Their ironic and experimental forms of attack on the violence of the U.S., and lyrical portrayal of ''the struggle of the underdeveloped and small peoples for their human dignity,'' as Alvarez has put it, place him among the leading innovators in art used for political persuasion.

As for narrative fiction features, other Cuban film makers have transcended the immediate political requirements. Best known abroad is Tomás Gutiérrez Alea, whose *Memories of Underdevelopment* (1968) was the first Cuban feature to achieve international recognition. Far from serving any obvious agitprop function, it chronicles the spiritual displacement of a bourgeois intellectual within the postrevolutionary Cuban culture with a kind of cinematic sophistication and emotional detachment that place it within the mainstream of modern world cinema. Humberto Solás's *Lucia* (1969) also eschews narrow political ends for a broad view of the historical role of women in Cuban society. Actually it is three films in one, and there are three Lucías: the first an aristocrat living in 1895 at the time of the struggle for Cuban independence from Spain; the second a factory worker in 1933, married to a revolutionary during Gerardo Machado's dictatorship; the third a spunky peasant newlywed in Castro's Cuba, whose husband considers her his property. Each historical period is re-created in a different cinematic style. Embedded within the formal pleasures the film offers is the point that, though social and political contexts may have changed over the years, women's struggle to establish independence from male dominance continues.

In Brazil, in an upsurge of nationalism at about the same time as the Cuban Revolution, a cooperative was formed by Glauber Rocha, Nelson Pereira dos Santos (*Barren Lives,* 1963), and Ruy Guerra (*The Guns,* 1963), which produced what they called Cinema Nôvo. This group offered a more applicable model than did Cuba for other

Memories of Underdevelopment (Cuba, 1968, Tomás Gutiérrez Alea). Museum of Modern Art/Film Stills Archive.

Latin American film makers on the left working independently within the entrenched capitalist regimes. Rocha was its leader and spokesman; *Black God, White Devil* (1964) and *Antonio das Mortes* (1969) are the two films of his which have received widest distribution outside Brazil. Both are set in the barren northeastern region of the country and explore the mythic folk roots of banditry and mystical religion that extreme poverty had bred. *Black God, White Devil,* particularly, is strange and haunting in its combination of severe naturalism and stylized ritual, in its portrayal of violence and madness. It lights up the screen with a kind of savage hallucination totally foreign to the cultural experience of most of us. We can see that it might have represented for the Brazilians a revolutionary scream. In any case, in the year of its release there was a reactionary military coup in Brazil. Following the release of *Antonio das Mortes* Rocha left Brazil and worked abroad. He made films in Europe and Africa which attempted to deal with the problems of a Third World—of underdevelopment, of neocolonialist exploitation—and of the possibilities for political action to bring about radical social change. In 1976 he returned to Brazil, but completed little of significance before his death in 1981.

Since the collapse of Cinema Nôvo, dos Santos's films have included *How Tasty Was My Little Frenchman* (1971), *Ogum's Amulet* (1975), and *Tent of Miracles* (1977). For the most part, revolutionary Brazilian film makers have blended into the commercial film industry, which has become increasingly visible following the international success

Black God, White Devil (Brazil, 1964, Glauber Rocha). Museum of Modern Art/Film Stills Archive.

of *Dona Flor and Her Two Husbands* (1978). Carlos Diegues's *Bye Bye Brazil* and *Xica,* and Argentine emigré Hector Babenco's *Pixote,* are more recent examples of Brazilian films which have gone out into the world.

In Argentina in the 1960s another group of political film makers set up an independent cooperative, in their case called Cine Liberacion. Its principal organizer was Fernando Solanas and its major work his *The Hour of the Furnaces* (1969, codirected with Octavio Getino). This huge documentary (nearly four-and-a-half hours long) is in three separate parts: ''Neo-Colonialism and Violence,'' ''An Act for Liberation,'' and ''Violence and Liberation.'' The first part presents a historical, geographical, economic, and social analysis of Argentina. The content of the second and third parts was developed out of points raised during audience discussion following the necessarily clandestine screenings of the first. Because of the time at which it appeared, its ambitious scope, its formal eclecticism, and the circumstances surrounding its production and distribution, *Hour of the Furnaces* has been regarded as the single most influential documentary to have come out of the entire new Latin American cinema movement. With the subsequent resumption of military rule in Argentina shortly after the release of *Hour of the Furnaces,* the films of the Cine Liberacion group were not only no longer smuggled abroad, they were not shown in Argentina itself, even clandestinely, because of the severe penalties attached to any activities critical of the government.

In Bolivia, since the nationalist government of Paz Estenssoro was overthrown in 1964, there have been a succession of military coups and dictatorships. Nonetheless, Jorge Sanjinés and his collaborators in the production group called Ukamau Films managed to produce several features, the best known of which is *Blood of the Condor* (1969). It deals, in semi-documentary fashion, with an alleged campaign of sterilization carried

The Hour of the Furnaces (Argentina, 1969, Fernando Solanas and Octavio Getino). Museum of Modern Art/Film Stills Archive London.

Blood of the Condor (Bolivia, 1969, Jorge Sanjinés). National Film Archive London.

out by members of the U.S. Peace Corps against the native Indians, and urges the preservation of the Indian heritage and cultural identity. Sanjinés's next feature, *The Night of San Juan* (1971), used survivors and witnesses to reconstruct a massacre of striking miners by the army. Soon after its release, in another shift of the government towards reaction and repression, film making in Bolivia virtually ceased and Sanjinés fled into exile in Chile. Subsequently he made *The Principal Enemy* (1974) in Peru.

In Chile, in the 1960s, a group of political film makers had developed in support of Salvador Allende's socialist movement. Their cooperative was called Cinematografia Tercer Mundo and its best known film is *The Jackal of Nahueltero* (1969), directed by Miguel Littín. This was another semi-documentary reconstruction, of a mass murder committed by a peasant brutalized and driven mad by hopeless poverty. After Allende's election in 1970, the Chilean cinema was nationalized and began producing a program of newsreels and documentaries following the Cuban pattern. (Of these, *The First Years,* 1971, made by Patricio Guzman [whose later *The Battle of Chile,* 1973, is even better known], received the widest distribution.) After the military coup of 1973, which deposed Allende, Littín left Chile and resumed work in Mexico.

The Battle of Chile (Chile, 1973, Patricio Guzman). National Film Archive London.

The climax of South American political film making, reached at the end of the sixties, receded into an unpromising denouement. In the seventies many of the principal film makers were working in exile abroad, without benefit of the strengths they had derived from their native cultures and the national political goals that had infused their work with revolutionary energy. Those at home are forced to remain silent or work within the noncommitted commercial film industries.

In Africa, there are only faint stirrings. In Algeria and other Arab countries a certain amount of noteworthy production is evident, but from below the Sahara only one film maker has reached out to world audiences. Ousmane Sembène, novelist and committed revolutionary from Senegal, has offered a genuine expression of certain facets of African culture and aspiration. With what is evidently deeply felt, painful irony, his first film, *Black Girl* (1966), attacked the exploitation and racism to which blacks were subjected by the French colonists. In *Xala* (1974), using satire and bawdy humor, he shows how the leaders of the new black state mimic the ways of their former colonial masters to the continued detriment of the people. With *Ceddo* (1977), Sembène maintained his preeminence as the father and leader of black African cinema.

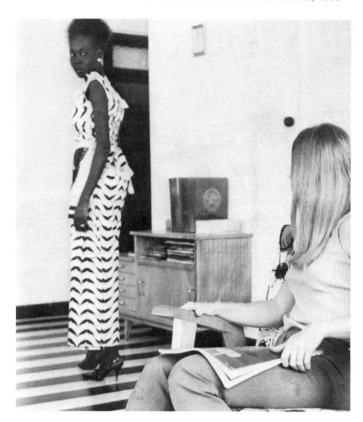

Black Girl (Senegal, 1966, Ousmane Sembène). Museum of Modern Art/Film Stills Archive.

WEST GERMANY

In Europe, West German film has experienced a resurgence and may require a chapter of its own in the next edition of this book. Like the films of the Third World, its successes have generally come from political positions on the left. Following the Oberhausen Film Festival of 1962, at which a group of young film makers presented a manifesto denouncing "Papa's cinema" and offering to make better films at half the cost, there appeared a group of directors who soon came to be regarded by the world at large and eventually in Germany itself as the new *Wunderkinder*. Under the leadership of Alexander Kluge, the group won government subsidy for the films of young directors and the establishment of a film school. Kluge's own features include *Yesterday Girl* (1966), *Artists at the Top of the Big Top: Disoriented* (1968), and *The Part-Time Work of a Domestic Slave* (1974). The last deals with a twenty-nine-year-old woman trying to achieve some order, meaning, and effectiveness in a life that includes roles as wife and mother, abortionist, and political militant.

Volker Schlöndorff, another member of the German new wave, also made his first feature (*Young Törless*) in 1966 and has remained active since. *The Lost Honor of Katharina Blum* (1975) was written and directed in collaboration with his wife,

Margarethe von Trotta. It concerns a young woman who spends the night with a fugitive political activist and is, as a result, hounded and exposed to humiliation by the authorities and the sensational press. *The Tin Drum* (1978), Schlöndorff's adaptation of Günter Grass's first novel, is his most substantial international success to date. Von Trotta has become quite active on her own with *The German Sisters* (1977), *Sisters or the Balance of Happiness* (1979), and *Friends and Husbands* (1981), exploring modern women's lives, and political matters.

Jean-Marie Straub is an Alsatian in exile from France for political reasons from 1958 on. He is both much more outspoken in his Marxism and more experimental in his exploration of cinema forms—in the development of a minimalist cinema—than his major colleagues. His later films have been made in collaboration with his wife, Danièle Huillet. *Not Reconciled* (1965) probed the ways in which the dominant Junkerism and Naziism of past generations carried over into contemporary German life, accompanied by lingering guilt and continuing need for explanations. *Chronicle of Anna Magdalena Bach* (1967) presents performances of Bach's music with reverence but also attempts to imply the feelings and social ambience that surrounded the life of the great composer. *History Lessons* (1973), a freely adapted version of a novel by Bertolt Brecht, combines a Marxist interpretation of the economic motives underlying the usual rendering of the history of ancient Rome with a slow automobile drive through the crowded streets of the present-day city. *Moses and Aaron* (1975) is a faithful rendition of Arnold Schönberg's twelve-tone opera with added ideological emphasis and characteristic straining of the formal conventions of narrative cinema. Of the modern German film makers Straub is the most "difficult," the least "accessible" to general audiences. At the same time he is valued by the few as the most innovative in his attempts to analyze and expose the medium itself, and to make it serve the purposes of truly radical, politically committed film making.

The two German film makers who seem most surely to speak to the pit as well as the gallery are Rainer Werner Fassbinder and Werner Herzog. Fassbinder, before his death in 1982, worked usually in the idiom of melodrama gone slightly askew, infusing the unfortunate plight of his characters with broad political meanings. *The Merchant of Four Seasons* (1971), for example, about a *lumpen* fruit peddler hounded by the women in his life (mother, girlfriend, wife) into drinking himself to death, is essentially a critique of bourgeois manners. In it wildly incongruous behavior becomes part of everyday reality. *The Bitter Tears of Petra von Kant* (1972), dealing with female homosexuality, explores various permutations of freedom and slavery evident in the women's relationship with each other in an extraordinarily bizarre and artificial visual style. *Ali: Fear Eats the Soul* (1974) is about a sixty-year-old German cleaning woman who falls in love with and marries a much younger immigrant Moroccan laborer and is ostracized by her family and the community because of racial prejudice. A subtitle suggests that "happiness is not always fun." Most widely popular among the forty-one features and television mini-series directed by the prodigious Fassbinder following his first in 1969 was *The Marriage of Maria Braun* (1979). It stars Hanna Schygulla as a woman buffeted by and adapting to the changing social conditions in Germany, from the stressful end of World War II to later affluence. The material success she achieves does not satisfy her hunger of spirit.

Werner Herzog first came to notice with *Even Dwarfs Started Small* (1970), in which he offers as political metaphor a ludicrously ineffectual revolt of prisoners, all played by dwarfs, whose hedonistic and anarchic impulses and inability to advance along any clear-cut line of collective action confines them in surrealistic chaos. *Aguirre, the Wrath of God* (1973) is a historical invention about one of Pizarro's conquistadors who leads an expedition into the Amazon jungle in search of El Dorado and ends as sole survivor lost in megalomaniacal fantasy. *The Mystery of Kaspar Hauser* (1974), originally entitled *Every Man for Himself and God Against All,* is about an actual nineteenth-century case of a young man who had been locked in solitary confinement in a dark cellar from childhood on. When he mysteriously appears on the streets of Nuremberg he is without language, without concepts—an instinctual and literally uncultured human animal.

Herzog's *Nosferatu* (1979), a reverent remake of Murnau's 1922 film, lacks the sort of individuality and passion we associate with its maker. *Fitzcarraldo* (1982), on the other hand, was as idiosyncratic and flamboyant a project as anyone could imagine. Huge, costly, beset with misadventures and interruptions, the making of the film in Peru was not unlike the events it chronicles, and Herzog not unlike its obsessed protagonist. It is about a nineteenth-century rubber tycoon who has a river steamer hauled over a mountain in the course of trying to satisfy his love for opera by building an opera house in the jungle. Of all the new German film makers Herzog is perhaps the most original and imaginative; certainly his work is the most varied.

Recently appearing on the international scene are Wim Wenders and Hans-Jürgen Syberberg. Wenders we know for *The Goalie's Anxiety at the Penalty Kick* (1972), *Alice in the Cities* (1974), *False Movement* (1975), *Kings of the Road* (1976), *The American Friend* (1977). All of these involve, to one degree or another, individual alienation from society, aimless wandering, cities, and a fascination with the U.S. One of the characters

The Marriage of Maria Braun (West Germany, 1979, Rainer Werner Fassbinder). Museum of Modern Art/Film Stills Archive.

in *Kings of the Road* says "The Americans have colonized our subconscious." Syberberg, for his part, is fascinated with Germany and Germanism. His *Ludwig: Requiem for a Virgin King* (1973) and *The Confessions of Winifred Wagner* (1975) were followed by the monumental (seven hours long), theatrical, and wildly experimental *Hitler, a Film from Germany* (1980), which provoked political outrage at home and aesthetic controversy abroad.

Taken together the contemporary directors discussed here have not only regained for German cinema something of the importance with which Murnau, Lang, and Pabst had earlier endowed it, they have brought it abreast of the modernist tendencies so strong in other leading national cinemas. An intelligence at work on political, social, and economic criticism, together with an aesthetic based on experimentation with the formal means of film expression informs their best work.

SPAIN

In Spain, Buñuel's native land, an easing of censorship that began in the early seventies has allowed for a newly serious and critical examination of the national culture. Following the death of dictator Francisco Franco in 1975, a variety of topics that had long been off limits—church, army, sexual relations, the Civil War—have been treated with candor and humor. Spanish politics, from the turn of the century to the present, is the note that recurs most frequently. Three Spanish film makers who stand out clearly are Carlos Saura, Victor Erice, and Jose Luis Borau.

Saura's *The Hunt* (1966) was one of the first Spanish films to return to the painful experience of the Civil War with an honesty designed to lay bare and perhaps to cauterize the old wounds. It proceeds obliquely, however, from a kind of allegory of a hunting expedition undertaken by a group of friends who had earlier fought together in that dreadful conflict. In *Cousin Angelica* (1974) Saura also looked back to the 1930s from a modern perspective, with a protagonist who revisits a town for the first time in thirty years and relives episodes of his childhood, especially those centering around his relationship with his cousin Angelica. *Blood Wedding* (1981) records a dance version of García Lorca's tragedy. In *Hurry, Hurry* (1982) Saura probes the lives of four young delinquents rushing headlong into tragedy.

Erice placed his best-known film, *The Spirit of the Beehive* (1973), in the period just after the Civil War. In it he evokes a strange dream world seen through the childhood games and fantasies of two sisters. There are what seem to be allusions to surrounding events (for example, a fugitive soldier hides in their barn), but mostly it is the mood of unstated tension and fragile unreality which conveys Erice's sense of what it was like living in those first years of fascist rule. Following *The Spirit of the Beehive*, the next film, *The South* (1983), is also about a Spanish provincial family, as seen through the childhood memories of a young woman. It is a tale of mystery and romance in which her father is the dominant figure.

Borau's very successful *Poachers* (1975) is another of the allegories about Spain during the Franco years which criticize indirectly but with remarkable force. It was followed by *La Sabina* (1980), set in contemporary times. It concerns an English writer and other foreigners caught up in passionate and desperate relationships and a legend from the Andalusian past.

The Spirit of the Beehive (Spain, 1973, Victor Erice). Museum of Modern Art/Film Stills Archive.

AUSTRALIA

The country to step into the spotlight most recently is Australia. To some extent its appearance was created by fiat. In 1970 the Australian government established an experimental fund for neophyte film makers, a film and television school, and a national development corporation that provides starting money for film productions. Before that time Australia had been known on the screen chiefly in a few films made by Britons and Americans. Once Australians were able to make their own films, they tended to feature the history and topography of their subcontinent.

In 1975 Ken Hannam's *Sunday Too Far Away,* an engaging film about the lives of itinerant Australian sheep shearers, was shown at the Cannes Film Festival. It was followed next year by Peter Weir's *Picnic at Hanging Rock* (1975), the first Australian film to achieve great commercial success both in Australia and abroad. It is a haunting story of a girls' boarding school outing on which a number of the girls disappear mysteriously. It evokes turn-of-the-century dress and manners and makes stunning use of its country's scenery. Its director, Peter Weir, has become one of the leaders in the new Australian cinema.

Weir's *The Last Wave* (1977) is about a white, middle-class Sydney lawyer who is required to learn the tribal mysteries of his aboriginal clients. *Gallipoli* (1981), a big-

Picnic at Hanging Rock (Australia, 1975, Peter Weir). Museum of Modern Art/Film Stills Archive.

budget spectacular, is about Australians fighting under English command in the Crimean War; it ends in senseless slaughter. *The Year of Living Dangerously* (1982) is set in Indonesia in the mid-1960s, around the time of Sukarno's fall from power. Its protagonist is an Australian journalist.

Films by other Australian film makers have achieved considerable international success as well. *Newsfront* (1978), directed by Phillip Noyce, is about two rival Australian newsreel companies in the pretelevision decade following World War II. Actual newsreel footage is ingeniously woven into its fictional plot. *The Chant of Jimmie Blacksmith* (1978), directed by Fred Schepisi, concerns a young half-caste aborigine in 1900 who, after being exploited by whites, turns to violence and revenge. *My Brilliant Career* (1979), directed by Gill Armstrong, is based on a novel published in 1901 about a spirited young woman from a poor farming family who persists in her resolution to become a writer. *Breaker Morant* (1980), directed by Bruce Beresford, is a powerful drama of court-martial for political reasons of Australian soldiers fighting under the English in the Boer War in South Africa.

This chapter surveying newly prominent film-producing countries began with Third World nations fired with revolutionary zeal, anticolonialism, anticapitalism, and nationalism. They were followed by West Germany, whose films also lean leftward politically but consist more of social, political and economic criticism, and examination of alienation and angst. In Spain the left-leanings are less pronounced and the view tends to be backward, over Spanish political history and cultural heritage of the past half century.

With Australia we come back into the mainstream of the international film industry. Australian films are not noticeably left politically; its contemplation of its own culture and past appears mainly nostalgic (with a few swipes at the former British Empire, to be sure). The problem for Australian films seems to be a familiar one of hanging into "Australianness" and international success at the same time, in the face of American competition and within the global industry dominated by the United States.

The dominant American industry has always faced the same problem, of course, and has solved it with sufficient success so that what comes from America is popular around the world. In these days of conglomerates and multinationals, financial balance sheets tend more than ever to demand a huge international audience. A film that might be distinctively American or especially personal may have considerable difficulty finding backing. If young American film makers come increasingly from university film departments, the young men and women who really call the shots (heads of studios) come increasingly from schools of business.

The next and final chapter of this history of film is devoted to the present state of the industry we call Hollywood, to a cycle of American films that examines a painful phase of our recent past, and to a few talented film makers who seem to have found ways to express themselves on film.

FILMS OF THE PERIOD

Argentina

1969
The Hour of the Furnaces (Fernando Solanas and Octavio Getino)

Australia

1975
Picnic at Hanging Rock (Peter Weir)
Sunday Too Far Away (Ken Hannam)

1977
The Last Wave (Weir)

1978
The Chant of Jimmie Blacksmith (Fred Schepisi)
Newsfront (Phillip Noyce)

1979
My Brilliant Career (Gill Armstrong)

1980
Breaker Morant (Bruce Beresford)

1981
Gallipoli (Weir)

1982
The Year of Living Dangerously (Weir)

Bolivia

1969
Blood of the Condor (Jorge Sanjinés)

Brazil

1963
Barren Lives (Nelson Pereira dos Santos)

1964
Black God, White Devil (Glauber Rocha)

1967
Terra em Transe (Rocha)

1969
Antonio das Mortes (Rocha)

1971
How Tasty Was My Little Frenchman (dos Santos)

1975
Ogum's Amulet (dos Santos)

1977
Tent of Miracles (dos Santos)

1979
Bye Bye Brazil (Carlos Diegues)

1981
Xica (Diegues)

1982
Pixote (Hector Babenco)

Chile

1969
The Jackal of Nahueltero (Miguel Littín)

1973
The Battle of Chile (Patricio Guzman)

Cuba

1968
Memories of Underdevelopment (Tomás Gutiérrez Alea)

1969
Lucia (Humberto Solás)

Senegal
1966
Black Girl (Ousmane Sembène)

1974
Xala (Sembène)

1977
Ceddo (Sembène)

Spain
1966
The Hunt (Carlos Saura)

1973
The Spirit of the Beehive (Victor Erice)

1974
Cousin Angelica (Saura)

1975
Poachers (Jose Luis Borau)

1980
La Sabina (Borau)

1983
The South (Erice)

West Germany
1965
Not Reconciled (Jean-Marie Straub and
    Danièle Huillet)

1966
Yesterday Girl (Alexander Kluge)
Young Törless (Volker Schlöndorff)

1967
Chronicle of Anna Magdalena Bach (Straub
    and Huillet)

1968
Artists at the Top of the Big Top: Disoriented
    (Kluge)

1970
Even Dwarfs Started Small (Werner Herzog)

1971
The Merchant of Four Seasons
    (Rainer Werner Fassbinder)

1972
The Bitter Tears of Petra von Kant
    (Fassbinder)
The Goalie's Anxiety at the Penalty Kick
    (Wim Wenders)

1973
Aguirre, the Wrath of God (Herzog)
Ludwig: Requiem for a Virgin King
    (Hans-Jürgen Syberberg)

1974
Ali: Fear Eats the Soul (Fassbinder)
Alice in the Cities (Wenders)
The Mystery of Kaspar Hauser (Herzog)
The Part-Time Work of a Domestic Slave
    (Kluge)

1975
False Movement (Wenders)
The Lost Honor of Katharina Blum
    (Schlöndorff and Margarethe
    von Trotta)

1976
Kings of the Road (Wenders)

1977
The American Friend (Wenders)
The German Sisters (von Trotta)

1978
The Tin Drum (Schlöndorff)

1979
The Marriage of Maria Braun (Fassbinder)
Nosferatu (Herzog)
Sisters or the Balance of Happiness
    (von Trotta)

1980
Hitler, a Film from Germany (Syberberg)

1981
Friends and Husbands (von Trotta)

1982
Fitzcarraldo (Herzog)

BOOKS ON THE PERIOD

CHANAN, MICHAEL, ed., *Chilean Cinema*. London: British Film Institute, 1977.

FOIX, VINCENTE MOLINA, *New Cinema in Spain*. London: British Film Institute, 1978.

FRANKLIN, JAMES C., *New German Cinema*. Boston: G. K. Hall & Co., 1983.

GABRIEL, TESHOME H., *Third Cinema in the Third World: The Aesthetics of Liberation*. Ann Arbor, Mich.: UMI Research Press, 1982. 160 pp.

JOHNSON, RANDAL and ROBERT STAM, eds., *Brazilian Cinema*. East Brunswick, N. J.: Fairleigh Dickinson University Press, 1982. 373 pp.

MANVELL, ROGER and HEINRICH FRAENKEL, *The German Cinema*. New York: Praeger Publishers, 1971. 159 pp.

MURRAY, SCOTT, ed., *The New Australian Cinema*. London: Elm Tree Books, 1981. 208 pp.

MYERSON, MICHAEL, ed., *Memories of Underdevelopment: The Revolutionary Films of Cuba*. New York: Grossman Publishers, 1973. 224 pp.

READE, ERIC, *History and Heartburn: The Saga of Australian Film, 1896–1978*. East Brunswick, N. J.: Fairleigh Dickinson University Press, 1980. 353 pp.

SANFORD, JOHN, *The New German Cinema*. Totowa, N. J.: Barnes & Noble Books, 1980. 180 pp.

STRATTON, DAVID, *The Last New Wave: The Australian Film Revival*. New York: Frederick Ungar Publishing Co., Inc., 1981. 356 pp.

23

Here and Now: U. S., 1977–

ECONOMICS AND TECHNOLOGY

The major Hollywood studios—Columbia, M-G-M, Paramount, Twentieth Century-Fox, United Artists, Universal, Warner Brothers—have tended to follow the merger model prevalent in American industry. For example, in 1981 Columbia Pictures was purchased by the Coca-Cola Company; United Artists, owned by Transamerica, Inc., was sold to Metro-Goldwyn-Mayer in the same year. Fewer and bigger tends to be the pattern for the pictures produced as well. A major studio that used to produce around fifty films a year now frequently releases no more than twelve to fifteen. What seems clear is that a few films on which a lot of money is spent can return huge profits; the studios and the independents try hard to make one of those few.

Super-spectacles and science fiction have been dominant among box office winners. *Star Wars* (1977) set the trend. Its record $185 million in domestic rentals surpassed even *The Godfather* (1972) and *Jaws* (1975). *Star Wars* was followed by its comparably successful sequels, *The Empire Strikes Back* (1980) and *Return of the Jedi* (1983), which completed a trilogy. *Close Encounters of the Third Kind* (1979), *Star Trek* (1979), and *Raiders of the Lost Ark* (1981) cost a lot and made a lot. *E. T.* (1982) is the biggest box office success to date—$400 million gross worldwide.

There have been, of course, extremely successful films that were neither sci-fi nor spectacular: *One Flew Over the Cuckoo's Nest* (1975), *Rocky* (1976), *Saturday Night Fever*

421

(1977), and *Grease* (1978); spectaculars that were biographical/historical: *Reds* (1981, which cost $30 million), *Gandhi* (1982, $20 million), and *The Right Stuff* (1983, $27 million); and others that were fictional/historical: *Ragtime* (1981, $25 million), *Heaven's Gate* (1981, $36 million). *Reds* and *Ragtime* were disappointing at the box office; *Heaven's Gate* was a much-publicized financial disaster that shook up the industry considerably.

The money being spent and returned (or not being returned) is up, and the technology being employed has reached a correspondingly high standard. Great advances have been made in special effects; it seems that George Lucas's Industrial Light and Magic company, which has created the sophisticated special effects for most of the science-fiction films mentioned above, can make almost anything appear to exist or happen. For live-action cinematography, the Steadycam, developed in 1977, permits a hand-held camera to move with the steadiness that formerly would have required tracks to be laid for a dolly. It was used to striking effect to follow Rocky running up the steps of the Philadelphia Museum of Art early in the morning. For the rest it can be noted that Arriflex cameras, Nagra tape recorders, and Elemack Spyder dollies are used almost everywhere.

Along with the economic and technological development within the film industry is the excitement and uncertainty of the new electronic means of producing and distributing the moving image accompanied by sound. Videotape, electronic cameras and editing machines are steadily replacing the chemical-optical system of the standard motion picture. Electronic transmission and playback possibilities already include—in addition to broadcast television—satellite, cable, and video cassette and disc recorders. With the use being made of fibre optics and the advances toward high definition television, in a comparatively short while the motion picture as art form, replete with computer graphics no doubt, will be part of the visual-audio material filling the walls of our living rooms with three-dimensional holographic images accompanied by stereophonic sound.

Motion pictures made with and for such new technologies, and audience expectations regarding them, will likely be quite different from what we have experienced to date. Another aesthetic jump—like that taken from silence to sound, from black and white to color, from almost square to very wide screen and stereophonic sound—is beginning. It may be bigger and more profound in its effects than any of the earlier technological leaps. Until it has been made and measured, the aesthetician can only conjecture about it. The historian as yet has nothing to say.

SOCIAL CONTENT

American movies frequently wait until after the tensions have somehow been resolved before dealing with large-scale stress and cultural dislocation, or deal with them obliquely. The film industry is loathe to offend segments of its audience by adopting a position on disturbing issues; the audience pays its admission to experience something other than the serious and worrisome actuality existing outside the theater.

But given this tendency, the Vietnam War is unique in having been absent from the screens of America until long after the event; even more puzzling was the sudden appearance of a number of films dealing with the subject five years after the last American troops had left Vietnam. The only earlier exception to prove the rule was *Green Berets* (1968). But for all of its patriotic intentions, it was more a military adventure than a film about our involvement in Vietnam. Not only was there no film that dealt directly and seriously with that war, the oblique acknowledgments of it must have been so heavily coded as to be undetected by most of us.

In 1978 there began a cycle of films about the Vietnam War that included *Go Tell the Spartans, Coming Home, Who'll Stop the Rain?,* and *The Deer Hunter.* In 1979 it reached its climax with *Apocalypse Now.*

Though not as popular as Vietnam films which followed it, *Go Tell the Spartans* (Ted Post) seems in many ways the most scrupulously accurate. Set in 1964, its point of view is that of a frustrated commander (Burt Lancaster) of a group of American military advisers at Penang who leads a platoon to an outpost that had been abandoned by the defeated French a decade before. *Go Tell the Spartans* portrays the shifting demands, the unclear loyalties, and the ethical dilemma that underlay the complex and irregular mode of warfare.

Coming Home (Hal Ashby) and *Who'll Stop the Rain?* (Karel Reisz) deal with those returning from Vietnam combat—the damage the experience has done to them emotionally and its effect on the lives of others at home. *Coming Home* concerns a paraplegic veteran (Jon Voight) who falls in love with the wife (Jane Fonda) of a pro-war Marine officer (Bruce Dern). Though involving no combat—and perhaps sentimental and unreal, as has been argued—it seems an honest attempt to confront the human wreckage left in the wake of war, the aftermath of the Vietnam War in particular. It does not question the war itself so much as the attitudes it had given rise to.

The opening ten minutes of *Who'll Stop the Rain?,* based on the novel *Dog Soldiers* by Robert Stone, offers some horrifying scenes of warfare in the Vietnamese countryside and of corruption in Saigon. Its narrative then centers on a war correspondent who has become so traumatized by the moral degradation he observed in the war that human decency and innocence have lost all meaning for him. He becomes a heroin smuggler. In "a world like this one," he says, "people are going to naturally want to get high."

It was *The Deer Hunter* (Michael Cimino) that seemed to touch the national nerve most directly. It deals with three buddies from a Pennsylvania steel town who volunteer for Vietnam. They experience dreadful violence and torture, physical and psychological. One dies in Saigon, one loses his legs, the other survivor has become truncated emotionally. The use of Russian roulette in prison camp and as a game for Saigon gambling created a furor; Cimino acknowledged that it probably didn't happen but insisted on his artist's prerogative to use it as a metaphor for the war. The ending of the film is ambiguous but exalting, even if it might be argued what exactly is being exalted. At a funeral breakfast the returned veterans begin to sing "God Bless America" as a dirge for their dead friend. As they continue the song becomes a hymn, to this country and to the values it traditionally holds, for which they and others had fought and died. This scene provides a catharsis of sorts; it is a sad moment but also curiously ennobling. Life goes on, it seems to mean, and we Americans may be, or can again become, the Americans we want to be.

Apocalypse Now (Francis Ford Coppola), with its effort to fuse the mystery and gloom of Joseph Conrad's *Heart of Darkness* with the known and awful actualities of the Vietnam War, was the first film to excoriate directly American involvement. The production of this film became something like a re-creation of the war it was portraying. Shot in the Phillipines, it ran over schedule and over budget; most critics and probably viewers found that it did not conclude satisfactorily. Yet it is a chilling and convincing vision of a kind of madness rampant in the American military command: homicidal, conspiratorial, megalomaniacal. The terrors of warfare and the disordered personalities encountered in that film must be like a drug-induced bad trip; they are frighteningly real and their reality is seen and heard from a heightened perception.

Apocalypse Now seems to have marked the end of our need to deal with that painful conflict, at least in such direct, sustained, and apocalyptic form. Possibly we have been purged of some of our feelings about what is, from whatever political position it is viewed, one of the unhappiest chapters in our history. The films have fixed the images and sounds of these feelings; they can be returned to if ever we forget them.

ARTISTRY

It is particularly arbitrary, and chancy, to attempt to pick film makers so close to the present in terms of the lasting artistic interest and value of their films. There is little difficulty, however, in deciding whose films have been widely popular during recent years. A list of that sort would include Woody Allen, Sydney Pollack, Brian De Palma, Alan J. Pakula, George Lucas, and Steven Spielberg, listed in the order in which they began directing.

With *Annie Hall* (1977) Woody Allen hit full stride with his own special and highly personal brand of humor. Based in New York City, it draws on Jewishness and

Annie Hall (U.S., 1977, Woody Allen). Museum of Modern Art/Film Stills Archive.

psychoanalysis, and offers in-jokes about other films. But most essential to it are the gentle, true, and amusing revelations about certain (male intellectual) sexual insecurities and inadequacies. *Manhattan* (1980), in black and white Panavision, is more of the same at the same high level of exact observation presented in the perfect nuances of Allen's and Diane Keaton's performances.

Zelig (1983) offered a new and bold line of comic invention. Allen plays Leonard Zelig, the "Chameleon Man," who takes on the identities and abilities of those around him—whatever groups he happens to be associating with at the moment; for example, physicians, politicians, black jazz musicians. It is a delicious satire of 1920s America with its flagpole sitters, home-run kings, movie stars, and gangsters. It is also a delightful parody of film styles and fashions, with re-created newsreels and home movies made and mixed so skillfully with the real thing that it's hard to tell them apart. *Zelig* is more than Allen's usual chic clowning; it is as if he had become a kindly Jonathan Swift trying to characterize an age and a culture.

Sydney Pollack also achieved a different sort of distinction during this recent period. (*They Shoot Horses, Don't They?*, 1969, and *Jeremiah Johnson*, 1972, are earlier Pollack films that stick in mind.) *The Electric Horseman* (1979) brings together a broken-down rodeo star (Robert Redford), whose image is refurbished and plastered across the country to sell Ranch Breakfast cereal, and an aggressive New York television reporter (Jane Fonda), involved in a bit of investigative journalism. *Absence of Malice* (1981) concerns the legal profession and the excesses of investigative journalism. Paul Newman plays an innocent businessman whose reputation is ruined by publicity. *Tootsie* (1982) represents

Tootsie (U.S., 1982, Sydney Pollack). Museum of Modern Art/Film Stills Archive.

the climax of Pollack's directorial career to date. An unusual tour de force, it stars Dustin Hoffman as an unemployed (and seemingly unemployable) actor (Pollack playing his agent) who achieves influential success in the role of heroine in a daytime television serial. As a woman, a role he must maintain off-tube as well as on, he leads a minor crusade for more dignity and equality of treatment for females. Given a subject that might have been played for easy laughs, *Tootsie* is especially impressive for its taste and intelligence. What is being laughed at is true of American male-female behavior (and also of those in theater and television), and all the funnier for that.

Brian De Palma is another kind of film maker altogether. His forte has been the skillfully made and highly manipulative thriller dealing with the bizarre and inexplicable—*The Fury* (1978), three people with occult powers—or the bizarre and explicable—*Dressed to Kill* (1980), a transvestite homicidal maniac. The latter, very successful commercially, was felt by many to be peculiarly nasty in the way it plays with violence to women. What else might be said of the film and of De Palma's work generally—and that of the other so-called movie brats (Francis Coppola, George Lucas, Martin Scorsese, Steven Spielberg, John Milius)—is that De Palma obviously has seen and understood thoroughly a lot of films. Movie genres and movie techniques seem to be what his films are about. His work includes many homages to Hitchcock; *Dressed to Kill* opens with Angie Dickinson in the shower, shot in a way to remind us of the shower scene in *Psycho*. Though with *Scarface* (1983) De Palma moved out of the thriller, it was to remake Howard Hawks's gangster film of 1932. It is the form of his movies more than their substance that seems to interest him. If his films are derivative, their fascination must be acknowledged. A lot of us respond to that form.

Alan J. Pakula began film making as a producer and generally produces the films he directs. They have been noteworthy for their sophistication, seeming to come from an especially modern sensibility and to be dealing with problems of deep current concern. Earlier Pakula films had as subjects loveless sexuality, violence, and fear, in *Klute* (1971); political assassination, in *The Parallax View* (1974); and political culpability, in *All the President's Men* (1976). During this final period he has made: *Comes a Horse-*

Dressed to Kill (U.S., 1980, Brian De Palma). Museum of Modern Art/Film Stills Archive.

man (1978), about pollution and destruction of the land; *Starting Over* (1979), divorce and a new life; *Rollover* (1981), international high finance and Arab oil money; and *Sophie's Choice* (1982), the effects of Nazi concentration camps on their survivors, and mental unbalance. Pakula's work is also noteworthy for the way in which a very sure sense of narrative and performance is combined with an elegant and precise visual sensitivity. *Sophie's Choice,* from the novel by William Styron, seems an ultimate achievement of type: a "literary" film that communicates its feeling for literature through affecting performances, images, and accompanying sounds. Artistic control, used to bring out most from the subject, is marked in all of Pakula's work.

George Lucas's career has been rather the other way round from Pakula's. Beginning as a director (*THX-1138,* 1971; *American Grafitti,* 1973; *Star Wars,* 1977), Lucas became a producer (*The Empire Strikes Back,* 1980; *Raiders of the Lost Ark,* 1981; *Return of the Jedi,* 1983). He heads his own company, Lucasfilm, Ltd., north of San Francisco, with its subsidiary company, Industrial Light and Magic, responsible for the special effects on his films and those of others. Whether he writes, directs, or produces, Lucas seems to control the conception of the films coming out of Lucasfilm. In the *Star Wars* trilogy his conception is of a mythical universe set in a future time but embodying elements from the past. In a sense the past of myth and fairy tale dominates; good rises to combat evil, voyages are undertaken, monsters are encountered and slain, magic is invoked, right overcomes might. Aside from the charm and the very great technical skill evident in the creation of this illusionary world, the most remarkable thing about these

Sophie's Choice (U.S., 1982, Alan J. Pakula). Museum of Modern Art/Film Stills Archive.

Star Wars (U.S., 1977, George Lucas). Museum of Modern Art/Film Stills Archive.

three films is the obvious appeal they have had for millions of people scattered around the globe. Taken together they have earned more money—that is to say, have been seen by more people—than any other three films ever made. The need for myths that confirm our values—not as readily available to us as they used to be—is clearly something a very great many of us have. The films Lucas has made seem designed to meet that need.

Steven Spielberg shares Lucas's predilection and talent for popular mythology. The phenomenal popularity of *Jaws* (1975), a dark myth about a white shark preying on a seaside community, fixed the direction his career would subsequently take. Its success was repeated with *Close Encounters of the Third Kind* (1977), about an average guy who comes in contact with creatures from another planet. His comedy *1941* (1979), set in California in the year we entered World War II, was unsuccessful—because it was unfunny, many said. With *Raiders of the Lost Ark* (1981), a rousing, globe-circling action-adventure full of derring-do, he was back on track. *E. T.* (1982), with its lovable extra-terrestrial in the midst of suburbia, achieved some sort of ultimate in popularity. The mythic content of the Spielberg films made within this last period is like that of Lucas's in its reassurance. If anything, the myths are even more benign; alien creatures who visit earth are well intentioned and pleasant company. A second point that might be made about Spielberg's films is that they grow out of the same sort of familiarity with movies that characterizes the "film generation," both the makers and the viewers. Spielberg seems quite content—thinks it proper, even necessary perhaps—to make his films within standard genres. Furthermore, he employs the familiar, the clichéd, with knowing and affectionate expertise; his films are full of "quotes" from other films. They are movie-movies, as a student film maker might say about them.

E.T. (U.S., 1982, Steven Spielberg). National Film Archive London.

It is not only salutary that we now have film makers and audiences who know film history; it is significant. Today artists in all the arts know what preceded them, and make use of it; even to reject the past we must know it. On the other hand, though historical knowledge clearly offers advantages, it has drawbacks too. Modern creators sometimes feel weighed down by the past; feeling that every artistic statement has been made, they are discouraged in their own efforts. This is one of the recognized aspects of modernism in the arts. It seems not yet to have happened in the newest art; there still is much joy in discovering the movies' past and making use of it, in telling movie stories in the ways they can best be told.

Not only are films from the past increasingly available for study, so also are those from present foreign cultures. The metaphor pursued in this book of a country stepping into the international spotlight with a particularly innovative national contribution to the evolution of film art has to be modified. Instead of more or less separable national developments, we now have films from any country reaching audiences in any other—if not always easily, certainly more readily than ever before.

As the old industry and old audiences give way to the new, individual artists are at last beginning to receive the recognition in film they have always had in the other arts. Still, the motion picture remains an awesomely difficult medium in which to create. The very characteristics that distinguish it from the older arts often impede the artist: the massive and complex technology, the demands of high finance, the necessity for a huge and diverse audience. But, as the film made for theaters has yielded to television its place as mass entertainer, and as the rigid production-distribution-exhibition systems have been shaken and cracked in many places, art of a new seriousness and difficulty, greater originality and individuality, has begun to appear.

The flexible and subtle eloquence of modern film has built upon those periods of great national creativity surveyed in this history. The capacity of the medium for handling widely varied personal expression has been added to, bit by bit. Along with the ever-growing richness of the new, it is a further boon that we are able to go back and review the old through the work of film archives and museums, film history courses, and retrospective series. In art there is rarely progress, only change. The works of Griffith, Murnau, and Eisenstein are no less valuable now than when they were created. Each generation of viewers can find something new in them, sometimes more than was seen by the original audiences; Kurosawa, Bergman, Resnais, Antonioni, Losey, Wajda, and Altman have replaced no one. Knowing as much as we can of the sum total of cinema helps us to better appreciate the work of every film maker and each individual work. That is the use of the history of film.

FILMS OF THE PERIOD

1977
Annie Hall (Woody Allen)
Bobby Deerfield (Sidney Pollack)
Close Encounters of the Third Kind
   (Steven Spielberg)
Star Wars (George Lucas)

1978
Comes a Horseman (Alan J. Pakula)
The Fury (Brian De Palma)
Interiors (Allen)

1979
The Electric Horseman (Pollack)
Home Movies (De Palma)
Manhattan (Allen)
1941 (Spielberg)
Starting Over (Pakula)

1980
Dressed to Kill (De Palma)

The Empire Strikes Back (Irvin Kershner)
Stardust Memories (Allen)

1981
Absence of Malice (Pollack)
Blow Out (De Palma)
Raiders of the Lost Ark (Spielberg)
Rollover (Pakula)

1982
E. T. (Spielberg)
A Midsummer Night's Sex Comedy
   (Allen)
Sophie's Choice (Pakula)
Tootsie (Pollack)

1983
Return of the Jedi (Richard Marquand)
Scarface (De Palma)
Zelig (Allen)

BOOKS ON THE PERIOD

ADAIR, GILBERT,   *Hollywood's Vietnam*. New York: Proteus, 1983. 192 pp.
BLUM, DANIEL,   *A New Pictorial History of the Talkies,* rev. and enlarged by John Kobal. New York:
   G. P. Putnam's Sons, 1982.

Keyser, Lester,   *Hollywood in the Seventies.* Cranbury, N. J.: A. S. Barnes & Co., Inc., 1981.

Kindem, Gorham, ed.,   *The American Movie Industry: The Business of Motion Pictures.* Carbondale and Edwardsville: Southern Illinois University Press, 1982. 448 pp.

Monaco, James,   *American Film Now: The People, The Power, The Money, The Movies.* New York: Oxford University Press, 1979. 540 pp.

Pye, Michael and Linda Miles,   *The Movie Brats: How the Film Generation Took Over Hollywood.* New York: Holt, Rinehart, & Winston, 1979.

INDEX

Abbott and Costello Meet Frankenstein, 191
Abbott and Costello Meet the Invisible Man, 191
Absence of Malice, 425
Abyss, The, 99
Academy of Film and Dramatic Art (Hungary), 351
Academy of Motion Picture Arts and Sciences, awards, 220, 223, 294, 312, 317, 355, 377, 383
Accatone!, 338
Accident, 373
Ace in the Hole, 218, 289
Actor's Revenge, An, 261
Actress, The, 286
Adam's Rib
    (1923), 137
    (1949), 286
Adventurer, The, 70
Adventures of Dollie, The, 43
Adventures of Robin Hood, The, 198, 231
Adventures of Robinson Crusoe, The, 309
Adventurous Automobile Trip, An, 66
Advise and Consent, 388
Affairs of Anatol, The, 137
Affair to Remember, An, 385
African Queen, The, 233–234, 363
Age d'or, L', 128, 309
Agee, James, 141–142, 233
Agnus Dei, 352
Aguirre, the Wrath of God, 413–414
Air Force, 218
Ajantrik, 267

Aldrich, Robert, 6, 392–394
Alea, Tomás Gutiérrez, 407
Alexander Nevsky, 117
Alice Adams, 287
Alice Doesn't Live Here Anymore, 402
Alice in the Cities, 414
Alice's Restaurant, 395
Ali: Fear Eats the Soul, 387, 413
Allegro Barbaro, 353
Allen, Dede, 5
Allen, Woody, 5, 142, 424–425
Allied Artists Pictures Corporation, 180
All Quiet on the Western Front, 159
All That Heaven Allows, 387
All That Jazz, 185
All the King's Men, 220–221
All the President's Men, 426
Almendros, Nestor, 5
Alone on the Pacific, 260–261
Alphaville, 319
Altered States, 372
Altman, Rick, 229
Altman, Robert, 385, 395, 399–400, 401
Alton, John, 96
Alvarez, Santiago, 406–407
Amarcord, 331
American Cinema: Directors and Directions 1929–1968, The, 199, 383–394
American Film Institute, 7
American Friend, The, 414–415
American Grafitti, 427
American in Paris, An, 294, 295, 389

American Pop, 197
Amidei, Sergio, 238
Amour en fuite, L', 316
Amour fou, L', 321
Anatahan, 384
Anderson, Joseph L., 252, 253
Anderson, Lindsay, 166, 311, 364, 365, 367
Anderson, Michael, 363
And God Created Woman, 312
Andrei Rublev, 344, 345
Andrews, Dana, 227
Anemic Cinema, 127
Anges du péché, Les, 303
Animal Crackers, 192
animated cartoon, 184, 195–198
Ankur, 267
Anna Boleyn. See Deception
Anna Christie, 158
Another Way, 353
À nous la liberté, 161, 165
Anschütz, Ottomar, 22
Antonio das Mortes, 408
Antonioni, Michelangelo, 4, 6, 246, 281, 327–328, 329, 333–335, 339
Apache, 394
Aparajito, 265
Apartment, The, 290–291
Apocalypse Now, 398, 423–424
À propos de Nice, 130
Arabian Nights, The, 338
Arbuckle, Roscoe "Fatty," 66, 182

Argent, L', 304
Argentina, films of, 409, 418, 420
Arletty, 168, 172
Armat, Thomas, 22, 26
Armstrong, Gill, 417
Arnheim, Rudolf, 155, 278
Arrival of a Train at the Station, The, 32
Arroseur arrosé, L', 26, 33–34
Arsenal, 110
Ars Magna Lucis et Umbrae, 11
Artaud, Antonin, 128
Arthur, Jean, 202, 288
Artists at the Top of the Big Top: Dis-oriented, 412
"Art of Cineplastics, The," 127
Aryan, The, 141
Ashby, Hal, 423
Ashes and Diamonds, 346–347
Asphalt Jungle, The, 189, 233
Asquith, Anthony, 104–105, 208
Assassination of the Duc de Guise, The, 48–49
Astaire, Fred, 187, 287, 294
Astor, Mary, 232
Astruc, Alexandre, 301, 311, 312
Atalante, L', 166, 167
Atlantic City, 323
Attack!, 392, 393, 394
Au hasard, Balthasar, 304
Aurenche, Jean, 300
Aurthur, Robert Alan, 273
Australia, films of, 416–417, 418, 420
Autant-Lara, Claude, 300
auteur theory, 6, 199, 300–303, 305, 311, 323–324, 382–394
Autobiography of a Princess, 268
Autumn Leaves, 393
Autumn Sonata, 5
avant-garde, 37, 89, 123, 124, 125, 126–130, 150, 156, 167–168, 309
Aviator's Wife, The, 322
Avventura, L', 4, 246, 327, 328, 333–335, 339
Awful Truth, The, 194
Aznavour, Charles, 314, 315

Babenco, Hector, 409
Baby Doll, 296
Bacall, Lauren, 223
Bachelor Party, The, 273
Backstairs, 91
Bacon, Lloyd, 185, 186
Bad and the Beautiful, The, 294, 389
Bad Timing, 378, 379
Bailiff, The. See Sansho Dayu
Baker's Wife, The, 167, 168, 171, 172
Bakshi, Ralph, 197
Balaban & Katz, 134
Balcon, Michael, 213–214
Ballad of a Soldier, 107
Ballad of Cable Hogue, The, 397
Ballad of Narayama, The, 260
Ballet mécanique, 127, 128
Ball of Fire, 194, 195, 289
Band of Outsiders, 281, 318, 319

Bandwagon, The, 294, 389
Bank Holiday, 208
Banky, Vilma, 158
Bara, Theda, 74
Baranovskaya, Vera, 119
Barber Shop, The, 193
Bardot, Brigitte, 312
Barkleys of Broadway, The, 187
Barney Oldfield's Race for Life, 68
Barnouw, Erik, 264
Barrault, Jean-Louis, 168
Barren Lives, 407
Barrier, 349
Barry Lyndon, 375
Barrymore, John, 151, 202
Barrymore, Lionel, 158–159
Bataan, 218
Battle, The, 60
Battle of Chile, The, 410, 411
Battle of San Pietro, The, 232–233
Battle of the River Plate, The, 363
Baur, Harry, 168, 171
Baxter, Warner, 185
Bazin, André, 2, 278, 302–303, 315, 382
Beatles, 376
Beau Serge, Le, 312, 313
Beauty and the Beast, 130
Beauty and the Bolshevik, The. See Kombrig Ivanov
Becker, Jacques, 301, 312
Becky Sharp, 198
Bed and Board, 316
Bed and Sofa, 107
Bed Sitting Room, The, 376
Beery, Wallace, 27, 158
Before the Revolution, 338
Beineix, Jean-Jacques, 323
Belle de jour, 310
Belle Équipe, La, 168, 170, 174
Bells of St. Mary's, The, 218
Belmondo, Jean-Paul, 315, 319
Benegal, Shyam, 267
Ben-Hur, 135, 147
Bennett, Charles, 70
Bennett, Joan, 219
Benoit-Levy, Jean, 165–166
Benton, Robert, 396
Beresford, Bruce, 417
Bergman, Ingmar, 4–5, 80, 81, 83, 84, 303, 304–308, 311, 312, 328, 332
Bergman, Ingrid, 4–5, 225, 231
Berkeley, Busby, 158, 185–186
Berlin: Symphony of a Great City, 129
Bernhardt, Sarah, 47–48
Bertolucci, Bernardo, 337, 338–339
Bessie, Alvah, 223
Best Years of Our Lives, The, 220, 227, 228
Bête humaine. See Human Beast, The
Betts, Ernest, 155
Bhumika, 267
Bhuvan Shome, 267
Biberman, Herbert, 223
Biches, Les, 320
Bicycle Thief, The, 241–243, 244, 245, 246, 247, 265, 331

Bidone, Il, 331
Big Carnival, The. See Ace in the Hole
Big City, The. See Mahanagar
Big Fisherman, The, 384
Big Knife, The, 394
Big Parade, The, 145
Big Red One, The, 392
Big Sleep, The, 219
Bill of Divorcement, A, 286
Billy Liar, 367
Biograph (American Mutoscope and Biograph Company), 53, 72
Birds, The, 384
Birinski, Leo, 101
Birth of a Nation, The, 28, 43, 45, 46, 53, 54–61, 63, 64, 84, 117, 133, 135, 228
Bitter Rice, 244
Bitter Tears of Petra von Kant, The, 413
Bitter Victory, 386
Bitzer, G. W. "Billy," 5, 46, 65
Black Girl, 411, 412
Black God, White Devil, 408
blacklisting, Hollywood, 224–225
Blackmail, 148, 161, 225
"Black Maria," 23–24
Black Orpheus, 312
Black Peter, 354
Black Pirate, The, 146
Black River, 261
Blanchar, Pierre, 168, 171
Blind Date, 372
Blind Husbands, 139
Blithe Spirit, 363
Blood of a Poet, The, 130
Blood of the Condor, 409–410
Blow-Up, 4, 281, 328–329
Blue Angel, The, 156, 161
Blue Bird, The, 385
Blum-Byrnes agreement, 311
Bluth, Don, 197
Boccaccio 70, 332
Body Snatcher, The, 5, 192
Boetticher, Budd, 204
Bogart, Humphrey, 176, 223, 231, 232, 233, 290
Bogdanovich, Peter, 311
Bolivia, films of, 409–410, 418, 420
Bombay Talkie, 268
Bond, James, cycle, 363
Bonnes Femmes, Les, 313, 321
Bonnie and Clyde, 189, 385, 394–395, 396
Boomerang, 220, 222, 296
Boorman, John, 372
Borau, Jose Luis, 415
Border, The, 372
Border Street, 346
Born Yesterday, 286
Borzage, Frank, 136, 384–385
Bost, Pierre, 300
Boucher, Le, 320
Boudu Saved from Drowning, 166, 172–173, 176
Bowie, David, 378
Boxcar Bertha, 401
Boy, 263

Boy Friend, The, 371
Bracken, Eddie, 228
Brackett, Charles, 194, 289
Brando, Marlon, 296
Brasseur, Pierre, 168
Brazil, films of, 407–409
Breaker Morant, 417
Breakfast at Sunrise, 143
Breathless, 313, 314, 315, 318, 319
Breen, Joseph I., 183
Brent, George, 185
Bresson, Robert, 6, 301, 303–305, 306, 311, 312
Brewster McCloud, 399, 400
Brides of Dracula, The, 369
Bride Wore Black, The, 315
Bridge on the River Kwai, The, 273, 280–281, 363
Brief Encounter, 363
Briel, Joseph Carl, 54, 63
Brigadoon, 294
Brighton School, 42, 43
Bringing Up Baby, 194–195, 202
Bring Me the Head of Alfredo Garcia, 397
Britannia Hospital, 367
British Sounds. See See You at Mao
Broken Blossoms, 53, 97
Brown, Clarence, 144
Brown, Joe E., 158, 290
Brute Force, 222
Buffalo Bill and the Indians, 400
Bugs Bunny, 197
Bunny, John, 74
Buñuel, Luis, 80, 125, 128, 129, 130, 303, 308–311
Burch, Noël, 250
Burgess, Anthony, 374
Burmese Harp, The, 260, 261
Burstyn, Ellen, 402
Bushman, Francis X., 74
Butch Cassidy and the Sundance Kid, 400
Butch Cassidy and the Sundance Kid—The Early Days, 376
Bwana Devil, 275
Bye Bye Brazil, 409
By the Law, 109

Cabinet of Dr. Caligari, The, 87, 89–90, 91, 97, 100, 124
Cabin in the Sky, 293
Cabiria, 48, 49
Cagney, James, 156, 190, 208, 231, 291
Cahiers du Cinéma, 199, 300–303, 305, 311, 312, 313, 315, 382
California Split, 400
Call Northside 777, 220, 222
Calm Before the Storm, The, 349
Camera Buff, 349
camera obscura, 11, 14, 15
Camille, 158, 286
Cammell, Donald, 378
Camouflage, 349, 350
Campbell, Eric, 70
Camus, Marcel, 312
Cannes International Film Festival, 249, 312–313, 327, 416

Cantata, 352
Canterbury Tales, The, 338
Canudo, Ricciotto, 126, 127
Capra, Frank, 159, 178, 194, 385, 200, 202–203
Captain Blood, 198, 231
Captains Courageous, 198
Carabiniers, Les, 317
Cardinal, The, 388
Carmen Comes Home, 259
Carnal Knowledge, 284
Carné, Marcel, 168–169, 171–172, 174–175, 177, 219, 300
Carnet de bal, 167, 168, 170, 171
Carnival in Flanders, 167, 169–170
Caron, Leslie, 294, 295
Carpenter, John, 192
Carrie, 227
Carry On series, 363
Casablanca, 217, 231, 232
Casanova. See Fellini's Casanova
Casino Royale, 367
Catered Affair, The, 273
Cat People, 5, 191–192
Cavalcanti, Alberto, 124–125, 129, 214
Cayrol, Jean, 317
Ceddo, 411
Celine and Julie Go Boating, 321, 322
censorship, U.S. See self-regulation, U.S.
Ceremony, The, 263
César, 165
Chabrol, Claude, 6, 311, 312, 313, 315, 320, 321
Chairy Tale, A, 19
Chaliapin, Fyodor, 156
Chance Meeting. See Blind Date
Chandler, Raymond, 218
Chang, 146
Chant of Jimmie Blacksmith, The, 417
Chapayev, 343
Chaplin, Charles, 53, 66, 69, 70–71, 74, 124, 133, 142, 156, 158, 171, 196, 265, 382, 383
Charge at Feather River, The, 275
Charge of the Light Brigade, The (1936), 231 (1968), 372
Chariots of Fire, 377
Charisse, Cyd, 294
Charulata, 266
Chase, The, 395
Chayefsky, Paddy, 273
Chess Players, The, 266
Chevalier, Maurice, 185
Cheyenne Autumn, 383
chien Andalou, Un, 124, 128, 129, 130, 309
Chienne, La, 172
Children Are Watching Us, The, 241
Children of Hiroshima, 260
Chile, films of, 410–411, 418, 420
Chimes at Midnight. See Falstaff
China, films of, 248, 249
China Doll, 384
China Gate, 392
Chinatown, 349

Chinoise, La, 319
Chloe in the Afternoon, 313
Chretien, Henri, 277
Christensen, Benjamin, 78, 79
Christie, Julie, 367, 378
Christ Stopped at Eboli, 336–337
Chronicle of Anna Magdalena Bach, 413
Chronicle of the Gray House, The, 97, 98
Churning, The. See Manthan
Chuvelyov, Ivan, 119
Chytilová, Věra, 354
Cimarron, 184
Cimino, Michael, 423
Cinderella, 35
cine-clubs, 124, 127
Cine Liberacion, 409
Cinema and Society, 101
Cinema Nôvo, 407–408
CinemaScope, 45, 65, 197, 277–278, 286
Cinémathèque Française, 7, 301
Cinematografia Tercer Mundo, 410
Cinématographe, Le, 25–26
cinéma vérité, 107
Cinerama, 125, 275, 276–277
Circumstance, The, 336
Citizen Kane, 217, 228–230, 294, 302, 333, 384
City Lights, 158
City of Women, 331
"city symphonies," 128–129
Clair, René, 130, 161, 165
Claire's Knee, 313
Clarke, Arthur, 374
Clarke, T. E. B., 214
classification/rating system, U.S. See self-regulation, U.S.
Clayton, Jack, 365
Clement, René, 300
Clift, Montgomery, 288, 293
Clock, The, 293
Clockmaker, The, 323
Clockwork Orange, A, 374, 375
Cloquet, Ghislain, 324
Close Encounters of the Third Kind, 421, 428
Closely Watched Trains, 355, 356
Close Quarters, 209
Clowns, The, 331
Coastal Command, 209
Cobb, Lee J., 296
Cobweb, The, 389
Cocoanuts, The, 192
Cocteau, Jean, 126, 130, 277, 301, 303
Coeur fidèle, 125
Cohl, Emile, 66
Cohn, Harry and Jack, 133
Colbert, Claudette, 194
Cold Days, 351
Cole, Lester, 223
Collins, Roy, 230
Colman, Ronald, 144
Color of Pomegranates, The, 345
Columbia Pictures, Inc., 133, 180, 273, 281, 421
Come Back to the Five & Dime Jimmy Dean, Jimmy Dean, 400

comedy
Ealing, 213–214
silent, U.S., 65–71, 139, 141–142, 148, 184
sound, U.S., 184, 192–195
"Comedy's Greatest Era," 141–142
Comes a Horseman, 426–427
Coming Home, 423
"Coming of Sound to the American Cinema: A History of the Transformation of an Industry, The," 151
Committee for the First Amendment, 223–224
communism, in Hollywood, 222–225
Concrete Jungle, The. See *Criminal, The*
Confessions of Winifred Wagner, The, 415
Confidence, 353
Conformist, The, 338–339
Confrontation, The, 352
Conklin, Chester, 66
Conquest of the Pole, The, 35
Contempt, 319
Contract, The, 349
Conversation, The, 398
Conversation Piece, 329–330
Cook, Elisha, Jr., 219
Cool Hand Luke, 394–395
Cooper, Gary, 156, 194, 202, 208, 223, 290, 293
Cooper, Merian C., 276
Coppola, Francis Ford, 126, 395, 398–399, 400–401, 402, 423, 426
Corman, Roger, 192, 398, 401
Cornelius, Henry, 214
Cossacks of the Don, 105
Cotton, Joseph, 225, 230
Courage for Everyday, 356
Courant, Kurt, 101
Cousin Angelica, 415
Cousins, The, 313
Coutard, Raoul, 5
Covered Wagon, The, 68, 141, 142
Coward, Noël, 209
Cranes Are Flying, The, 107
Crawford, Joan, 231, 286
Crichton, Charles, 214
Cries and Whispers, 307
Crime of Monsieur Lange, The, 173, 176
Criminal, The, 372–373
Crisis, 305
Cromwell, John, 158
Crosby, Floyd, 292
Crosland, Alan, 153
Crossfire, 220, 222
Cross of Iron, 397
Crowd, The, 144, 154
Crown Film Unit, 209, 214
Cruel Sea, The, 363
Crusades, The, 87–88
Cruze, James, 136, 141, 142
Cry of the City, 219
Cuba, films of, 406–407, 418–419, 420
Cukor, George, 158, 286–287, 385
Cul de Sac, 349
Cure, The, 70, 71
Curse of Frankenstein, The, 368–369

Curtis, Tony, 290
Curtiss, Thomas Quinn, 139
Curtiz, Michael, 219, 225, 231–232, 234
Cushing, Peter, 369
Cutter's Way, 357
Cybulski, Zbigniew, 347
Czechoslovakia, films of, 197, 346, 354–357, 359

Daffy Duck, 197
Dagover, Lil, 99
Daguerre, Louis, 16
daguerreotype, 16–17
Daie Motion Picture Company, 250
Daisies, 354
Dali, Salvador, 128, 129, 130, 309
Dam Busters, The, 363
Dames du bois de Boulogne, Les, 303
Damned, The
(1961), 373
(1969), 329
Dance of the Seven Veils: A Comic Strip in Seven Episodes in the Life of Richard Strauss, The, 370
Daniels, Bebe, 185
D'Annunzio, Gabriele, 49
Dante's Inferno
(1911), 49
(1967), 370
Danton, 351
Daring Youth, 143
Darling, 324, 367
David Copperfield, 198, 286
Davis, Bette, 156, 208
Dawn Patrol, The, 201–202
Daybreak. See *Jour se lève, Le*
Day for Night, 315, 316
Day in the Country, A, 166, 171, 282
Day of Wrath, 79, 80
Days and Nights in the Forest, 266
Days of Heaven, 5
Dead End, 227
Deadly Companions, 396
Dean, James, 296, 386
Death by Hanging, 262, 263
Death in Venice, 329
Death of a Salesman, 221
Death Watch, 323
Debussy Film, The, 370
Decameron, The, 338
Deception, 87, 139
Deep End, 349
Deep Throat, 284
Deer Hunter, The, 423
de Forest, Lee, 151
Delaney, Shelagh, 365
Delannoy, Jean, 300
Deliverance, 372
Delluc, Louis, 123–124, 125, 127, 128, 382
Demarest, William, 227
Dementia 13, 398, 401
De Mille, Cecil B., 27, 49, 81, 87–88, 136–138, 139, 142, 146–147, 384

Demy, Jacques, 323
Deneuve, Catherine, 316
De Niro, Robert, 401, 402–403
Denmark, films of, 77–81, 84, 85, 99
De Palma, Brian, 192, 424, 426
Depardieu, Gérard, 316
Depart, Le, 349
de Putti, Lya, 101
Deren, Maya, 129–130
Dern, Bruce, 423
de Rochemont, Louis, 221–222, 276
Dersu Uzala, 256
Destination Moon, 188
Destiny, 88
Detective Story, 227
Devi, 266
Devil in the Flesh, 300
Devil Is a Woman, The, 200, 310
Devil Rides Out, The, 369, 370
Devils, The, 349, 371
Devil's Bride, The. See *Devil Rides Out, The*
Devil's Canyon, 275
de Wilde, Brandon, 288
Dial M for Murder, 275
Diamond, I. A. L., 290
Diamonds of the Night, 354
Diary for Timothy, A, 210
Diary of a Chambermaid, 310
Diary of a Country Priest, 303–304, 305
Diary of a Shinjuku Thief, 262–263
Dickinson, Angie, 426
Dickson, W. K. L., 22–24, 151
Diegues, Carlos, 409
Dietrich, Marlene, 156, 200, 201
Dinner at Eight, 286
Directors Guild of America, 6
Dirty Dozen, The, 394
Discreet Charm of the Bourgeoisie, The, 310
Dishonored, 200
Disney, Walt, 196–198, 224. See also Walt Disney Productions
Distant Thunder, 267
distribution, U.S., 75, 133–134, 179–182, 271, 272, 279, 281–282
Diva, 323
Dmytryk, Edward, 219, 220, 223
Doctor Zhivago, 278
documentary, 107–108, 121, 146, 188, 208, 209, 214–215, 367–368
Dolce Vita, La, 327, 328, 331–332, 333
Dona Flor and Her Two Husbands, 409
Donald Duck, 196
Donat, Robert, 22
Donen, Stanley, 301, 324
Don Giovanni, 374
Doniol-Valcroze, Jacques, 311
Don Juan
(1926), 151, 152
(c. 1954), 282
Don Quixote, 156
Don't Change Your Husband, 137
Don't Look Now, 378

dos Santos, Nelson Pereira, 407–408
Double Indemnity, 102, 218–219, 289
Double Life, A, 286
Double Suicide, 260
Douglas, Kirk, 218, 294
Dovzhenko, Alexander, 110–112, 113, 117
Dracula
  (1931), 102, 191
  (1957), 369
Draughtsman's Contract, The, 377
Dream of a Rarebit Fiend, The, 42
Dressed to Kill, 426
Dressler, Marie, 70, 158
Dreyer, Carl Theodor, 79–81, 82–83, 304
Dr. Mabuse, the Gambler, 124
Dr. Strangelove, or: How I Learned to Stop Worrying and Love the Bomb, 374
Duchamp, Marcel, 127, 130
Dulac, Germaine, 124, 128, 130
Dunne, Irene, 194
Dunne, Philip, 223
Dupont, E. A., 94, 101
Duport, Catherine, 349
Durante, Jimmy, 158
Duras, Marguerite, 313, 317
Duvivier, Julien, 165–166, 167, 168, 170–171
Dwan, Alan, 146

Ealing Studios, 209, 213–214, 378
Earth, 110–112
Eastman, George, 22
Eastman Color, 250, 271
Eastman House, George, 7
East of Eden, 277, 296
Easy Rider, 395
Easy Street, 70
Eclipse, The, 328, 333
Eddy, Nelson, 185
Edge of the City, 273
Edinburgh International Film Festival, 249, 387, 392
Edison, Thomas A., 14, 22–26, 150–151
Edison Manufacturing Company, 32–34, 37, 40, 47, 66, 72
Educating Rita, 377
Edwards, Blake, 389–390
Eggeling, Viking, 89, 127
8½, 328, 331, 332, 339, 343
Eisenstein, Sergei, 4, 5, 65, 108–110, 113–117, 119–120, 126, 157, 230, 278, 301, 329, 334–335
Eisner, Lotte, 91
El, 309
El Dorado (1967), 384
Eldorado (1921), 124
Electric Horseman, The, 425
Elusive Corporal, The, 384
Emak Bakia, 130
Emperor of the North Pole, 393
Empire Strikes Back, The, 421, 427
End of St. Petersburg, The, 113, 119
Enjo, 260

Enoch Arden, 45
Entertainer, The, 365
Entr'acte, 130
Epstein, Jean, 124, 125, 309
Erice, Victor, 415
Ericson, Leif, 296
Eroica, 348
Erotikon, 81
Essanay Film Manufacturing Company, 72
E.T., 429
Étoile de mer, L', 130
Eureka, 378
Europeans, The, 268
Europe 51, 330
Even Dwarfs Started Small, 413
Every Day Except Christmas, 365
Every Man for Himself. See *Sauve qui peut . . . La Vie*
Everything for Sale, 347
Eviction, The, 142
Ewell, Tom, 290
Ex-Convict, The, 105
Execution of Mary Queen of Scots, The, 146
exhibition, U.S., 75, 133–134, 179–182, 271–272
Exodus, 388
Exorcist, The, 249
Expressionism, 87, 88–91, 96, 97, 101, 124
Exterminating Angel, The, 309–310

Fábri, Zoltán, 351
Face in the Crowd, A, 296
Fahrenheit 451, 378
Fairbanks, Douglas, 71, 74, 133, 146, 382
Fairbanks, Douglas, Jr., 189
Falcons, The, 351
Fallen Angel, 219
Fallen Idol, The, 363
Fall of Babylon, The, 64
Fall of the House of Usher, The
  (1928), 125
  (1960), 192
Fall of Troy, The, 49
False Movement, 414
Falstaff, 384
Family Life, 349
Family Plot, 384
Famous Players Film Company, 48
Famous Players-Lasky Corporation, 133, 141
Fanny, 165
Fanny and Alexander, 307–308
Fantasia, 197
Fantomas, 124
Far Country, The, 390
Far from the Madding Crowd, 378
Fassbinder, Rainer Werner, 387, 413, 414
Father of the Bride, 293
Faure, Elie, 127
Fear and Desire, 374
Feeding the Baby, 32
Fellini, Federico, 6, 238, 241, 246, 282,

306, 327, 328, 329, 330–332, 333, 334, 335, 339, 343
Fellini Satyricon, 331
Fellini's Casanova, 331
Fellini's Roma, 331
Femme de nulle part, La, 124
Femme infidèle, La, 320
Fernandel, 171
Fête espagnole, La, 124
Feuillade, Louis, 124
FEX (Factory of the Eccentric Actor), 109–110
Feyder, Jacques, 168–170
F for Fake, 384
Fiancés, The, 246, 336
Fields, W. C., 5, 158, 192, 193
Fièvre, 124
Fille de l'eau, La, 130
Film Acting, 113
Film Answers Back, The, 100
Film as Art, 155
Film Culture, 382, 383
Film Daily, 220
film d'art, 47–48, 106, 124
Film Form, 119
film noir, 102, 218–220, 234, 289
Film Sense, The, 119–120
Film Technique, 113, 117, 118–119, 120
Film Till Now, The, 202–203, 383
Finch, Peter, 293
Fin du jour, La, 171
Finian's Rainbow, 398
Finis Terrae, 125
Finler, Joel, W., 139
Finney, Albert, 367
Fire!, 42
Firemen's Ball, The, 355
Fires on the Plain, 260
Fires Were Started, 209, 210–212, 213
First National Exhibitors' Circuit, 71, 134, 155
First Years, The, 410
Fisher, Terence, 369, 370
Fitzcarraldo, 414
Five Boys from Barska Street, 346
Flaherty, Robert J., 136, 139, 214, 265, 292, 383
Flaming Youth, 143
Flashdance, 185
Flesh and Fantasy, 171
Flesh and the Devil, 144, 145
Fletcher, John, 365–366
Flight of the Phoenix, 392, 394
Floating Clouds, 259
Flowers and Trees, 196, 197
Flying Down to Rio, 187
Flynn, Errol, 231
Folie du Docteur Tube, La, 125
Fonda, Henry, 227
Fonda, Jane, 423, 425
Foolish Wives, 68, 139
Fool's Paradise, 137
For Better or Worse, 137
Forbidden Fruit, 137
Forbidden Games, 300
Forbidden Paradise, 141
Ford, Aleksander, 346

Ford, John, 6, 136, 141, 147, 159–161, 200, 203–205, 253, 265, 301, 383
Foreign Correspondent, 225
Foreign Friend, The, 249
Foreman, Carl, 293
Foreman Went to France, The, 209
For Ladies Only, 143
Forman, Henry James, 183
Forman, Miloš, 354, 355, 357
Forsyth, Bill, 377–378
Forty Guns, 392
42nd Street, 185–187
Four Chimneys, 259
Four Friends, 395–396
400 Blows, The, 312–313, 315, 316
Four Nights of a Dreamer, 304
Fourteen Hours, 221
Fox, William, 133, 152, 155
Fox Film Corporation, 133, 134, 152, 155
Foy, Bryan, 154
France, films of
   silent, 32, 33–37, 47–50, 105, 123–131, 132, 150
   sound, 80, 161, 164–177, 219, 300–304, 309–326
Franju, Georges, 312
Frankenheimer, John, 274
Frankenstein, 102, 191, 192
Frederick, Pauline, 74
Fred Ott's Sneeze, 66
Free Cinema, 363, 364–366, 367
Freed, Arthur, 294
French Cancan, 383
French Lieutenant's Woman, The, 372
French They Are a Funny Race, The, 385
Frend, Charles, 214, 363
Frenzy, 4, 384
Freshman, The, 142
Freund, Karl, 5, 96, 101
Friedman v. Maryland, 283
Friends and Husbands, 413
Friese-Greene, William, 22
Fritz the Cat, 197
Frogmen, The, 222
From Caligari to Hitler: A Psychological History of the German Film, 92, 94, 100–101
From Here to Eternity, 293
Fuller, Samuel, 6, 301, 391–392
Fun in a Chinese Laundry, 32, 66
Funny Thing Happened on the Way to the Forum, A, 376
Furthman, Jules, 159
Fury, The, 426

Gaál, István, 351
Gabin, Jean, 168, 171–172, 174, 175–176
Gai Savoir, Le, 319
Gallipoli, 416–417
Game of Cards, A, 34
Gance, Abel, 53, 124, 125–126, 301
Gandhi, 377, 422
gangster film, 184, 187–190, 191, 192

Gangster Film: Emergence, Variation and Decay of a Genre, 1930-1940, The, 188–189
Garbo, Greta, 5, 81, 99, 144, 145, 158, 208, 286
Gardener, The, 81
Garfunkel, Art, 378
Garland, Judy, 286–287
Garner, James, 274
Garnett, Tay, 158
Gaslight, 286
Gate of Hell, 250, 251, 252, 259
Gauguin, 313
Gaumont Company, 34, 164
Gaynor, Janet, 286
General, The, 142, 143
General della Rovere, 246
General Film Company, 72
General Line, The, 108, 117, 329
General Post Office Film Unit, 214
General Teleradio, 273
Generation, A, 346–347
Genevieve, 214
genres, 73–74, 141–148, 184–199
Gentle Creature, A, 304
Gentleman's Agreement, 220, 222, 296
Gentlemen Prefer Blondes, 147, 277
Gerald McBoing Boing, 197
Gerlach, Arthur von, 97, 98
German Sisters, The, 413
Germany, films of
   silent, 77, 78, 79, 81–82, 83–84, 85, 86–105, 120–121, 123–124, 126, 132, 139, 150, 154, 174, 190–191
   sound, 161, 412–415, 419, 420
Germi, Pietro, 330
Gertie the Dinosaur, 196
Gertrud, 79, 80
Getaway, The, 397
Getino, Octavio, 409
Ghatak, Ritwik, 267
Giannini, Giancarlo, 340
Giant, 288–289
Gibson, Hoot, 141
Gigi, 294
Gilbert, John, 144, 145, 158
Girl from Lorraine, A, 323
Girl from the Marsh Croft, The, 83
Gish, Lillian, 45, 53, 56, 60–61, 62, 99
Goalie's Anxiety at the Penalty Kick, The, 414
Go-Between, The, 373–374
Godard, Jean-Luc, 5, 43, 281, 305, 311, 313, 314–315, 317, 318–320, 321, 349
Goddess, The (India). See *Devi*
Goddess, The (U.S.), 273
Godfather, The, 189, 398, 399, 421
God Needs Men, 300
Going My Way, 218
Gold Diggers series, 186
Golden Coach, The, 383
Gold Rush, The, 142
Goldwyn, Samuel, 5, 133, 143, 227, 276. See also Goldwyn Pictures Corporation; Samuel Goldwyn Productions

Goldwyn Pictures Corporation, 133. See also Goldwyn, Samuel; Samuel Goldwyn Productions
Golem, The, 90, 91, 97, 190
Golovnya, Anatoli, 109
Gomery, Douglas, 151
Gone with the Wind, 147, 285
Good Marriage, A, 322
Goofy, 196
Gordon, Ruth, 286
Goretta, Claude, 323, 365
Gosho, Heinosuke, 259
Gospel According to St. Matthew, The, 338
Go Tell the Spartans, 423
Gould, Elliott, 400
Graduate, The, 394–395
Grand Café, 25–26, 32
Grand Hotel, 158
Grand Illusion, The, 167, 173, 174, 176, 177
Grant, Cary, 194, 195, 202, 225
Grass, 146
Grease, 422
Great Britain. See United Kingdom
Great Dictator, The, 156
Greatest Show on Earth, The, 384
Greatest Story Ever Told, The, 385
Great Expectations, 363
Great McGinty, The, 227
Great Race, The, 390
Great Train Robbery, The, 39–41, 42, 44, 75, 95, 141, 167
Greed, 138–139, 140
Green Berets, The, 422–423
Greene, Graham, 363
Green Room, The, 317
Greenstreet, Sydney, 232
Gregory's Girl, 377
Grido, Il, 333
Grierson, John, 201, 208, 214, 244, 368
Griffith, Corinne, 158
Griffith, David Wark, 4, 5, 27, 42–46, 47, 48, 49, 53–65, 66, 68, 69, 70, 71, 73, 77, 78, 79, 83, 84, 95, 97, 98, 99, 100, 105, 112–113, 117, 120, 124, 125, 126, 133, 136, 139, 146, 147, 150, 230, 301, 383
Griffith, Richard, 202–203
Grim Reaper, The, 338
Grissom Gang, The, 393
Group 3, 214
Gruault, Jean, 317
Grune, Karl, 92
Guernica, 313
Guerra, Ruy, 407–408
Guerre est finie, La, 317
Guinness, Alec, 214
Gun Fighter, The (1916), 141
Gunfighter, The (1950), 204
Gunga Din, 287
Gunnar Hede's Saga, 81
Guns, The, 407
Guns of Navarone, The, 278
Guru, The, 268
Guy-Blaché, Alice, 34
Guzman, Patricio, 410, 411

Hackman, Gene, 378
Hail the Conquering Hero, 217, 228, 229
Hair, 357
Hallelujah!, 159
Hamlet, 363
Hammer Films, 368-370
Hammid, Alexander, 130
Hands Over the City, 246, 336, 337
Hands Up!, 349
Hannam, Ken, 416
Hanson, Einar, 92-94
Hanson, Lars, 81
Harakiri, 262
Hard Day's Night, A, 324, 376, 377
Hardy, Oliver, 69, 142, 158
Harlow, Jean, 194
Hart, William S., 73, 141
Harvest, 167, 171
Hatari!, 384
Hatful of Rain, A, 293
Hathaway, Henry, 219
Haunted Castle, The, 35
Haunted Screen: Expressionism in the German Cinema and the Influence of Max Reinhardt, The, 91
Haver, Ronald, 287
Hawks, Howard, 6, 136, 147, 194, 195, 200, 201-202, 203, 204, 219, 289, 301, 384, 426
Hawks and the Sparrows, The, 338
Hays, Will H., 151, 182
Heat and Dust, 268
Heaven's Gate, 422
Heavy Traffic, 197
Hecht, Ben, 194
Heflin, Van, 288
Heiress, The, 227
Hellinger, Mark, 222
Help!, 324, 376
Henry V, 212, 363
Hepburn, Audrey, 290, 293
Hepburn, Katharine, 194, 195, 202, 233, 286, 288
Hepworth, Cecil, 42
Heraclitus; or The Future of Films, 155
Heritage of Horror: The English Gothic Cinema, 1946-1972, A, 369
Herzog, Werner, 413-414
Heyl, Henry Renno, 19
High and Dry. See *Maggie, The*
High Noon, 204, 292-293
Hiroshima, mon amour, 313, 317, 318
His Girl Friday, 194
History Lessons, 413
His Trust, 46
Hitchcock, Alfred, 4, 5, 147-148, 161, 208, 219, 225-226, 227, 231, 234, 275, 301, 315, 320, 384, 426
Hitler, a Film from Germany, 415
Hoaxters, The, 223
Holden, William, 218, 289-290
Hole in the Head, A, 385
Holiday, 286
Holliday, Judy, 286
Holloway, Stanley, 214
Hollywood in Transition, 271, 297

Hollywood Revue of 1929, The, 185
"Hollywood Ten," 223-225
Holt, Tim, 233
Home from the Hill, 389
Home of the Brave, 221, 222
Hong Kong, films of, 248, 249
Horne, Denis, 364
Horner, William George, 14
horror film, 101-102, 184, 190-192, 368-370
Horse Soldiers, The, 383
Hour of the Furnaces, The, 409
Houseman, John, 294
House of Bamboo, 392
House of Wax, 275, 276
House of Youth, The, 143
House on 92nd Street, The, 221-222
House Un-American Activities Committee (HUAC), 223-225, 234, 293, 296
How I Won the War, 376
How Tasty Was My Little Frenchman, 408
How to Marry a Millionaire, 277
Hu, King, 249
Huaco, George, 101
Hudson, Rock, 288, 387
Hue and Cry, 214
Hughes, Howard, 273
Hui, Ann, 249
Huillet, Danièle, 413
Hullabaloo Over Georgie and Bonnie's Pictures, 268
Human, Too Human, 323
Human Beast, The, 174
Human Condition, The, 261-262
Human Factor, The, 389
Hungarian Rhapsody, 353
Hungary, films of, 346, 351-353, 359
Hunt, The, 415
Hurry, Hurry, 415
Hurry Sundown, 388
Husbands for Rent, 143
Hush, Hush . . . Sweet Charlotte, 393, 394
Hustle, 394
Huston, John, 219, 223, 225, 232-234, 265, 363
Huston, Walter, 231, 233

I Am Curious, 357
ICAIC (Instituto Cubano del Arte y Industria Cinematográficos), 406
Ichikawa, Kon, 259, 260-261, 262
Identification Marks: None, 349
Identification of a Woman, 333
I Even Met Some Happy Gypsies, 357
If . . . , 166, 367
Ikiru, 247, 250, 254, 255-256
I Live in Fear, 249
Illumination, 349
Imai, Tadashi, 259
Imitation of Life, 388
Immediate Experience, The, 184, 204
Immigrant, The, 70
Immortal Story, The, 384
Impossible Voyage, An, 35
impressionism, 128-129

Impressionists, 124-126, 128, 130, 150, 309, 382
Inagaki, Hiroshi, 251, 252
Ince, Thomas H., 53, 72-73, 77, 124, 135, 141, 382
India, films of, 247, 248-249, 264-268
Indian Film, 264
Indiscretion of an American Wife, 234
Industrial Light and Magic Company, 422, 427
Informer, The, 159-161, 203
Ingeborg Holm, 82
Ingram, Rex, 136
In Harm's Way, 388
Inhumaine, L', 124
Innocence Unprotected, 357
In Old Arizona, 159
In Search of Famine, 267
In the Name of the Law, 330
In the Realm of the Senses, 263
Intimate Lighting, 355
Intolerance, 46, 53, 55, 61-65, 71, 79, 112-113, 117, 147, 333
Intruder in the Dust, 221, 222
In Which We Serve, 209
Iron Horse, The, 28, 141
Isadora Duncan, The Biggest Dancer in the World, 370
Island, The, 247, 260
Islanders, The, 214
Italian Cinema, The, 238
Italy, films of
silent, 48-49, 50, 51, 150
sound, 102, 141, 237-247, 324, 327-342
It Happened One Night, 194, 202
It's a Mad, Mad, Mad, Mad World, 277
It's a Wonderful Life, 203
It Should Happen to You, 286
Ivan's Childhood. See *My Name Is Ivan*
Ivan the Terrible, 117
Ivens, Joris, 129
Ivory, James, 267-268
I Walked with a Zombie, 192
I Was a Communist for the FBI, 223
Iwerks, Ub, 197

Jackal of Nahueltoro, The, 410
Jackson, Pat, 212-213
Jacobs, Lewis, 136, 139, 383
Jagger, Mick, 378
Jakubowska, Wanda, 346
Jancsó, Miklós, 351-352, 353
Jannings, Emil, 92, 94, 99-100, 101, 156, 158
Janowitz, Hans, 89
Japan, films of, 130, 141, 247, 248-264
Japanese Cinema: Film Style and National Character, 252-253, 259
"Japanese Swordfighters and American Gunfighters," 252
Japanese Tragedy, A, 259-260
Jarratt, Vernon, 238
Jaws, 421, 428
Jazz Singer, The, 150, 152-153, 184, 276
Jeanson, Henri, 168

Jenkins, C. Francis, 26
Jennings, Humphrey, 210–212
Jeremiah Johnson, 425
Je t'aime, je t'aime, 317
Jewison, Norman, 274
Jezebel, 227
Jhabvala, Ruth Prawer, 267–268
Jin, Xie, 249
Jireš, Jaromil, 354
Joffroy, 171, 282
Johnston, Eric, 223, 285
Jolson, Al, 152
Jonah Who Will Be 25 in the Year 2000, 323
Jones, Buck, 141
Jones, Chuck, 197
Joseph Kilián, 354
Jour se lève, Le, 168, 171, 174
Jouvet, Louis, 168, 170, 171
Joyless Street, The, 81, 92–94, 99
Judith of Bethulia, 46, 53, 54
Jules and Jim, 314, 315, 316, 317
Juliet of the Spirits, 328
Junior Bonner, 397
Juráček, Pavel, 354
Just Before Nightfall, 320

Kadár, Ján, 354–355, 357
Kagemusha, 256
Kalem Company, Inc., 72
Kameradschaft, 161
Kammerspielfilm ("chamber play film"), 91–92, 93, 94, 95, 96, 97, 98
Kanal, 346–347, 348
Kanchanjungha, 266
Kanin, Garson, 286
Karina, Anna, 318, 319
Karloff, Boris, 191
Karpf, Stephen, 188–189
Kawalerowicz, Jerzy, 349
Kaye, Danny, 142, 223
Kazan, Elia, 277, 286, 295–297
Keaton, Buster, 69, 124, 136, 142, 143, 158, 383
Keaton, Diane, 425
Keeler, Ruby, 185
Keighley, William, 231
Keitel, Harvey, 401
Kelly, Gene, 223, 294, 301
Kermesse héroïque, La. See *Carnival in Flanders*
Kerr, Deborah, 293
Kessel, Adam, 70
Keystone comedies, 66–69
Keystone Film Company, 66, 70
Keystone Kops, 66–67
Kibee, Guy, 185
Kid, The, 142
Kieslowski, Krzysztof, 349
Killer Elite, The, 397
Killers, The, 219–220
Killer's Kiss, 374
Killing, The, 374
Killing of Sister George, The, 393
Kimiko, 259
Kind of Loving, A, 367

Kinetograph, 22–25
Kinetoscope, 14, 22–26, 66
King, Henry, 136, 204
King, Queen, Knave, 349
King and Country, 373
King of Comedy, 402–403
King of Kings, The, 137, 138, 147
Kings of the Road, 414–415
Kino-Pravda, 107–108
Kinoshita, Keisuke, 259–260
Kinugasa, Teinosuke, 250, 259
Kircher, Athanasius, 11
Kiss, The, 144
Kiss Me Deadly, 394
Kiss Me Kate, 275
Kiss of Death, 219, 220
Kitses, Jim, 390–391
Klos, Elmar, 354–355
Kluge, Alexander, 412
Klute, 426
Knack, The, 376
Knife in the Water, 349
Kobayashi, Masaki, 260, 261–262
Kombrig, Ivanov, 107
Körklaren. See *Phantom Chariot, The*
Korte, Walter, 239
Koster, Henry, 278
Koster and Bial's Music Hall, 26, 32
Koszarski, Richard, 139
Kovács, András, 351
Kozintsev, Grigori, 109–110
Kracauer, Siegfried, 32, 92, 94, 100–101, 102, 104, 174, 278
Kramer, Stanley, 222, 292
Kraus, Werner, 99
Kriemhild's Revenge, 88. See also *Nibelungen, Die*
Krishnaswamy, S., 264
Kubrick, Stanley, 374–376
Kuleshov, Lev, 108–109, 112, 113, 117–118
Kurant, Willy, 349
Kurosawa, Akira, 227, 247, 248, 249, 250, 251, 253–256, 264
Kwaidan, 261
Kyo, Machiko, 250, 251

La Cava, Gregory, 194, 385
Lacemaker, The, 323
Lacombe, Lucien, 323
Ladd, Alan, 288
Lady Eve, The, 194, 227
Lady from Shanghai, The, 231
Ladykillers, The, 214
Lady Vanishes, The, 208, 225
Lady Windermere's Fan, 141
Laemmle, Carl, 133
Lagerlöf, Selma, 81, 82–84
Lancaster, Burt, 330, 423
Lancelot of the Lake, 304
Land of the Pharaohs, 147
Landscape After Battle, 348
Land Without Bread, 309
Lang, Fritz, 88–89, 97–98, 101, 102, 124, 161, 219, 301, 319, 320, 383

Langdon, Harry, 69, 142, 158
Lardner, Ring, Jr., 223
Lasky, Jesse, 133
Lassally, Walter, 365–366
Last Command, The, 154
Last Days of Pompeii, The
  (1908), 48
  (1913), 49
Last Laugh, The, 91–92, 93, 95–96, 97, 100
Last Metro, The, 316
Last Stage, The, 346
Last Tango in Paris, 339
Last Wave, The, 416
Last Year at Marienbad, 314, 317
Late Autumn, 258–259
Late Matthew Pascal, The, 124–125
Lattuada, Alberto, 330
Laura, 219
Laurel, Stan, 69, 142, 158
Lavender Hill Mob, The, 214
Lawrence of Arabia, 278, 280–281
Lawson, John Howard, 223, 296
L. B. J., 406–407
Lean, David, 209, 363
Léaud, Jean-Pierre, 313, 316, 349
Leaves from Satan's Book, 79
Lee, Christopher, 369
Leenhardt, Roger, 301, 311
Left-Handed Gun, The, 395
Legend of Lylah Clare, The, 393
Legend of the Mountain, 249
Léger, Fernand, 124, 127, 130
Legion of Decency, 183, 285
Legion of the Condemned, The, 145
Lemmon, Jack, 290
Leni, Paul, 91, 101
Leopard, The, 329, 330
Le Prince, Louis, 21–22
Lerner, Alan Jay, 294
LeRoy, Mervyn, 189, 190
Lester, Richard, 324, 376–377, 378
Letter, The, 227
Lewis, Jerry, 142, 402–403
Lewton, Val, 5, 191–192
L'Herbier, Marcel, 124–125, 127
Library of Congress, 7
Lies My Father Told Me, 357
Lifeboat, 218
Life of an American Fireman, 38–39, 40, 42, 107
Lightning Over Water, 386
Lights of New York, The, 153–154
Lilac Time, 145
Limelight, 383
Linder, Max, 66
Listen to Britain, 210
Lisztomania, 372
Littín, Miguel, 410
Little Big Man, 395
Little Caesar, 188–190
Little Foxes, The, 227
Little Match Girl, The, 130
Little Women, 286
Lives of a Bengal Lancer, 198
Lloyd, Frank, 199
Lloyd, Harold, 69, 142, 158

Local Hero, 377, 378
Lodger, The, 148, 225
Lodz, Polish film school at, 346
Loew, Marcus, 133
Loew's, Inc., 133, 134, 180
Lola, 323
Lola Montès, 384
Lolita, 374
Lombard, Carole, 194, 202
Lone Eagle, The, 145
Loneliness of the Long Distance Runner, The, 366
Longest Day, The, 278
Longest Yard, The, 394
Long Goodbye, The, 400
Look Back in Anger, 363, 365
Lord, Daniel, S. J., 182
Lorentz, Pare, 178, 292
Lorre, Peter, 232
Losey, Joseph, 372-374, 376, 385
Lost Boundaries, 222
Lost Honor of Katharina Blum, The, 412-413
Lost Weekend, The, 218, 222, 289
Louis B. Mayer Pictures Corporation, 133. See also Mayer, Louis B.
Love, 145
Love Affair, or The Case of the Missing Switchboard Operator, 357-358
Love and Anarchy, 339
Love and Journalism, 81
Love at Twenty, 316
Love in the Afternoon, 290
Love Is a Many-Splendored Thing, 280
Love Me Tonight, 185
Love on the Run. See Amour en fuite, L'
Love Parade, The, 185
Lovers, The, 312
Loves of a Blonde, 354, 355
Lower Depths, The, 166, 173, 176
Lubitsch, Ernst, 81, 87-88, 101, 136-137, 139-140, 185, 192, 289, 290, 383
Lucas, George, 422, 424, 426, 427-428
Lucasfilm, Ltd., 427
Lucia, 407
Ludwig, 329
Ludwig: Requiem for a Virgin King, 415
Lumet, Sidney, 274
Lumière, Louis and Auguste, 22, 24-26, 32-34, 35, 105, 151
Luna, 339
Lust for Life, 294

M, 161
Macbeth
(1948), 231
(1971), 349
McCabe and Mrs. Miller, 399-400
MacCann, Richard Dyer, 271, 297
McCarey, Leo, 158, 194, 223-224, 385
McCay, Winsor, 196
McCord, Ted, 277
McCoy, Tim, 141
McCrea, Joel, 396
MacDonald, Jeanette, 185

Mackendrick, Alexander, 214, 215
McLaglen, Victor, 159-161
MacLaine, Shirley, 290
McLaren, Norman, 19, 197
McLuhan, Marshall, 30
MacMurray, Fred, 218, 290
McNamara, Maggie, 284
McQueen, Steve, 274
Madame Bovary, 172
Madame de Barry. See Passion
Made in USA, 319
Mad Whirl, The, 143
Maggie, The, 214
Magic Box, The, 22
Magician, The, 307
magic lantern, 11, 12
Magnani, Anna, 238, 282
Magnascope, 275
Magnificent Ambersons, The, 217, 231
Magnificent Seven, The, 253
Mahanagar, 266
Mahler, 371-372
Major and the Minor, The, 289
Major Dundee, 396
Makavejev, Dušan, 357-359
Making a Living, 70
Makk, Károly, 353
Male and Female, 137
Malle, Louis, 312, 322-323
Maltese Falcon, The, 219, 232
Maltz, Albert, 223
Mamoulian, Rouben, 158, 185
Man Escaped, A, 304, 312
Man from Laramie, The, 390
Manhattan, 425
Man in the White Suit, The, 214
Man is Not a Bird, 357
Mankiewicz, Herman J., 229
Mann, Anthony, 204, 301, 390-391
Mann, Delbert, 273, 274
Man of Aran, 214
Man of Iron, 350, 351
Man of Marble, 351
Man of the West, 390, 391
Man on a Tightrope, 296
Man on the Track, 348
Man's Favorite Sport?, 384
Manslaughter, 137
Manthan, 267
Man Who Fell to Earth, The, 378
Man Who Knew Too Much, The, 225
Man Who Shot Liberty Valance, The, 383
Man with the Golden Arm, The, 284
March, Fredric, 227, 286
March of Time series, The, 221, 229
Marey, Etienne Jules, 21, 22
Marius, 165
Marius trilogy, 171
Marker, Chris, 312
Mark of Zoro, The, 146
Marquise of O . . ., The, 322
Marriage Circle, The, 140, 141
Marriage of Maria Braun, The, 413, 414
Married Woman, A, 281
Marrying Kind, The, 286
Marseillaise, La, 174
Marsh, Mae, 56, 58-59, 60, 65, 99

Marty, 273, 274
Marx Brothers, 158, 192, 193
Masculine-Feminine, 349
M*A*S*H, 399, 400
Masina, Giulietta, 331
Mason, James, 286-287
Masque of the Red Death, The, 192
Mastroianni, Marcello, 332
Maternelle, La, 165-166
Mattei Affair, The, 336
Matter of Time, A, 389
Mauvaises rencontres, Les, 312
Mayer, Carl, 5, 89, 91, 100, 157, 243
Mayer, Louis B., 133, 158, 224, 280. See also Louis B. Mayer Pictures Corporation
Mayerling, 167
Maynard, Ken, 141
Mazetti, Lorenza, 364
Mean Streets, 401, 402
Mechanics of the Brain, 105
Medea, 338
Medium Cool, 395
Meet Me in St. Louis, 218, 293, 389
Méliès, Georges, 34-37, 38, 39, 42, 44, 45, 46, 47, 66, 68, 165
Member of the Wedding, The, 293
Memories of Underdevelopment, 407
Memphis Belle, 227
Men, The, 221, 292
Menjou, Adolphe, 223
Menschen am Sonntag. See People on Sunday
Men Who Tread on the Tiger's Tail, The, 251
Menzel, Jiři, 355, 356
Mephisto, 353
Mercanton, Louis, 47-48
Mercer, David, 317
Merchant, Ismail, 267-268
Merchant of Four Seasons, The, 413
Merkel, Una, 185
Merrill's Marauders, 392
Merry Christmas, Mr. Lawrence, 263
Merry-Go-Round, 351
Merry Widow, The
(1925), 139, 184
(1934), 185
Meshes of the Afternoon, 129-130
Messidor, 323
Messter, Oskar, 22
Metro Pictures Corporation, 133
Metropolis, 88, 98, 99, 187
Mexican Bus Ride. See Subida al Cielo
M-G-M (Metro-Goldwyn-Mayer), 73, 102, 133, 134, 135, 154, 158, 180, 185, 187, 188, 273, 275, 279, 280, 281, 292, 293, 294, 389, 421
Michi, Maria, 238
Mickey Mouse, 196
Mickey One, 324, 395, 396
Midnight Cowboy, 285, 372
Midsummer Night's Dream, A, 198
Mifune, Toshiro, 250, 256
Mildred Pierce, 219, 231
Milestone, Lewis, 159

Milhaud, Darius, 124
Milius, John, 426
Miller, Merle, 273
Million, Le, 161, 165
Million and One Nights, A, 23-24
Millions Like Us, 209
Mill on the Po, 330
Minnelli, Liza, 402
Minnelli, Vincente, 286, 293-295, 301, 389
Minnie Mouse, 196
Miracle, The, 171, 282, 283
Miracle in Milan, 244
Miracle of Morgan's Creek, The, 194, 217-218, 228
Miracle Worker, The, 395
Mirror, 344
Mischief Makers, The, 312
Mission to Moscow, 223
Missouri Breaks, The, 395-396
Mister Shome. See Bhuvan Shome
Mix, Tom, 141
Mizoguchi, Kenji, 250, 251, 253, 256-258
Moana, 146
Moby Dick, 363
Modern Times, 158
Momma Don't Allow, 364
Monaco, Paul, 101
Monika, 305
Monogram Pictures Corporation, 180
Mon Oncle d'Amérique, 317, 319
Monroe, Marilyn, 286, 290
montage, 38, 65, 109, 117-120, 154, 157
Montenegro, 358
Montgomery, Robert, 223
Moon Is Blue, The, 284
Moon is Down, The, 218
Moonlighting, 349
Moore, Colleen, 158
Moorehead, Agnes, 230
Moreau, Jeanne, 315
More the Merrier, The, 288
Morgan, Michèle, 168, 172
Morocco, 200
Moscow Institute of Cinematography, 106, 108
Moscow International Film Festival, 343, 344
Moses and Aaron, 413
Mother, 65, 113, 119, 188
Mother and Daughter, 81
Mother and the Law, The, 61, 64, 83
Mother Joan of the Angels, 349
Motion Picture Association of America (MPAA), 151, 180, 223, 282, 284-285
Motion Picture Herald, 182
Motion Picture Patents Company, 72, 133, 134
Motion Picture Producers and Distributors of America (MPPDA), 151, 180, 181, 182, 183
Motion Pictures and Youth, 183
Mouchette, 304
Moulin Rouge, 363

Movie magazine, 199, 382, 389
Movietone, 155
Mozhukin, Ivan, 118, 120, 125
Mr. Arkadin, 302, 384
Mr. Deeds Goes to Town, 178, 202
Mr. Klein, 374
Mr. Magoo, 197
Mrs. Miniver, 218, 227
Mr. Smith Goes to Washington, 178, 202, 203
Muddy Waters, 259
Mulligan, Robert, 274
Muni, Paul, 190
Munk, Andrzej, 348-349
Murder, My Sweet, 219, 220
Muriel, 317
Murmer of the Heart, 323
Murnau, F. W., 4, 5, 90-91, 101, 136, 157, 301, 383
Murphy, George, 223
Museum of Modern Art, 7, 151
musical, 141, 148, 184-187, 188, 189, 190, 192
Music Lovers, The, 371
Music Room, The, 266
Musketeers of Pig Alley, The, 83
Mutiny on the Bounty, 198, 199
Mutual Film Corporation, 54, 71
Mutual Film Corporation v. Ohio, 282
Muybridge, Eadweard, 19-21, 22
My Brilliant Career, 417
My Darling Clementine, 204
My Dinner with André, 323
My Fair Lady, 278
My Life to Live, 314, 318, 319, 320
My Man Godfrey, 194
My Name Is Ivan, 344
My Night at Maud's, 313, 321-322, 323
My Son John, 223
Mystères du Château du Dé, Les, 127
Mysterious X, The, 78
Mystery of Kaspar Hauser, The, 414
My Way Home, 351, 352

Nagata, Masaichi, 250
Naked City, The, 220, 222
Naked Night, The, 84, 305
Naked Spur, The, 390
Nanook of the North, 146, 188, 265
Napoléon, 53, 125-126
Naruse, Mikio, 259
Nashville, 400, 401
National Board of Review of Motion Pictures, awards, 220, 223
National Catholic Office of Motion Pictures, 285
National Film Board of Canada, 197
National Film Finance Corporation, U.K., 281
Natural Vision, 275
Naughty Marietta, 185
Navigator, The, 142
Negri, Pola, 88, 101, 144, 158
Neighbors, 19
Nelson, Ralph, 274
Němec, Jan, 354, 356

neorealism, 166, 188, 213, 234, 237-247, 327, 329, 330-331, 333
Neue Sachlichkeit (new realism), 94
New Faces, 185
Newman, David, 396
Newman, Paul, 425
Newsfront, 417
New Wave, 177, 246, 311-322, 323-326, 327-329, 349, 382
New Year's Eve, 100
New York Film Bulletin, 382
New York Film Critics, awards, 167, 220
New York, New York, 401, 402
New York State Board of Regents, 282
Next of Kin, 209
Nibelungen, Die, 88, 97-98. See also *Kriemhild's Revenge* and *Siegfried*
Niblo, Fred, 147
Nice Time, 365
Nichols, Dudley, 159-161, 194-195, 203-204
Nichols, Mike, 284
nickelodeon, 49, 74-75
Nielsen, Asta, 99
Niépce, Nicéphore, 16
Night and Fog, 313, 317
Night Drum, 259
Night Moves, 395, 396
Night of San Juan, The, 410
Night of the Shooting Stars, 340
Nights of Cabiria, The, 331
Nine Men, 209
1941, 428
1900, 339
Ninotchka, 158, 289
Niven, David, 284
Noble, Peter, 139
No Greater Love, 261-262
Nordisk Films Kompagni, 77, 79, 81
Normand, Mabel, 70, 74
North by Northwest, 384
North Star, The, 223
Nosferatu
  (1922), 90-91, 190
  (1979), 414
Nostalgia, 345
"Notes on the Auteur Theory in 1962," 383
Nothing Sacred, 194
Notorious, 225
Not Reconciled, 413
Notte, La, 328, 333
Now About These Women, 307
No Way Out, 221
Noyce, Phillip, 417
Numéro deux, 319
Nun's Story, The, 293
Nureyev, Rudolf, 372

Oberhausen Film Festival, 412
Oboler, Arch, 275
October, 117 .
Odd Obsession, 260
O Dreamland, 364
Oedipus Rex, 338

Ogum's Amulet, 408
Oklahoma!, 293
Old and New. See *General Line, The*
Old Mill, The, 196
Oliver Twist, 363
Olivier, Laurence, 22, 29, 212, 363, 365
Olmi, Ermanno, 246, 335–336
O Lucky Man!, 367
Olvidados, Los, 309
On a Clear Day You Can See Forever, 295, 389
One A.M., 70
One Fine Day, 336
One Flew Over the Cuckoo's Nest, 357, 421
One from the Heart, 398
One of Our Aircraft is Missing, 209
One, Two, Three, 290, 291
Onibaba, 260
Only Angels Have Wings, 201–202
Only Game in Town, The, 385
On the Town, 187, 188
On the Waterfront, 296, 297
Open City, 188, 237–238, 239, 240, 244, 245, 246, 330
Ophüls, Max, 301, 312, 384
Ordet, 79, 80
Ornitz, Samuel, 223
Orphans of the Storm, 55, 147
Orpheus, 130
Osborne, John, 365
Oshima, Nagisa, 260, 262–264
Ossessione, 166, 239, 241, 329
Our Dancing Daughters, 143
Our Movie-Made Children, 183
Outcry, 244
Outlaw and His Wife, The, 82
Out One: Spectre, 321
Outrage, The, 253
Outsiders, The, 398
Overlanders, The, 209
Ozu, Yasujiro, 253, 258–259

Pabst, G. W., 81, 92–94, 105, 156, 161
Padre Padrone, 340
Page of Madness, A, 259
Pagliero, Marcello, 238
Pagnol, Marcel, 165, 168, 171, 282
Painting with Light, 96
Paisan, 240–241, 330
Pakula, Alan J., 424, 426–427
Palance, Jack, 288
Pale Flower, 260
Palm Beach Story, The, 194, 227
Panavision, 277
Pangborn, Franklin, 227
Panic in the Streets, 221, 296
Paradine Case, The, 219
Paradjanov, Sergo, 345
Parain, Brice, 319
Parallax View, The, 426
Paramount Pictures, 48, 101, 102, 133–134, 141, 155, 180, 185, 227, 273, 277, 279, 421
Paris, John Ayrton, 12
Paris Does Strange Things, 383

Paris nous appartient, 313, 317, 320
Paris qui dort, 130
Park Row, 392
Parson's Widow, The, 79, 80
Part-Time Work of a Domestic Slave, The, 412
Pasolini, Piero Paolo, 337, 338
Passenger (1963), 348–349
Passenger, The (1975), 328, 329
Passer, Ivan, 355, 357
Passion, 87, 88, 139, 319
Passion of Anna, The, 307
Passion of Joan of Arc, The, 79, 80, 304
Passport to Pimlico, 214
Pastrone, Giovanni, 48, 49
Pat and Mike, 286
Pat Garrett and Billy the Kid, 397
Pathé Frères, 105, 164
Pather Panchali, 247, 249, 265, 266, 267
Pathetic Fallacy, See *Ajantrik*
Paths of Glory, 374
Patterns, 188
Paul, Robert, 22, 26, 35, 42
Pauline at the Beach, 322
Pavlović, Živojin, 357
Pawnshop, The, 70
Payne Fund, 183
Peckinpah, Sam, 204, 274, 395, 396–398
Penn, Arthur, 5, 324, 385, 395–396
Pension Mimosas, 168
People on Sunday, 291–292
Pépé le Moko, 170–171, 174
Perceval, 322
Performance, 378
Perkins, Victor F., 388
persistence of vision, 11–12
Persona, 307
Petit Soldat, Le, 319
Petrović, Aleksander, 357
Petulia, 324, 376, 378
Phantom Chariot, The, 82–84
Phantom India series, 323
Phantom Lady, 102, 219
Phantom of Liberty, The, 310, 311
Pharoah, 349
Phenakistiscope, 13, 14
Philadelphia Story, The, 286
Photoplay magazine, 134
Pick, Lupu, 91
Pickford, Mary, 71, 74, 133, 158
Pickpocket, 304
Pickup on South Street, 392
Picnic at Hanging Rock, 416, 417
Picnic on the Grass, 383–384
Pierrot le fou, 314, 319
Pigpen, 338
Pink Panther, The, 390
Pinky, 221, 222, 296
Pinter, Harold, 373–374
Pirate, The, 293, 389
Pirie, David, 369
Pixote, 409
Place in the Sun, A, 288
Plainsman, The, 184
Plateau, Joseph, 13–14
Playtime, 323

Plow that Broke the Plains, The, 178
Plucked from the Burning, 42
Pluto, 196
Poachers, 415
Pocketful of Miracles, 385
Poil de carotte, 165–166
Point Blank, 372
Pointe courte, La, 312
Poland, films of, 197, 346–351, 359
Polanski, Roman, 349
Pollack, Sydney, 424, 425–426
Polyvision, 125–126
Pommer, Erich, 101
Pont du Nord, Le, 321
Ponti, Carlo, 5
Porter, Edwin S., 37–42, 43, 44, 45, 46, 66, 68, 95, 105, 107
Port of Shadows. See *Quai des brumes*
Post, Ted, 423
Posto, Il, 246, 336
Potemkin, 115–116, 117, 121, 188, 228, 333
Powell, Dick, 185, 219
Powell, Michael, 363
Praxinoscope, 14
Preminger, Otto, 219, 284, 302, 319, 388–389
President, The, 79
Pressburger, Emeric, 363
Pretty Baby, 323
Prévert, Jacques, 168, 171–172, 174–175, 177, 219, 300
Principal Enemy, The, 410
Prisoner of Shark Island, The, 203
"problem picture," 142–143, 188, 213, 222, 234, 244
production, Hollywood studio system
silent, 71–75, 134–136
sound, 156, 179–182, 271, 272, 279–282
Production Code, U.S. See self-regulation, U.S.
Professor Hannibal, 351
Promised Land, 349
Providence, 317
Psycho, 384, 426
Public Enemy, The, 188
Pudovkin, V. I., 65, 105, 108–109, 110, 112–113, 117–120
Pumpkin Race, The, 66
Punishment Island, 260
Purviance, Edna, 70
Puttnam, David, 377
Pygmalion, 208

Quai des brumes, 171, 174–175, 300
Queen Christina, 158
Queen Elizabeth, 47–48, 49
Queen Kelly, 139
Quiet Man, The, 383
Quigley, Martin, 182
Quo Vadis? (1912), 49

Raft, George, 290
Raging Bull, 402
Ragtime, 357

Rahn, Bruno, 92
Raider, The. See *Western Approaches*
Raiders of the Lost Ark, 421, 427, 428
Raimu, 168, 171
Rain, 129
Raines, Ella, 219
Raining in the Mountain, 249
Rain People, The, 398, 402
Rains, Claude, 225
Rally Round the Flag, Boys!, 385
Ramsaye, Terry, 23–24
Rashomon, 247, 248, 250, 251, 252, 253, 254, 264
Ray, Man, 127, 130
Ray, Nicholas, 302, 385–386
Ray, Satyajit, 227, 247, 249, 264–266, 267
RCA (Radio Corporation of America), 155
Reagan, Ronald, 223
Realm of Passion, 263
Rear Window, 384
Rebecca, 225, 226, 234
Rebel Without a Cause, 188, 386
Red and the White, The, 352
Red Badge of Courage, The, 233
Red Beard, 256
Red Desert, The, 4, 333
Redford, Robert, 425
Red Line 7000, 384
Red Psalm, 352
Red River, 204
Reds, 422
Reed, Carol, 208, 363
Regain. See *Harvest*
Reimann, Walter, 89
Reinhardt, Max, 87, 91, 96, 139, 198
Reisz, Karel, 311, 364, 365, 366–367, 372, 423
Religieuse, La, 317, 320
Renoir, Jean, 4, 130, 166, 167, 168, 171, 172–174, 176–177, 265, 282, 301, 306, 307, 310, 313, 315, 383–384
Report on the Party and the Guests, 356
Republic Pictures Corporation, 180
Repulsion, 349
Requiem for a Heavyweight, 273
Rescued by Rover, 42
Rescued from an Eagle's Nest, 42
Resnais, Alain, 312, 313, 314, 315, 317–318, 319, 322, 378
Return of the Jedi, 159, 421, 427
Return of the Prodigal Son, The, 356
Revenge of Frankenstein, The, 369
Rex, "King of the Wild Horses," 146
Reynaud, Emile, 14, 16
Reynolds, Burt, 5
Rhythmus 21, 89, 127
Rialto Theatre, 134, 135
Rice, 259
Rich and Famous, 385
Richardson, Tony, 324, 364, 365, 366, 372
Richard III, 363
Richie, Donald, 251, 252–253, 256, 259

Richter, Hans, 89, 127
Rickshaw Boy, 249
Ride the High Country, 204, 396
Rien que les heures, 124, 129
Rieupeyrout, Jean-Louis, 141
Right Stuff, The, 422
Rink, The, 70
Rin-Tin-Tin, 146
Rio Bravo, 384
Rio Lobo, 384
Rip van Winkle, 32
Rise and Fall of Free Speech in America, The, 61
Rise of Louis XIV, The, 317
Rise of the American Film, The, 136, 383
Riskin, Robert, 159, 194
Ritt, Martin, 253
River, The
(1937), 178
(1951), 265
Rivette, Jacques, 311, 313, 315, 317, 320–321, 322
RKO (RKO Radio Pictures, Inc.), 155, 180, 231, 273, 279
Road Runner, 197
Roads of Exile, 323
Road to Eternity, 261–262
Robbe-Grillet, Alain, 317
Robbery of the Mail Coach, The, 42
Robe, The, 277, 278
Robin and Marian, 376
Robin Hood, 146
Robinson, Edward G., 189, 190, 219
Robinson, John Stuart, 136
Robson, E. W. and M. M., 100
Rocco and his Brothers, 239, 327, 329
Rocha, Glauber, 407–408
Rocky, 421, 422
Roeg, Nicolas, 377, 378–379
Rogers, Ginger, 185, 187, 287
Rogers, Will, 158
Roget, Peter Mark, 11–12
Rohmer, Eric, 311, 313, 315, 321–322, 323
Röhrig, Walter, 89
Role, The. See *Bhumika*
Rollover, 427
Roma. See *Fellini's Roma*
Romantic Englishwoman, The, 374
Rome, Eleven O'Clock, 244
Romeo and Juliet, 286
Roof, The, 246
Room, Abram, 107
Room at the Top, 363, 365, 367
Room in Town, A, 323
Rope, 219
Rosay, Françoise, 168, 170, 171
Rose, Reginald, 273
Rosemary's Baby, 349
Rosenblum, Ralph, 5
Rosi, Francesco, 246, 336–337
Rossellini, Roberto, 171, 237–238, 239, 240–241, 243, 246, 282, 283, 317, 329, 330
Rotha, Paul, 383
Rouch, Jean, 107
Roue, La, 125

Round-Up, The, 352
Rules of the Game, The, 167, 172, 173, 174
Rumble Fish, 398
Run for Your Money, A, 214
Running, Jumping, and Standing-Still Film, 376
Run of the Arrow, 392
Russell, Harold, 227
Russell, Ken, 349, 370–372
Russell, Rosalind, 194
Russell, Theresa, 378
Russia. See Soviet Union
Ruttmann, Walther, 129

Sabina, La, 415
Saboteur, 225
Sabrina, 290
Sadoul, Georges, 42
Safety Last, 142
Saint Joan, 319
Salò or the 120 Days of Sodom, 338
Salvatore Giuliano, 246, 336
Samuel Goldwyn Productions, 180. See also Goldwyn Pictures Corporation and Goldwyn, Samuel
Samurai, 251
San Demetrio, London, 209
Sandra, 329
Sanjinés, Jorge, 409–410
Sanjuro, 253
Sansho Dayu, 253
Sarris, Andrew, 199, 289, 382–394
Satan Never Sleeps, 385
Saturday Night, 137
Saturday Night and Sunday Morning, 366–367
Saturday Night Fever, 185, 421
Satyricon. See *Fellini Satyricon*
Saura, Carlos, 415
Sauve qui peut . . . La Vie, 319
Savage Messiah, 371
Sawdust and Tinsel. See *Naked Night, The*
Sayonara, 280
Scandalous Adventures of Buraikan, The, 260
Scarface
(1932), 188, 202
(1983), 426
Scarlet Empress, The, 200
Scarlet Letter, The, 82
Scarlet Street, 102, 219
Scenes from a Marriage, 307
Schepisi, Fred, 417
Schlesinger, John, 324, 365, 367, 372, 378
Schlöndorff, Volker, 412–413
Schmidt, Jan, 354
Schorm, Evald, 355–356
Schrader, Paul, 311
Schulberg, Budd, 296
Schygulla, Hanna, 413
Scorsese, Martin, 395, 400–403, 426
Scott, Adrian, 223
Scott, Randolph, 396
Screen Gems, 273

"screwball comedy," 194-195
Sea Hawk, The, 231
Sea of Grass, 296
Search, The, 292
Searchers, The, 383
Seashell and the Clergyman, The, 128, 130
Seastrom, Victor. See Sjöström, Victor
Seberg, Jean, 319
Secret, The, 249
Secret of Nimh, 197
Secrets of a Soul, 105
Secrets of Women, 305
Seduction of Mimi, The, 339
Seedling, The. See *Ankur*
See You at Mao, 319
self-regulation, U.S., 182-184, 189, 282, 284-285, 293
Selig Polyscope Company, 72
Sellers, Coleman, 19
Selznick, David O., 5, 180, 225, 226, 234, 286
Sembène, Ousmane, 411-412
semi-documentary
  U.K., 208-213, 214, 244
  U.S., 213, 221-222, 244
Semprin, Jorge, 317
Sen, Mrinal, 267
Senegal, films of, 411, 412, 419, 420
Sennett, Mack, 27-28, 53, 65-70, 73, 77, 100, 142, 167, 196, 382
Senso, 329
Serling, Rod, 273
Servant, The, 373, 374
Set-Up, The, 219
Seven Beauties, 339-340
Seven Brides for Seven Brothers, 277
Seven Samurai, 250, 251, 253-256
Seventh Seal, The, 83, 305-307
79 Springtimes, 406-407
Seven Year Itch, The, 290
Shadow of a Doubt, 219, 225-226
Shadows of Our Forgotten Ancestors, 345
Shadow Warrior, The. See *Kagemusha*
Shakespeare-Wallah, 268
Shall We Dance, 187
Shane, 204, 288
Shanghai Express, 200
Shattered, 91, 100
Shearer, Norma, 286
Sherwood, Robert E., 227, 296
Shimura, Takashi, 254
Shindo, Kaneto, 247, 260
Shining, The, 375-376
Shinoda, Masahiro, 260
Shock Corridor, 392
Shoeshine, 188, 241, 242, 245, 313
Shoot the Piano Player, 313, 314, 315, 316
Shop on Main Street, The, 354-355
Shot in the Dark, A, 390
Shoulder Arms, 70-71
Shout, The, 349
Shriek of Araby, The, 69
Siegel, Don, 6
Siegfried, 88, 89. See also *Nibelungen, Die*
Signe du lion, Le, 313
Sign of Leo, The. See *Signe du lion, Le*
Signs and Meaning in the Cinema, 202, 204

Silence, The, 306, 307
Silence and Cry, 352
Sillitoe, Alan, 366
Silly Symphonies, 196-197
Sim, Alistair, 214
Simon, Michel, 125, 168
Sinatra, Frank, 293
Sinclair, Upton, 155
Singin' in the Rain, 154
Siodmak, Robert, 102, 219, 291-292
Sir Arne's Treasure, 81
Sirk, Douglas, 302, 387-388
Sisters or the Balance of Happiness, 413
Six Moral Tales, 321-322
Sjöberg, Alf, 305
Sjöman, Vilgot, 357
Sjöström, Victor, 79, 81, 82-84, 124, 136
Skeleton Dance, 196
Skelton, Red, 142
Skladanowsky, Max, 22
Skolimowski, Jerzy, 349
Skouras, Spyros, 277
Smiles of a Summer Night, 305-306, 307
Smith, George Albert, 42
Snake Pit, The, 220, 222
Snow White and the Seven Dwarfs, 197
socialist realism, 107, 117, 343
social-realist features, U.K., 246, 363-368
Sociology of Film Art, The, 101
Solanas, Fernando, 409
Solaris, 344
Solás, Humberto, 407
Soldier's Prayer, A, 261-262
Solomon and Sheba, 385
Some Came Running, 389
Some Like It Hot, 290
Something to Think About, 137
Song of Bernadette, The, 218
Song of Russia, 223
Sophie's Choice, 427
sound, transition to, 129, 130, 148, 150-163, 274
Sound of Music, The, 278
Sounds from the Mountains, 259
Sous les toits de Paris, 161, 165
South, The, 415
Southern, Terry, 374
Southerner, The, 265
Soviet Union, films of
  silent, 95, 102, 104-121, 123, 125, 132, 150, 154, 188
  sound, 343-345
Sovkino Trust, 106
Spaak, Charles, 168-169, 173
Spain, films of, 415-416, 419, 420
Sparkuhl, Theodore, 101
Spartacus, 374
Speedy Gonzalez, 197
Spellbound, 218, 225
Spider's Stratagem, The, 339
Spiegel, Sam, 234
Spielberg, Steven, 424, 426, 428-429
Spiral Staircase, The, 102, 219
Spirit of St. Louis, The, 290
Spirit of the Beehive, The, 415, 416

Splendor in the Grass, 296
Spooky Bunch, The, 249
Squaw Man, The, 137
Stagecoach, 184, 203-204
Stage to Screen, 27, 29-30
Stalag 17, 289-290
Stalker, 344-345
Stampfer, Simon Ritter von, 13
Stanwyck, Barbara, 194, 218, 227
Star Film Company, 35
Star Is Born, A
  (1937), 286
  (1954), 277, 286-287
Starting Over, 427
Star Trek, 421
Star Wars, 421, 427, 428
Star Wars trilogy, 427-428
State of the Union, 220
Stavisky, 317
Steadycam, 422
Steamboat 'Round the Bend, 203
Steamboat Willie, 196, 198
Steinbeck, John, 296
stereophonic sound, 197, 275-276, 277, 278
stereoscopic projection (3-D), 151, 275, 276
Sterling, Ford, 70
Stern, Seymour, 54
Sternberg, Jacques, 317
Sternberg, Josef von, 136, 156, 157, 159, 161, 187-188, 200-201, 203, 310, 384
Stevens, George, 6, 188, 204, 286-289, 385
Stewart, James, 194, 202
Stiller, Mauritz, 81-82, 84, 124
Stolen Kisses, 316
Storey, David, 367
Storm Over Asia, 113
Story of Adele H., The, 317
Story of G. I. Joe, The, 218
Story of Gösta Berling, The, 81, 82
Story of Woo Viet, The, 249
Strada, La, 246, 328, 330-331
Strand, Paul, 292
Stranger, The, 329
Strangers on a Train, 225
Straub, Jean-Marie, 413
Straw Dogs, 397
Streamers, 400
Street, The, 92
Streetcar Named Desire, A, 296
"street film," 92-93, 94, 95, 96, 97, 98
Streisand, Barbra, 5
Strike, 110, 113, 114-116
Stroheim, Erich von, 68, 136, 138-139, 141, 184, 218, 384-385
Strong Man, The, 142
Sturges, John, 253
Sturges, Preston, 194, 217-218, 225, 227-229, 231, 234, 385
Subida al Cielo, 309
Sullivan's Travels, 217, 228
Summer Interlude, 305
Summertime, 363
Summerville, Slim, 66

Sunday Bloody Sunday, 372
Sunday Too Far Away, 416
Sundowners, The, 293
Sunrise, 157
Sunset Boulevard, 145, 218, 220, 289
Superman II and *III,* 376
Supreme Court, U.S., 271, 272, 282–284, 285
surrealism, 127–128, 308–311
Suspicion, 225
Sutherland, Donald, 378
Svensk Filmindustri, 77, 79
Swain, Mack, 66, 70
Swanson, Gloria, 27, 144, 145, 218
Sweden, films of, 77, 78, 79, 80, 81–85, 99, 102, 132, 150, 305
Sweet Movie, 357–358
Swept Away, 339
Swing Time, 188, 287
Syberberg, Hans-Jürgen, 414, 415
Sympathy for the Devil, 318
Symphonie diagonale, 89, 127
Symphonie pastorale, La, 300
Szabó, István, 351, 353

Tabu, 383
Talbot, W. H. Fox, 15–16
Tales of Manhattan, 171
Talk of the Town, The, 288
Talmadge, Norma, 158
Tanner, Alain, 323, 365
Target for Tonight, 209–210, 212, 213
Tarkovsky, Andrei, 344–345
Tarzan of the Apes, 146
Taste of Honey, A, 365–366
Tati, Jacques, 301, 323
Tavernier, Bertrand, 323
Taviani, Paolo and Vittorio, 339, 340
Taxi Driver, 402
Taylor, Elizabeth, 288
Taylor, John Russell, 362
Taylor, Robert, 223
Taylor, Rod, 274
Taylor, William Desmond, 182
Technicolor, 197, 198, 212, 274, 286, 288
Teddy at the Throttle, 27
television, effects on motion picture industry, U.S., 271, 272–274
Tellegen, Lou, 47–48
Telsen v. Chicago, 283
"Temptation of Dr. Antonio, The," 332
"10," 390
Ten Commandments, The
(1923), 28, 137, 147
(1956), 137–138, 147, 384
Ten Days that Shook the World. See October
Tent of Miracles, 408
Teorema, 338
Teresa, 292
Terje Vigen, 82
Terra Trema, La, 239, 240, 244, 329
Teshigahara, Hiroshi, 260
Tess, 349
Testament of Orpheus, The, 130

Texas Rangers, The, 184
Thalberg, Irving, 135, 179, 280
That Obscure Object of Desire, 310
That Sinking Feeling, 377
Thaumatrope, 12–13
Théâtre Optique, 14, 16
Théâtre Robert-Houdin, 35
Theory of Film: The Redemption of Physical Reality, 32, 278
Thérèse Raquin, 168
These Are the Damned. See Damned, The
They Live by Night, 385
They Shoot Horses, Don't They?, 425
Thief of Bagdad, The, 146
Thieves Like Us, 385, 400
Thing, The, 147
Third Man, The, 363
13 Rue Madeleine, 222
Thirty-Nine Steps, The, 161, 225
Thirty Seconds Over Tokyo, 218
This Is Cinerama, 275, 276
This Sporting Life, 367
Thomas, Lowell, 276
Thomas Graal's Best Film, 81
Thousand Eyes of Dr. Mabuse, The, 383
Three Brothers, 337
Three Coins in a Fountain, 280
Three Foolish Weeks, 68
Three Little Pigs, 196–197
Three Musketeers, The
(1921), 146
(1974), 376
Threepenny Opera, The, 161
Three Strange Loves, 305
3 Women, 400
Throne of Blood, 254
Through a Glass Darkly, 306
THX-1138, 427
Tight Little Island, 214, 215, 377
Tillie's Punctured Romance, 70, 71
Times Film Corporation, 282–283
Time Without Pity, 372
Tin Drum, The, 413
Tissé, Edward, 5, 109
Titfield Thunderbolt, The, 214
Todd, Michael, 276
Todd A-O, 277
Toeplitz, Jerzy, 346
Together, 364
Tokyo Olympiad, 261
Toland, Gregg, 5, 227, 230
To Live in Peace, 244
Tom Jones, 324, 366
Tommy, 371
"Tomorrow the World: Some Reflections on the un-Englishness of English Films," 362
Toni, 166, 172, 174
Tonnere, Le, 125
Too Late the Hero, 392–393
Tootsie, 425–426
Toot, Whistle, Plunk, and Boom, 197
Torment, 305
To the Distant Observer, 250
Touch of Evil, 384
Touch of Zen, A, 249
Toute la memoire du monde, 313

Tout va bien, 319
Tracy, Spencer, 286, 288
Traffic, 323
Tragedy of a Ridiculous Man, 339
Tragedy of a Street, 92
Tragic Hunt, The, 244, 245, 333
Tramp, The, 70
Tramp, Tramp, Tramp, 142
Trauberg, Leonid, 109
Treasure of the Sierra Madre, The, 233
Tree Grows in Brooklyn, A, 295–296
Tree of the Wooden Clogs, The, 336
Trial, The, 384
Trial Marriage, 143
Trial of Joan of Arc, The, 304
Triangle Film Corporation, 73
"trick film," 35, 37, 66
Trip to the Moon, A, 35–37, 40
Trotta, Margarethe von, 413
Trouble in Paradise, 184, 192
True Heart Susie, 53
True Story of Ah Q, The, 249
Truffaut, François, 5, 6, 300–301, 302, 303, 311, 312–313, 314–316, 317, 318, 320, 322
Trumbo, Dalton, 223
Tumbleweeds, 141
Turpin, Ben, 69
Tweetie Pie, 197
Twelve Angry Men, 273
Twentieth Century, 194, 202
Twentieth Century-Fox Film Corporation, 155, 180, 277, 279, 421
25 Fireman's Street, 351
Twenty-four Eyes, 260
Twilight's Last Gleaming, 394
Two Cents Worth of Hope, 244
Two English Girls, 317
Two for the Road, 324
Two Rode Together, 383
Two Stage Sisters, 249
2001: A Space Odyssey, 374
Two Weeks in Another Town, 389
Two Women, 246
Tyrant's Heart, The, 353

Ufa (Universum Film A. G.), 95, 98, 101, 102
Ugetsu, 250, 251, 253, 256–257
Ukamau Films, 409–410
Ulmer, Edgar, 291–292
Ulzana's Raid, 393
Umberto D, 244, 245, 246
Umbrellas of Cherbourg, The, 323
Uncle Tom's Cabin, 42
Uncovered Wagon, The, 68
Under the Paris Sky, 171
Underworld, 157, 188
United Artists, 71, 133, 180, 273, 279, 284–285, 421
United Kingdom, films of
silent, 42, 49–51, 150
sound, 102, 130, 161, 207-216, 362–381
United States, films of
silent, 32–33, 37–46, 48, 49–50, 51,

52–76, 77, 79, 81, 82, 83, 84,
85, 86, 87, 96, 99, 100, 101–
102, 104, 123–124, 132–149,
150–151
sound, 129–130, 178–206, 217–238,
271–299, 382–405, 417–418,
421–431
Universal Pictures, 101–102, 133, 134,
180, 190, 421
Unsuspected, The, 219
UPA (United Productions of America),
197
Upton Sinclair Presents William Fox, 155
USSR. See Soviet Union

Vadim, Roger, 312
Valenti, Jack, 285
Valentino, Rudolph, 69, 144, 372
Vampyr, 79, 80
Van Dyke, Dick, 274
Van Gogh, 313
Vanishing Lady, The, 35
Varda, Agnes, 312
Vardac, A. Nicholas, 26–27, 29–30
Variety, 94, 96, 97, 101, 147
Variety (trade journal), 218, 272, 276
Variety Lights, 330, 331
Veidt, Conrad, 99, 101
Venice International Film Festival, 247,
327, 329, 340–341
Vernon, Bobbie, 27
Vertigo, 384
Vertov, Dziga, 107–108, 109
Victor/Victoria, 390
Vidor, King, 136, 144, 145, 159, 385
Vie est un roman, La, 317
Vietnam War, U.S. films about, 422–
424
Vigo, Jean, 130, 166, 167
Virgin Spring, The, 81
Viridiana, 309, 310
Visconti, Luchino, 166, 238–239, 241,
327, 328, 329–330, 331, 334,
335, 338
VistaVision, 277, 288
Vitagraph Company of America, 72,
151
Vitam et Sanguinerm, 353
Vitaphone, 151–152, 155
Vitascope, 26, 35
Vitelloni, I, 330, 331
Viva Zapata!, 296
Vivre sa vie. See *My Life to Live*
Voight, Jon, 423
Voyage to Italy, 246

Wajda, Andrzej, 346–348, 349–351
Wake Island, 218
Walkabout, 378
Walker, Robert, 225
Walking Down Broadway, 384–385
Walk in the Sun, A, 220
Walkover, 349
Waller, Fred, 275
Wallis, Hal, 179

Walsh, Raoul, 136, 145, 159, 219, 301,
384, 385
Walt Disney Productions, 180, 196–
198, 272. See also Disney, Walt
Walthall, Henry B., 58–59, 60–61
Wanger, Walter, 5, 180, 225
Warm, Hermann, 89
Warner, Jack L., 133, 224
Warner Brothers Pictures, 133, 150,
151–153, 154, 155, 180, 185,
190, 197, 232, 273, 274, 279,
286–287, 421
Warshow, Robert, 184, 204
Watt, Harry, 209–210, 212, 214
Wave, The, 292
Way Ahead, The, 209
Ways of Love, The, 171, 282
We Are the Lambeth Boys, 365
Wedding, A, 400
Wedding March, The, 139
We Dive at Dawn, 209
Weekend, 319
Wegener, Paul, 90, 91
Weir, Peter, 416–417
Welles, Orson, 5, 29, 217, 225, 228–
231, 234, 301, 302, 384
Wellman, William, 194, 286, 302
Wells Fargo, 184
Wenders, Wim, 386, 414–415
Wertmüller, Lina, 339–340
West, Mae, 158, 192, 193–194
western, 39–41, 141, 184, 189, 203–205
Western Approaches, 209, 212–213
Western Electric, 155
Westerner, The, 227
Westfront 1918, 161
Whale, James, 192
What Did You Do in the War, Daddy?, 390
Whatever Happened to Baby Jane?, 393, 394
What is Cinema?, 2, 278
What Price Glory?, 145
When I'm Dead and White, 357
Whiskey Galore. See *Tight Little Island*
Whitaker, Rodney, 174–175, 176
White, Pearl, 382
White Dog, 392
White Heat, 189, 219
White Nights, 329
White Sheik, The, 330, 331, 333
Who'll Stop the Rain?, 372, 423
Who's Afraid of Virginia Woolf?, 285
Who's That Knocking at My Door?, 401,
402
Why Change Your Wife?, 137
Why We Fight series, 203
wide screen, 151, 271, 275–278, 280
Wiene, Robert, 89–90
Wild Bunch, The, 396–397
Wild Child, The, 317
Wilde, Hagar, 194–195
Wilder, Billy, 102, 194, 218, 265, 279,
286, 289–291, 292
Wild River, 296
Wild Strawberries, 81, 83, 305–306, 307,
308
Williamson, James A., 42
Wilson, Dooley, 231

Wily Coyote, 197
Winchester 73, 390
Wind, The, 82, 154
Wine of Youth, 143
Wings, 145
Winter Light, 306
Winters, Shelley, 288
Winter Wind, 352
Wise, Robert, 219, 302
Witchcraft Through the Ages, 78, 79
With Beauty and Sorrow, 260
Without Anesthetic, 349
Without Pity, 244, 330
Witness for the Prosecution, 290
Wollen, Peter, 202, 204
Woman in the Window, The, 102, 219
Woman Is a Woman, A, 315, 318, 319
Woman of Affairs, A, 145
Woman of the Dunes, 260
Woman of the Year, 288
Women, The, 286
Women in Love, 371
Wood, Sam, 223
Woodfall Productions, 365
Workers Leaving the Factory, 34
World of Apu, The, 265–266
Wright, Basil, 208
Wright, Teresa, 225
Wringing Good Joke, A, 66
WR: Mysteries of the Organism, 357–358
Wuthering Heights, 227
Wyatt, Jane, 223
Wyler, William, 5, 223, 225–226, 231,
234, 265, 302
Wyman, Jane, 387

Xala, 411
Xica, 409

Yankee Doodle Dandy, 218, 231
Year of Living Dangerously, The, 417
Yesterday Girl, 412
Yojimbo, 253
Yoshimura, Kimisaburo, 259
You Can't Take It with You, 202
Young, Loretta, 87–88
Young Mr. Lincoln, 203
Young Törless, 412
You Only Live Twice, 367
You're a Big Boy Now, 398
Yugoslavia, films of, 197, 346, 357–359
Yutkevich, Sergei, 109–110

Zabriskie Point, 4, 281, 328, 395
Zanuck, Darryl F., 179
Zanussi, Krzysztof, 349, 350
Zavattini, Cesare, 5, 241–244, 246,
265, 313
Zecca, Ferdinand, 66
Zelig, 425
Zéro de conduite, 166, 167
Ziegfeld Follies, 185
Zinnemann, Fred, 204, 286, 291–293
Zoetrope, 14, 15
Zukor, Adolph, 48, 106, 133, 134
Zvenigora, 110